Contents

www.philips-maps.co.uk

First published in 1998 by Philip's, a division of
Octopus Publishing Group Ltd
www.octopusbooks.co.uk
Endeavour House, 189 Shaftesbury Avenue, London WC2H 8JY
An Hachette UK Company
www.hachette.co.uk

Nineteenth edition 2010, first impression 2010

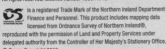 Ordnance Survey® This product includes mapping data licensed from
Ordnance Survey®, with the permission of the
Controller of Her Majesty's Stationery Office © Crown copyright 2010.
All rights reserved. Licence number 100011710.

OS is a registered Trade Mark of the Northern Ireland Department of
Finance and Personnel. This product includes mapping data
licensed from Ordnance Survey of Northern Ireland®,
reproduced with the permission of Land and Property Services under
delegated authority from the Controller of Her Majesty's Stationery
Office © Crown Copyright 2010.

publication, some of this information is subject to change and the Publisher
cannot guarantee its correctness or completeness.

The information in this atlas is provided without any representation or
warranty, express or implied and the Publisher cannot be held liable for any
loss or damage due to any use or reliance on the information in this atlas,
nor for any errors, omissions or subsequent changes in such information.

The representation in this atlas of any road, drive or track is not evidence of
the existence of a right of way.

The mapping on page 134 and the town plans of Edinburgh and London are
based on mapping data licenced from Ordnance Survey with the permission
of the Controller of Her Majesty's Stationery Office, © Crown Copyright
2010. All rights reserved. Licence number 100011710.

The maps of Ireland on pages 18 to 21 and the urban area map and town
plan of Dublin are based on Ordnance Survey Ireland by permission of
the Government Permit Number 8621 © Ordnance Survey Ireland and
Government of Ireland, and Land and Property Services under delegated
authority from the Controller of Her Majesty's Stationery Office
© Crown Copyright 2010 Permit Number 90163

Cartography by Philip's, Copyright © Philip's 2010

Photographic acknowledgements: Alamy page II column 2 top
iStockphoto.com page II top right, column 1 top and bottom, column 3
top, column 4 top and bottom; page III column 1 top and bottom, column 2
top, column 3 top and bottom, column 4 top and bottom; page VII top right.
Dreamstime.com page II column 2 bottom, column 3 bottom, column 4 top
right • page III column 1 middle, column 2 bottom, column 3 top.

Printed in China

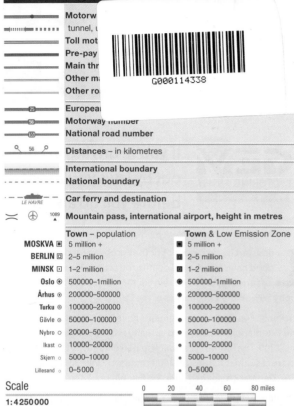

Legend to route planning maps pages 2–16

	Motorway
	tunnel, under construction
	Toll motorway
	Pre-pay motorway
	Main through route
	Other main road
	Other road
25	European road number
50	Motorway number
55	National road number
56	Distances – in kilometres
	International boundary
	National boundary
LE HAVRE	Car ferry and destination
1089	Mountain pass, international airport, height in metres

	Town – population		Town & Low Emission Zone
MOSKVA	5 million +		5 million +
BERLIN	2–5 million		2–5 million
MINSK	1–2 million		1–2 million
Oslo	500000–1million		500000–1million
Århus	200000–500000		200000–500000
Turku	100000–200000		100000–200000
Gävle	50000–100000		50000–100000
Nybro	20000–50000		20000–50000
Ikast	10000–20000		10000–20000
Skjern	5000–10000		5000–10000
Lillesand	0–5000		0–5000

Scale
1:4250000
1cm = 42.5km 1 inch = 67 miles

0 20 40 60 80 miles
0 20 40 60 80 100 120 140 km

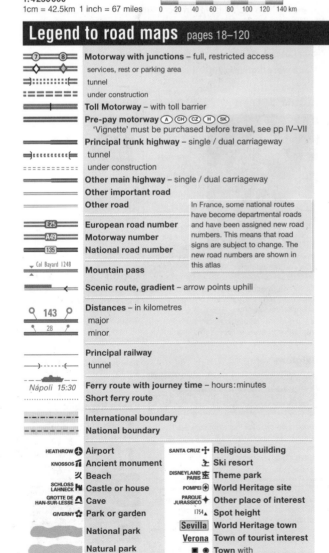

Legend to road maps pages 18–120

7 8	Motorway with junctions – full, restricted access
	services, rest or parking area
	tunnel
	under construction
	Toll Motorway – with toll barrier
	Pre-pay motorway (A) (CH) (CZ) (H) (SK)
	'Vignette' must be purchased before travel, see pp IV–VII
	Principal trunk highway – single / dual carriageway
	tunnel
	under construction
	Other main highway – single / dual carriageway
	Other important road
	Other road
E25	European road number
A49	Motorway number
135	National road number
Col Bayard 1248	Mountain pass
	Scenic route, gradient – arrow points uphill
143	Distances – in kilometres
	major
28	minor
	Principal railway
	tunnel
Nápoli 15:30	Ferry route with journey time – hours:minutes
	Short ferry route
	International boundary
	National boundary

In France, some national routes have become departmental roads and have been assigned new road numbers. This means that road signs are subject to change. The new road numbers are shown in this atlas

HEATHROW	Airport	SANTA CRUZ	Religious building
KNOSSOS	Ancient monument		Ski resort
	Beach	DISNEYLAND PARIS	Theme park
SCHLOSS LAHNECK	Castle or house	POMPEI	World Heritage site
GROTTE DE HAN-SUR-LESSE	Cave	PARQUE JURASSICO	Other place of interest
GIVERNY	Park or garden	1754	Spot height
	National park	Sevilla	World Heritage town
	Natural park	Verona	Town of tourist interest
			Town with Low Emission Zone

Scales

1:1000000 • Pages 18–110 and 120
1cm = 10km 1 inch = 16 miles

0 5 10 15 20 miles
0 5 10 15 20 25 30 35 km

1:2000000 • Pages 111–119
1cm = 20km, 1 inch = 32 miles

0 10 20 30 40 miles
0 10 20 30 40 50 60 70 km

The A to Z of Driving in Europe

If you're driving in Europe this year, don't be caught out by laws you're not used to. Do your homework before you go and ensure a stress-free journey.

Let's start by taking a look at the European road safety picture, and the good news is that road deaths and serious injuries continue to fall in just about every European country. Since 2001, road deaths have been cut by 36% in the 27 countries of the EU.

The most significant improvements have been in Latvia, Spain, Portugal and Estonia, who all achieved casualty reductions above 50% between 2001 and 2009. The biggest year-on-year percentage reductions were in Slovakia, where casualties fell 36% in 2009 compared with 2008. Lithuania achieved 26%, Denmark managed 25% and Estonia saw 24%.

Ten more people were killed on the roads in Belgium in 2009 than in 2008. France, which took the lead in reducing road deaths earlier in the decade, has lost its lead role. In 2009, 4,262 people lost their lives on French roads, almost as many as in 2008. The pace of reduction has also slowed down in Switzerland, the UK and the Netherlands, while road deaths in Romania and Malta were higher in 2009 than in 2001.

Austria

Although the drink-drive limit is generally 50mg, Austria has an almost zero tolerance of alcohol for bus drivers, truck drivers, moped riders aged under 20, learner drivers and their supervisors.

Following problems with collision in ice and snow, it was decided during the winter of 2007/08 to make the use of winter tyres on cars compulsory.

There's an interesting quirk in Austria's traffic light operation: before the green light of a traffic signal ends, it flashes four times.

Be aware, there's no shortage of traffic cops in Austria. Every uniformed police officer carries out traffic surveillance.

Belgium

If you are driving a car that is not registered to you, make sure you have a letter signed by the owner which makes clear you have his/her permission to be driving it.

If you are caught drink-driving with a reading between 50mg and 80mg BAC, you will be fined 125 euros on the spot and may lose your licence for three hours while you sober up. Above 80mg and the fines soar to 10,000 euros, with the possibility of a six-month prison sentence and a five-year driving ban. Belgium has also introduced roadside saliva screening for drugs.

By the way, always have a few coins to hand when you're driving in Belgium. You'll pay to use any public toilet, including the ones at motorway service areas (though the more generous ones will give you a credit against a cup of coffee you might buy afterwards).

Bulgaria

In Bulgaria, the cop's the star. Daily traffic reports are delivered on Bulgarian TV from a uniformed police officer, giving details of current road conditions, heavy traffic, and any specific dangers.

In large cities, they don't leave you guessing and drumming your fingers at traffic lights. Many junctions have been installed with special devices indicating the time left before the lights will change to green and back to red.

Don't drink and drive. The limit is 50mg BAC, but if you are caught at 120mg or above, you could be imprisoned for up to a year.

Cyprus

Police are authorised to give you an on-the-spot penalty. They have a special catalogue where offences and the amount of the fine are determined. Where offences are not included in the fixed penalty system, you can expect to be brought before a court.

Cyprus used to have one of the most generous drink-drive limits in Europe (90mg BAC compared with the UK's 80mg). However, this has now been reduced to 50mg, to align with most of Europe.

Czech Republic

City road space (both normal tarmac and potentially lethal cobblestone) is shared by cars, buses and trams. Don't let the gentle-sounding 'ding-ding' of a Prague tram fool you into thinking the driver's being friendly. He's not. He means 'Get out of the way now!' Tram drivers are known for showing no mercy to other users of the road.

Bear in mind it is also an offence to overtake a stationary tram on the inside.

If you are involved in a collision, don't move your vehicle until the police have arrived and inspected it. In fact, you could be prosecuted for moving it without their permission.

You need to buy a vignette, or permit, for driving on the motorway. These are available at petrol stations. If you are caught without one, the fine will be substantial.

Denmark

In 2009 it became mandatory for all car occupants, front and rear, to wear seatbelts. There are good reasons for being polite to the Danish police. That's because in 2007 they received new powers to test abusive drivers suspected to be under the influence of drugs.

Danish law permits police officers to issue and collect on-the-spot fines to foreign citizens who must pay the fine before they can proceed. If you can't pay up, your car may be taken into custody until the fine has been settled.

Estonia

Police have achieved significant successes dealing with drink-driving in Estonia. In 2009, road deaths dropped by 24%, following a 33% decrease in 2008. There are now fewer than 60 road deaths per million inhabitants, compared with nearly 140 in 2001.

In the capital city, Tallinn, before the green light of a traffic signal changes to amber, the light flashes twice.

Finland

Fines for traffic offences in Finland are calculated based on an individual's income and number of dependants. Small wonder, then, that a bachelor millionaire was once fined 170,000 euros for driving at 80km/h in a 40 zone. The Finnish National Traffic Police website has a page which allows drivers to choose the offence they plan to commit. They also enter their monthly income and the number of their dependants. The system then calculates how much it will cost them to commit the offence.

France

France's penalty points system is the opposite of our own. When a driver first gets a licence, it will have 12 points on it. Points are then deducted for offences. Minor infringements mean a one point deduction. More serious violations can see up to six points being removed.

The old *libertaire* days, in which high-speed French motorway journeys were the norm for many foreign drivers, are long gone. Speeds are strictly controlled and penalties for exceeding the limit are harsh. The Gendarmerie Nationale are responsible for surveillance of 95% of the road network, using marked and unmarked patrol cars, motorcycles, static speed cameras and even helicopters to detect offending drivers.

Germany

◄ German speed cameras may not be easy to spot.

Around 25% of the German motorway network is still without a formal speed limit. There is a recommended limit of 130km/h. Many German insurers will refuse to pay for damage to cars involved in collisions if they were being driven at speeds above this recommended limit.

The German police are severe on drivers who close-follow (or 'tailgate') on the motorway. Officers in unmarked cars use video surveillance to measure how closely a vehicle is following another vehicle. They can issue a summons which will be dealt with by a local court and could lead to a fine of several hundred euros and possible disqualification.

One other point to remember: you will receive a ticket and fine if you run out of fuel on a motorway in Germany.

Greece

The drink-drive limit in Greece is 50mg BAC, though for novice drivers, motorcyclists, taxi drivers and ambulance drivers the limit is 20mg.

Drivers detected with more than 80mg of alcohol will have their licence withdrawn.

In Greece, police officers are authorised to give fines on the spot. They have a special catalogue where the offences and the amount of the fine are determined.

Many trucks use the roads and motorways of Greece in transit between Europe and Asia. Collisions involving trucks were commonplace, but fatalities and serious injuries have fallen considerably in recent years.

Hungary

There is a zero-tolerance policy on drink-driving, which means that no amount of alcohol should be consumed before taking a vehicle on to the roads. Since January 2008, police have had the power to confiscate your licence on the spot if alcohol is detected in your system. It will only be returned after any driving-ban period decided by the authorities has expired.

In spite of recent road safety improvements, more vehicles exceed the speed limit than in any other European country. Police officers are authorised to issue on-the-spot fines. However, you cannot pay the fine by cash or bank card. Fines issued on the spot must be paid by using the special 'yellow cheques' you will be given by the police officer.

Ireland

In 2010, Ireland received a prestigious EU award for its sustained successful strategies in reducing road deaths. Ireland now has the lowest number of vehicles exceeding the speed limit. Tougher enforcement of regulations on trucks and new police powers to conduct random breath tests have helped drive down casualty rates, whilst secondary school pupils all have road-safety lessons as part of the curriculum. It's an offence to drive an animal-drawn vehicle while intoxicated. Of more practical importance are laws relating to leaving your car and locking it. For example, you must not leave a stationary vehicle with its engine running. You must also not leave a stationary vehicle unattended without locking the vehicle or removing the key. Getting into a moving vehicle is against the law, as is refusing the assistance of the police if you're involved in a collision. Lastly, don't reverse onto a major road, as you could receive a ticket.

Italy

In theory, if you don't have the money to pay an Italian motorway toll, you can request that an invoice be sent to you. Bear in mind that the police (Caribinieri) have the power to stop you for a document check, even if you have not committed any offence. The Caribinieri can issue, and collect, on-the-spot fines for minor traffic offences.

You must use dipped headlights during the day while travelling on motorways and major roads outside cities. You should carry at least one reflective safety jacket in your vehicle and wear it when standing with, inspecting or repairing your vehicle if you are on a public highway.

Latvia

Latvia achieved an outstanding 54% reduction in road fatalities between 2001 and 2009, better than any other European country. However, you should still be extra vigilant for pedestrians who step out without looking and slow moving vehicles in traffic. In towns, it is forbidden to overtake stationary vehicles. You must also give way to pedestrians, even at marked intersections.

Road quality tends to deteriorate rapidly once you are away from the cities and major routes.

Lithuania

Seatbelt enforcement is strict. You can be disqualified if you are seen driving without wearing a seatbelt.

Drink-drive restrictions are severe. The general limit is 40mg BAC. However, a limit of 20mg applies to novice drivers, drivers of large vehicles and drivers of vehicles with more than nine seats.

There are seasonal motorway speed limits. In summer (1 April to 31 October), the limit is 130km/h. This drops to 110km/h between November and March.

Luxembourg

Traffic law prohibits the use of a car horn except in emergency situations. The drink-drive limit was recently reduced from 80 to 50mg BAC, in line with most European countries. However, a 10mg limit applies to learners and their supervisors, as well s to bus, taxi and truck drivers. Police are empowered to levy substantial on-the-spot fines to violators. For more serious drink-drive offences, expect a prison sentence.

Malta

Yes, there ARE places outside the UK where you drive on the left, and Malta is one of them. Malta is part of the European Union; the seatbelt law is always strictly enforced. Drivers and all passengers should wear their seatbelts at all times. However, the use of child safety seats is not mandatory (though, it is highly recommended). Drink-driving is taken much more seriously these days. If you are found to be over the legal alcohol limit, you can lose your licence on the spot.

Netherlands

If you lose your licence through drink-driving, you will be required to pay for and attend an obligatory three-day course to study alcohol and traffic issues.

Minor traffic violations are part of the administrative law, the 'Mulder Act'. If you are fined, you can only appeal once you have paid the fine.

All 'Mulder violations' are listed in a book with corresponding descriptions and fixed penalty charges. When 'Mulder violations' are detected automatically by photographing the licence plate of a vehicle, the owner of the vehicle is responsible for the offence, regardless of who might have been driving the vehicle at the specific time of the violation.

Norway

Norwegian laws on drink-driving are amongst the strictest in Europe. The general blood alcohol content limit is 20mg BAC and above this limit, various levels of disqualification and heavy penalties of fines and imprisonment apply.

There is a legal requirement of 3mm tread depth on tyres between October and March. Depending on where you are, studded tyres are recommended, although bear in mind these are illegal for the rest of the year. Snow chains are recommended to be carried everywhere in Norway during winter, and if you do not carry and fit them when conditions demand, the police can prevent you continuing your journey.

Poland

The drink-drive limit is 20mg BAC. For minor infringements, you can expect a ban of at least six months and a fine. Above 50mg and you face loss of licence for up to 10 years and also a prison sentence.

Speed limits in towns are 50 km/h from 5am to 11pm, rising to 60 km/h overnight.

If you break a traffic law, you may find it's not a police officer who deals with you. That's because representatives of the Road Transport Inspectorate and the Municipal Guard have the same powers to stop drivers for traffic violations.

Portugal

It's illegal to wear headphones connected to a sound system while you're driving.

If you're driving, make sure everyone in the car wears a seatbelt, because you are responsible for paying fines for anyone not properly belted.

The motorway system includes 'Via Verde' lanes for frequent travellers. Don't use these lanes unless you subscribe to the Via Verde system. If you get to the end of your motorway journey without a valid toll ticket, you will have to pay a fine as well as a toll fee covering the entire motorway, not just the stretch you have used.

Romania

In spite of a 9% reduction in road fatalities in 2009 compared with 2008, more people died on the roads of Romania than in 2001. Major trunk roads and main streets in large Romanian cities are generally in good condition. However, many other roads are in poor repair, so expect potholes, poor lighting and faded or non-existent lane markings.

Enforcement of traffic law is strict. Police can confiscate any form of driving licence or permit for up to three months. Payment of fines may be requested at the time of the offence.

Slovakia

Slovakia operates a zero-tolerance policy for drink-driving with a blood alcohol content limit of 0mg BAC. The same policy also applies to the use of drugs, and drivers are prohibited from driving when under the influence of drugs.

Above right: Road hazards vary around Europe. In northern Scandinavia, you may find yourself sharing a tunnel with a herd of reindeer.

Police can issue and collect on-the-spot fines. They are empowered to decide the size of the on-the-spot traffic fine you will pay them, based on the nature of the offence you have committed, but also paying regard to your personal circumstances. If you can't pay, you will have your driving licence confiscated and will receive a certificate entitling you to drive for the next 15 days. The certificate is valid only for driving in Slovakia.

Slovenia

If you are detected driving above the drink-drive limit (50mg BAC), it is now mandatory that you will be arrested.

Winter tyres are mandatory between 15 November and 15 March. If you do not have them, you can be fined 125 euros. Even worse, if you block the road by not having them, the fine rises to 417 euros.

There is a 'vignette' system in use for motorways in Slovenia. You can buy a weekly, monthly or annual pass at petrol stations and motorway offices. Failure to display a valid vignette will cost you 800 euros.

Spain

Traffic police officers (the Civil Guard and local police) are authorised to issue on-the-spot fines for a range of minor offences for which there is a pre-set fine.

You must carry not one but TWO warning triangles, to be placed behind and in front of your vehicle in the event of a breakdown or accident.

If you have to get out of your car, you must wear a reflective jacket at all times. Therefore, make sure you have it to hand and not stored in the boot.

Talking on a mobile phone while driving is an offence, as is the use of an earpiece. The only permitted use of a mobile phone is if it is installed in a fully hands-free system.

Sweden

In cities, trams have priority. You must give way to passengers leaving a tram if there is no pedestrian island for them.

Use of dipped headlights is compulsory at all times. But don't use the horn in town unless there is a genuine emergency. Out of town, it's common practice to toot the horn or flash headlights before overtaking.

Police are not empowered to collect fines on the spot.

Switzerland

If using the motorway, you will need to buy an annual vignette costing 40 CHF. Failure to display a vignette can bring a hefty fine.

Bear in mind that a lot of your motorway driving in Switzerland will be underground, as the Swiss motorway network has a high proportion of tunnels. Every ninth kilometre of motorway runs underground.

The information above relating to legal requirements is provided for general information only and may not be fully accurate in particular cases.

Driving regulations

A national vehicle identification plate is always required when taking a vehicle abroad.

It is important for your own safety and that of other drivers to fit headlamp converters or beam deflectors when taking a right-hand drive car to a country where driving is on the right (every country in Europe except the UK and Ireland). When the headlamps are dipped on a right-hand drive car, the lenses of the headlamps cause the beam to shine upwards to the left – and so, when driving on the right, into the eyes of oncoming motorists.

In countries that require visibility vests, these must be kept within reach, not in the boot. Within the EU, if driving your own car it is compulsory to have either Europlates or a GB sticker; outside the EU (and in Andorra), if driving your own car, a GB sticker is compulsory, even with Europlates.

The symbols used are:

- 🏛 Motorway
- ⚠ Dual carriageway
- ⚠ Single carriageway
- 🚗 Surfaced road
- 🚜 Unsurfaced / gravel road
- 🏙 Urban area
- ⏱ Speed limit in kilometres per hour (kph). These are the maximum speeds for the types of roads listed. In some places and under certain conditions they may be considerably lower. Always obey local signs.
- 🛡 Seat belts
- 👶 Children
- 🍷 Blood alcohol level
- △ Warning triangle
- ⊞ First aid kit
- 💡 Spare bulb kit
- 🔥 Fire extinguisher
- ⛑ Motorcycle helmet
- ⊖ Minimum driving age
- 📋 Additional documents required
- 📱 Mobile phones
- **LEZ** Low Emission Zone
- ★ Other information

All countries require that you carry a driving licence, green card/insurance documentation, registration document or hire certificate, and passport.

In some countries, vignettes are being replaced by electronic tags. See country details.

The penalties for infringements of regulations vary considerably from one country to another. In many countries the police have the right to impose on-the-spot fines (you should always request a receipt for any fine paid). Penalties can be severe for serious infringements, particularly for drinking when driving which in some countries can lead to immediate imprisonment. Insurance is important, and you may be forced to take out cover at the frontier if you cannot produce acceptable proof that you are insured.

Please note that driving regulations often change.

Andorra Principat d'Andorra (AND)

Area 468 sq km (181 sq miles) **Population** 84,525 **Capital** Andorra la Vella (22,884) **Languages** Catalan (official), French, Castilian and Portuguese **Currency** Euro = 100 cents **Website** www.andorra.ad

🏛	⚠	⚠	🏙
n/a	90	60/90	60

- 🛡 Compulsory
- 👶 Over 10 only allowed in front seats if over 150cm; under 10 not allowed in front seat
- 🍷 0.05%
- △ Compulsory ⊞ Recommended
- 💡 Compulsory 🔥 Recommended
- ⛑ Compulsory for all riders
- ⊖ 18
- 📋 International driving permit if driving licence has no photograph; green card recommended
- 📱 Not permitted whilst driving
- ★ Winter tyres and snow chains compulsory

Austria Österreich (A)

Area 83,859 sq km (32,377 sq miles) **Population** 8,214,160 **Capital** Vienna / Wien (2,268,656) **Languages** German (official) **Currency** Euro = 100 cents **Website** www.austria.gv.at

🏛	⚠	⚠	🏙
130	100	100	50

If towing trailer under 750kg / over 750 kg

100	100	100/80	50

- 🛡 Compulsory
- 👶 Under 12 and under 150cm cannot travel as a front or rear passenger unless they use a suitable child restraint; under 12 over 150cm must wear adult seat belt
- 🍷 0.049%
- △ Compulsory ⊞ Compulsory
- 💡 Recommended 🔥 Recommended
- ⛑ Compulsory for all riders
- ⊖ 18 (16 for mopeds)
- 📋 Third party insurance; photo identity if driving licence has no photograph
- 📱 Only allowed with hands-free kit
- **LEZ** On A12 motorway, non-compliant vehicles banned, certain substances banned, night-time restrictions, overtaking bans and speed limits on others. LEZ for Graz planned.
- ★ If you intend to drive on motorways or expressways, a motorway vignette must be purchased at the border. These are available for 10 days, 2 months or 1 year. Vehicles 3.5 tonnes and over must purchase an electronic tag.
- ★ Winter tyres and snow chains compulsory
- ★ Dipped headlights must be used during the day by all road users.
- ★ Visibility vest compulsory

Belarus (BY)

Area 207,600 sq km (80,154 sq miles) **Population** 9,612,232 **Capital** Minsk (3,000,000) **Languages** Belarusian, Russian (both official) **Currency** Belarusian ruble = 100 kopek **Website** www.mfa.gov.by/eng

🏛	⚠	⚠	🏙
110	90	90	60

If towing trailer under 750kg

90	70	70	

Vehicle towing another vehicle 50 kph limit • If full driving licence held for less than two years, must not exceed 70 kph

- 🛡 Compulsory in front seats, and rear seats if fitted
- 👶 Under 12 not allowed in front seat
- 🍷 0.00%
- △ Compulsory ⊞ Compulsory
- 💡 Recommended 🔥 Compulsory
- ⛑ Compulsory for all riders
- ⊖ 18 (16 for motorbikes)
- 📋 Third party insurance; visa (ensure it's specific to driving); vehicle technical check stamp; international driving permit
- 📱 Only allowed with hands-free kit
- ★ Belarus insurance and temporary vehicle import certificate must be purchased on entry, and driver must be registered
- ★ Dipped headlights compulsory at all times from Nov to Mar
- ★ Fees payable for driving on highways
- ★ Winter tyres and snow chains recommended

Belgium Belgique (B)

Area 30,528 sq km (11,786 sq miles) **Population** 10,423,493 **Capital** Brussels/Bruxelles (1,080,790) **Languages** Dutch, French, German (all official) **Currency** Euro = 100 cents **Website** www.belgium.be/en

🏛	⚠	⚠	🏙
120*	120*	90	50**

If towing trailer

⏱			
90	90	60	50

Over 3.5 tonnes

⏱			
90	90	60	50

*Minimum speed of 70kph may be applied in certain conditions on motorways and some dual carriageways **Near schools, hospitals and churches the limit may be 30kph

- 🛡 Compulsory
- 👶 Children under 12 must use an appropriate child restraint front and rear
- 🍷 0.05%
- △ Compulsory ⊞ Compulsory
- 💡 Recommended 🔥 Compulsory
- ⛑ Compulsory for all riders
- ⊖ 18 (16 for motorbikes under 50cc)
- 📋 Third party insurance
- 📱 Only allowed with a hands-free kit
- ★ Cruise control is not permitted on motorways
- ★ Dipped headlights compulsory for motorcycles during the day and other vehicles during poor daytime visibility
- ★ Sticker indicating maximum recommended speed for winter tyres must be displayed on dashboard if using them
- ★ Use of radar-detecting equipment is illegal
- ★ Visibility vest compulsory

Bulgaria Bulgariya (BG)

Area 110,912 sq km (42,822 sq miles) **Population** 7,148,785 **Capital** Sofia (1,449,277) **Languages** Bulgarian (official), Turkish **Currency** Lev = 100 stotinki **Website** www.president.bg/en/index.php

🏛	⚠	⚠	🏙
130	90	90	50

If towing trailer

⏱			
100	70	70	50

- 🛡 Compulsory in front and rear seats
- 👶 Under 10 not allowed in front seats
- 🍷 0.05% △ Compulsory ⊞ Compulsory
- 💡 Recommended 🔥 Compulsory
- ⛑ Compulsory for all riders
- ⊖ 18 (16 for mopeds)
- 📋 Driving licence with translation or international driving permit, third party insurance
- 📱 Only allowed with a hands-free kit
- ★ Fee at border
- ★ GPS systems that indicate the position of speed cameras must have this function deactivated
- ★ Radar-detection equipment is prohibited
- ★ Vignette system in operation, can be purchased from all border-crossing points and available annually, monthly and weekly. Write your vehicle registration number on the vignette before displaying it.

Czech Republic

Česka Republica (CZ)

Area 78,864 sq km (30,449 sq miles) **Population** 10,201,797 **Capital** Prague/Praha (1,900,000) **Languages** Czech (official), Moravian **Currency** Czech Koruna = 100 haler **Website** www.czech.cz

🏛	⚠	⚠	🏙
130	130	90	50

If towing

⏱			
80	80	80	50

- 🛡 Compulsory in front seats and, if fitted, in rear
- 👶 Under 12 or under 150cm not allowed in front seats
- 🍷 0.00%
- △ Compulsory ⊞ Compulsory
- 💡 Compulsory 🔥 Compulsory
- ⛑ Compulsory for all riders
- ⊖ 18 (16 for motorcycles under 125 cc)
- 📋 International driving permit
- 📱 Only allowed with a hands-free kit
- **LEZ** All vehicles above 3.5 tonnes banned from Prague LEZ.
- ★ Dipped headlights compulsory at all times
- ★ GPS systems that indicate the position of speed cameras must have this function deactivated
- ★ Radar-detection equipment is prohibited
- ★ Vignette needed for motorway driving, available for 1 year, 60 days, 15 days. Toll specific to lorries introduced 2006, those over 12 tonnes must buy an electronic tag

---

- ★ Visibility vest compulsory
- ★ Wearers of spectacles or contact lenses must carry a spare pair in their vehicle at all times
- ★ Winter tyres or snow chains compulsory between Nov and Apr

Denmark Danmark (DK)

Area 43,094 sq km (16,638 sq miles) **Population** 5,515,575 **Capital** Copenhagen / København (1,899,427) **Languages** Danish (official) **Currency** Krone = 100 øre **Website** www.denmark.dk/en

🏛	⚠	⚠	🏙
130	80	80	50

If towing

⏱			
80	70	70	50

- 🛡 Compulsory in front seats and, if fitted, in rear
- 👶 Children under 12 must use an appropriate child restraint front and rear
- 🍷 0.05%
- △ Compulsory ⊞ Recommended
- 💡 Recommended 🔥 Recommended
- ⛑ Compulsory for all riders
- ⊖ 18
- 📋 Third party insurance
- 📱 Only allowed with a hands-free kit
- **LEZ** Aalborg, Arhus, Copenhagen, Frederiksberg and Odense. Proofs of emissions compliance/compliant filter needed to obtain sticker. Non-compliant vehicles banned.
- ★ Dipped headlights must be used at all times
- ★ Tolls apply on the Storebaeltsbroen and Oresundsbron bridges.

Estonia Eesti (EST)

Area 45,100 sq km (17,413 sq miles) **Population** 1,291,170 **Capital** Tallinn (409,661) **Languages** Estonian (official), Russian **Currency** Kroon = 100 sents **Website** www.riik.ee/en

🏛	⚠	⚠	🏙
n/a	90*	70	50

If full driving licence held for less than two years

⏱			
90	90	70	50

*In summer, the speed limit on some dual carriageways may be raised to 100/110 kph

- 🛡 Compulsory in front seats and if fitted in rear seats
- 👶 Under 12 not allowed in front seats; under 7 must have child safety seat in rear
- 🍷 0.00%
- △ Compulsory ⊞ Compulsory
- 💡 Recommended 🔥 Compulsory
- ⛑ Compulsory for all riders
- ⊖ 18 (16 for motorcycles, 14 for mopeds)
- 📋 International driving permit recommended
- 📱 Only allowed with a hands-free kit
- ★ Winter tyres are compulsory Dec–Feb but illegal from May–Sep.

Finland Suomi (FIN)

Area 338,145 sq km (130,557 sq miles) **Population** 5,255,068 **Capital** Helsinki (1,313,574) **Languages** Finnish, Swedish (both official) **Currency** Euro = 100 cents **Website** www.government.fi

🏛	⚠	⚠	🏙
120	100	80*	30/60

If towing

⏱			
80	80	80	30/60

*100 in summer •If towing a vehicle by rope, cable or rod, max speed limit 60 kph. •Maximum of 80 kph for vans and lorries •Speed limits are often lowered in winter

- 🛡 Compulsory in front and rear
- 👶 Children use a safety belt or special child's seat
- 🍷 0.05%
- △ Compulsory ⊞ Recommended
- 💡 Recommended 🔥 Recommended
- ⛑ Compulsory for all riders
- ⊖ 18
- 📋 Third party insurance
- 📱 Only allowed with hands-free kit
- ★ Radar-detection equipment is prohibited.
- ★ Dipped headlights must be used at all times
- ★ Winter tyres compulsory Dec–Feb

France (F)

Area 551,500 sq km (212,934 sq miles) **Population** 64,057,792 **Capital** Paris (11,746,000) **Languages** French (official), Breton, Occitan **Currency** Euro = 100 cents **Website** www.francetourism.com

	130	110	90	50
On wet roads or if full driving licence held for less than 2 years				
	110	90	80	50
If towing below 3.5 tonnes gross / above 3.5 tonnes gross				
	110/90	100/90	90/80	50

50kph on all roads if fog reduces visibility to less than 50m • Licence will be lost and driver fined for exceeding speed limit by over 40kph

- Compulsory in front seats and, if fitted, in rear
- Under 10 not allowed in front seats; in rear, if 4 or under, must have a child safety seat (rear facing if up to 9 months); if 5 to 10 must use an appropriate restraint system
- 0.05%
- Compulsory Recommended
- Recommended Compulsory for all riders
- 18 (16 for light motorcycles, 14 for mopeds)
- Use not permitted whilst driving
- ★ Radar-detection equipment is prohibited
- ★ Tolls on motorways. Electronic tag needed if using automatic tolls.
- ★ Visibility vest compulsory

Germany Deutschland (D)

Area 357,022 sq km (137,846 sq miles) **Population** 82,282,998 **Capital** Berlin (3,439,100) **Languages** German (official) **Currency** Euro = 100 cents **Website** www.deutschland.de

	*	*	100	50
If towing				
	80	80	80	50

*no limit, 130 kph recommended

- Compulsory
- Children under 12 and under 150cm must have a child safety seat, in front and rear
- 0.05%, 0.0% for young and newly qualified drivers
- Compulsory Compulsory
- Recommended Recommended
- Compulsory for all riders
- 18 (motorbikes: 16 if under 50cc)
- Third party insurance
- Use permitted only with hands-free kit – also applies to drivers of motorbikes and bicycles
- LEZ More than 40 cities have or are planning LEZs. Proof of compliance needed to acquire sticker. Non-compliant vehicles banned.
- ★ Carrying snow chains recommended in winter.
- ★ GPS systems that indicate the position of speed cameras must have this function deactivated
- ★ Motorcyclists must use dipped headlights at all times; other vehicles must use dipped headlights during poor daytime visibility.
- ★ Radar-detection equipment is prohibited
- ★ Tolls on autobahns for lorries

Greece Ellas (GR)

Area 131,957 sq km (50,948 sq miles) **Population** 11,749,943 **Capital** Athens / Athina (3,686,371) **Languages** Greek (official) **Currency** Euro = 100 cents **Website** www.primeminister.gr/english

	120	110	110	50
If towing				
	90	70	70	40

- Compulsory in front seats and, if fitted, in rear
- Under 12 not allowed in front seats except with suitable safety seat; under 10 not allowed in front seats
- 0.025% breath, 0.05 blood, 0.02% for drivers with less than 2 years experience, motorcyclists and drivers of business or commercial vehicles
- Compulsory Compulsory
- Recommended Compulsory
- Compulsory for all riders
- 18 (16 for low cc motorcycles)
- Third party insurance
- Not permitted.
- ★ Radar-detection equipment is prohibited
- ★ Tolls on several newer motorways.

Hungary Magyarország (H)

Area 93,032 sq km (35,919 sq miles) **Population** 9,880,059 **Capital** Budapest (3,271,100) **Languages** Hungarian (official) **Currency** Forint = 100 filler **Website** www.parlament.hu/parl_en.htm

	130	110	90	50
If towing				
	80	70	70	50

- Compulsory in front seats and if fitted in rear seats
- Under 12 or under 140cm not allowed in front seats
- 0.00% Compulsory Compulsory
- Compulsory Recommended
- Compulsory for all riders
- 18 Third party insurance
- Only allowed with a hands-free kit
- ★ All motorways are toll and operate electronic vignette system with automatic number plate recognition, tickets are available for 4 days, 7 days, 1 month, 1 year
- ★ Dipped headlights are compulsory during daylight hours (cars exempted in built-up areas)

Iceland Ísland (IS)

Area 103,000 sq km (39,768 sq miles) **Population** 308,910 **Capital** Reykjavik (201,847) **Languages** Icelandic **Currency** Krona = 100 aurar **Website** http://government.is

	n/a	90	80	50

- Compulsory in front and rear seats
- Under 12 or under 140cm not allowed in front seats
- 0.05% Compulsory Compulsory
- Compulsory Compulsory for all riders
- 18; 21 to drive a hire car; 25 to hire a jeep
- Third party insurance
- Only allowed with a hands-free kit
- ★ Driving off marked roads is forbidden
- ★ Headlights are compulsory at all times
- ★ Highland roads are not suitable for ordinary cars
- ★ Winter tyres compulsory c.1 Nov–14 Apr (variable)

Ireland, Republic of Eire (IRL)

Area 70,273 sq km (27,132 sq miles) **Population** 4,250,163 **Capital** Dublin (1,661,185) **Languages** Irish, English (both official) **Currency** Euro = 100 cents **Website** www.gov.ie/en/

	120	100	80	50
If towing				
	80	80	80	50

- Compulsory where fitted. Driver responsible for ensuring passengers under 17 comply
- Under 3 not allowed unless restrained in an appropriate child restraint when travelling in cars fitted with seatbelts
- 0.08% Recommended Recommended
- Recommended Recommended
- Compulsory for all riders
- 17 (16 for motorbikes up to 125cc; 18 for over 125cc; 18 for lorries; 21 bus/minibus)
- Third party insurance; international driving permit for non-EU drivers
- Only allowed with a hands-free kit
- ★ Dipped headlights are compulsory during daylight hours
- ★ Driving is on the left
- ★ GPS systems that indicate the position of speed cameras must have this function deactivated
- ★ Radar-detection equipment is prohibited
- ★ Tolls are being introduced on some motorways

Italy Italia (I)

Area 301,318 sq km (116,338 sq miles) **Population** 58,090,061 **Capital** Rome / Roma (2,731,996) **Languages** Italian (official) **Currency** Euro = 100 cents **Website** www.enit.it

	130	110	90	50
When wet				
	100	90	80	50
If towing				
	80	70	70	50

Some motorways with emergency lanes have speed limit of 150 kph

- Compulsory in front seats and, if fitted, in rear
- Under 12 not allowed in front seats except in child safety seat; children under 3 must have special seat in the back
- 0.05% Compulsory Recommended
- Compulsory Recommended
- Compulsory for all motorcylists
- 18 (14 for mopeds, 16 up to 125cc, 20 up to 350cc)
- International Driving Licence unless you have photocard licence
- Only allowed with hands-free kit
- LEZ Piemonte, Emilia-Romagna, Lombardia, Bolzano, Veneto operate LEZs in winter for some hours each day. A22 motorway, Milan and Palermo have full-time LEZs. Fees charged for non-compliant vehicles. Many Italian towns and cities operate ZTLs, in which no vehicles are allowed at certain times or odd and even number plates are banned on different days.
- ★ Dipped headlights compulsory for motorcycles at all times, and other vehicles in poor daytime visibility and tunnels, and on motorways, dual carriageways and out of town roads
- ★ Radar-detection equipment is prohibited
- ★ Tolls on motorways. Blue lanes accept credit cards; yellow lanes restricted to holders of Telepass pay-toll device.
- ★ Visibility vest compulsory
- ★ Winter tyres recommended; these or snow chains are compulsory in the Val d'Aosta 15 Oct–15 Apr

Latvia Latvija (LV)

Area 64,589 sq km (24,942 sq miles) **Population** 2,217,969 **Capital** Riga (709,145) **Languages** Latvian (official), Russian **Currency** Lats = 100 santims **Website** www.lv

	90/100	90	90	50
If towing				
	90/100	90	90	50

In residential areas limit is 20kph • If full driving licence held for less than two years, must not exceed 80 kph

- Compulsory in front seats and if fitted in rear
- If under 12 years and 150cm must use child restraint in front and rear seats
- 0.05%, 0.02% with less than 2 years experience
- Compulsory Compulsory
- Recommended Compulsory
- Compulsory for all riders
- 18 (14 for mopeds, 16 up to 125cc, 21 up to 350cc)
- International driving permit if licence is not in accordance with Vienna Convention
- Only allowed with hands-free kit
- ★ Dipped headlights must be used at all times all year round
- ★ Pedestrians have priority
- ★ Winter tyres compulsory Dec–Feb, but illegal May–Sep

Lithuania Lietuva (LT)

Area 65,200 sq km (25,173 sq miles) **Population** 3,545,319 **Capital** Vilnius (558,165) **Languages** Lithuanian (official), Russian, Polish **Currency** Litas = 100 centai **Website** www.lrvk.lt/en

	130	110	90	50
If towing				
	n/a	70	70	50

- Compulsory in front seats and if fitted in rear seats
- Under 12 not allowed in front seats unless in a child safety seat
- 0.04% Compulsory Compulsory
- Recommended Compulsory
- Compulsory for all riders
- 18 (14 for mopeds)
- Visa for some non-EU citizens; green card if taking your own vehicle into the country
- Only allowed with a hands-free kit
- ★ Dipped headlights must be used at all times

Luxembourg (L)

Area 2,586 sq km (998 sq miles) **Population** 497,538 **Capital** Luxembourg (88,586) **Languages** Luxembourgian / Letzeburgish (official), French, German **Currency** Euro = 100 cents **Website** www.ont.lu

	130/110	90	90	50
If towing				
	90	75	75	50

If full driving licence held for less than two years, must not exceed 75 kph

- Compulsory
- Under 12 or 150cm not allowed in front seats unless in a child restraint system; under 3 must have child safety seat in rear seats; 3-11 must have child restraint system if under 150cm
- 0.05%, 0.02 for young drivers, drivers with less than 2 years experience and drivers of taxis and commercial vehicles
- Compulsory Compulsory (buses)
- Compulsory Compulsory (buses, transport of dangerous goods)
- Compulsory 18 Third party insurance
- Use permitted only with hands-free kit
- ★ Dipped headlights at all times.

Macedonia Makedonija (MK)

Area 25,713 sq km (9,927 sq miles) **Population** 2,072,086 **Capital** Skopje (668,518) **Languages** Macedonian (official), Albanian **Currency** Denar = 100 deni **Website** www.vlada.mk/english/index_en.htm

	120	100	60	60
If towing				
	80	70	50	50

- Compulsory in front seats; compulsory if fitted in rear seats
- Under 12 not allowed in front seats
- 0.05%, 0.00% for business, commercial and professional drivers
- Compulsory Compulsory
- Compulsory Recommended
- Compulsory for all riders
- 18 (mopeds 16)
- International driving permit; visa
- Use not permitted whilst driving
- ★ GPS systems that indicate the position of speed cameras must have this function deactivated
- ★ Headlights must be used at all times
- ★ Radar-detection equipment is prohibited
- ★ Tolls apply on many roads
- ★ Winter tyres or snow chains compulsory 15 Nov–15 Mar

Moldova (MD)

Area 33,851 sq km (13,069 sq miles) **Population** 4,317,483 **Capital** Chisinau (596,355) **Languages** Moldovan / Romanian (official) **Currency** Leu = 100 bani **Website** www.parliament.md/en.html

	90	90	90	60
If towing or if licence held under 1 year				
	70	70	70	60

- Compulsory in front seats and, if fitted, in rear seats
- Under 12 not allowed in front seats
- 0.00%
- Compulsory Compulsory
- Recommended Compulsory
- Compulsory for all riders
- 18 (mopeds and motorbikes, 16; vehicles with more than eight passenger places, taxis or towing heavy vehicles, 21)
- International driving permit (preferred), third party insurance, visa
- Only allowed with hands-free kit
- ★ Motorcyclists must use dipped headlights at all times
- ★ Winter tyres recommended Nov–Feb

Montenegro Crna Gora (MNE)

Area 13,812 sq km (5,333 sq miles) **Population** 666,730 **Capital** Podgorica (160,100) **Languages** Serbian (of the Ijekavian dialect) **Currency** Euro = 100 cents **Website** www.visit-montenegro.com

	n/a	100	80	60

80kph speed limit if towing a caravan

- Compulsory in front and rear seats
- Under 12 not allowed in front seats
- 0.05%
- Compulsory Compulsory
- Recommended Compulsory
- Compulsory
- 18 (16 for motorbikes less than 125cc; 14 for mopeds)
- International driving permit; visa; green card recommended
- Prohibited
- ★ An 'eco' tax vignette must be obtained when crossing the border and displayed in the upper right-hand corner of the windscreen
- ★ Dipped headlights must be used at all times
- ★ Tolls on some primary roads and in the Sozina tunnel between Lake Skadar and the sea
- ★ Visibility vest compulsory

The Netherlands
Nederland (NL)

Area 41,526 sq km (16,033 sq miles) **Population** 16,783,092 **Capital** Amsterdam (city 762,057; urban 1,364,422); administrative capital 's-Gravenhage (The Hague) (488,370) **Languages** Dutch (official), Frisian **Currency** Euro = 100 cents **Website** www.government.nl

	🛣	⩓	△	🏙
⏲	120/100	80/100	80/100	50

💺 Compulsory in front seats and, if fitted, rear

👶 Under 12 not allowed in front seats except in child restraint; in rear, 0-3 child safety restraint, 4-12 child restraint or seat belt

🍷 0.05%

△ Recommended ✚ Recommended

💡 Recommended 🧯 Recommended

⛑ Compulsory

⊖ 18

📄 Third party insurance

📱 Only allowed with a hands-free kit

LEZ About 20 cities operate or are planning LEZs. Permit system/number plate recognition.

★ Dipped headlights compulsory for motorcycles

★ Radar-detection equipment is prohibited

Norway Norge (N)

Area 323,877 sq km (125,049 sq miles) **Population** 4,676,305 **Capital** Oslo (907,288) **Languages** Norwegian (official), Lappish, Finnish **Currency** Krone = 100 øre **Website** www.norge.no

	🛣	⩓	△	🏙
⏲	90/100	80	80	30/50
If towing trailer with brakes				
⏲	80	80	80	50
If towing trailer without brakes				
⏲	60	60	60	50

💺 Compulsory in front seats and, if fitted, in rear

👶 Children less than 150cm tall must use appropriate child restraint where available. Children under 4 must use child safety seat or safety restraint (cot)

🍷 0.01%

△ Compulsory ✚ Recommended

💡 Recommended 🧯 Recommended

⛑ Compulsory for all riders

⊖ 18 (heavy vehicles 18/21)

📱 Only allowed with a hands-free kit

LEZ Due to begin operating in Bergen, Oslo and Trondheim

★ At least 3mm of tread Oct–Mar; winter tyres Nov–Mar if in a hire car registered in Norway

★ Dipped headlights must be used at all times

★ Radar-detection equipment is prohibited

★ Tolls apply on some bridges, tunnels and access roads into major cities. Several use electronic fee collection only.

★ Visibility vest compulsory

Poland Polska (PL)

Area 323,250 sq km (124,807 sq miles) **Population** 38,463,689 **Capital** Warsaw / Warszawa (1,711,466) **Languages** Polish (official) **Currency** Zloty = 100 groszy **Website** www.poland.gov.pl

	🛣	⩓	△	🏙
Motor-vehicle only roads[1], under/over 3.5 tonnes				
⏲	130[2]/80[2]	110/80	100/80	n/a
Motor-vehicle only roads[1] if towing				
⏲	n/a	80	80	n/a
Other roads, under 3.5 tonnes				
⏲	n/a	100	90	50/60[3]
Other roads, 3.5 tonnes or over				
⏲	n/a	80	70	50/60[3]
Other roads, if towing				
⏲	n/a	60	60	30

[1]Indicated by signs with white car on blue background. [2]Minimum speed 40 kph. [3]50 kph 05.00–23.00; 60 kph 23.00–05.00; 20 kph in marked residential areas

💺 Compulsory in front seats and, if fitted, in rear

👶 Under 12 not allowed in front seats unless in a child safety seat; in rear seats children under 12 and less than 150 cm must use child safety seat

🍷 0.00%

△ Compulsory ✚ Recommended

💡 Recommended 🧯 Compulsory

⛑ Compulsory for all riders

⊖ 18 (mopeds and motorbikes – 16)

📄 International permit (recommended); originals of insurance certificate and registration document must be carried, not photocopies

📱 Only allowed with a hands-free kit

★ Dipped headlights compulsory at all times

★ Radar-detection equipment is prohibited

Portugal (P)

Area 88,797 sq km (34,284 sq miles) **Population** 10,735,765 **Capital** Lisbon / Lisboa (564,477 municipality; urban 2,824,000) **Languages** Portuguese (official) **Currency** Euro = 100 cents **Website** www.visitportugal.com

	🛣	⩓	△	🏙
⏲	120*	100	90	50
If towing				
⏲	100*	90	80	50

*40kph minimum; 90kph maximum if licence held under 1 year

💺 Compulsory in front seats; compulsory if fitted in rear seats

👶 Under 3 not allowed in front seats unless in a child seat; 3–12 not allowed in front seats except in approved restraint system

🍷 0.05%

△ Compulsory ✚ Recommended

💡 Recommended 🧯 Recommended

⛑ Compulsory for all riders

⊖ 18 (motorcycles under 50cc 16)

📄 MOT certificate for vehicles over three years old; letter of permission from the owner of any borrowed car

📱 Only allowed with hands-free kit

★ Visibility vest compulsory

★ Wearers of spectacles or contact lenses must carry a spare pair in their vehicle at all times

★ Dipped headlights compulsory for motorcycles, and for other vehicles in poor daytime visibility

★ Tolls on motorways; do not use green lanes, these are reserved for auto-payment users

★ Drivers with less than a year's experience should display a yellow 90 sticker obtainable from the ACP motoring club

★ Radar-detection equipment is prohibited

Romania (RO)

Area 238,391 sq km (92,042 sq miles) **Population** 22,181,287 **Capital** Bucharest / Bucuresti (1,944,367) **Languages** Romanian (official), Hungarian **Currency** Romanian leu = 100 bani **Website** www.gov.ro

	🛣	⩓	△	🏙
Cars and motorcycles				
⏲	120/130	100	90	50
Vans				
⏲	110	90	80	50
Motorcycles				
⏲	100	80	80	50

For motor vehicles with trailers or if full driving licence has been held for less than one year, speed limits are 20kph lower than those listed above •Jeep-like vehicles: 70kph outside built-up areas but 60kph in all areas if diesel

💺 Compulsory in front seats and, if fitted, in rear

👶 Under 12 not allowed in front seats

🍷 0.00%

△ Recommended ✚ Compulsory

💡 Recommended 🧯 Compulsory

⛑ Compulsory for all riders

⊖ 18 (16 for mopeds)

📄 Registration certificate (only if stay over 90 days for EU citizens); third party insurance

📱 Only allowed with hands-free kit

★ Compulsary vignette (rovinieta) valid for variety of periods available at customs points, petrol stations; price depends on emissions category. Write your vehicle registration number on the vignette before displaying it.

★ Winter tyres or snow chains compulsory in wintry weather

★ Tolls on motorways

Russia Rossiya (RUS)

Area 17,075,000 sq km (6,592,800 sq miles) **Population** 139,390,205 **Capital** Moscow / Moskva (10,562,099) **Languages** Russian (official), and many others **Currency** Russian ruble = 100 kopeks **Website** www.visitrussia.org.uk

	🛣	⩓	△	🏙
⏲	110	90	90	60
If licence held for under 2 years				
⏲	70	70	70	60

💺 Compulsory in front seats

👶 Under 12 not allowed in front seats

🍷 0.00%

△ Compulsory ✚ Compulsory

💡 Recommended 🧯 Compulsory

⛑ Compulsory ⊖ 18

📄 International driving licence with Russian translation; visa

📱 Only allowed with a hands-free kit

★ Dipped headlights compulsory during the day

★ Picking up hitchhikers is prohibited

Serbia Srbija (SRB)

Area 88,412 sq km (34,137 sq miles), including Kosovo **Population** 7,344,847 **Capital** Belgrade / Beograd (1,182,000) **Languages** Serbian **Currency** Dinar = 100 paras **Website** www.srbija.gov.rs

	🛣	⩓	△	🏙
⏲	120	100	80	60

💺 Compulsory in front and rear seats

👶 Under 12 not allowed in front seats

🍷 0.03%, 0.00% for commercial, business and professional drivers

△ Compulsory ✚ Compulsory

💡 Compulsory 🧯 Compulsory

⛑ Compulsory

⊖ 18 (16 for motorbikes less than 125cc; 14 for mopeds)

📄 International driving permit

📱 No legislation

★ 80km/h speed limit if towing a caravan

★ Tolls on motorways and some primary roads

★ Winter tyres or snow chains compulsory in poor winter weather conditions

Slovak Republic
Slovenska Republika (SK)

Area 49,012 sq km (18,923 sq miles) **Population** 5,470,306 **Capital** Bratislava (428,791) **Languages** Slovak (official), Hungarian **Currency** Euro = 100 cents **Website** www.prezident.sk

	🛣	⩓	△	🏙
⏲	130	90	90	60

💺 Compulsory in front seats and, if fitted, in rear

👶 Under 12 not allowed in front seats unless in a child safety seat

🍷 0.0

△ Compulsory ✚ Compulsory

💡 Compulsory 🧯 Recommended

⛑ Compulsory for motorcyclists

⊖ 18 (15 for mopeds)

📄 International driving permit

📱 Only allowed with a hands-free kit

★ Dipped headlights compulsory at all times

★ Radar-detection equipment is prohibited

★ Tow rope recommended

★ Vignette required for motorways, car valid for 1 year, 30 days, 7 days; lorry vignettes carry a higher charge.

★ Winter tyres recommended

Slovenia Slovenija (SLO)

Area 20,256 sq km (7,820 sq miles) **Population** 2,003,136 **Capital** Ljubljana (280,000) **Languages** Slovene **Currency** Euro = 100 cents **Website** www.gov.si

	🛣	⩓	△	🏙
⏲	130	100*	90*	50
If towing				
⏲	80	80*	80*	50

*70kph in urban areas

💺 Compulsory in front seats and, if fitted, in rear

👶 Under 12 only allowed in the front seats with special seat; babies must use child safety seat

🍷 0.05%

△ Compulsory ✚ Compulsory

💡 Compulsory 🧯 Recommended

⛑ Compulsory for all riders

⊖ 18 (motorbikes up to 125cc – 16, up to 350cc – 18)

📱 Only allowed with hands-free kit

★ At least 4mm of tread in winter; winter tyres and snow chains necessary but not compulsory

★ Dipped headlights must be used at all times

★ Vignettes valid for variety of periods compulsory for vehicles below 3.5 tonnes for toll roads. Write your vehicle registration number on the vignette before displaying it. For heavier vehicles electronic tolling system applies; several routes are cargo-traffic free during high tourist season.

★ Visibility vest compulsory

Spain España (E)

Area 497,548 sq km (192,103 sq miles) **Population** 40,548,753 **Capital** Madrid (6,386,932) **Languages** Castilian Spanish (official), Catalan, Galician, Basque **Currency** Euro = 100 cents **Website** www.la-moncloa.es/index.htm

	🛣	⩓	△	🏙
⏲	120	100	90	50
If towing				
⏲	80	80	70	50

💺 Compulsory in front seats and if fitted in rear seats

👶 Under 12 not allowed in front seats except in a child safety seat; in rear children under 135cm must use child restraint system

🍷 0.05% (0.3% if vehicle over 3.5 tonnes or carries more than 9 passengers; 0.01% for drivers with less than 2 years' experience)

△ Two compulsory (one for in front, one for behind)

✚ Recommended

💡 Compulsory 🧯 Recommended

⛑ Compulsory for all riders

⊖ 18 (18/21 heavy vehicles; 18 for motorbikes over 125cc; 16 for motorbikes up to 125cc; 14 for mopeds up to 75cc)

📄 Third party insurance

📱 Only allowed with hands-free kit

★ Radar-detection equipment is prohibited

★ Snow chains recommended for mountainous areas in winter

★ Tolls on motorways

★ Visibility vest compulsory

★ Wearers of spectacles or contact lenses must carry a spare pair in their vehicle at all times.

Sweden Sverige (S)

Area 449,964 sq km (173,731 sq miles) **Population** 9,074,055 **Capital** Stockholm (2,019,182) **Languages** Swedish (official), Finnish **Currency** Swedish krona = 100 ore **Website** www.sweden.gov.se

	🛣	⩓	△	🏙
⏲	110	90	70	50
If towing trailer with brakes				
⏲	80	80	70	50

💺 Compulsory in front and rear seats

👶 Under 7 must have safety seat or other suitable restraint

🍷 0.02%

△ Compulsory ✚ Recommended

💡 Recommended 🧯 Recommended

⛑ Compulsory for all riders

⊖ 18 📄 Third party insurance

📱 No legislation

LEZ Gothenberg, Helsingborg, Lund, Malmo and Stockholm have LEZs. Sticker system.

★ Dipped headlights must be used at all times

★ New, more variable and often lower, speed limits introduced during 2009

★ Radar-detection equipment is prohibited

Switzerland Schweiz (CH)

Area 41,284 sq km (15,939 sq miles) **Population** 7,623,438 **Capital** Bern (122,925) **Languages** French, German, Italian, Romansch (all official) **Currency** Swiss Franc = 100 centimes / rappen **Website** www.admin.ch

	🛣	⩓	△	🏙
⏲	120	80	80	50/30
If towing up to 1 tonne / over 1 tonne				
⏲	80	80	60/80	30/50

💺 Compulsory in front and, if fitted, in rear

👶 Under 7 not allowed in front seats unless in child restraint; between 7 and 12 must use child restraint or seatbelt

🍷 0.05% △ Compulsory ✚ Recommended

💡 Recommended 🧯 Recommended

⛑ Compulsory for all riders

⊖ 18 (mopeds up to 50cc – 16)

📄 Third party insurance

📱 Only allowed with a hands-free kit

★ Wearers of spectacles or contact lenses must carry a spare pair in their vehicle at all times

★ Motorways are all toll and for vehicles below 3.5 tonnes a vignette must be purchased at the border. The vignette is valid for one calendar year. Vehicles over 3.5 tonnes must have an electronic tag for travel on any road.

★ Winter tyres recommended Nov–Mar; snow chains compulsory in designated areas in poor winter weather

★ Radar-detection equipment is prohibited

★ GPS systems that indicate the position of speed cameras must have this function deactivated

★ Picking up hitchhikers is prohibited on motorways and main roads

Turkey Türkiye (TR)

Area 774,815 sq km (299,156 sq miles)
Population 77,804,122 **Capital** Ankara (3,763,591) **Languages** Turkish (official), Kurdish **Currency** New Turkish lira = 100 kurus
Website www.tbmm.gov.tr

	120	90	90	50
If towing				
	70	70	70	40

Compulsory in front seats
Under 10 not allowed in front seats
0.05% for private cars not towing, 0.0% for all other drivers
Two compulsory (one in front, one behind)
Compulsory Compulsory Compulsory
Compulsory for all riders
18
International driving permit advised; note that Turkey is in both Europe and Asia
Prohibited
★ Tow rope and tool kit must be carried
★ Several motorways, and the Bosphorus bridges are toll roads
★ Dipped headlights compulsory in daylight hours

Ukraine Ukraina (UA)

Area 603,700 sq km (233,088 sq miles)
Population 45,415,596 **Capital** Kiev / Kyviv (2,819,566) **Languages** Ukrainian (official), Russian **Currency** Hryvnia = 100 kopiykas
Website www.president.gov.ua/en

	130	90	90	60
If towing				
	80	80	80	60

Speed limit in pedestrian zone 20 kph
Compulsory in front and rear seats
Under 12 not allowed in front seats
0.0%
Compulsory Compulsory
Optional Compulsory
Compulsory for all riders
18 cars; 16 motorbikes
International driving permit; visa; International Registration Certificate recommended.
No legislation
★ A road tax is payable on entry to the country.
★ Tow rope and tool kit recommended

United Kingdom (GB)

Area 241,857 sq km (93,381 sq miles)
Population 61,284,806 **Capital** London (8,505,000) **Languages** English (official), Welsh (also official in Wales), Gaelic **Currency** Sterling (pound) = 100 pence
Website www.direct.gov.uk

	112	112	96	48
If towing				
	96	96	80	48

Compulsory in front seats and if fitted in rear seats
Under 3 not allowed in front seats except with appropriate restraint, and in rear must use child restraint if available; 3–12 and under 150cm must use appropriate restraint or seat belt in front seats, and in rear if available
0.08%
Recommended Recommended
Recommended Recommended
Compulsory for all riders
17 (16 for mopeds)
Only allowed with hands-free kit
LEZ London's LEZ operates by number-plate recognition; non-compliant vehicles face hefty daily charges. Foreign-registered vehicles must register.
★ Driving is on the left
★ Smoking is banned in all commercial vehicles
★ Some toll motorways and bridges

Ski Resorts

The resorts listed are popular ski centres, therefore road access to most is normally good and supported by road clearing during snow falls. However, mountain driving is never predictable and drivers should make sure they take suitable snow chains as well as emergency provisions and clothing. Listed for each resort are: the atlas page and grid square; the altitude; the number of lifts (the total for directly linked resorts); the season start and end dates; the nearest town (with its distance in km) and the telephone number of the local tourist information centre or ski centre ('00' prefix required for calls from the UK).

Andorra

Pyrenees

Pas de la Casa / Grau Roig 91 A4 2640m 67 lifts Dec–Apr •Andorra La Vella (30km) +376 855292 http://pas-de-la-casa-grau-roig.andorramania.com *Access via Envalira Pass (2407m), highest in Pyrenees, snow chains essential.*

Austria

Alps

A 24-hour driving conditions information line is provided by the Tourist Office of Austria www.austria.info 0845 1011818

Bad Gastein 72 A3 1002m 51 lifts Dec–Mar •St Johann im Pongau (45km) +43 6432 85044 www.skigastein.com *Snow report: +43 6432 64555.*

Bad Hofgastein 72 A3 860m 51 lifts Dec–Apr •St Johann im Pongau (40km) +43 6432 3393260 www.badhofgastein.com

Bad Kleinkirchheim 72 B3 1100m 25 lifts Dec–Mar •Villach (35km) +43 4240 8212 www.badkleinkirchheim.at *Snowfone:+43 4240 8222.*

Ehrwald 71 A5 1000m 24 lifts Dec–Apr •Imst (30km) +43 512 5351 553 www.tiscover.at/ehrwald *Weather report: +43 5673 3329*

Innsbruck 71 A6 574m 78 lifts Dec–Apr •Innsbruck +43 5125 9850 www.ski-innsbruck.at *Motorway normally clear. The motorway through to Italy and through the Arlberg Tunnel are both toll roads.*

Ischgl 71 A5 1400m 41 lifts Dec–May •Landeck (25km) +43 50990 100 www.ischgl.com *Car entry to resort prohibited between 2200hrs and 0600hrs.*

Kaprun 72 A2 885m, 25 lifts Nov–Apr •Zell am See (10km) +43 6542 770 www.zellamsee-kaprun.com *Snowfone:+43 6547 73684.*

Kirchberg in Tirol 72 A2 860m 55 lifts Nov–Apr •Kitzbühel (6km) +43 5357 2000 www.kirchberg.at *Easily reached from Munich International Airport (120 km)*

Kitzbühel (Brixen im Thale) 72 A2 800m 55 lifts Nov–Apr •Wörgl (40km) +43 5334 84330 www.kitzbuehel-alpen.com

Lech/Oberlech 71 A5 1450m 80 lifts Dec–Apr •Bludenz (50km) +43 5583 21610 www.lech-zuers.at *Roads normally cleared but keep chains accessible because of altitude. Road conditions report tel +43 5583 1515.*

Mayrhofen 72 A1 630m 51 lifts Dec–Apr •Jenbach (35km) +43 5285 67600 www.mayrhofen.at *Chains rarely required.*

Obertauern 72 A3 1740m 26 lifts Dec–Apr •Radstadt (20km) +43 6456 7252 www.obertauern.com *Roads normally cleared but chain accessibility recommended. Camper vans and caravans not allowed; park these in Radstadt*

Saalbach Hinterglemm 72 A2 1003m 55 lifts Nov–Apr •Zell am See (19km) +43 6541 6800 68 www.saalbach.com *Both village centres are pedestrianised and there is a good ski bus service during the daytime*

St Anton am Arlberg 71 A5 1304m 80 lifts Dec–Apr •Innsbruck (104km) +43 5446 22690 www.stantonamarlberg.com *Snow report tel +43 5446 2565*

Schladming 72 A3 2708m 88 lifts Dec–Mar •Schladming + 43 36 87 233 10 www.schladming-dachstein.at

Serfaus 71 A5 1427m 70 lifts Dec–Apr •Landeck (30km) +43 5476 6239 www.serfaus-fiss-ladis.at *Private vehicles banned from village, use world's only 'hover'-powered underground railway.*

Sölden 71 B6 1377m, 33 lifts Sep-Apr (glacier); Nov-Apr (main area) •Imst (50km) +43 572 000 200 www.soelden.com *Roads normally cleared but snow chains recommended because of altitude. The route from Italy and the south over the Timmelsjoch via Obergurgl is closed Oct-May and anyone arriving from the south should use the Brenner Pass motorway. Snow information tel +43 5254 2666.*

Zell am See 72 A2 758m 28 lifts Dec–Mar •Zell am See +43 6542 770 www.zellamsee-kaprun.com *Snowfone +43 6542 73694 Low altitude, so good access and no mountain passes to cross.*

Zell im Zillertal (Zell am Ziller) 72 A1 580m 51 lifts Dec–Apr •Jenbach (25km) +43 5282 2281 www.zell.at *Snowfone +43 5282 716526.*

Zürs 71 A5 1720m 80 lifts Dec–Apr •Bludenz (30km) +43 5583 2245 www.lech-zuers.at *Roads normally cleared but keep chains accessible because of altitude. Village has garage with 24-hour self-service gas/petrol, breakdown service and wheel chains supply.*

France

Alps

Alpe d'Huez 79 A5 1860m 85 lifts Dec–Apr •Grenoble (63km) +33 4 76 11 44 44 www.alpedhuez.com *Snow chains may be required on access road to resort. Road report tel +33 4 76 11 44 50.*

Avoriaz 70 B1 2277m 34 lifts Dec–May •Morzine (14km) +33 4 50 74 02 11 www.avoriaz.com *Chains may be required for access road from Morzine. Car-free resort, park on edge of village. Horse-drawn sleigh service available.*

Chamonix-Mont-Blanc 70 C1 1035m 47 lifts Dec–May •Martigny (38km) +33 4 50 53 00 24 www.chamonix.com

Chamrousse 79 A4 1700m 26 lifts Dec–Apr •Grenoble (30km) +33 4 76 89 92 65 www.chamrousse.com *Roads normally cleared, keep chains accessible because of altitude.*

Châtel 70 B1 2200m 45 lifts Dec–Apr •Thonon-Les-Bains (35km) +33 4 50 73 22 44 http://info.chatel.com/english-version.html

Courchevel 70 C1 1850m 62 lifts Dec–Apr •Moûtiers (23km) +33 4 79 08 00 29 www.courchevel.com *Roads normally cleared but keep chains accessible. Traffic 'discouraged' within the four resort bases. Traffic info: +33 4 79 37 73 37.*

Flaine 70 B1 1800m 29 lifts Dec–Apr •Cluses (25km) +33 4 50 90 80 01 www.flaine.com *Keep chains accessible for D6 from Cluses to Flaine. Car access for depositing luggage and passengers only. 1500-space car park outside resort. Road conditions report tel +33 4 50 25 20 50. Near Sixt-Fer-á-Cheval.*

La Clusaz 69 C6 1100m 55 lifts Dec–Apr •Annecy (32km) +33 4 50 32 65 00 www.laclusaz.com *Roads normally clear but keep chains accessible for final road from Annecy.*

La Plagne 70 C1 2100m 102 lifts Dec–Apr Moûtiers (32km) +33 4 79 09 79 79 www.la-plagne.com *Ten different centres up to 2100m altitude. Road access via Bozel, Landry or Aime normally cleared. Linked to Les Arcs by cablecar*

Les Arcs 70 C1 2600m 77 lifts Dec–May •Bourg-St-Maurice (15km) +33 4 79 07 12 57 www.lesarcs.com *Three base areas up to 2000 metres; keep chains accessible. Pay parking at edge of each base resort. Linked to La Plagne by cablecar*

Les Carroz d'Araches 70 B1 1140m 80 lifts Dec–Apr •Cluses (13km) +33 50 90 00 04 www.lescarroz.com

Les Deux-Alpes 79 B5 1650m 55 lifts Dec–Apr •Grenoble (75km) +33 4 76 79 22 00 www.les2alpes.com *Roads normally cleared, however snow chains recommended for D213 up from valley road (D1091).*

Les Gets 70 B1 1172m 52 lifts Dec–Apr •Cluses (18km) +33 4 50 75 80 80 www.lesgets.com

Les Ménuires 69 C6 1815m 40 lifts Dec–Apr •Moûtiers (27km) +33 4 79 00 73 00 www.lesmenuires.com *Keep chains accessible for D117 from Moûtiers.*

Les Sept Laux 69 C6 1350m, 24 lifts Dec–Apr •Grenoble (38km) +33 4 76 08 17 86 www.les7laux.com *Roads normally cleared, however keep chains accessible for mountain road up from the A41 motorway. Near St Sorlin d'Arves.*

Megève 69 C6 2350m 79 lifts Dec–Apr •Sallanches (12km) +33 4 50 21 29 52 www.megeve.com *Horse-drawn sleigh rides available.*

Méribel 69 C6 1400m 61 lifts Dec–May •Moûtiers (18km) +33 4 79 08 60 01 www.meribel.net *Keep chains accessible for 18km to resort on D90 from Moûtiers.*

Morzine 70 B1 1000m 67 lifts, Dec–Apr •Thonon-Les-Bains (30km) +33 4 50 74 72 72 www.morzine-avoriaz.com

Pra Loup 79 B5 1600m 53 lifts Dec–Apr •Barcelonnette (10km) +33 4 92 84 10 04 www.praloup.com *Roads normally cleared but chains accessibility recommended.*

Risoul 79 B5 1850m 59 lifts Dec–Apr •Briançon (40km) +33 4 92 46 02 60 www.risoul.com *Keep chains accessible. Near Guillestre. Linked with Vars Les Claux*

St-Gervais Mont-Blanc 70 C1 850m 27 lifts Dec–Apr •Sallanches (10km) +33 4 50 47 76 08 www.st-gervais.com

Serre Chevalier 79 B5 1350m 77 lifts Dec–Apr •Briançon (10km) + 33 4 92 24 98 98 www.serre-chevalier.com *Made up of 13 small villages along the valley road, which is normally cleared.*

Tignes 70 C1 2100m 47 lifts Jan–Dec •Bourg St Maurice (26km) +33 4 79 40 04 40 www.tignes.net *Keep chains accessible because of altitude. Parking information tel +33 4 79 06 39 45.*

Val d'Isère 70 C1 1850m 50 lifts Nov–May •Bourg-St-Maurice (30km) +33 4 79 06 06 60 www.valdisere.com *Roads normally cleared but keep chains accessible.*

Val Thorens 69 C6 2300m 29 lifts Dec–Apr •Moûtiers (37km) +33 4 79 00 08 08 www.valthorens.com *Chains essential – highest ski resort in Europe. Obligatory paid parking on edge of resort.*

Valloire 69 C6 1430m 33 lifts Dec–Apr •Modane (20km) +33 4 79 59 03 96 www.valloire.net *Road normally clear up to the Col du Galbier, to the south of the resort, which is closed from 1st November to 1st June. Linked to Valmeinier.*

Valmeinier 69 C6 2600m 34 lifts Dec–Apr •St Michel de Maurienne (47km) +33 4 79 59 53 69 www.valmeinier.com *Access from north on D1006 / D902. Col du Galbier, to the south of the resort closed from 1st November to 1st June. Linked to Valloire.*

Valmorel 69 C6 1400m 38 lifts Dec–Apr •Moûtiers (15km) +33 4 79 09 85 55 www.valmorel.com *Near St Jean-de-Belleville. Linked with ski areas of Doucy-Combelouvière and St François-Longchamp.*

Vars Les Claux 79 B5 1850m 59 lifts Dec–Apr •Briançon (40km) +33 4 92 46 51 31 www.vars-ski.com *Four base resorts up to 1850 metres. Keep chains accessible. Road and weather information tel +33 4 36 68 02 05 and +33 4 91 78 78 78. Snowfone +33 492 46 51 04. Linked with Risoul.*

Villard de Lans 79 A4 1050m 28 lifts Dec–Apr •Grenoble (32km) ☎+33 4 76 95 10 38 🖳www.villarddelans.com

Pyrenees

Font-Romeu 91 A5 1800m 25 lifts Nov–Apr •Perpignan (87km) ☎+33 4 68 30 68 30 🖳www.font-romeu.fr *Roads normally cleared but keep chains accessible.*

St Lary-Soulan 77 D3 830m 32 lifts Dec–Mar •Tarbes (75km) ☎+33 5 62 39 50 81 🖳www.saintlary.com *Access roads constantly cleared of snow.*

Vosges

La Bresse-Hohneck 60 B2 900m 33 lifts Dec–Mar •Cornimont (6km) ☎+33 3 29 25 41 29 🖳www.labresse.net

Germany

Alps

Garmisch-Partenkirchen 71 A6 702m 39 lifts Dec–Apr •Munich (95km) ☎+49 8821 180 700 🖳www.gapa.de *Roads usually clear, chains rarely needed.*

Oberaudorf 62 C3 483m 22 lifts Dec–Apr •Kufstein (15km) ☎+49 8033 301 20 🖳www.oberaudorf.de *Motorway normally kept clear. Near Bayrischzell.*

Oberstdorf 71 A5 815m 27 lifts Dec–Apr •Sonthofen (15km) ☎+49 8322 7000 🖳http://oberstdorf.de *Snow information on tel +49 8322 3035 or 1095 or 5757.*

Rothaargebirge

Winterberg 51 B4 700m 19 lifts Dec–Mar •Brilon (30km) ☎+49 2981 925 00 🖳www.winterberg.de *Roads usually cleared, chains rarely required.*

Greece

Central Greece

Mount Parnassos: Kelaria-Fterolakka 116 D4 1750–1950m 13 lifts Dec–Apr •Amfiklia ☎Kelaria +30 22340 22693-5, Fterolakka 22340 22373 🖳www.parnassos-ski.gr/en

Mount Parnassos: Gerondovrahos 116 D4 1800–2390m 3 lifts Dec–Apr •Amfiklia ☎+30 29444 70371

Ipiros

Mount Pindos: Karakoli 116 C3 1350–1700m 1 lift Dec–Mar •Metsovo ☎+30 2656 41211

Mount Pindos: Profitis Ilias 116 C3 1500–1700m 3 lifts Dec–Mar •Metsovo ☎+30 26560 41095

Peloponnisos

Mount Helmos: Kalavrita Ski Centre 117 D4 1650–2340m 7 lifts Dec–Mar •Kalavrita ☎+30 2692 2261

Mount Menalo: Ostrakina 117 E4 1600m 3 lifts Dec–Mar •Tripoli ☎+30 27960 22227

Macedonia

Mount Falakro: Agio Pneuma 116 A6 1720m 2 lifts Dec–Apr •Drama ☎+30 25210 62224 🖳www.falakro.gr (Greek only)

Mount Vasilitsa: Vasilitsa 116 B3 1750m 3 lifts Dec–Mar •Konitsa ☎+30 24620 84100 🖳www.vasilitsa.com (Greek only)

Mount Vermio: Seli 116 B4 1500m 7 lifts Dec–Mar •Kozani ☎+30 23310 71234 🖳www.seli-ski.gr (in Greek)

Mount Vermio: Tria-Pente Pigadia 116 B3 1420–2005m 4 lifts Dec–Mar •Ptolemaida ☎+30 23320 44464

Mount Verno: Vigla 116 B3 1650–1900m 3 lifts Dec–Mar •Florina ☎+30 23850 22354 🖳www.vigla-ski.gr (in Greek)

Mount Vrondous: Lailias 116 A5 1847m 2 lifts Dec–Mar •Serres ☎+30 23210 53790

Thessalia

Mount Pilio: Agriolefkes 116 C5 1500m 4 lifts Dec–Mar •Volos ☎+30 24280 73719 🖳www.skipilio.gr (Greek only)

Italy

Alps

Bardonecchia 79 A5 1312m 21 lifts Dec–Apr •Bardonecchia ☎+39 122 99032 Snowfone +39 122 907778 🖳www.bardonecchiaski.com *Resort reached through the 11km Frejus tunnel from France, roads normally cleared.*

Bórmio 71 B5 1225m 24 lifts Dec–Apr •Tirano (40km) ☎+39 342 902424 🖳www.bormio.com *Tolls payable in Ponte del Gallo Tunnel, open 0800hrs–2000hrs.*

Breuil-Cervinia 70 C2 2050m 21 lifts Jan–Dec •Aosta (54km) ☎+39 166 9444311 🖳www. cervinia.it *Snow chains strongly recommended. Bus from Milan airport.*

Courmayeur 70 C1 1224m 21 lifts Dec–Apr •Aosta (40km) ☎+39 165 842060 🖳www.turismo.courmayeur. ao.it *Access through the Mont Blanc tunnel from France. Roads constantly cleared.*

Limone Piemonte 80 B1 1050m 29 lifts Dec–Apr •Cuneo (27km) ☎+39 171 925280 🖳www.limonepiemonte.com *Roads normally cleared, chains rarely required. Snow report tel +39 171 926254.*

Livigno 71 B5 1816m 31 lifts Nov–May •Zernez (CH) (27km) ☎+39 342 052200 🖳www.livigno.com *Keep chains accessible. La Drosa Tunnel from Zernez, Switzerland, is open only from 0800hrs to 2000hrs.*

Sestrière 79 B5 2035m 92 lifts Dec–Apr •Oulx (22km) ☎+39 122 755444 🖳www.sestriere.it *One of Europe's highest resorts; although roads are normally cleared keep chains accessible.*

Appennines

Roccaraso – Aremogna 103 B7 1285m 24 lifts Dec–Apr •Castel di Sangro (7km) ☎+39 864 62210 🖳www.roccaraso.net

Dolomites

Andalo – Fai della Paganella 71 B5 1042m 19 lifts Dec–Apr •Trento (40km) 🖳www.paganella.net ☎+39 461 585588

Arabba 72 B1 2500m 29 lifts Dec–Apr •Brunico (45km) ☎+39 436 780019 🖳www.arabba.it *Roads normally cleared but keep chains accessible.*

Cortina d'Ampezzo 72 B2 1224m 37 lifts Dec–Apr •Belluno (72km) ☎+39 436 3231 🖳www.dolomiti.org/ dengl/cortina/index.html *Access from north on route 51 over the Cimabanche Pass may require chains.*

Corvara (Alta Badia) 72 B1 1568m 56 lifts Dec–Apr •Brunico (38km) ☎+39 471 836176 🖳www.altabadia.it *Roads normally clear but keep chains accessible.*

Madonna di Campiglio 71 B5 1550m 24 lifts Dec–Apr •Trento (60km) ☎+39 465 447501 🖳www.campiglio.net *Roads normally cleared but keep chains accessible. Linked to Folgarida and Marilleva.*

Moena di Fassa (Sorte/Ronchi) 72 B1 1184m 8 lifts Dec–Apr •Bolzano (40km) ☎+39 462 609500 🖳www.fassa.com

Selva di Val Gardena/Wolkenstein Groden 72 B1 1563m 81 lifts Dec–Apr •Bolzano (40km) ☎+39 471 777777 🖳www.valgardena.it *Roads normally cleared but keep chains accessible.*

Norway

Hemsedal 32 B5 650m 14 lifts Nov–May •Honefoss (150km) ☎+47 32 055030 🖳www.hemsedal.com *Be prepared for extreme weather conditions.*

Trysil (Trysilfjellet) 34 A4 465m 32 lifts Nov–Apr •Elverum (100km) 🖳www.trysilresort.com ☎+47 62 451000 *Be prepared for extreme weather conditions.*

Slovak Republic

Chopok (Jasna-Chopok) 65 B5 2024m 14 lifts Dec–Apr •Jasna ☎+421 907 886644 🖳www.jasna.sk

Donovaly 65 B5 1360m 14 lifts Nov–Apr •Ruzomberok ☎+421 48 4199900 🖳www.parksnow.sk/donovaly

Martinské Hole 65 A4 1456m 8 lifts Nov–May •Zilina ☎+421 43 430 6000 🖳www.martinky.com

Plejsy 65 B6 912m 9 lifts Dec–Mar •Krompachy ☎+421 53 429 8015 🖳www.plejsy.com

Strbske Pleso 65 A6 1915m 6 lifts Dec–Mar •Poprad ☎+421 52 449 2455 🖳www.parksnow.sk/tatry

Rohace 65 A5 1450m 6 lifts Dec–Apr •Liptovsky Mikulas ☎+421 43 5320777 🖳www.zuberec.sk

Slovenia

Julijske Alpe

Kanin (Bovec) 72 B3 2289m 4 lifts Dec–Apr •Bovec ☎+386 5 3841 919 🖳www.boveckanin.si/eng

Kobla (Bohinj) 72 B3 1480m 6 lifts Dec–Mar •Bohinjska Bistrica ☎+386 4 5747 100 🖳www.bohinj.si/kobla

Kranjska Gora 72 B3 1620m 20 lifts Dec–Mar •Kranjska Gora ☎+386 4 5809 440 🖳www.kranjska-gora.si

Vogel 72 B3 1800m 8 lifts Dec–Apr •Bohinjska Bistrica ☎+386 4 5729 712 🖳www.vogel.si

Kawiniske Savinjske Alpe

Krvavec 73 B4 1970m 13 lifts Dec–Apr •Kranj ☎+386 4 2525 930 🖳www.rtc-krvavec.si

Pohorje

Rogla 73 B5 1517m 13 lifts Dec–Apr •Slovenska Bistrica ☎+386 3 75 76 000 🖳www.rogla.si

Spain

Pyrenees

Baqueira-Beret/Bonaigua 90 A3 1500m 33 lifts Dec–Apr •Vielha (15km) ☎+34 973 639010 🖳www.baqueira.es *Roads normally clear but keep chains accessible. Snowfone tel +34 973 639025. Near Salardú.*

Sistema Penibetico

Sierra Nevada 100 B2 2102m 20 lifts Dec–May •Granada (32km) ☎+34 958 249100 🖳www.sierranevadaski.com (in Spanish) *Access road designed to be avalanche safe and is snow cleared. Snowfone +34 958 249119.*

Sweden

Idre Fjäll 115 F9 710m 33 lifts Nov–Apr •Mora (140km) ☎+46 253 41000 🖳www.idrefjall.se *Be prepared for extreme weather conditions.*

Sälen 34 A5 360m 100 lifts Nov–Apr •Malung (70km) ☎+46 280 880 50 🖳www.skistar.com/salen *Be prepared for extreme weather conditions.*

Switzerland

Alps

Adelboden 70 B2 1353m 55 lifts Dec–Apr •Frutigen (15km) ☎+41 33 673 80 80 🖳www.adelboden.ch *Linked with Lenk.*

Arosa 71 B4 1800m 16 lifts Dec–Apr •Chur (30km) ☎+41 81 378 70 20 🖳www.arosa.ch *Roads cleared but keep chains accessible because of high altitude (1800m).*

Crans Montana 70 B2 1500m 34 lifts Dec–Apr, Jul–Oct •Sierre (15km) ☎+41 27 485 04 04 🖳www.crans-montana.ch *Roads normally cleared, however keep chains accessible for ascent from Sierre.*

Davos 71 B4 1560m 38 lifts Nov–Apr •Davos ☎+41 81 415 21 21 🖳www.davos.ch

Engelberg 70 B3 1000m 26 lifts Nov–May •Luzern (39km) ☎+41 41 639 77 77 🖳www.engelberg.ch *Straight access road normally cleared.*

Flums (Flumserberg) 71 A4 1400m 17 lifts Dec–Apr •Buchs (25km) ☎+41 81 720 18 18 🖳www.flumsberg.ch *Roads normally cleared, but 1000-metre vertical ascent; keep chains accessible.*

Grindelwald 70 B3 1034m 20 lifts Dec–Apr •Interlaken (20km) ☎+41 33 854 12 12 🖳www.grindelwald.travel/en/welcome.cfm

Gstaad – Saanenland 70 B2 1050m 20 lifts Dec–Apr •Gstaad ☎+41 33 748 81 81 🖳www.gstaad.ch *Linked to Anzère.*

Klosters 71 B4 1191m 52 lifts Dec–Apr •Davos (10km) ☎+41 81 410 20 20 🖳www.klosters.ch *Roads normally clear but keep chains accessible.*

Leysin 70 B2 1263m 16 lifts Dec–Apr •Aigle (6km) ☎+41 24 493 33 00 🖳www.leysin.ch

Mürren 70 B2 1650m 12 lifts Dec–Apr •Interlaken (18km) ☎+41 33 856 86 86 🖳www.mymuerren.ch/en/welcome.cfm *No road access. Park in Strechelberg (1500 free places) and take the two-stage cable car.*

Nendaz 70 B2 1365m 20 lifts Nov–Apr •Sion (16km) ☎+41 27 289 55 89 🖳www.nendaz.ch *Roads normally cleared, however keep chains accessible for ascent from Sion. Near Vex.*

Saas-Fee 70 B2 1800m 23 lifts Jan–Dec •Brig (35km) ☎+41 27 958 18 58 🖳www.saas-fee.ch *Roads normally cleared but keep chains accessible because of altitude.*

St Moritz 71 B4 1856m 24 lifts Nov–May •Chur (89km) ☎+41 81 837 33 33 🖳www.stmoritz.ch *Roads normally cleared but keep chains accessible.*

Samnaun 71 B5 1846m 40 lifts Dec–May •Scuol (30km) ☎+41 81 868 58 58 🖳www.samnaun.ch *Roads normally cleared but keep chains accessible.*

Verbier 70 B2 1500m 17 lifts Nov–Apr, Jun–Jul •Martigny (27km) ☎+41 27 775 38 88 🖳www.verbier.ch *Roads normally cleared.*

Villars 70 B2 1253m 16 lifts Dec–Apr, Jun–Jul •Montreux (35km) ☎+41 24 495 32 32 🖳www.villars.ch *Roads normally cleared but keep chains accessible for ascent from N9. Near Bex.*

Wengen 70 B2 1270m 19 lifts Dec–Apr •Interlaken (12km) ☎+41 33 856 85 85 🖳www.mywengen.ch/en/welcome.cfm *No road access. Park at Lauterbrunnen and take mountain railway.*

Zermatt 70 B2 1620m 40 lifts all year •Brig (42km) ☎+41 27 966 81 00 🖳www.zermatt.ch *Cars not permitted in resort, park in Täsch (3km) and take shuttle train.*

Turkey

North Anatolian Mountains

Uludag 118 B4 2543m 13 lifts Dec–March •Bursa (36km) ☎+90 224 285 21 11

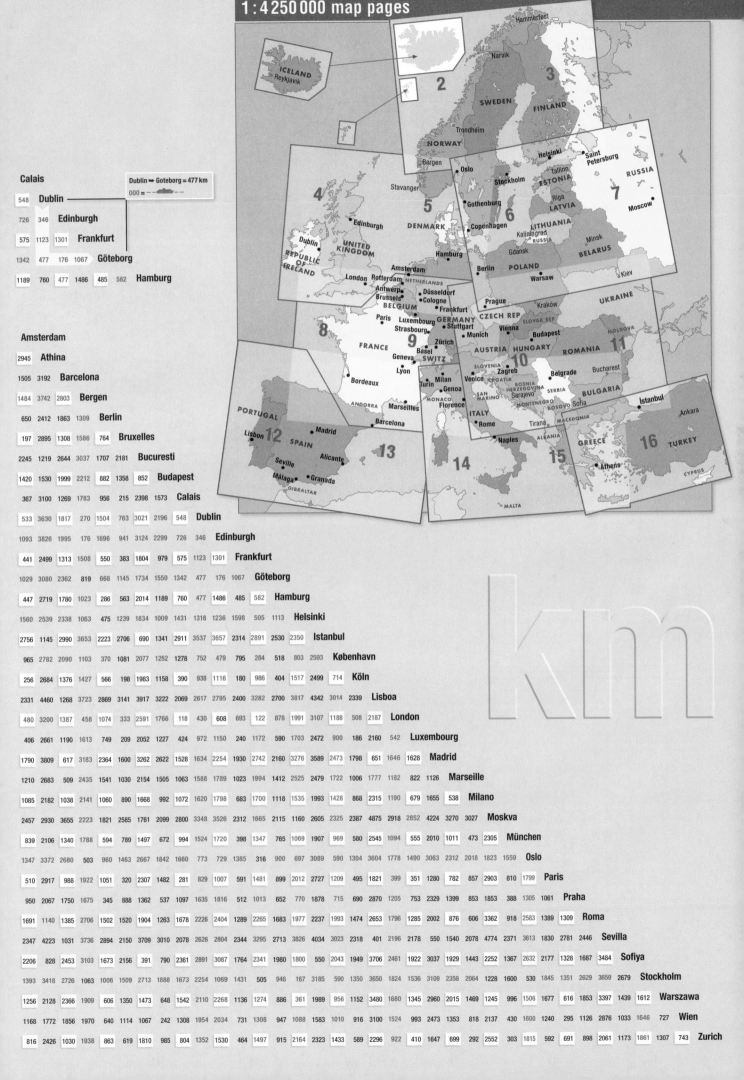

1:4 250 000 map pages

Dublin ⤳ Goteborg = 477 km

Calais					
548	**Dublin**				
726	346	**Edinburgh**			
575	1123	1301	**Frankfurt**		
1342	477	176	1067	**Göteborg**	
1189	760	477	1486	485	582 **Hamburg**

km

Amsterdam	Athina	Barcelona	Bergen	Berlin	Bruxelles	Bucuresti	Budapest	Calais	Dublin	Edinburgh	Frankfurt	Göteborg	Hamburg	Helsinki	Istanbul	København	Köln	Lisboa	London	Luxembourg	Madrid	Marseille	Milano	Moskva	München	Oslo	Paris	Praha	Roma	Sevilla	Sofiya	Stockholm	Warszawa	Wien	
2945	**Athina**																																		
1505	3192	**Barcelona**																																	
1484	3742	2803	**Bergen**																															
650	2412	1863	1309	**Berlin**																														
197	2895	1308	1586	764	**Bruxelles**																													
2245	1219	2644	3037	1707	2181	**Bucuresti**																												
1420	1530	1999	2212	882	1358	852	**Budapest**																											
367	3100	1269	1783	956	215	2398	1573	**Calais**																										
533	3630	1817	270	1504	763	3021	2196	548	**Dublin**																									
1093	3826	1995	176	1696	941	3124	2299	726	346	**Edinburgh**																								
441	2499	1313	1508	550	383	1804	979	575	1123	1301	**Frankfurt**																							
1029	3080	2362	819	668	1145	1734	1550	1342	477	176	1067	**Göteborg**																						
447	2719	1780	1023	286	563	2014	1189	760	477	1486	485	582	**Hamburg**																					
1560	2539	2338	1063	475	1239	1834	1009	1431	1318	1236	1598	505	1113	**Helsinki**																				
2756	1145	2990	3653	2223	2706	690	1341	2911	3537	3657	2314	2891	2530	2350	**Istanbul**																			
965	2782	2090	1103	370	1081	2077	1252	1278	752	479	795	284	518	803	2593	**København**																		
256	2684	1376	1427	566	198	1983	1158	390	938	1116	180	986	404	1517	2499	714	**Köln**																	
2331	4460	1268	3723	2869	3141	3917	3222	2069	2617	2795	2400	3282	2700	3817	4342	3014	2339	**Lisboa**																
480	3200	1387	458	1074	333	2591	1766	118	430	608	693	122	878	1991	3107	1188	508	2187	**London**															
406	2661	1190	1613	749	209	2052	1227	424	972	1150	240	1172	590	1703	2472	900	186	2160	542	**Luxembourg**														
1790	3809	617	3183	2364	1600	3262	2622	1528	1634	2254	1930	2742	2160	3276	3589	2473	1798	651	1646	1628	**Madrid**													
1210	2683	509	2435	1541	1030	2154	1505	1063	1588	1789	1023	1994	1412	2525	2479	1722	1006	1777	1182	822	1126	**Marseille**												
1085	2182	1038	2141	1060	890	1668	992	1072	1620	1798	683	1700	1118	1535	1993	1428	868	2315	1190	679	1655	538	**Milano**											
2457	2930	3655	2223	1821	2585	1761	2099	2800	3348	3526	2312	1665	2115	1160	2605	2325	2387	4875	2918	2852	4224	3270	3027	**Moskva**										
839	2106	1340	1788	594	789	1497	672	994	1524	1720	398	1347	765	1069	1907	969	580	2545	1094	555	2010	1011	473	2305	**München**									
1347	3372	2680	503	960	1463	2667	1842	1660	773	729	1385	316	900	697	3089	590	1304	3604	1778	1490	3063	2312	2018	1823	1559	**Oslo**								
510	2917	988	1922	1051	320	2307	1482	281	829	1007	591	1481	899	2012	2727	1209	495	1821	399	351	1280	782	857	2903	810	1799	**Paris**							
950	2067	1750	1675	345	888	1362	537	1097	1635	1816	512	1013	652	770	1878	715	690	2870	1205	753	2329	1399	853	1853	388	1305	1061	**Praha**						
1691	1140	1385	2706	1502	1520	1904	1263	1678	2226	2404	1289	2265	1683	1977	2237	1993	1474	2653	1796	1285	2002	876	606	3362	918	2583	1389	1309	**Roma**					
2347	4223	1031	3736	2894	2150	3709	3010	2078	2626	2804	2344	3295	2713	3826	4034	3023	2318	401	2196	2178	550	1540	2078	4774	2371	3613	1830	2781	2446	**Sevilla**				
2206	828	2453	3103	1673	2156	391	790	2361	2891	3087	1764	2341	1980	1800	550	2043	1949	3706	2461	1922	3037	1929	1443	2252	1367	2632	2177	1328	1687	3484	**Sofiya**			
1393	3418	2726	1063	1006	1509	2713	1888	1673	2254	1069	1431	505	946	167	3185	590	1350	3650	1824	1536	3109	2358	2064	1228	1600	530	1845	1351	2629	3659	2679	**Stockholm**		
1256	2128	2366	1909	606	1350	1473	648	1542	2110	2268	1136	1274	886	361	1989	956	1152	3480	1680	1345	2960	2015	1469	1245	996	1506	1677	616	1853	3397	1439	1612	**Warszawa**	
1168	1772	1856	1970	640	1114	1067	242	1308	1954	2034	731	1308	947	1088	1583	1010	916	3100	1524	993	2473	1353	818	2137	430	1600	1240	295	1126	2876	1033	1646	727	**Wien**
816	2426	1030	1938	863	619	1810	985	804	1352	1530	464	1497	915	2164	2323	1433	589	2296	922	410	1647	699	292	2552	303	1815	592	691	898	2061	1173	1861	1307	743 **Zurich**

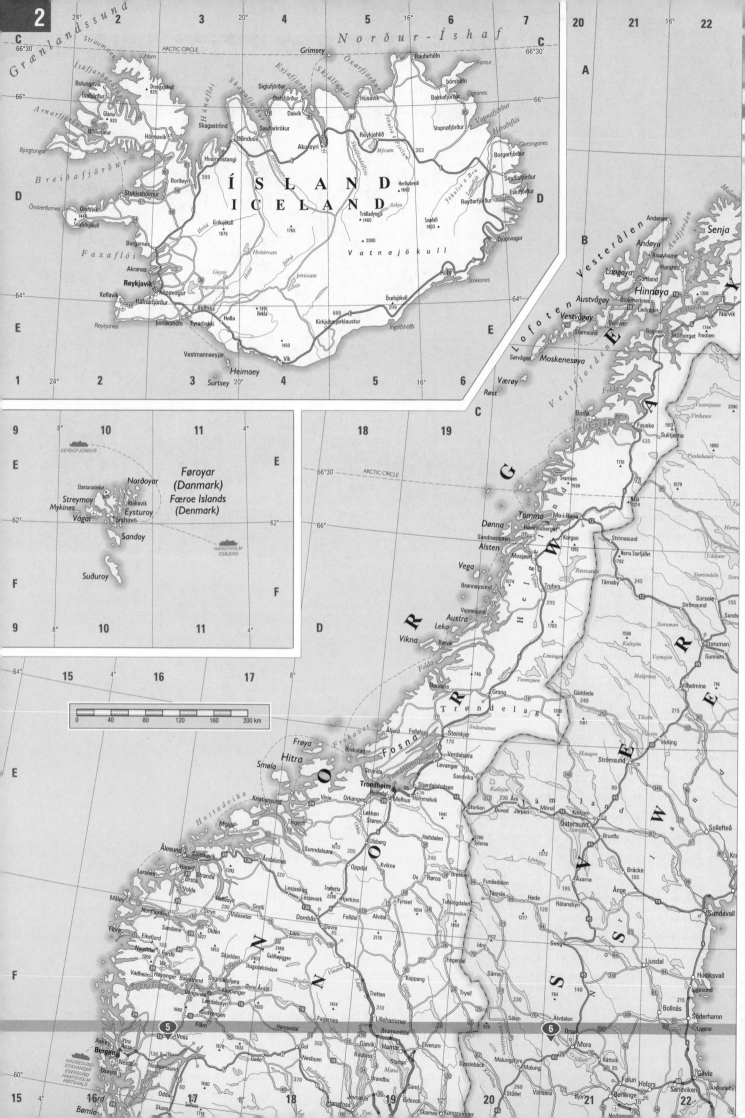

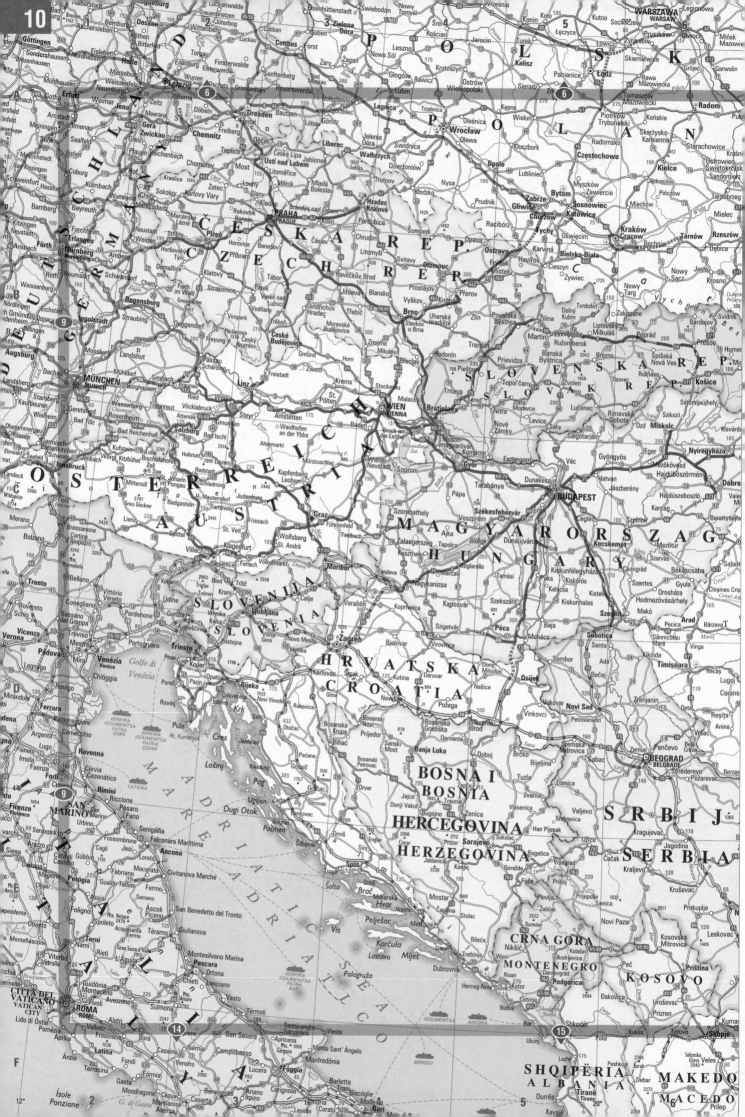

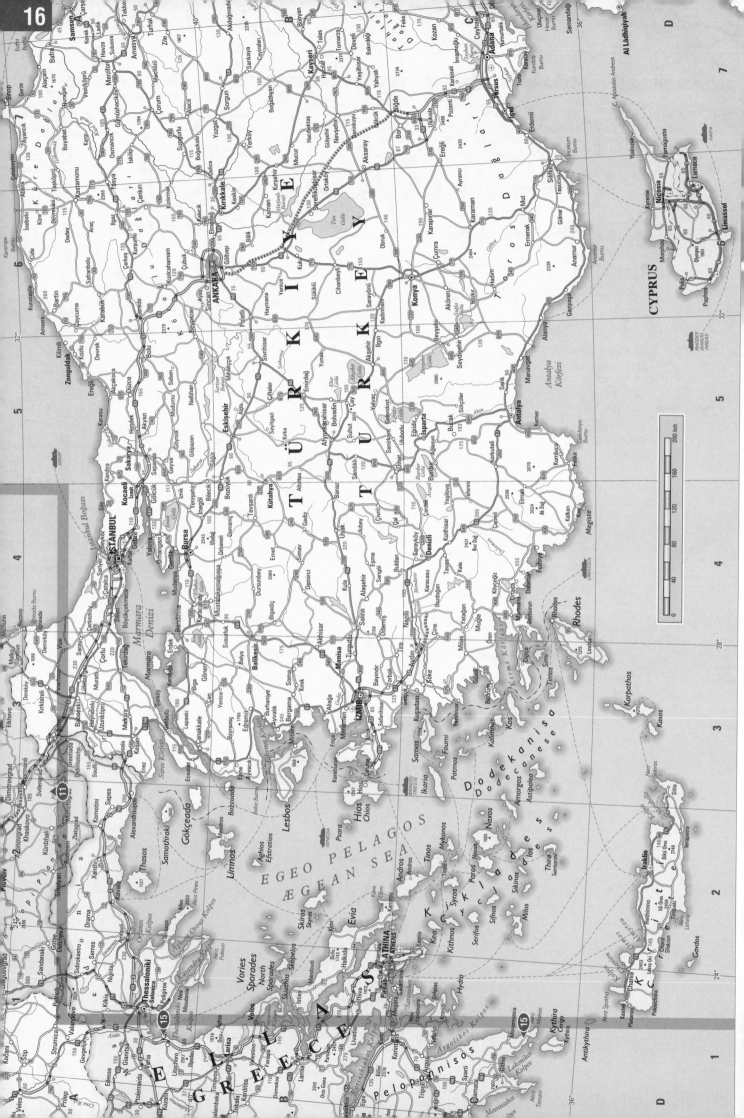

Key to road map pages

- ● **Florence** *Firenze* — City plan
- ☐ **İstanbul** — City approach map
- ■ **Milan** *Milano* — City plan and approach map

See pages 121–148 for city plans and approach maps

- **97** Map pages at 1:1 000 000
- **114** Map pages at 1:2 000 000

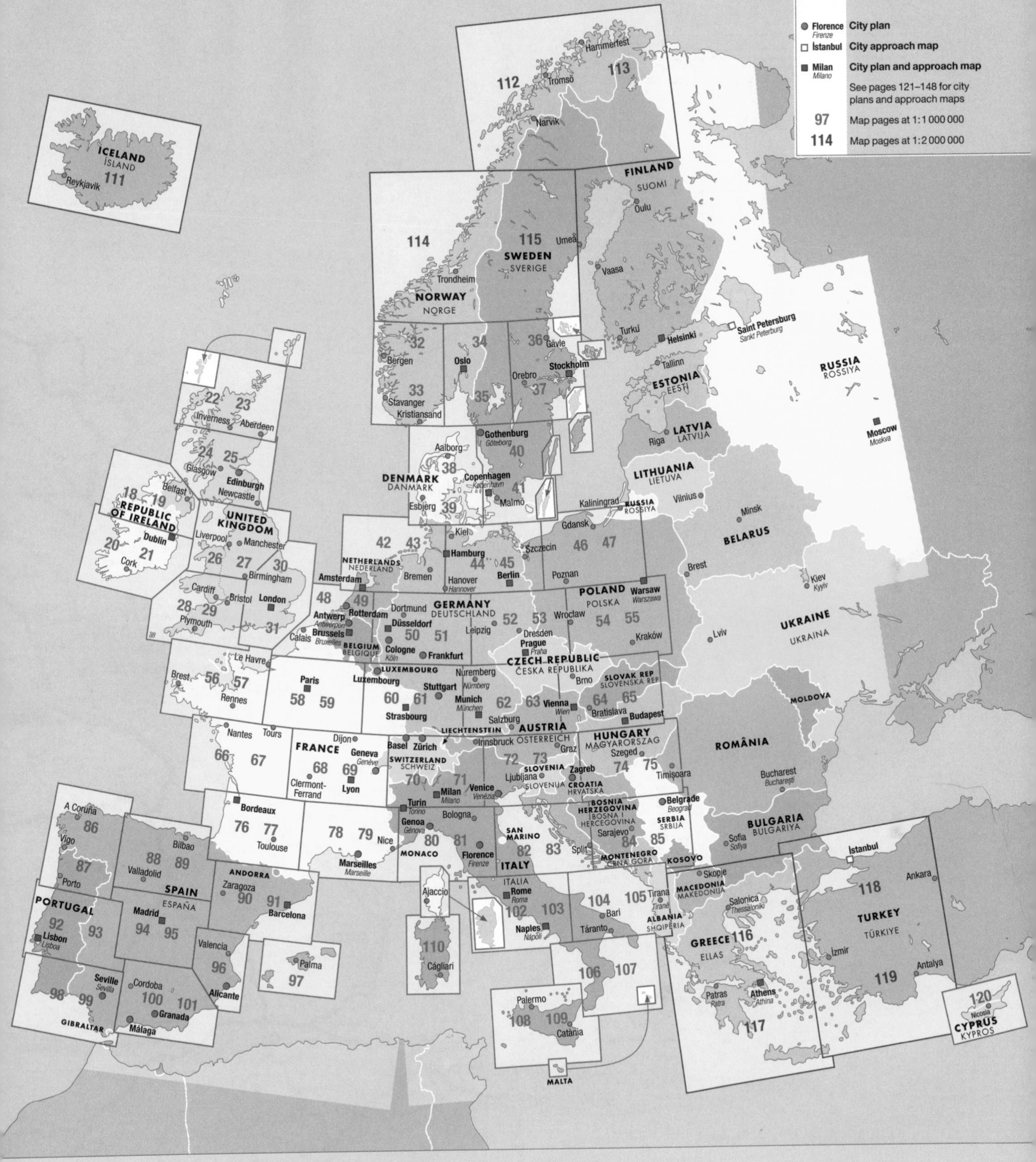

ICELAND ÍSLAND **111**
Reykjavik

112 Tromsö
113 Hammerfest
Narvik

FINLAND SUOMI
Oulu

114
115 **SWEDEN** SVERIGE
Umeå
Vaasa

NORWAY NORGE
Trondheim
32 Bergen
34 Oslo
36 Gävle
Turku
Helsinki
Saint Petersburg Sankt Peterburg
RUSSIA ROSSIYA

33 Stavanger
Kristiansand
35
37 Örebro
Stockholm

ESTONIA EESTI
Tallinn

38 Aalborg
40 Gothenburg Göteborg
Riga
LATVIA LATVIJA
Moscow Moskva

22 23 Inverness Aberdeen
24 25 Glasgow Edinburgh Newcastle
DENMARK DANMARK
Copenhagen København
41 Malmö
39 Esbjerg
Kaliningrad
RUSSIA ROSSIYA
Vilnius
Minsk
LITHUANIA LIETUVA
BELARUS

18 19 **REPUBLIC OF IRELAND** Belfast
UNITED KINGDOM
Liverpool Manchester
Kiel
Gdansk
Brest
Kiev Kyyiv

20 21 Dublin Cork
26 27 30 Birmingham
42 43 **Hamburg**
44 45 **Berlin**
Szczecin
46 47 Poznan
POLAND POLSKA
Warsaw Warszawa
Lviv
UKRAINE UKRAINA

28 29 Cardiff Bristol London
31
48 49 **NETHERLANDS** NEDERLAND Amsterdam
Bremen Hanover Hannover
52 53 Wroclaw
54 55
Kraków
MOLDOVA

Plymouth
Antwerp Antwerpen **Rotterdam** Dortmund **GERMANY** DEUTSCHLAND
Leipzig
Dresden
Brno
Prague Praha
CZECH REPUBLIC ČESKÁ REPUBLIKA
SLOVAK REP SLOVENSKÁ REP
ROMÂNIA

56 57 Brest Rennes
Calais Bruxelles **BELGIUM** BELGIQUE
Düsseldorf 50 51 Cologne Köln Frankfurt
62 61 60 Stuttgart
Munich München
63 **Vienna** Wien
64 65 Bratislava Budapest
Bucharest Bucuresti

Le Havre
LUXEMBOURG
Luxembourg
Nuremberg Nürnberg
Salzburg
HUNGARY MAGYARORSZAG
Sofia Sofiya

58 59 **Paris**
FRANCE
Strasbourg
LIECHTENSTEIN
AUSTRIA ÖSTERREICH
Innsbruck Graz
72 73 **SLOVENIA** SLOVENIJA Zagreb
74 75 Szeged
Timişoara
BULGARIA BULGARIYA

66 67 Nantes Tours
Dijon
Basel Zürich
68 69 Geneva Genève
SWITZERLAND SCHWEIZ
70 71 Ljubljana **CROATIA** HRVATSKA
Venice Venezia
Milan Milano
Turin Torino
ISTANBUL

Clermont-Ferrand Lyon
76 77 Bordeaux Toulouse
78 79 Nice
80 81 Bologna
Genoa Génova
MONACO
82 83 Split
SAN MARINO
BOSNIA HERZEGOVINA BOSNA HERCEGOVINA Sarajevo
Belgrade Beograd
SERBIA SRBIJA
84 85
MONTENEGRO CRNA GORA
KOSOVO
Skopje
MACEDONIA MAKEDONIJA
118 Ankara

A Coruña 86
Vigo 87 Porto
88 89 Bilbao
Valladolid
90 91 Zaragoza Barcelona
ANDORRA
Marseilles Marseille
Ajaccio
Florence Firenze
ITALY ITALIA
Rome Roma
104 105 Bari
Táranto
Tirana Tiranë
ALBANIA SHQIPERIA
Salonica Thessaloniki
TURKEY TÜRKİYE
İzmir

PORTUGAL
Lisbon Lisboa
92 93
94 95 **Madrid**
SPAIN ESPAÑA
Valencia
96
110 Cágliari
102 103
Naples Nápoli
106 107
GREECE ELLAS 116
119 Antalya

98 99 Seville Sevilla
100 101 Cordoba Granada
Alicante
97 Palma
Palermo
108 109 Catània
Patras Patra
Athens Athína
117
120 Nicosia
CYPRUS KYPROS

GIBRALTAR
Málaga
MALTA

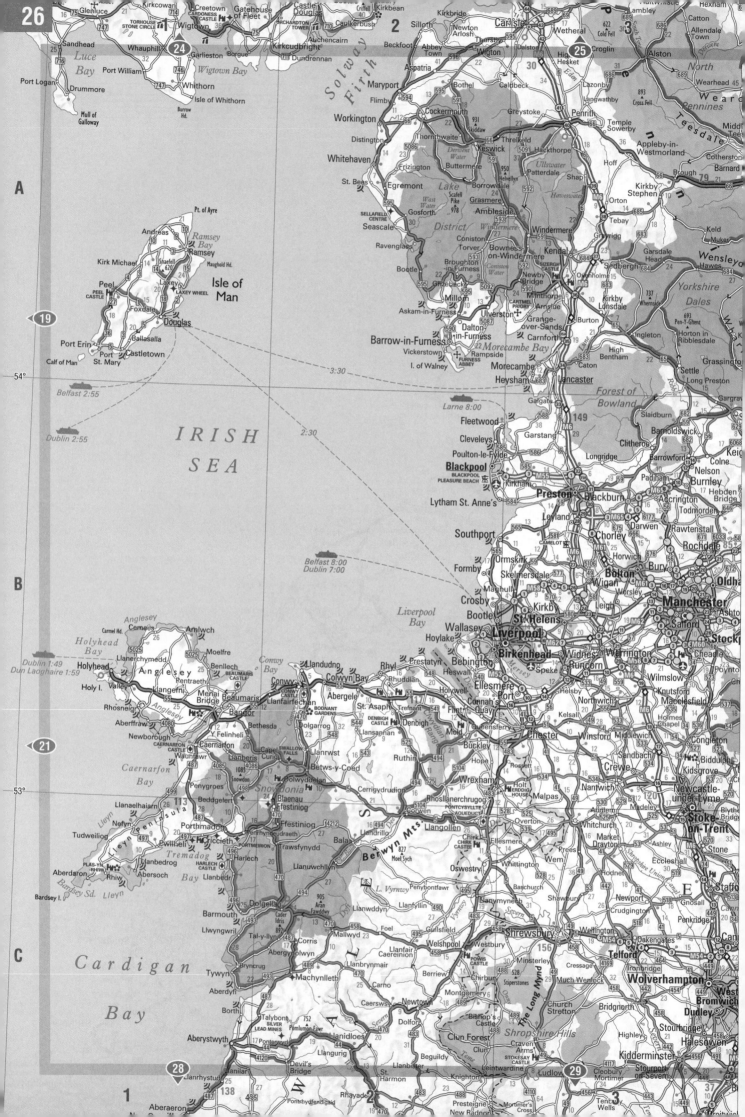

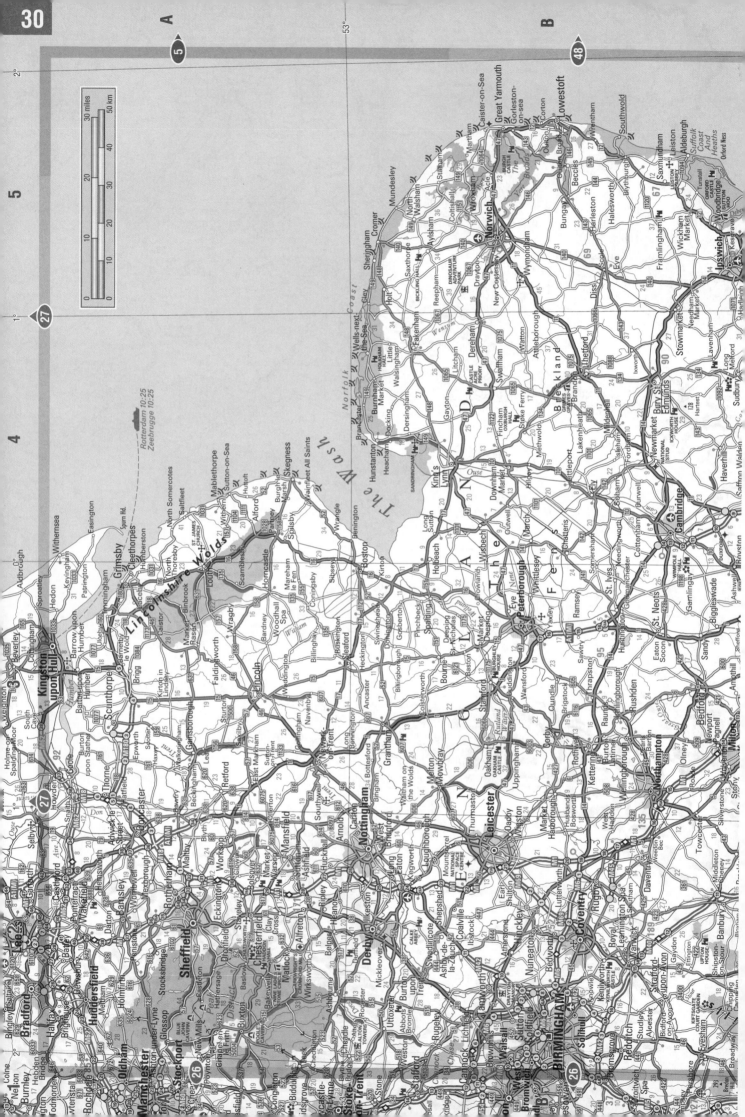

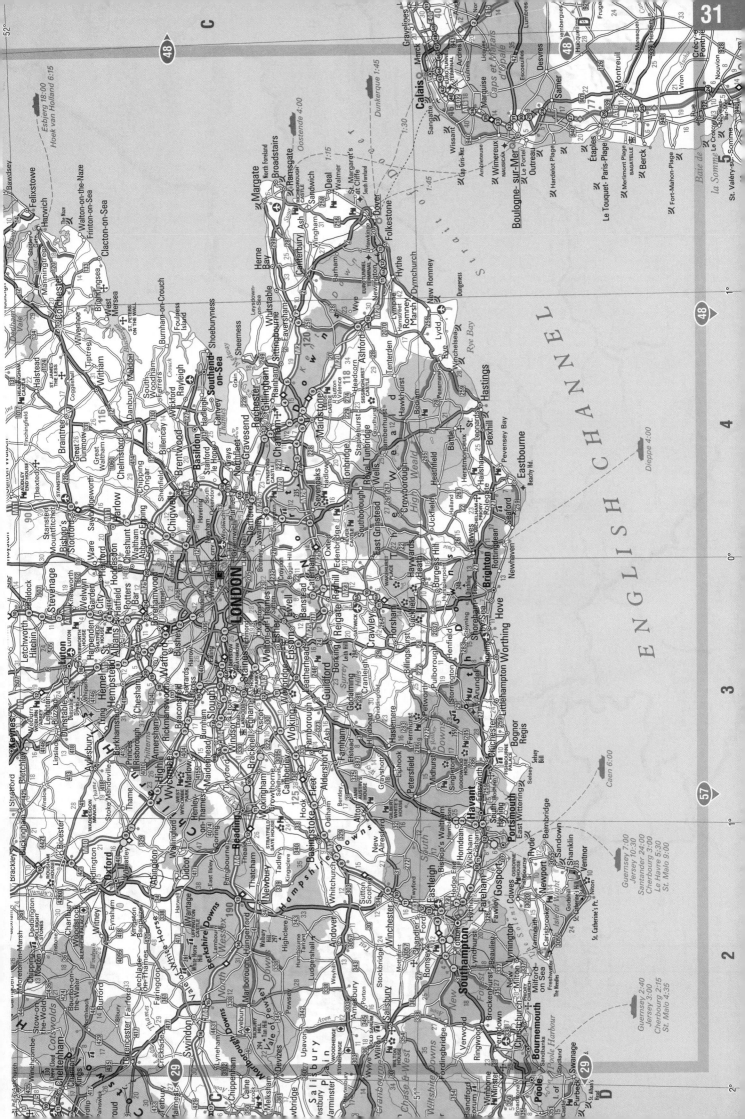

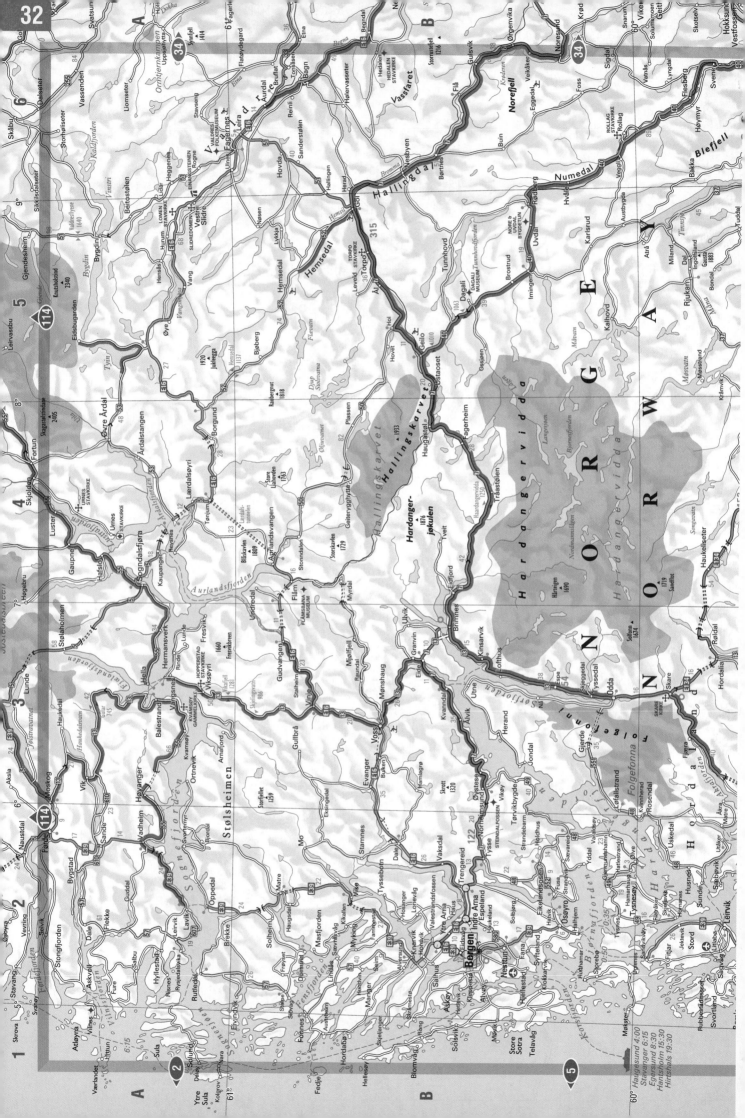

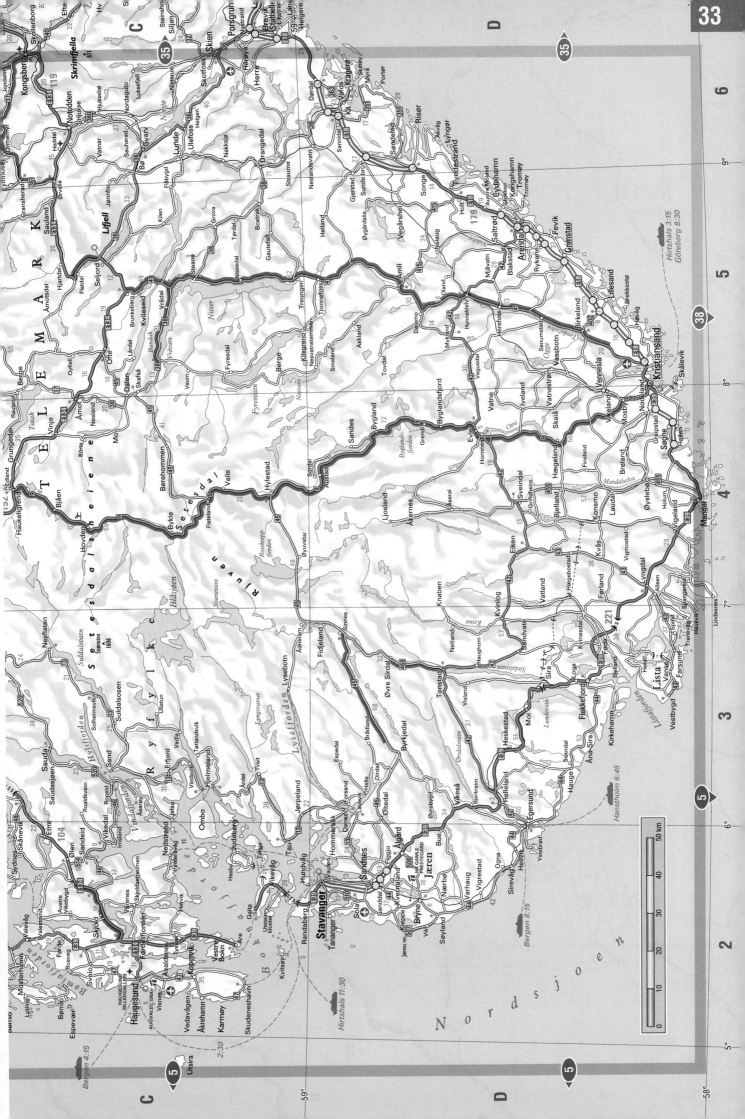

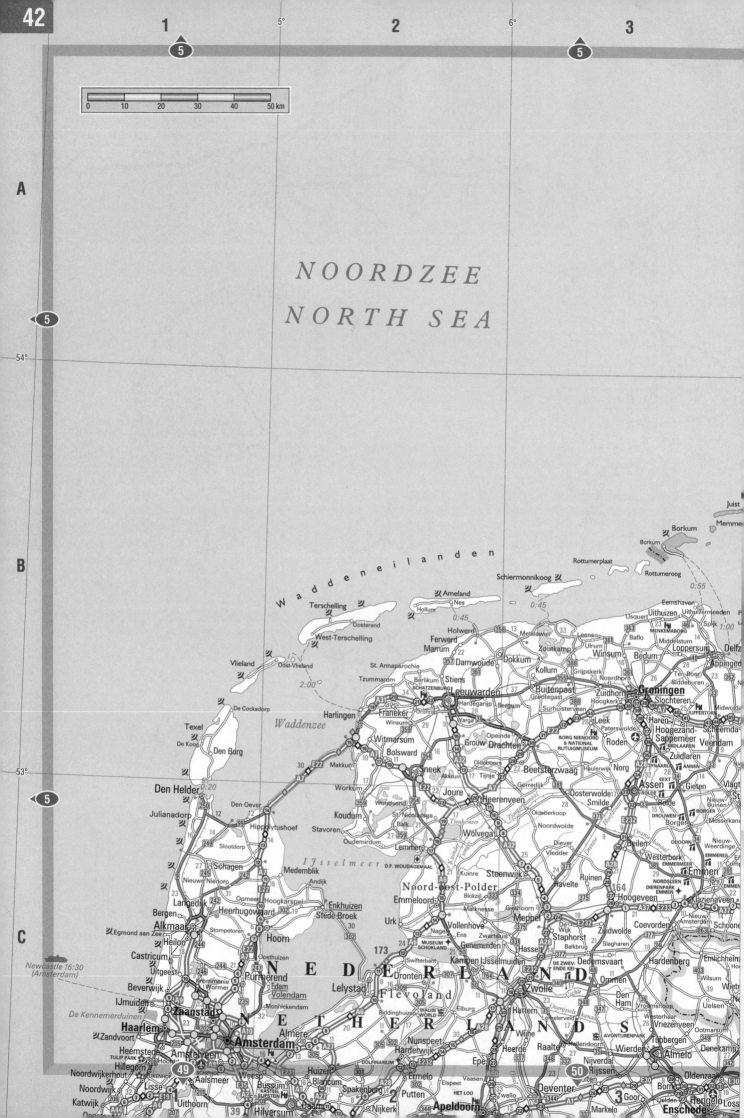

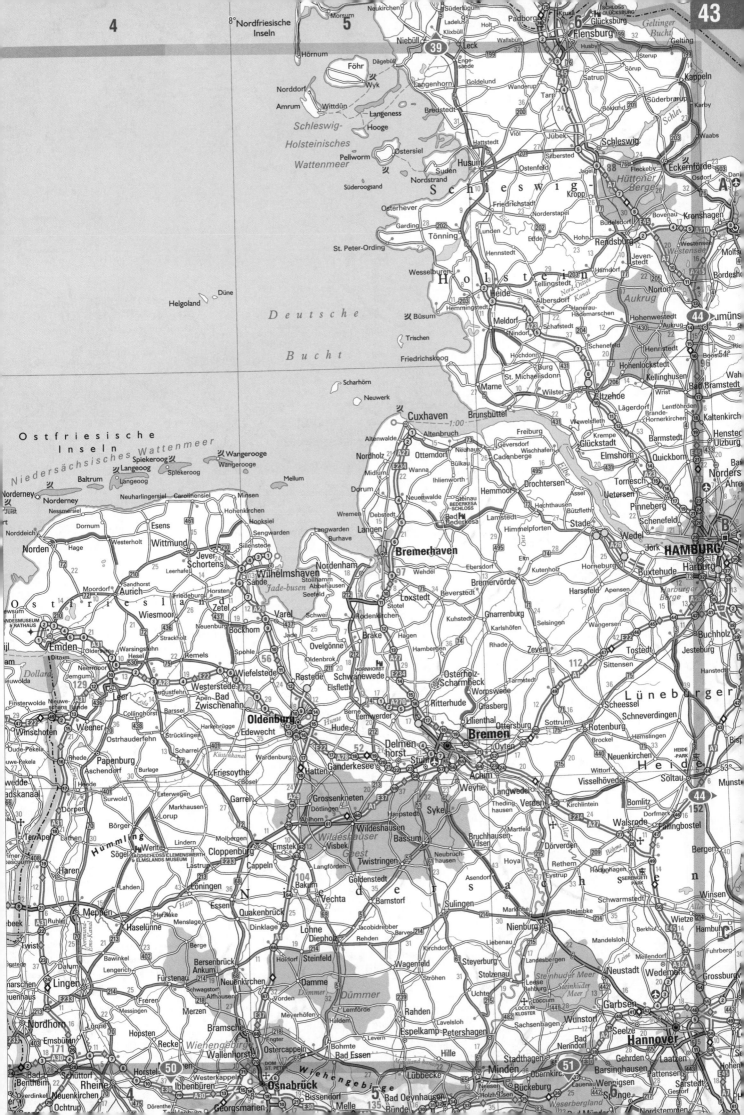

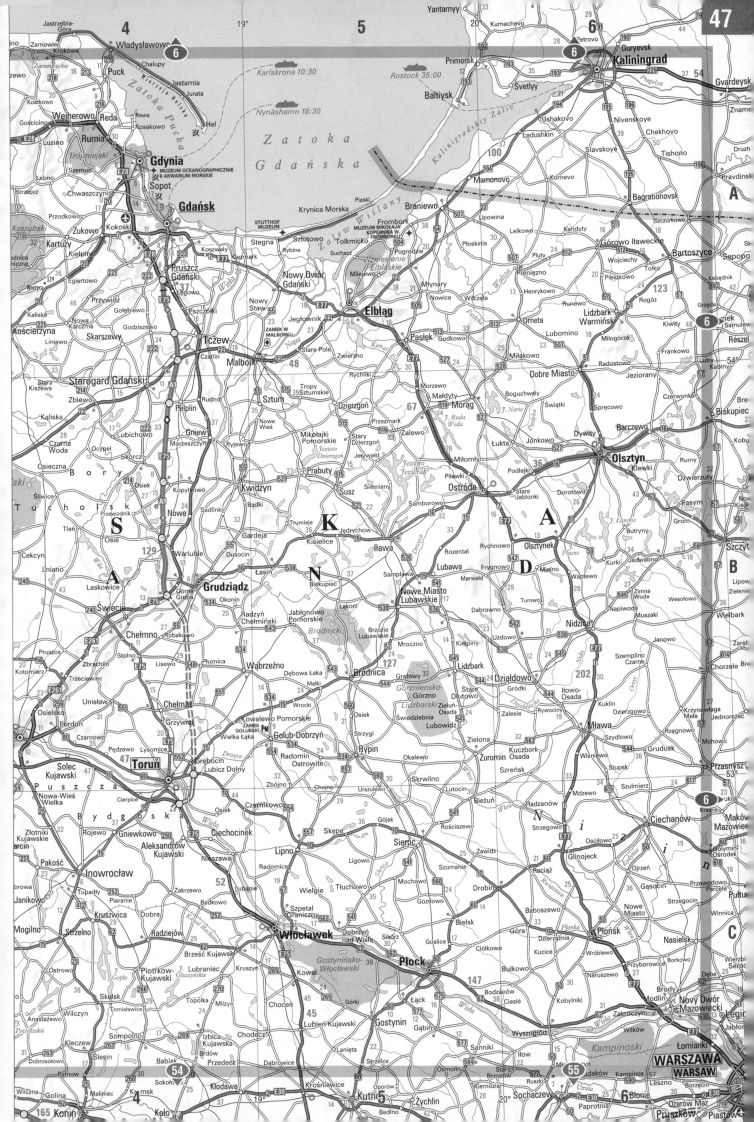

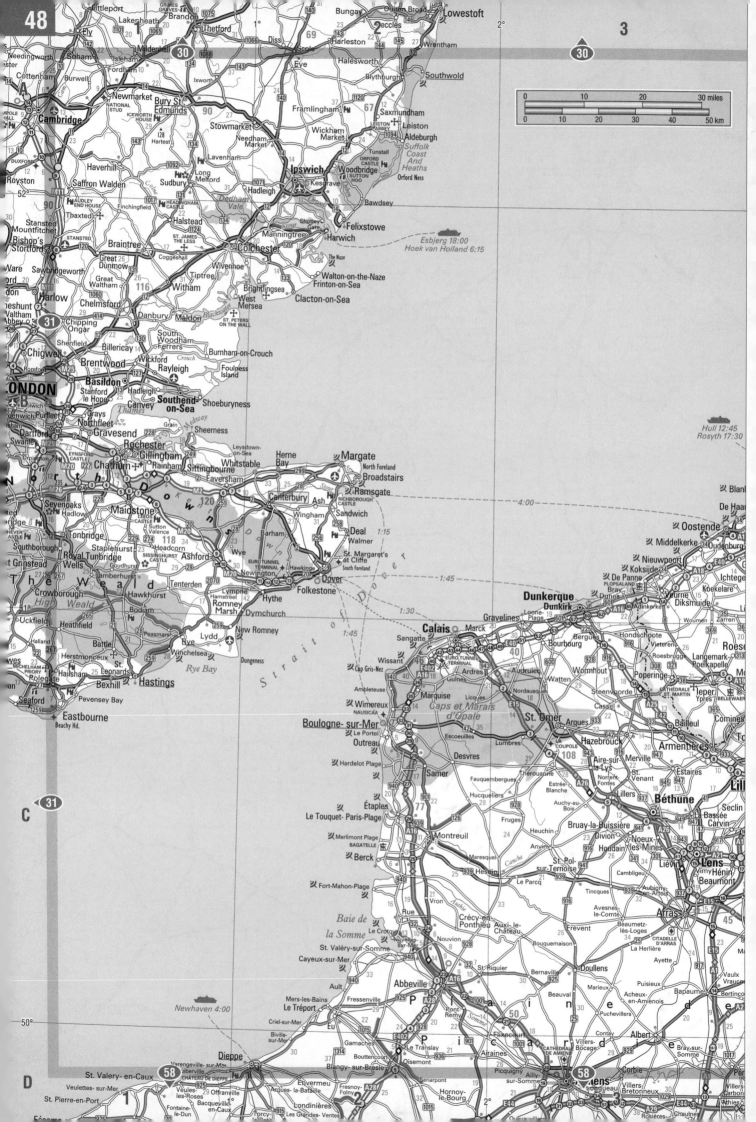

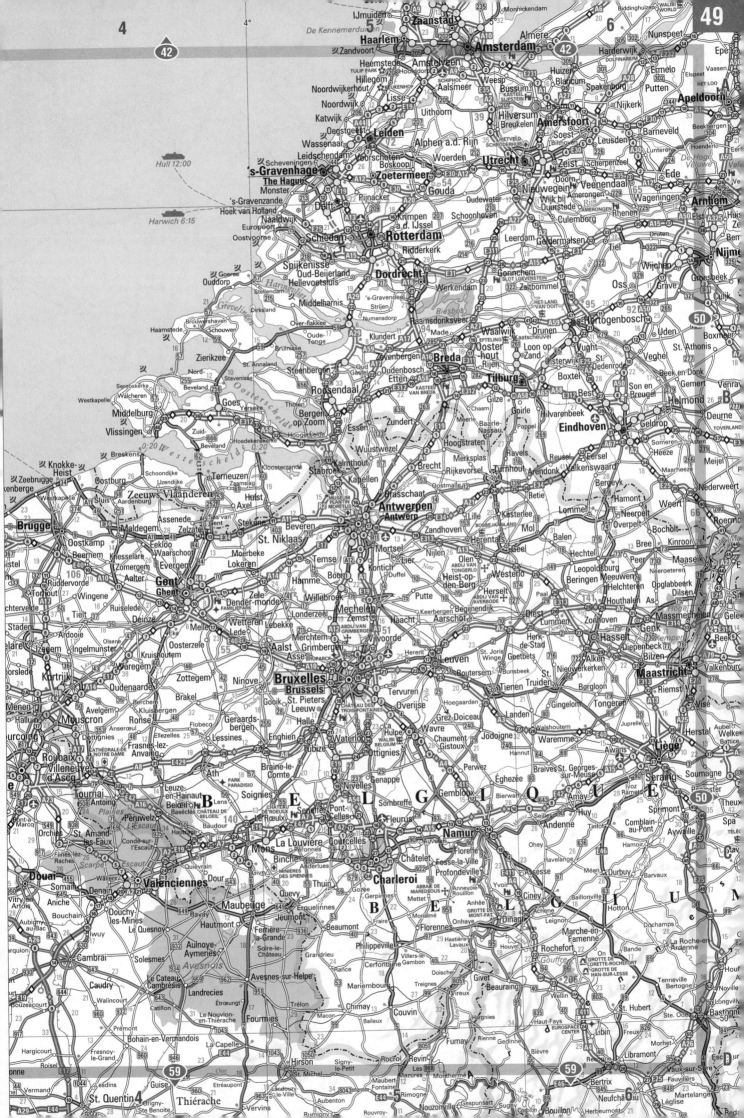

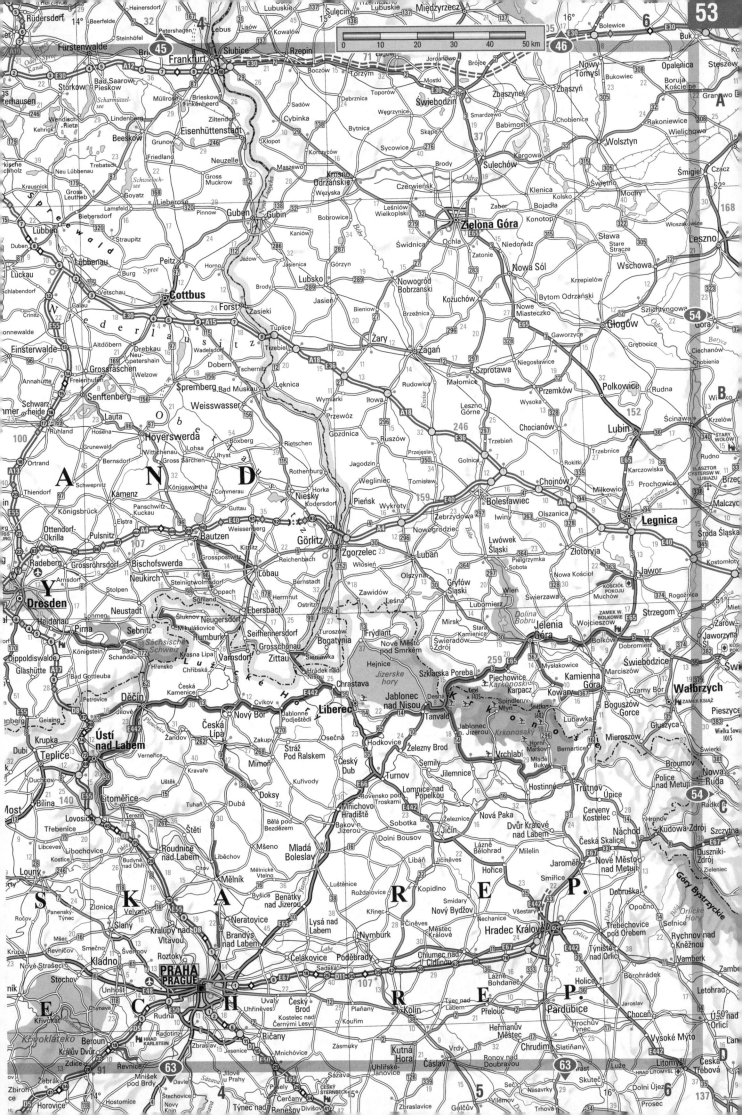

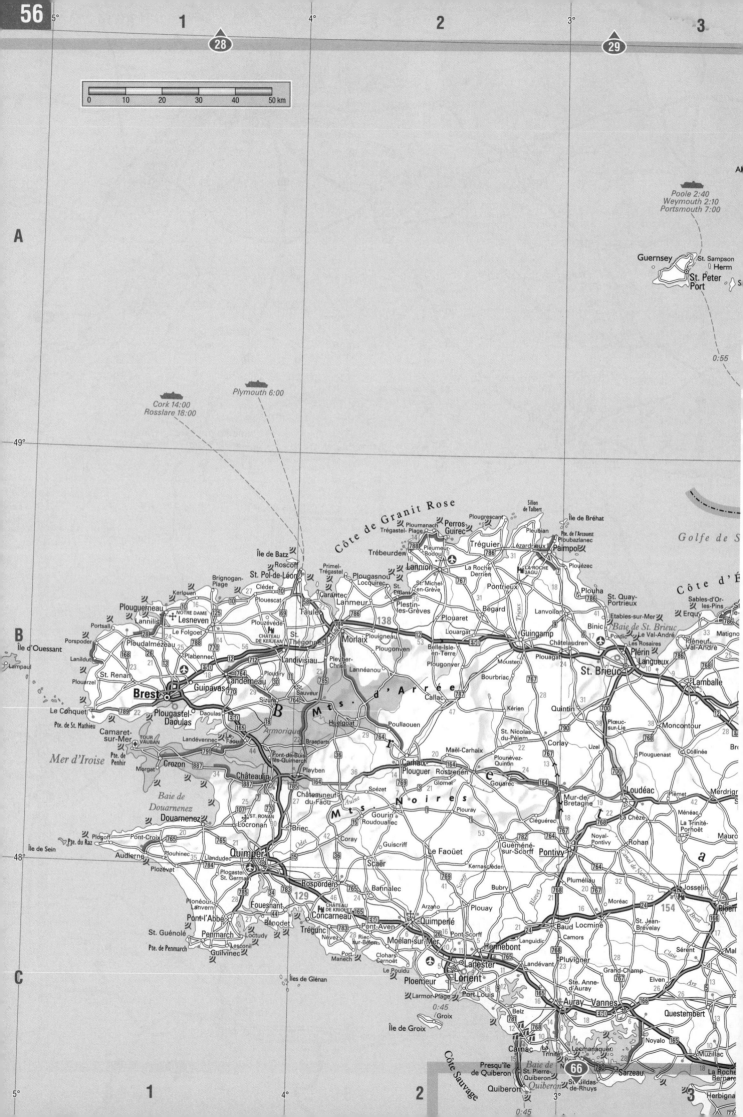

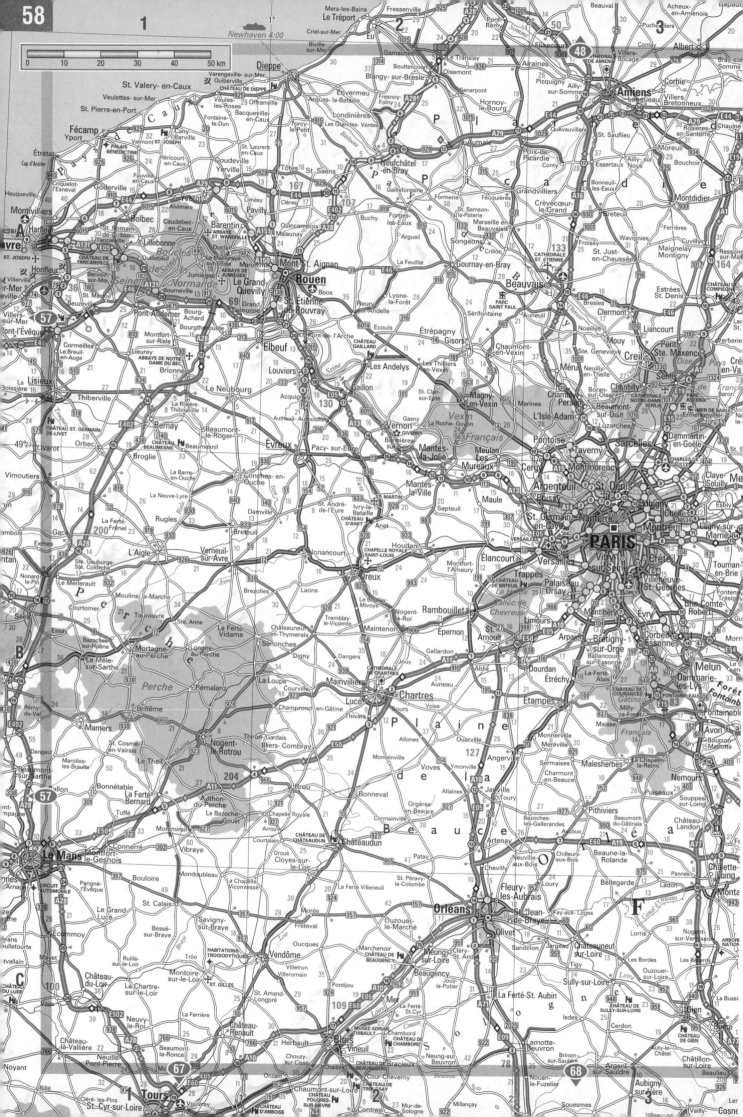

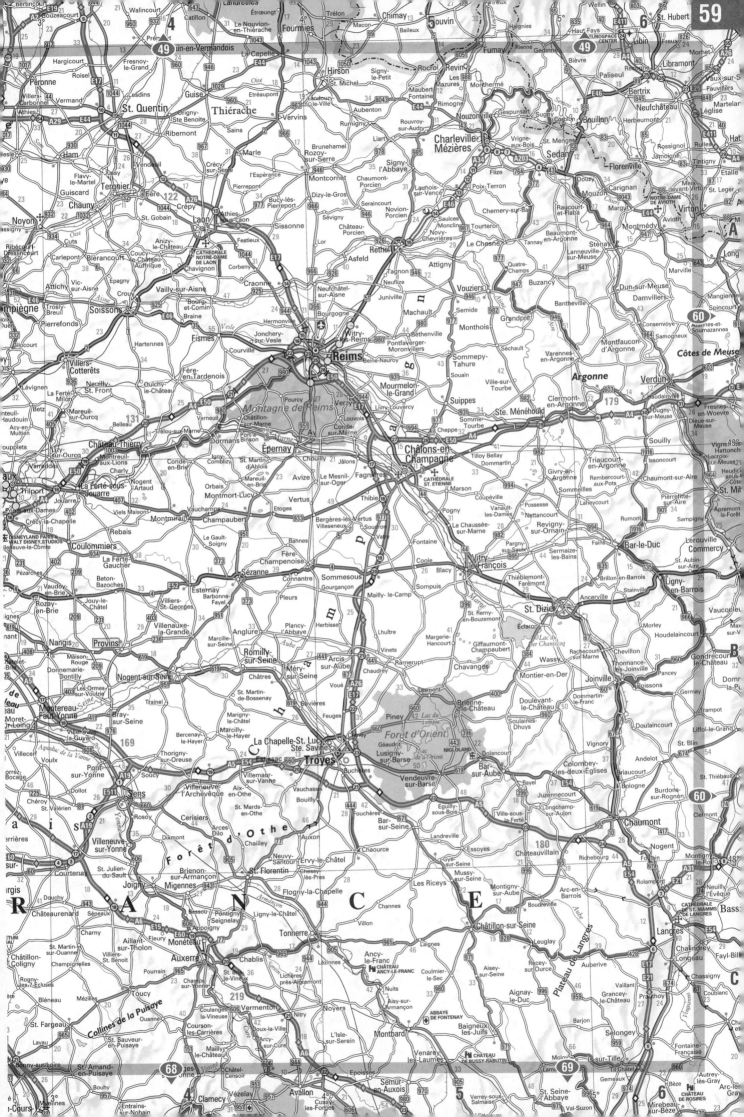

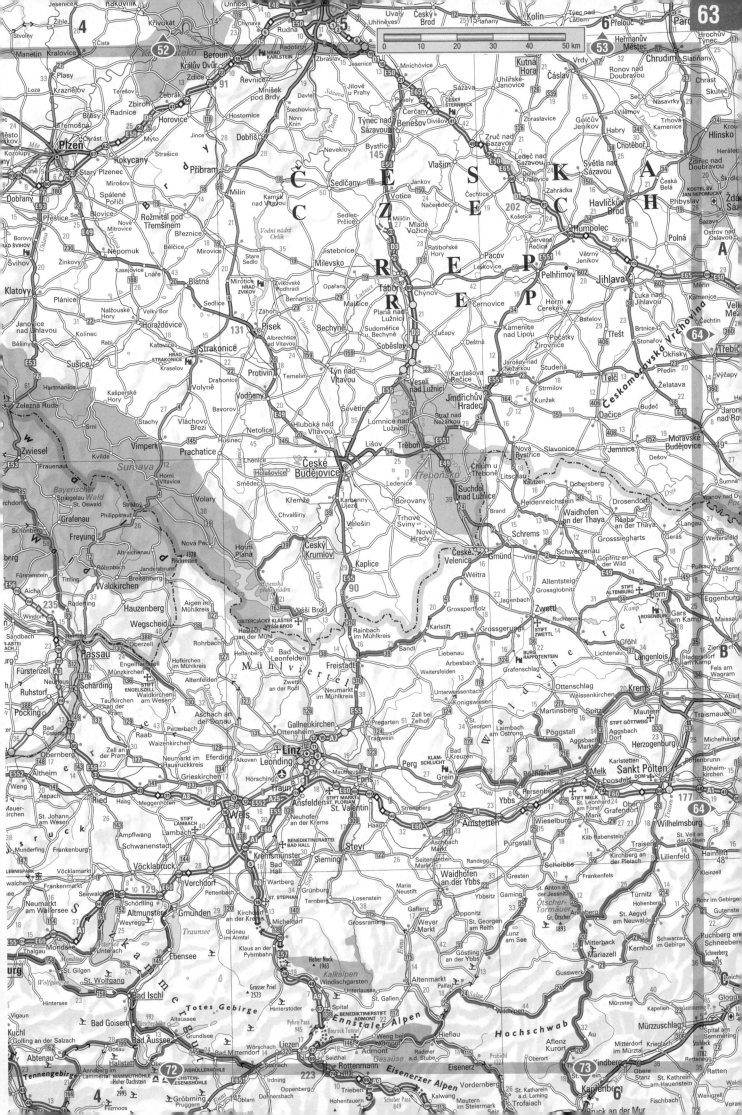

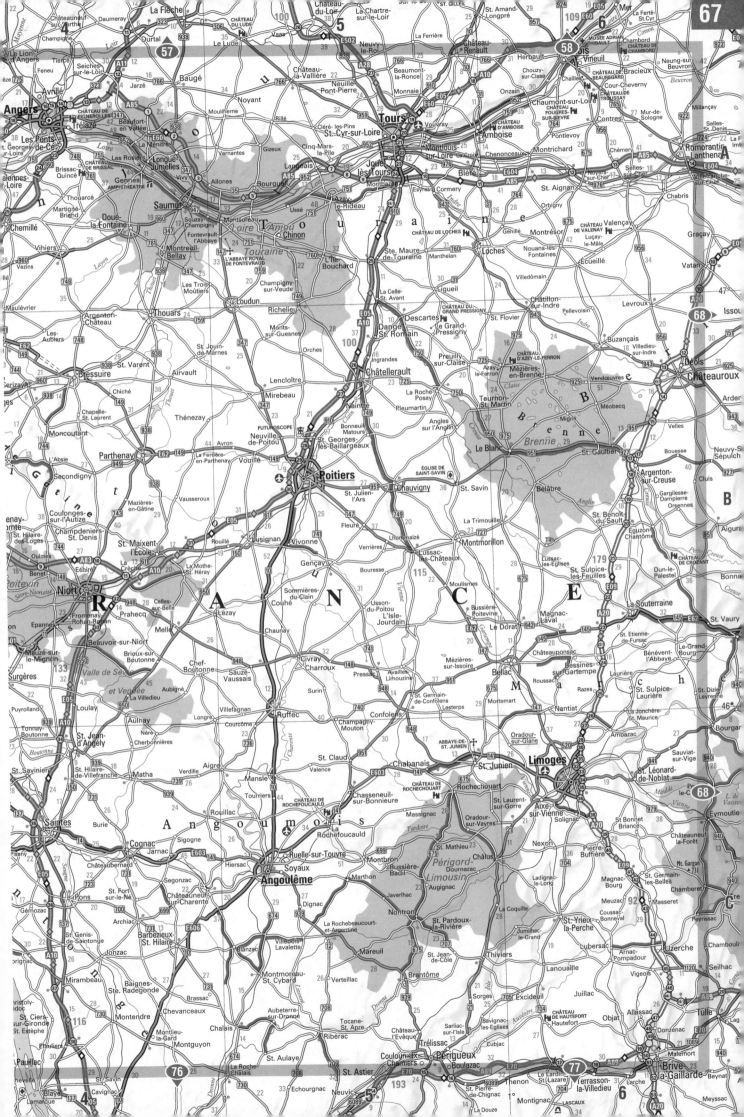

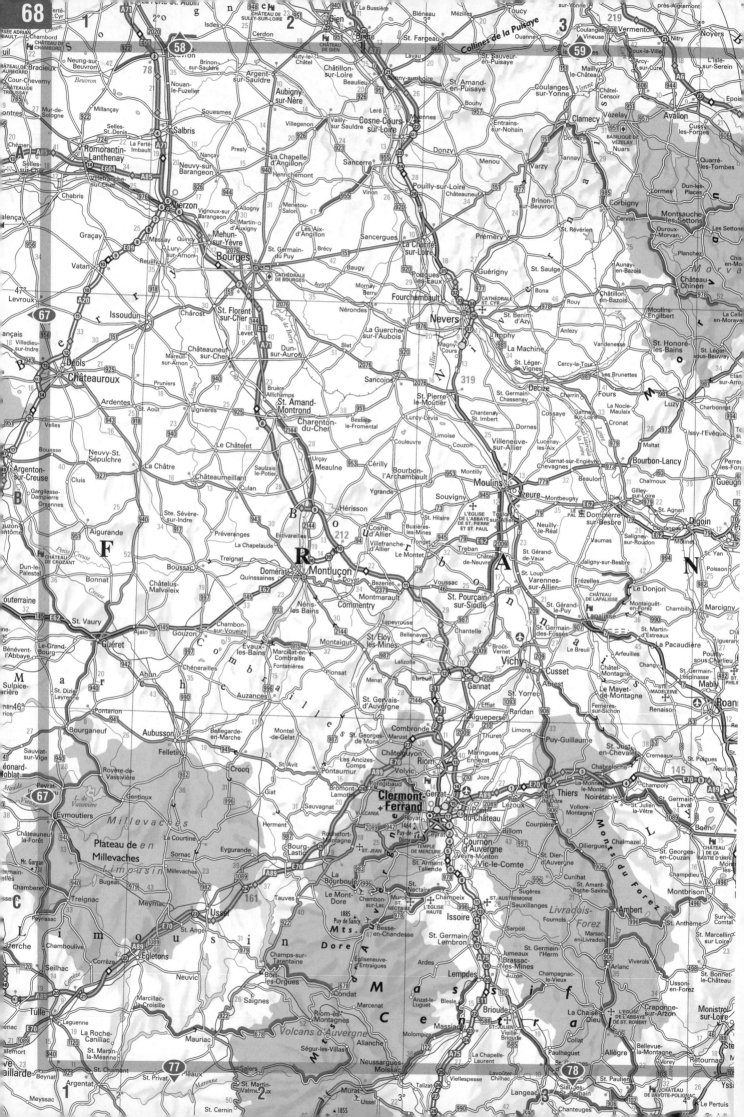

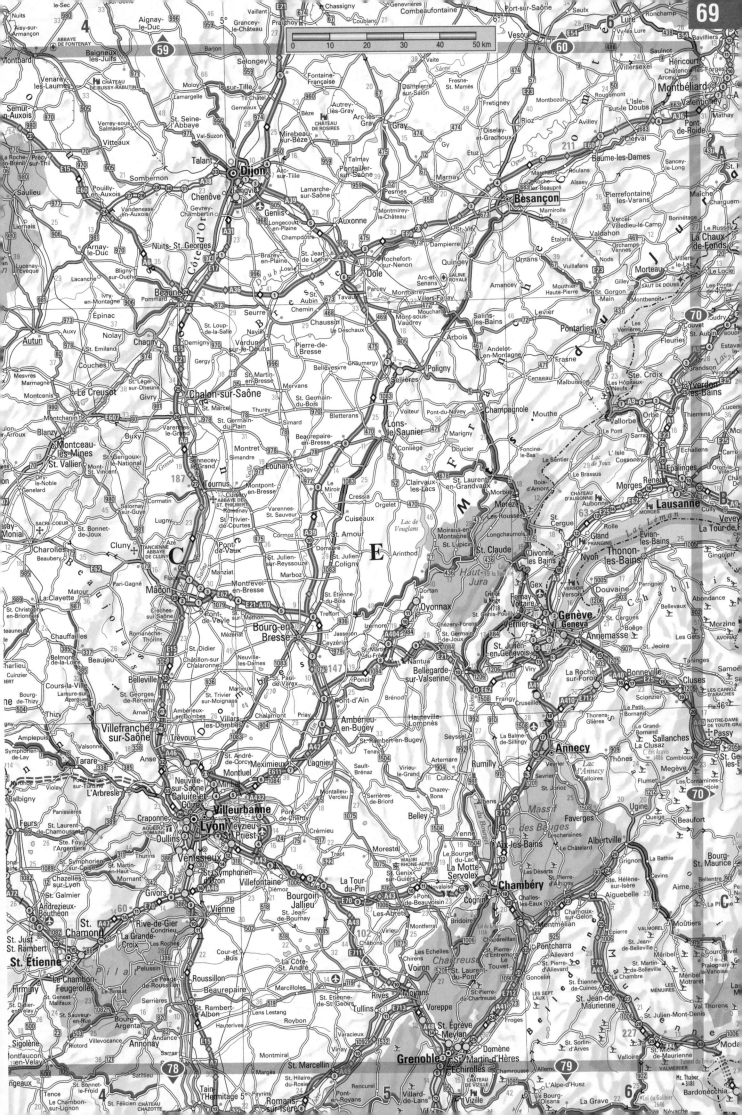

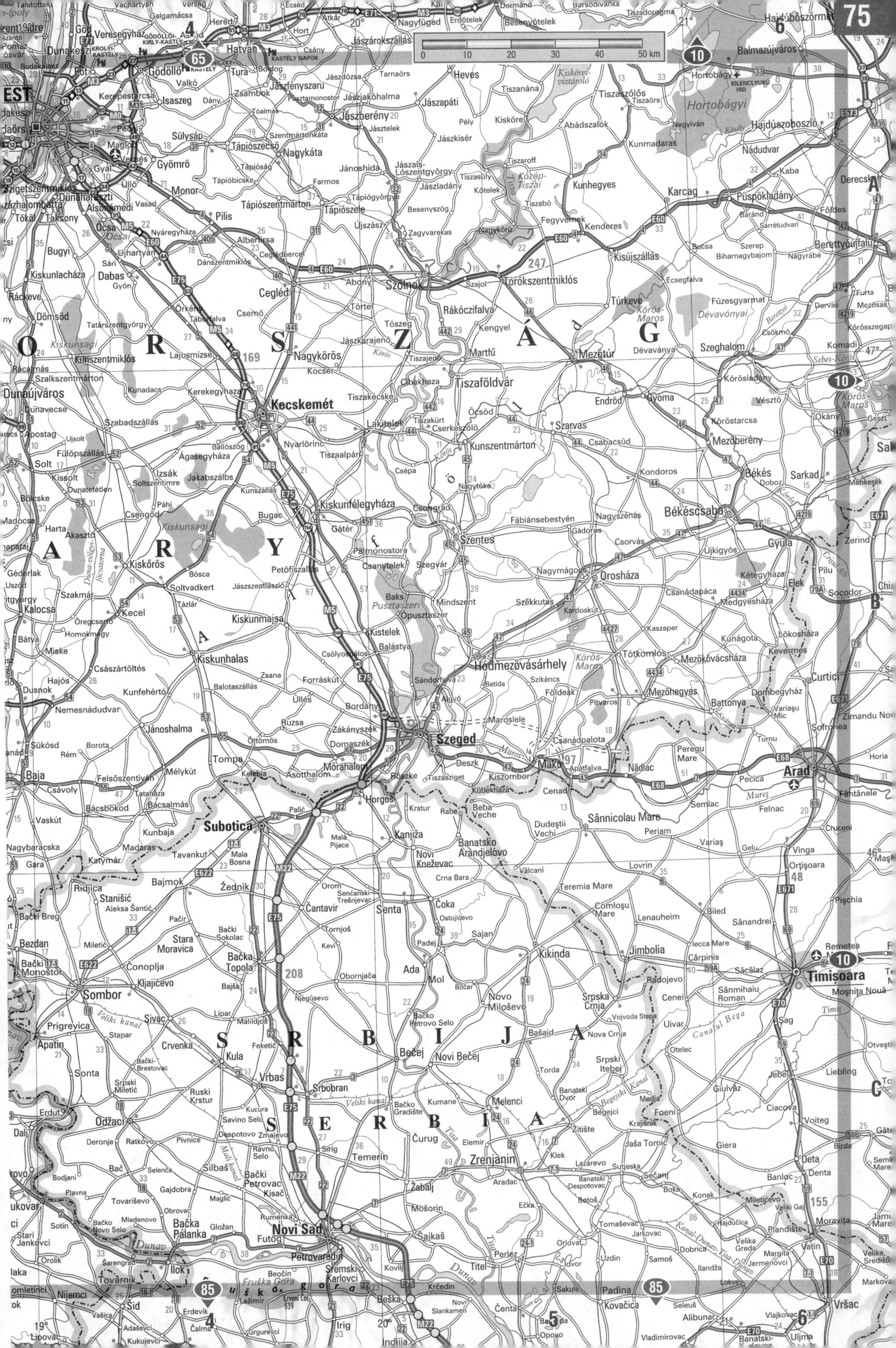
0 10 20 30 40 50 km
Gödöllő
Hatvan
Gyöngyös
Heves
Jászberény
Jászapáti
Tiszanána
Kisköre
Abádszalók
Tiszafüred
Hortobágy
Hortobágyi
Balmazújváros
Hajdúböszörmény
Hajdúszoboszló
Nádudvar
Kaba
Püspökladány
Karcag
Kunhegyes
Kenderes
Fegyvernek
Kisújszállás
Berettyóújfalu
Derecske
Földes
Túrkeve
Dévaványa
Szeghalom
Füzesgyarmat
Dévavónyai
Törökszentmiklós
Szolnok
Abony
Cegléd
Monor
Pilis
Albertirsa
Dabas
Gyömrő
Üllő
Vecsés
Maglód
Pécel
Isaszeg
Sülysáp
Tápiószecső
Nagykáta
Tápiószele
Tápiószentmárton
Szigetszentmiklós
Dunaharaszti
Taksony
Ócsa
Bugyi
Kiskunlacháza
Ráckeve
Dömsöd
Kunszentmiklós
Lajosmizse
Nagykőrös
Kecskemét
Dunaújváros
Dunavecse
Solt
Kalocsa
Kiskőrös
Soltvadkert
Kecel
Kiskunmajsa
Kiskunhalas
Kiskunfélegyháza
Csongrád
Szentes
Tiszaföldvár
Martfű
Kunszentmárton
Szarvas
Mezőtúr
Gyoma
Endrőd
Békés
Békéscsaba
Gyula
Orosháza
Hódmezővásárhely
Mezőhegyes
Battonya
Szeged
Makó
Mórahalom
Kistelek
Csongrád
Jánoshalma
Baja
Tompa
Horgoš
Subotica
Kanjiža
Senta
Ada
Bačka Topola
Kikinda
Novi Bečej
Bečej
Zrenjanin
Sombor
Apatin
Kula
Vrbas
Srbobran
Novi Sad
Petrovaradin
Sremski Karlovci
Bačka Palanka
Ilok
Šid
Beška
Titel
Kovačica
Vršac
Temerin
Žabalj
Čurug
Arad
Timişoara
Nădlac
Sânnicolau Mare
Jimbolia
Deta
Vinga
Lovrin
Curtici
Pecica
O R S Z Á G
A R Y
S R B I J A
S E R B I A
Fruška Gora
Dunav
Tisza
Mureş
Kanal Dunav-Tisa-Dunav
E60
E75
E70
E68
E671
E573
M3
M5
M22
10
65
85
169
208
247
155
6
4
5
A
B
C
20°
21°
19°
46°
47°

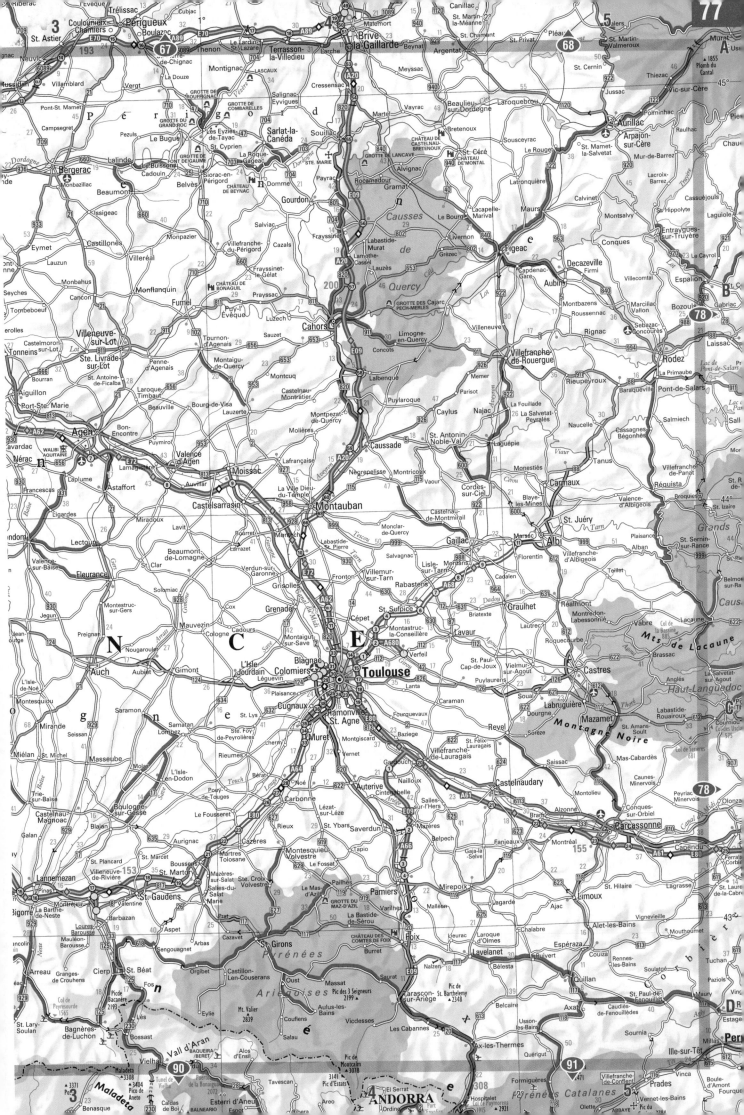

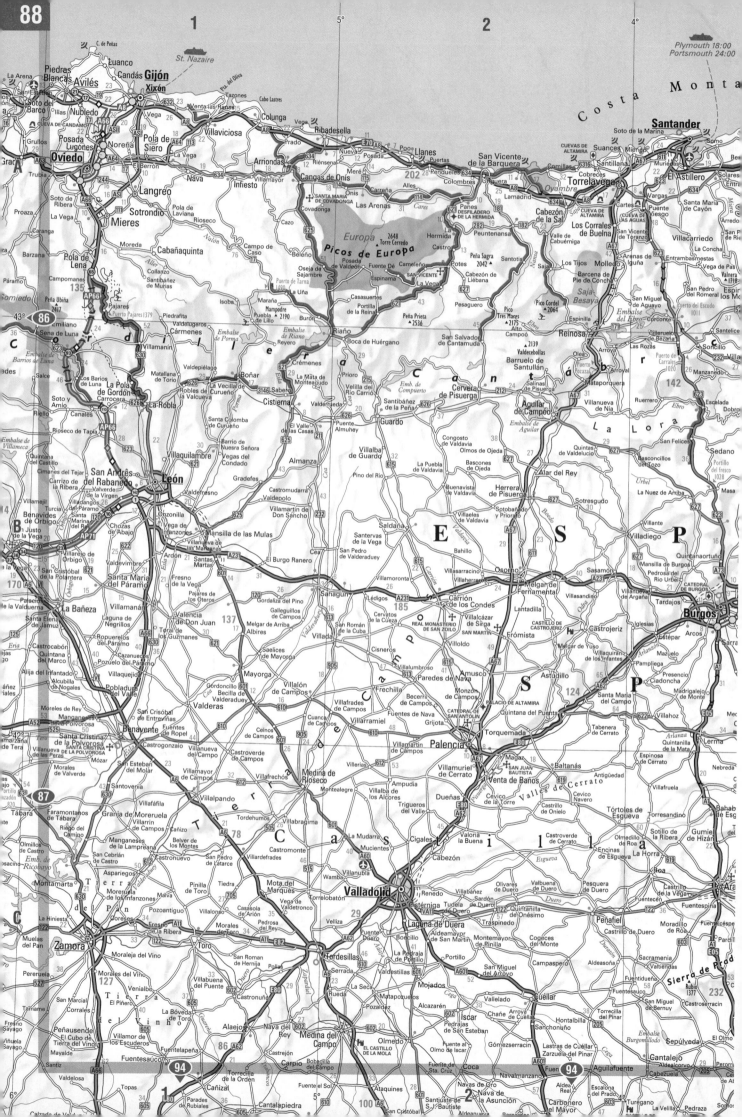

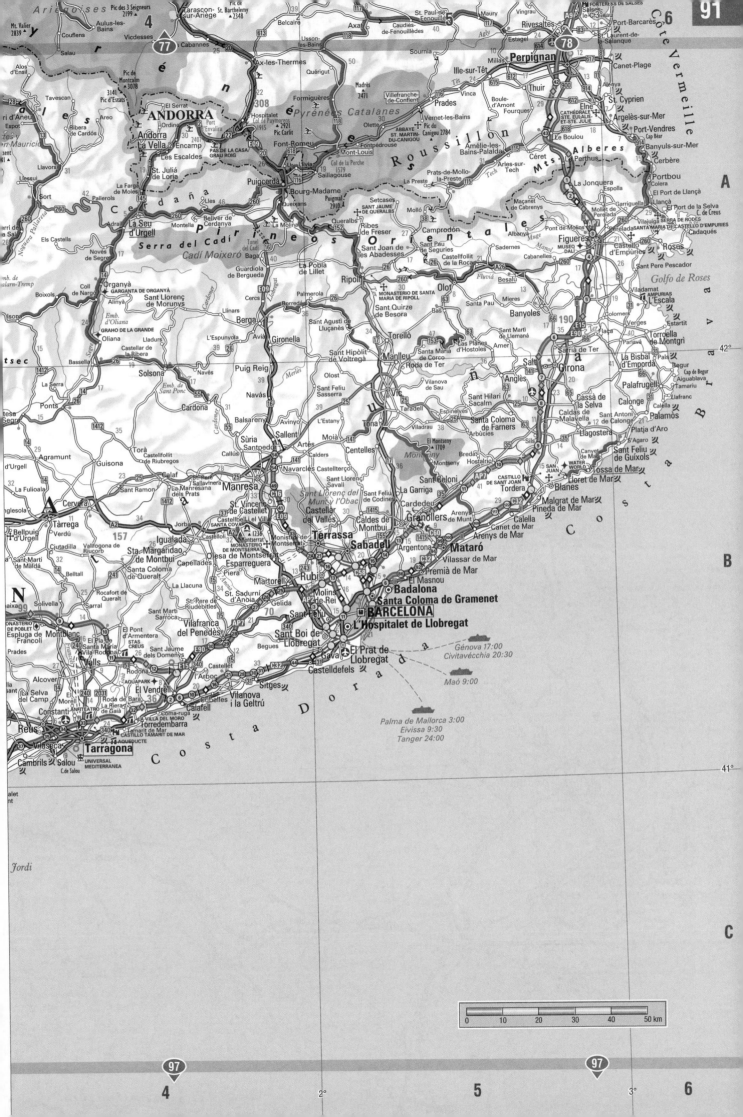

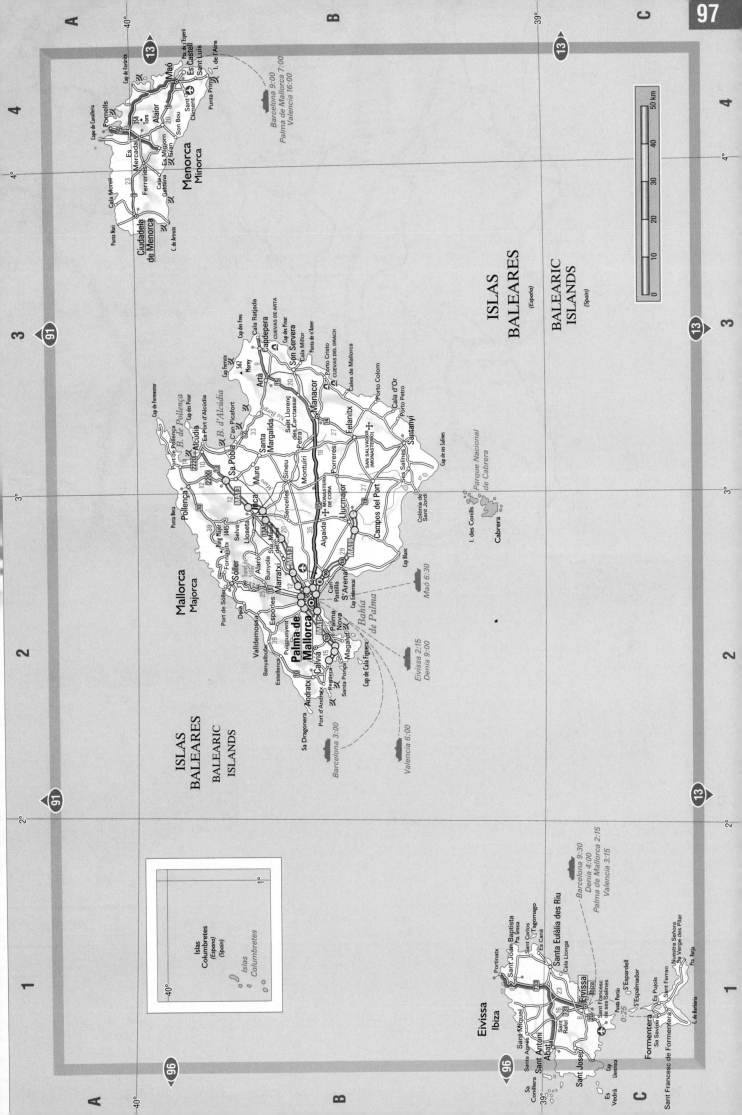

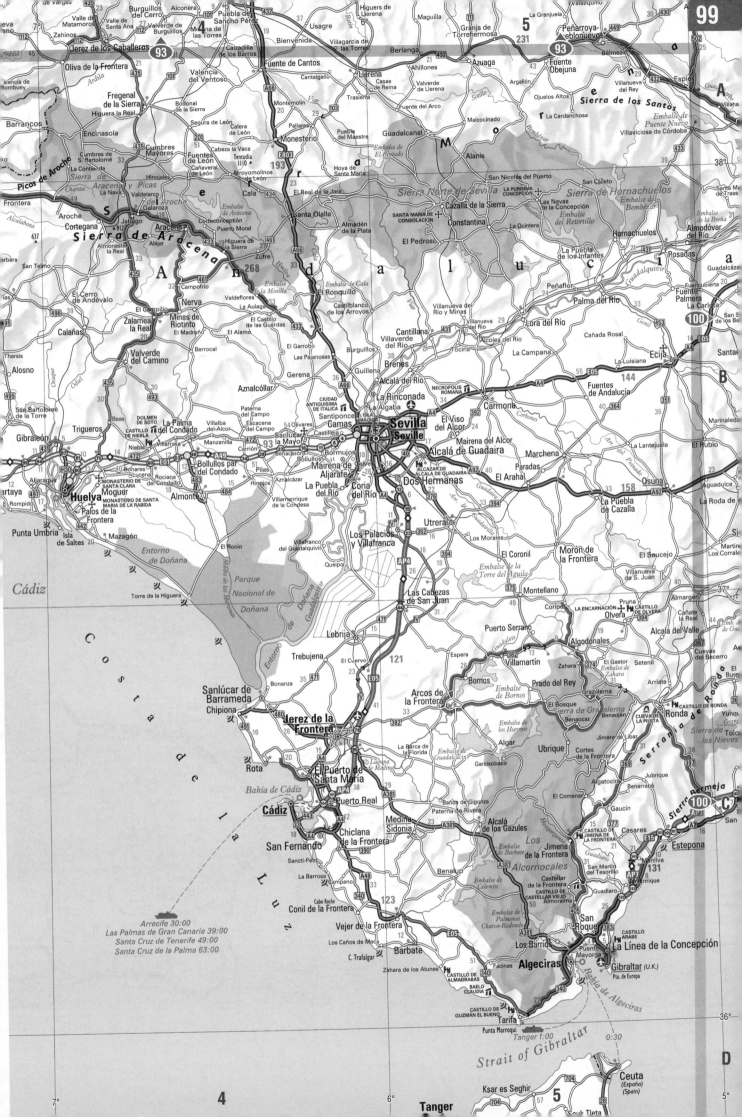

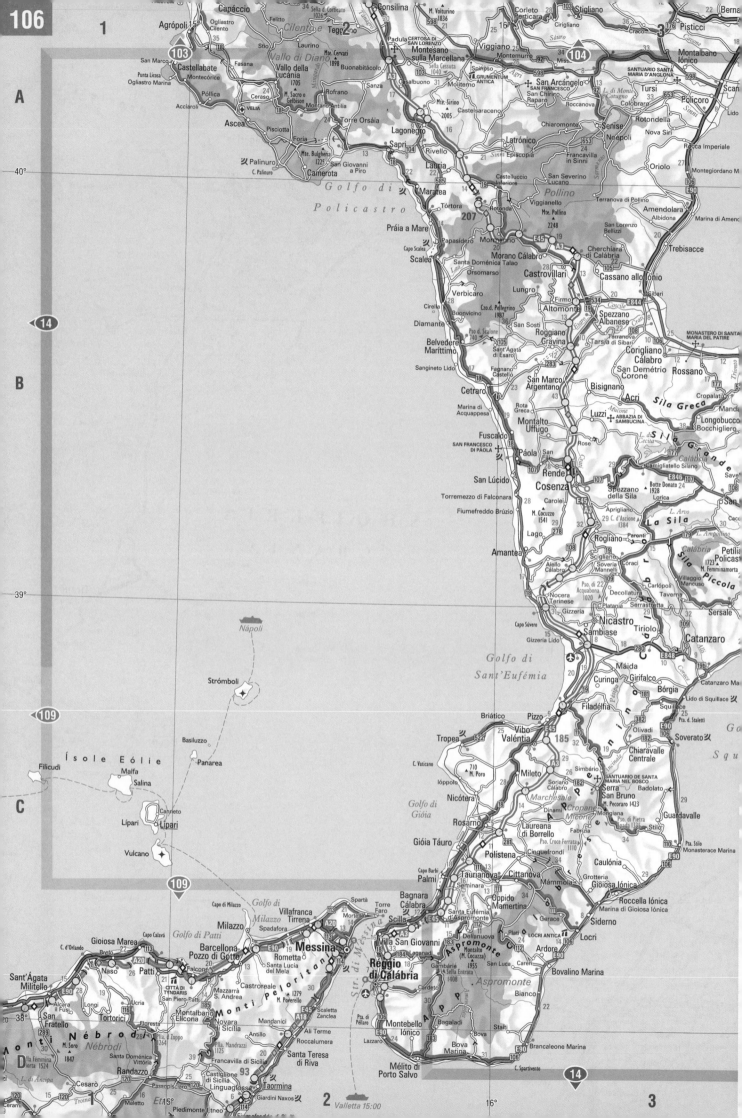

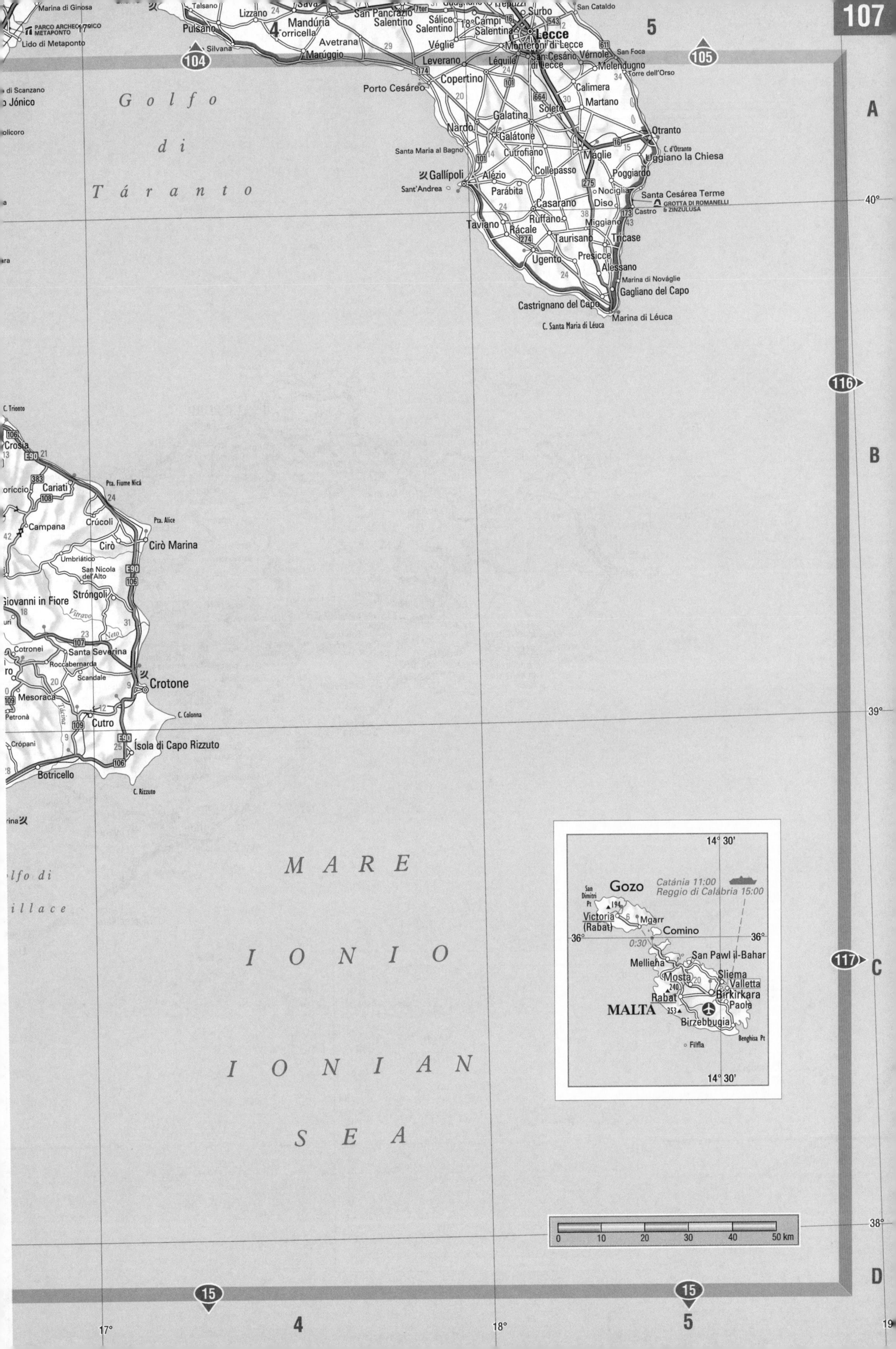

Talsano
Lizzano 24
Sava
San Pancrazio Salentino
Campi Salentina
Surbo
San Cataldo
Pulsano
Manduria
Torricella
Sálice Salentino
Véglie
Lecce
5
Marina di Ginosa
PARCO ARCHEO ICO METAPONTO
Lido di Metaponto
Silvana
104
Marúggio
Avetrana
Leverano
Copertino
Monteroni di Lecce
San Cesário di Lecce
Vérnole
San Foca
105

di Scanzano
o Jónico

Torre dell'Orso
Melendugno
A

Porto Cesáreo
174
101
Calimera
Martano
34
Galatina
664
Soleto
30

olicoro
G o l f o

d i

Nardò
Galátone
Cutrofiano
Máglie
Otranto
C. d'Otranto
Uggiano la Chiesa

a
Santa Maria al Bagno
101
14
Collepasso
16
15
Poggiardo

T á r a n t o
Gallípoli
Sant'Andrea
Alézio
Parábita
Casarano
Ruffano
Taviano
Rácale
Diso
275
173
Nociglia
Castro
Santa Cesárea Terme
GROTTA DI ROMANELLI & ZINZULUSA
40°

24
38
Miggiano
43

274
Taurisano
Tricase

Ugento
Presicce
Alessano
Marina di Nováglie
Castrignano del Capo
Gagliano del Capo
24

Marina di Léuca
C. Santa Maria di Léuca

116

C. Trionto
106
Crosia
13
E90
21

oríccio
Cariati
383
24
108
Pta. Fiume Nicá

Campana
Crúcoli
Pta. Alice

42
Cirò
Cirò Marina

Umbriático
San Nicola del Alto
E90
106

Giovanni in Fiore
Stróngoli
18
Vúravo
31

uri
23
107
Neto

Cotronei
Santa Severina
Roccabernarda
Scandale

Mesoraca
109
9
Crotone

Petronà
39°
C. Colonna

Crópani
109
Cutro
E90
25
Ísola di Capo Rizzuto

28
Botricello
106

C. Rizzuto

rina

olfo di
illace
M A R E

I O N I O

I O N I A N

S E A

Catánia 11:00
14° 30'
San Dimitri Pt
Gozo
Reggio di Calábria 15:00
194
Victoria (Rabat)
Mgarr
Comino
36°
0:30
San Pawl il-Bahar
Mellieha
Mosta
240
20
Sliema
Valletta
Rabat
Birkirkara
Paola
MALTA
253
Birzebbugia
14° 30'
Filfla
Benghisa Pt
117
C

38°
0   10   20   30   40   50 km

15
15
D

17°
4
18°
5
19°

0 10 20 30 40 50 km

12°   1   13°   2

14   14

Ústica

2:20

Nápoli 4:00
Livorno 17:00
Génova 20:00

Cágliari 13:30

A

14   Cágliari 11:30

C. San Vito   Golfo di
Castellammare

Isola delle
Fémmine   C. Gallo
Mondello

Terrasini   Capaci
Carini   Palermo   Golfo di
Términi Imerese

San Vito
lo Capo   M. Sparagio
1110   Scopello

Pizzolungo   Balestrate   Monreale   Ficarazzi
Érice   Montelepre   Altofonte   Bagheria
38°   Trápani   Valdérice   Castellammare   Partinico   Misilmeri   Casteldáccia   Trabia   Campofelice
del Golfo   Alcamo   Riana degli   Términi   di Roccella
Lévanzo   Paceco   Fulgatore   San Cipirello   Albanesi   Bolognetta   Imerese   Cerda
Ísole Égadi   Calatafimi   San Gúiseppe   Marineo   Cáccamo
Jato   Villafrati   Ciminna   Caltavuturo
Maréttimo   Rilievo   TEMPIO GRECO   Camporeale   Mezzojuso   Montemaggiore
di SEGESTA   Roccamena   Belsito
Favignana   Vita   Salemi   Gibellina   Corleone   Rca. Busambra   Vicari   Roccapalumba   Ália
Favignana   Nuova   1613   Leonardo
Stagnone   Santa Ninfa   Prizzi   Lercara   Valledolmo
CASE   Partanna   Campofiorito   Friddi
ROMANA   Salaparuta   Bisacquino   Vallelunga
Marsala   Santa Margherita   Pratameno   Villalba
Strasatti   di Belice   Chiusa   Santo Stéfano   Cammarata
Sclafani   Quisquina
Mazara   Sambuca   Palazzo   Mussomeli   Marianópoli
Menfi   di Sicilia   Adriano   Alessándria   Campofránco
Castelvetrano   della Rocca   CASTELLO DEI
Mazara   Caltabellotta   Búrgio   Casteltérmini   CHIAROMONTE
del Vallo   Bivona   San Cat
Campobello   Cianciana   San Biágio   Serradifalco   Santa
di Mazára   Ribera   Pláteni   Villarm
Granitola-Torretta   Menfi   Sciacca   Cattólica   Montedoro   Racalmuto   San Cat
CITTÀ GRECO DI   Eráclea   Canicattì
C. Granitola   SEILINUNTE   Marinella   Raffadali   Aragona   Racalmuto   Castrofilippo
Montallegro   Siculiana   Favara   Camastra   Campob
HERACLEA   Agrigento   di Licata
MINOA   Porto Empédocle   Naro   Naro   Licat
AGRIGENTO   Palma
di Montechiaro

Linosa 5:45
Lampedusa 8:15

Tunis 7:00

Pantelleria 4:45

Trápani 4:45   36°   13°

Porto Empédocle
5:45

Linosa

Pantelleria   Ísole
Pelágie
(Italia)   (Italia)
(Italy)   (Italy)   1:45

Pantelleria
(Italia)
(Italy)   836

Lampione   Lampedusa

C   12°   13°
1   14   14   2

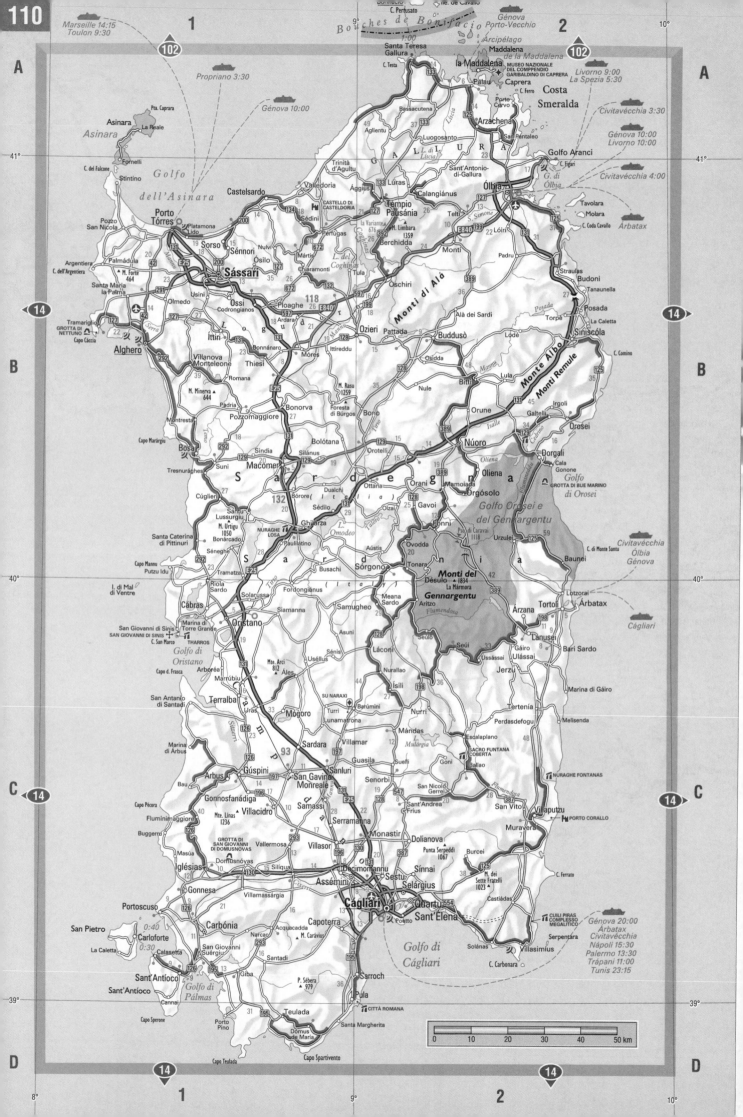

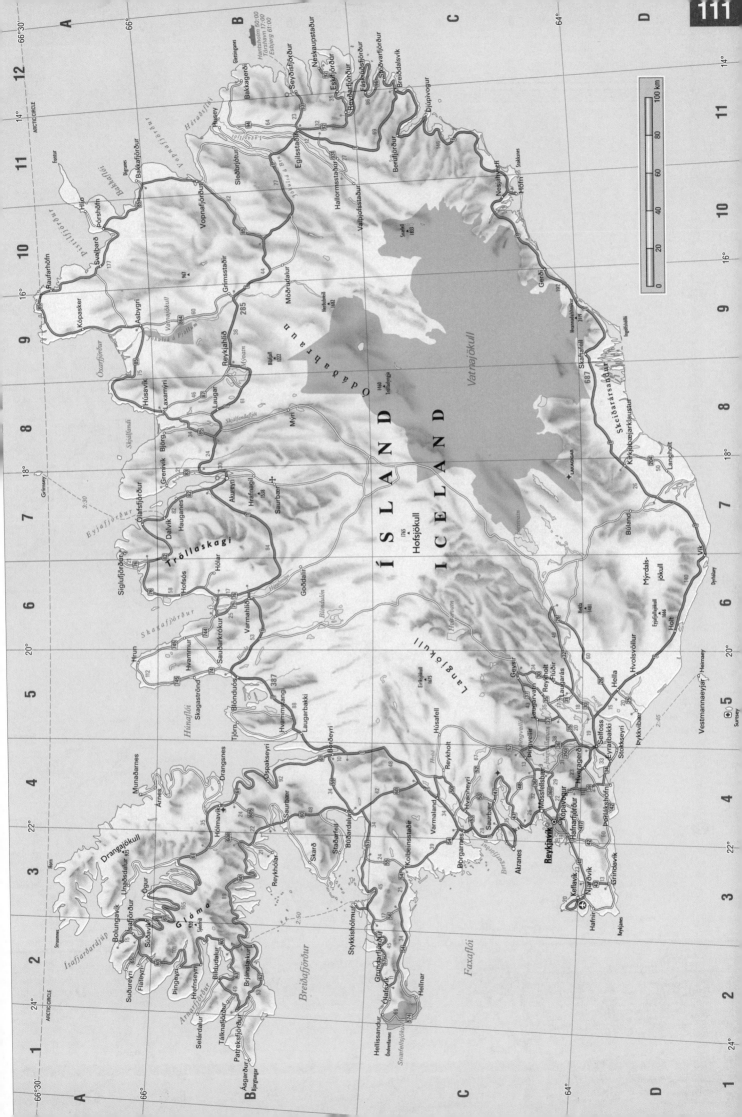

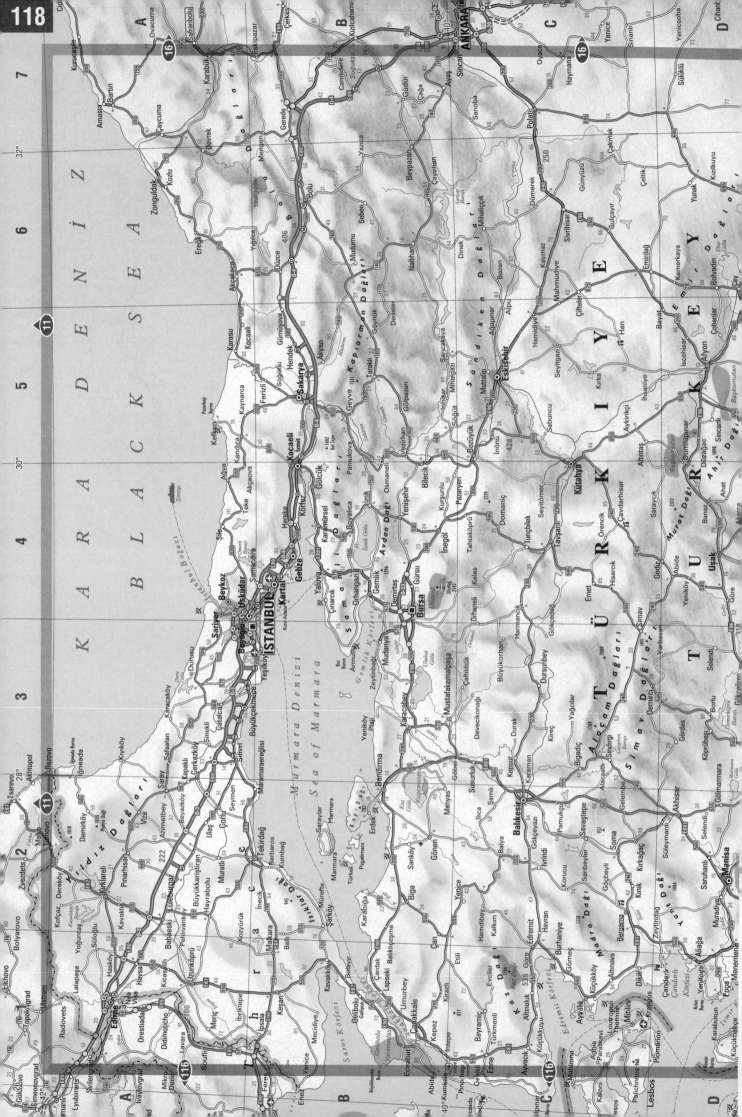

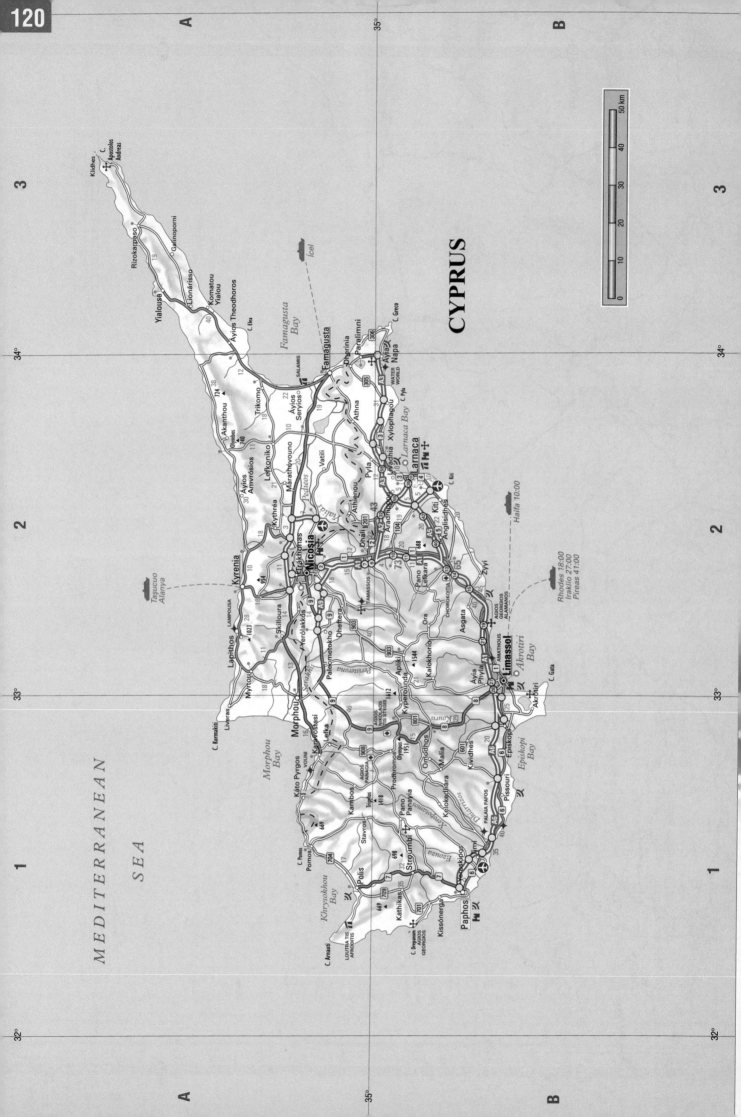

CYPRUS

City plans • Plans de villes
Stadtpläne • Piante di città

Motorway	Autoroute	Autobahn	Autostrada
Major through route	Route principale majeur	Hauptstrecke	Strada di grande comunicazione
Through route	Route principale	Schnellstrasse	Strada d'importanza regionale
Secondary road	Route secondaire		
Dual carriageway	Chaussées séparées	Nebenstrasse	Strada d'interesse locale
Other road	Autre route	Zweispurig Schnellstrasse	Strada a carreggiate doppie
Tunnel	Tunnel	Nebenstrasse	Altra strada
Limited access / pedestrian road	Rue réglementée / rue piétonne	Tunnel	Galleria stradale
One-way street	Sens unique	Beschränkter Zugang / Fussgängerzone	Strada pedonale / a accesso limitato
Parking	Parc de stationnement	Einbahnstrasse	Senso unico
Motorway number A7	Numéro d'autoroute	Parkplatz P	Parcheggio
National road number 447	Numéro de route nationale	Autobahnnummer A7	Numero di autostrada
European road number E45	Numéro de route européenne	Nationalstrassen-nummer 447	Numero di strada nazionale
Destination GENT	Destination	Europäische Strassennummer E45	Numero di strada europea
Car ferry	Bac passant les autos	Ziel GENT	Destinazione
Railway	Chemin de fer	Autofähre	Traghetto automobili
Rail / bus station	Gare / gare routière	Eisenbahn	Ferrovia
Underground, metro station	Station de métro	Bahnhof / Busstation	Stazione ferrovia / pullman
Cable car	Téléférique	U-Bahnstation	Metropolitano
Abbey, cathedral	Abbaye, cathédrale	Drahtseilbahn	Funivia
Church of interest	Église intéressante	Abtei, Kloster, Kathedrale	Abbazia, duomo
Synagogue	Synagogue	Interessante Kirche	Chiesa da vedere
Hospital	Hôpital	Synagoge	Sinagoga
Police station	Police	Krankenhaus	Ospedale
Post office	Bureau de poste	Polizeiwache POL	Polizia
Tourist information	Office de tourisme	Postamt	Ufficio postale
Place of interest Theatre	Autre curiosité	Informationsbüro	Ufficio informazioni turistiche
		Sonstige Sehenswürdigkeit Theatre	Luogo da vedere

Approach maps • Agglomérations
Carte régionale • Regionalkarte

Toll motorway – with motorway number A10	Autoroute à péage – avec numéro d'autoroute	Gebührenpflichtige Autobahn – mit Autobahnnummer A10	Autostrada a pedaggio – con numero
Toll-free motorway – with European road number E51	Autoroute – avec numéro de route européenne	Gebührenfreie Autobahn – Europäische Strassennummer E51	Autostrada – con numero di strada europea
Pre-pay motorway – vignette required	Autoroute – 'vignette'	Autobahn – 'vignette'	Autostrada – 'vignette'
Motorway services	Aire de service	Autobahnservice	Area di servizio autostradale
Motorway junction full access, restricted access	Échangeur d'autoroute – accès libre, accès reglémenté	Autobahnkreuz – voller/begrenzter Zugang	Raccordi autostradali – completo/parziali
Under construction	En construction	Im Bau	In construzione
Tunnel	Tunnel	Tunnel	Galleria stradale
Major route dual carriageway 14 single carriageway 14	Route principale chaussées séparées chausée sans séparation	Hauptstrecke – zweispurige 14 Schnellstrasse 14	Strada di grande comunicazione carreggiata doppia carreggiata unica
Secondary route dual carriageway 96 single carriageway 96	Route secondaire chaussées séparées chausée sans séparation	Nebenstrasse – zweispurige 96 Schnellstrasse 96	Strada d'interesse locale – carreggiata doppia carreggiata unica
Other road	Autre route	Nebenstrecke	Altra strada
Car ferry	Bac passant les autos	Autofähre	Traghetto automobili
Destination GIRONA	Destination	Ziel GIRONA	Destinazione
Railway	Chemin de fer	Eisenbahn	Ferrovia
Railway station Estación Central	Gare	Hauptbahnhof Estación Central	Stazione ferrovia
Height – in metres 234	Altitude – en mètres	Höhe – über dem Meeresspiegel 234	Altezza in metri
Airport	Aéroport principal	Flughafen	Aeroporto
Airfield	Autre aéroport	Flugplatz	Aerodromo / campo d'aviazione
City plan coverage area	Région de plan de ville	Vom Stadtplan abgedecktes Gebiet	Area della pianta della città

Alicante
0 km 0.5

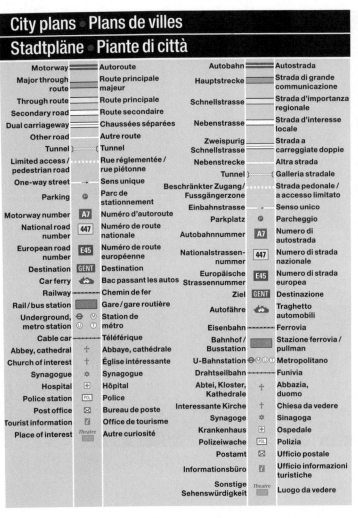
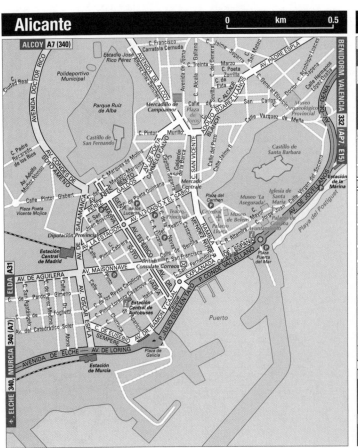

Antwerpen Antwerp
0 km 1

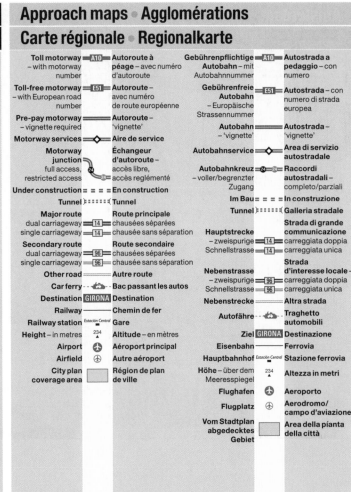
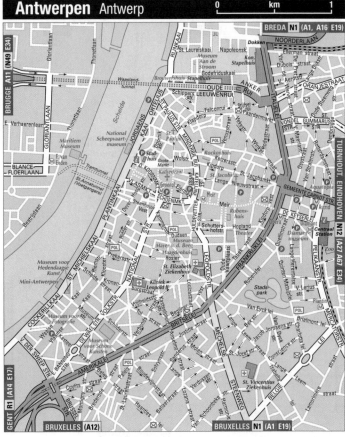

Amsterdam

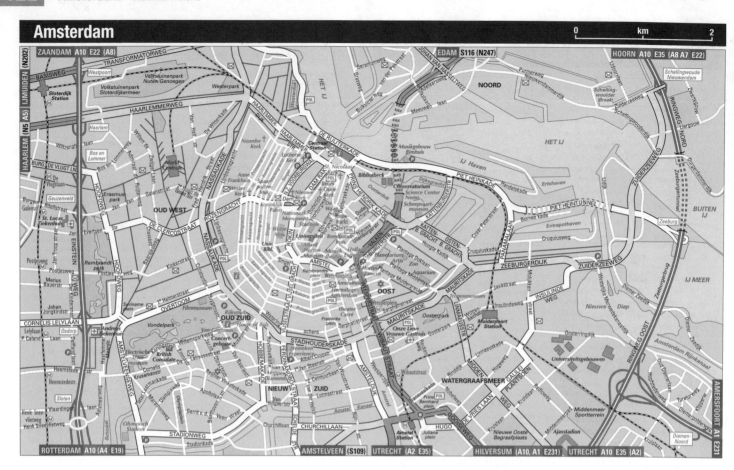

Amsterdam

Athina Athens

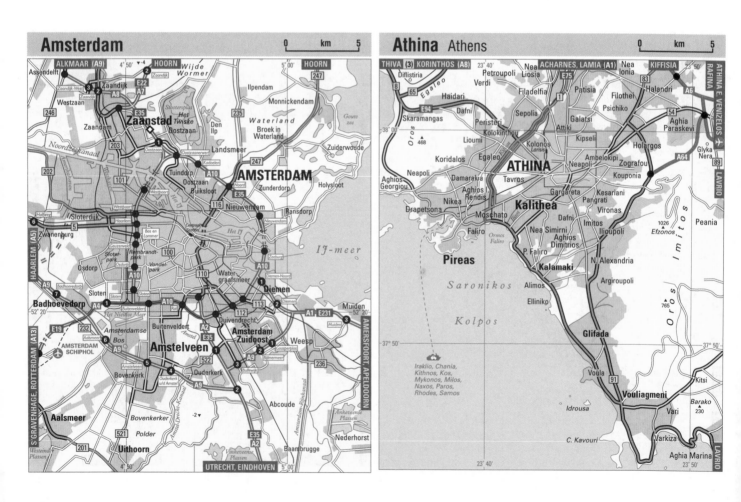

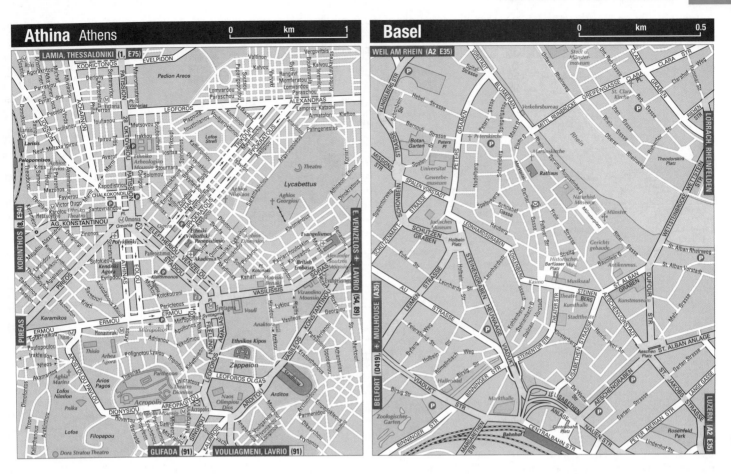

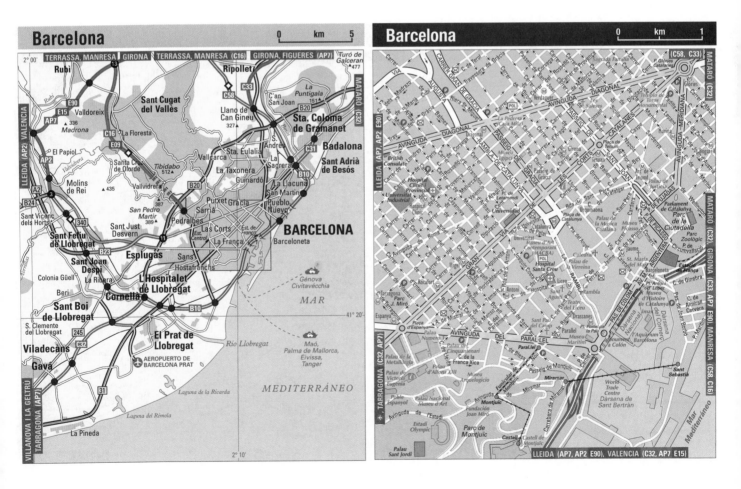

Berlin

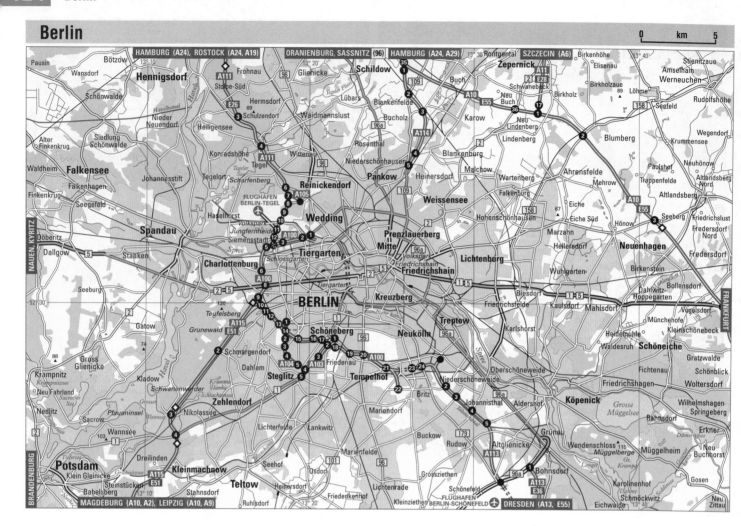

Berlin

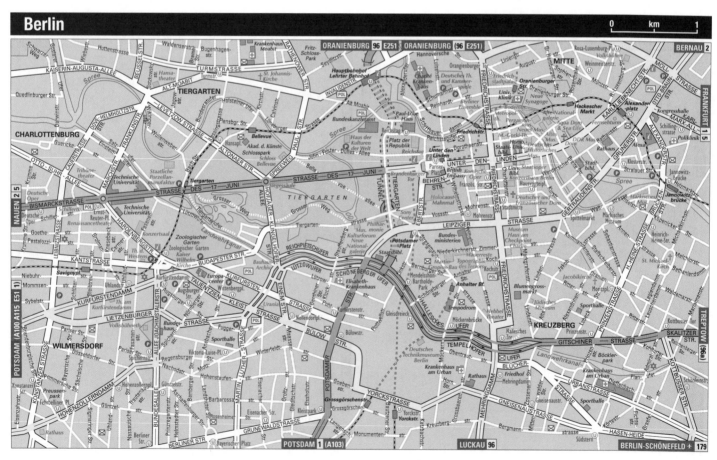

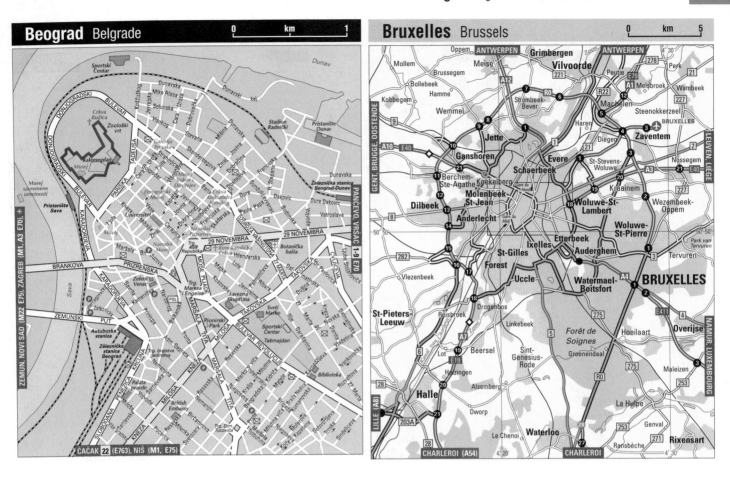

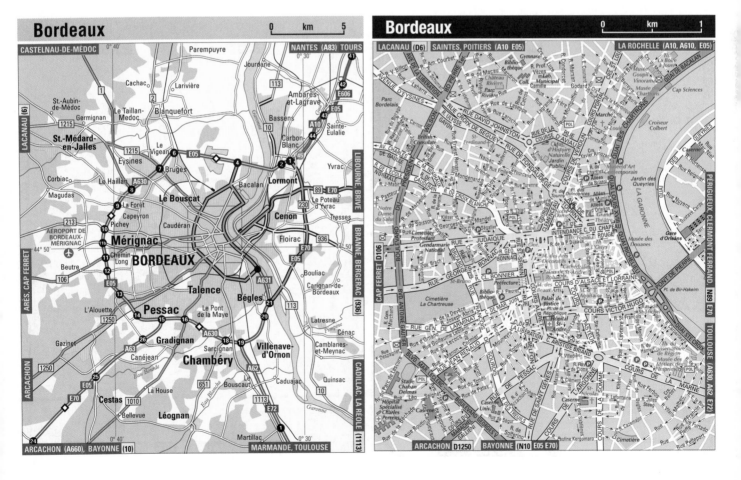

Bruxelles Brussels

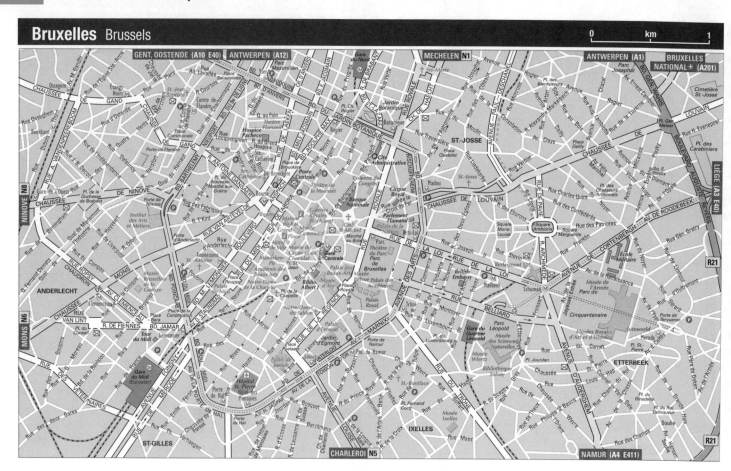

Budapest

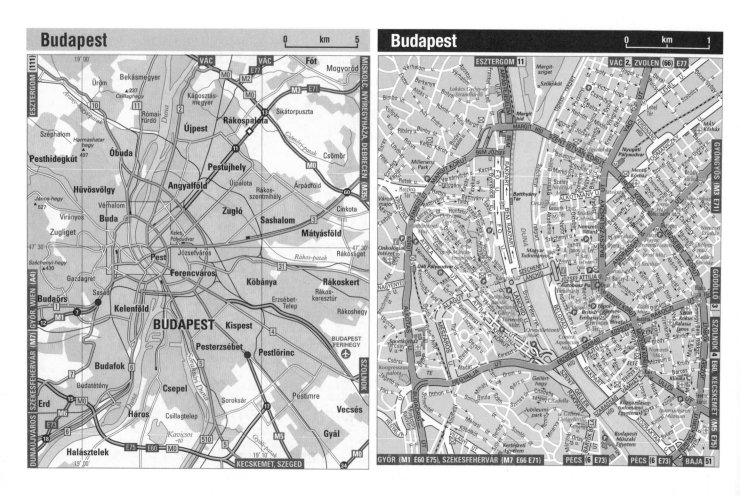

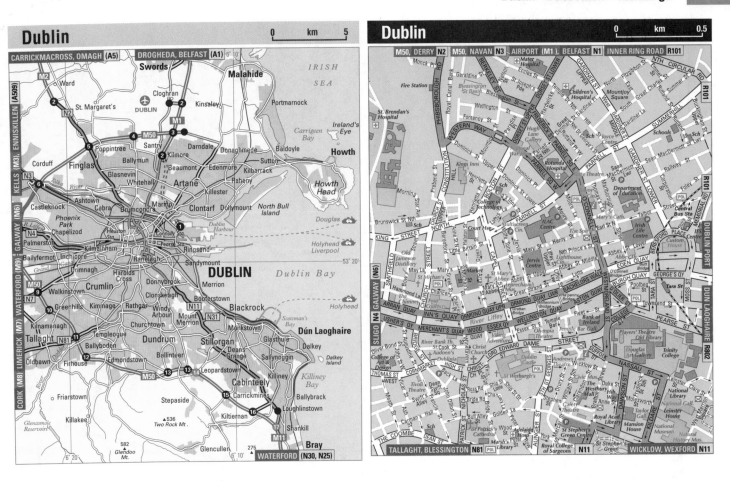

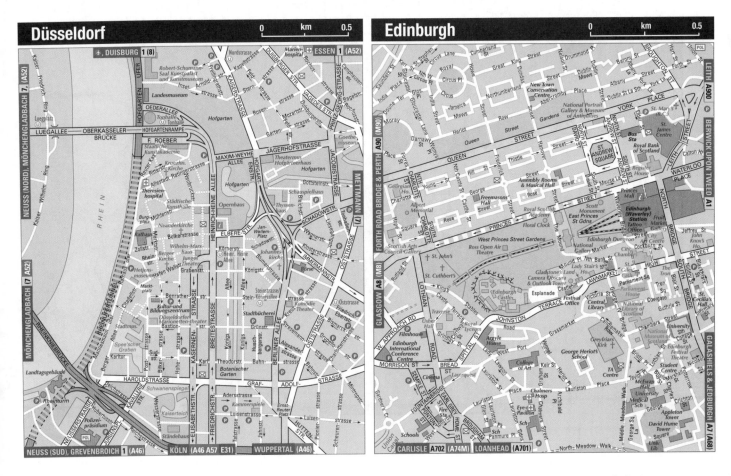

For **Cologne** see page 132

For **Copenhagen** see page 132

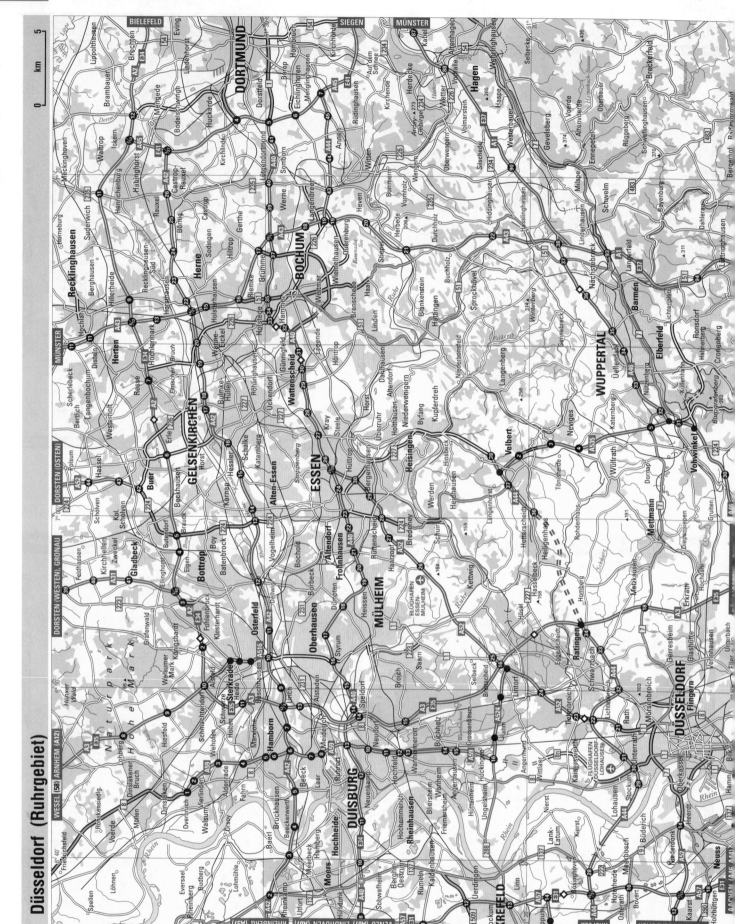

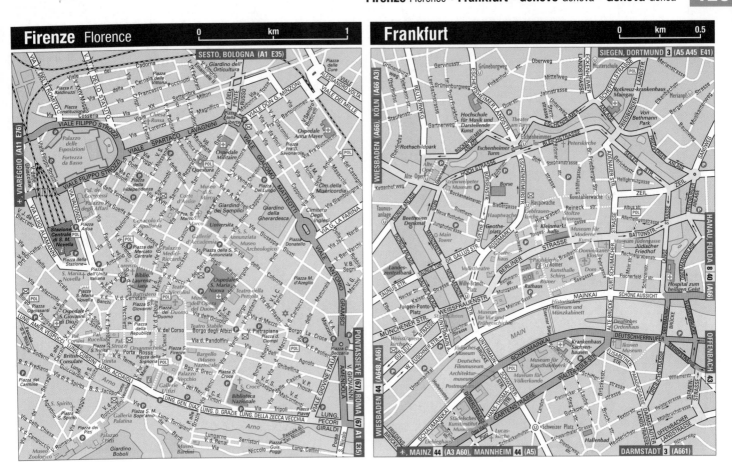

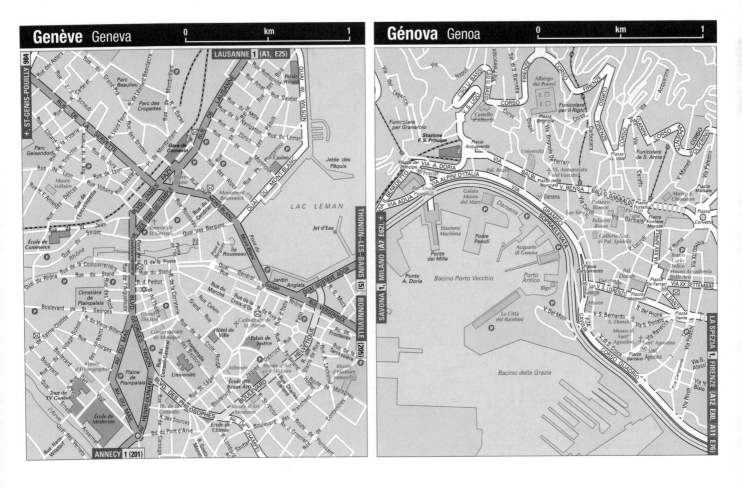

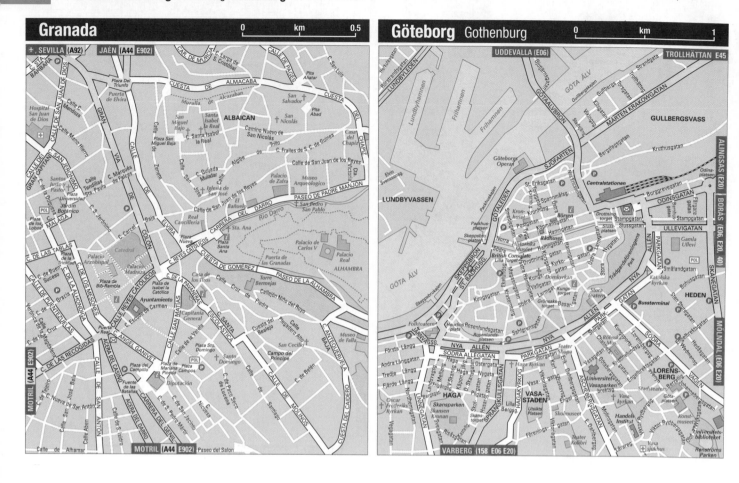

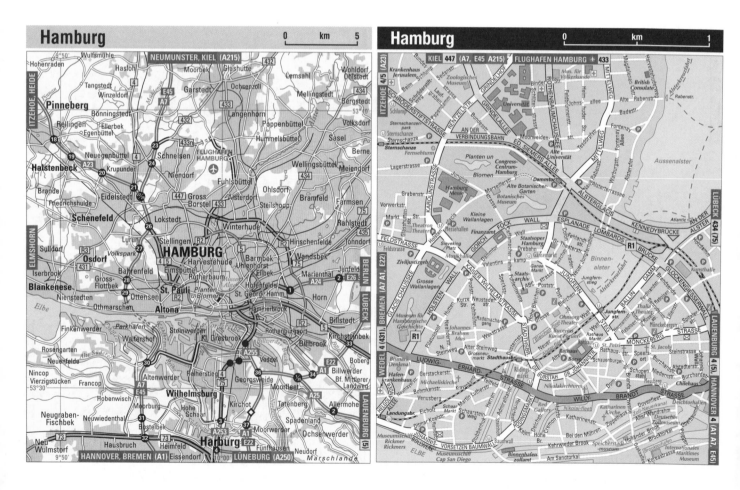

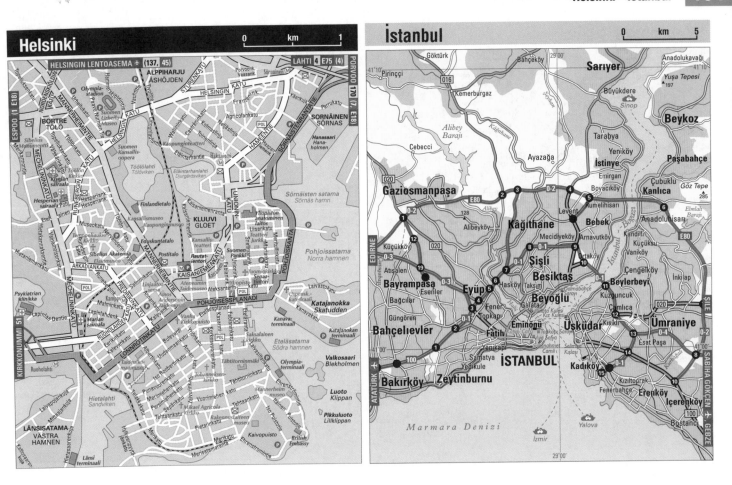

Helsinki

İstanbul

Helsinki

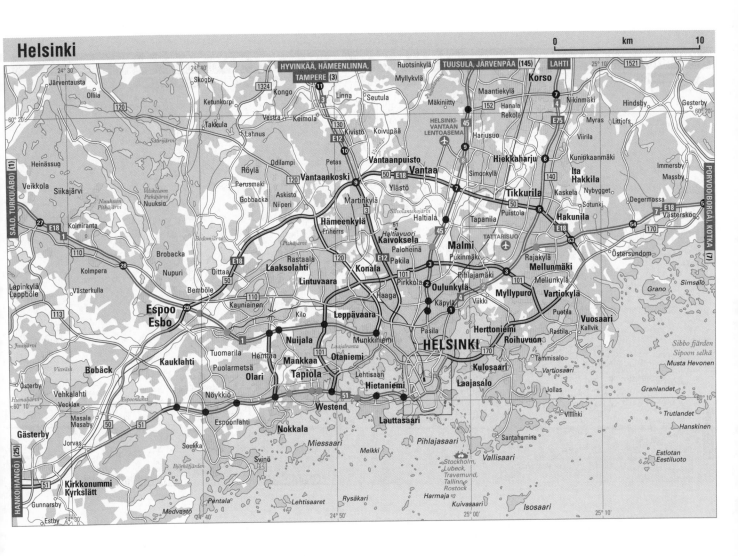

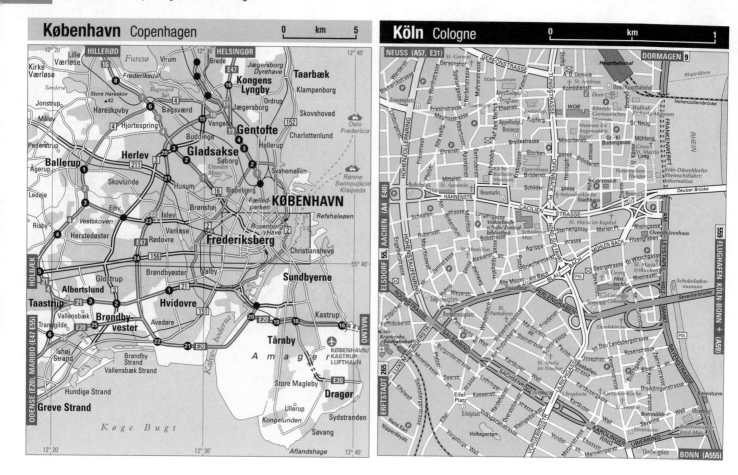

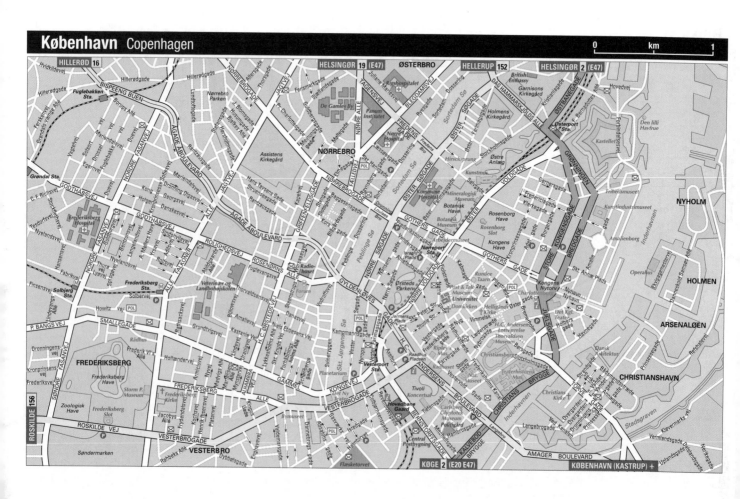

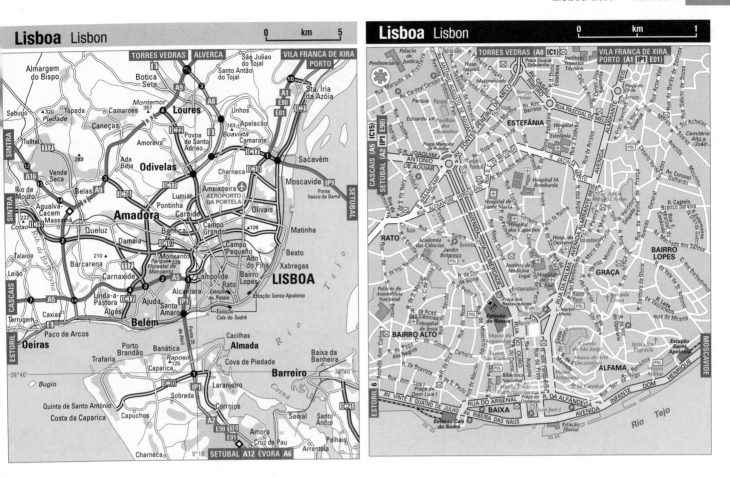

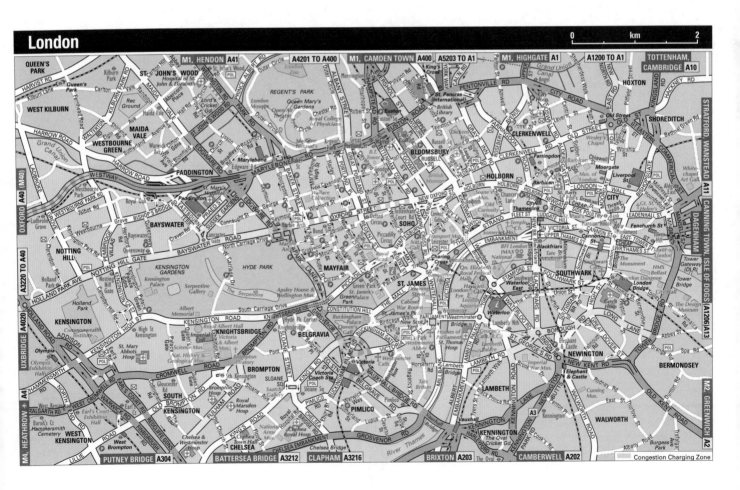

London

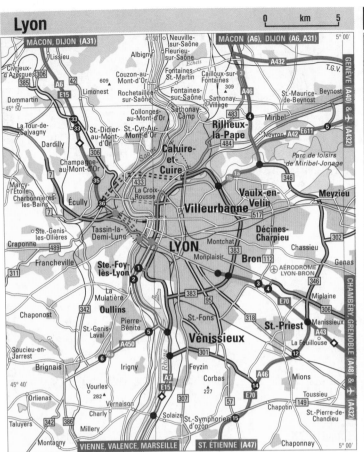

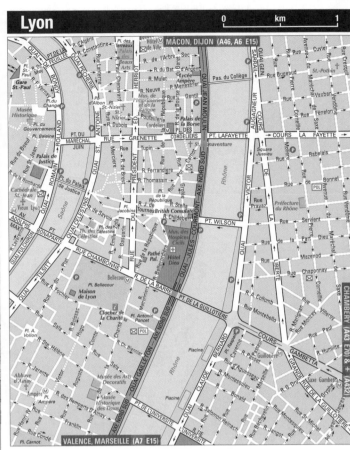

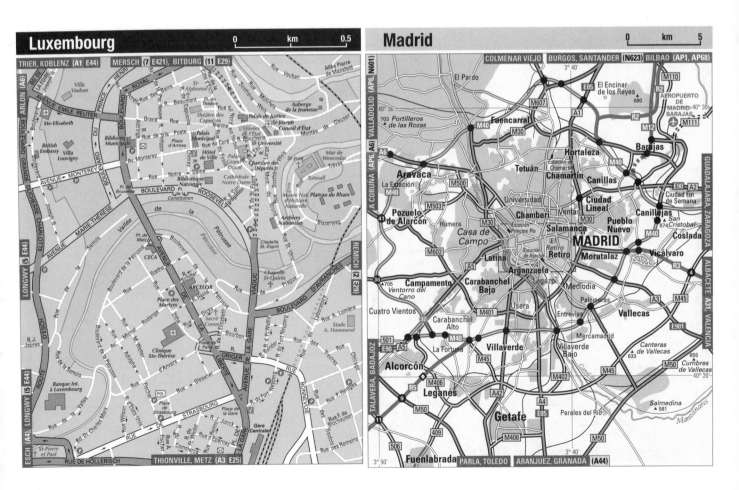

Madrid

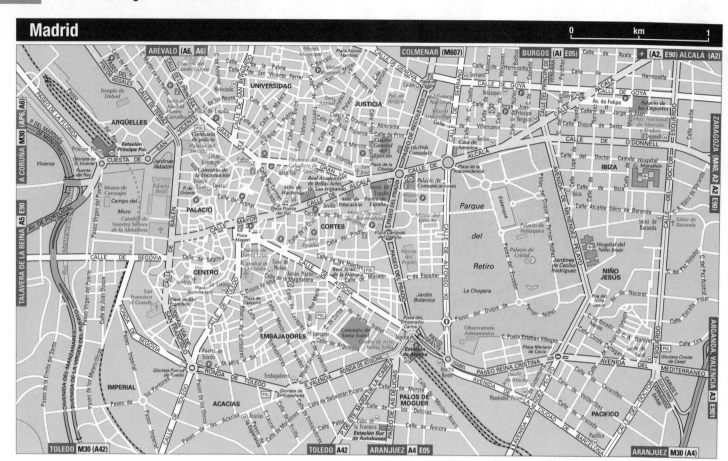

Málaga

Marseille Marseilles

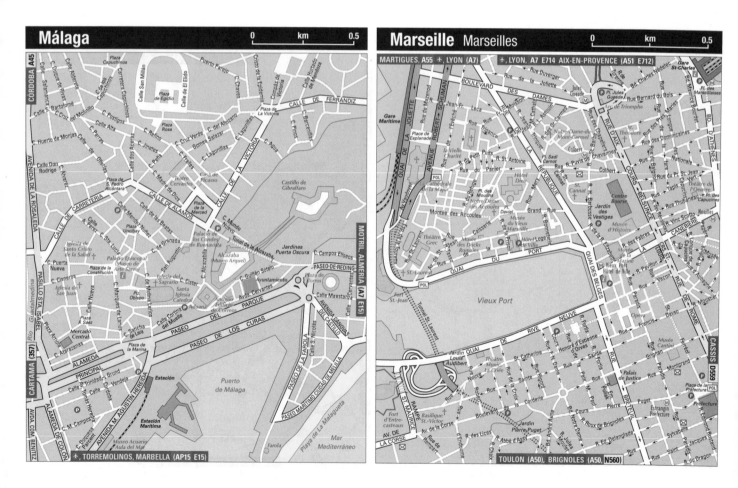

Milano

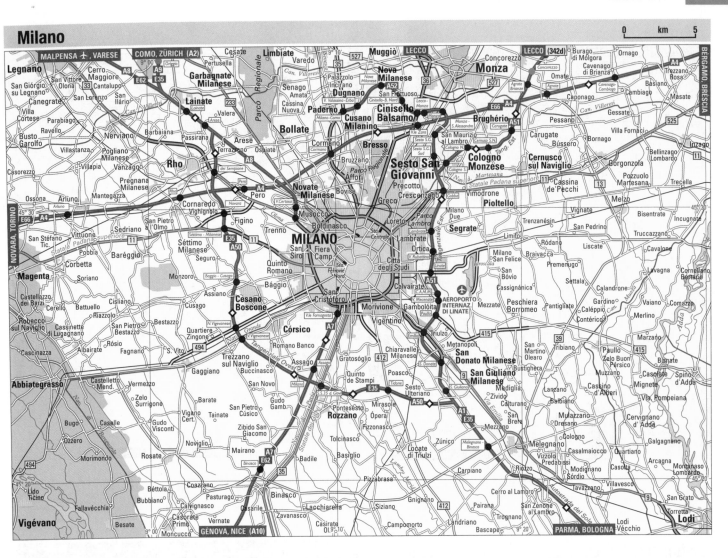

Milano Milan

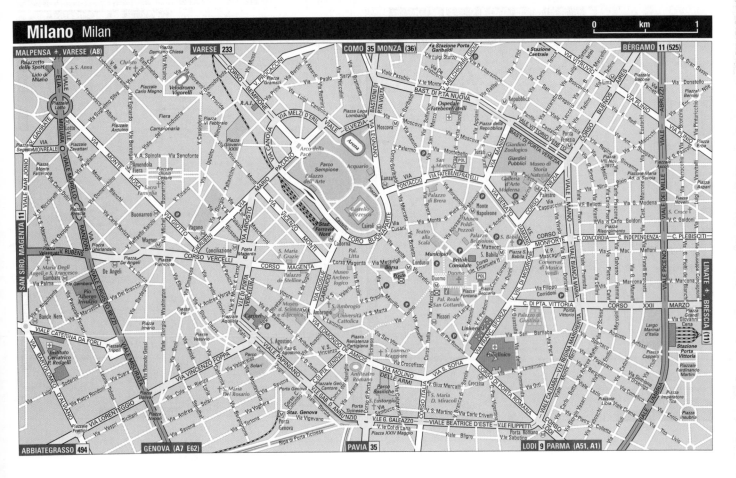

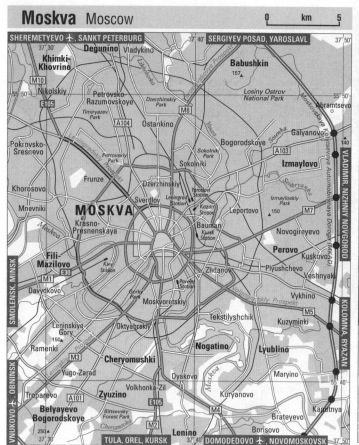

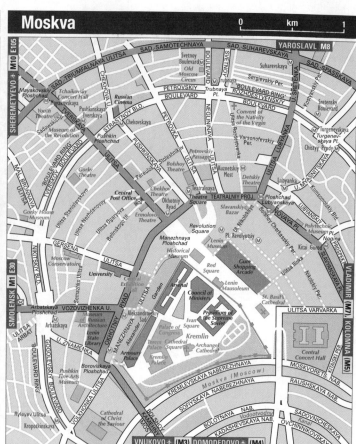

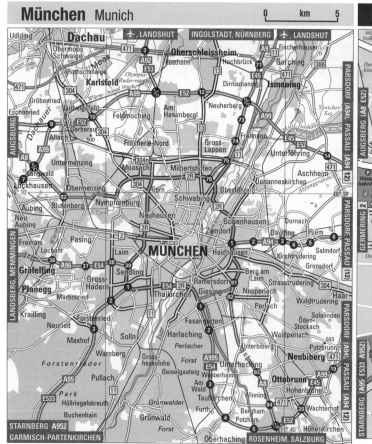

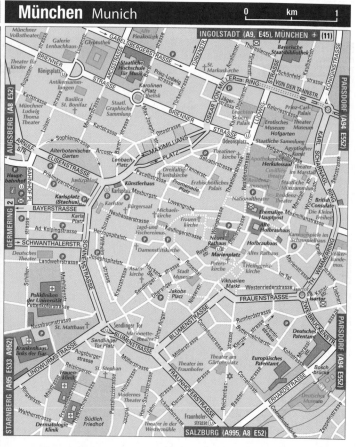

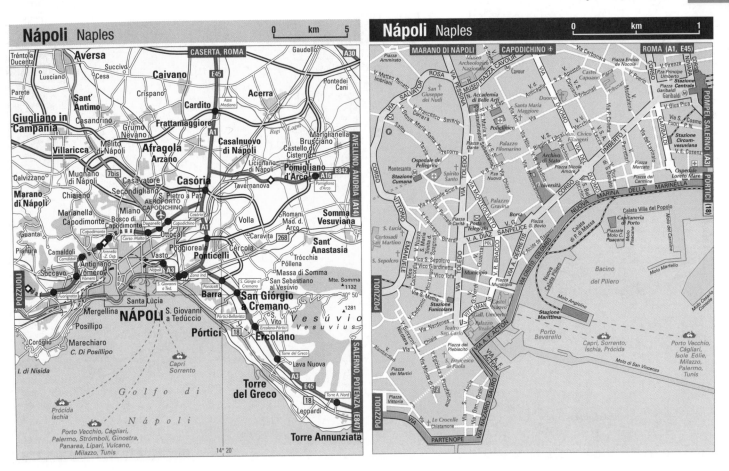

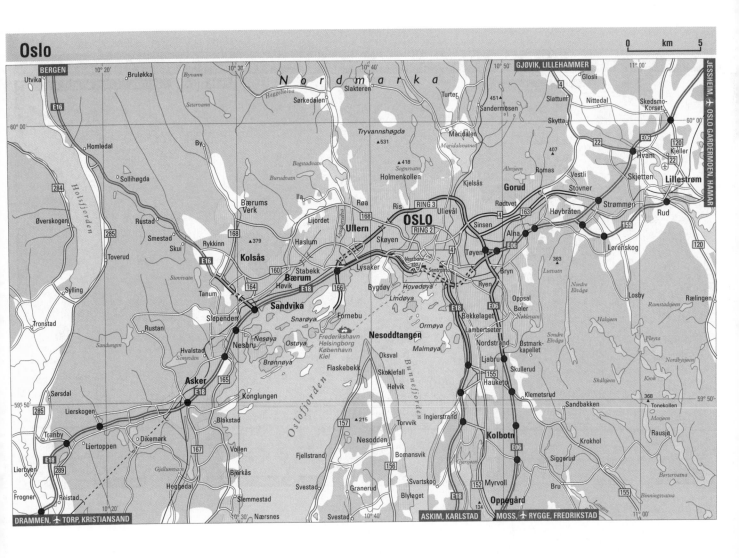

Oslo

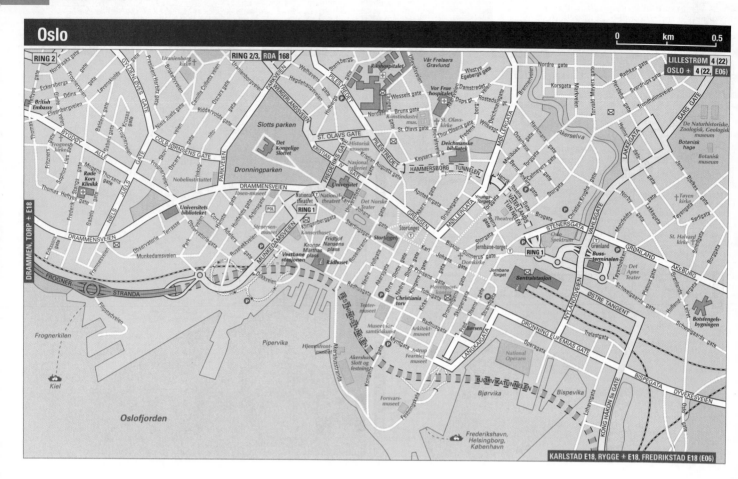

Paris

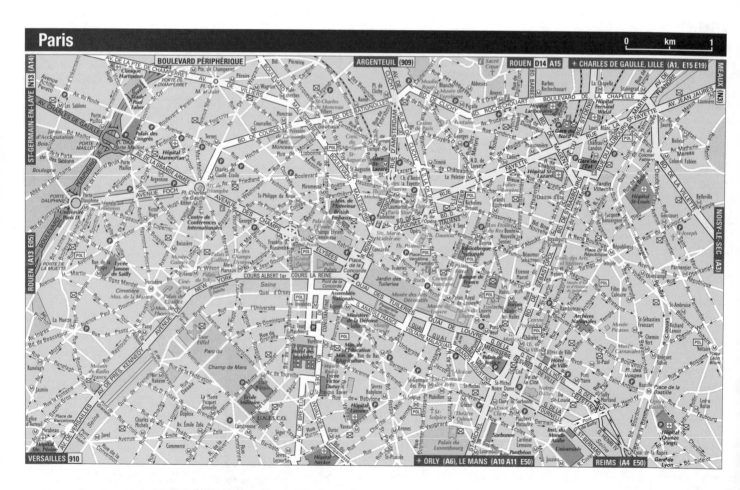

Paris

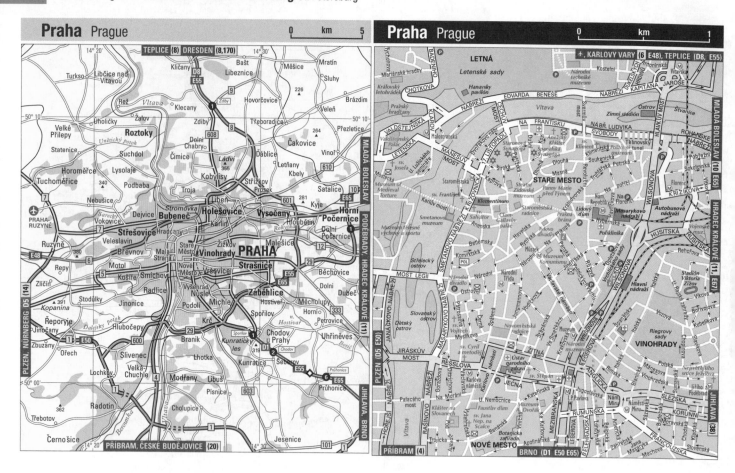

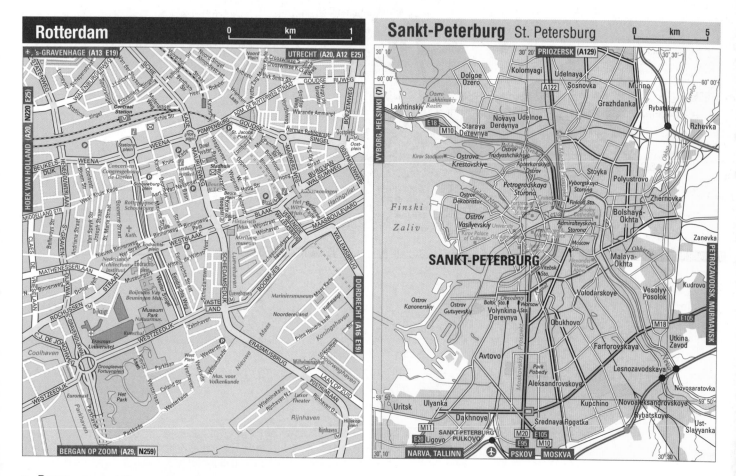

For **Rome** see page 143

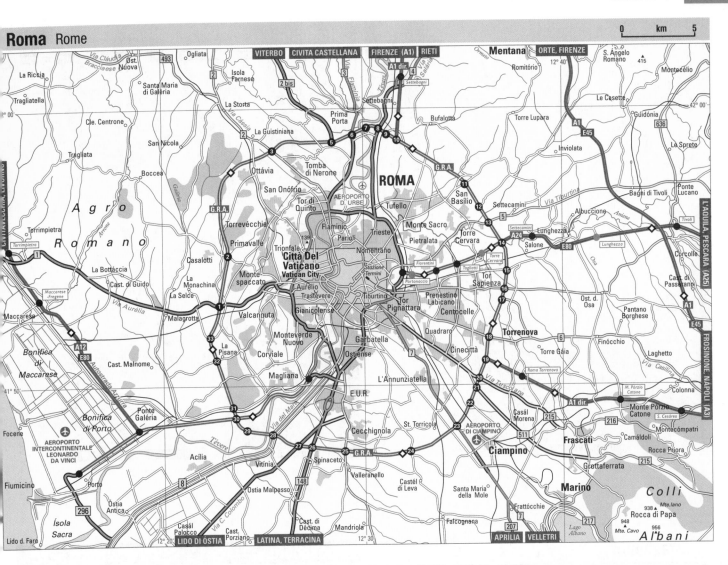

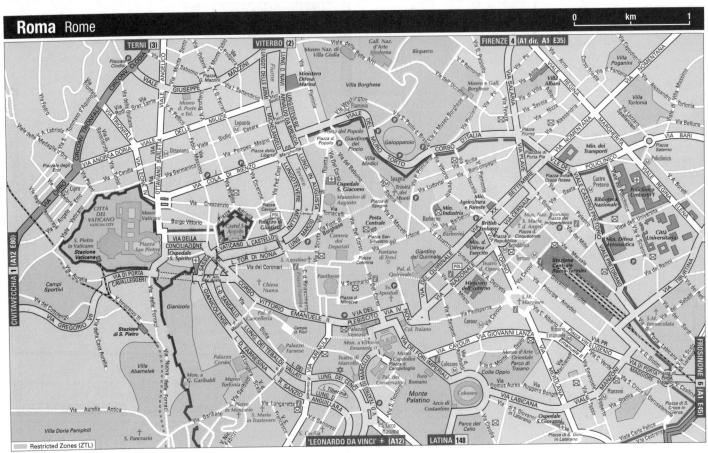

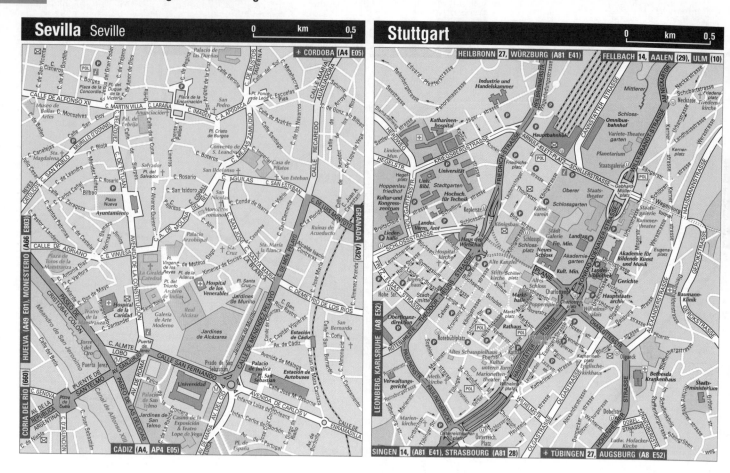

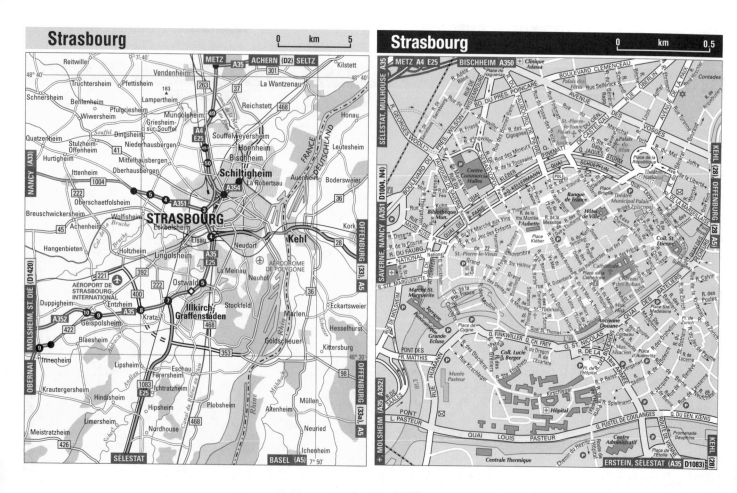

Stockholm

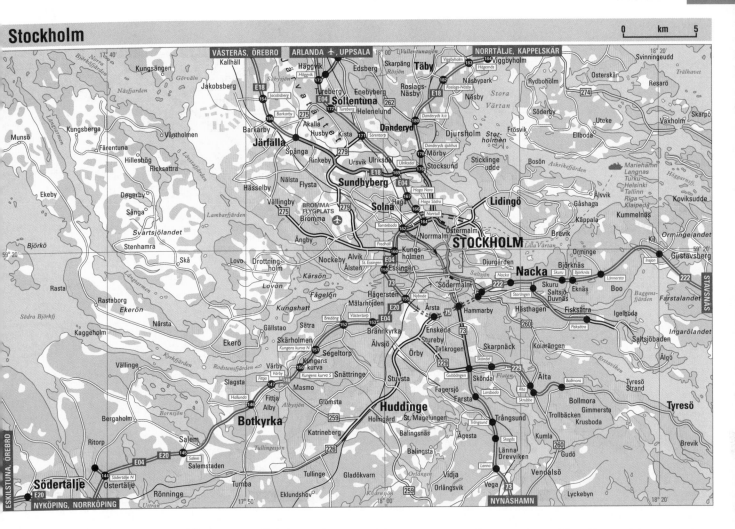

0 km 5

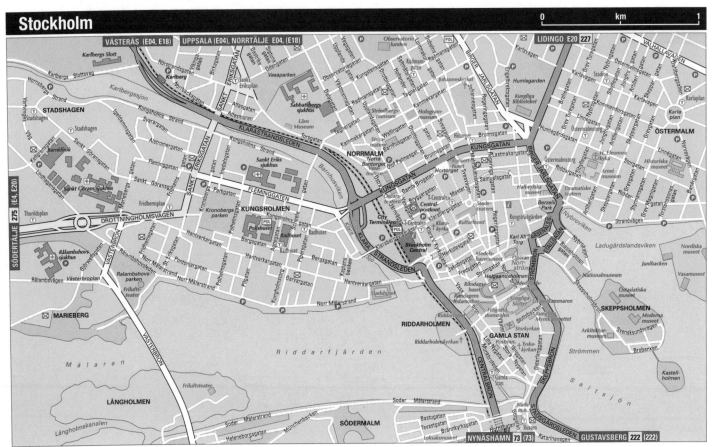

Stockholm

0 km 1

Torino Turin

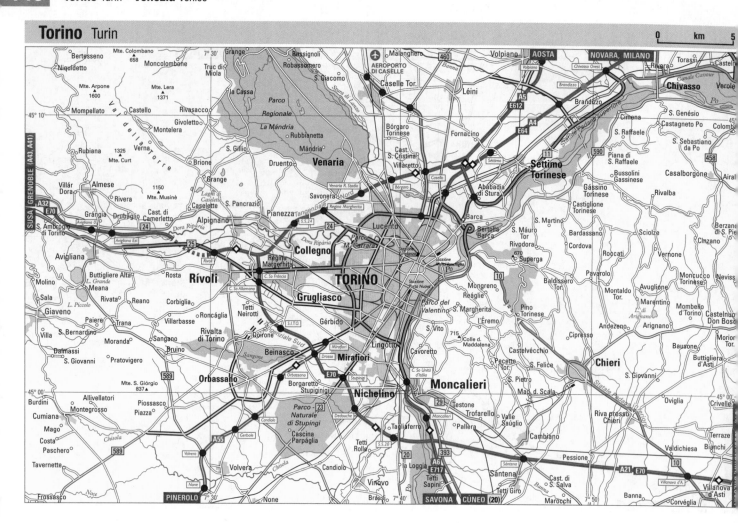

Venézia Venice

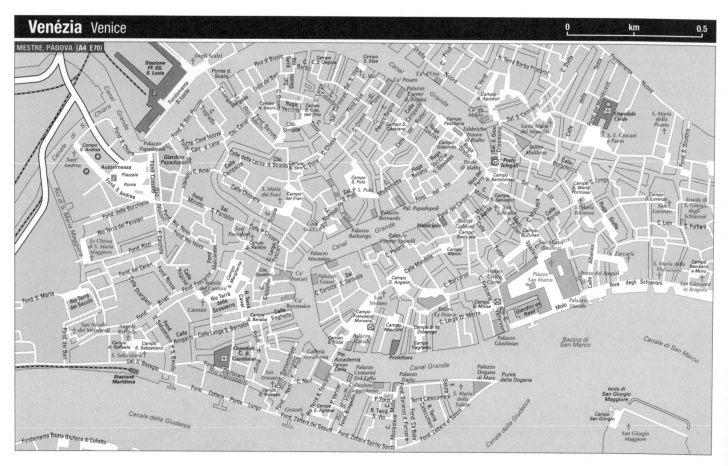

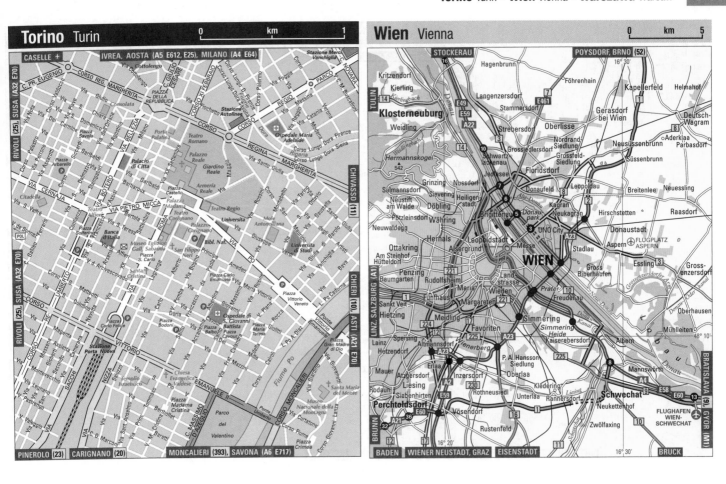

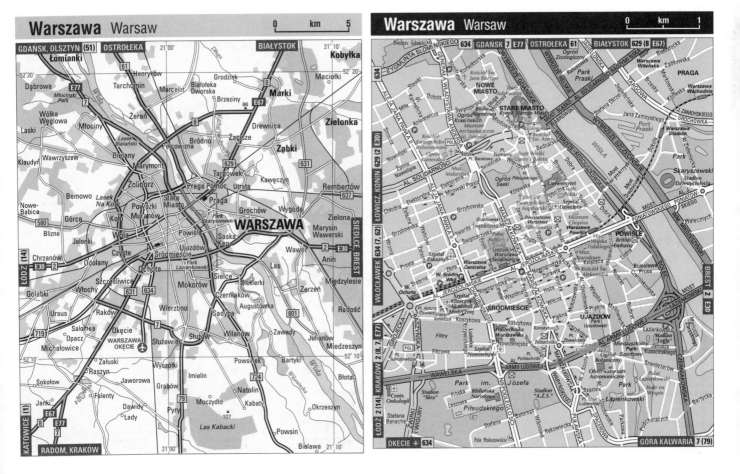

Wien Vienna

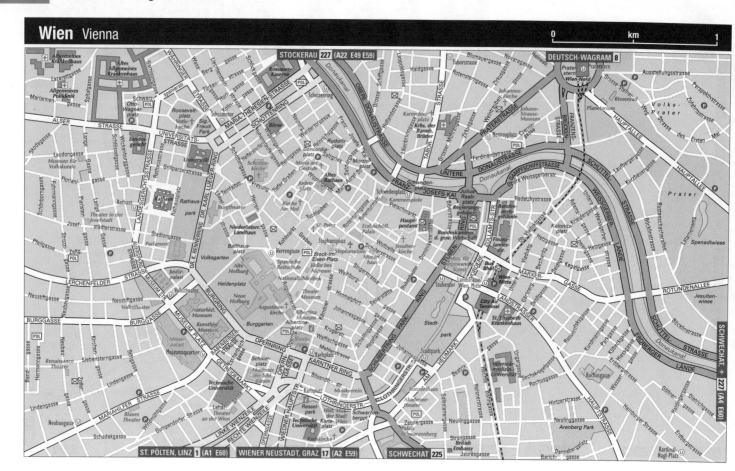

Zagreb

Zürich

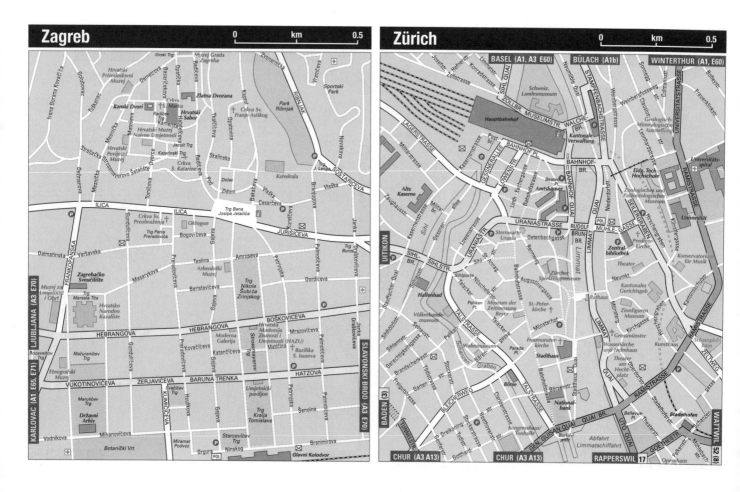

	GB	F	D	I
A	Austria	Autriche	Österreich	Austria
AL	Albania	Albanie	Albanien	Albania
AND	Andorra	Andorre	Andorra	Andorra
B	Belgium	Belgique	Belgien	Belgio
BG	Bulgaria	Bulgarie	Bulgarien	Bulgaria
BIH	Bosnia-Herzegovin	Bosnia-Herzegovine	Bosnien-Herzegowina	Bosnia-Herzegovina
BY	Belarus	Belarus	Weissrussland	Bielorussia
CH	Switzerland	Suisse	Schweiz	Svizzera
CY	Cyprus	Chypre	Zypern	Cipro
CZ	Czech Republic	République Tchèque	Tschechische Republik	Repubblica Ceca
D	Germany	Allemagne	Deutschland	Germania
DK	Denmark	Danemark	Dänemark	Danimarca
E	Spain	Espagne	Spanien	Spagna
EST	Estonia	Estonie	Estland	Estonia
F	France	France	Frankreich	Francia
FIN	Finland	Finlande	Finnland	Finlandia
FL	Liechtenstein	Liechtenstein	Liechtenstein	Liechtenstein
FO	Faeroe Islands	Îles Féroé	Färoër-Inseln	Isole Faroe
GB	United Kingdom	Royaume Uni	Grossbritannien und Nordirland	Regno Unito
GBZ	Gibraltar	Gibraltar	Gibraltar	Gibilterra
GR	Greece	Grèce	Greichenland	Grecia
H	Hungary	Hongrie	Ungarn	Ungheria
HR	Croatia	Croatie	Kroatien	Croazia
I	Italy	Italie	Italien	Italia
IRL	Ireland	Irlande	Irland	Irlanda
IS	Iceland	Islande	Island	Islanda
KOS	Kosovo	Kosovo	Kosovo	Kosovo
L	Luxembourg	Luxembourg	Luxemburg	Lussemburgo
LT	Lithuania	Lituanie	Litauen	Lituania
LV	Latvia	Lettonie	Lettland	Lettonia
M	Malta	Malte	Malta	Malta
MC	Monaco	Monaco	Monaco	Monaco
MD	Moldova	Moldavie	Moldawien	Moldavia
MK	Macedonia	Macédoine	Makedonien	Macedonia
MNE	Montenegro	Monténégro	Montenegro	Montenegro
N	Norway	Norvège	Norwegen	Norvegia
NL	Netherlands	Pays-Bas	Niederlande	Paesi Bassi
P	Portugal	Portugal	Portugal	Portogallo
PL	Poland	Pologne	Polen	Polonia
RO	Romania	Roumanie	Rumanien	Romania
RSM	San Marino	Saint-Marin	San Marino	San Marino
RUS	Russia	Russie	Russland	Russia
S	Sweden	Suède	Schweden	Svezia
SK	Slovak Republic	République Slovaque	Slowak Republik	Repubblica Slovacca
SLO	Slovenia	Slovénie	Slowenien	Slovenia
SRB	Serbia	Serbie	Serbien	Serbia
TR	Turkey	Turquie	Türkei	Turchia
UA	Ukraine	Ukraine	Ukraine	Ucraina

A

A Baña E 86 B2
A Bola E 87 B3
A Cañiza E 87 B2
A Capela E 86 A2
A Coruña E 86 A2
A Estrada E 86 B2
A Fonsagrada E 86 A3
A Guarda E 87 C2
A Gudiña E 87 B3
A Merca E 87 B3
A Peroxa E 86 B3
A Pontenova E 86 A3
A Rúa E 87 B3
A Teixeira E 87 B3
A Veiga E 87 B3
A-Ver-o-Mar P 87 C2
Aabenraa DK 39 D2
Aabybro DK 38 B2
Aach D 71 A4
Aachen D 50 C2
Aalborg DK 38 B2
Aalen D 61 B6
Aalestrup DK 38 C2
Aalsmeer NL 49 A5
Aalst B 49 C5
Aalten NL 50 B2
Aalter B 49 B4
Äänekoski FIN 3 E26
Aapajärvi FIN 113 E16
Aarau CH 70 A3
Aarberg CH 70 A2
Aarburg CH 70 A2
Aardenburg NL 49 B4
Aars DK 38 C2
Aarschot B 49 C5
Aarup DK 39 D3
Aba H 74 A3
Abádanes E 95 B4
Abades E 94 B2
Abadin E 86 A3
Abádszalók H 75 A5
Abaliget H 74 B3
Abana TR 16 A7
Abanilla E 101 A4
Abano Terme I 72 C1
Abarán E 101 A4
Abasár H 65 C6
Abbadia San Salvatore I 81 D5
Abbaue D 45 B5
Abbehausen D 43 B5
Abbekäs S 41 D3
Abbeville F 48 C2
Abbey IRL 20 A3
Abbey Town GB 25 D4
Abbeydorney IRL 20 B2
Abbeyfeale IRL 20 B2
Abbeyleix IRL 21 B4
Abbiategrasso I 70 C3
Abborrträsk S 115 B16
Abbots Bromley GB 27 C4
Abbotsbury GB 29 C5
Abda H 64 C3
Abejar E 89 C4
Abela P 98 B2
Abelvær N 114 C8
Abenberg D 62 A1
Abenójar E 100 A1
Abensberg D 62 B2
Aberaeron GB 28 A3
Abercarn GB 29 B4
Aberchirder GB 23 D6
Aberdare GB 29 B4
Aberdaron GB 26 C1
Aberdeen GB 23 D6
Aberdulais GB 28 B4
Aberdyfi GB 26 C1
Aberfeldy GB 25 B4
Aberffraw GB 26 B1
Aberfoyle GB 24 B3
Abergavenny GB 29 B4
Abergele GB 26 B2
Abergynolwyn GB 26 C2
Aberporth GB 28 A3
Abersoch GB 26 C1
Abertillery GB 29 B4
Abertura E 93 B5
Aberystwyth GB 26 C1
Abetone I 81 B4
Abfaltersbach A 72 B2
Abide, *Çanakkale* TR 118 B1
Abide, *Kütahya* TR 118 D4
Abiego E 90 A2
Abild DK 39 E1
Abingdon GB 31 C2
Abington GB 25 C4
Abisko S 112 D7
Abiul P 92 B2
Abla E 101 B3
Ablis F 58 B2
Abondance F 70 B1
Abony H 75 A5
Aboyne GB 23 D6
Abrantes P 92 B2
Abreiro P 87 C3
Abreschviller F 60 B3
Abrest F 68 B3
Abriès F 79 B5
Abrud RO 11 C7
Absdorf A 64 B1
Abtenau A 72 A3
Abtsgmünd D 61 B5
Abusejo E 93 A4
Åby, *Kronoberg* S 40 B4
Åby, *Östergötland* S 37 D3
Åbyggeby S 36 B4
Åbytorp S 37 C2
Acate I 109 B3
Accadía I 103 B8
Accéglio I 79 B5
Accettura I 104 C2
Acciaroli I 106 A2
Accous F 76 D2
Accrington GB 26 B3
Accúmoli I 82 D2
Acedera E 93 B5
Acehuche E 93 B4
Acered E 95 A5
Acerenza I 104 C1
Acerno I 103 C8
Acerra I 103 C7
Aceuchal E 93 C4
Acharacle GB 24 B2
Acharnes GR 117 D5
Achavanich GB 23 C5
Achene B 49 C6
Achenkirch A 72 A1
Achensee A 72 A1
Achenthal A 72 A1
Achentrias GR 117 H7
Achern D 61 B4
Acheux-en-Amienois F 48 C3
Achiltibuie GB 22 C3
Achim D 43 B6
Achladokambos GR 117 E4
Achnasheen GB 22 D3
Achnashellach GB 22 D3
Achosnich GB 24 B1
Aci Castello I 109 B4
Aci Catena I 109 B4
Acilia I 102 B5
Acıpayam TR 119 E4
Acireale I 109 B4
Acle GB 30 B5
Acqua Doria F 102 B1
Acquacadda I 110 C1
Acquanegra sul Chiese I 71 C5
Acquapendente I 81 D5
Acquasanta Terme I 82 D2
Acquasparta I 102 A5
Acquaviva I 81 C5
Acquaviva delle Fonti I 104 C2
Acquaviva Picena I 82 D2
Ácqui Terme I 80 B2
Acquigny F 58 A2
Acri I 106 B3
Acs H 64 C4
Acsa H 65 C5
Ácsteszér H 74 A2
Acy-en-Multien F 59 A3
Ada SRB 75 C5
Adak S 115 B15
Ådalsbruk N 34 B3
Adamas GR 117 F6
Adamsfjord N 113 B15
Adamuz E 100 A1
Adana TR 16 C7
Ádánd H 74 B3
Adanero E 94 B2
Adare IRL 20 B3
Adaševci SRB 85 A4
Adeanueva de Ebro E 89 B5
Adelboden CH 70 B2
Adelebsen D 51 B5
Adélfia I 104 B2
Adelmannsfelden D 61 B6
Adelsheim D 61 A5
Adelsö S 37 C4
Ademuz E 96 A1
Adenau D 50 C2
Adendorf D 44 B2
Adinkerke B 48 B3
Adjud RO 11 C9
Adliswil CH 70 A3
Admont A 63 C5
Ådneram N 33 C3
Adolfsström S 115 A13
Adony H 74 A3
Adorf, *Hessen* D 51 B4
Adorf, *Sachsen* D 52 C2
Adra E 100 C2
Adradas E 89 C4
Adrall E 91 A4
Adrano I 109 B3
Ádria I 82 A1
Adrigole IRL 20 C2
Adwick le Street GB 27 B4
Adzaneta E 96 A2
Ærøskøbing DK 39 E3
Aesch CH 70 A2
Afandou GR 119 F3
Åfarnes N 114 E4
Affing D 62 B1
Affoltern CH 70 A3
Affric Lodge GB 22 D3
Åfjord N 114 D7
Aflenz Kurort A 73 A5
Afragóla I 103 C7
Afritz A 72 B3
Afyon TR 118 D5
Ağapınar TR 118 C5
Ágasegyháza H 75 B4
Agay F 79 C5
Agazzano I 80 B3
Agde F 78 C2
Agdenes N 114 D6
Agen F 77 B3
Ager E 90 B3
Agerbæk DK 39 D1
Agerskov DK 39 D2
Ageyevo RUS 7 D14
Agger DK 38 C1
Aggersund DK 38 B2
Ággius I 110 B2
Aggsbach Dorf A 63 B6
Aggsbach Markt A 63 B6
Aggtelek H 65 B6
Aghalee GB 19 B5
Aghia GR 116 C4
Aghia Anna GR 116 D5
Aghia Galini GR 117 G6
Aghia Marina, *Dodekanisa* GR 119 G1
Aghia Marina, *Dodekanisa* GR 119 E1
Aghia Paraskevi GR 118 C1
Aghia Pelagia GR 117 F4
Aghia Triada GR 117 E3
Aghio Theodori GR 117 E5
Aghiokambos GR 116 C4
Aghios Efstratios GR 116 C6
Aghios Kirikos GR 119 E1
Aghios Matheos GR 116 C1
Aghios Mironas GR 117 G7
Aghios Nikolaos GR 117 G7
Aghios Petros GR 116 D2
Agiči BIH 83 B5
Agira I 109 B3
Ağlasun TR 119 E5
Aglientu I 110 A2
Agnières F 79 B4
Agno CH 70 C3
Agnone I 103 B7
Agolada E 86 B2
Agon Coutainville F 57 A4
Ágordo I 72 B2
Agost E 96 C2
Agramón E 101 A4
Agramunt E 91 B4
Agreda E 89 C5
Agria GR 116 C5
Agrigento I 108 B2
Agrinio GR 116 D3
Agrón E 100 B2
Agrópoli I 103 C7
Agua Longa P 87 C2
Aguadulce, *Almería* E 101 C3
Aguadulce, *Sevilla* E 100 B1
Agualada E 86 A2
Aguarón E 89 C5
Aguas E 90 A2
Aguas Belas P 92 B2
Aguas de Busot E 96 C2
Aguas de Moura P 92 C2
Águas Frias P 87 C3
Aguas Santas P 87 C2
Aguaviva E 90 C2
Aguaviva de la Vega E 89 C4
Agudo E 94 D2
Águeda P 92 A2
Aguessac F 78 B2
Agugliano I 82 C2
Aguiar P 92 C3
Aguiàr da Beira P 87 D3
Aguilafuente E 94 A2
Aguilar de Campóo E 88 B2
Aguilar de la Frontera E 100 B1
Aguilas E 101 B4
Agunnaryd S 40 C4
Ağva TR 118 A4
Ahat TR 118 D4
Ahaus D 50 A2
Åheim N 114 E2
Ahigal E 93 A4
Ahigal de Villarino E 87 C4
Ahillones E 99 A5
Ahlbeck, *Mecklenburg-Vorpommern* D 45 B6
Ahlbeck, *Mecklenburg-Vorpommern* D 45 B6
Ahlen D 50 B3
Ahlhorn D 43 C5
Ahmetbey TR 118 A2
Ahmetler TR 119 D4
Ahmetli TR 119 D2
Ahoghill GB 19 B5
Ahrensbök D 44 A2
Ahrensburg D 44 B2
Ahrenshoop D 44 A4
Ahun F 68 B2
Åhus S 41 D4
Ahvenselkä FIN 113 F17
Aibar E 89 B5
Aich D 62 B3
Aicha D 63 B4
Aichach D 62 B2
Aidone I 109 B3
Aiello Cálabro I 106 B3
Aigen im Mühlkreis A 63 B4
Aigle CH 70 B1
Aignan F 76 C3
Aignay-le-Duc F 59 C5
Aigre F 67 C5
Aigrefeuille-d'Aunis F 66 B4
Aigrefeuille-sur-Maine F 66 A3
Aiguablava E 91 B6
Aiguebelle F 69 C6
Aigueperse F 68 B3
Aigues-Mortes F 78 C3
Aigues-Vives F 78 C1
Aiguilles F 79 B5
Aiguillon F 77 B3
Aigurande F 68 B1
Ailefroide F 79 B5
Aillant-sur-Tholon F 59 C4
Ailly-sur-Noye F 58 A3
Ailly-sur-Somme F 58 A3
Aimargues F 78 C3
Aime F 70 C1
Ainaži LV 6 C8
Ainet A 72 B2
Ainhoa F 76 C1
Ainsa E 90 A3
Airaines F 48 D2
Aird GB 24 B2
Aird Asaig Tairbeart GB 22 D2
Airdrie GB 25 C4
Aire-sur-la-Lys F 48 C3
Aire-sur-l'Adour F 76 C2
Airole I 80 C1
Airolo CH 70 B3
Airvault F 67 B4
Aisey-sur-Seine F 59 C5
Aïssey F 69 A6
Aisy-sur-Armançon F 59 C5
Aiterhofen D 62 B3
Aith, *Orkney* GB 23 B6
Aith, *Shetland* GB 22 A7
Aitona E 90 B3
Aitrach D 61 C6
Aiud RO 11 C7
Aix-en-Othe F 59 B4
Aix-en-Provence F 79 C4
Aix-les-Bains F 69 C5
Aixe-sur-Vienne F 67 C6
Aizenay F 66 B3
Aizkraukle LV 7 C8
Aizpute LV 6 C6
Ajac F 77 C5
Ajaccio F 102 B1
Ajain F 68 B1
Ajaureforsen S 115 B12
Ajdovščina SLO 72 C3
Ajka H 74 A2
Ajo E 89 A3
Ajofrin E 94 C3
Ajuda P 93 C3
Akanthou CY 120 A2
Akarca TR 118 D4
Akasztó H 75 B4
Akçakoca TR 118 A6
Akçaova TR 118 A4
Akçay TR 119 F4
Aken D 52 B2
Åkerby S 36 B4
Åkernes N 33 D4
Åkers styckebruk S 37 C4
Åkersberga S 37 C5
Åkervik N 115 B10
Akhisar TR 118 D2
Åkirkeby DK 41 D4
Akköy TR 119 E2
Akkrum NL 42 B2
Akören TR 119 E7
Åkra N 32 C3
Akranes IS 111 C3
Åkrehamn N 33 C2
Akrotiri CY 120 B1
Aksaray TR 16 B7
Akşehir TR 119 D6
Akseki TR 119 E6
Aksla N 32 A3
Aksu TR 119 F5
Aktsyabrski BY 7 E10
Akureyri IS 111 B7
Åkvåg N 33 D6
Akyazı TR 118 B5
Ål N 32 B5
Ala I 71 C6
Alà dei Sardi I 110 B2
Ala di Stura I 70 C2
Ala-Nampa FIN 113 F15
Alaca TR 16 A7
Alacaatlı TR 118 C3
Alaçam TR 16 A7
Alaçatı TR 119 D1
Alaejos E 88 C1
Alagna Valsésia I 70 C2
Alagón E 90 B1
Alaior E 97 B4
Alájar E 99 B4
Alakurtti RUS 3 C29
Alakylä FIN 113 E13
Alameda E 100 B1
Alameda de la Sagra E 94 B3
Alamedilla E 100 B2
Alamillo E 100 A1
Alaminos E 95 B4
Alanäs S 115 C12
Alandroal P 92 C3
Alange E 93 C4
Alanís E 99 A5
Alanno I 103 A6
Ålansbro S 115 E14
Alanya TR 119 F7
Alap H 74 B3
Alaquáso E 96 B2
Alar del Rey E 88 B2
Alaraz E 94 B1
Alarcón E 95 C4
Alaró E 97 B2
Alaşehir TR 119 D3
Alássio I 80 B2
Alatoz E 96 B1
Alatri I 103 B6
Alavus FIN 3 E25
Alba E 95 B5
Alba I 80 B2
Alba Adriática I 82 D2
Alba de Tormes E 94 B1
Alba de Yeltes E 93 A4
Alba-Iulia RO 11 C7
Albacete E 95 D5
Albæk DK 38 B3
Albaida E 96 C2
Albala del Caudillo E 93 B4
Albaladejo E 101 A3
Albalat E 96 B2
Albalate de Cinca E 90 B3
Albalate de las Nogueras E 95 B4
Albalate del Arzobispo E 90 B2
Albalete de Zorita E 95 B4
Alban F 77 C5
Albánchez E 101 B3
Albanchez de Ubeda E 100 B2
Albano Laziale I 102 B5
Albanyà E 91 A5
Albaredo d'Adige I 71 C6
Albares E 95 B3
Albarracín E 95 B5
Albatana E 101 A4
Albatarrec E 90 B3
Albatera E 101 A5
Albbruck D 61 C4
Albedin E 100 B1
Albelda de Iregua E 89 B4
Albenga I 80 B2
Albens F 69 C5
Ålberga, *Södermanland* S 37 D3
Ålberga, *Södermanland* S 37 C3
Albergaria-a-Nova P 87 D2
Albergaria-a-Velha P 92 A2
Albergaria dos Doze P 92 B2
Alberge P 92 C2
Alberic E 96 B2
Albernoa P 98 B3
Alberobello I 104 C3
Alberoni I 72 C2
Albersdorf D 43 A6
Albersloh D 50 B3
Albert F 48 C3
Albertirsa H 75 A4
Albertville F 69 C6
Alberuela de Tubo E 90 B2
Albi F 77 C5
Albidona I 106 B3
Albínia I 102 A4
Albino I 71 C4
Albinshof D 45 B5
Albires E 88 B1
Albisola Marina I 80 B2
Albocácer E 90 C3
Albolote E 100 B2
Albondón E 100 C2
Alborea E 96 B1
Albox E 101 B3
Albrechtice nad Vitavou CZ 63 A5
Albstadt D 61 B5
Albufeira P 98 B2
Albuñol E 100 C2
Albuñuelas E 100 C2
Alburquerque E 93 B3
Alby, *Öland* S 41 C6
Alby, *Västernorrland* S 115 E12
Alcácer do Sal P 92 C2
Alcáçovas P 92 C2
Alcadozo E 101 A4
Alcafoces P 93 B3
Alcains P 92 B3
Alcalá de Guadaira E 99 B5
Alcalá de Gurrea E 90 A2
Alcalá de Henares E 95 B3
Alcalá de la Selva E 90 C2
Alcalá de los Gazules E 99 C5
Alcalá de Xivert E 90 C3
Alcalá del Júcar E 96 B1
Alcalá del Río E 99 B5
Alcalá del Valle E 99 C5
Alcalá la Real E 100 B2
Álcamo I 108 B1
Alcampell E 90 B3
Alcanadre E 89 B4
Alcanar E 90 C3
Alcanede P 92 B2
Alcanena P 92 B2
Alcañices E 87 C4
Alcántara E 93 B4
Alcantarilha P 98 B2
Alcantarilla E 101 B4
Alcañiz E 90 B2
Alcara il Fusi I 109 A3
Alcaracejos E 100 A1
Alcaraz E 101 A3
Alcaria Ruiva P 98 B3
Alcarraz E 90 B3
Alcaudete E 100 B1
Alcaudete de la Jara E 94 C2
Alcázar de San Juan E 95 C3
Alcazarén E 88 C2
Alcester GB 29 A6
Alcoba E 94 C2
Alcobaça P 92 B1
Alcobendas E 94 B3
Alcocer E 95 B4
Alcochete P 92 C2
Alcoentre P 92 B2
Alcolea, *Almería* E 100 C3
Alcolea, *Córdoba* E 100 B1
Alcolea de Calatrava E 94 D2
Alcolea de Cinca E 90 B3
Alcolea de Tajo E 93 B5
Alcolea del Pinar E 95 A4
Alcolea del Rio E 99 B5
Alcollarin E 93 B5
Alconchel E 93 C3
Alconera E 93 C4
Alcontar E 101 B3
Alcora E 96 A2
Alcorcón E 94 B3
Alcorisa E 90 C2
Alcossebre E 96 A3
Alcoutim P 98 B3
Alcover E 91 B4
Alcoy E 96 C2
Alcsútdoboz H 74 A3
Alcubierre E 90 B2
Alcubilla de Avellaneda E 89 C3
Alcubilla de Nogales E 88 B1

Alcubillas E 100 A2
Alcublas E 96 B2
Alcúdia E 97 B3
Alcudia de Guadix E 100 B2
Alcuéscar E 93 B4
Aldbrough GB 27 B5
Aldea de Trujillo E 93 B5
Aldea del Cano E 93 B4
Aldea del Fresno E 94 B2
Aldea del Obispo E 87 D4
Aldea del Rey E 100 A2
Aldea Real E 94 A2
Aldeacentenera E 93 B5
Aldeadávila de la Ribera E 87 C4
Aldealcorvo E 94 A3
Aldealuenga de Santa Maria E 89 C3
Aldeamayor de San Martin E 88 C2
Aldeanueva de Barbarroya E 94 C1
Aldeanueva de San Bartolomé E 94 C1
Aldeanueva del Camino E 93 A5
Aldeanueva del Codonal E 94 A2
Aldeapozo E 89 C4
Aldeaquemada E 100 A2
Aldearrubia E 94 A1
Aldeaseca de la Frontera E 94 B1
Aldeasoña E 88 C2
Aldeatejada E 94 B1
Aldeavieja E 94 B2
Aldeburgh GB 30 B5
Aldehuela E 96 A1
Aldehuela de Calatañazor E 89 C4
Aldeia da Serra P 92 C3
Aldeia do Bispo P 93 A4
Aldeia do Mato P 92 B2
Aldeia Gavinha P 92 B1
Aldeire E 100 B2
Aldenhoven D 50 C2
Aldersbach D 62 B4
Aldershot GB 31 C3
Aldudes F 76 C1
Åled S 40 C2
Aledo E 101 B4
Alegria E 89 B4
Aleksa Šantić SRB 75 C4
Aleksandrovac, *Srbija* SRB 85 B6
Aleksandrovac, *Srbija* SRB 85 C6
Aleksandrów Kujawski PL 47 C4
Aleksandrów Łódźki PL 55 B4
Aleksin RUS 7 D14
Ålem S 40 C6
Alençon F 57 B6
Alenquer P 92 B1
Alenya F 91 A5
Aléria F 102 A2
Alès F 78 B3
Áles I 110 C1
Alessándria I 80 B2
Alessándria della Rocca I 108 B2
Alessano I 107 B5
Ålesund N 114 E3
Alet-les-Bains F 77 D5
Alexandria GB 24 C3
Alexandria GR 116 B4
Alexandria RO 11 E8
Alexandroupoli GR 116 B7
Aleyrac F 78 B3
Alézio I 107 A5
Alfacar E 100 B2
Alfaiates P 93 A4
Alfajarin E 90 B2
Alfambra E 90 C1
Alfambra P 98 B2
Alfândega da Fé P 87 C4
Alfarela de Jafes P 87 C3
Alfarelos P 92 A2
Alfarim P 92 C1
Alfarnate E 100 C1
Alfaro E 89 B5
Alfarrás E 90 B3
Alfaz del Pi E 96 C2
Alfedena I 103 B7
Alfeizarão P 92 B1
Alfeld, *Bayern* D 62 A2
Alfeld, *Niedersachsen* D 51 B5
Alfena P 87 C2
Alferce P 98 B2
Alfhausen D 43 C4
Alfonsine I 81 B6
Alford, *Aberdeenshire* GB 23 D6
Alford, *Lincolnshire* GB 27 B6
Alforja E 90 B3
Alfoz E 86 A3
Alfreton GB 27 B4
Alfta S 36 A3
Alfundão P 98 A2
Algaida E 97 B2
Algar E 99 C5
Älgarås S 35 D6
Ålgård N 33 D2
Algarinejo E 100 B1
Algarrobo E 100 C1
Algatocin E 99 C5
Algeciras E 99 C5
Algemesí E 96 B2
Algés P 92 C1
Algete E 95 B3
Alghero I 110 B1
Älghult S 40 B5
Alginet E 96 B2
Algodonales E 99 C5
Algodor E 94 C3
Algodor P 98 B3
Algora E 95 B4
Algoso P 87 C4
Algoz P 98 B2
Älgsjö S 115 C14
Alguaire E 90 B3
Alguazas E 101 A4
Algutsrum S 41 C6
Algyö H 75 B5
Alhama de Almería E 101 C3
Alhama de Aragón E 89 C5
Alhama de Granada E 100 C2
Alhama de Murcia E 101 B4
Alhambra E 100 A2
Alhandra P 92 C1
Alhaurín de la Torre E 100 C1
Alhaurín el Grande E 100 C1
Alhendín E 100 B2
Alhóndiga E 95 B4
Ali Terme I 109 A4
Alia E 93 B5
Ália I 108 B2
Aliaga E 90 C2
Aliağa TR 118 D1
Alibunar SRB 85 A5
Alicante E 96 C2
Alicún de Ortega E 100 B2
Alife I 103 B7
Alija del Infantado E 88 B1
Alijó P 87 C3
Alimena I 109 B3
Alingsås S 40 B2
Alinyà E 91 A4
Aliseda E 93 B4
Aliveri GR 116 D6
Alixan F 79 B4
Aljaraque E 99 B3
Aljezur P 98 B2
Aljorra E 101 B4
Aljubarrota P 92 B2
Aljucen E 93 B4
Aljustrel P 98 B2
Alken B 49 C6
Alkmaar NL 42 C1
Alkoven A 63 B5
Allaines F 58 B2
Allaire F 57 C3
Allanche F 68 C2
Alland A 64 B2
Allariz E 87 B3
Allassac F 67 C6
Allauch F 79 C4
Alleen N 33 D4
Allègre F 68 C3
Allemont F 69 C6
Allendale Town GB 25 D5
Allendorf D 51 C4
Allentsteig A 63 B6
Allepuz E 90 C2
Allersberg D 62 A2
Allershausen D 62 B2
Alles E 88 A2
Allevard F 69 C6
Allgunnen S 40 B5
Allihies IRL 20 C1
Allingåbro DK 38 C3
Allmannsdorf D 61 C5
Allo E 89 B4
Alloa GB 25 B4
Allogny F 68 A2
Ålloluokta S 112 E8
Allones, *Eure et Loire* F 58 B2
Allones, *Maine-et-Loire* F 67 A5
Allonnes F 57 C6
Allons F 76 B2
Allos F 79 B5
Allstedt D 52 B1
Alltwalis GB 28 B3
Allumiere I 102 A4
Almaceda P 92 B3
Almacelles E 90 B3
Almachar E 100 C1
Almada P 92 C1
Almadén E 100 A1
Almadén de la Plata E 99 B4
Almadenejos E 100 A1
Almadrones E 95 B4
Almagro E 100 A2
Almajano E 89 C4
Almansa E 96 C1
Almansil P 98 B2
Almanza E 88 B1
Almaraz E 93 B5
Almargen E 99 C5
Almarza E 89 C4
Almásfüzitö H 64 C4
Almassora E 96 B2
Almazán E 89 C4
Almazul E 89 C4
Alme D 51 B4
Almedina E 100 A3
Almedinilla E 100 B1
Almeida E 87 C4
Almeida P 93 A4
Almeirim P 92 B2
Almelo NL 42 C3
Almenar E 90 B3
Almenar de Soria E 89 C4
Almenara E 96 B2
Almendra P 87 D3
Almendral E 93 C4
Almendral de la Cañada E 94 B2
Almendralejo E 93 C4
Almenno San Bartolomeo I 71 C4
Almere NL 42 C2
Almería E 101 C3
Almerimar E 101 C3
Almese I 70 C2
Almexial P 98 B3
Älmhult S 40 C4
Almiropotamos GR 117 D6
Almiros GR 116 C4
Almodôvar P 98 B2
Almodóvar del Campo E 100 A1
Almodóvar del Pinar E 95 C5
Almodóvar del Río E 99 B5
Almofala P 87 D3
Almogia E 100 C1
Almoharin E 93 B4
Almonacid de la Sierra E 89 C5
Almonacid de Toledo E 94 C3
Almonaster la Real E 99 B4
Almondsbury GB 29 B5
Almonte E 99 B4
Almoradí E 101 A5
Almoraima E 99 C5
Almorox E 94 B2
Almoster P 92 B2
Almsele S 115 C14
Älmsta S 36 C5
Almudena E 101 A4
Almudévar E 90 A2
Almuñécar E 100 C2
Almunge S 36 C5
Almuradiel E 100 A2
Almussafes E 96 B2
Almvik S 40 B6
Alness GB 23 D4
Alnmouth GB 25 C6
Alnwick GB 25 C6
Åloppe S 36 C4
Álora E 100 C1
Alos d'Ensil E 91 A4
Alosno E 99 B3
Alozaina E 100 C1
Alpbach A 72 A1
Alpedrete de la Sierra E 95 B3
Alpedrinha P 92 A3
Alpen D 50 B2
Alpera E 96 C1
Alphen aan de Rijn NL 49 A5
Alpiarça P 92 B2
Alpignano I 70 C2
Alpirsbach D 61 B4
Alpu TR 118 C5
Alpuente E 96 B1
Alqueva P 98 A3
Alquézar E 90 A3
Als DK 38 C3
Alsasua E 89 B4
Alsdorf D 50 C2
Alselv DK 39 D1
Alsfeld D 51 C5
Alsike S 36 C4
Alskog S 37 E5
Alsleben D 52 B1
Alsónémedi H 75 A4
Alsótold H 65 C5
Alsóújlak H 74 A1
Alstad N 112 E4
Alstätte D 50 A2
Alsterbro S 40 C5
Alstermo S 40 C5
Alston GB 25 D5
Alsvåg N 112 D4
Alsvik N 112 E3
Alt Ruppin D 45 C4
Alta N 113 C12
Älta S 37 C5
Altamura I 104 C2
Altarejos E 95 C4
Altaussee A 63 C4
Altavilla Irpina I 103 B7
Altavilla Silentina I 103 C8
Altdöbern D 53 B4
Altdorf CH 70 B3
Altdorf D 62 B3
Altdorf bei Nürnberg D 62 A2
Alte P 98 B2
Altea E 96 C2
Altedo I 81 B5
Alten-weddingen D 52 A1
Altena D 50 B3
Altenau D 51 B6
Altenberg D 53 C3
Altenberge D 50 A3
Altenbruch D 43 B5
Altenburg D 52 C2
Altenfelden A 63 B4
Altengronau D 51 C5
Altenheim D 60 B3
Altenhundem D 50 B4
Altenkirchen, *Mecklenburg-Vorpommern* D 45 A5
Altenkirchen, *Radom* D 50 C3
Altenkunstadt D 52 C1
Altenmarkt A 63 C5
Altenmarkt D 62 B3
Altenmarkt im Pongall A 72 A3
Altensteig D 61 B4
Altentreptow D 45 B5
Altenwalde D 43 B5
Alter do Chão P 92 B3
Altfraunhofen D 62 B3
Altheim A 63 B4
Altheim D 61 A5
Althofen A 73 B4
Altinoluk TR 118 C1
Altinova TR 118 C1
Altıntaş TR 118 C5
Altınyaka TR 119 F5
Altınyayla TR 119 E4
Altkirch F 60 C3
Altlandsberg D 45 C5
Altlewin D 45 C6
Altmannstein D 62 B2
Altmorschen D 51 B5
Altmunster A 63 C4
Altnaharra GB 23 C4
Alto Campoó E 88 A2
Altofonte I 108 A2
Altomonte I 106 B3
Alton, *Hampshire* GB 31 C3
Alton, *Staffordshire* GB 27 C4
Altopáscio I 81 C4
Altötting D 62 B3
Altreichenau D 63 B4
Altshausen D 61 C5
Altstätten CH 71 A4
Altura E 96 B2
Altusried D 61 C6
Alūksne LV 7 C9
Alunda S 36 B5
Alustante E 95 B5
Alva GB 25 B4
Alvaiázere P 92 B2
Alvalade P 98 B2
Älvängen S 38 B5
Alvarenga P 87 D2
Alvares P 92 A2
Alvdal N 114 E7
Älvdalen S 34 A6
Alverca P 92 C1
Alversund N 32 B2
Alvesta S 40 C4
Alvignac F 77 B4
Alvignano I 103 B7
Ålvik N 32 B3
Alvik S 36 B1
Alvimare F 58 A1
Alviobeira P 92 B2
Alvito P 98 A3
Älvkarleby S 36 B4
Älvkarleö bruk S 36 B4
Alvor P 98 B2
Alvorge P 92 B2
Alvøy N 32 B2
Älvros S 115 E11
Alvsbacka S 35 C5
Älvsbyn S 3 D24
Älvsered S 40 B2
Alwernia PL 55 C4
Alwinton GB 25 C5
Alyth GB 25 B4
Alytus LT 6 D8
Alzénau D 51 C5
Alzey D 61 A4
Alzira E 96 B2
Alzonne F 77 C5
Amadora P 92 C1
Åmål S 35 C4
Amalfi I 103 C7
Amaliada GR 117 E3
Amance F 60 C2
Amancey F 69 A6
Amándola I 82 D2
Amantea I 106 B3
Amarante P 87 C2
Amareleja P 98 A3
Amares P 87 C2
Amaseno I 103 B6
Amasra TR 118 A7
Amasya TR 16 A8
Amatrice I 103 A6
Amay B 49 C6
Ambarnyy RUS 3 D30
Ambazac F 67 C6
Ambelonas GR 116 C4
Amberg D 62 A2
Ambérieu-en-Bugey F 69 C5
Ambérieux-en-Dombes F 69 B4
Ambert F 68 C3
Ambés F 76 A2
Ambjörby S 34 B5
Ambjörnarp S 40 B3
Amble GB 25 C6
Ambleside GB 26 A3
Ambleteuse F 48 C2
Amboise F 67 A5
Ambrières-les-Vallées F 57 B5
Amden CH 71 A4
Amel B 50 C2
Amélia I 102 A5
Amélie-les-Bains-Palalda F 91 A5
Amelinghausen D 44 B2
Amendoa P 92 B2
Amendoeira P 98 B3
Améndola I 104 B1
Amendolara I 106 B3
Amer E 91 A5
Amerongen NL 49 A6
Amersfoort NL 49 A6
Amersham GB 31 C3
Ames E 86 B2
Amesbury GB 29 B6
Amfiklia GR 116 D4
Amfilochia GR 116 D3
Amfipoli GR 116 B5
Amfissa GR 116 D4
Amièira, *Évora* P 98 A3
Amieira, *Portalegre* P 92 B3
Amieiro P 92 A2
Amiens F 58 A3
Amindeo GR 116 B3
Åminne S 40 B3
Åmli N 33 D5
Amlwch GB 26 B1
Ammanford GB 28 B4
Ammarnäs S 115 B13
Åmmeberg S 37 D1
Amorbach D 61 A5
Amorebieta E 89 A4
Amorgos GR 117 F7
Amorosa P 87 C2
Amorosi I 103 B7
Åmot, *Buskerud* N 34 C1
Åmot, *Telemark* N 33 C4
Åmot S 36 B3
Åmotfors S 34 C4
Åmotsdal N 33 C5
Amou F 76 C2
Ampezzo I 72 B2
Ampfing D 62 B3
Ampflwang A 63 B4
Amplepuis F 69 C4
Amposta E 90 C3
Ampthill GB 30 B3
Ampudia E 88 C2
Ampuero E 89 A3
Amriswil CH 71 A4
Åmsele S 115 C16
Amstelveen NL 49 A5
Amsterdam NL 42 C1
Amstetten A 63 B5
Amtzell D 61 C5
Amulree GB 25 B4
Amurrio E 89 A4
Amusco E 88 B2
An t-Ob GB 22 D1
Åna-Sira N 33 D3
Anacapri I 103 C7
Anadia P 92 A2
Anadon E 90 C1
Anafi GR 117 F7
Anagni I 102 B6
Anamur TR 16 C6
Ananyiv UA 11 C10
Anascaul IRL 20 B1
Ånäset S 3 D24
Anastażewo PL 47 C4
Anaya de Alba E 94 B1
Ança P 92 A2
Ancaster GB 27 C5
Ancede P 87 C2
Ancenis F 66 A3
Ancerville F 59 B6
Anchuras E 94 C2
Ancona I 82 C2
Ancora P 87 C2
Ancrum GB 25 C5
Ancy-le-Franc F 59 C5
Andalo I 71 B5
Åndalsnes N 114 E4
Andance F 69 C4
Andau A 64 C3
Andebu N 35 C2
Andeer CH 71 B4
Andelfingen CH 61 C4
Andelot F 59 B6
Andelot-en-Montagne F 69 B5
Andenes N 112 C5
Andenne B 49 C6
Anderlues B 49 C5
Andermatt CH 70 B3
Andernach D 50 C3
Andernos-les-Bains F 76 B1
Anderslöv S 41 D3
Anderstorp S 40 B3
Andijk NL 42 C2
Andoain E 89 A4
Andocs H 74 B2
Andolsheim F 60 B3
Andorra E 90 C2
Andorra La Vella AND 91 A4
Andosilla E 89 B5
Andover GB 31 C2
Andratx E 97 B2
Andreapol RUS 7 C12
Andreas GB 26 A1
Andréspol PL 55 B4
Andrest F 76 C3
Andretta I 103 C8
Andrezieux-Bouthéon F 69 C4
Ándria I 104 B2
Andrijevica MNE 85 D4
Andritsena GR 117 E3
Andros GR 117 E6
Andrychów PL 65 A5
Andselv N 112 C7
Andújar E 100 A1
Anduze F 78 B2
Åneby N 34 B2
Aneby S 40 B4
Añes E 89 A3
Anet F 58 B2
Anfo I 71 C5
Ang S 40 B4
Anga S 37 E5
Angaïs F 76 C2
Änge, *Jämtland* S 115 D11
Ånge, *Västernorrland* S 115 E12
Angeja P 92 A2
Ängelholm S 41 C2
Angeli FIN 113 D14
Ängelsberg S 36 C3
Anger A 73 A5
Angera I 70 C3
Angermünde D 45 B6
Angern A 64 B2
Angers F 67 A4
Angerville F 58 B3
Anghiari I 82 C1
Angle GB 28 B2
Anglès E 91 B5
Anglés, *Tarn* F 77 C5
Angles, *Vendée* F 66 B3
Angles sur l'Anglin F 67 B5
Anglesola E 91 B4
Anglet F 76 C1
Anglisidhes CY 120 B2
Anglure F 59 B4
Angoulême F 67 C5
Angoulins F 66 B3
Angsö S 37 C3
Angueira P 87 C4
Angües E 90 A2
Anguiano E 89 B4
Anguillara Sabazia I 102 A5
Anguillara Véneta I 72 C1
Anhée B 49 C5
Anholt DK 38 C4
Aniane F 78 C2
Aniche F 49 C4
Ånimskog S 35 D4
Anina RO 10 D6
Anixi GR 116 C3
Anizy-le-Château F 59 A4
Anjalankoski FIN 3 F27
Anjan S 115 D9
Ankara TR 118 C7
Ankaran SLO 72 C3
Ankarsrum S 40 B6
Ankerlia N 112 C9
Anklam D 45 B5
Ankum D 43 C4
Anlauftal A 72 A3
Anlezy F 68 B3
Ånn S 115 D9
Annaberg A 63 C6
Annaberg-Buchholz D 52 C3
Annaberg im Lammertal A 72 A3
Annaburg D 52 B3
Annahütte D 53 B3
Annalong GB 19 B6
Annan GB 25 D4
Anndalsvågen N 115 B9
Anneberg, *Halland* S 38 B5
Anneberg, *Jönköping* S 40 B4
Annecy F 69 C6
Annelund S 40 B3
Annemasse F 69 B6
Annenskiy Most RUS 7 A14
Annerstad S 40 C3
Annestown IRL 21 B4
Annevoie-Rouillon B 49 C5
Annonay F 69 C4
Annot F 79 C5
Annweiler D 60 A3
Ano Poroia GR 116 A5
Ano Siros GR 117 E6
Añora E 100 A1
Anould F 60 B2
Anquela del Ducado E 95 B4
Anröchte D 51 B4
Ans DK 39 C2
Ansager DK 39 D1
Ansbach D 62 A1
Anse F 69 C4
Anseroeul B 49 C4
Ansfelden A 63 B5
Ansião P 92 B2
Ansó E 76 D2
Ansoain E 76 D1
Anstruther GB 25 B5
Antalya TR 119 F5
Antas E 101 B4
Antegnate I 71 C4
Antequera E 100 B1
Anterselva di Mezzo I 72 B2
Antibes F 79 C6
Antigüedad E 88 C2
Antillo I 109 B4
Antirio GR 117 D3
Antoing B 49 C4
Antonin PL 54 B2
Antrain F 57 B4
Antrim GB 19 B5
Antrodoco I 102 A6
Antronapiana I 70 B3
Anttis S 113 E11
Antuzede P 92 A2
Antwerp = Antwerpen B 49 B5
Antwerpen = Antwerp B 49 B5
Anversa d'Abruzzi I 103 B6
Anvin F 48 C3
Anzat-le-Luguet F 68 C3
Anzi I 104 C1
Ánzio I 102 B5
Anzola d'Emilia I 81 B5
Anzón E 89 C5
Aoiz E 76 D1
Aosta I 70 C2
Apalhão P 92 B3
Apátfalva H 75 B5
Apatin SRB 75 C4
Apatity RUS 3 C30
Apc H 65 C5
Apécchio I 82 C1
Apeldoorn NL 50 A1
Apen D 43 B4
Apenburg D 44 C3
Apensen D 43 B6
Apiro I 82 C2
Apliki CY 120 B2
Apolda D 52 B1
Apolonia GR 117 F6
Apostag H 75 B3
Äppelbo S 34 B6
Appennino I 82 D2
Appenzell CH 71 A4
Appiano I 71 B6
Appingedam NL 42 B3
Appleby-in-Westmorland GB 26 A3
Applecross GB 22 D3
Appledore GB 28 B3
Appoigny F 59 C4
Apremont-la-Forêt F 60 B1
Aprica I 71 B5
Apricena I 103 B8
Aprigliano I 106 B3
Aprília I 102 B5
Apt F 79 C4
Apúlia P 87 C2
Aquiléia I 72 C3
Aquilónia I 103 C8
Aquino I 103 B6
Ar S 37 E5
Arabayona E 94 A1
Arabba I 72 B1
Araç TR 16 A6
Aracena E 99 B4
Arachova GR 116 D4
Arad RO 75 B6
Aradac SRB 75 C5
Aradhippou CY 120 B2
Aragnouet F 76 D3
Aragona I 108 B2
Aramits F 76 C2
Aramon F 78 C3
Aranda de Duero E 88 C3
Aranda de Moncayo E 89 C5
Arandjelovac SRB 85 B5
Aranjuez E 95 B3
Arantzazu E 89 B4
Aranzueque E 95 B3
Aras de Alpuente E 96 B1
Arauzo de Miel E 89 C3
Arazede P 92 A2
Arbas F 77 D3
Árbatax I 110 C2
Arbeca E 90 B3
Arberg D 62 A1
Arbesbach A 63 B6
Arboga S 37 C2
Arbois F 69 B5
Arbon CH 71 A4
Arboréa I 110 C1
Arbório I 70 C3
Årbostad N 112 D6
Arbrå S 36 A3
Arbroath GB 25 B5
Arbùcies E 91 B5
Arbuniel E 100 B2
Arbus I 110 C1
Arc-en-Barrois F 59 C5
Arc-et-Senans F 69 A5
Arc-lès-Gray F 69 A5
Arc-sur-Tille F 69 A5
Arcachon F 76 B1
Arce I 103 B6
Arcen NL 50 B2
Arces-Dilo F 59 B4
Arcévia I 82 C1
Arcey F 70 A1
Archanes GR 117 G7
Archangelos GR 119 F3
Archena E 101 A4
Archez E 100 C2
Archiac F 67 C4
Archidona E 100 B1
Archiestown GB 23 D5
Archivel E 101 A4
Arcidosso I 81 D5
Arcille I 81 D5
Arcis-sur-Aube F 59 B5
Arco I 71 C5
Arcones E 94 A3
Arcos E 88 B3
Arcos de Jalón E 95 A4
Arcos de la Frontera E 99 C5
Arcos de la Sierra E 95 B4
Arcos de las Salinas E 96 B1
Arcos de Valdevez P 87 C2
Arcozelo P 92 A3
Arcusa E 90 A3
Arcy-sur-Cure F 59 C4
Ardagh IRL 20 B2
Årdal N 33 C3
Ardala S 35 D5
Ardales E 100 C1
Årdalstangen N 32 A4
Ardara I 110 B1
Ardara IRL 18 B3
Ardarroch GB 22 D3
Ardbeg GB 24 C1
Ardcharnich GB 22 D3
Ardchyle GB 24 B3
Ardee IRL 19 C5
Arden DK 38 C2
Ardentes F 68 B1
Ardenza I 81 C4
Ardersier GB 23 D4
Ardes F 68 C3
Ardessie GB 22 D3
Ardez CH 71 B5
Ardfert IRL 20 B2
Ardgay GB 23 D4
Ardglass GB 19 B6
Ardgroom IRL 20 C2
Ardhasig GB 22 D2
Ardino BG 116 A7

Ardisa E 90 A2
Ardkearagh IRL 20 C1
Ardlui GB 24 B3
Ardlussa GB 24 B2
Ardón E 88 B1
Ardooie B 49 C4
Ardore I 106 C3
Ardre S 37 E5
Ardres F 48 C2
Ardrishaig GB 24 B2
Ardrossan GB 24 C3
Are N 33 C2
Åre S 115 D10
Areia Branca P 92 B1
Aremark N 35 C3
Arenales de San Gregorio E 95 C3
Arenas E 100 C1
Arenas de Iguña E 88 A2
Arenas de San Juan E 95 C3
Arenas de San Pedro E 94 B1
Arenas del Rey E 100 C2
Arendal N 33 D5
Arendonk B 49 B6
Arengosse F 76 B2
Arentorp S 35 D4
Arenys de Mar E 91 B5
Arenys de Munt E 91 B5
Arenzano I 80 B2
Areo E 91 A4
Areopoli GR 117 F4
Ares E 86 A2
Arès F 76 B1
Ares del Maestrat E 90 C2
Aresvika N 114 D5
Arette F 76 C2
Aretxabaleta E 89 A4
Arevalillo E 93 A5
Arévalo E 94 A2
Arez P 92 B3
Arezzo I 81 C5
Arfeuilles F 68 B3
Argalasti GR 116 C5
Argallón E 99 A5
Argamasilla de Alba E 95 C3
Argamasilla de Calatrava E 100 A1
Arganda E 95 B3
Arganil P 92 A2
Argasion GR 117 E2
Argegno I 71 C4
Argelès-Gazost F 76 C2
Argelès-sur-Mer F 91 A6
Argent-sur-Sauldre F 68 A2
Argenta I 81 B5
Argentan F 57 B5
Argentat F 77 A4
Argentera I 79 B5
Argenteuil F 58 B3
Argenthal D 50 D3
Argentiera I 110 B1
Argenton-Château F 67 B4
Argenton-sur-Creuse F 67 B6
Argentona E 91 B5
Argentré F 57 B5
Argentré-du-Plessis F 57 B4
Argirades GR 116 C1
Argithani TR 119 D6
Argos GR 117 E4
Argos Orestiko GR 116 B3
Argostoli GR 117 D2
Argote E 89 B4
Arguedas E 89 B5
Argueil F 58 A2
Arholma S 36 C6
Århus DK 39 C3
Ariano Irpino I 103 B8
Ariano nel Polésine I 82 B1
Aribe E 76 D1
Aridea GR 116 B4
Arienzo I 103 B7
Arild S 41 C2
Arileod GB 24 B1
Arilje SRB 85 C5
Arinagour GB 24 B1
Ariño E 90 B2
Arinthod F 69 B5
Arisaig GB 24 B2
Arisgotas E 94 C3
Aritzo I 110 C2
Ariza E 89 C4
Årjäng S 35 C4
Arjeplog S 115 A14
Arjona E 100 B1
Arjonilla E 100 B1
Arkasa GR 119 G2
Arkelstorp S 41 C4
Arklow IRL 21 B5
Arkösund S 37 D3
Ärla S 37 C3
Arlanc F 68 C3
Arlanzón E 89 B3
Arlebosc F 78 A3
Arlena di Castro I 102 A4
Arles F 78 C3
Arles-sur-Tech F 91 A5
Arló H 65 B6
Arlon B 60 A1
Armação de Pera P 98 B2
Armadale, *Highland* GB 22 D3
Armadale, *West Lothian* GB 25 C4
Armagh GB 19 B5
Armamar P 87 C3
Armenistis GR 117 E8
Armeno I 70 C3
Armenteros E 93 A5
Armentières F 48 C3
Armilla E 100 B2
Armiñón E 89 B4
Armoy GB 19 A5
Armuña de Tajuña E 95 B3
Armutlu, *Bursa* TR 118 B3
Armutlu, *İzmir* TR 119 D2
Arnac-Pompadour F 67 C6
Arnafjord N 32 A3
Arnage F 57 C6
Arnas F 69 B4
Årnäs S 35 D5
Arnay-le-Duc F 69 A4
Arnborg DK 39 C2
Arnbruck D 62 A3
Arnea GR 116 B5
Arneberg, *Hedmark* N 34 B4
Arneberg, *Hedmark* N 34 A2
Arneburg D 44 C4
Arnedillo E 89 B4
Arnedo E 89 B4
Arneguy F 76 C1
Arnés E 90 C3
Árnes IS 111 A4
Årnes, *Akershus* N 34 B3
Årnes, *Troms* N 112 C7
Arnfels A 73 B5
Arnhem NL 50 B1
Arnissa GR 116 B3
Arno S 37 D4
Arnold GB 27 B4
Arnoldstein A 72 B3
Arnsberg D 50 B4
Arnschwang D 62 A3
Arnsdorf D 53 B3
Årnset N 114 D6
Arnside GB 26 A3
Arnstadt D 51 C6
Arnstein D 51 D5
Arnstorf D 62 B3
Arnum DK 39 D1
Aroche E 99 B4
Arolla CH 70 B2
Arolsen D 51 B5
Arona I 70 C3
Åros N 35 C2
Arosa CH 71 B4
Arosa P 87 C2
Ærøsund DK 39 D3
Arouca P 87 D2
Årøysund N 35 C2
Arpajon F 58 B3
Arpajon-sur-Cère F 77 B5
Arpino I 103 B6
Arquata del Tronto I 82 D2
Arques F 48 C3
Arques-la-Bataille F 58 A2
Arquillos E 100 A2
Arraia-Maeztu E 89 B4
Arraiolos P 92 C2
Arrancourt F 60 B2
Arras F 48 C3
Arrasate E 89 A4
Årre DK 39 D1
Arreau F 77 D3
Arredondo E 89 A3
Arrens-Marsous F 76 D2
Arriate E 99 C5
Arrifana P 98 B2
Arrigorriaga E 89 A4
Arriondas E 88 A1
Arroba de los Montes E 94 C2
Arrochar GB 24 B3
Arromanches-les-Bains F 57 A5
Arronches P 92 B3
Arroniz E 89 B4
Arrou F 58 B2
Arroya E 88 B2
Arroya de Cuéllar E 88 C2
Arroyal E 88 B2
Arroyo de la Luz E 93 B4
Arroyo de San Servan E 93 C4
Arroyo del Ojanco E 100 A3
Arroyomolinos de León E 99 A4
Arroyomolinos de Montánchez E 93 B4
Arruda dos Vinhos P 92 C1
Ars-en-Ré F 66 B3
Ars-sur-Moselle F 60 A2
Arsac F 76 B2
Arsiè I 72 C1
Arsiero I 71 C6
Årslev DK 39 D3
Ársoli I 102 A6
Årsunda S 36 B3
Artà E 97 B3
Arta GR 116 C3
Artajona E 89 B5
Artegna I 72 B3
Arteixo E 86 A2
Artemare F 69 C5
Arten I 72 B1
Artena I 102 B5
Artenay F 58 B2
Artern D 52 B1
Artés E 91 B4
Artesa de Segre E 91 B4
Arth CH 70 A3
Arthez-de-Béarn F 76 C2
Arthon-en-Retz F 66 A3
Arthurstown IRL 21 B5
Artieda E 90 A2
Artix F 76 C2
Artotina GR 116 D4
Artsyz UA 11 C10
Artziniega E 89 A3
Arudy F 76 C2
Arundel GB 31 D3
Arveyres F 76 B2
Arvidsjaur S 115 B16
Arvieux F 79 B5
Arvika S 35 C4
Åryd, *Blekinge* S 41 C5
Åryd, *Kronoberg* S 40 C4
Arzachena I 110 A2
Arzacq-Arraziguet F 76 C2
Árzana I 110 C2
Arzano F 56 C2
Aržano HR 84 C1
Arzberg D 52 C2
Arzignano I 71 C6
Arzila P 92 A2
Arzl im Pitztal A 71 A5
Arzúa E 86 B2
As B 49 B6
Aš CZ 52 C2
Ås N 35 C2
As Neves E 87 B2
As Nogais E 86 B3
As Pontes de García Rodríguez E 86 A3
Åsa S 40 B2
Asaa DK 38 B3
Aşağıçiğil TR 119 D6
Ašanja SRB 85 B5
Åsarøy N 33 C3
Åsarp S 40 A3
Asasp F 76 C2
Åsbro S 37 C2
Åsby, *Halland* S 40 B2
Åsby, *Östergötland* S 40 B5
Asbygri IS 111 A9
Ascain F 76 C1
Ascea I 106 A2
Ascha D 62 A3
Aschach an der Donau A 63 B5
Aschaffenburg D 51 D5
Aschbach Markt A 63 B5
Ascheberg, *Nordrhein-Westfalen* D 50 B3
Ascheberg, *Schleswig-Holstein* D 44 A2
Aschendorf D 43 B4
Aschersleben D 52 B1
Asciano I 81 C5
Ascó E 90 B3
Asco F 102 A2
Áscoli Piceno I 82 D2
Áscoli Satriano I 104 B1
Ascona CH 70 B3
Ascot GB 31 C3
Ascoux F 58 B3
Åse N 112 C4
Åseda S 40 B5
Åsele S 115 C14
Åsen N 114 D8
Åsen S 34 A5
Asendorf D 43 C6
Asenovgrad BG 11 E8
Åsensbruk S 35 D4
Åseral N 33 D4
Asfeld F 59 A5
Ásgarður IS 111 B1
Åsgårdstrand N 35 C2
Asgate CY 120 B2
Ash, *Kent* GB 31 C5
Ash, *Surrey* GB 31 C3
Åshammar S 36 B3
Ashbourne GB 27 B4
Ashbourne IRL 21 A5
Ashburton GB 28 C4
Ashby-de-la-Zouch GB 27 C4
Ashchurch GB 29 B5
Åsheim N 114 F8
Ashford GB 31 C4
Ashington GB 25 C6
Ashley GB 26 C3
Ashmyany BY 7 D8
Ashton Under Lyne GB 26 B3
Ashwell GB 30 B3
Asiago I 71 C6
Asipovichy BY 7 E10
Aska FIN 113 E15
Askam-in-Furness GB 26 A2
Askeaton IRL 20 B3
Asker N 34 C2
Askersund S 37 D1
Åskilje S 115 C14
Askim N 35 C3
Askland N 33 D5
Äsköping S 37 C3
Askvoll N 32 A2
Åsljunga S 41 C3
Asnæs DK 39 D4
Ásola I 71 C5
Asolo I 72 C1
Asos GR 116 D2
Asotthalom H 75 B4
Aspach A 63 B4
Aspang Markt A 64 C2
Aspariegos E 88 C1
Asparn an der Zaya A 64 B2
Aspatria GB 26 A2
Aspberg S 35 C5
Aspe E 101 A5
Aspet F 77 C3
Äspö S 41 C5
Aspres-sur-Buëch F 79 B4
Aspsele S 115 D15
Assafora P 92 C1
Asse B 49 C5
Assebakte N 113 C14
Assel D 43 B6
Asselborn L 50 C1
Assémini I 110 C1
Assen NL 42 C3
Assenede B 49 B4
Assens, *Aarhus Amt.* DK 38 C3
Assens, *Fyns Amt.* DK 39 D2
Assesse B 49 C6
Assisi I 82 C1
Åsskard N 114 D5
Assling D 62 C3
Asso I 71 C4
Asson F 76 C2
Ássoro I 109 B3
Assumar P 92 B3
Åsta N 34 A3
Astaffort F 77 B3
Astakos GR 116 D3
Asten NL 50 B1
Asti I 80 B2
Astipalea GR 119 F1
Astorga E 86 B4
Åstorp S 41 C2
Åsträsk S 115 C16
Astudillo E 88 B2
Asuni I 110 C1
Asványráró H 64 C3
Aszód H 65 C5
Aszófő H 74 B2
Atabey TR 119 E5
Atalaia P 92 B3
Atalandi GR 116 D4
Atalho P 92 C2
Átány H 65 C6
Atanzón E 95 B3
Ataquines E 94 A2
Atarfe E 100 B2
Atça TR 119 E3
Ateca E 89 C5
Atella I 104 C1
Atessa I 103 A7
Ath B 49 C4
Athboy IRL 19 C5
Athea IRL 20 B2
Athenry IRL 20 A3
Athens = Athina GR 117 E5
Atherstone GB 27 C4
Athienou CY 120 A2
Athies F 59 A3
Athies-sous-Laon F 59 A4
Athina = Athens GR 117 E5
Athleague IRL 20 A3
Athlone IRL 21 A4
Athna CY 120 A2
Athy IRL 21 B5
Atienza E 95 A4
Atina I 103 B6
Atkár H 65 C5
Atlantı TR 119 D7
Atna N 114 F7
Åtorp S 35 C6
Åtrå N 32 C5
Ätran S 40 B2
Atri I 103 A6
Atripalda I 103 C7
Atsiki GR 116 C7
Attendorn D 50 B3
Attichy F 59 A4
Attigliano I 102 A5
Attigny F 59 A5
Attleborough GB 30 B5
Åtvidaberg S 37 D2
Atzendorf D 52 B1
Au, *Steiermark* A 63 C6
Au, *Vorarlberg* A 71 A4
Au, *Bayern* D 62 C2
Au, *Bayern* D 62 B2
Aub D 61 A6
Aubagne F 79 C4
Aubange B 60 A1
Aubel B 50 C1
Aubenas F 78 B3
Aubenton F 59 A5
Auberive F 59 C6
Aubeterre-sur-Dronne F 67 C5
Aubiet F 77 C3
Aubigné F 67 B4
Aubigny F 66 B3
Aubigny-au-Bac F 49 C4
Aubigny-en-Artois F 48 C3
Aubigny-sur-Nère F 68 A2
Aubin F 77 B5
Aubonne CH 69 B6
Aubrac F 78 B1
Aubusson F 68 C2
Auch F 77 C3
Auchencairn GB 25 D4
Auchinleck GB 24 C3
Auchterarder GB 25 B4
Auchtermuchty GB 25 B4
Auchtertyre GB 22 D3
Auchy-au-Bois F 48 C3
Audenge F 76 B1
Auderville F 57 A4
Audierne F 56 B1
Audincourt F 70 A1
Audlem GB 26 C3
Audruicq F 48 C3
Audun-le-Roman F 60 A1
Audun-le-Tiche F 60 A1
Aue, *Nordrhein-Westfalen* D 50 B4
Aue, *Sachsen* D 52 C2
Auerbach, *Bayern* D 62 A2
Auerbach, *Sachsen* D 52 C2
Auffach A 72 A2
Augher GB 19 B4
Aughnacloy GB 19 B5
Aughrim IRL 21 B5
Augignac F 67 C5
Augsburg D 62 B1
Augusta I 109 B4
Augusten-borg DK 39 E2
Augustfehn D 43 B4
Augustów PL 6 E7
Aukrug D 44 A1
Auktsjaur S 115 B16
Auldearn GB 23 D5
Aulendorf D 61 C5
Auletta I 103 C8
Aulla I 81 B3
Aullène F 102 B2
Aulnay F 67 B4
Aulnoye-Aymeries F 49 C4
Ault F 48 C2
Aultbea GB 22 D3
Aulum DK 39 C1
Aulus-les-Bains F 77 D4
Auma D 52 C1
Aumale F 58 A2
Aumetz F 60 A1
Aumont-Aubrac F 78 B2
Aunay-en-Bazois F 68 A3
Aunay-sur-Odon F 57 A5
Aune N 115 C10
Auneau F 58 B2
Auneuil F 58 A2
Auning DK 39 C3
Aunsetra N 115 C9
Aups F 79 C5
Aura D 51 C5
Auray F 56 C3
Aurdal N 32 B6
Aure N 114 D5
Aurich D 43 B4
Aurignac F 77 C3
Aurillac F 77 B5
Auriol F 79 C4
Auritz-Burguette E 76 D1
Aurlandsvangen N 32 B4
Auronzo di Cadore I 72 B2
Auros F 76 B2
Auroux F 78 B2
Aurskog N 34 C3
Aursmoen N 34 C3
Ausónia I 103 B6
Ausservillgraton A 72 B2
Austad N 33 D4
Austbygda N 32 B5
Aústis I 110 B2
Austmarka N 34 B4
Austre Moland N 33 D5
Austre Vikebygd N 33 C2
Austrheim N 32 B1
Auterive F 77 C4
Autheuil-Authouillet F 58 A2
Authon F 79 B5
Authon-du-Perche F 58 B1
Autol E 89 B5
Autreville F 60 B1
Autrey-lès-Gray F 69 A5
Autun F 69 B4
Auty-le-Châtel F 58 C3
Auvelais B 49 C5
Auvillar F 77 B3
Auxerre F 59 C4
Auxi-le-Château F 48 C3
Auxon F 59 B4
Auxonne F 69 A5
Auxy F 69 B4
Auzances F 68 B2
Auzon F 68 C3
Availles-Limouzine F 67 B5
Avaldsnes N 33 C2
Avallon F 68 A3
Avantas GR 116 B7
Avaviken S 115 B15
Avebury GB 29 B6
Aveiras de Cima P 92 B2
Aveiro P 92 A2
Avelgem B 49 C4
Avellino I 103 C7
Avenches CH 70 B2
Aversa I 103 C7
Avesnes-le-Comte F 48 C3
Avesnes-sur-Helpe F 49 C4
Avesta S 36 B3
Avetrana I 105 C3
Avezzano I 103 A6
Avià E 91 A4
Aviano I 72 B2
Aviemore GB 23 D5
Avigliana I 80 A1
Avigliano I 104 C1
Avignon F 78 C3
Ávila E 94 B2
Avilés E 88 A1
Avilley F 69 A6
Avintes P 87 C2
Avinyo E 91 B4
Àvio I 71 C5
Avioth F 59 A6
Avis P 92 B3
Avize F 59 B5
Avlonari GR 116 D6
Ávola I 109 C4
Avon F 58 B3
Avonmouth GB 29 B5
Avord F 68 A2
Avranches F 57 B4
Avril F 60 A1
Avrillé F 67 A4
Avtovac BIH 84 C3
Awans B 49 C6
Ax-les-Thermes F 77 D4
Axams A 71 A6
Axat F 77 D5
Axbridge GB 29 B5
Axel NL 49 B4
Axmarby S 36 B4
Axmarsbruk S 36 A4
Axminster GB 29 C4
Axvall S 35 D5
Ay F 59 A5
Aya E 89 A4
Ayamonte E 98 B3
Ayancık TR 16 A7
Ayaş TR 118 B7
Aydın TR 119 E2
Ayelo de Malferit E 96 C2
Ayer CH 70 B2
Ayerbe E 90 A2
Ayette F 48 C3
Ayia Napa CY 120 B2
Áyia Phyla CY 120 B2
Áyios Amvrósios CY 120 A2
Áyios Seryios CY 120 A2
Áyios Theodhoros CY 120 A3
Aykirikçi TR 118 C5
Aylesbury GB 31 C3
Ayllón E 89 C3
Aylsham GB 30 B5
Ayna E 101 A3
Ayódar E 96 B2
Ayora E 96 B1
Ayr GB 24 C3
Ayrancı TR 16 C6
Ayrancılar TR 119 D2
Ayron F 67 B5
Aysgarth GB 27 A4
Ayton GB 25 C5
Aytos BG 11 E9
Ayvacık TR 118 C1
Ayvalık TR 118 C1
Aywaille B 49 C6
Azaila E 90 B2
Azambuja P 92 B2
Azambujeira P 92 B2
Azanja SRB 85 B5
Azannes-et-Soumazannes F 60 A1
Azanúy-Alins E 90 B3
Azaruja P 92 C3
Azay-le-Ferron F 67 B6
Azay-le-Rideau F 67 A5
Azcoitia E 89 A4
Azé F 69 B4
Azeiteiros P 92 B3
Azenhas do Mar P 92 C1
Azinhaga P 92 B2
Azinhal P 98 B3
Azinheira dos Bairros P 98 A2
Aznalcázar E 99 B4
Aznalcóllar E 99 B4
Azóia P 92 B2
Azpeitia E 89 A4
Azuaga E 99 A5
Azuara E 90 B2
Azuqueca de Henares E 95 B3
Azur F 76 C1
Azzano Décimo I 72 C2

B

Baad A 71 A5
Baamonde E 86 A3
Baar CH 70 A3
Baarle-Nassau B 49 B5
Baarn NL 49 A6
Babadag RO 11 D10
Babadağ TR 119 E3
Babaeski TR 118 A2
Babayevo RUS 7 B13
Babenhausen, *Bayern* D 61 B6
Babenhausen, *Hessen* D 51 D4
Babiak PL 54 A3
Babice PL 55 C4
Babigoszcz PL 45 B6
Babimost PL 53 A5
Babina Greda HR 84 A3
Babócsa H 74 B2
Bábolma H 64 C3
Baborów PL 54 C2
Baboszewo PL 47 C6
Babót H 64 C3
Babruysk BY 7 E10
Babsk PL 55 B5
Bac GB 22 C2
Bač MNE 85 D5
Bač SRB 75 C4
Bacares E 101 B3
Bacău RO 11 C9
Baccarat F 60 B2
Bacharach D 50 C3
Bačina SRB 85 C6
Backa S 36 B2
Bačka Palanka SRB 75 C4
Bačka Topola SRB 75 C4
Backaryd S 41 C5
Backe S 115 D13
Bäckebo S 40 C6
Bäckefors S 35 D4
Bäckhammar S 35 C6
Bački Breg SRB 75 C3
Bački-Brestovac SRB 75 C4
Bački Monoštor SRB 75 C3
Bački Petrovac SRB 75 C4
Bački Sokolac SRB 75 C4
Backnang D 61 B5
Bačko Gradište SRB 75 C5
Bačko Novo Selo SRB 75 C4
Bačko Petrovo Selo SRB 75 C5
Bácoli I 103 C7
Bacqueville-en-Caux F 58 A2
Bácsalmás H 75 B4
Bácsbokod H 75 B4
Bad Abbach D 62 B3
Bad Aibling D 62 C3
Bad Aussee A 63 C4
Bad Bederkesa D 43 B5
Bad Bentheim D 50 A3
Bad Bergzabern D 60 A3
Bad Berka D 52 C1
Bad Berleburg D 51 B4
Bad Berneck D 52 C1
Bad Bevensen D 44 B2
Bad Bibra D 52 B1
Bad Birnbach D 62 B4
Bad Blankenburg D 52 C1
Bad Bleiberg A 72 B3
Bad Brambach D 52 C2
Bad Bramstedt D 44 B1
Bad Breisig D 50 C3
Bad Brückenau D 51 C5
Bad Buchau D 61 B5
Bad Camberg D 50 C4
Bad Doberan D 44 A3
Bad Driburg D 51 B5
Bad Düben D 52 B2
Bad Dürkheim D 61 A4
Bad Dürrenberg D 52 B2
Bad Dürrheim D 61 B4
Bad Elster D 52 C2
Bad Ems D 50 C3
Bad Endorf D 62 C3
Bad Essen D 50 A4
Bad Fischau A 64 C2
Bad Frankenhausen D 52 B1
Bad Freienwalde D 45 C6
Bad Friedrichshall D 61 A5
Bad Füssing D 63 B4
Bad Gandersheim D 51 B6
Bad Gastein A 72 A3
Bad Gleichenberg A 73 B5
Bad Goisern A 63 C4
Bad Gottleuba D 53 C3
Bad Grund D 51 B6
Bad Hall A 63 B5
Bad Harzburg D 51 B6
Bad Herrenalb D 61 B4
Bad Hersfeld D 51 C5
Bad Hofgastein A 72 A3
Bad Homburg D 51 C4
Bad Honnef D 50 C3
Bad Hönningen D 50 C3
Bad Iburg D 50 A4
Bad Inner-laterns A 71 A4
Bad Ischl A 63 C4
Bad Karlshafen D 51 B5
Bad Kemmeriboden CH 70 B2
Bad Kissingen D 51 C6
Bad Kleinen D 44 B3
Bad Kohlgrub D 62 C2
Bad König D 61 A5
Bad Königshofen D 51 C6
Bad Köstritz D 52 C2
Bad Kreuzen A 63 B5
Bad Kreuznach D 60 A3
Bad Krozingen D 60 C3
Bad Laasphe D 51 C4
Bad Langensalza D 51 B6
Bad Lauchstädt D 52 B1
Bad Lausick D 52 B2
Bad Lauterberg D 51 B6
Bad Leonfelden A 63 B5
Bad Liebenwerda D 52 B3
Bad Liebenzell D 61 B4
Bad Lippspringe D 51 B4
Bad Meinberg D 51 B4
Bad Mergentheim D 61 A5
Bad Mitterndorf A 72 A3
Bad Münder D 51 A5
Bad Münstereifel D 50 C2
Bad Muskau D 53 B4
Bad Nauheim D 51 C4
Bad Nenndorf D 43 C6
Bad Neuenahr-Ahrweiler D 50 C3
Bad Neustadt D 51 C6
Bad Oeynhausen D 51 A4
Bad Oldesloe D 44 B2
Bad Orb D 51 C5
Bad Peterstal D 61 B4
Bad Pyrmont D 51 B5
Bad Radkersburg A 73 B5
Bad Ragaz CH 71 B4
Bad Rappenau D 61 A5
Bad Reichenhall D 62 C3
Bad Saarow-Pieskow D 53 A4
Bad Sachsa D 51 B6
Bad Säckingen D 70 A2
Bad Salzdetfurth D 51 A6
Bad Salzig D 50 C3
Bad Salzuflen D 51 A4
Bad Salzungen D 51 C6
Bad Sankt Leonhard A 73 B4
Bad Sassendorf D 50 B4
Bad Schandau D 53 C4
Bad Schmiedeberg D 52 B2
Bad Schönborn D 61 A4
Bad Schussenried D 61 B5
Bad Schwalbach D 50 C4
Bad Schwartau D 44 B2
Bad Segeberg D 44 B2
Bad Soden D 51 C4
Bad Soden-Salmünster D 51 C5

Bogadmindszent H 74 C3
Bogajo E 87 D4
Bogarra E 101 A3
Bogarre E 100 B2
Bogatić SRB 85 B4
Bogatynia PL 53 C4
Boğazkale TR 16 A7
Boğazlıyan TR 16 B7
Bogdaniec PL 45 C7
Bogë AL 105 A5
Boge S 37 E5
Bogen D 62 B3
Bogen, *Nordland* N 112 E4
Bogen, *Nordland* N 112 D5
Bogen S 34 B4
Bogense DK 39 D3
Bogetići MNE 84 D3
Bognanco Fonti I 70 B3
Bognelv N 113 B11
Bognes N 112 D5
Bogno CH 70 B4
Bognor Regis GB 31 D3
Bogoria PL 55 C6
Bograngen S 34 B4
Boguchwaly PL 47 B6
Bogumiłowice PL 55 B4
Boguslav UA 11 B11
Boguszów-Gorce PL 53 C6
Bogutovac SRB 85 C5
Bogyiszló H 74 B3
Bohain-en-Vermandois F 49 D4
Böheimkirchen A 64 B1
Bohinjska Bistrica SLO 72 B3
Böhlen D 52 B2
Böhmenkirch D 61 B5
Bohmte D 43 C5
Bohonal de Ibor E 93 B5
Böhönye H 74 B2
Bohumin CZ 65 A4
Boiro E 86 B2
Bois-d'Amont F 69 B6
Boisseron F 78 C3
Boitzenburg D 45 B5
Boixols E 91 A4
Boizenburg D 44 B2
Bojadła PL 53 B5
Bojano I 103 B7
Bojanowo PL 54 B1
Bøjden DK 39 D3
Bojkovice CZ 64 A3
Bojná SK 64 B4
Bojnice SK 65 B4
Boka SRB 75 C5
Böklund D 43 A6
Bokod H 74 A3
Böksholm S 40 B4
Boksitogorsk RUS 7 B12
Bol HR 83 C5
Bolaños de Calatrava E 100 A2
Bolayır TR 118 B1
Bolbec F 58 A1
Bölcske H 75 B3
Bolderslev DK 39 E2
Boldog H 65 C5
Boldva H 65 B6
Bolea E 90 A2
Bolekhiv UA 11 B7
Bolesławiec PL 53 B5
Boleszkowice PL 45 C6
Bolewice PL 46 C2
Bólgheri I 81 C4
Bolhrad UA 11 D10
Boliden S 3 D24
Bolimów PL 55 A5
Boliqueime P 98 B2
Boljevci SRB 85 B5
Boljkovci SRB 85 B5
Bolkhov RUS 7 E14
Bolków PL 53 C6
Bollebygd S 40 B2
Bollène F 78 B3
Bólliga E 95 B4
Bollnäs S 36 A3
Bollstabruk S 115 E14
Bollullos E 99 B4
Bollullos par del Condado E 99 B4
Bologna I 81 B5
Bologne F 59 B6
Bolognetta I 108 B2
Bolognola I 82 D2
Bologoye RUS 7 C13
Bolótana I 110 B1
Bolsena I 102 A4
Bolshaya Vradiyevka UA 11 C11
Bolsover GB 27 B4
Bolstad S 35 D4
Bolsward NL 42 B2
Boltaña E 90 A3
Boltenhagen D 44 B3
Boltigen CH 70 B2
Bolton GB 26 B3
Bolu TR 118 B6
Bolungavík IS 111 A2
Bolvadin TR 118 D6
Bóly H 74 C3
Bolzaneto I 80 B2
Bolzano I 71 B6
Bomba I 103 A7
Bombarral P 92 B1
Bömenzien D 44 C3
Bomlitz D 43 C6
Bømlo N 33 C2
Bøn N 34 B3
Bon-Encontre F 77 B3
Bona F 68 A3
Bonaduz CH 71 B4
Bonanza E 99 C4
Boñar E 88 B1
Bonarbridge GB 23 D4
Bonárcado I 110 B1
Bonares E 99 B4
Bonäs S 36 A1
Bonassola I 80 B3
Bonawe GB 24 B2
Bondal N 32 C5
Bondeno I 81 B5
Bondorf D 61 B4
Bondstorp S 40 B3
Bo'ness GB 25 B4
Bonete E 101 A4
Bonifacio F 102 B2
Bonigen CH 70 B2
Bonin PL 46 A2
Bonn D 50 C3
Bonnánaro I 110 B1
Bonnåsjøen N 112 E4
Bonnat F 68 B1
Bonndorf D 61 C4
Bonnétable F 58 B1
Bonnétage F 70 A1
Bonneuil-les-Eaux F 58 A3
Bonneuil-Matours F 67 B5
Bonneval F 58 B2
Bonneval-sur-Arc F 70 C2
Bonneville F 69 B6
Bonnières-sur-Seine F 58 A2
Bonnieux F 79 C4
Bönnigheim D 61 A5
Bonny-sur-Loire F 68 A2
Bonnyrigg GB 25 C4
Bono E 90 A3
Bono I 110 B2
Bonorva I 110 B1
Bønsnes N 34 B2
Bonyhád H 74 B3
Boom B 49 B5
Boos F 58 A2
Boostedt D 44 A2
Bootle, *Cumbria* GB 26 A2
Bootle, *Merseyside* GB 26 B2
Bopfingen D 61 B6
Boppard D 50 C3
Boqueixón E 86 B2
Bor CZ 62 A3
Bor S 40 B4
Bor SRB 11 D7
Bor TR 16 C7
Boran-sur-Oise F 58 A3
Borås S 40 B2
Borba P 92 C3
Borbona I 102 A4
Borča SRB 85 B5
Borci BIH 84 C3
Borculo NL 50 A2
Bordány H 75 B4
Bordeaux F 76 B2
Bordeira P 98 B2
Bordesholm D 44 A2
Borðeyri IS 111 B4
Bordighera I 80 C1
Bording DK 39 C2
Bordón E 90 C2
Bore I 81 B3
Borehamwood GB 31 C3
Borek Strzeliński PL 54 C2
Borek Wielkopolski PL 54 B2
Boreland GB 25 C4
Borello I 82 B1
Borensberg S 37 D2
Borgafjäll S 115 C12
Borgarnes IS 111 C4
Borgentreich D 51 B5
Börger D 43 C4
Borger NL 42 C3
Borggård S 37 D2
Borghamn S 37 D1
Borghetta di Vara I 81 B3
Borghetto d'Arróscia I 80 B1
Borghetto Santo Spirito I 80 B2
Borgholm S 41 C6
Borghorst D 50 A3
Bórgia I 106 C3
Borgloon B 49 C6
Børglum DK 38 B2
Borgo F 102 A2
Borgo a Mozzano I 81 C4
Borgo alla Collina I 81 C5
Borgo Pace I 82 C1
Borgo San Dalmazzo I 80 B1
Borgo San Lorenzo I 81 C5
Borgo Val di Taro I 81 B3
Borgo Valsugana I 71 B6
Borgo Vercelli I 70 C3
Borgoforte I 81 A4
Borgofranco d'Ivrea I 70 C2
Borgomanero I 70 C3
Borgomasino I 70 C2
Borgonovo Val Tidone I 80 A3
Borgorose I 102 A6
Borgosésia I 70 C3
Borgstena S 40 B3
Borgue GB 24 D3
Borgund N 32 A4
Borgvik S 35 C4
Borisovka RUS 7 F14
Borja E 89 C5
Bork D 50 B3
Borken D 50 B2
Borkenes N 112 D5
Børkop DK 39 D2
Borkowice PL 55 B5
Borkowo PL 47 C6
Borkum D 42 B3
Borlänge S 36 B2
Borlu TR 118 D3
Bormes-les-Mimosas F 79 C5
Bórmio I 71 B5
Bormujos E 99 B4
Borna D 52 B2
Borne NL 50 A2
Borne Sulinowo PL 46 B2
Bornes P 87 C3
Bornheim D 50 C2
Bornhöved D 44 A2
Börnicke D 45 C4
Bornos E 99 C5
Borobia E 89 C5
Borodino RUS 7 D13
Borohrádek CZ 53 C6
Boronów PL 54 C3
Bórore I 110 B1
Borosźow PL 54 C3
Borota H 75 B4
Boroughbridge GB 27 A4
Borovany CZ 63 B5
Borovichi RUS 7 B12
Borovnica SLO 73 C4
Borovo HR 75 C3
Borovsk RUS 7 D14
Borovy CZ 63 A4
Borowa PL 54 B2
Borowie PL 55 B6
Borox E 94 B3
Borrby S 41 D4
Borre DK 41 D2
Borre N 35 C2
Borredá E 91 A4
Borrenes E 86 B4
Borriol E 96 A2
Borris DK 39 D1
Borris IRL 21 B5
Borris-in-Ossory IRL 21 B4
Borrisokane IRL 20 B3
Borrisoleigh IRL 21 B4
Borrowdale GB 26 A2
Børrud N 34 C4
Borşa RO 11 C8
Borsdorf D 52 B2
Børselv N 113 B14
Borsfa H 74 B1
Borský Mikuláš SK 64 B3
Borsodivánka H 65 C6
Borsodnádasd H 65 B6
Bort-les-Orgues F 68 C2
Börte N 33 C4
Borth GB 26 C1
Börtnan S 115 E10
Børtnes N 32 B6
Boruja Kościelne PL 54 A1
Borup DK 39 D4
Boryslav UA 11 B7
Boryspil UA 11 A11
Boryszyn PL 46 C1
Borzęciczki PL 54 B2
Borzęcin PL 55 A5
Borzna UA 7 F12
Borzonasca I 80 B3
Borzyszkowy PL 46 A3
Borzytuchom PL 46 A3
Bosa I 110 B1
Bošáca SK 64 B3
Bosanci HR 73 C5
Bosanska Dubica BIH 74 C1
Bosanska Gradiška BIH 74 C2
Bosanska Kostajnica BIH 74 C1
Bosanska Krupa BIH 83 B5
Bosanski Brod BIH 84 A2
Bosanski Novi BIH 83 A5
Bosanski Petrovac BIH 83 B5
Bosanski Šamac BIH 84 A3
Bosansko Grahovo BIH 83 B5
Bošany SK 64 B4
Bősárkány H 64 C3
Bosau D 44 A2
Bósca H 75 B4
Boscastle GB 28 C3
Bosco I 80 B2
Bosco Chiesanuova I 71 C6
Bösdorf D 44 A2
Bösel D 43 B4
Bosham GB 31 D3
Bösingfeld D 51 A5
Bosjön S 34 C5
Boskoop NL 49 A5
Boskovice CZ 64 A2
Bošnjaci HR 84 A3
Bošnjane SRB 85 C6
Bossast E 77 D3
Bossolasco I 80 B2
Boštanj SLO 73 B5
Boston GB 27 C5
Bostrak N 33 C5
Böszénfa H 74 B2
Bot E 90 B3
Botajica BIH 84 B3
Bøte By DK 44 A3
Bothel GB 26 A2
Boticas P 87 C3
Botilsäter S 35 C5
Botngård N 114 D6
Botoš SRB 75 C5
Botoşani RO 11 C9
Botricello I 107 C3
Bottendorf D 51 B4
Bottesford GB 27 C5
Bottnaryd S 40 B3
Bottrop D 50 B2
Botunje SRB 85 B6
Boturić SRB 85 C5
Bötzingen D 60 B3
Bouaye F 66 A3
Bouça P 87 C3
Boucau F 76 C1
Bouchain F 49 C4
Bouchoir F 58 A3
Boudreville F 59 C5
Boudry CH 70 B1
Bouesse F 67 B6
Bouguenais F 66 A3
Bouhy F 68 A3
Bouillargues F 78 C3
Bouillon B 59 A6
Bouilly F 59 B4
Bouin F 66 B3
Boulay-Moselle F 60 A2
Boulazac F 67 C5
Boule-d'Amont F 91 A5
Bouligny F 60 A1
Boulogne-sur-Gesse F 77 C3
Boulogne-sur-Mer F 48 C2
Bouloire F 58 C1
Bouquemaison F 48 C3
Bourbon-Lancy F 68 B3
Bourbon-l'Archambault F 68 B3
Bourbonne-les-Bains F 60 C1
Bourbourg F 48 C3
Bourbriac F 56 B2
Bourcefranc-le-Chapus F 66 C3
Bourdeaux F 79 B4
Bouresse F 67 B5
Bourg F 76 A2
Bourg-Achard F 58 A1
Bourg-Argental F 69 C4
Bourg-de-Péage F 79 A4
Bourg-de-Thizy F 69 B4
Bourg-de-Visa F 77 B3
Bourg-en-Bresse F 69 B5
Bourg-et-Comin F 59 A4
Bourg-Lastic F 68 C2
Bourg-Madame F 91 A4
Bourg-St. Andéol F 78 B3
Bourg-St. Maurice F 70 C1
Bourganeuf F 68 C1
Bourges F 68 A2
Bourgneuf-en-Retz F 66 A3
Bourgogne F 59 A5
Bourgoin-Jallieu F 69 C5
Bourgtheroulde F 58 A1
Bourgueil F 67 A5
Bourmont F 60 B1
Bourne GB 30 B3
Bournemouth GB 29 C6
Bourneville F 58 A1
Bournezeau F 66 B3
Bourran F 77 B3
Bourret F 77 C4
Bourron-Marlotte F 58 B3
Bourton-on-The-Water GB 29 B6
Boussac F 68 B2
Boussens F 77 C3
Boutersem B 49 C5
Bouttencourt F 48 D2
Bouvières F 79 B4
Bouvron F 66 A3
Bouxwiller F 60 B3
Bouzas E 87 B2
Bouzonville F 60 A2
Bova I 106 D2
Bova Marina I 106 D2
Bovalino Marina I 106 C3
Bovallstrand S 35 D3
Bovec SLO 72 B3
Bóveda E 86 B3
Bóvegno I 71 C5
Bovenau D 44 A1
Bovenden D 51 B5
Bøverdal N 114 F5
Bóves I 80 B1
Bovey Tracey GB 28 C4
Bovino I 103 B8
Bøvlingbjerg DK 38 C1
Bovolenta I 72 C1
Bovolone I 71 C6
Bowes GB 27 A4
Bowmore GB 24 C1
Bowness-on-Windermere GB 26 A3
Box GB 29 B5
Boxberg, *Baden-Württemberg* D 61 A5
Boxberg, *Sachsen* D 53 B4
Boxholm S 37 D2
Boxmeer NL 50 B1
Boxtel NL 49 B6
Boyabat TR 16 A7
Boyalıca TR 118 B4
Boyle IRL 18 C3
Bozan TR 118 C6
Božava HR 83 B3
Bozburun TR 119 F3
Bozcaada TR 116 C8
Bozdoğan TR 119 E3
Bożepole Wielkie PL 46 A3
Boževac SRB 85 B6
Boži Dar CZ 52 C2
Božice CZ 64 B2
Bozkır TR 119 E7
Bozouls F 78 B1
Bozova TR 119 E5
Bozüyük TR 118 C5
Bózzolo I 81 A4
Bra I 80 B1
Braås S 40 B5
Brabrand DK 39 C3
Bracadale GB 22 D2
Bracciano I 102 A5
Bracieux F 67 A6
Bräcke S 115 E12
Brackenheim D 61 A5
Brackley GB 30 B2
Bracklin IRL 19 C5
Bracknell GB 31 C3
Brackwede D 51 B4
Braco GB 25 B4
Brad RO 11 C7
Bradford GB 27 B4
Bradford on Avon GB 29 B5
Bradina BIH 84 C3
Brådland N 33 D3
Brae GB 22 A7
Brædstrup DK 39 D2
Braemar GB 23 D5
Braemore GB 22 D3
Braga P 87 C2
Bragança P 87 C4
Brăila RO 11 D9
Braine F 59 A4
Braine-le-Comte B 49 C5
Braintree GB 31 C4
Braives B 49 C6
Brake D 43 B5
Brakel B 49 C4
Brakel D 51 B5
Bräkne-Hoby S 41 C5
Brålanda S 35 D4
Bralin PL 54 B2
Brallo di Pregola I 80 B3
Bram F 77 C5
Bramafan F 79 C5
Bramberg am Wildkogel A 72 A2
Bramdrupdam DK 39 D2
Bramming DK 39 D1
Brampton GB 25 D5
Bramsche D 43 C4
Branca I 82 C1
Brancaleone Marina I 106 D3
Brancaster GB 30 B4
Brand, *Nieder Österreich* A 63 B6
Brand, *Vorarlberg* A 71 A4
Brand-Erbisdorf D 52 C3
Brandbu N 34 B2
Brande DK 39 D2
Brande-Hornerkirchen D 43 B6
Brandenberg A 72 A1
Brandenburg D 45 C4
Brandis D 52 B2
Brando F 102 A2
Brandomil E 86 A2
Brandon GB 30 B4
Brandshagen D 45 A5
Brandval N 34 B4
Brandýs nad Labem CZ 53 C4
Branice PL 54 C2
Braničevo SRB 85 B6
Braniewo PL 47 A5
Branik SLO 72 C3
Brankovina SRB 85 B4
Branky CZ 64 A3
Branne F 76 B2
Brannenburg-Degerndorf D 62 C3
Brantôme F 67 C5
Branzi I 71 B4
Bras d'Asse F 79 C5
Braskereidfoss N 34 B3
Braslaw BY 7 D9
Braşov RO 11 D8
Brasparts F 56 B2
Brassac, *Charente* F 67 C4
Brassac, *Tarn* F 77 C5
Brassac-les-Mines F 68 C3
Brasschaat B 49 B5
Brastad S 35 D3
Břasy CZ 63 A4
Brąszewice PL 54 B3
Brataj AL 105 C5
Bratislava SK 64 B3
Brattfors S 35 C6
Brattvåg N 114 E3
Bratunac BIH 85 B4
Braubach D 50 C3
Braunau A 62 B4
Braunfels D 51 C4
Braunlage D 51 B6
Braunsbedra D 52 B1
Braunschweig D 51 A6
Bray IRL 21 A5
Bray Dunes F 48 B3
Bray-sur-Seine F 59 B4
Bray-sur-Somme F 48 D3
Brazatortas E 100 A1
Brazey-en-Plaine F 69 A5
Brbinj HR 83 B4
Brčko BIH 84 B3
Brdani SRB 85 C5
Brdów PL 47 C4
Brea de Tajo E 95 B3
Brécey F 57 B4
Brechen D 50 C4
Brechin GB 25 B5
Brecht B 49 B5
Brecketfeld D 50 B3
Břeclav CZ 64 B2
Brecon GB 29 B4
Brécy F 68 A2
Breda E 91 B5
Breda NL 49 B5
Bredaryd S 40 B3
Bredbyn S 115 D15
Breddin D 44 C4
Bredebro DK 39 D1
Bredelar D 51 B4
Bredenfelde D 45 B5
Bredsjö S 36 C1
Bredstedt D 43 A5
Bredsten DK 39 D2
Bredträsk S 115 D15
Bredviken S 115 A11
Bree B 49 B6
Bregana HR 73 C5
Breganze I 72 C1
Bregenz A 71 A4
Bréhal F 57 B4
Brehna D 52 B2
Breidenbach F 60 A3
Breiðdalsvík IS 111 C11
Breil-sur-Roya F 80 C1
Breisach D 60 B3
Breitenbach CH 70 A2
Breitenbach D 51 C5
Breitenberg D 63 B4
Breitenfelde D 44 B2
Breitengussbach D 51 D6
Breivikbotn N 113 B11
Brejning DK 39 D2
Brekke N 32 A2
Brekken N 114 E8
Brekkestø N 33 D5
Brekkvasselv N 115 C10
Brekstad N 114 D6
Breland N 33 D4
Brem-sur-Mer F 66 B3
Bremanger N 114 F1
Bremen D 43 B5
Bremerhaven D 43 B5
Bremervörde D 43 B6
Bremgarten CH 70 A3
Bremsnes N 114 D4
Brenderup DK 39 D2
Brenes E 99 B5
Brengova SLO 73 B5
Brenna PL 65 A4
Breno I 71 C5
Brénod F 69 B5
Brensbach D 61 A4
Brentwood GB 31 C4
Brescello I 81 B4
Bréscia I 71 C5
Breskens NL 49 B4
Bresles F 58 A3
Bresnica SRB 85 C5
Bressana I 80 A3
Bressanone I 72 B1
Bressuire F 67 B4
Brest BY 6 E7
Brest F 56 B1
Brest HR 72 C3
Brestač SRB 85 B4
Brestanica SLO 73 B5
Brestova HR 82 A3
Brestovac HR 74 C2
Bretenoux F 77 B4
Breteuil, *Eure* F 58 B1
Breteuil, *Oise* F 58 A3
Brétigny-sur-Orge F 58 B3
Bretten D 61 A4
Bretteville-sur-Laize F 57 A5
Brettheim D 61 A6
Breuil-Cervínia I 70 C2
Breukelen NL 49 A6
Brevik N 35 C1
Brevik, *Stockholm* S 37 C5
Brevik, *Västra Götaland* S 37 D1
Breza BIH 84 B3
Brežice SLO 73 C5
Bréziers F 79 B5
Brezna SRB 85 C5
Breznica HR 73 B6
Breznica Našička HR 74 C3
Březnice CZ 63 A4
Brezno SK 65 B5
Brezojevice MNE 85 D4
Brezolles F 58 B2
Březová nad Svitavou CZ 64 A2
Brezová pod Bradlom SK 64 B3
Brezovica SK 65 A6
Brezovica SLO 73 B4
Brezovo Polje Selo BIH 84 B3
Briançon F 79 B5
Brianconnet F 79 C5
Briare F 58 C3
Briatexte F 77 C4
Briático I 106 C3
Briaucourt F 59 B6
Bribir HR 73 C4
Bricquebec F 57 A4
Bridge of Cally GB 25 B4
Bridge of Don GB 23 D6
Bridge of Earn GB 25 B4
Bridge of Orchy GB 24 B3
Bridgend, *Argyll & Bute* GB 24 C1
Bridgend, *Bridgend* GB 29 B4
Bridgnorth GB 26 C3
Bridgwater GB 29 B5
Břidličná CZ 64 A3
Bridlington GB 27 A5
Bridport GB 29 C5
Brie-Comte-Robert F 58 B3
Briec F 56 B1
Brienne-le-Château F 59 B5
Brienon-sur-Armançon F 59 C4
Brienz CH 70 B3
Brienza I 104 C1
Briesen D 45 C6
Brieskow Finkenheerd D 53 A4
Brietlingen D 44 B2
Brieva de Cameros E 89 B4
Briey F 60 A1
Brig CH 70 B3
Brigg GB 27 B5
Brighouse GB 27 B4
Brightlingsea GB 31 C5
Brighton GB 31 D3
Brignogan-Plage F 56 B1
Brignoles F 79 C5
Brigstock GB 30 B3
Brihuega E 95 B4
Brijuni HR 82 B2
Brillon-en-Barrois F 59 B6
Brilon D 51 B4
Brimnes N 32 B3
Brinches P 98 A3
Bríndisi I 105 C3
Brinje HR 83 A4
Brinon-sur-Beuvron F 68 A3
Brinon-sur-Sauldre F 68 A2
Brinyan GB 23 B5
Brión E 86 B2
Briones E 89 B4
Brionne F 58 A1
Brioude F 68 C3
Brioux-sur-Boutonne F 67 B4
Briouze F 57 B5
Briscous F 76 C1
Brisighella I 81 B5
Brissac-Quincé F 67 A4
Brissago CH 70 B3
Bristol GB 29 B5
Brive-la-Gaillarde F 67 C6
Briviesca E 89 B3
Brixham GB 29 C4
Brixlegg A 72 A1
Brjánslækur IS 111 B2
Brka BIH 84 B3
Brnaze HR 83 C5
Brněnec CZ 64 A2
Brno CZ 64 A2
Bro S 37 C4
Broad Haven GB 28 B2
Broadclyst GB 29 C4
Broadford GB 22 D3
Broadford IRL 20 B3
Broadstairs GB 31 C5
Broadstone GB 29 C5
Broadway GB 29 A6
Broager DK 39 E2
Broaryd S 40 B3
Broby S 41 C4
Brobyværk DK 39 D3
Bročanac BIH 84 C2
Broćanac MNE 84 D3
Brocas F 76 B2
Brock D 50 A3
Brockel D 43 B6
Brockenhurst GB 31 D2
Broczyno PL 46 B2
Brod MK 116 A3
Brod na Kupi HR 73 C4
Brodalen S 35 D3
Brodarevo SRB 85 C4
Broddbo S 36 C3
Brodek u Přerova CZ 64 A3
Broden-bach D 50 C3
Brodick GB 24 C2
Brodnica PL 47 B5
Brodnica Graniczna PL 47 A4
Brody, *Lubuskie* PL 53 B4
Brody, *Lubuskie* PL 53 A5
Brody, *Mazowieckie* PL 47 C6
Brody UA 11 A8
Broglie F 58 B1
Brójce PL 53 A5
Brokind S 37 D2
Brolo I 109 A3
Brome D 44 C2
Bromley GB 31 C4
Bromölla S 41 C4
Bromont-Lamothe F 68 C2
Brömsebro S 41 C5
Bromsgrove GB 29 A5
Bromyard GB 29 A5
Bronchales E 95 B5
Bronco E 93 A4
Brønderslev DK 38 B2
Broni I 80 A3
Brønnøysund N 114 B9
Brøns DK 39 D1
Bronte I 109 B3
Bronzani Mejdan BIH 84 B1
Bronzolo I 71 B6
Broons F 57 B3
Broquies F 78 B1
Brora GB 23 C5
Brørup DK 39 D2
Brösarp S 41 D4
Brostrud N 32 B5
Brotas P 92 C2
Brötjärna S 36 B2
Broto E 90 A2
Brottby S 37 C5
Brøttum N 34 A2
Brou F 58 B2
Brouage F 66 C3
Brough GB 26 A3
Broughshane GB 19 B5
Broughton GB 25 C4
Broughton-in-Furness GB 26 A2
Broumov CZ 53 C6
Broût-Vernet F 68 B3
Brouvelieures F 60 B2
Brouwershaven NL 49 B4

Brovary UA 11 A11
Brovst DK 38 B2
Brownhills GB 27 C4
Brozas E 93 B4
Brozzo I 71 C5
Brtnice CZ 63 A6
Brtonigla HR 72 C3
Bruay-la-Buissière F 48 C3
Bruchhausen-Vilsen D 43 C6
Bruchsal D 61 A4
Bruck, *Bayern* D 62 A3
Brück, *Brandenburg* D 52 A2
Bruck an der Grossglocknerstrasse A 72 A2
Bruck an der Leitha A 64 B2
Bruck an der Mur A 73 A5
Brückl A 73 B4
Bruckmühl D 62 C2
Brue-Auriac F 79 C4
Brüel D 44 B3
Bruen CH 70 B3
Bruère-Allichamps F 68 B2
Bruff IRL 20 B3
Bruflat N 32 B6
Brugg CH 70 A3
Brugge B 49 B4
Brüggen D 50 B2
Brühl D 50 C2
Bruinisse NL 49 B5
Brûlon F 57 C5
Brumano I 71 C4
Brumath F 60 B3
Brummen NL 50 A2
Brumov-Bylnice CZ 64 A4
Brumunddal N 34 B2
Brunau D 44 C3
Brunehamel F 59 A5
Brünen D 50 B2
Brunete E 94 B2
Brunflo S 115 D11
Brunico I 72 B1
Brunkeberg N 33 C5
Brunn D 45 B5
Brunnen CH 70 B3
Brunsbüttel D 43 B6
Brunssum NL 50 C1
Bruntál CZ 54 D2
Brus SRB 85 C6
Brušane HR 83 B4
Brusasco I 70 C3
Brusio CH 71 B5
Brusno SK 65 B5
Brusque F 78 C1
Brussels = Bruxelles B 49 C5
Brusson I 70 C2
Brüssow D 45 B6
Brusy PL 46 B3
Bruton GB 29 B5
Bruvno HR 83 B4
Bruvoll N 34 B3
Bruxelles = Brussels B 49 C5
Bruyères F 60 B2
Bruz F 57 B4
Bruzaholm S 40 B5
Brwinów PL 55 A5
Bryansk RUS 7 E13
Brynamman GB 28 B4
Bryncrug GB 26 C1
Bryne N 33 D2
Brynmawr GB 29 B4
Bryrup DK 39 C2
Brzeće SRB 85 C5
Brzeg PL 54 C2
Brzeg Dolny PL 54 B1
Brześć Kujawski PL 47 C4
Brzesko PL 55 D5
Brzeszcze PL 55 D4
Brzezie PL 46 B2
Brzeziny, *Łódzkie* PL 55 B4
Brzeziny, *Wielkopolskie* PL 54 B3
Brzeźnica PL 53 B5
Brzeźnica Nowa PL 55 B4
Brzeżno PL 46 B1
Brzotin SK 65 B6
Brzozie Lubawskie PL 47 B5
Bua S 40 B2
Buarcos P 92 A2
Buaveg N 33 C2
Bubbio I 80 B2
Bubry F 56 C2
Buca TR 119 D2
Bucak TR 119 E5
Bučany SK 64 B3
Buccheri I 109 B3
Buccino I 103 C8
Bucelas P 92 C1
Buch, *Bayern* D 61 B6
Buch, *Bayern* D 62 B3
Buchach UA 11 B8
Bucharest = Bucureşti RO 11 D9
Buchbach D 62 B3
Buchboden A 71 A4
Buchen, *Baden-Württemberg* D 61 A5
Büchen, *Schleswig-Holstein* D 44 B2
Buchenberg D 61 C6
Buchères F 59 B5
Buchholz D 44 B1
Buchloe D 62 B1
Buchlovice CZ 64 A3
Buchlyvie GB 24 B3
Bucholz D 44 B4
Buchs CH 71 A4
Buchy F 58 A2
Bückeburg D 51 A5
Buckfastleigh GB 28 C4
Buckhaven GB 25 B4
Buckie GB 23 D6
Buckingham GB 31 B3
Buckley GB 26 B2
Bückwitz D 44 C4
Bučovice CZ 64 A3
Bucsa H 75 A6
Bucureşti = Bucharest RO 11 D9
Bucy-lés-Pierreport F 59 A4
Buczek PL 55 B4
Bud N 114 E3
Budakalasz H 65 C5
Budakeszi H 75 A3
Budal N 114 E7
Budaörs H 75 A3
Budapest H 75 A4
Budča SK 65 B5
Buddusò I 110 B2
Bude GB 28 C3
Budeč CZ 63 A6
Büdelsdorf D 43 A6
Budens P 98 B2
Búðardalur IS 111 B4
Budia E 95 B4
Budimlić-Japra BIH 83 B5
Büdingen D 51 C5
Budinšćina HR 73 B6
Budišov CZ 64 A3
Budleigh Salterton GB 29 C4
Budmerice SK 64 B3
Budoni I 110 B2
Búdrio I 81 B5
Budva MNE 105 A4
Budyně nad Ohří CZ 53 C4
Budziszewice PL 55 B4
Budzyń PL 46 C2
Bue N 33 D2
Bueña E 95 B5
Buenache de Alarcón E 95 C4
Buenache de la Sierra E 95 B5
Buenaventura E 94 B2
Buenavista de Valdavia E 88 B2
Buendia E 95 B4
Bueu E 87 B2
Buezo E 89 B3
Bugac H 75 B4
Bugarra E 96 B2
Bugeat F 68 C1
Buggerru I 110 C1
Bugojno BIH 84 B2
Bugøyfjord N 113 C18
Bugøynes N 113 C18
Bugyi H 75 A4
Buharkent TR 119 E3
Bühl, *Baden-Württemberg* D 61 B4
Bühl, *Bayern* D 61 C6
Bühlertal D 61 B4
Bühlertann D 61 A5
Buia I 72 B3
Builth Wells GB 29 A4
Buin N 32 B6
Buis-les-Baronnies F 79 B4
Buitenpost NL 42 B3
Buitrago del Lozoya E 94 B3
Bujalance E 100 B1
Bujaraloz E 90 B2
Buje HR 72 C3
Bujedo E 89 B3
Bük H 74 A1
Buk PL 46 C2
Bükkösd H 74 B3
Bükkzsérc H 65 C6
Bukovci SLO 73 B5
Bukowiec PL 53 A6
Bukowina Tatrzańska PL 65 A6
Bukownica PL 54 B3
Bukowno PL 55 C4
Bülach CH 70 A3
Búland IS 111 D7
Buldan TR 119 D3
Bulgnéville F 60 B1
Bulgurca TR 119 D2
Bülkau D 43 B5
Bulken N 32 B3
Bulkowo PL 47 C6
Bullas E 101 A4
Bulle CH 70 B2
Büllingen B 50 C2
Bulqizë AL 116 A2
Buna BIH 84 C2
Bunahowen IRL 18 B2
Bunbeg IRL 18 A3
Bunclody IRL 21 B5
Buncrana IRL 19 A4
Bunde, *Niedersachsen* D 43 B4
Bünde, *Nordrhein-Westfalen* D 51 A4
Bundoran IRL 18 B3
Bunessan GB 24 B1
Bungay GB 30 B5
Bunge S 37 E6
Bunić HR 83 B4
Bunmahon IRL 21 B4
Bunnyconnellan IRL 18 B2
Buño E 86 A2
Buñol E 96 B2
Bunratty IRL 20 B3
Bunsbeek B 49 C5
Buñuel E 89 C5
Bünyan TR 16 B7
Bunyola E 97 B2
Buonabitácolo I 104 C1
Buonalbergo I 103 B7
Buonconvento I 81 C5
Buonvicino I 106 B2
Burano I 72 C2
Burbach D 50 C4
Burcei I 110 C2
Burdons-sur-Rognon F 59 B6
Burdur TR 119 E5
Bureå S 3 D24
Burela E 86 A3
Büren D 51 B4
Büren an der Aare CH 70 A2
Burford GB 29 B6
Burg, *Cottbus* D 53 B4
Burg, *Magdeburg* D 52 A1
Burg, *Schleswig-Holstein* D 43 B6
Burg auf Fehmarn D 44 A3
Burg Stargard D 45 B5
Burgas BG 11 E9
Burgau A 73 A6
Burgau D 61 B6
Burgau P 98 B2
Burgbernheim D 61 A6
Burgdorf CH 70 A2
Burgdorf D 44 C2
Burgebrach D 62 A1
Bürgel D 52 C1
Burgess Hill GB 31 D3
Burgh le Marsh GB 27 B6
Burghaslach D 61 A6
Burghausen D 62 B3
Burghead GB 23 D5
Burgheim D 62 B2
Búrgio I 108 B2
Burgkirchen D 62 B3
Burgkunstadt D 52 C1
Burglengenfeld D 62 A3
Burgo P 87 D2
Burgoberbach D 61 A6
Burgohondo E 94 B2
Burgos E 88 B3
Burgsinn D 51 C5
Burgstädt D 52 C2
Burgstall D 44 C3
Burgsvik S 37 E5
Burgui E 76 D2
Burguillos E 99 B5
Burguillos de Toledo E 94 C3
Burguillos del Cerro E 93 C4
Burhaniye TR 118 C1
Burhave D 43 B5
Burie F 67 C4
Burjassot E 96 B2
Burk D 61 A6
Burkhardtsdorf D 52 C2
Burlada E 76 D1
Burladingen D 61 B5
Burlage D 43 B4
Burness GB 23 B6
Burnham GB 31 C3
Burnham Market GB 30 B4
Burnham-on-Crouch GB 31 C4
Burnham-on-Sea GB 29 B5
Burniston GB 27 A5
Burnley GB 26 B3
Burntisland GB 25 B4
Burón E 88 A1
Buronzo I 70 C3
Burovac SRB 85 B6
Burow D 45 B5
Burravoe GB 22 A7
Burrel AL 105 B6
Burret F 77 D4
Burriana E 96 B2
Burry Port GB 28 B3
Bürs A 71 A4
Bursa TR 118 B4
Burseryd S 40 B3
Bürstadt D 61 A4
Burton GB 26 A3
Burton Agnes GB 27 A5
Burton Bradstock GB 29 C5
Burton Latimer GB 30 B3
Burton upon Stather GB 27 B5
Burton upon Trent GB 27 C4
Burujón E 94 C2
Burwell GB 30 B4
Burwick GB 23 C6
Bury GB 26 B3
Bury St. Edmunds GB 30 B4
Buryn UA 7 F12
Burzenin PL 54 B3
Busachi I 110 B1
Busalla I 80 B2
Busana I 81 B4
Busano I 70 C2
Busca I 80 B1
Busch D 44 C3
Buševec HR 73 C6
Bushat AL 105 B5
Bushey GB 31 C3
Bushmills GB 19 A5
Bušince SK 65 B5
Buskhyttan S 37 D3
Busko-Zdrój PL 55 C5
Busot E 96 C2
Busovača BIH 84 B2
Busquistar E 100 C2
Bussang F 60 C2
Busseto I 81 B4
Bussière-Badil F 67 C5
Bussière-Poitevine F 67 B5
Bussolengo I 71 C5
Bussoleno I 70 C2
Bussum NL 49 A6
Busto Arsízio I 70 C3
Büsum D 43 A5
Butera I 109 B3
Butgenbach B 50 C2
Butler's Bridge IRL 19 B4
Butryny PL 47 B6
Bütschwil CH 70 A4
Buttermere GB 26 A2
Buttevant IRL 20 B3
Buttle S 37 E5
Buttstädt D 52 B1
Butzbach D 51 C4
Bützfleth D 43 B6
Bützow D 44 B3
Buxières-les-Mines F 68 B2
Buxtehude D 43 B6
Buxton GB 27 B4
Buxy F 69 B4
Büyükçekmece TR 118 A3
Büyükkariştiran TR 118 A2
Büyükorhan TR 118 C3
Buzançais F 67 B6
Buzancy F 59 A5
Buzău RO 11 D9
Buzet HR 72 C3
Buzsák H 74 B2
Buzy F 76 C2
By S 36 B3
Byala BG 11 E8
Byaroza BY 6 E8
Byczyna PL 54 B3
Bydalen S 115 D10
Bydgoszcz PL 47 B4
Bygdin N 32 A5
Bygland N 33 D4
Byglandsfjord N 33 D4
Bygstad N 32 A2
Bykhaw BY 7 E11
Bykle N 33 C4
Bylderup-Bov DK 39 E2
Byrkjedal N 33 D3
Byrkjelo N 114 F3
Byrum DK 38 B3
Byšice CZ 53 C4
Byske S 3 D24
Býškovice CZ 64 A3
Bysław PL 46 B3
Bystré CZ 64 A2
Bystrice, *Středočeský* CZ 65 A4
Bystřice, *Středočeský* CZ 63 A5
Bystřice nad Pernštejnem CZ 64 A2
Bystřice pod Hostýnem CZ 64 A3
Bystrzyca Kłodzka PL 54 C1
Bytča SK 65 A4
Bytnica PL 53 A5
Bytom PL 54 C3
Bytom Odrzański PL 53 B5
Bytów PL 46 A3
Byxelkrok S 41 B7
Bzenec CZ 64 B3
Bzince SK 64 B3

C

Cabacos P 92 B2
Cabaj-Čápor SK 64 B4
Cabana E 86 A2
Cabanac-et-Villagrains F 76 B2
Cabañaquinta E 88 A1
Cabanas P 98 B3
Cabañas de Yepes E 95 C3
Cabañas del Castillo E 93 B5
Cabanelles E 91 A5
Cabanes E 96 A3
Cabanillas E 89 B5
Čabar HR 73 C4
Cabasse F 79 C5
Cabdella E 91 A4
Cabeceiras de Basto P 87 C2
Cabeço de Vide P 92 B3
Cabella Ligure I 80 B3
Cabeza del Buey E 93 C5
Cabeza la Vaca E 99 A4
Cabezamesada E 95 C3
Cabezarados E 100 A1
Cabezarrubias del Puerto E 100 A1
Cabezas del Villar E 94 B1
Cabezas Rubias E 98 B3
Cabezón E 88 C2
Cabezón de la Sal E 88 A2
Cabezón de Liébana E 88 A2
Cabezuela E 94 A3
Cabezuela del Valle E 93 A5
Cabo de Gata E 101 C3
Cabo de Palos E 101 B5
Cabolafuenta E 95 A4
Cabourg F 57 A5
Cabra E 100 B1
Cabra P 92 A3
Cabra del Santo Cristo E 100 B2
Cabrach GB 23 D5
Cábras I 110 C1
Cabreiro P 87 C2
Cabreiros E 86 A3
Cabrejas E 95 B4
Cabrela P 92 C2
Cabrillas E 87 D4
Cabuna HR 74 C2
Cacabelos E 86 B4
Čačak SRB 85 C5
Cáccamo I 108 B2
Caccuri I 107 B3
Cacela P 98 B3
Cacém P 92 C1
Cáceres E 93 B4
Cachafeiro E 86 B2
Cachopo P 98 B3
Čachtice SK 64 B3
Cacin E 100 B2
Čačinci HR 74 C2
Cadafais P 92 C1
Cadalen F 77 C5
Cadalso E 93 A4
Cadaqués E 91 A6
Cadaval P 92 B1
Cadavedo E 86 A4
Čadavica BIH 84 B1
Čadca SK 65 A4
Cadéac F 77 D3
Cadelbosco di Sopra I 81 B4
Cadenazzo CH 70 B3
Cadenberge D 43 B6
Cadenet F 79 C4
Cadeuil F 66 C4
Cádiar E 100 C2
Cadillac F 76 B2
Cádiz E 99 C4
Čadjavica HR 74 C2
Cadouin F 77 B3
Cadours F 77 C4
Cadrete E 90 B2
Caen F 57 A5
Caerleon GB 29 B5
Caernarfon GB 26 B1
Caerphilly GB 29 B4
Caersws GB 26 C2
Cafede P 92 B3
Çağa TR 118 B7
Caggiano I 104 C1
Cagli I 82 C1
Cágliari I 110 C2
Čaglin HR 74 C2
Cagnano Varano I 104 B1
Cagnes-sur-Mer F 79 C6
Caher IRL 21 B4
Caherciveen IRL 20 C1
Caherdaniel IRL 20 C1
Cahors F 77 B4
Cahul MD 11 D10
Caiazzo I 103 B7
Caion E 86 A2
Cairndow GB 24 B3
Cairnryan GB 24 D2
Cairo Montenotte I 80 B2
Caister-on-Sea GB 30 B5
Caistor GB 27 B5
Caivano I 103 C7
Cajarc F 77 B4
Čajetina SRB 85 C4
Čajniče BIH 84 C4
Çakırlar TR 119 F5
Çakmak TR 118 C6
Čakovec HR 73 B6
Çakran AL 105 C5
Çal TR 119 D4
Cala E 99 B4
Cala d'Or E 97 B3
Cala Galdana E 97 B3
Cala Gonone I 110 B2
Cala Llonga E 97 C1
Cala Millor E 97 B3
Cala Morell E 97 A3
Cala Ratjada E 97 B3
Calabritto I 103 C8
Calaceite E 90 C3
Calacuccia F 102 A2
Calaf E 91 B4
Calafat RO 11 D7
Calafell E 91 B4
Calahonda, *Granada* E 100 C2
Calahonda, *Málaga* E 100 C1
Calahorra E 89 B5
Calais F 48 C2
Calalzo di Cadore I 72 B2
Calamocha E 95 B5
Calamonte E 93 C4
Calanais GB 22 C2
Calañas E 99 B4
Calanda E 90 C2
Calangiánus I 110 B2
Călăraşi RO 11 D9
Calascibetta I 109 B3
Calasetta I 110 C1
Calasparra E 101 A4
Calatafimi I 108 B1
Calatayud E 89 C5
Calatorao E 89 C5
Calau D 53 B3
Calbe D 52 B1
Calcena E 89 C5
Calcinelli I 82 C1
Calco I 71 C4
Caldaro sulla strada del Vino I 71 B6
Caldarola I 82 C2
Caldas da Rainha P 92 B1
Caldas de Boì E 90 A3
Caldas de Malavella E 91 B5
Caldas de Reis E 86 B2
Caldas de San Jorge P 87 D2
Caldas de Vizela P 87 C2
Caldaso de los Vidrios E 94 B2
Caldbeck GB 26 A2
Caldearenas E 90 A2
Caldelas P 87 C2
Calders E 91 B4
Caldes de Montbui E 91 B5
Caldicot GB 29 B5
Caldirola I 80 B3
Caledon GB 19 B5
Calella, *Barcelona* E 91 B5
Calella, *Girona* E 91 B6
Calenzana F 102 A1
Calera de León E 99 A4
Calera y Chozas E 94 C2
Caleruega E 89 C3
Caleruela E 93 B5
Cales de Mallorca E 97 B3
Calestano I 81 B4
Calfsound GB 23 B6
Calgary GB 24 B1
Calimera I 105 C4
Calitri I 103 C8
Calizzano I 80 B2
Callac F 56 B2
Callan IRL 21 B4
Callander GB 24 B3
Callas F 79 C5
Calliano, *Piemonte* I 80 A2
Calliano, *Trentino Alto Adige* I 71 C6
Callington GB 28 C3
Callosa de Ensarriá E 96 C2
Callosa de Segura E 101 A5
Callús E 91 B4
Čalma SRB 85 A4
Calmbach D 61 B4
Calne GB 29 B6
Calolziocorte I 71 C4
Calonge E 91 B6
Čalovec SK 64 C3
Calpe E 96 C3
Caltabellotta I 108 B2
Caltagirone I 109 B3
Caltanissetta I 109 B3
Caltavuturo I 108 B2
Çaltılıbük TR 118 C3
Caltojar E 89 C4
Caluire-et-Cuire F 69 C4
Caluso I 70 C2
Calvello I 104 C1
Calvi F 102 A1
Calviá E 97 B2
Calvinet F 77 B5
Calvisson F 78 C3
Calvörde D 44 C3
Calw D 61 B4
Calzada de Calatrava E 100 A2
Calzada de Valdunciel E 94 A1
Calzadilla de los Barros E 93 C4
Cam GB 29 B5
Camaiore I 81 C4
Camarasa E 90 B3
Camarena E 94 B2
Camarès F 78 C1
Camaret-sur-Aigues F 78 B3
Camaret-sur-Mer F 56 B1
Camarillas E 90 C2
Camariñas E 86 A1
Camarma E 95 B3
Camarzana de Tera E 87 B4
Camas E 99 B4
Camastra I 108 B2
Cambados E 86 B2
Cambarinho P 92 A2
Camberley GB 31 C3
Cambil E 100 B2
Cambligeu F 48 C3
Cambo-les-Bains F 76 C1
Camborne GB 28 C2
Cambrai F 49 C4
Cambre E 86 A2
Cambridge GB 30 B4
Cambrils E 91 B4
Cambs D 44 B3
Camburg D 52 B1
Camden GB 31 C3
Cameleño E 88 A2
Camelford GB 28 C3
Çameli TR 119 E4
Camelle E 86 A1
Camerano I 82 C2
Camerino I 82 C2
Camerota I 106 A2
Camigliatello Silano I 106 B3
Caminha P 87 C2
Caminomorisco E 93 A4
Caminreal E 95 B5
Camisano Vicentino I 72 C1
Camlıdere TR 118 B7
Cammarata I 108 B2
Camogli I 80 B3
Camors F 56 C3
Camp IRL 20 B2
Campagna I 103 C8
Campagnano di Roma I 102 A5
Campagnático I 81 D5
Campan F 76 C3
Campana I 107 B3
Campanario E 93 C5
Campanillas E 100 C1
Campano E 99 C4
Campaspero E 88 C2
Campbeltown GB 24 C2
Campello E 96 C2
Campelos P 92 B1
Campi Bisénzio I 81 C5
Campi Salentina I 105 C4
Campico López E 101 B4
Campíglia Maríttima I 81 C4
Campillo de Altobuey E 95 C5
Campillo de Aragón E 95 A5
Campillo de Arenas E 100 B2
Campillo de Llerena E 93 C5
Campillos E 100 B1
Câmpina RO 11 D8
Campli I 82 D2
Campo E 90 A3
Campo da Feira E 86 A3
Campo de Bacerros E 87 B3
Campo de Caso E 88 A1
Campo de Criptana E 95 C3
Campo Ligure I 80 B2
Campo Lugar E 93 B5
Campo Maior P 93 B3
Campo Molino I 79 B6
Campo Real E 95 B3
Campo Túres I 72 B1
Campobasso I 103 B7
Campobello di Licata I 108 B2
Campobello di Mazara I 108 B1
Campodársego I 72 C1
Campodolcino I 71 B4
Campofelice di Roccella I 108 B2
Campofiorito I 108 B2
Campofórmido I 72 B3
Campofranco I 108 B2
Campofrio E 99 B4
Campogalliano I 81 B4
Campolongo I 72 B2
Campomanes E 88 A1
Campomarino I 103 B8
Campomono F 102 B1
Camporeale I 108 B2
Camporeggiano I 82 C1
Camporrells E 90 B3
Camporrobles E 96 B1
Campos P 87 C3
Campos del Port E 97 B3
Camposa P 87 C2
Camposampiero I 72 C1
Camposanto I 81 B5
Camposines E 90 B3
Campotéjar E 100 B2
Campotosto I 103 A6
Camprodón E 91 A5
Campsegret F 77 B3
Camrose GB 28 B2
Camuñas E 95 C3
Çamyolu TR 119 F7
Çan TR 118 B2
Can Pastilla E 97 B2
C'an Picafort E 97 B3
Cana I 81 D5
Cañada del Hoyo E 95 C5
Cañada Rosal E 99 B5
Cañadajuncosa E 95 C4
Čanak HR 83 B4
Çanakkale TR 118 B1
Canal San Bovo I 72 B1
Canale I 80 B1
Canales, *Asturias* E 88 B1
Canales, *Castellón de la Plana* E 96 B2
Canals E 96 C2
Cañamares E 95 B4
Cañamero E 93 B5
Cañar E 100 C2
Cañate la Real E 99 C5
Cañaveral E 93 B4
Cañaveral de León E 99 A4
Cañaveras E 95 B4
Cañaveruelas E 95 B4
Canazei I 72 B1
Cancale F 57 B4
Cancellara I 104 C1
Cancello ed Arnone I 103 B7
Cancon F 77 B3
Canda E 87 B4
Candamil E 86 A3
Candanchu E 76 D2
Çandarlı TR 118 D1
Candas E 88 A1
Candasnos E 90 B3
Candé F 66 A3
Candela I 104 B1
Candelario E 93 A5
Candeleda E 93 A5
Cándia Lomellina I 70 C3
Candide Casamazzagno I 72 B2
Candín E 86 B4
Candosa P 92 A3
Canecas P 92 C1
Canelli I 80 B2
Canena E 100 A2
Canencia E 94 B3
Canero E 86 A4
Canet F 78 C2
Canet de Mar E 91 B5
Canet d'en Berenguer E 96 B2
Canet-Plage F 91 A6
Cañete E 95 B5
Cañete de las Torres E 100 B1
Canfranc E 76 D2
Cangas, *Lugo* E 86 A3
Cangas, *Pontevedra* E 87 B2
Cangas de Narcea E 86 A4
Cangas de Onís E 88 A1
Canha P 92 C2
Canhestros P 98 A2
Canicattì I 108 B2
Canicattini Bagni I 109 B4
Canicosa de la Sierra E 89 C3
Caniles E 101 B3
Canillas de Aceituno E 100 C1
Canino I 102 A4
Canisy F 57 A4
Cañizal E 94 A1
Cañizo E 88 C1
Canjáyar E 101 C3
Çankırı TR 16 A6
Cannai I 110 C1
Cannara I 82 C1
Cánnero Riviera I 70 B3

Cannes F 79 C6
Canneto, *Sicilia* I 106 C1
Canneto, *Toscana* I 81 C4
Canneto sull'Oglio I 71 C5
Cannich GB 22 D4
Cannóbio I 70 B3
Cannock GB 26 C3
Canonbie GB 25 C5
Canosa di Púglia I 104 B2
Cantalapiedra E 94 A1
Cantalejo E 94 A3
Cantalgallo E 99 A4
Cantalice I 102 A5
Cantalpino E 94 A1
Cantalupo in Sabina I 102 A5
Cantanhede P 92 A2
Cantavieja E 90 C2
Čantavir SRB 75 C4
Canterbury GB 31 C5
Cantiano I 82 C1
Cantillana E 99 B5
Cantiveros E 94 B2
Cantoria E 101 B3
Cantù I 71 C4
Canvey GB 31 C4
Cany-Barville F 58 A1
Canyet de Mar E 91 B5
Caol GB 24 B2
Cáorle I 72 C2
Caorso I 81 A3
Cap-de-Pin F 76 B2
Cap Ferret F 76 B1
Capáccio I 103 C8
Capaci I 108 A2
Capálbio I 102 A4
Capánnori I 81 C4
Caparde BIH 84 B3
Caparroso E 89 B5
Capbreton F 76 C1
Capdenac-Gare F 77 B5
Capdepera E 97 B3
Capel Curig GB 26 B2
Capellades E 91 B4
Capena I 102 A5
Capendu F 77 C5
Capestang F 78 C2
Capestrano I 103 A6
Capileira E 100 C2
Capinha P 92 A3
Ca'Pisani I 82 B1
Capistrello I 103 B6
Capizzi I 109 B3
Čaplje BIH 83 B5
Čapljina BIH 84 C2
Capo di Ponte I 71 B5
Caposile I 72 C2
Capoterra I 110 C1
Cappamore IRL 20 B3
Cappeln D 43 C5
Cappoquin IRL 21 B4
Capracotta I 103 B7
Capránica I 102 A5
Caprarola I 102 A5
Capretta I 82 D1
Capri I 103 C7
Capriati a Volturno I 103 B7
Caprino Veronese I 71 C5
Captieux F 76 B2
Cápua I 103 B7
Capurso I 104 B2
Capvern F 77 C3
Carabaña E 95 B3
Carabias E 88 C3
Caracal RO 11 D8
Caracenilla E 95 B4
Caráglio I 80 B1
Caraman F 77 C4
Caramánico Terme I 103 A7
Caranga E 86 A4
Caranguejeira P 92 B2
Caransebeş RO 11 D7
Carantec F 56 B2
Carapelle I 104 B1
Carasco I 80 B3
Carate Brianza I 71 C4
Caravaca de la Cruz E 101 A4
Caravággio I 71 C4
Carbajal E 100 C1
Carbajo E 93 B3
Carballeda E 86 B3
Carballeda de Avia E 87 B2
Carballo E 86 A2
Carbis Bay GB 28 C2
Carbon-Blanc F 76 B2
Carbonera de Frentes E 89 C4
Carboneras E 101 C4
Carboneras de Guadazaón E 95 C5
Carbonero el Mayor E 94 A2
Carboneros E 100 A2
Carbónia I 110 C1
Carbonin I 72 B2
Carbonne F 77 C4
Carbost, *Highland* GB 22 D2
Carbost, *Highland* GB 22 D2
Carcaboso E 93 A4
Carcabuey E 100 B1
Carcaixent E 96 B2
Carcans F 76 A1
Carcans-Plage F 76 A1
Carção P 87 C4
Carcar E 89 B5
Cárcare I 80 B2
Carcassonne F 77 C5
Carcastillo E 89 B5
Carcedo de Burgos E 89 B3
Carcelén E 96 B1
Carcès F 79 C5
Carchelejo E 100 B2
Çardak, *Çanakkale* TR 118 B1
Çardak, *Denizli* TR 119 E4
Cardedeu E 91 B5
Cardeña E 100 A1
Cardenete E 95 C5
Cardeñosa E 94 B2
Cardeto I 109 A4
Cardiff GB 29 B4
Cardigan GB 28 A3
Cardona E 91 B4
Cardosos P 92 B2
Carei RO 11 C7
Carentan F 57 A4
Carentoir F 57 C3
Careri I 106 C3
Carevdar HR 74 B1
Cargèse F 102 A1
Carhaix-Plouguer F 56 B2
Caria P 92 A3
Cariati I 107 B3
Carignan F 59 A6
Carignano I 80 B1
Cariñena E 90 B1
Carini I 108 A2
Cariño E 86 A3
Carínola I 103 B6
Carisbrooke GB 31 D2
Carlabhagh GB 22 C2
Carlepont F 59 A4
Carlet E 96 B2
Carlingford IRL 19 B5
Carlisle GB 25 D5
Carloforte I 110 C1
Carlópoli I 106 B3
Carlow D 44 B2
Carlow IRL 21 B5
Carlton GB 27 C4
Carluke GB 25 C4
Carmagnola I 80 B1
Carmarthen GB 28 B3
Carmaux F 77 B5
Carmena E 94 C2
Cármenes E 88 B1
Carmine I 80 B1
Carmona E 99 B5
Carmonita E 93 B4
Carmyllie GB 25 B5
Carnac F 56 C2
Carndonagh IRL 19 A4
Carnew IRL 21 B5
Carnforth GB 26 A3
Cárnia I 72 B3
Carnlough GB 19 B6
Carno GB 26 C2
Carnon Plage F 78 C2
Carnota E 86 B1
Carnoustie GB 25 B5
Carnwath GB 25 C4
Carolei I 106 B3
Carolinensiel D 43 B4
Carolles F 57 B4
Carona I 71 B4
Caronía I 109 A3
Carovigno I 104 C3
Carovilli I 103 B7
Carpaneto Piacentino I 81 B3
Carpegna I 82 C1
Carpenédolo I 71 C5
Carpentras F 79 B4
Carpi I 81 B4
Carpignano Sésia I 70 C3
Carpineti I 81 B4
Carpineto Romano I 102 B6
Cărpiniş RO 75 C5
Carpino I 104 B1
Carpinone I 103 B7
Carpio E 94 A1
Carquefou F 66 A3
Carqueiranne F 79 C5
Carral E 86 A2
Carranque E 94 B3
Carrapichana P 92 A3
Carrara I 81 B4
Carraroe IRL 20 A2
Carrascalejo E 93 B5
Carrascosa del Campo E 95 B4
Carratraca E 100 C1
Carrazeda de Ansiães P 87 C3
Carrazedo de Montenegro P 87 C3
Carrbridge GB 23 D5
Carregal do Sal P 92 A2
Carreña E 88 A2
Carrick IRL 18 B3
Carrick-on-Shannon IRL 18 C3
Carrick-on-Suir IRL 21 B4
Carrickart IRL 19 A4
Carrickfergus GB 19 B6
Carrickmacross IRL 19 C5
Carrigallen IRL 19 C4
Carrión E 99 B4
Carrión de Calatrava E 94 C3
Carrión de los Condes E 88 B2
Carrizo de la Ribera E 88 B1
Carrizosa E 100 A3
Carro F 79 C4
Carrocera E 88 B1
Carros F 79 C6
Carrouge CH 70 B1
Carrouges F 57 B5
Carrù I 80 B1
Carry-le-Rouet F 79 C4
Carryduff GB 19 B6
Carsóli I 102 A6
Carsphairn GB 24 C3
Cartagena E 101 B5
Cártama E 100 C1
Cartaxo P 92 B2
Cartaya E 98 B3
Carteret F 57 A4
Cartes E 88 A2
Carúnchio I 103 B7
Carviçães P 87 C4
Carvin F 48 C3
Carvoeira P 92 B1
Carvoeiro P 98 B2
Casa Branca, *Portalegre* P 92 C3
Casa Branca, *Setúbal* P 98 A2
Casa Castalda I 82 C1
Casa l'Abate I 105 C4
Casabermeja E 100 C1
Casacalenda I 103 B7
Casaio E 87 B4
Casàl di Principe I 103 B7
Casalarreina E 89 B4
Casalbordino I 103 A7
Casalborgone I 70 C2
Casalbuono I 104 C1
Casalbuttano ed Uniti I 71 C4
Casale Monferrato I 70 C3
Casalécchio di Reno I 81 B5
Casalina I 82 D1
Casalmaggiore I 81 B4
Casalnuovo Monterotaro I 103 B8
Casaloldo I 71 C5
Casalpusterlengo I 71 C4
Casamássima I 104 C2
Casamicciola Terme I 103 C6
Casamozza F 102 A2
Casar de Cáceres E 93 B4
Casar de Palomero E 93 A4
Casarabonela E 100 C1
Casarano I 107 A5
Casarejos E 89 C3
Casares E 99 C5
Casares de las Hurdes E 93 A4
Casariche E 100 B1
Casarrubios del Monte E 94 B2
Casas de Don Pedro E 93 B5
Casas de Fernando Alonso E 95 C4
Casas de Haro E 95 C4
Casas de Juan Gil E 96 B1
Casas de Millán E 93 B4
Casas de Reina E 99 A5
Casas de Ves E 96 B1
Casas del Juan Núñez E 95 C5
Casas del Puerto E 101 A4
Casas del Rio E 96 B1
Casas-Ibáñez E 96 B1
Casas Nuevas E 101 B4
Casasimarro E 95 C4
Casasola E 94 B2
Casasola de Arión E 88 C1
Casasuertes E 88 A2
Casatejada E 93 B5
Casavieja E 94 B2
Casazza I 71 C4
Cascais P 92 C1
Cascante E 89 C5
Cascante del Rio E 96 A1
Cáscia I 82 D2
Casciana Terme I 81 C4
Cáscina I 81 C4
Cáseda E 89 B5
Casekow D 45 B6
Casella I 80 B3
Caselle Torinese I 70 C2
Casemurate I 82 B1
Casenove I 82 D1
Caseres E 90 B3
Caserío Benali E 96 B2
Caserta I 103 B7
Casével P 98 B2
Cashel IRL 21 B4
Casillas E 94 B2
Casillas de Coria E 93 B4
Casina I 81 B4
Casinos E 96 B2
Čáslav CZ 63 A6
Cásola Valsénio I 81 B5
Cásole d'Elsa I 81 C5
Cásoli I 103 A7
Casória I 103 C7
Caspe E 90 B2
Cassà de la Selva E 91 B5
Cassagnas F 78 B2
Cassagnes-Bégonhès F 77 B5
Cassano allo Iónio I 106 B3
Cassano d'Adda I 71 C4
Cassano delle Murge I 104 C2
Cassano Magnago I 70 C3
Cassano Spinola I 80 B2
Cassel F 48 C3
Cassíbile I 109 C4
Cassine I 80 B2
Cassino I 103 B6
Cassis F 79 C4
Cassolnovo I 70 C3
Cassuéjouls F 78 B1
Častá SK 64 B3
Castagnaro I 71 C6
Castagneto Carducci I 81 C4
Castagnola CH 70 B3
Castalla E 96 C2
Castañar de Ibor E 93 B5
Castanheira de Pêra P 92 A2
Cástano Primo I 70 C3
Castasegna CH 71 B4
Castéggio I 80 A3
Casteição P 87 D3
Castejón E 89 B5
Castejón de Monegros E 90 B2
Castejón de Sos E 90 A3
Castejón de Valdejasa E 90 B2
Castèl Baronia I 103 B8
Castel Bolognese I 81 B5
Castel d'Aiano I 81 B4
Castel d'Ario I 71 C5
Castel de Cabra E 90 C2
Castél del Monte I 103 A6
Castel del Piano I 81 D5
Castel di Iúdica I 109 B3
Castel di Rio I 81 B5
Castèl di Sangro I 103 B7
Castél di Tora I 102 A5
Castèl Frentano I 103 A7
Castel San Gimignano I 81 C5
Castèl San Giovanni I 80 A3
Castèl San Pietro Terme I 81 B5
Castél Sant'Elia I 102 A5
Castél Volturno I 103 B6
Castelbuono I 109 B3
Casteldáccia I 108 A2
Casteldelfino I 79 B6
Castelfidardo I 82 C2
Castelfiorentino I 81 C4
Castelforte I 103 B6
Castelfranco Emília I 81 B5
Castelfranco in Miscano I 103 B8
Castelfranco Véneto I 72 C1
Casteljaloux F 76 B3
Castell Arquato I 81 B3
Castell de Cabres E 90 C3
Castell de Castells E 96 C2
Castell de Ferro E 100 C2
Castellabate I 103 C7
Castellammare del Golfo I 108 A1
Castellammare di Stábia I 103 C7
Castellamonte I 70 C2
Castellana Grotte I 104 C3
Castellane F 79 C5
Castellaneta I 104 C2
Castellaneta Marina I 104 C2
Castellar E 100 A2
Castellar de la Frontera E 99 C5
Castellar de la Ribera E 91 A4
Castellar de Santiago E 100 A2
Castellar del Vallés E 91 B5
Castellarano I 81 B4
Castell'Azzara I 81 D5
Castellbell i Villar E 91 B4
Castelldans E 90 B3
Castelldefels E 91 B4
Castelleone I 71 C4
Castellet E 91 B4
Castelletto di Brenzone I 71 C5
Castellfollit de la Roca E 91 A5
Castellfollit de Riubregos E 91 B4
Castellfort E 90 C2
Castellina in Chianti I 81 C5
Castellina Marittima I 81 C4
Castelló de Farfaña E 90 B3
Castelló de la Plana E 96 B2
Castello d'Empùries E 91 A6
Castello di Fiemme I 71 B6
Castello Tesino I 72 B1
Castelloli E 91 B4
Castellón de Rugat E 96 C2
Castellote E 90 C2
Castellterçol E 91 B5
Castellúcchio I 71 C5
Castellúccio de'Sáuri I 103 B8
Castelluccio Inferiore I 106 B3
Castelmassa I 81 A5
Castelmáuro I 103 B7
Castelmoron-sur-Lot F 77 B3
Castelnau-de-Médoc F 76 A2
Castelnau-de-Montmirail F 77 C4
Castelnau-Magnoac F 77 C3
Castelnau-Montratier F 77 B4
Castelnaudary F 77 C4
Castelnou E 90 B2
Castelnovo ne'Monti I 81 B4
Castelnuovo Berardenga I 81 C5
Castelnuovo della Dáunia I 103 B8
Castelnuovo di Garfagnana I 81 B4
Castelnuovo di Val di Cécina I 81 C4
Castelnuovo Don Bosco I 80 A1
Castelnuovo Scrivia I 80 B2
Castelo Branco, *Bragança* P 87 C4
Castelo Branco, *Castelo Branco* P 92 B3
Castelo de Paiva P 87 C2
Castelo de Vide P 92 B3
Castelo do Neiva P 87 C2
Castelo Mendo P 93 A4
Castelraimondo I 82 C2
Castelsantángelo I 82 D2
Castelsaraceno I 106 A2
Castelsardo I 110 B1
Castelsarrasin F 77 B4
Castelserás E 90 C2
Casteltérmini I 108 B2
Castelvecchio Subéquo I 103 A6
Castelvetrano I 108 B1
Castenédolo I 71 C5
Castets F 76 C1
Castiádas I 110 C2
Castiglion Fibocchi I 81 C5
Castiglion Fiorentino I 81 C5
Castiglioncello I 81 C4
Castiglione I 102 A6
Castiglione Chiavarese I 80 B3
Castiglione d'Adda I 71 C4
Castiglione dei Pepoli I 81 B5
Castiglione del Lago I 81 C6
Castiglione della Pescáia I 81 D4
Castiglione delle Stiviere I 71 C5
Castiglione di Sicilia I 109 B4
Castiglione d'Órcia I 81 C5
Castiglione Messer Marino I 103 B7
Castiglione Messer Raimondo I 103 A6
Castil de Peones E 89 B3
Castilblanco E 94 C1
Castilblanco de los Arroyos E 99 B5
Castilfrío de la Sierra E 89 C4
Castilgaleu E 90 A3
Castilisar E 90 A1
Castilleja E 99 B4
Castillejar E 101 B3
Castillejo de Martin Viejo E 93 A4
Castillejo de Mesleón E 89 C3
Castillejo de Robledo E 89 C3
Castillo de Bayuela E 94 B2
Castillo de Locubín E 100 B2
Castillon-la-Bataille F 76 B2
Castillon-Len-Couserans F 77 D4
Castillonès F 77 B3
Castillonroy E 90 B3
Castilruiz E 89 C4
Castione CH 70 B4
Castions di Strada I 72 C3
Castirla F 102 A2
Castle Cary GB 29 B5
Castle Douglas GB 25 D4
Castlebar IRL 18 C2
Castlebellingham IRL 19 C5
Castleblaney IRL 19 B5
Castlebridge IRL 21 B5
Castlecomer IRL 21 B4
Castlederg GB 19 B4
Castledermot IRL 21 B5
Castleford GB 27 B4
Castleisland IRL 20 B2
Castlemaine IRL 20 B2
Castlemartyr IRL 20 C3
Castlepollard IRL 19 C4
Castlerea IRL 18 C3
Castleton GB 27 B4
Castletown, *Highland* GB 23 C5
Castletown, *Isle of Man* GB 26 A1
Castletown Bearhaven IRL 20 C2
Castletownroche IRL 20 B3
Castlewellan GB 19 B6
Casto I 71 C5
Castrejón E 88 C1
Castrelo del Valle E 87 C3
Castres F 77 C5
Castricum NL 42 C1
Castries F 78 C2
Castrignano del Capo I 107 B5
Castril E 101 B3
Castrillo de Duero E 88 C3
Castrillo de la Vega E 88 C3
Castrillo de Onielo E 88 C2
Castro E 88 A2
Castro I 107 A5
Castro-Caldelas E 87 B3
Castro Daire P 87 D3
Castro de Rey E 86 A3
Castro dei Volsci I 103 B6
Castro del Río E 100 B1
Castro Laboreiro P 87 B2
Castro Marim P 98 B3
Castro-Urdiales E 89 A3
Castro Verde P 98 B2
Castrocabón E 88 B1
Castrocaro Terme I 81 B5
Castrocontrigo E 87 B4
Castrofilippo I 108 B2
Castrogonzaio E 88 B1
Castrojeriz E 88 B2
Castromonte E 88 C1
Castromudarra E 88 B1
Castronuevo E 88 C1
Castronuño E 88 C1
Castropol E 86 A3
Castroreale I 109 A4
Castroserracin E 88 C3
Castroverde E 86 A3
Castroverde de Campos E 88 C1
Castroverde de Cerrato E 88 C2
Castrovillari I 106 B3
Castuera E 93 C5
Catadau E 96 B2
Cataéggio I 71 B4
Çatalca TR 118 A3
Catallar TR 119 F5
Çatalzeytin TR 16 A7
Catánia I 109 B4
Catanzaro I 106 C3
Catanzaro Marina I 106 C3
Catarroja E 96 B2
Catarruchos P 92 A2
Catcleugh GB 25 C5
Catenanuova I 109 B3
Caterham GB 31 C3
Cati E 90 C3
Čatići BIH 84 B3
Catignano I 103 A6
Catillon F 49 C4
Catoira E 86 B2
Caton GB 26 A3
Catral E 101 A5
Catterick GB 27 A4
Cattólica I 82 C1
Cattólica Eraclea I 108 B2
Catton GB 25 D5
Caudebec-en-Caux F 58 A1
Caudete E 101 A5
Caudete de las Fuentes E 96 B1
Caudiel E 96 B2
Caudiès-de-Fenouillèdes F 77 D5
Caudry F 49 C4
Caulkerbush GB 25 D4
Caulnes F 57 B3
Caulónia I 106 C3
Caumont-l'Evente F 57 A5
Caunes-Minervois F 77 C5
Cauro F 102 B1
Caussade F 77 B4
Causse-de-la-Selle F 78 C2
Cauterets F 76 D2
Cava de Tirreni I 103 C7
Cavaglia I 70 C3
Cavaillon F 79 C4
Cavalaire-sur-Mer F 79 C5
Cavaleiro P 98 B2
Cavalese I 71 B6
Cavallermaggiore I 80 B1
Cavallino I 72 C2
Cavan IRL 19 C4
Cavárzere I 72 C2
Çavdarhisar TR 118 C4
Çavdır TR 119 E4
Cavernais P 87 D3
Cavezzo I 81 B5
Cavignac F 76 A2
Čavle HR 73 C4
Cavo I 81 D4
Cavour I 80 B1
Cavtat HR 84 D3
Cawdor GB 23 D5
Çay TR 118 D6
Çaycuma TR 118 A7
Cayeux-sur-Mer F 48 C2
Cayiralan TR 16 B7
Çayırhan TR 118 B6
Caylus F 77 B4
Cayres F 78 B2
Cazalilla E 100 B2
Cazalla de la Sierra E 99 B5
Cazals F 77 B4
Cazanuecos E 88 B1
Cazaubon F 76 C2
Cazaux F 76 B1
Cazavet F 77 C4
Cazères F 77 C4
Cazin BIH 83 B4
Cazis CH 71 B4
Čazma HR 74 C1
Cazo E 88 A1
Cazorla E 100 B3
Cazouls-lès-Béziers F 78 C2
Cea, *León* E 88 B1
Cea, *Orense* E 86 B3
Ceánuri E 89 A4
Ceauce F 57 B5
Cebolla E 94 C2
Čebovce SK 65 B5
Cebreros E 94 B2
Čečava BIH 84 B2
Ceccano I 103 B6
Cece H 74 B3
Cecenowo PL 46 A3
Čechtice CZ 63 A6
Čechtín CZ 64 A1
Cécina I 81 C4
Ceclavín E 93 B4
Cedégolo I 71 B5
Cedeira E 86 A2
Cedillo E 92 B3
Cedillo del Condado E 94 B3
Cedrillas E 90 C2
Cedynia PL 45 C6
Cée E 86 B1
Cefalù I 109 A3
Céggia I 72 C2
Cegléd H 75 A4
Ceglédbercel H 75 A4
Céglie Messápica I 104 C3
Cehegín E 101 A4
Ceilhes-et-Rocozels F 78 C2
Ceinos de Campos E 88 B1
Ceira P 92 A2
Čejč CZ 64 B2
Cekcyn PL 47 B4
Cela BIH 83 B5
Čelákovice CZ 53 C4
Celano I 103 A6
Celanova E 87 B3
Celbridge IRL 21 A5
Čelebič BIH 83 C5
Celenza Valfortore I 103 B7
Čelić BIH 84 B3
Čelinac BIH 84 B2
Celje SLO 73 B5
Cella E 95 B5
Celldömölk H 74 A2
Celle D 44 C2
Celle Ligure I 80 B2
Celles B 49 C5
Celles-sur-Belle F 67 B4
Cellino San Marco I 105 C3
Celorico da Beira P 92 A3
Celorico de Basto P 87 C2
Çeltik TR 118 C6
Çeltikçi TR 119 E5
Cemaes GB 26 B1
Cembra I 71 B6
Čemerno BIH 84 C3
Cenad RO 75 B5
Cencenighe Agordino I 72 B1
Cenei RO 75 C5
Ceneselli I 81 A5
Cenicero E 89 B4
Cenicientos E 94 B2
Censeau F 69 B6
Čenta SRB 85 A5
Centallo I 80 B1
Centelles E 91 B5
Cento I 81 B5
Centúripe I 109 B3
Cepeda la Mora E 94 B1
Cépet F 77 C4
Čepin HR 74 C3
Čepinski Martinci HR 74 C3
Cepovan SLO 72 B3
Ceprano I 103 B6
Čeralije HR 74 C2
Cerami I 109 B3
Cerano I 70 C3
Cérans Foulletourte F 57 C6
Ceraso I 106 A2
Cerbaia I 81 C5
Cerbère F 91 A6
Cercadillo E 95 A4
Cercal, *Lisboa* P 92 B1
Cercal, *Setúbal* P 98 B2
Čerčany CZ 63 A5
Cerceda E 94 B3
Cercedilla E 94 B2
Cercemaggiore I 103 B7
Cercs E 91 A4
Cercy-la-Tour F 68 B3
Cerda I 108 B2
Cerdedo E 86 B2
Cerdeira P 93 A3
Cerdon F 58 C3
Cerea I 71 C6
Ceres GB 25 B5
Ceres I 70 C2
Cerese I 81 A4
Ceresole-Reale I 70 C2
Cereste F 79 C4
Céret F 91 A5
Cerezo de Abajo E 95 A3
Cerezo de Riotirón E 89 B3
Cerfontaine B 49 C5
Cergy F 58 A3
Cerignola I 104 B1
Cérilly F 68 B2
Cerisiers F 59 B4
Cerizay F 67 B4
Çerkeş TR 16 A6
Çerkezköy TR 118 A3
Cerkije SLO 73 B4
Cerknica SLO 73 C4
Cerkno SLO 72 B3
Cerkwica PL 45 A7
Çermë-Proshkë AL 105 B5
Černa HR 74 C3
Černá Hora CZ 64 A2
Cernavodă RO 11 D10
Cernay F 60 C3
Cerne Abbas GB 29 C5
Cernégula E 89 B3
Cernik HR 74 C2
Cernóbbio I 70 C4
Černošin CZ 62 A3
Cernovice CZ 63 A5
Cérons F 76 B2
Cerovlje HR 73 C4
Cerovo SK 65 B5
Cerqueto I 82 D1
Cerralbo E 87 D4
Cerreto d'Esi I 82 C1
Cerreto Sannita I 103 B7
Cerrigydrudion GB 26 B2
Cërrik AL 105 B5
Cerro Muriano E 100 A1
Certaldo I 81 C5
Certosa di Pésio I 80 B1
Cerva P 87 C3
Cervaro I 103 B6
Cervatos de la Cueza E 88 B2
Červena Řečice CZ 63 A6
Červená-Skala SK 65 B6
Cervená Voda CZ 54 C1
Cerveny Kostelec CZ 53 C6
Cervera E 91 B4
Cervera de la Cañada E 89 C5
Cervera de Pisuerga E 88 B2
Cervera del Llano E 95 C4
Cervera del Río Alhama E 89 B5
Cervéteri I 102 B5

Cérvia I 82 B1
Cerviá de les Garriques E 90 B3
Cervignano del Friuli I 72 C3
Cervinara I 103 B7
Cervione F 102 A2
Cervo E 86 A3
Cervon F 68 A3
Cesana Torinese I 79 B5
Cesarica HR 83 B4
Cesarò I 109 B3
Cesena I 82 B1
Cesenático I 82 B1
Cēsis LV 7 C8
Česká Belá CZ 63 A6
Česká Kamenice CZ 53 C4
Česká Lípa CZ 53 C4
Česká Skalice CZ 53 C6
Česká Třebová CZ 64 A2
České Budějovice CZ 63 B5
České Velenice CZ 63 B5
Český Brod CZ 53 C4
Český Dub CZ 53 C4
Český Krumlov CZ 63 B5
Český Těšín CZ 65 A4
Češljeva Bara SRB 85 B6
Çeşme TR 119 D1
Cessenon F 78 C2
Cesson-Sévigné F 57 B4
Cestas F 76 B2
Čestobrodica SRB 85 C5
Cesuras E 86 A2
Cetin Grad HR 73 C5
Cetina E 89 C5
Cetinje MNE 105 A4
Cetraro I 106 B2
Ceuta E 99 D5
Ceuti E 101 A4
Ceva I 80 B2
Cevico de la Torre E 88 C2
Cevico Navero E 88 C2
Cevins F 69 C6
Cévio CH 70 B3
Cevizli TR 119 E6
Čevo MNE 105 A4
Cewice PL 46 A3
Ceyhan TR 16 C7
Ceylan TR 119 F4
Ceyrat F 68 C3
Ceyzériat F 69 B5
Chaam NL 49 B5
Chabanais F 67 C5
Chabeuil F 79 B4
Chabielice PL 55 B4
Chablis F 59 C4
Châbons F 69 C5
Chabówka PL 65 A5
Chabreloche F 68 C3
Chabris F 67 A6
Chagford GB 28 C4
Chagny F 69 B4
Chagoda RUS 7 B13
Chaherrero E 94 B2
Chailland F 57 B5
Chaillé-les-Marais F 66 B3
Chailles F 67 A6
Chailley F 59 B4
Chalabre F 77 D5
Chalais F 67 C5
Chalamont F 69 C5
Châlette-sur-Loing F 58 B3
Chalindrey F 59 C6
Challacombe GB 28 B4
Challans F 66 B3
Challes-les-Eaux F 69 C5
Chalmazel F 68 C3
Chalmoux F 68 B3
Chalon-sur-Saône F 69 B4
Chalonnes-sur-Loire F 66 A4
Châlons-en-Champagne F 59 B5
Chalupy PL 47 A4
Châlus F 67 C5
Cham CH 70 A3
Cham D 62 A3
Chamberet F 68 C1
Chambéry F 69 C5
Chambilly F 68 B4
Chambley F 60 A1
Chambly F 58 A3
Chambois F 57 B6
Chambon-sur-Lac F 68 C2
Chambon-sur-Voueize F 68 B2
Chambord F 58 C2
Chamborigaud F 78 B2
Chamboulive F 68 C1
Chamerau D 62 A3
Chamonix-Mont Blanc F 70 C1
Chamoux-sur-Gelon F 69 C6
Champagnac-le-Vieux F 68 C3
Champagney F 60 C2
Champagnole F 69 B5
Champagny-Mouton F 67 B5
Champaubert F 59 B4
Champdeniers-St. Denis F 67 B4
Champdieu F 68 C4
Champdôtre F 69 A5
Champeix F 68 C3
Champéry CH 70 B1
Champigne F 57 C5
Champignelles F 59 C4
Champigny-sur-Veude F 67 A5
Champlitte-et-le-Prelot F 60 C1
Champoluc I 70 C2
Champoly F 68 C3
Champorcher I 70 C2
Champrond-en-Gâtine F 58 B2
Champs-sur-Tarentaine F 68 C2
Champs-sur-Yonne F 59 C4
Champtoceaux F 66 A3
Chamrousse F 69 C5
Chamusca P 92 B2
Chanac F 78 B2
Chanaleilles F 78 B2
Chandler's Ford GB 31 D2
Chandra GR 117 G8
Chandrexa de Queixa E 87 B3
Chañe E 88 C2
Changy F 68 B3
Chania GR 117 G6
Channes F 59 C5
Chantada E 86 B3
Chantelle F 68 B3
Chantenay-St. Imbert F 68 B3
Chanteuges F 78 A2
Chantilly F 58 A3
Chantonnay F 66 B3
Chão de Codes P 92 B2
Chaource F 59 B5
Chapa E 86 B2
Chapareillan F 69 C5
Chapel en le Frith GB 27 B4
Chapelle Royale F 58 B2
Chapelle-St. Laurent F 67 B4
Charbonnat F 68 B4
Chard GB 29 C5
Charenton-du-Cher F 68 B2
Charlbury GB 31 C2
Charleroi B 49 C5
Charlestown GB 28 C3
Charlestown IRL 18 C3
Charlestown of Aberlour GB 23 D5
Charleville IRL 20 B3
Charleville-Mézières F 59 A5
Charlieu F 68 B4
Charlottenberg S 34 C4
Charlton Kings GB 29 B5
Charly F 59 B4
Charmes F 60 B2
Charmes-sur-Rhône F 78 B3
Charmey CH 70 B2
Charminster GB 29 C5
Charmont-en-Beauce F 58 B3
Charny F 59 C4
Charolles F 69 B4
Chârost F 68 B2
Charquemont F 70 A1
Charrin F 68 B3
Charroux F 67 B5
Chartres F 58 B2
Charzykow PL 46 B3
Chasseneuil-sur-Bonnieure F 67 C5
Chassigny F 59 C6
Château-Arnoux F 79 B5
Château-Chinon F 68 A3
Château-d'Oex CH 70 B2
Château-d'Olonne F 66 B3
Château-du-Loir F 58 C1
Château-Gontier F 57 C5
Château-la-Vallière F 67 A5
Château-Landon F 58 B3
Château-l'Evêque F 67 C5
Château-Porcien F 59 A5
Château-Renault F 58 C1
Château-Salins F 60 B2
Château-Thierry F 59 A4
Châteaubernard F 67 C4
Châteaubourg F 57 B4
Châteaubriant F 57 C4
Châteaudun F 58 B2
Châteaugiron F 57 B4
Châteaulin F 56 B1
Châteaumeillant F 68 B2
Châteauneuf, *Nièvre* F 68 A3
Châteauneuf, *Saône-et-Loire* F 69 B4
Châteauneuf-de-Randon F 78 B2
Châteauneuf-d'Ille-et-Vilaine F 57 B4
Châteauneuf-du-Faou F 56 B2
Châteauneuf-du-Pape F 78 B3
Châteauneuf-en-Thymerais F 58 B2
Châteauneuf la-Forêt F 67 C6
Châteauneuf-le-Rouge F 79 C4
Châteauneuf-sur-Charente F 67 C4
Châteauneuf-sur-Cher F 68 B2
Châteauneuf-sur-Loire F 58 C3
Châteauneuf-sur-Sarthe F 57 C5
Châteauponsac F 67 B6
Châteauredon F 79 B5
Châteaurenard, *Bouches du Rhône* F 78 C3
Châteaurenard, *Loiret* F 59 C3
Châteauroux F 68 B1
Châteauroux-les-Alpes F 79 B5
Châteauvillain F 59 B5
Châtel F 70 B1
Châtel-Censoir F 68 A3
Châtel-de-Neuvre F 68 B3
Châtel-Montagne F 68 B3
Châtel-St. Denis CH 70 B1
Châtel-sur-Moselle F 60 B2
Châtelaillon-Plage F 66 B3
Châtelaudren F 56 B3
Châtelet B 49 C5
Châtelguyon F 68 C3
Châtellerault F 67 B5
Châtelus-Malvaleix F 68 B2
Châtenois F 60 B1
Châtenois-les-Forges F 70 A1
Chatham GB 31 C4
Châtillon I 70 C2
Châtillon-Coligny F 59 C3
Châtillon-en-Bazois F 68 A3
Châtillon-en-Diois F 79 B4
Châtillon-sur Chalaronne F 69 B4
Châtillon-sur-Indre F 67 B6
Châtillon-sur-Loire F 58 C3
Châtillon-sur-Marne F 59 A4
Châtillon-sur-Seine F 59 C5
Châtres F 59 B4
Chatteris GB 30 B4
Chatton GB 25 C6
Chauchina E 100 B2
Chaudes-Aigues F 78 B2
Chaudrey F 59 B5
Chauffailles F 69 B4
Chaulnes F 58 A3
Chaument Gistoux B 49 C5
Chaumergy F 69 B5
Chaumont F 59 B6
Chaumont-en-Vexin F 58 A2
Chaumont-Porcien F 59 A5
Chaumont-sur-Aire F 59 B6
Chaumont-sur-Loire F 67 A6
Chaunay F 67 B5
Chauny F 59 A4
Chaussin F 69 B5
Chauvigny F 67 B5
Chavagnes-en-Paillers F 66 B3
Chavanges F 59 B5
Chaves P 87 C3
Chavignon F 59 A4
Chazelles-sur-Lyon F 69 C4
Chazey-Bons F 69 C5
Cheadle, *Greater Manchester* GB 26 B3
Cheadle, *Staffordshire* GB 27 C4
Cheb CZ 52 C2
Chebsara RUS 7 B15
Checa E 95 B5
Chęciny PL 55 C5
Cheddar GB 29 B5
Cheddleton GB 26 B3
Chef-Boutonne F 67 B4
Chekalin RUS 7 D14
Chekhovo RUS 47 A6
Cheles E 93 C3
Chella E 96 B2
Chelles F 58 B3
Chełm PL 11 A7
Chełmno, *Kujawsko-Pomorskie* PL 47 B4
Chełmno, *Wielkopolskie* PL 54 A3
Chelmsford GB 31 C4
Chełmża PL 47 B4
Cheltenham GB 29 B5
Chelva E 96 B1
Chémery F 67 A6
Chemery-sur-Bar F 59 A5
Chemillé F 67 A4
Chemin F 69 B5
Chemnitz D 52 C2
Chénerailles F 68 B2
Cheniménil F 60 B2
Chenonceaux F 67 A6
Chenôve F 69 A4
Chepelare BG 116 A6
Chepstow GB 29 B5
Chera E 96 B2
Cherasco I 80 B1
Cherbonnières F 67 C4
Cherbourg F 57 A4
Cherchiara di Calábria I 106 B3
Cherepovets RUS 7 B14
Cherkasy UA 11 B12
Chernihiv UA 7 F11
Chernivtsi UA 11 B8
Chernobyl = Chornobyl UA 7 F11
Chernyakhovsk RUS 6 D6
Chéroy F 59 B3
Cherven BY 7 E10
Chervonohrad UA 11 A8
Cherykaw BY 7 E11
Chesham GB 31 C3
Cheshunt GB 31 C3
Chessy-lès-Pres F 59 B4
Cheste E 96 B2
Chester GB 26 B3
Chester-le-Street GB 25 D6
Chesterfield GB 27 B4
Chevagnes F 68 B3
Chevanceaux F 67 C4
Chevillon F 59 B6
Chevilly F 58 B2
Chew Magna GB 29 B5
Chézery-Forens F 69 B5
Chialamberto I 70 C2
Chiampo I 71 C6
Chianale I 79 B6
Chianciano Terme I 81 C5
Chiaramonte Gulfi I 109 B3
Chiaramonti I 110 B1
Chiaravalle I 82 C2
Chiaravalle Centrale I 106 C3
Chiaréggio I 71 B4
Chiari I 71 C4
Chiaromonte I 106 A3
Chiasso CH 70 C4
Chiávari I 80 B3
Chiavenna I 71 B4
Chiché F 67 B4
Chichester GB 31 D3
Chiclana de la Frontera E 99 C4
Chiclana de Segura E 100 A2
Chiddingfold GB 31 C3
Chieri I 80 A1
Chiesa in Valmalenco I 71 B4
Chieti I 103 A7
Chieti Scalo I 103 A7
Chiéuti I 103 B8
Chigirin UA 11 B12
Chigwell GB 31 C4
Chiliomodi GR 117 E4
Chillarón de Cuenca E 95 B4
Chillarón del Rey E 95 B4
Chilleurs-aux-Bois F 58 B3
Chillón E 100 A1
Chilluevar E 100 B2
Chiloeches E 95 B3
Chimay B 49 C5
Chimeneas E 100 B2
Chinchilla de Monte Aragón E 96 C1
Chinchón E 95 B3
Chingford GB 31 C4
Chinon F 67 A5
Chióggia I 72 C2
Chiomonte I 79 A5
Chipiona E 99 C4
Chippenham GB 29 B5
Chipping Campden GB 29 A6
Chipping Norton GB 31 C2
Chipping Ongar GB 31 C4
Chipping Sodbury GB 29 B5
Chirac F 78 B2
Chirbury GB 26 C2
Chirens F 69 C5
Chirivel E 101 B3
Chirk GB 26 C2
Chirnside GB 25 C5
Chişinău = Khisinev MD 11 C10
Chişineu Criş RO 10 C6
Chissey-en-Morvan F 69 A4
Chiusa I 71 B6
Chiusa di Pésio I 80 B1
Chiusa Scláfani I 108 B2
Chiusaforte I 72 B3
Chiusi I 81 C5
Chiva E 96 B2
Chivasso I 70 C2
Chlewiska PL 55 B5
Chludowo PL 46 C2
Chlum u Třeboně CZ 63 B5
Chlumec nad Cidlinou CZ 53 C5
Chmielnik PL 55 C5
Chobienia PL 54 B1
Chobienice PL 53 A5
Choceň CZ 53 D6
Choceń PL 47 C5
Chochołow PL 65 A5
Chocianów PL 53 B5
Chociw PL 55 B4
Chociwel PL 46 B1
Choczewo PL 46 A3
Chodaków PL 55 A5
Chodecz PL 47 C5
Chodov CZ 52 C2
Chodzież PL 46 C2
Chojna PL 45 C6
Chojnice PL 46 B3
Chojno, *Kujawsko-Pomorskie* PL 47 C5
Chojno, *Wielkopolskie* PL 46 C2
Chojnów PL 53 B5
Cholet F 66 A4
Chomérac F 78 B3
Chomutov CZ 52 C3
Chop UA 11 B7
Chora GR 117 E3
Chora Sfakion GR 117 G6
Chorges F 79 B5
Chorley GB 26 B3
Chornobyl = Chernobyl UA 7 F11
Chortkiv UA 11 B8
Chorzew PL 54 B3
Chorzów PL 54 C3
Choszczno PL 46 B1
Chotcza-Józefów PL 55 B6
Chotěboř CZ 63 A6
Chouilly F 59 A5
Chouto P 92 B2
Chouzy-sur-Cisse F 67 A6
Chozas de Abajo E 88 B1
Chrast, *Vychodočeský* CZ 64 A1
Chrást, *Západočeský* CZ 63 A4
Chrastava CZ 53 C4
Chřibská CZ 53 C4
Christchurch GB 29 C6
Christiansfeld DK 39 D2
Chroberz PL 55 C5
Chropyně CZ 64 A3
Chrudim CZ 53 D5
Chrzanów PL 55 C4
Chtelnica SK 64 B3
Chudovo RUS 7 B11
Chueca E 94 C3
Chulmleigh GB 28 C4
Chur CH 71 B4
Church Stretton GB 26 C3
Churriana E 100 C1
Churwalden CH 71 B4
Chvalšiny CZ 63 B5
Chwaszczyno PL 47 A4
Chynava CZ 53 C4
Chýnov CZ 63 A5
Ciacova RO 75 C6
Ciadîr-Lunga MD 11 C10
Ciadoncha E 88 B3
Cianciana I 108 B2
Ciano d'Enza I 81 B4
Ciążen PL 54 A2
Cibakhaza H 75 B5
Ciborro P 92 C2
Cicagna I 80 B3
Cicciano I 103 C7
Cičevac SRB 85 C6
Ciciliano I 102 B5
Cicognolo I 71 C5
Cidadelhe P 87 D3
Cide TR 16 A6
Cidones E 89 C4
Ciechanów, *Dolnośląskie* PL 54 B1
Ciechanów, *Mazowieckie* PL 47 C6
Ciechocinek PL 47 C4
Cielądz PL 55 B5
Ciemnik PL 46 B1
Ciempozuelos E 95 B3
Ciepielów PL 55 B6
Čierny Balog SK 65 B5
Cierp F 77 D3
Cierpice PL 47 C4
Ciervana E 89 A3
Cierznie PL 46 B3
Cieslé PL 47 C6
Cieszyn PL 65 A4
Cieutat F 76 C3
Cieza E 101 A4
Cifer SK 64 B3
Çifteler TR 118 C6
Cifuentes E 95 B4
Cigales E 88 C2
Cigliano I 70 C3
Cihanbeyli TR 16 B6
Čilipi HR 105 A4
Cillas E 95 B5
Cilleros E 93 A4
Cilleruelo de Arriba E 88 C3
Cilleruelo de Bezana E 88 B3
Cimalmotto CH 70 B3
Cimanes del Tejar E 88 B1
Ciminna I 108 B2
Cimişlia MD 11 C10
Cimoláis I 72 B2
Cîmpulung RO 11 D8
Çınarcık TR 118 B4
Cinctorres E 90 C2
Cinderford GB 29 B5
Çine TR 119 E3
Činěves CZ 53 C5
Ciney B 49 C6
Cinfães P 87 C2
Cingia de Botti I 81 A4
Cíngoli I 82 C2
Cinigiano I 81 D5
Cinobaňa SK 65 B5
Cinq-Mars-la-Pile F 67 A5
Cinquefrondí I 106 C3
Cintegabelle F 77 C4
Cintruénigo E 89 B5
Ciółkowo PL 47 C5
Ciperez E 87 D4
Cirat E 96 A2
Cirella I 106 B2
Cirencester GB 29 B6
Cirey-sur-Vezouze F 60 B2
Ciria E 89 C5
Ciriè I 70 C2
Cirigliano I 104 C2
Cirò I 107 B4
Cirò Marina I 107 B4
Ciry-le-Noble F 69 B4
Cislău RO 11 D9
Cismon del Grappa I 72 C1
Cisneros E 88 B2
Cissac-Médoc F 66 C4
Čista CZ 52 C3
Cisterna di Latina I 102 B5
Cistérniga E 88 C2
Cisternino I 104 C3
Cistierna E 88 B1
Čitluk BIH 84 C2
Citov CZ 53 C4
Città del Vaticano = Vatican City I 102 B5
Città della Pieve I 81 D6
Città di Castello I 82 C1
Città Sant'Angelo I 103 A7
Cittadella I 72 C1
Cittaducale I 102 A5
Cittanova I 106 C3
Ciudad Real E 94 D3
Ciudad Rodrigo E 93 A4
Ciudadela de Menorca E 97 B3
Cividale del Friuli I 72 B3
Cívita I 102 A6
Cívita Castellana I 102 A5
Civitanova Alta I 82 C2
Civitanova Marche I 82 C2
Civitavécchia I 102 A4
Civitella di Romagna I 81 B5
Civitella di Tronto I 82 D2
Civitella Roveto I 103 B6
Civray F 67 B5
Çivril TR 119 D4
Cizur Mayor E 76 D1
Cjutadilla E 91 B4
Clabhach GB 24 B1
Clachan GB 22 D2
Clachan na Luib GB 22 D1
Clacton-on-Sea GB 31 C5
Cladich GB 24 B2
Claggan GB 24 B2
Clairvaux-les-Lacs F 69 B5
Clamecy F 68 A3
Claonaig GB 24 C2
Clarecastle IRL 20 B3
Claregalway IRL 20 A3
Claremorris IRL 18 C2
Clarinbridge IRL 20 A3
Clashmore GB 23 D4
Clashmore IRL 21 B4
Claudy GB 19 B4
Clausthal-Zellerfeld D 51 B6
Cláut I 72 B2
Clay Cross GB 27 B4
Claye-Souilly F 58 B3
Cléder F 56 B1
Cleethorpes GB 27 B5
Clefmont F 60 B1
Cléguérec F 56 B2
Clelles F 79 B4
Clenze D 44 C2
Cleobury Mortimer GB 29 A5
Cléon-d'Andran F 78 B3
Cléré-les-Pins F 67 A5
Clères F 58 A2
Clermont F 58 A3
Clermont-en-Argonne F 59 A6
Clermont-Ferrand F 68 C3
Clermont-l'Hérault F 78 C2
Clerval F 69 A6
Clervaux L 50 C2
Clèry-St. André F 58 C2
Cles I 71 B6
Clevedon GB 29 B5
Cleveleys GB 26 B2
Cley GB 30 B5
Clifden IRL 18 C1
Clifford GB 29 A4
Clisson F 66 A3
Clitheroe GB 26 B3
Clogh IRL 21 B4
Cloghan, *Donegal* IRL 19 B4
Cloghan, *Offaly* IRL 21 A4
Clogheen IRL 21 B4
Clogher GB 19 B4
Cloghjordan IRL 20 B3
Clohars-Carnoët F 56 C2
Clonakilty IRL 20 C3
Clonaslee IRL 21 A4
Clondalkin IRL 21 A5
Clones IRL 19 B4
Clonmany IRL 19 A4
Clonmel IRL 21 B4
Clonmellon IRL 19 C4
Clonord IRL 21 A4
Clonroche IRL 21 B5
Cloone IRL 19 C4
Cloppenburg D 43 C5
Closeburn GB 25 C4
Clough GB 19 B6
Clova GB 25 B4
Clovelly GB 28 C3
Clowne GB 27 B4
Cloyes-sur-le-Loir F 58 C2
Cloyne IRL 20 C3
Cluis F 68 B1
Cluj-Napoca RO 11 C7
Clun GB 26 C2
Clunes GB 24 B3
Cluny F 69 B4
Cluses F 69 B6
Clusone I 71 C4
Clydach GB 28 B4
Clydebank GB 24 C3
Coachford IRL 20 C3
Coagh GB 19 B5
Coalisland GB 19 B5
Coalville GB 27 C4
Coaña E 86 A4
Çobanlar TR 118 D5
Cobas E 86 A2
Cobertelade E 89 C4
Cobeta E 95 B4
Cóbh IRL 20 C3
Cobreces E 88 A2
Coburg D 51 C6
Coca E 94 A2
Cocentaina E 96 C2
Cochem D 50 C3
Cockburnspath GB 25 C5
Cockermouth GB 26 A2
Codigoro I 82 B1
Codogno I 71 C4
Codos E 89 C5
Codróipo I 72 C2
Codrongianos I 110 B1
Coelhoso P 87 C4
Coesfeld D 50 B3
Coevorden NL 42 C3
Cofrentes E 96 B1
Cogeces del Monte E 88 C2
Coggeshall GB 31 C4
Cognac F 67 C4
Cogne I 70 C2
Cognin F 69 C5
Cogolin F 79 C5
Cogollos de Guadix E 100 B2
Cogollos-Vega E 100 B2
Cogolludo E 95 B3
Coimbra P 92 A2
Coín E 100 C1
Coirós E 86 A2
Čoka SRB 75 C5
Col SLO 73 C4
Colares P 92 C1
Cölbe D 51 C4
Colbitz D 52 A1
Colchester GB 31 C4
Coldingham GB 25 C5
Colditz D 52 B2
Coldstream GB 25 C5
Colebrooke GB 28 C4
Colera E 91 A6
Coleraine GB 19 A5
Colfiorito I 82 C1
Cólico I 71 B4
Coligny F 69 B5
Colindres E 89 A3
Coll de Nargó E 91 A4
Collado-Mediano E 94 B2
Collado Villalba E 94 B3
Collagna I 81 B4
Collanzo E 88 A1
Collat F 68 C3
Colle di Val d'Elsa I 81 C5
Colle Isarco I 71 B6
Colle Sannita I 103 B7
Collécchio I 81 B4
Colledimezzo I 103 B7
Colleferro I 102 B6
Collelongo I 103 B6
Collepasso I 107 A5
Collepepe I 82 D1
Collesalvetti I 81 C4
Collesano I 108 B2
Colli a Volturno I 103 B7
Collin GB 25 C4
Collinée F 56 B3
Collingham, *Nottinghamshire* GB 27 B5
Collingham, *West Yorkshire* GB 27 B4
Collinghorst D 43 B4
Cóllio I 71 C5
Collobrières F 79 C5
Collon IRL 19 C5
Collooney IRL 18 B3
Colmar F 60 B3
Colmars F 79 B5
Colmenar E 100 C1
Colmenar de la Sierra E 95 A3
Colmenar de Oreja E 95 B3
Colmenar Viejo E 94 B3
Colmonel GB 24 C3
Colne GB 26 B3
Colobraro I 106 A3
Cologna Véneta I 71 C6
Cologne = Köln D 50 C2
Cologne F 77 C3
Cologne al Serio I 71 C4
Colombey-les-Belles F 60 B1
Colombey-les-deux-Églises F 59 B5
Colombres E 88 A2
Colomera E 100 B2
Colomers E 91 A5
Colomiers F 77 C4
Colònia de Sant Jordi E 97 B3
Colorno I 81 B4
Colos P 98 B2
Cölpin D 45 B5
Colpy GB 23 D6
Colsterworth GB 30 B3
Coltishall GB 30 B5
Colunga E 88 A1
Colwell GB 25 C5
Colwyn Bay GB 26 B2
Colyford GB 29 C4
Coma-ruga E 91 B4
Comácchio I 82 B1
Combarros E 86 B4
Combeaufontaine F 60 C1
Comber GB 19 B6
Comblain-au-Pont B 49 C6
Combloux F 70 C1
Combourg F 57 B4
Combronde F 68 C3
Comeglians I 72 B2
Comillas E 88 A2
Comines F 49 C4
Cómiso I 109 C3
Comloşu Mare RO 75 C5
Commensacq F 76 B2
Commentry F 68 B2
Commerau D 53 B4
Commercy F 60 B1
Como I 71 C4
Cómpeta E 100 C2
Compiègne F 58 A3
Comporta P 92 C2
Comps-sur-Artuby F 79 C5
Comrat MD 11 C10
Comrie GB 25 B4
Comunanza I 82 D2
Cona, *Emilia Romagna* I 81 B5
Cona, *Veneto* I 72 C2
Concarneau F 56 C2
Conceição P 98 B2
Conches-en-Ouche F 58 B1
Concordia Sagittária I 72 C2
Concordia sulla Sécchia I 81 B4
Concots F 77 B4
Condat F 68 C2

Condé-en-Brie F 59 B4
Condé-sur-l'Escaut F 49 C4
Conde-sur-Marne F 59 A5
Condé-sur-Noireau F 57 B5
Condeixa P 92 A2
Condemios de Abajo E 95 A3
Condemios de Arriba E 95 A3
Condino I 71 C5
Condom F 77 C3
Condove I 70 C2
Condrieu F 69 C4
Conegliano I 72 C2
Conflans-sur-Lanterne F 60 C2
Confolens F 67 B5
Conforto E 86 A3
Cong IRL 18 C2
Congleton GB 26 B3
Congosto E 86 B4
Congosto de Valdavia E 88 B2
Congostrina E 95 A3
Conil de la Frontera E 99 C4
Coningsby GB 27 B5
Coniston GB 26 A2
Conlie F 57 B5
Conliège F 69 B5
Conna IRL 20 B3
Connah's Quay GB 26 B2
Connantre F 59 B4
Connaugh IRL 20 B3
Connaux F 78 B3
Connel GB 24 B2
Connerré F 58 B1
Cononbridge GB 23 D4
Čonoplja SRB 75 C4
Conques F 77 B5
Conques-sur-Orbiel F 77 C5
Conquista E 100 A1
Conquista de la Sierra E 93 B5
Consándolo I 81 B5
Consélice I 81 B5
Conselve I 72 C1
Consenvoye F 59 A6
Consett GB 25 D6
Consolacão P 92 B1
Constancia P 92 B2
Constanco E 86 A2
Constanța RO 11 D10
Constanti E 91 B4
Constantina E 99 B5
Consuegra E 95 C3
Consuma I 81 C5
Contarina I 82 A1
Contay F 48 D3
Conthey CH 70 B2
Contigliano I 102 A5
Contis-Plage F 76 B1
Contrada I 103 C7
Contres F 67 A6
Contrexéville F 60 B1
Controne I 103 C8
Contursi Termi I 103 C8
Conty F 58 A3
Conversano I 104 C3
Conwy GB 26 B2
Cookstown GB 19 B5
Coole F 59 B5
Coolgreany IRL 21 B5
Cooneen GB 19 B4
Cootehill IRL 19 B4
Cope E 101 B4
Copenhagen = København DK 41 D2
Copertino I 105 C4
Copparo I 81 B5
Coppenbrugge D 51 A5
Corabia RO 11 E8
Córaci I 106 B3
Coralići BIH 83 B4
Corato I 104 B2
Coray F 56 B2
Corbeil-Essonnes F 58 B3
Corbeny F 59 A4
Corbera E 96 B2
Corbie F 58 A3
Corbigny F 68 A3
Corbion B 59 A5
Corbridge GB 25 D5
Corby GB 30 B3
Corconte E 88 A3
Corcubión E 86 B1
Corcumello I 103 A6
Cordenòns I 72 C2
Cordes-sur-Ciel F 77 B4
Córdoba E 100 B1
Cordobilla de Lácara E 93 B4
Cordovado I 72 C2
Corella E 89 B5
Coreses E 88 C1
Corfe Castle GB 29 C5
Corga de Lobão P 87 D2
Cori I 102 B5
Coria E 93 B4
Coria del Río E 99 B4
Corigliano Cálabro I 106 B3
Corinaldo I 82 C1
Corinth = Korinthos GR 117 E4
Cório I 70 C2
Coripe E 99 C5
Cork IRL 20 C3
Corlay F 56 B2
Corleone I 108 B2
Corleto Monforte I 103 C8
Corleto Perticara I 104 C2
Çorlu TR 118 A2
Cormainville F 58 B2
Cormatin F 69 B4
Cormeilles F 58 A1
Cormery F 67 A5
Cormòns I 72 C3
Cormoz F 69 B5
Cornago E 89 B4
Cornberg D 51 B5
Cornellana E 86 A4
Cornești MD 11 C10
Corníglio I 81 B4
Cornimont F 60 C2
Corniolo I 81 C5
Cornuda I 72 C2
Cornudella de Montsant E 90 B3
Cornudilla E 89 B3
Cornus F 78 C2
Çorovodë AL 116 B2
Corpach GB 24 B2
Corps F 79 B4
Corps Nuds F 57 C4
Corral de Almaguer E 95 C3
Corral de Ayllon E 89 C3
Corral de Calatrava E 100 A1
Corral-Rubio E 101 A4
Corrales E 88 C1
Corran GB 24 B2
Corredoiras E 86 A2
Corréggio I 81 B4
Corrèze F 68 C1
Corridónia I 82 C2
Corris GB 26 C2
Corrubedo E 86 B1
Córsico I 71 C4
Corsock GB 25 C4
Corte F 102 A2
Corte de Peleas E 93 C4
Corte Pinto P 98 B3
Corteconcepción E 99 B4
Cortegaca P 87 D2
Cortegada E 87 B2
Cortegana E 99 B4
Cortemaggiore I 81 B3
Cortemilia I 80 B2
Cortes E 89 C5
Cortes de Aragón E 90 C2
Cortes de Arenoso E 96 A2
Cortes de Baza E 101 B3
Cortes de la Frontera E 99 C5
Cortes de Pallás E 96 B2
Cortiçadas P 92 C2
Cortico P 87 C3
Cortijo de Arriba E 94 C2
Cortijos Nuevos E 101 A3
Cortina d'Ampezzo I 72 B2
Corton GB 30 B5
Cortona I 81 C5
Coruche P 92 C2
Corullón E 86 B4
Çorum TR 16 A7
Corvara in Badia I 72 B1
Corvera E 101 B4
Corwen GB 26 C2
Cosenza I 106 B3
Cosham GB 31 D2
Coslada E 95 B3
Cosne-Cours-sur-Loire F 68 A2
Cosne d'Allier F 68 B2
Cospeito E 86 A3
Cossato I 70 C3
Cossaye F 68 B3
Cossé-le-Vivien F 57 C5
Cossonay CH 69 B6
Costa da Caparica P 92 C1
Costa de Santo André P 98 A2
Costa Nova P 92 A2
Costalpino I 81 C5
Costaros F 78 B2
Costești RO 11 D8
Costigliole d'Asti I 80 B2
Costigliole Saluzzo I 80 B1
Coswig, *Sachsen-Anhalt* D 52 B2
Coswig, *Sachsen* D 52 B3
Cotherstone GB 27 A4
Cotronei I 107 B3
Cottbus D 53 B4
Cottenham GB 30 B4
Cottingham GB 27 B5
Coublanc F 60 C1
Couches F 69 B4
Couço P 92 C2
Coucouron F 78 B2
Coucy-le-Château-Auffrique F 59 A4
Couëron F 66 A3
Couflens F 77 D4
Couhé F 67 B5
Couiza F 77 D5
Coulags GB 22 D3
Coulanges F 68 B3
Coulanges-la-Vineuse F 59 C4
Coulanges-sur-Yonne F 68 A3
Couleuvre F 68 B2
Coulmier-le-Sec F 59 C5
Coulommiers F 59 B4
Coulonges-sur-l'Autize F 67 B4
Coulounieix-Chamiers F 67 C5
Coulport GB 24 B3
Coupar Angus GB 25 B4
Coupéville F 59 B5
Couptrain F 57 B5
Cour-Cheverny F 67 A6
Cour-et-Buis F 69 C4
Coura P 87 C2
Courcelles B 49 C5
Courcelles-Chaussy F 60 A2
Courchevel F 70 C1
Courcôme F 67 C5
Courçon F 66 B4
Courgenay CH 70 A2
Courmayeur I 70 C1
Courniou F 78 C1
Cournon-d'Auvergne F 68 C3
Cournonterral F 78 C2
Courpière F 68 C3
Cours-la-Ville F 69 B4
Coursan F 78 C2
Courseulles-sur-Mer F 57 A5
Courson-les-Carrières F 59 C4
Courtalain F 58 B2
Courtenay F 59 B4
Courtomer F 58 B1
Courville, *Eure-et-Loire* F 58 B2
Courville, *Marne* F 59 A4
Coussac-Bonneval F 67 C6
Coutances F 57 A4
Couterne F 57 B5
Coutras F 76 A2
Couvet CH 70 B1
Couvin B 49 C5
Couzon F 68 B3
Covadonga E 88 A1
Covaleda E 89 C4
Covarrubias E 89 B3
Covas P 87 C2
Cove GB 22 D3
Coventry GB 30 B2
Coverack GB 28 C2
Covigliáio I 81 B5
Covilhã P 92 A3
Cowbridge GB 29 B4
Cowdenbeath GB 25 B4
Cowes GB 31 D2
Cox F 77 C4
Cózar E 100 A2
Cozes F 66 C4
Cozzano F 102 B2
Craco I 104 C2
Cracow = Kraków PL 55 C4
Craibstone GB 23 D6
Craighouse GB 24 C2
Craignure GB 24 B2
Crail GB 25 B5
Crailsheim D 61 A6
Craiova RO 11 D7
Cramlington GB 25 C6
Cranleigh GB 31 C3
Craon F 57 C5
Craonne F 59 A4
Craponne F 69 C4
Craponne-sur-Arzon F 68 C3
Crathie GB 23 D5
Crato P 92 B3
Craughwell IRL 20 A3
Craven Arms GB 26 C3
Crawford GB 25 C4
Crawinkel D 51 C6
Crawley GB 31 C3
Creag Ghoraidh GB 22 D1
Crecente E 87 B2
Crèches-sur-Saône F 69 B4
Crécy-en-Ponthieu F 48 C2
Crécy-la-Chapelle F 59 B3
Crécy-sur-Serre F 59 A4
Crediton GB 29 C4
Creeslough IRL 19 A4
Creetown GB 24 D3
Creeve GB 19 B5
Creglingen D 61 A6
Creil F 58 A3
Creissels F 78 B2
Crema I 71 C4
Cremeaux F 68 C3
Crémenes E 88 B1
Crémieu F 69 C5
Cremlingen D 51 A6
Cremona I 81 A4
Creney F 59 B5
Črenšovci SLO 73 B6
Créon F 76 B2
Crepaja SRB 85 A5
Crépey F 60 B1
Crépy F 59 A4
Crépy-en-Valois F 59 A3
Cres HR 83 B3
Crescentino I 70 C3
Crespino I 81 B5
Crespos E 94 B2
Cressage GB 26 C3
Cressensac F 77 A4
Cressia F 69 B5
Crest F 79 B4
Cresta CH 71 B4
Créteil F 58 B3
Creully F 57 A5
Creussen D 62 A2
Creutzwald F 60 A2
Creuzburg D 51 B6
Crevalcore I 81 B5
Crèvecœur-le-Grand F 58 A3
Crevillente E 101 A5
Crévola d'Ossola I 70 B3
Crewe GB 26 B3
Crewkerne GB 29 C5
Criales E 89 B3
Crianlarich GB 24 B3
Criccieth GB 26 C1
Crickhowell GB 29 B4
Cricklade GB 29 B6
Crieff GB 25 B4
Criel-sur-Mer F 48 C2
Crikvenica HR 73 C4
Crillon F 58 A2
Crimmitschau D 52 C2
Crimond GB 23 D7
Crinitz D 53 B3
Cripán E 89 B4
Criquetot-l'Esneval F 57 A6
Crispiano I 104 C3
Crissolo I 79 B6
Cristóbal E 93 A5
Crivitz D 44 B3
Črna SLO 73 B4
Crna Bara, *Srbija* SRB 85 B4
Crna Bara, *Vojvodina* SRB 75 C5
Crnac HR 74 C2
Crnča SRB 85 B4
Crni Lug BIH 83 B5
Crni Lug HR 73 C4
Črni Vrh SLO 73 C4
Crnjelovo Donje BIH 85 B4
Črnomelj SLO 73 C5
Crocketford GB 25 C4
Crocq F 68 C2
Crodo I 70 B3
Croglin GB 25 D5
Crolly IRL 18 A3
Cromarty GB 23 D4
Cromer GB 30 B5
Cronat F 68 B3
Crookhaven IRL 20 C2
Crookstown IRL 20 C3
Croom IRL 20 B3
Cropalati I 106 B3
Crópani I 107 C3
Crosbost GB 22 C2
Crosby GB 26 B2
Crosía I 106 B3
Cross-Hands GB 28 B3
Crosskiel IRL 19 C4
Crosshaven IRL 20 C3
Crosshill GB 24 C3
Crossmolina IRL 18 B2
Crotone I 107 B4
Crottendorf D 52 C2
Crouy F 59 A4
Crowborough GB 31 C4
Crowland GB 30 B3
Crowthorne GB 31 C3
Croyde GB 28 B3
Croydon GB 31 C3
Crozon F 56 B1
Cruas F 78 B3
Cruceni RO 75 B6
Crúcoli I 107 B4
Cruden Bay GB 23 D7
Crudgington GB 26 C3
Cruis F 79 B4
Crumlin GB 19 B5
Cruseilles F 69 B6
Crusheen IRL 20 B3
Cruz de Incio E 86 B3
Crvenka SRB 75 C4
Črveny Kamen SK 64 A4
Csabacsüd H 75 B5
Csabrendek H 74 A2
Csákánydoroszló H 74 B1
Csákvár H 74 A3
Csanádapáca H 75 B5
Csanádpalota H 75 B5
Csány H 65 C5
Csanytelek H 75 B5
Csapod H 74 A1
Császár H 74 A3
Császártöltés H 75 B4
Csávoly H 75 B4
Csemö H 75 A4
Csengöd H 75 B4
Csépa H 75 B5
Csepreg H 74 A1
Cserkeszölö H 75 B5
Csernely H 65 B6
Csesztreg H 74 B1
Csökmö H 75 A6
Csököly H 74 B2
Csokonyavisonta H 74 B2
Csólyospálos H 75 B4
Csongrád H 75 B5
Csopak H 74 B2
Csorna H 64 C3
Csorvás H 75 B5
Csurgo H 74 B2
Cuacos de Yuste E 93 A5
Cualedro E 87 C3
Cuanca de Campos E 88 B1
Cuba P 98 A3
Cubel E 95 A5
Cubelles E 91 B4
Cubillos E 89 C4
Cubillos del Sil E 86 B4
Cubjac F 67 C5
Cubo de la Solana E 89 C4
Çubuk TR 16 A6
Cuckfield GB 31 C3
Cucuron F 79 C4
Cudillero E 86 A4
Cuéllar E 88 C2
Cuenca E 95 B4
Cuers F 79 C5
Cuerva E 94 C2
Cueva de Agreda E 89 C5
Cuevas Bajas E 100 B1
Cuevas de San Clemente E 89 B3
Cuevas de San Marcos E 100 B1
Cuevas del Almanzora E 101 B4
Cuevas del Becerro E 99 C5
Cuevas del Campo E 100 B3
Cuevas del Valle E 94 B1
Cuges-les-Pins F 79 C4
Cúglieri I 110 B1
Cugnaux F 77 C4
Cuijk NL 50 B1
Cuinzier F 69 B4
Cuiseaux F 69 B5
Cuisery F 69 B5
Culan F 68 B2
Culemborg NL 49 B6
Cúllar E 101 B3
Cullaville GB 19 B5
Cullera E 96 B2
Cullivoe GB 22 A7
Cullompton GB 29 C4
Cully CH 70 B1
Culoz F 69 C5
Cults GB 23 D6
Cumbernauld GB 25 C4
Cumbres de San Bartolomé E 99 A4
Cumbres Mayores E 99 A4
Cumiana I 80 B1
Čumić SRB 85 B5
Cumnock GB 24 C3
Çumra TR 16 C6
Cúneo I 80 B1
Cunlhat F 68 C3
Čunski HR 83 B3
Cuntis E 86 B2
Cuorgnè I 70 C2
Cupar GB 25 B4
Cupello I 103 A7
Cupra Maríttima I 82 C2
Cupramontana I 82 C2
Čuprija SRB 85 C6
Curinga I 106 C3
Currelos E 86 B3
Currie GB 25 C4
Curtea de Argeș RO 11 D8
Curtici RO 75 B6
Curtis E 86 A2
Curtis Santa Eulalia E 86 A2
Čurug SRB 75 C5
Cusano Mutri I 103 B7
Cushendall GB 19 A5
Cusset F 68 B3
Cussy-les-Forges F 68 A4
Custines F 60 B2
Cutanda E 90 C1
Cutro I 107 B3
Cutrofiano I 107 A5
Cuts F 59 A4
Cuvilly F 58 A3
Cuxhaven D 43 B5
Cvikov CZ 53 C4
Cwmbran GB 29 B4
Cybinka PL 53 A4
Czacz PL 54 A1
Czajków PL 54 B3
Czaplinek PL 46 B2
Czarlin PL 47 A4
Czarna-Dąbrówka PL 46 A3
Czarna Woda PL 47 B4
Czarnca PL 55 C4
Czarne PL 46 B2
Czarnków PL 46 C2
Czarnowo PL 47 B4
Czarnozyly PL 54 B3
Czarny Bór PL 53 C6
Czarny-Dunajec PL 65 A5
Czarny Las PL 54 B2
Czchow PL 65 A6
Czechowice-Dziedzice PL 65 A4
Czempiń PL 54 A1
Czermno PL 55 B5
Czernichow PL 55 D4
Czerniejewo PL 46 C3
Czernikowo PL 47 C4
Czersk PL 46 B3
Czerwieńsk PL 53 A5
Czerwionka-Leszczyny PL 54 C3
Czerwonka PL 47 B6
Częstochowa PL 55 C4
Czeszewo PL 46 C3
Człopa PL 46 B2
Człuchów PL 46 B3
Czołpino PL 46 A3

D

Daaden D 50 C3
Dabas H 75 A4
Dąbie PL 54 A3
Dąbki PL 46 A2
Dabo F 60 B3
Dabrowa PL 46 C3
Dąbrowa Górnicza PL 55 C4
Dąbrowa Tarnowska PL 55 C5
Dąbrowice PL 55 A4
Dabrowno PL 47 B6
Dachau D 62 B2
Dačice CZ 63 A6
Daday TR 16 A6
Dağ TR 119 E5
Dagali N 32 B5
Dägebüll D 39 E1
Dagmersellen CH 70 A2
Dahlen D 52 B2
Dahlenburg D 44 B2
Dahme D 52 B3
Dahn D 60 A3
Dähre D 44 C2
Daikanvik S 115 B13
Dail bho Dheas GB 22 C2
Dailly GB 24 C3
Daimiel E 95 C3
Daingean IRL 21 A4
Đakovica KOS 10 E6
Đakovo HR 74 C3
Dal, *Akershus* N 34 B3
Dal, *Telemark* N 32 C5
Dala-Floda S 36 B1
Dala-Husby S 36 B2
Dala-Järna S 36 B1
Dalaas A 71 A5
Dalabrog GB 22 D1
Dalaman TR 119 F3
Dalarö S 37 C5
Dalbeattie GB 25 D4
Dalby DK 39 D3
Dalby, *Skåne* S 41 D3
Dalby, *Uppsala* S 37 C4
Dalby, *Värmland* S 34 B4
Dale, *Pembrokeshire* GB 28 B2
Dale, *Shetland* GB 22 A7
Dale, *Hordaland* N 32 B2
Dale, *Sogn og Fjordane* N 32 A2
Dalen, *Akershus* N 34 C3
Dalen, *Telemark* N 33 C5
Daleszyce PL 55 C5
Dalhalvaig GB 23 C5
Dalheim L 60 A2
Dalhem S 37 E5
Dalias E 100 C3
Dalj HR 75 C3
Dalkeith GB 25 C4
Dalkey IRL 21 A5
Dalmally GB 24 B3
Dalmellington GB 24 C3
Dalmose DK 39 D4
Daløy N 32 A1
Dalry, *Dumfries & Galloway* GB 24 C3
Dalry, *North Ayrshire* GB 24 C3
Dalrymple GB 24 C3
Dals Långed S 35 D4
Dals Rostock S 35 D4
Dalseter N 32 A6
Dalsjöfors S 40 B3
Dalskog S 35 D4
Dalston GB 25 D5
Dalstorp S 40 B3
Dalton-in-Furness GB 26 A2
Daluis F 79 B5
Dalum D 43 C4
Dalum S 40 B3
Dalvík IS 111 B7
Dalwhinnie GB 24 B3
Dalyan TR 119 F3
Damasi GR 116 C4
Damasławek PL 46 C3
Damazan F 76 B3
Damës AL 105 C5
Dammarie-les-Lys F 58 B3
Dammartin-en-Goële F 58 A3
Damme D 43 C5
Damnica PL 46 A3
Dampierre F 69 A5
Dampierre-sur-Salon F 69 A5
Damüls A 71 A4
Damville F 58 B2
Damvillers F 59 A6
Damwoude NL 42 B2
Danasjö S 115 B13
Danbury GB 31 C4
Dangé-St. Romain F 67 B5
Dängebo S 40 C5
Dangers F 58 B2
Dangeul F 57 B6
Danilovgrad MNE 105 A5
Danischenhagen D 44 A2
Daniszyn PL 54 B2
Danjoutin F 60 C2
Dannas S 40 B3
Dannemarie F 60 C3
Dannemora S 36 B4
Dannenberg D 44 B3
Dánszentmiklós H 75 A4
Dány H 75 A4
Daoulas F 56 B1
Darabani RO 11 B9
Darány H 74 C2
Darda HR 74 C3
Dardesheim D 51 B6
Darfeld D 50 A3
Darfo I 71 C5
Dargiń PL 46 A2
Dargun D 45 B4
Darlington GB 27 A4
Darłowo PL 46 A2
Darmstadt D 61 A4
Darney F 60 B2
Daroca E 95 A5
Darque P 87 C2
Darragh IRL 20 B2
Dartford GB 31 C4
Dartington GB 28 C4
Dartmouth GB 29 C4
Darton GB 27 B4
Daruvar HR 74 C2
Darvas H 75 A6
Darvel GB 24 C3
Darwen GB 26 B3
Dassel D 51 B5
Dassow D 44 B2
Datça TR 119 F2
Datteln D 50 B3
Dattenfeld D 50 C3
Daugard DK 39 D2
Daugavpils LV 7 D9
Daumeray F 57 C5
Daun D 50 C2
Daventry GB 30 B2
Davle CZ 63 A5
Davor HR 84 A2
Davos CH 71 B4
Davutlar TR 119 E2
Davyd Haradok BY 7 E9
Dawlish GB 29 C4
Dax F 76 C1
Dazkırı TR 119 E4
De Cocksdorp NL 42 B1
De Haan B 49 B4
De Koog NL 42 B1
De Panne B 48 B3
De Wijk NL 42 C3
Deal GB 31 C5
Deauville F 57 A6
Deba E 89 A4
Debar MK 116 A2
Debe Wielkie PL 55 A6
Dębica PL 55 C6
Dębnica Kaszubska PL 46 A3
Dębno PL 45 C6
Dęboleka PL 54 B3
Dębowa Łaka PL 47 B5
Debrc SRB 85 B4
Debrecen H 10 C6
Debrznica PL 53 A5
Debrzno PL 46 B3
Debstedt D 43 B5
Decazeville F 77 B5
Dechtice SK 64 B3
Decima I 102 B5
Decimomannu I 110 C1
Děčín CZ 53 C4
Decize F 68 B3
Decollatura I 106 B3
Decs H 74 B3
Dedaj AL 105 A5
Deddington GB 31 C2
Dedeler TR 118 B5
Dedelow D 45 B5
Dedemli TR 119 E7
Dedemsvaart NL 42 C3
Dédestapolcsány H 65 B6
Dedovichi RUS 7 C10
Deeping St. Nicholas GB 30 B3
Dég H 74 B3
Degaña E 86 B4
Degeberga S 41 D4
Degerby FIN 36 B7
Degerfors S 37 C1
Degerhamn S 41 C6
Degernes N 35 C3
Deggendorf D 62 B3
Deggingen D 61 B5
Dego I 80 B2
Degolados P 93 B3
Dehesas de Guadix E 100 B2
Dehesas Viejas E 100 B2
Deia E 97 B2
Deining D 62 A2
Deinze B 49 C4
Déiva Marina I 80 B3
Dej RO 11 C7
Deje S 35 C5
Delabole GB 28 C3
Delary S 40 C3
Delbrück D 51 B4
Delden NL 50 A2
Deleitosa E 93 B5
Delekovec HR 74 B1
Delémont CH 70 A2
Delft NL 49 A5
Delfzijl NL 42 B3
Délia I 108 B2
Delianuova I 106 C2
Deliblato SRB 85 B6
Delice TR 16 B6
Deliceto I 103 B8
Delitzsch D 52 B2
Dellach A 72 B3
Delle F 70 A2
Delme F 60 B2
Delmen-horst D 43 B5
Delnice HR 73 C4
Delsbo S 115 F13
Delvin IRL 19 C4
Delvinë AL 116 C2
Demandice SK 65 B4
Demen D 44 B3
Demidov RUS 7 D11
Demigny F 69 B4
Demirci TR 118 C3
Demirköy TR 118 A2
Demirtaş TR 118 B4
Demmin D 45 B5
Demonte I 79 B6
Demyansk RUS 7 C12
Den Burg NL 42 B1
Den Ham NL 42 C3
Den Helder NL 42 C1
Den Oever NL 42 C2
Denain F 49 C4
Denbigh GB 26 B2
Dender-monde B 49 B5
Denekamp NL 42 C3
Denholm GB 25 C5
Denia E 96 C3
Denizli TR 119 E4
Denkendorf D 62 B2
Denklingen D 50 C3
Denny GB 25 B4
Denta RO 75 C6
Déols F 68 B1
Derbent TR 119 D3

Derby GB 27 C4
Dereköy TR 118 A2
Derenberg D 51 B6
Derinkuyu TR 16 B7
Dermbach D 51 C6
Dermulo I 71 B6
Deronje SRB 75 C4
Derrygonnelly GB 19 B4
Derrylin GB 19 B4
Derry/Londonderry GB 19 B4
Dersingham GB 30 B4
Deruta I 82 D1
Dervaig GB 24 B1
Derval F 57 C4
Derveni GR 117 D4
Derventa BIH 84 B2
Dervock GB 19 A5
Desana I 70 C3
Descartes F 67 B5
Desenzano del Garda I 71 C5
Deset N 34 A3
Deševa BIH 84 C3
Desfina GR 116 D4
Desimirovac SRB 85 B5
Désio I 71 C4
Deskati GR 116 C3
Deskle SLO 72 B3
Desná CZ 53 C5
Dešov CZ 63 B6
Despotovac SRB 85 B6
Despotovo SRB 75 C4
Dessau D 52 B2
Deštná CZ 63 A5
Destriana E 87 B4
Désulo I 110 B2
Desvres F 48 C2
Deszk H 75 B5
Deta RO 75 C6
Detmold D 51 B4
Dětřichov CZ 64 A3
Dettelbach D 61 A6
Dettingen, *Baden-Württemberg* D 61 B5
Dettingen, *Baden-Württemberg* D 61 C5
Dettwiller F 60 B3
Detva SK 65 B5
Deurne NL 50 B1
Deutsch Wagram A 64 B2
Deutschkreutz A 64 C2
Deutschlandsberg A 73 B5
Deva RO 11 D7
Dévaványa H 75 A5
Devecikonağı TR 118 C3
Devecser H 74 A2
Develi TR 16 B7
Deventer NL 50 A2
Devil's Bridge GB 28 A4
Devin BG 116 A6
Devinska Nova Ves SK 64 B2
Devizes GB 29 B6
Devonport GB 28 C3
Devrek TR 118 A6
Devrekâni TR 16 A6
Đevrske HR 83 C4
Dewsbury GB 27 B4
Deza E 89 C4
Dežanovac HR 74 C2
Dezzo I 71 C5
Dhali CY 120 A2
Dheftera CY 120 A2
Dherinia CY 120 A2
Dhërmi AL 105 C5
Diamante I 106 B2
Dianalund DK 39 D4
Diano d'Alba I 80 B2
Diano Marina I 80 C2
Dicomano I 81 C5
Didcot GB 31 C2
Didimoticho GR 118 A1
Die F 79 B4
Diebling F 60 A2
Dieburg D 61 A4
Diego del Carpio E 93 A5
Diekirch L 60 A2
Diélette F 57 A4
Diémoz F 69 C5
Dienten am Hochkönig A 72 A2
Diepenbeck B 49 C6
Diepholz D 43 C5
Dieppe F 58 A2
Dierberg D 45 B4
Dierdorf D 50 C3
Dieren NL 50 A2
Dierhagen D 44 A4
Diesdorf D 44 C2
Diessen D 62 C2
Diest B 49 C6
Dietenheim D 61 B6
Dietfurt D 62 A2
Dietikon CH 70 A3
Dietzenbach D 51 C4
Dieue-sur-Meuse F 60 A1
Dieulefit F 79 B4
Dieulouard F 60 B2
Dieuze F 60 B2
Diever NL 42 C3
Diez D 50 C4
Diezma E 100 B2
Differdange L 60 A1
Digermulen N 112 D4
Dignac F 67 C5
Dignano I 72 B2
Digne-les-Bains F 79 B5
Digny F 58 B2
Digoin F 68 B3
Dijon F 69 A5
Dikanäs S 115 B13
Dikili TR 118 C1
Diksmuide B 48 B3
Dilar E 100 B2
Dillenburg D 50 C4
Dillingen, *Bayern* D 61 B6
Dillingen, *Saarland* D 60 A2
Dilsen B 50 B1
Dimaro I 71 B5
Dimitrovgrad BG 11 E8
Dimitsana GR 117 E4
Dinami I 106 C3
Dinan F 57 B3
Dinant B 49 C5
Dinar TR 119 D5
Dinard F 57 B3
Dinek TR 118 C6
Dingden D 50 B2
Dingelstädt D 51 B6
Dingle IRL 20 B1
Dingle S 35 D3
Dingolfing D 62 B3
Dingtuna S 37 C3
Dingwall GB 23 D4
Dinkelsbühl D 61 A6
Dinkelscherben D 62 B1
Dinklage D 43 C5
Dinslaken D 50 B2
Dinxperlo NL 50 B2
Diö S 40 C4
Diósgyör H 65 B6
Diósjeno H 65 C5
Diou F 68 B3
Dippen GB 24 C2
Dipperz D 51 C5
Dippoldiswalde D 53 C3
Dirdal N 33 D3
Dirksland NL 49 B5
Dirlewang D 61 C6
Dischingen D 61 B6
Disentis CH 70 B3
Diso I 107 A5
Diss GB 30 B5
Dissen D 50 A4
Distington GB 26 A2
Ditzingen D 61 B5
Ditzum D 43 B4
Divača SLO 72 C3
Dives-sur-Mer F 57 A6
Divín SK 65 B5
Divion F 48 C3
Divišov CZ 63 A5
Divjakë AL 105 C5
Divonne les Bains F 69 B6
Dixmont F 59 B4
Dizy-le-Gros F 59 A5
Djúpivogur IS 111 C11
Djupvasshytta N 114 E4
Djura S 36 B1
Djurås S 36 B2
Djurmo S 36 B2
Djursdala S 40 B5
Dlouhá Loucka CZ 64 A3
Długowola PL 55 B6
Dmitriyev Lgovskiy RUS 7 E13
Dmitrov RUS 7 C14
Dmitrovsk-Orlovskiy RUS 7 E13
Dno RUS 7 C10
Doade E 86 B3
Dobanovci SRB 85 B5
Dobbertin D 44 B4
Dobbiaco I 72 B2
Dobczyce PL 65 A6
Dobele LV 6 C7
Döbeln D 52 B3
Doberlug-Kirchhain D 52 B3
Dobern D 53 B4
Dobersberg A 63 B6
Dobiegniew PL 46 C1
Dobieszyn PL 55 B6
Doboj BIH 84 B3
Dobošnica BIH 84 B3
Doboz H 75 B6
Dobrá CZ 65 A4
Dobra, *Wielkopolskie* PL 54 B3
Dobra, *Zachodnio-Pomorskie* PL 45 B7
Dobra, *Zachodnio-Pomorskie* PL 45 B6
Dobrá Niva SK 65 B5
Dobřany CZ 63 A4
Dobre, *Kujawsko-Pomorskie* PL 47 C4
Dobre, *Mazowieckie* PL 55 A6
Dobre Miasto PL 47 B6
Dobreta-Turnu-Severin RO 11 D7
Dobri H 74 B1
Dobri Do SRB 85 D6
Dobrica SRB 75 C5
Dobrich BG 11 E9
Dobříš CZ 63 A5
Dobro E 89 B3
Dobrodzień PL 54 C3
Döbrököz H 74 B3
Dobromierz PL 53 C6
Dobrosołowo PL 47 C4
Dobroszyce PL 54 B2
Dobrota MNE 105 A4
Dobrovnik SLO 73 B6
Dobrush BY 7 E11
Dobruška CZ 53 C6
Dobrzany PL 46 B1
Dobrzen Wielki PL 54 C2
Dobrzyca, *Wielkopolskie* PL 46 B2
Dobrzyca, *Wielkopolskie* PL 54 B2
Dobrzyca, *Zachodnio-Pomorskie* PL 46 A1
Dobrzyń nad Wisłą PL 47 C5
Dobšiná SK 65 B6
Dobwalls GB 28 C3
Dochamps B 49 C6
Docking GB 30 B4
Docksta S 115 D15
Doddington GB 25 C5
Döderhult S 40 B6
Doesburg NL 50 A2
Doetinchem NL 50 B2
Doğanhisar TR 119 D6
Dogliani I 80 B1
Dogueno P 98 B3
Dois Portos P 92 B1
Doische B 49 C5
Dojč SK 64 B3
Dokka N 34 B2
Dokkedal DK 38 C3
Dokkum NL 42 B2
Dokležovje SLO 73 B6
Doksy CZ 53 C4
Dokuz TR 119 D7
Dol-de-Bretagne F 57 B4
Dolancourt F 59 B5
Dolceácqua I 80 C1
Dole F 69 A5
Dølemo N 33 D5
Dolenja vas SLO 73 C4
Dolenjske Toplice SLO 73 C5
Dolfor GB 26 C2
Dolgarrog GB 26 B2
Dolgellau GB 26 C2
Doliana GR 116 C2
Dolianova I 110 C2
Dolice PL 45 B7
Doljani HR 83 B5
Döllach im Mölltal A 72 B2
Dolle D 44 C3
Dollnstein D 62 B2
Dollot F 59 B4
Döllstadt D 51 B6
Dolná Strehová SK 65 B5
Dolné Saliby SK 64 B3
Dolni Benešov CZ 64 A4
Dolni Bousov CZ 53 C5
Dolni Kounice CZ 64 A2
Dolni Kralovice CZ 63 A6
Dolni Újezd CZ 64 A2
Dolni Žandov CZ 52 C2
Dolný Kubín SK 65 A5
Dolo I 72 C2
Dolores E 96 C2
Dolovo SRB 85 B5
Dölsach A 72 B2
Dolsk PL 54 B2
Dolwyddelan GB 26 B2
Dolynska UA 11 B12
Domaljevac BIH 84 A3
Domaniç TR 118 C4
Domaniža SK 65 A4
Domanovići BIH 84 C2
Domašov CZ 54 C2
Domaszék H 75 B4
Domaszków PL 54 C1
Domaszowice PL 54 B2
Domat-Ems CH 71 B4
Domažlice CZ 62 A3
Dombås N 114 E6
Dombasle-sur-Meurthe F 60 B2
Dombegyház H 75 B6
Dombóvár H 74 B3
Domène F 69 C5
Domérat F 68 B2
Domfessel F 60 B3
Domfront F 57 B5
Domfront-en-Champagne F 57 B6
Domingão P 92 B2
Domingo Pérez, *Granada* E 100 B2
Domingo Pérez, *Toledo* E 94 C2
Dömitz D 44 B3
Dommartin F 59 B5
Dommartin-le-Franc F 59 B5
Domme F 77 B4
Dommitzsch D 52 B2
Domodóssola I 70 B3
Domokos GR 116 C4
Domoszló H 65 C6
Dompaire F 60 B2
Dompierre-du-Chemin F 57 B4
Dompierre-sur-Besbre F 68 B3
Dompierre-sur-Mer F 66 B3
Domrémy-la-Pucelle F 60 B1
Dömsöd H 75 A4
Domsure F 69 B5
Dómus de Maria I 110 D1
Domusnóvas I 110 C1
Domvena GR 117 D4
Domžale SLO 73 B4
Don Alvaro E 93 C4
Don Benito E 93 C5
Doña Mencía E 100 B1
Donado E 87 B4
Donaghadee GB 19 B6
Donaueschingen D 61 C4
Donauwörth D 62 B1
Doncaster GB 27 B4
Donegal IRL 18 B3
Donestebe-Santesteban E 76 C1
Donges F 66 A2
Dongo I 71 B4
Donington GB 30 B3
Doniños E 86 A2
Donja Bebrina HR 84 A3
Donja Brela HR 84 C1
Donja Dubica BIH 84 A3
Donja Dubrava HR 74 B1
Donja Kupčina HR 73 C5
Donja Mutnica SRB 85 C6
Donja Šatornja SRB 85 B5
Donja Stubica HR 73 C5
Donje Brišnik BIH 84 C2
Donje Ljupče KOS 85 D6
Donje Stative HR 73 C5
Donji-Andrijevci HR 74 C3
Donji Kazanci BIH 83 C5
Donji Koričáni BIH 84 B2
Donji Lapac HR 83 B4
Donji Malovan BIH 84 C2
Donji Miholjac HR 74 C3
Donji Mosti HR 74 B1
Donji Poloj HR 73 C5
Donji-Rujani BIH 83 C5
Donji Srb HR 83 B5
Donji Svilaj BIH 84 A3
Donji Tovarnik SRB 85 B4
Donji Vakuf BIH 84 B2
Donnalucata I 109 C3
Donnemarie-Dontilly F 59 B4
Donnersbach A 73 A4
Donnersbachwald A 73 A4
Donnerskirchen A 64 C2
Donorático I 81 C4
Donostia-San Sebastián E 76 C1
Donovaly SK 65 B5
Donzenac F 67 C6
Donzère F 78 B3
Donzy F 68 A3
Doonbeg IRL 20 B2
Doorn NL 49 A6
Dor E 86 A1
Dorchester GB 29 C5
Dørdal N 33 D6
Dordrecht NL 49 B5
Dörenthe D 50 A3
Dores GB 23 D4
Dorf Mecklenburg D 44 B3
Dorfen D 62 B3
Dorfgastein A 72 A3
Dorfmark D 43 C6
Dorgali I 110 B2
Dorking GB 31 C3
Dormagen D 50 B2
Dormánd H 65 C6
Dormans F 59 A4
Dornava SLO 73 B5
Dornbirn A 71 A4
Dornburg D 52 B1
Dorndorf D 51 C6
Dornecy F 68 A3
Dornes F 68 B3
Dornhan D 61 B4
Dornie GB 22 D3
Dornoch GB 23 D4
Dornum D 43 B4
Dorog H 65 C4
Dorogobuzh RUS 7 D12
Dorohoi RO 11 C9
Dorotea S 115 C13
Dorotowo PL 47 B6
Dörpen D 43 C4
Dorsten D 50 B2
Dortan F 69 B5
Dortmund D 50 B3
Doruchów PL 54 B3
Dorum D 43 B5
Dörverden D 43 C6
Dörzbach D 61 A5
Dos Aguas E 96 B2
Dos Hermanas E 99 B5
Dos-Torres E 100 A1
Dosbarrios E 95 C3
Döşemealtı TR 119 E5
Dospat BG 116 A6
Dötlingen D 43 C5
Dottignies B 49 C4
Döttingen CH 70 A3
Douai F 49 C4
Douarnenez F 56 B1
Douchy F 59 C4
Douchy-les-Mines F 49 C4
Doucier F 69 B5
Doudeville F 58 A1
Doué-la-Fontaine F 67 A4
Douglas, *Isle of Man* GB 26 A1
Douglas, *South Lanarkshire* GB 25 C4
Doulaincourt F 59 B6
Doulevant-le-Château F 59 B5
Doullens F 48 C3
Dounby GB 23 B5
Doune GB 24 B3
Dounreay GB 23 C5
Dour B 49 C4
Dourdan F 58 B3
Dourgne F 77 C5
Dournazac F 67 C5
Douro Calvo P 87 D3
Douvaine F 69 B6
Douvres-la-Délivrande F 57 A5
Douzy F 59 A6
Dover GB 31 C5
Dovje SLO 72 B3
Dovre N 114 F6
Downham Market GB 30 B4
Downhill GB 19 A5
Downpatrick GB 19 B6
Dowra IRL 18 B3
Doxato GR 116 A6
Doyet F 68 B2
Dozule F 57 A5
Drača SRB 85 B5
Dračevo BIH 84 D3
Drachten NL 42 B3
Draga SLO 73 C4
Drăgășani RO 11 D8
Dragatuš SLO 73 C5
Dragichyn BY 7 E8
Draginja SRB 85 B4
Dragobi AL 105 A5
Dragocvet SRB 85 C6
Dragolovci BIH 84 B2
Dragoni I 103 B7
Dragør DK 41 D2
Dragotina HR 73 C6
Dragotinja BIH 83 A5
Dragozetići HR 82 A3
Draguignan F 79 C5
Drahnsdorf D 52 B3
Drahonice CZ 63 A5
Drahovce SK 64 B3
Drama GR 116 A6
Drammen N 35 C2
Drangedal N 33 C6
Drangsnes IS 111 B4
Dransfeld D 51 B5
Dranske D 45 A5
Draperstown GB 19 B5
Drassburg A 64 C2
Drávaszabolcs H 74 C3
Dravograd SLO 73 B5
Drawno PL 46 B1
Drawsko Pomorskie PL 46 B1
Drayton GB 30 B5
Draženov CZ 62 A3
Draževac SRB 85 B5
Dražice HR 73 C4
Drebkau D 53 B4
Dreieich D 51 C4
Dreisen D 61 A4
Dren KOS 85 C5
Drenovac SRB 85 B6
Drenovci HR 84 B3
Drensteinfurt D 50 B3
Dresden D 53 B3
Dretyń PL 46 A3
Dreux F 58 B2
Dřevohostice CZ 64 A3
Drevsjø N 114 F9
Drewitz D 52 A2
Drezdenko PL 46 C1
Drežnica HR 83 A4
Drežnik-Grad HR 83 B4
Drietona SK 64 B3
Driffield GB 27 A5
Drimnin GB 24 B2
Drimoleague IRL 20 C2
Dringenberg D 51 B5
Drinić BIH 83 B5
Drinjača BIH 85 B4
Drinovci BIH 84 C2
Driopida GR 117 E6
Drivstua N 114 E6
Drlače SRB 85 B4
Drnholec CZ 64 B2
Drniš HR 83 C5
Drnje HR 74 B1
Drnovice CZ 64 A2
Dro I 71 C5
Drøbak N 35 C2
Drobin PL 47 C6
Drochia MD 11 B9
Drochtersen D 43 B6
Drogheda IRL 19 C5
Drohobych UA 11 B7
Droitwich Spa GB 29 A5
Drołtowice PL 54 B2
Dromahair IRL 18 B3
Dromcolliher IRL 20 B3
Dromore, *Down* GB 19 B5
Dromore, *Tyrone* GB 19 B4
Dromore West IRL 18 B3
Dronero I 79 B6
Dronfield GB 27 B4
Drongan GB 24 C3
Dronninglund DK 38 B3
Dronrijp NL 42 B2
Dronten NL 42 C2
Drosendorf A 63 B6
Drösing A 64 B2
Drottningholm S 37 C4
Droué F 58 B2
Drulingen F 60 B3
Drumbeg GB 22 C3
Drumcliff IRL 18 B3
Drumgask GB 23 D4
Drumkeeran IRL 18 B3
Drummore GB 24 D3
Drumnadrochit GB 23 D4
Drumquin GB 19 B4
Drumshanbo IRL 18 B3
Drumsna IRL 19 C4
Drunen NL 49 B6
Druskininkai LT 6 D7
Druten NL 49 B6
Druya BY 7 D9
Družetići SRB 85 B5
Drvar BIH 83 B5
Drvenik HR 84 C2
Drwalew PL 55 B6
Drymen GB 24 B3
Drynoch GB 22 D2
Drzewce PL 54 A2
Drzewiany PL 46 B2
Drzewica PL 55 B5
Dualchi I 110 B1
Duas Igrejas P 87 C4
Dub SRB 85 C4
Dubá CZ 53 C4
Dubăsari MD 11 C10
Duben D 53 B3
Dübendorf CH 70 A3
Dubi CZ 53 C3
Dubica HR 74 C1
Dublin IRL 21 A5
Dubna RUS 7 C14
Dubňany CZ 64 B3
Dubnica nad Váhom SK 64 B4
Dubnik SK 65 C4
Dubno UA 11 A8
Dubodiel SK 64 B4
Dubona SRB 85 B5
Dubovac SRB 85 B6
Dubovic BIH 83 B5
Dubranec HR 73 C5
Dubrava HR 74 C1
Dubrave BIH 84 B3
Dubravica HR 73 C5
Dubravica SRB 85 B6
Dubrovnik HR 84 D3
Dubrovytsya UA 7 F9
Ducey F 57 B4
Duchcov CZ 53 C3
Ducherow D 45 B5
Dučina SRB 85 B5
Duclair F 58 A1
Dudar H 74 A2
Duddington GB 30 B3
Duderstadt D 51 B6
Dudeştii Vechi RO 75 B5
Dudley GB 26 C3
Dueñas E 88 C2
Duesund N 32 B2
Dueville I 72 C1
Duffel B 49 B5
Duffield GB 27 C4
Dufftown GB 23 D5
Duga Poljana SRB 85 C5
Duga Resa HR 73 C5
Dugi Rat HR 83 C5
Dugny-sur-Meuse F 59 A6
Dugo Selo HR 73 C6
Dugopolje HR 83 C5
Duino I 72 C3
Duisburg D 50 B2
Dukat AL 105 C5
Dukhovshchina RUS 7 D12
Dukovany CZ 64 A2
Duleek IRL 19 C5
Dülken D 50 B2
Dülmen D 50 B3
Dulovo BG 11 E9
Dulpetorpet N 34 B4
Dulverton GB 29 B4
Dumbarton GB 24 C3
Dümerek TR 118 C6
Dumfries GB 25 C4
Dumlupınar TR 118 D4
Dümpelfeld D 50 C2
Dun Laoghaire IRL 21 A5
Dun-le-Palestel F 67 B6
Dun-les-Places F 68 A4
Dun-sur-Auron F 68 B2
Dun-sur-Meuse F 59 A6
Dunaalmás H 65 C4
Dunabogdány H 65 C5
Dunafalva H 74 B3
Dunaföldvár H 74 B3
Dunaharaszti H 75 A4
Dunajská Streda SK 64 C3
Dunakeszi H 65 C5
Dunakiliti H 64 C3
Dunakömlöd H 74 B3
Dunapataj H 75 B3
Dunaszekcső H 74 B3
Dunaszentgyorgy H 74 B3
Dunatetétlen H 75 B4
Dunaújváros H 74 B3
Dunavecse H 75 B3
Dunbar GB 25 B5
Dunbeath GB 23 C5
Dunblane GB 25 B4
Dunboyne IRL 21 A5
Dundalk IRL 19 B5
Dundee GB 25 B5
Dundrennan GB 25 D4
Dundrum GB 19 B6
Dunfanaghy IRL 19 A4
Dunfermline GB 25 B4
Dungannon GB 19 B5
Dungarvan IRL 21 B4
Dungiven GB 19 B5
Dunglow IRL 18 B3
Dungourney IRL 20 C3
Duninowo PL 46 A2
Đunis SRB 85 C6
Dunkeld GB 25 B4
Dunker S 37 C3
Dunkerque = Dunkirk F 48 B3
Dunkineely IRL 18 B3
Dunkirk = Dunkerque F 48 B3
Dunlavin IRL 21 A5
Dunleer IRL 19 C5
Dunlop GB 24 C3
Dunloy GB 19 A5
Dunmanway IRL 20 C2
Dunmore IRL 18 C3
Dunmore East IRL 21 B5
Dunmurry GB 19 B5
Dunnet GB 23 C5
Dunningen D 61 B4
Dunoon GB 24 C3
Duns GB 25 C5
Dunscore GB 25 C4
Dunsford GB 28 C4
Dunshaughlin IRL 21 A5
Dunstable GB 31 C3
Dunster GB 29 B4
Dunvegan GB 22 D2
Duplek SLO 73 B5
Dupnitsa BG 11 E7
Durach D 61 C6
Durağan TR 16 A7
Durak TR 118 C3
Đurakovac KOS 85 D5
Durana E 89 B4
Durance F 76 B3
Durango E 89 A4
Durankulak BG 11 E10
Duras F 76 B3
Durban-Corbières F 78 D1
Dürbheim D 61 B4
Durbuy B 49 C6
Dúrcal E 100 C2
Đurdjenovac HR 74 C3
Đurdjevac HR 74 B2
Đurdjevik BIH 84 B3
Düren D 50 C2
Durham GB 25 D6
Đurinci SRB 85 B5
Durlach D 61 B4
Đurmanec HR 73 B5
Durness GB 22 C4
Dürnkrut A 64 B2
Dürrboden CH 71 B4
Dürrenboden CH 70 B3
Durrës AL 105 B5
Durrow IRL 21 B4
Durrus IRL 20 C2
Dursunbey TR 118 C3
Durtal F 57 C5
Durup DK 38 C1
Durusu TR 118 A3
Dusina BIH 84 C2
Dusnok H 75 B3
Dusocin PL 47 B4
Düsseldorf D 50 B2
Dusslingen D 61 B5
Duszniki PL 46 C2
Duszniki-Zdrój PL 54 C1
Dutovlje SLO 72 C3
Duvebo S 40 A4
Duved S 115 D9
Düzağac TR 118 D5
Düzce TR 118 B6
Dvärsätt S 115 D11
Dvor HR 83 A5
Dvorce CZ 64 A3
Dvorníky SK 64 B3
Dvory nad Žitavou SK 64 C4
Dvůr Králové nad Labem CZ 53 C5
Dyatkovo RUS 7 E13
Dybvad DK 38 B3
Dyce GB 23 D6
Dygowo PL 46 A1
Dykehead GB 25 B4
Dymchurch GB 31 C5
Dymer UA 11 A11
Dyrnes N 114 D4
Dywity PL 47 B6
Džanići BIH 84 C2
Dziadowa Kłoda PL 54 B2
Działdowo PL 47 B6
Działoszyce PL 55 C5
Działoszyn PL 54 B3
Dziemiany PL 46 A3
Dzierzążnia PL 47 C6
Dzierzgoń PL 47 B5
Dzierzgowo PL 47 B6
Dzierżoniów PL 54 C1
Dzisna BY 7 D10
Dziwnów PL 45 A6
Dzyarzhynsk BY 7 E9
Dzyatlava BY 7 E8

E

Ea E 89 A4
Eaglesfield GB 25 C4
Ealing GB 31 C3
Eardisley GB 29 A4
Earl Shilton GB 30 B2
Earls Barton GB 30 B3
Earlston GB 25 C5
Easington GB 27 B6
Easky IRL 18 B3
East Calder GB 25 C4
East Dereham GB 30 B4
East Grinstead GB 31 C4
East Ilsley GB 31 C2
East Kilbride GB 24 C3
East Linton GB 25 C5
East Markham GB 27 B5
East Wittering GB 31 D3
Eastbourne GB 31 D4
Easter Skeld GB 22 A7
Eastleigh GB 31 D2
Easton GB 29 C5
Eaton Socon GB 30 B3
Eaux-Bonnes F 76 D2
Eauze F 76 C3
Ebberup DK 39 D2
Ebbs A 62 C3
Ebbw Vale GB 29 B4

Ebeleben D 51 B6
Ebeltoft DK 39 C3
Eben im Pongau A 72 A3
Ebene Reichenau A 72 B3
Ebensee A 63 C4
Ebensfeld D 51 C6
Eberbach D 61 A4
Ebergötzen D 51 B6
Ebermann-Stadt D 62 A2
Ebern D 51 C6
Eberndorf A 73 B4
Ebersbach D 53 B4
Ebersberg D 62 B2
Ebersdorf, *Bayern* D 52 C1
Ebersdorf, *Niedersachsen* D 43 B6
Eberstein A 73 B4
Eberswalde D 45 C5
Ebnat-Kappel CH 71 A4
Éboli I 103 C8
Ebrach D 61 A6
Ebreichsdorf A 64 C2
Ebreuil F 68 B3
Ebstorf D 44 B2
Ecclefechan GB 25 C4
Eccleshall GB 26 C3
Eceabat TR 118 B1
Echallens CH 69 B6
Echauri E 76 D1
Echinos GR 116 A7
Echiré F 67 B4
Échirolles F 69 C5
Echourgnac F 76 A3
Echt NL 50 B1
Echte D 51 B6
Echternach L 60 A2
Ecija E 99 B5
Ečka SRB 75 C5
Eckartsberga D 52 B1
Eckelshausen D 51 C4
Eckental D 62 A2
Eckernförde D 44 A1
Eckerö FIN 36 B6
Eckington GB 27 B4
Éclaron F 59 B5
Écommoy F 58 C1
Écouché F 57 B5
Ecouis F 58 A2
Ecséd H 65 C4
Ecsegfalva H 75 A5
Écueillé F 67 A6
Ed S 35 D3
Eda S 34 C4
Eda glasbruk S 34 C4
Edam NL 42 C2
Edane S 35 C4
Edderton GB 23 D4
Ede NL 49 A6
Edebäck S 34 B5
Edebo S 36 B5
Edelény H 65 B6
Edelschrott A 73 A5
Edemissen D 44 C2
Edenbridge GB 31 C4
Edenderry IRL 21 A4
Edenkoben D 61 A4
Edesheim D 61 A4
Edessa GR 116 B4
Edewecht D 43 B4
Edgeworthstown IRL 19 C4
Edinburgh GB 25 C4
Edineţ MD 11 B9
Edirne TR 118 A1
Edland N 33 C4
Edolo I 71 B5
Edøy N 114 D5
Edremit TR 118 C2
Eds bruk S 40 A6
Edsbro S 36 C5
Edsbyn S 36 A2
Edsele S 115 D13
Edsleskog S 35 C4
Edsvalla S 35 C5
Eekloo B 49 B4
Eemshaven NL 42 B3
Eerbeek NL 50 A2
Eersel NL 49 B6
Eferding A 63 B5
Effiat F 68 B3
Efteløt N 35 C1
Egeln D 52 B1
Eger H 65 C6
Egerbakta H 65 C6
Egernsund DK 39 E2
Egersund N 33 D3
Egerszólát H 65 C6
Egervár H 74 B1
Egg A 71 A4
Egg D 61 B6
Eggby S 35 D5
Eggedal N 32 B6
Eggenburg A 64 B1
Eggenfelden D 62 B3
Eggesin D 45 B6
Eggum N 112 D2
Egham GB 31 C3
Éghezée B 49 C5
Egiertowo PL 47 A4
Egilsstaðir IS 111 B11
Egina GR 117 E5
Eginio GR 116 B4
Egio GR 117 D4
Égletons F 68 C2
Egling D 62 C2
Eglinton GB 19 A4
Eglisau CH 61 C4
Égliseneuve-d'Entraigues F 68 C2
Eglofs D 61 C5
Egmond aan Zee NL 42 C1
Egna I 71 B6
Egosthena GR 117 D5
Egremont GB 26 A2
Eğridir TR 119 E5
Egtved DK 39 D2
Eguilles F 79 C4
Eguilly-sous-Bois F 59 B5
Éguzon-Chantôme F 67 B6
Egyek H 65 C6
Egyházasrádóc H 74 A1
Ehekirchen D 62 B2
Ehingen D 61 B5
Ehra-Lessien D 44 C2
Ehrang D 60 A2
Ehrenfriedersdorf D 52 C2
Ehrenhain D 52 C2
Ehrenhausen A 73 B5
Ehringshausen D 51 C4
Ehrwald A 71 A5
Eibar E 89 A4
Eibelstadt D 61 A6
Eibenstock D 52 C2
Eibergen NL 50 A2
Eibiswald A 73 B5
Eichenbarleben D 52 A1
Eichendorf D 62 B3
Eichstätt D 62 B2
Eickelborn D 50 B4
Eide, *Hordaland* N 32 B3
Eide, *Møre og Romsdal* N 114 E4
Eidet N 112 C7
Eidfjord N 32 B4
Eidsberg N 35 C3
Eidsbugarden N 32 A5
Eidsdal N 114 E4
Eidsfoss N 35 C2
Eidskog N 34 B4
Eidsvåg, *Hordaland* N 32 B2
Eidsvåg, *Møre og Romsdal* N 114 E5
Eidsvoll N 34 B3
Eikefjord N 114 F2
Eikelandsosen N 32 B2
Eiken N 33 D4
Eikesdal N 114 E5
Eikstrand N 35 C1
Eilenburg D 52 B2
Eilsleben D 52 A1
Eina N 34 B2
Einbeck D 51 B5
Eindhoven NL 49 B6
Einsiedeln CH 70 A3
Einville-au-Jard F 60 B2
Eisenach D 51 C6
Eisenberg, *Rheinland-Pfalz* D 61 A4
Eisenberg, *Thüringen* D 52 C1
Eisenerz A 73 A4
Eisenhüttenstadt D 53 A4
Eisenkappel A 73 B4
Eisenstadt A 64 C2
Eisentratten A 72 B3
Eisfeld D 51 C6
Eisleben D 52 B1
Eislingen D 61 B5
Eitensheim D 62 B2
Eiterfeld D 51 C5
Eitorf D 50 C3
Eivindvik N 32 B2
Eivissa = Ibiza E 97 C1
Eixo P 92 A2
Ejby DK 39 D2
Ejea de los Caballeros E 90 A1
Ejstrupholm DK 39 D2
Ejulve E 90 C2
Eke B 49 C4
Ekeby, *Gotland* S 37 E5
Ekeby, *Skåne* S 41 D2
Ekeby, *Uppsala* S 36 B5
Ekeby-Almby S 37 C2
Ekenäs S 35 D5
Ekenässjön S 40 B5
Ekerö S 37 C4
Eket S 41 C3
Eketorp S 41 C6
Ekevik S 40 A6
Ekkerøy N 113 B19
Ekshärad S 34 B5
Eksingedal N 32 B2
Eksjö S 40 B4
Eksta S 37 E5
Ekträsk S 115 C16
El Alamo, *Madrid* E 94 B3
El Alamo, *Sevilla* E 99 B4
El Algar E 101 B5
El Almendro E 98 B3
El Alquián E 101 C3
El Arahal E 99 B5
El Arenal E 94 B1
El Arguellite E 101 A3
El Astillero E 88 A3
El Ballestero E 101 A3
El Barco de Ávila E 93 A5
El Berrón E 88 A1
El Berrueco E 95 B3
El Bodón E 93 A4
El Bonillo E 95 D4
El Bosque E 99 C5
El Bullaque E 94 C2
El Burgo E 100 C1
El Burgo de Ebro E 90 B2
El Burgo de Osma E 89 C3
El Burgo Ranero E 88 B1
El Buste E 89 C5
El Cabaco E 93 A4
El Callejo E 89 A3
El Campillo E 99 B4
El Campillo de la Jara E 94 C1
El Cañavete E 95 C4
El Carpio E 100 B1
El Carpio de Tajo E 94 C2
El Casar E 95 B3
El Casar de Escalona E 94 B2
El Castillo de las Guardas E 99 B4
El Centenillo E 100 A2
El Cerro E 93 A5
El Cerro de Andévalo E 99 B4
El Comenar E 99 C5
El Coronil E 99 B5
El Crucero E 86 A4
El Cubo de Tierra del Vino E 88 C1
El Cuervo E 99 C4
El Ejido E 101 C3
El Escorial E 94 B2
El Espinar E 94 B2
El Frago E 90 A2
El Franco E 86 A4
El Frasno E 89 C5
El Garrobo E 99 B4
El Gastor E 99 C5
El Gordo E 93 B5
El Grado E 90 A3
El Granado E 98 B3
El Grao de Castelló E 96 B3
El Grau E 96 C2
El Higuera E 100 B1
El Hijate E 101 B3
El Hontanar E 96 A1
El Hoyo E 100 A2
El Madroño E 99 B4
El Maillo E 93 A4
El Masnou E 91 B5
El Mirón E 93 A5
El Molar E 95 B3
El Molinillo E 94 C2
El Morell E 91 B4
El Muyo E 89 C3
El Olmo E 88 C3
El Palo E 100 C1
El Pardo E 94 B3
El Payo E 93 A4
El Pedernoso E 95 C4
El Pedroso E 99 B5
El Peral E 95 C5
El Perelló, *Tarragona* E 90 C3
El Perelló, *Valencia* E 96 B2
El Picazo E 95 C4
El Pinell de Bray E 90 B3
El Piñero E 88 C1
El Pla de Santa Maria E 91 B4
El Pobo E 90 C2
El Pobo de Dueñas E 95 B5
El Pont d'Armentera E 91 B4
El Port de la Selva E 91 A6
El Port de Llançà E 91 A6
El Port de Sagunt E 96 B2
El Prat de Llobregat E 91 B5
El Provencio E 95 C4
El Puente E 89 A3
El Puente del Arzobispo E 93 B5
El Puerto E 86 A4
El Puerto de Santa María E 99 C4
El Real de la Jara E 99 B4
El Real de San Vincente E 94 B2
El Robledo E 94 C2
El Rocio E 99 B4
El Rompido E 99 B3
El Ronquillo E 99 B4
El Royo E 89 C4
El Rubio E 100 B1
El Sabinar E 101 A3
El Saler E 96 B2
El Salobral E 101 A4
El Saucejo E 99 B5
El Serrat AND 91 A4
El Temple E 90 B2
El Tiemblo E 94 B2
El Toboso E 95 C4
El Tormillo E 90 B2
El Torno E 93 A5
El Valle de las Casas E 88 B1
El Vellón E 95 B3
El Vendrell E 91 B4
El Villar de Arnedo E 89 B4
El Viso E 100 A1
El Viso del Alcor E 99 B5
Élancourt F 58 B2
Elassona GR 116 C4
Elati GR 116 C3
Elbasan AL 116 A2
Elbeuf F 58 A1
Elbingerode D 51 B6
Elbląg PL 47 A5
Elburg NL 42 C2
Elche E 96 C2
Elche de la Sierra E 101 A3
Elchingen D 61 B6
Elda E 101 A5
Eldena D 44 B3
Eldingen D 44 C2
Elefsina GR 117 D5
Elek H 75 B6
Elemir SRB 75 C5
Eleutheroupoli GR 116 B6
Elgå N 114 E8
Elgin GB 23 D5
Elgoibar E 89 A4
Elgol GB 22 D2
Elgshøa N 34 A4
Elie GB 25 B5
Elizondo E 76 C1
Ełk PL 6 E7
Elkhovo BG 11 E9
Ellenberg D 61 A6
Ellesmere GB 26 C3
Ellesmere Port GB 26 B3
Ellezelles B 49 C4
Ellingen D 62 A1
Ellmau A 72 A2
Ellon GB 23 D6
Ellös S 35 D3
Ellrich D 51 B6
Ellwangen D 61 B6
Elm CH 71 B4
Elm D 43 B6
Elmadağ TR 16 B6
Elmalı TR 119 F4
Elmshorn D 43 B6
Elmstein D 60 A3
Elne F 91 A5
Elnesvågen N 114 E4
Elorrio E 89 A4
Elöszállás H 74 B3
Elouda GR 117 G7
Éloyes F 60 B2
Elphin GB 22 C3
Els Castells E 91 A4
Elsdorf D 50 C2
Elsenfeld D 61 A5
Elsfleth D 43 B5
Elspeet NL 50 A1
Elst NL 50 B1
Elstead GB 31 C3
Elster D 52 B2
Elsterberg D 52 C2
Elsterwerda D 52 B3
Elstra D 53 B4
Eltmann D 51 D6
Eltville D 50 C4
Elvas P 93 C3
Elvebakken N 113 C12
Elven F 56 C3
Elverum N 34 B3
Elvington GB 27 B5
Elxleben D 51 B6
Ely GB 30 B4
Elzach D 61 B4
Elze D 51 A5
Emådalen S 36 A1
Embleton GB 25 C6
Embonas GR 119 F2
Embrun F 79 B5
Embún E 90 A2
Emden D 43 B4
Emecik TR 119 F2
Emet TR 118 C4
Emirdağ TR 118 C6
Emlichheim D 42 C3
Emmaboda S 40 C5
Emmaljunga S 41 C3
Emmeloord NL 42 C2
Emmen CH 70 A3
Emmen NL 42 C3
Emmendingen D 60 B3
Emmer-Compascuum NL 43 C4
Emmerich D 50 B2
Emmern D 51 A5
Emöd H 65 C6
Émpoli I 81 C4
Emsbüren D 43 C4
Emsdetten D 50 A3
Emsfors S 40 B6
Emskirchen D 62 A1
Emstek D 43 C5
Emsworth GB 31 D3
Emyvale IRL 19 B5
Enafors S 115 D9
Enånger S 115 F14
Encamp AND 91 A4
Encarnaçao P 92 C1
Encinas de Abajo E 94 B1
Encinas de Esgueva E 88 C2
Encinas Reales E 100 B1
Encinasola E 99 A4
Encio E 89 B3
Enciso E 89 B4
Enden N 114 F7
Endingen D 60 B3
Endrinal E 93 A5
Endröd H 75 B5
Enebakk N 34 C3
Eneryda S 40 C4
Enese H 64 C3
Enez TR 116 B8
Enfield IRL 21 A5
Eng A 72 A1
Enge-sande D 39 E1
Engelberg CH 70 B3
Engelhartszell A 63 B4
Engelskirchen D 50 C3
Engen D 61 C4
Enger N 34 B2
Engerdal N 114 F8
Engerneset N 34 A4
Engesvang DK 39 C2
Enghien B 49 C5
Engstingen D 61 B5
Engter D 43 C5
Enguera E 96 C2
Enguidanos E 95 C5
Enkenbach D 60 A3
Enkhuizen NL 42 C2
Enklinge FIN 36 B7
Enköping S 37 C4
Enna I 109 B3
Ennezat F 68 C3
Ennigerloh D 50 B4
Enningdal N 35 D3
Ennis IRL 20 B3
Enniscorthy IRL 21 B5
Enniskean IRL 20 C3
Enniskillen GB 19 B4
Ennistimon IRL 20 B2
Enns A 63 B5
Eno FIN 3 E29
Enontekiö FIN 113 D12
Ens NL 42 C2
Enschede NL 50 A2
Ensdorf D 62 A2
Ensisheim F 60 C3
Enstaberga S 37 D3
Enstone GB 31 C2
Entlebuch CH 70 A3
Entrácque I 80 B1
Entradas P 98 B2
Entrains-sur-Nohain F 68 A3
Entrambasaguas E 88 A3
Entrambasmestas E 88 A3
Entraygues-sur-Truyère F 77 B5
Entre-os-Rios P 87 C2
Entrevaux F 79 C5
Entrin Bajo E 93 C4
Entroncamento P 92 B2
Entzheim F 60 B3
Envermeu F 58 A2
Enviken S 36 B2
Enying H 74 B3
Enzingerboden A 72 A2
Enzklösterle D 61 B4
Épagny F 59 A4
Epalinges CH 70 B1
Epannes F 67 B4
Epanomi GR 116 B4
Epe D 50 A3
Epe NL 42 C2
Épernay F 59 A4
Épernon F 58 B2
Epfig F 60 B3
Epierre F 69 C6
Épila E 90 B1
Épinac F 69 B4
Épinal F 60 B2
Episcopia I 106 A3
Episkopi CY 120 B1
Epitalio GR 117 E3
Epoisses F 69 A4
Eppenbrunn D 60 A3
Eppendorf D 52 C3
Epping GB 31 C4
Eppingen D 61 A4
Epsom GB 31 C3
Epworth GB 27 B5
Eraclea I 72 C2
Eraclea Mare I 72 C2
Erba I 71 C4
Erbach, *Baden-Württemberg* D 61 B5
Erbach, *Hessen* D 61 A4
Erbalunga F 102 A2
Erbendorf D 62 A3
Érchie I 105 C3
Ercolano I 103 C7
Ercsi H 74 A3
Érd H 74 A3
Erdek TR 118 B2
Erdemli TR 16 C7
Erdevik SRB 85 A4
Erding D 62 B2
Erdötelek H 65 C6
Erdut HR 75 C4
Erdweg D 62 B2
Ereğli, *Konya* TR 16 C7
Ereğli, *Zonguldak* TR 118 A6
Erenkaya TR 119 E7
Eresfjord N 114 E5
Eresos GR 116 C7
Eretria GR 116 D5
Erfde D 43 A6
Erfjord N 33 C3
Erfstadt D 50 C2
Erfurt D 52 C1
Ergli LV 7 C8
Ergoldsbach D 62 B3
Eriboll GB 22 C4
Érice I 108 A1
Ericeira P 92 C1
Eriksberg S 115 B12
Eriksmåla S 40 C5
Eringsboda S 40 C5
Eriswil CH 70 A2
Erithres GR 117 D5
Erkelenz D 50 B2
Erkner D 45 C5
Erkrath D 50 B2
Erla E 90 A2
Erlangen D 62 A2
Erli I 80 B2
Erlsbach A 72 B2
Ermelo NL 49 A6
Ermenak TR 16 C6
Ermenonville F 58 A3
Ermezinde P 87 C2
Ermidas P 98 A2
Ermioni GR 117 E5
Ermoupoli GR 117 E6
Ermsleben D 52 B1
Erndtebrück D 50 C4
Ernée F 57 B5
Ernestinovo HR 74 C3
Ernstbrunn A 64 B2
Erolzheim D 61 B6
Erquelinnes B 49 C5
Erquy F 56 B3
Erra P 92 C2
Erratzu E 76 C1
Errindlev DK 44 A3
Erro E 76 D1
Ersa F 102 A2
Érsekcsanád H 75 B3
Ersekë AL 116 B2
Érsekvadkert H 65 C5
Erstein F 60 B3
Erstfeld CH 70 B3
Ertebølle DK 38 C2
Ertingen D 61 B5
Ervedal, *Coimbra* P 92 A2
Ervedal, *Portalegre* P 92 B3
Ervenik HR 83 B4
Ervidel P 98 B2
Ervy-le-Châtel F 59 B4
Erwitte D 51 B4
Erxleben D 52 A1
Erzsébet H 74 B3
Es Caná E 97 B1
Es Castell E 97 B4
Es Mercadal E 97 B4
Es Migjorn Gran E 97 B4
Es Port d'Alcúdia E 97 B3
Es Pujols E 97 C1
Es Soleràs E 90 B3
Esbjerg DK 39 D1
Esbly F 58 B3
Escacena del Campo E 99 B4
Escairón E 86 B3
Escalada E 88 B3
Escalante E 89 A3
Escalaplano I 110 C2
Escalona E 94 B2
Escalona del Prado E 94 A2
Escalonilla E 94 C2
Escalos de Baixo P 92 B3
Escalos de Cima P 92 B3
Escamilla E 95 B4
Escañuela E 100 B1
Escatrón E 90 B2
Esch-sur-Alzette L 60 A1
Esch-sur-Sûre L 60 A1
Eschach D 61 C5
Eschau D 61 A5
Eschede D 44 C2
Eschenau D 62 A2
Eschenbach D 62 A2
Eschenz CH 61 C4
Eschershausen D 51 B5
Eschwege D 51 B6
Eschweiler D 50 C2
Escobasa de Almazán E 89 C4
Escoeuilles F 48 C2
Escombreras E 101 B5
Escos F 76 C1
Escource F 76 B1
Escragnolles F 79 C5
Escrick GB 27 B4
Escurial E 93 B5
Escurial de la Sierra E 93 A5
Esens D 43 B4
Esgos E 87 B3
Esher GB 31 C3
Eskdalemuir GB 25 C4
Eskifjörður IS 111 B12
Eskilhem S 37 E5
Eskilsäter S 35 D5
Eskilstrup DK 39 E4
Eskilstuna S 37 C3
Eskipazar TR 118 B7
Eskişehir TR 118 C5
Eslarn D 62 A3
Eslava E 89 B5
Eslida E 96 B2
Eslohe D 50 B4
Eslöv S 41 D3
Eşme TR 119 D3
Espa N 34 B3
Espalion F 78 B1
Esparragalejo E 93 C4
Esparragosa del Caudillo E 93 C5
Esparragossa de la Serena E 93 C5
Esparreguera E 91 B4
Esparron F 79 C4
Espe N 32 B3
Espedal N 33 D3
Espejo, *Alava* E 89 B3
Espejo, *Córdoba* E 100 B1
Espeland N 32 B2
Espelkamp D 43 C5
Espeluche F 78 B3
Espeluy E 100 A2
Espera E 99 C5
Esperança P 93 B3
Espéraza F 77 D5
Espéria I 103 B6
Espevær N 33 C2
Espiel E 99 A5
Espinama E 88 A2
Espiñaredo E 86 A3
Espinasses F 79 B5
Espinelves E 91 B5
Espinhal P 92 A2
Espinho P 87 C2
Espinilla E 88 A2
Espinosa de Cerrato E 88 C3
Espinosa de los Monteros E 89 A3
Espinoso del Rey E 94 C2
Espirito Santo P 98 B3
Espluga de Francolí E 91 B4
Esplús E 90 B3
Espolla E 91 A5
Espoo FIN 6 A8
Esporles E 97 B2
Esposende P 87 C2
Espot E 91 A4
Esquedas E 90 A2
Esquivias E 94 B3
Essay F 57 B6
Essen B 49 B5
Essen, *Niedersachsen* D 43 C4
Essen, *Nordrhein-Westfalen* D 50 B3
Essenbach D 62 B3
Essertaux F 58 A3
Essingen D 61 B6
Esslingen D 61 B5
Essoyes F 59 B5
Estacas E 87 B2
Estadilla E 90 A3
Estagel F 78 D1
Estaires F 48 C3
Estang F 76 C2
Estarreja P 87 D2
Estartit E 91 A6
Estavayer-le-Lac CH 70 B1
Este I 72 C1
Esteiro E 86 A2
Estela P 87 C2
Estella E 89 B4
Estellencs E 97 B2
Estepa E 100 B1
Estépar E 88 B3
Estepona E 99 C5
Esternay F 59 B4
Esterri d'Aneu E 91 A4
Esterwegen D 43 C4
Estissac F 59 B4
Estivadas E 87 B3
Estivareilles F 68 B2
Estivella E 96 B2
Estói P 98 B3
Estopiñán E 90 B3
Estoril P 92 C1
Estoublon F 79 C5
Estrée-Blanche F 48 C3
Estrées-St. Denis F 58 A3
Estrela P 98 A3
Estremera E 95 B3
Estremoz P 92 C3
Estuna S 36 C5
Esyres F 67 A5
Esztergom H 65 C4
Etables-sur-Mer F 56 B3
Étain F 60 A1
Étalans F 69 A6
Etalle B 60 A1
Étampes F 58 B3
Etang-sur-Arroux F 69 B4
Étaples F 48 C2
Etauliers F 67 C4
Etili TR 118 C1
Etna N 34 B1
Etne N 33 C2
Etoges F 59 B4
Etoliko GR 116 D3
Eton GB 31 C3
Etréaupont F 59 A4
Étréchy F 58 B3
Étrépagny F 58 A2
Étretat F 57 A6
Étroeungt F 49 C4
Étroubles I 70 C2
Ettal D 62 C2
Ettelbruck L 60 A2
Etten NL 49 B5
Ettenheim D 60 B3
Ettington GB 29 A6
Ettlingen D 61 B4
Ettringen D 62 B1
Etuz F 69 A5
Etxarri-Aranatz E 89 B4
Etyek H 74 A3
Eu F 48 C2
Euerdorf D 51 C6
Eulate E 89 B4
Eupen B 50 C2
Europoort NL 49 B5
Euskirchen D 50 C2
Eutin D 44 A2
Evanger N 32 B3
Évaux-les-Bains F 68 B2
Evciler, *Afyon* TR 119 D4
Evciler, *Çanakkale* TR 118 C1
Evenskjær N 112 D5
Evenstad N 34 A3
Evercreech GB 29 B5
Evergem B 49 B4
Everöd S 41 D4
Eversberg D 51 B4
Everswinkel D 50 B3
Evertsberg S 34 A5
Evesham GB 29 A6
Évian-les-Bains F 69 B6
Evisa F 102 A1
Evje N 33 D4
Evolène CH 70 B2
Évora P 92 C3
Evoramonte P 92 C3
Evran F 57 B4
Evrecy F 57 A5
Évreux F 58 A2
Évron F 57 B5
Évry F 58 B3
Ewell GB 31 C3
Ewersbach D 50 C4
Excideuil F 67 C6

Freyung D 63 B4
Frias de Albarracin E 95 B5
Fribourg CH 70 B2
Frick CH 70 A3
Fridafors S 41 C4
Fridaythorpe GB 27 A5
Friedberg A 73 A6
Friedberg, *Bayern* D 62 B1
Friedberg, *Hessen* D 51 C4
Friedeburg D 43 B4
Friedewald D 51 C5
Friedland, *Brandenburg* D 53 A4
Friedland, *Mecklenburg-Vorpommern* D 45 B5
Friedland, *Niedersachsen* D 51 B5
Friedrichroda D 51 C6
Friedrichsdorf D 51 C4
Friedrichshafen D 61 C5
Friedrichskoog D 43 A5
Friedrichstadt D 43 A6
Friedrichswalde D 45 B5
Friesach A 73 B4
Friesack D 45 C4
Friesenheim D 60 B3
Friesoythe D 43 B4
Friggesund S 115 F13
Frigiliana E 100 C2
Frihetsli N 112 D8
Frillesås S 40 B2
Frinnaryd S 40 B4
Frinton-on-Sea GB 31 C5
Friockheim GB 25 B5
Friol E 86 A3
Fristad S 40 B2
Fritsla S 40 B2
Fritzlar D 51 B5
Frizington GB 26 A2
Frödinge S 40 B6
Froges F 69 C5
Frohburg D 52 B2
Frohnhausen D 50 C4
Frohnleiten A 73 A5
Froissy F 58 A3
Frombork PL 47 A5
Frome GB 29 B5
Frómista E 88 B2
Fröndenberg D 50 B3
Fronsac F 76 B2
Front I 70 C2
Fronteira P 92 B3
Frontenay-Rohan-Rohan F 67 B4
Frontenhausen D 62 B3
Frontignan F 78 C2
Fronton F 77 C4
Fröseke S 40 C5
Frosinone I 103 B6
Frosolone I 103 B7
Frosta N 114 D7
Frøstrup DK 38 B1
Frosunda S 37 C5
Frouard F 60 B2
Frövi S 37 C2
Frøyset N 32 B2
Fruges F 48 C3
Frutigen CH 70 B2
Frýdek-Místek CZ 65 A4
Frýdlant CZ 53 C5
Frydlant nad Ostravicí CZ 65 A4
Frygnowo PL 47 B6
Fryšták CZ 64 A3
Fucécchio I 81 C4
Fuencaliente, *Ciudad Real* E 100 A1
Fuencaliente, *Ciudad Real* E 94 C3
Fuencemillán E 95 B3
Fuendejalón E 89 C5
Fuengirola E 100 C1
Fuenlabrada E 94 B3
Fuenlabrada de los Montes E 94 C2
Fuensalida E 94 B2
Fuensanta E 101 B4
Fuensanta de Martos E 100 B2
Fuente al Olmo de Iscar E 88 C2
Fuente-Alamo E 101 A4
Fuente-Álamo de Murcia E 101 B4
Fuente Dé E 88 A2
Fuente de Cantos E 99 A4
Fuente de Santa Cruz E 94 A2
Fuente del Arco E 99 A5
Fuente del Conde E 100 B1
Fuente del Maestre E 93 C4
Fuente el Fresno E 94 C3
Fuente el Saz de Jarama E 95 B3
Fuente el Sol E 94 A2
Fuente Obejuna E 99 A5
Fuente Palmera E 99 B5
Fuente-Tójar E 100 B1
Fuente Vaqueros E 100 B2
Fuentealbilla E 96 B1
Fuentecén E 88 C3
Fuenteguinaldo E 93 A4
Fuentelapeña E 88 C1
Fuentelcésped E 89 C3
Fuentelespino de Haro E 95 C4
Fuentelespino de Moya E 95 C5
Fuentenovilla E 95 B3
Fuentepelayo E 94 A2
Fuentepinilla E 89 C4
Fuenterroble de Salvatierra E 93 A5
Fuenterrobles E 96 B1
Fuentes E 95 C4
Fuentes de Andalucía E 99 B5
Fuentes de Ebro E 90 B2
Fuentes de Jiloca E 89 C5
Fuentes de la Alcarria E 95 B4
Fuentes de León E 99 A4
Fuentes de Nava E 88 B2
Fuentes de Oñoro E 93 A4
Fuentes de Ropel E 88 B1
Fuentesauco, *Segovia* E 88 C2
Fuentesaúco, *Zamora* E 94 A1
Fuentespalda E 90 C3
Fuentespina E 88 C3
Fuentidueña E 88 C3
Fuentidueña de Tajo E 95 B3
Fuerte del Rey E 100 B2
Fügen A 72 A1
Fuglebjerg DK 39 D4
Fuglevik N 35 C2
Fuhrberg D 44 C1
Fulda D 51 C5
Fulgatore I 108 B1
Fully CH 70 B2
Fulnek CZ 64 A3
Fülöpszállás H 75 B4
Fulpmes A 71 A6
Fulunäs S 34 A5
Fumay F 49 D5
Fumel F 77 B3
Funäsdalen S 115 E9
Fundão P 92 A3
Funzie GB 22 A8
Furadouro P 87 D2
Fure N 32 A2
Fürstenau, *Niedersachsen* D 43 C4
Furstenau, *Nordrhein-Westfalen* D 51 B5
Fürstenberg D 45 B5
Fürstenfeld A 73 A6
Fürstenfeldbruck D 62 B2
Fürstenstein D 63 B4
Fürstenwalde D 45 C6
Fürstenwerder D 45 B5
Fürstenzell D 63 B4
Fürth, *Bayern* D 62 A1
Fürth, *Hessen* D 61 A4
Furth im Wald D 62 A3
Furtwangen D 61 B4
Furuby S 40 C5
Furudal S 36 A2
Furuflaten N 112 C9
Furulund S 41 D3
Furusjö S 40 B3
Fusa N 32 B2
Fuscaldo I 106 B3
Fusch an der Grossglocknerstrasse A 72 A2
Fushë Arrëz AL 105 A6
Fushë-Krujë AL 105 B5
Fusina I 72 C2
Fusio CH 70 B3
Füssen D 62 C1
Fustiñana E 89 B5
Futog SRB 75 C4
Futrikelv N 112 C8
Füzesabony H 65 C6
Füzesgyarmat H 75 A6
Fužine HR 73 C4
Fyllinge S 40 C2
Fynshav DK 39 E2
Fyresdal N 33 C5

G

Gaaldorf A 73 A4
Gabaldón E 95 C5
Gabarret F 76 C3
Gabčíkovo SK 64 C3
Gąbin PL 47 C5
Gabriac F 78 B1
Gabrovo BG 11 E8
Gaby I 70 C2
Gacé F 58 B1
Gacko BIH 84 C3
Gäddede S 115 C11
Gadebusch D 44 B3
Gadmen CH 70 B3
Gádor E 101 C3
Gádoros H 75 B5
Gael F 57 B3
Gærum DK 38 B3
Găești RO 11 D8
Gaeta I 103 B6
Gafanhoeira P 92 C2
Gaflenz A 63 C5
Gagarin RUS 7 D13
Gaggenau D 61 B4
Gagliano Castelferrato I 109 B3
Gagliano del Capo I 107 B5
Gagnet S 36 B2
Gaibanella I 81 B5
Gaildorf D 61 B5
Gaillac F 77 C4
Gaillefontaine F 58 A2
Gaillon F 58 A2
Gainsborough GB 27 B5
Gairloch GB 22 D3
Gairlochy GB 24 B3
Gáiro I 110 C2
Gaj HR 74 C2
Gaj SRB 85 B6
Gaja-la-Selve F 77 C4
Gajanejos E 95 B4
Gajary SK 64 B2
Gajdobra SRB 75 C4
Galan F 77 C3
Galanta SK 64 B3
Galapagar E 94 B2
Galápagos E 95 B3
Galaroza E 99 B4
Galashiels GB 25 C5
Galatas GR 117 E5
Galați RO 11 D10
Galatina I 107 A5
Galatista GR 116 B5
Galatone I 107 A5
Galaxidi GR 117 D4
Galdakao E 89 A4
Galeata I 81 C5
Galende E 87 B4
Galera E 101 B3
Galéria F 102 A1
Galgamácsa H 65 C5
Galgate GB 26 B3
Galgon F 76 B2
Galices P 92 A3
Galinduste E 93 A5
Galinoporni CY 120 A3
Galisteo E 93 B4
Galków PL 55 B4
Gallarate I 70 C3
Gallardon F 58 B2
Gallegos de Argañán E 93 A4
Gallegos del Solmirón E 93 A5
Galleguillos de Campos E 88 B1
Galleno I 81 C4
Galliate I 70 C3
Gallicano I 81 B4
Gállio I 72 C1
Gallípoli I 107 A4
Gallipoli = Gelibolu TR 118 B1
Gällivare S 112 E9
Gallizien A 73 B4
Gallneukirchen A 63 B5
Gällö S 115 E12
Gallocanta E 95 B5
Gällstad S 40 B3
Gallur E 90 B1
Galmisdale GB 24 B1
Galmpton GB 29 C4
Galston GB 24 C3
Galta N 33 C2
Galtelli I 110 B2
Galten DK 39 C2
Galtür A 71 B5
Galve de Sorbe E 95 A3
Galveias P 92 B2
Gálvez E 94 C2
Galway IRL 20 A2
Gamaches F 48 D2
Gámbara I 71 C5
Gambárie I 106 C2
Gambassi Terme I 81 C4
Gambatesa I 103 B7
Gambolò I 70 C3
Gaming A 63 C6
Gamla Uppsala S 36 C4
Gamleby S 40 B6
Gamlingay GB 30 B3
Gammelgarn S 37 E5
Gammelstad S 3 D25
Gammertingen D 61 B5
Gams CH 71 A4
Gamvik, *Finnmark* N 113 B11
Gamvik, *Finnmark* N 113 A17
Gan F 76 C2
Gáname E 87 C4
Ganda di Martello I 71 B5
Gandarela P 87 C2
Ganddal N 33 D2
Ganderkesee D 43 B5
Gandesa E 90 B3
Gandía E 96 C2
Gandino I 71 C4
Gandrup DK 38 B3
Ganges F 78 C2
Gånghester S 40 B3
Gangi I 109 B3
Gangkofen D 62 B3
Gannat F 68 B3
Gannay-sur-Loire F 68 B3
Gänserndorf A 64 B2
Ganzlin D 44 B4
Gap F 79 B5
Gara H 75 B4
Garaballa E 96 B1
Garaguso I 104 C2
Garbayuela E 94 C1
Garbhallt GB 24 B2
Garbsen D 43 C6
Garching D 62 B3
Garciaz E 93 B5
Garcihernández E 94 B1
Garcillán E 94 B2
Garcinarro E 95 B4
Garcisobaco E 99 C5
Garda I 71 C5
Gardanne F 79 C4
Gärdås S 34 B5
Gårdby S 41 C6
Gardeja PL 47 B4
Gardelegen D 44 C3
Gardermoen N 34 B3
Gardiki GR 116 D3
Garding D 43 A5
Gardone Riviera I 71 C5
Gardone Val Trómpia I 71 C5
Gárdony H 74 A3
Gardouch F 77 C4
Gårdsjö S 37 D1
Gårds Köpinge S 41 D4
Gårdskär S 36 B4
Garein F 76 B2
Garelochhead GB 24 B3
Garéoult F 79 C5
Garešnica HR 74 C1
Garéssio I 80 B2
Garforth GB 27 B4
Gargaliani GR 117 E3
Gargaligas E 93 B5
Gargallo E 90 C2
Garganta la Olla E 93 A5
Gargantiel E 100 A1
Gargellen A 71 B4
Gargilesse-Dampierre F 67 B6
Gargnano I 71 C5
Gargnäs S 115 B14
Gárgoles de Abajo E 95 B4
Gargrave GB 26 B3
Garitz D 52 B2
Garlasco I 70 C3
Garlieston GB 24 D3
Garlin F 76 C2
Garlitos E 94 D1
Garmisch-Partenkirchen D 71 A6
Garnat-sur-Engièvre F 68 B3
Garpenberg S 36 B3
Garphyttan S 37 C1
Garray E 89 C4
Garrel D 43 C5
Garriguella E 91 A6
Garrison GB 18 B3
Garrovillas E 93 B4
Garrucha E 101 B4
Gars-am-Kamp A 63 B6
Garsås S 36 B1
Garsdale Head GB 26 A3
Gärsnäs S 41 D4
Garstang GB 26 B3
Gartow D 44 B3
Gartz D 45 B6
Garvagh GB 19 B5
Garvão P 98 B2
Garve GB 22 D4
Garwolin PL 55 B6
Garz D 45 A5
Garzyn PL 54 B1
Gąsawa PL 46 C3
Gåsborn S 34 C6
Gaschurn A 71 B5
Gascueña E 95 B4
Gasny F 58 A2
Gąsocin PL 47 C6
Gastes F 76 B1
Gastouni GR 117 E3
Gastouri GR 116 C1
Gata E 93 A4
Gata HR 83 C5
Gata de Gorgos E 96 C3
Gatchina RUS 7 B11
Gatehouse of Fleet GB 24 D3
Gátér H 75 B4
Gateshead GB 25 D6
Gátova E 96 B2
Gattendorf A 64 B2
Gatteo a Mare I 82 B1
Gattinara I 70 C3
Gattorna I 80 B3
Gaucín E 99 C5
Gaulstad N 114 D9
Gaupne N 32 A4
Gautefall N 33 C5
Gauting D 62 B2
Gauto S 115 A13
Gava E 91 B5
Gavardo I 71 C5
Gavarnie F 76 D2
Gavi I 80 B2
Gavião P 92 B3
Gavirate I 70 C3
Gävle S 36 B4
Gavoi I 110 B2
Gavorrano I 81 D4
Gavray F 57 B4
Gavrio GR 117 E6
Gävunda S 34 B6
Gaweinstal A 64 B2
Gaworzyce PL 53 B5
Gawroniec PL 46 B2
Gaydon GB 30 B2
Gayton GB 30 B4
Gazipaşa TR 119 F7
Gazoldo degli Ippoliti I 71 C5
Gazzuolo I 81 A4
Gbelce SK 65 C4
Gdańsk PL 47 A4
Gdinj HR 84 C1
Gdov RUS 7 B9
Gdów PL 65 A6
Gdynia PL 47 A4
Gea de Albarracin E 95 B5
Geary GB 22 D2
Géaudot F 59 B5
Geaune F 76 C2
Gebesee D 51 B6
Gebiz TR 119 E5
Gebze TR 118 B4
Géderlak H 75 B3
Gedern D 51 C5
Gedinne B 49 D5
Gediz TR 118 D4
Gèdre F 76 D3
Gedser DK 44 A3
Gedsted DK 38 C2
Geel B 49 B5
Geesthacht D 44 B2
Geetbets B 49 C6
Gefell D 52 C1
Gehrden D 51 A5
Gehren D 52 C1
Geilenkirchen D 50 C2
Geilo N 32 B5
Geinsheim D 61 A4
Geisa D 51 C5
Geiselhöring D 62 B3
Geiselwind D 61 A6
Geisenfeld D 62 B2
Geisenhausen D 62 B3
Geisenheim D 50 D4
Geising D 53 C3
Geisingen D 61 C4
Geislingen D 61 B5
Geistthal A 73 A5
Geiterygghytta N 32 B4
Geithain D 52 B2
Geithus N 34 C1
Gela I 109 B3
Geldermalsen NL 49 B6
Geldern D 50 B2
Geldrop NL 49 B6
Geleen NL 50 C1
Gelembe TR 118 C2
Gelendost TR 119 D6
Gelibolu = Gallipoli TR 118 B1
Gelida E 91 B4
Gelnhausen D 51 C5
Gelnica SK 65 B6
Gelsa E 90 B2
Gelse H 74 B1
Gelsenkirchen D 50 B3
Gelsted DK 39 D2
Geltendorf D 62 B2
Gelterkinden CH 70 A2
Gelting D 39 E2
Gelu RO 75 B6
Gelves E 99 B4
Gembloux B 49 C5
Gemeaux F 69 A5
Gémenos F 79 C4
Gemerská Poloma SK 65 B6
Gemerská Ves SK 65 B6
Gemert NL 50 B1
Gemla S 40 C4
Gemlik TR 118 B4
Gemmenich B 50 C1
Gemona del Friuli I 72 B3
Gémozac F 67 C4
Gemund D 50 C2
Gemünden, *Bayern* D 51 C5
Gemünden, *Hessen* D 51 C4
Gemünden, *Rheinland-Pfalz* D 60 A3
Genappe B 49 C5
Génave E 101 A3
Genazzano I 102 B5
Gençay F 67 B5
Gencsapáti H 74 A1
Gendringen NL 50 B2
Genelard F 68 B4
Genemuiden NL 42 C3
Generalski Stol HR 73 C5
Geneva = Genève CH 69 B6
Genevad S 40 C3
Genève = Geneva CH 69 B6
Genevriéres F 60 C1
Gengenbach D 61 B4
Genillé F 67 A6
Genk B 49 C6
Genlis F 69 A5
Gennep NL 50 B1
Genner DK 39 D2
Gennes F 67 A4
Genoa = Génova I 80 B2
Genola I 80 B1
Génova = Genoa I 80 B2
Genowefa PL 54 A3
Gensingen D 60 A3
Gent = Ghent B 49 B4
Genthin D 44 C4
Gentioux F 68 C1
Genzano di Lucánia I 104 C2
Genzano di Roma I 102 B5
Georgenthal D 51 C6
Georgsmarien-hütte D 50 A4
Gera D 52 C2
Geraards-bergen B 49 C4
Gerace I 106 C3
Geraci Siculo I 109 B3
Geraki GR 117 F4
Gérardmer F 60 B2
Geras A 63 B6
Gerbéviller F 60 B2
Gerbini I 109 B3
Gerbstedt D 52 B1
Gerði IS 111 C9
Gerede TR 118 B7
Gerena E 99 B4
Geretsried D 62 C2
Gérgal E 101 B3
Gergy F 69 B4
Gerindote E 94 C2
Gerjen H 74 B3
Gerlos A 72 A2
Germay F 59 B6
Germencik TR 119 E2
Germering D 62 B2
Germersheim D 61 A4
Gërneç AL 105 C5
Gernika-Lumo E 89 A4
Gernrode D 52 B1
Gernsbach D 61 B4
Gernsheim D 61 A4
Geroda D 51 C5
Gerola Alta I 71 B4
Geroldsgrun D 52 C1
Gerolsbach D 62 B2
Gerolstein D 50 C2
Gerolzhofen D 61 A6
Gerovo HR 73 C4
Gerpinnes B 49 C5
Gerrards Cross GB 31 C3
Gerri de la Sal E 91 A4
Gersfeld D 51 C5
Gerstetten D 61 B6
Gersthofen D 62 B1
Gerstungen D 51 C6
Gerswalde D 45 B5
Gerzat F 68 C3
Gerze TR 16 A7
Gerzen D 62 B3
Gescher D 50 B3
Geseke D 51 B4
Geslau D 61 A6
Gespunsart F 59 A5
Gesté F 66 A3
Gestorf D 51 A5
Gesualda I 103 C8
Gesunda S 36 B1
Geta FIN 36 B6
Getafe E 94 B3
Getinge S 40 C2
Getxo E 89 A4
Geversdorf D 43 B6
Gevgelija MK 116 A4
Gevora del Caudillo E 93 C4
Gevrey-Chambertin F 69 A4
Gex F 69 B6
Gey D 50 C2
Geyikli TR 118 C1
Geysir IS 111 C5
Geyve TR 118 B5
Gföhl A 63 B6
Ghedi I 71 C5
Ghent = Gent B 49 B4
Gheorgheni RO 11 C8
Ghigo I 79 B6
Ghilarza I 110 B1
Ghisonaccia F 102 A2
Ghisoni F 102 A2
Gialtra GR 116 D4
Gianitsa GR 116 B4
Giardinetto Vécchio I 103 B8
Giardini Naxos I 109 B4
Giarratana I 109 B3
Giarre I 109 B4
Giat F 68 C2
Giaveno I 80 A1
Giazza I 71 C6
Giba I 110 C1
Gibellina Nuova I 108 B1
Gibostad N 112 C7
Gibraleón E 99 B4
Gibraltar GBZ 99 C5
Gic H 74 A2
Gideå S 115 D16
Gideåkroken S 115 C14
Gidle PL 55 C4
Giebelstadt D 61 A5
Gieboldehausen D 51 B6
Gielniów PL 55 B5
Gielow D 45 B4
Gien F 58 C3
Giengen D 61 B6
Giens F 79 C5
Giera RO 75 C5
Gieselwerder D 51 B5
Giessen D 51 C4
Gieten NL 42 B3
Giethoorn NL 42 C3
Giffaumont-Champaubert F 59 B5
Gifford GB 25 C5
Gifhorn D 44 C2
Gige H 74 B2
Giglio Porto I 102 A3
Gignac F 78 C2
Gijón = Xixón E 88 A1
Gilena E 100 B1
Gilford GB 19 B5
Gillberga S 35 C4
Gilleleje DK 41 C2
Gilley F 69 A6
Gilley-sur-Loire F 68 B3
Gillingham, *Dorset* GB 29 B5
Gillingham, *Medway* GB 31 C4
Gilocourt F 59 A3
Gilserberg D 51 C5
Gilsland GB 25 D5
Gilze NL 49 B5
Gimåt S 115 D15
Gimo S 36 B5
Gimont F 77 C3
Ginasservis F 79 C4
Gingelom B 49 C6
Gingst D 45 A5
Ginosa I 104 C2
Ginzling A 72 A1
Giões P 98 B3
Gióia dei Marsi I 103 B6
Gióia del Colle I 104 C2
Gióia Sannitica I 103 B7
Gióia Táuro I 106 C2
Gioiosa Iónica I 106 C3
Gioiosa Marea I 109 A3
Giosla GB 22 C2
Giovinazzo I 104 B2
Girifalco I 106 C3
Giromagny F 60 C2
Girona E 91 B5
Gironcourt-sur-Vraine F 60 B1
Gironella E 91 A4
Gironville-sous-les-Côtes F 60 B1
Girvan GB 24 C3
Gislaved S 40 B3
Gislev DK 39 D3
Gisors F 58 A2
Gissi I 103 A7
Gistad S 37 D2
Gistel B 48 B3
Gistrup DK 38 C3
Giswil CH 70 B3
Githio GR 117 F4
Giugliano in Campania I 103 C7
Giulianova I 82 D2
Giulvăz RO 75 C5
Giurgiu RO 11 E8
Give DK 39 D2
Givet F 49 C5
Givors F 69 C4
Givry B 49 C5
Givry F 69 B4
Givry-en-Argonne F 59 B5
Givskud DK 39 D2
Giżalki PL 54 A2
Gizeux F 67 A5
Giżycko PL 6 D6
Gizzeria I 106 C3
Gizzeria Lido I 106 C3
Gjedved DK 39 D2
Gjegjan AL 105 B6
Gjendesheim N 32 A5
Gjerde N 32 B3
Gjerlev DK 38 C3
Gjermundshamn N 32 B2
Gjerrild DK 38 C3
Gjerstad N 33 D6
Gjesås N 34 B4
Gjesvær N 113 A14
Gjirokastër AL 116 B2
Gjøfjell N 35 C2
Gjøl DK 38 B2
Gjøra N 114 E6
Gjøvik N 34 B2
Gladbeck D 50 B2
Gladenbach D 51 C4
Gladstad N 114 B8
Glamis GB 25 B5
Glamoč BIH 84 B1
Glamsbjerg DK 39 D3
Gland CH 69 B6
Glandorf D 50 A3
Glanegg A 73 B4
Glanshammar S 37 C2
Glarus CH 70 A4
Glasgow GB 24 C3
Glashütte, *Bayern* D 62 C2
Glashütte, *Sachsen* D 53 C3
Glastonbury GB 29 B5
Glatzau A 73 B5
Glauchau D 52 C2
Glava S 35 C4
Glavatičevo BIH 84 C3
Glavičice BIH 85 B4
Glavnik KOS 85 D6
Gledica SRB 85 C5
Glein A 73 A4
Glein N 115 A9
Gleinstätten A 73 B5
Gleisdorf A 73 A5
Glenamoy IRL 18 B2
Glenarm GB 19 B6
Glenavy GB 19 B5
Glenbarr GB 24 C2
Glenbeigh IRL 20 B2
Glenbrittle GB 22 D2
Glencoe GB 24 B2
Glencolumbkille IRL 18 B3
Glendalough IRL 21 A5
Glenealy IRL 21 B5
Glenelg GB 22 D3
Glenfinnan GB 24 B2
Glengarriff IRL 20 C2
Glenluce GB 24 D3
Glennamaddy IRL 18 C3
Glenrothes GB 25 B4
Glenties IRL 18 B3
Glesborg DK 38 C3
Glesien D 52 B2
Gletsch CH 70 B3
Glewitz D 45 A4
Glifada GR 117 E5
Glimåkra S 41 C4
Glin IRL 20 B2
Glina HR 73 C6
Glinde D 44 B2
Glinojeck PL 47 C6
Glinsk IRL 20 A1
Gliwice PL 54 C3
Glödnitz A 73 B4
Gloggnitz A 64 C1
Głogoczów PL 65 A5
Glogonj SRB 85 B5
Glogovac SRB 85 B6
Głogów PL 53 B6
Głogówek PL 54 C2
Glomel F 56 B2
Glomfjord N 112 F2
Glommen S 40 C2
Glommersträsk S 115 B16
Glonn D 62 C2
Glorenza I 71 B5
Gloria P 92 B2

Glosa GR 116 C5
Glossop GB 27 B4
Gloucester GB 29 B5
Głowaczów PL 55 B6
Główczyce PL 46 A3
Glöwen D 44 C4
Głowno PL 55 B4
Gložan SRB 75 C4
Głubczyce PL 54 C2
Głuchołazy PL 54 C2
Głuchów PL 55 B5
Głuchowo PL 54 A1
Glücksburg D 39 E2
Glückstadt D 43 B6
Glumina BIH 84 B4
Glumsø DK 39 D4
Glušci SRB 85 B4
Glusk BY 7 E10
Głuszyca PL 53 C6
Glyn Neath GB 29 B4
Glyngøre DK 38 C1
Gmünd, *Karnten* A 72 B3
Gmünd, *Nieder Östereich* A 63 B5
Gmund D 62 C2
Gmunden A 63 C4
Gnarp S 115 E14
Gnarrenburg D 43 B6
Gnesau A 72 B3
Gnesta S 37 C4
Gnięchowice PL 54 B1
Gniew PL 47 B4
Gniewkowo PL 47 C4
Gniezno PL 46 C3
Gnoien D 45 B4
Gnojnice BIH 84 C2
Gnojno PL 55 C5
Gnosall GB 26 C3
Gnosjö S 40 B3
Göbel TR 118 B3
Göçbeyli TR 118 C2
Goch D 50 B2
Gochsheim D 51 C6
Göd H 65 C5
Godalming GB 31 C3
Godby FIN 36 B6
Goddelsheim D 51 B4
Gódega di Sant'Urbano I 72 C2
Godegård S 37 D2
Godelheim D 51 B5
Goderville F 58 A1
Goðdalir IS 111 B6
Godiasco I 80 B3
Godič SLO 73 B4
Godkowo PL 47 A5
Godmanchester GB 30 B3
Gödöllö H 65 C5
Gödre H 74 B2
Godshill GB 31 D2
Godzikowice PL 54 C2
Godziszewo PL 47 A4
Goes NL 49 B4
Goetzenbrück F 60 B3
Góglio I 70 B3
Gogolin PL 54 C3
Göhren D 45 A5
Goirle NL 49 B6
Góis P 92 A2
Góito I 71 C5
Goizueta E 76 C1
Gojna Gora SRB 85 C5
Gójsk PL 47 C5
Gökçedağ TR 118 C3
Gökçen TR 119 D2
Gökçeören TR 119 D3
Gökçeyazı TR 118 C2
Göktepe TR 119 E3
Gol N 32 B5
Gola HR 74 B2
Gola N 34 A1
Gołańcz PL 46 C3
Gölbaşı TR 16 B6
Gölby FIN 36 B6
Gölcük, *Kocaeli* TR 118 B4
Gölcük, *Niğde* TR 16 B7
Golčův Jenikov CZ 63 A6
Gołczewo PL 45 B6
Goldach CH 71 A4
Goldbach D 51 C5
Goldbeck D 44 C3
Goldberg D 44 B4
Goldelund D 43 A6
Goldenstedt D 43 C5
Gołębiewo PL 47 A4
Golegã P 92 B2
Goleniów PL 45 B6
Golfo Aranci I 110 B2
Gölhisar TR 119 E4
Golina PL 54 A3
Gölle H 74 B3
Göllersdorf A 64 B2
Golling an der Salzach A 63 C4
Gölmarmara TR 118 D2
Golnice PL 53 B5
Golnik SLO 73 B4
Gölova TR 119 F5
Gölpazarı TR 118 B5
Gols A 64 C2
Golspie GB 23 D5
Golssen D 52 B3
Golub-Dobrzyń PL 47 B5
Golubac SRB 85 B6
Golubinci SRB 85 B5
Golubovci MNE 105 A5
Gołuchów PL 54 B2
Golzow D 52 A2
Gomagoi I 71 B5
Gómara E 89 C4
Gomaringen D 61 B5
Gömbe TR 119 F4
Gömeç TR 118 C1
Gomel = Homyel BY 7 E11
Gomes Aires P 98 B2
Gómezserracin E 88 C2
Gommern D 52 A1
Gomulin PL 55 B4
Gonäs S 36 B2
Goncelin F 69 C5
Gończyce PL 55 B6
Gondomar E 87 B2
Gondomar P 87 C2
Gondrecourt-le-Château F 60 B1
Gondrin F 76 C3
Gönen, *Balıkesir* TR 118 B2
Gönen, *Isparta* TR 119 E5
Gonfaron F 79 C5
Goñi E 76 D1
Goni GR 116 C4
Goni I 110 C2
Gonnesa I 110 C1
Gonnosfanádiga I 110 C1
Gönyü H 64 C3
Gonzaga I 81 B4
Goodrich GB 29 B5
Goodwick GB 28 A2
Gooik B 49 C5
Goole GB 27 B5
Goor NL 50 A2
Göpfritz an der Wild A 63 B6
Goppenstein CH 70 B2
Göppingen D 61 B5
Gor E 100 B3
Góra, *Dolnośląskie* PL 54 B1
Góra, *Mazowieckie* PL 47 C6
Góra Kalwaria PL 55 B6
Gorafe E 100 B2
Gorawino PL 46 B1
Goražde BIH 84 C3
Gordaliza del Pino E 88 B1
Gördes TR 118 D3
Gørding DK 39 D1
Górdola CH 70 B3
Gordon GB 25 C5
Gordoncillo E 88 B1
Gorebridge GB 25 C4
Gorenja Vas SLO 73 B4
Gorenje Jelenje HR 73 C4
Gorey GB 57 A3
Gorey IRL 21 B5
Gorgonzola I 71 C4
Gorica HR 83 B4
Gorican HR 74 B1
Gorinchem NL 49 B5
Goring GB 31 C2
Goritsy RUS 7 C14
Göritz D 45 B5
Gorízia I 72 C3
Górki PL 47 C5
Gorleben D 44 B3
Gorleston-on-sea GB 30 B5
Gørlev DK 39 D4
Görlitz D 53 B4
Górliz E 89 A4
Görmin D 45 B5
Górna Grupa PL 47 B4
Gorna Oryakhovitsa BG 11 E8
Gornja Gorevnica SRB 85 C5
Gornja Klina KOS 85 D5
Gornja Ploča HR 83 B4
Gornja Radgona SLO 73 B5
Gornja Sabanta SRB 85 C6
Gornja Trešnjevica SRB 85 B5
Gornja Tuzla BIH 84 B3
Gornje Polje MNE 84 D3
Gornje Ratkovo BIH 84 B1
Gornji Grad SLO 73 B4
Gornji Humac HR 83 C5
Gornji Jasenjani BIH 84 C2
Gornji Kamengrad BIH 83 B5
Gornji Kneginec HR 73 B6
Gornji Kokoti MNE 105 A5
Gornji Kosinj HR 83 B4
Gornji Milanovac SRB 85 B5
Gornji Podgradci BIH 84 A2
Gornji Ravno BIH 84 C2
Gornji Sjenicak HR 73 C5
Gornji Vakuf BIH 84 C2
Górno PL 55 C5
Görömböly H 65 B6
Górowo Iławeckie PL 47 A6
Gorran Haven GB 28 C3
Gorredijk NL 42 B3
Gorron F 57 B5
Gorseinon GB 28 B3
Gort IRL 20 A3
Gortin GB 19 B4
Görzke D 52 A2
Gorzkowice PL 55 B4
Górzno, *Kujawsko-Pomorskie* PL 47 B5
Górzno, *Zachodnio-Pomorskie* PL 46 B1
Gorzów Śląski PL 54 B3
Gorzów Wielkopolski PL 45 C7
Górzyca PL 45 C6
Gorzyce PL 54 D3
Górzyn, *Lubuskie* PL 53 B4
Gorzyń, *Wielkopolskie* PL 46 C1
Gorzyno PL 46 A3
Gosaldo I 72 B1
Gosau A 63 C4
Gosberton GB 30 B3
Gościcino PL 47 A4
Gościęcin PL 54 C3
Gościm PL 46 C1
Gościno PL 46 A1
Gosdorf A 73 B5
Gosforth GB 26 A2
Goslar D 51 B6
Goslice PL 47 C5
Gospič HR 83 B4
Gosport GB 31 D2
Goss Ilsede D 51 A6
Gössäter S 35 D5
Gossau CH 71 A4
Gössnitz D 52 C2
Gössweinstein D 62 A2
Gostimë AL 105 C6
Gostkow PL 55 B4
Göstling an der Ybbs A 63 C5
Gostomia PL 46 B2
Gostycyn PL 46 B3
Gostyń PL 54 B2
Gostynin PL 47 C5
Goszczyn PL 55 B5
Göta S 35 D4
Göteborg = Gothenburg S 38 B4
Götene S 35 D5
Gotha D 51 C6
Gothem S 37 E5
Gothenburg = Göteborg S 38 B4
Gotse Delchev BG 116 A5
Gottersdorf D 62 B3
Göttingen D 51 B5
Gottne S 115 D15
Götzis A 71 A4
Gouarec F 56 B2
Gouda NL 49 A5
Goudhurst GB 31 C4
Goumenissa GR 116 B4
Goura GR 117 E4
Gourdon F 77 B4
Gourgançon F 59 B5
Gourin F 56 B2
Gournay-en-Bray F 58 A2
Gourock GB 24 C3
Gouveia P 92 A3
Gouvy B 50 C1
Gouzeacourt F 49 C4
Gouzon F 68 B2
Govedari HR 84 D2
Govérnolo I 81 A4
Gowarczów PL 55 B5
Gowerton GB 28 B3
Gowidlino PL 46 A3
Gowran IRL 21 B4
Goyatz D 53 A4
Göynük, *Antalya* TR 119 F5
Göynük TR 118 B5
Gozdnica PL 53 B5
Gozdowo PL 47 C5
Gozee B 49 C5
Graal-Müritz D 44 A4
Grab BIH 84 D3
Grabenstätt D 62 C3
Grabhair GB 22 C2
Gråbo S 38 B5
Grabovac HR 84 C1
Grabovac SRB 85 B5
Grabovci SRB 85 B4
Grabow D 44 B3
Grabów PL 55 A4
Grabow nad Pilicą PL 55 B6
Grabów nad Prosną PL 54 B3
Grabowno PL 46 B3
Grabs CH 71 A4
Gračac HR 83 B4
Gračanica BIH 84 B3
Gračanica KOS 85 D6
Graçay F 68 A1
Gracen AL 105 B5
Grad SLO 73 B6
Gradac BIH 84 D3
Gradac HR 84 C2
Gradac MNE 85 C4
Gradac SRB 85 C5
Gradačac BIH 84 B3
Gradec HR 74 C1
Gradefes E 88 B1
Grades A 73 B4
Gradil P 92 C1
Gradina HR 74 C2
Gradina MNE 85 C4
Gradisca d'Isonzo I 72 C3
Gradište HR 74 C3
Grado E 86 A4
Grado I 72 C3
Grærup Strand DK 39 D1
Græsted DK 41 C2
Grafenau D 63 B4
Gräfenberg D 62 A2
Gräfenhainichen D 52 B2
Grafenschlag A 63 B6
Grafenstein A 73 B4
Gräfenthal D 52 C1
Grafentonna D 51 B6
Grafenwöhr D 62 A2
Grafing D 62 B2
Grafling D 62 B3
Gräfsnäs S 40 A2
Gragnano I 103 C7
Grahovo MNE 84 D3
Grahovo SLO 72 B3
Graiguenamanagh IRL 21 B5
Grain GB 31 C4
Grainau D 71 A6
Graja de Iniesta E 95 C5
Grajera E 89 C3
Gram DK 39 D2
Gramais A 71 A5
Gramat F 77 B4
Gramatneusiedl A 64 B2
Grambow D 45 B6
Grammichele I 109 B3
Gramsh AL 116 B2
Gramzow D 45 B6
Gran N 34 B2
Granada E 100 B2
Granard IRL 19 C4
Grañas E 86 A3
Granátula de Calatrava E 100 A2
Grancey-le-Château F 59 C6
Grand-Champ F 56 C3
Grand Couronne F 58 A2
Grand-Fougeray F 57 C4
Grandas de Salime E 86 A4
Grandcamp-Maisy F 57 A4
Grândola P 98 A2
Grandpré F 59 A5
Grandrieu B 49 C5
Grandrieu F 78 B2
Grandson CH 70 B1
Grandvillars F 70 A1
Grandvilliers F 58 A2
Grañén E 90 B2
Grangärde S 36 B1
Grange IRL 18 B3
Grange-over-Sands GB 26 A3
Grangemouth GB 25 B4
Granges-de Crouhens F 77 D3
Granges-sur-Vologne F 60 B2
Gängesberg S 36 B1
Gräningen D 44 C4
Granitola-Torretta I 108 B1
Granja, *Évora* P 98 A3
Granja, *Porto* P 87 C2
Granja de Moreruela E 88 C1
Granja de Torrehermosa E 93 C5
Gränna S 40 A4
Grannäs, *Västerbotten* S 115 B13
Grannäs, *Västerbotten* S 115 B14
Granö S 115 C16
Granollers E 91 B5
Granowiec PL 54 B2
Granowo PL 54 A1
Gransee D 45 B5
Gransherad N 33 C6
Grantham GB 27 C5
Grantown-on-Spey GB 23 D5
Grantshouse GB 25 C5
Granville F 57 B4
Granvin N 32 B3
Gräsås S 40 C2
Grasbakken N 113 B17
Grasberg D 43 B6
Grasmere GB 26 A2
Gräsmyr S 115 D16
Grasö S 36 B5
Grassano I 104 C2
Grassau D 62 C3
Grasse F 79 C5
Grassington GB 27 A4
Gråsten DK 39 E2
Grästorp S 35 D4
Gratkorn A 73 A5
Gråträsk S 115 B16
Gratwein A 73 A5
Graulhet F 77 C4
Graus E 90 A3
Grávalos E 89 B5
Gravberget N 34 B4
Grave NL 50 B1
Gravedona I 71 B4
Gravelines F 48 B3
Gravellona Toce I 70 C3
Gravendal S 36 B1
's-Gravendeel NL 49 B5
's-Gravenhage = The Hague NL 49 A5
Gravens DK 39 D2
's-Gravenzande NL 49 B5
Gravesend GB 31 C4
Graveson F 78 C3
Gravina in Púglia I 104 C2
Gray F 69 A5
Grayrigg GB 26 A3
Grays GB 31 C4
Grayshott GB 31 C3
Grayvoron RUS 7 F13
Graz A 73 A5
Grazalema E 99 C5
Grążawy PL 47 B5
Grazzano Visconti I 80 B3
Greåker N 35 C3
Great Dunmow GB 31 C4
Great Malvern GB 29 A5
Great Torrington GB 28 C3
Great Waltham GB 31 C4
Great Yarmouth GB 30 B5
Grebbestad S 35 D3
Grebenstein D 51 B5
Grębocice PL 53 B6
Grębocin PL 47 B4
Greding D 62 A2
Gredstedbro DK 39 D1
Greenhead GB 25 D5
Greenisland GB 19 B6
Greenlaw GB 25 C5
Greenock GB 24 C3
Greenway GB 28 B3
Greenwich GB 31 C4
Grefrath D 50 B2
Greifenburg A 72 B3
Greiffenberg D 45 B5
Greifswald D 45 A5
Grein A 63 B5
Greipstad N 33 D4
Greiz D 52 C2
Grenaa DK 39 C3
Grenade F 77 C4
Grenade-sur-l'Adour F 76 C2
Grenchen CH 70 A2
Grendi N 33 D4
Grenivík IS 111 B7
Grenoble F 69 C5
Gréoux-les-Bains F 79 C4
Gresenhorst D 44 A4
Gressoney-la-Trinité I 70 C2
Gressoney-St.-Jean I 70 C2
Gressthal D 51 C6
Gressvik N 35 C2
Gresten A 63 C6
Gretna GB 25 D4
Greussen D 51 B6
Greve in Chianti I 81 C5
Greven, *Mecklenburg-Vorpommern* D 44 B2
Greven, *Nordrhein-Westfalen* D 50 A3
Grevena GR 116 B3
Grevenbroich D 50 B2
Grevenbrück D 50 B4
Grevenmacher L 60 A2
Grevesmühlen D 44 B3
Grevestrand DK 41 D2
Grevie S 41 C2
Greystoke GB 26 A3
Greystones IRL 21 A5
Grez-Doiceau B 49 C5
Grez-en-Bouère F 57 C5
Grèzec F 77 B4
Grezzana I 71 C6
Grgar SLO 72 B3
Grgurevci SRB 85 A4
Gries A 71 A6
Gries in Sellrain A 71 A6
Griesbach D 63 B4
Griesheim D 61 A4
Grieskirchen A 63 B4
Griffen A 73 B4
Grignan F 78 B3
Grignano I 72 C3
Grigno I 72 B1
Grignols F 76 B2
Grignon F 69 C6
Grijota E 88 B2
Grijpskerk NL 42 B3
Gril AL 105 A5
Grillby S 37 C4
Grimaud F 79 C5
Grimbergen B 49 C5
Grimma D 52 B2
Grimmen D 45 A5
Grimmialp CH 70 B2
Grimsås S 40 B3
Grimsby GB 27 B5
Grimslöv S 40 C4
Grímsstaðir IS 111 B9
Grimstad N 33 D5
Grimstorp S 40 B4
Grindavík IS 111 D3
Grindelwald CH 70 B3
Grindheim N 33 D4
Grindsted DK 39 D1
Griñón E 94 B3
Gripenberg S 40 B4
Gripsholm S 37 C4
Grisolles F 77 C4
Grisslehamn S 36 B5
Gritley GB 23 C6
Grizebeck GB 26 A2
Grndina BIH 84 B1
Gröbming A 72 A3
Gröbzig D 52 B1
Grocka SRB 85 B5
Gröditz D 52 B3
Gródki PL 47 B6
Grodków PL 54 C2
Grodziec PL 54 A3
Grodzisk Mazowiecki PL 55 A5
Groenlo NL 50 A2
Groesbeek NL 50 B1
Grohote HR 83 C5
Groitzsch D 52 B2
Groix F 56 C2
Grójec PL 55 B5
Grom PL 47 B6
Gromiljca BIH 84 C3
Grömitz D 44 A2
Gromnik PL 65 A6
Gromo I 71 C4
Gronau, *Niedersachsen* D 51 A5
Gronau, *Nordrhein-Westfalen* D 50 A3
Grønbjerg DK 39 C1
Grönenbach D 61 C6
Grong N 114 C9
Grönhögen S 41 C6
Groningen D 52 B1
Groningen NL 42 B3
Grønnestrand DK 38 B2
Grono CH 71 B4
Grönskåra S 40 B5
Grootegast NL 42 B3
Gropello Cairoli I 70 C3
Grorud N 34 C2
Grósio I 71 B5
Grošnica SRB 85 C5
Gross Beeren D 45 C5
Gross Berkel D 51 A5
Gross-botwar D 61 B5
Gross-Dölln D 45 B5
Gross-Gerau D 61 A4
Gross-hartmansdorf D 52 C3
Gross Kreutz D 45 C4
Gross Lafferde D 51 A6
Gross Leutheb D 53 A4
Gross Muckrow D 53 A4
Gross Oesingen D 44 C2
Gross Reken D 50 B3
Gross Sarau D 44 B2
Gross Särchen D 53 B4
Gross Schönebeck D 45 C5
Gross Umstadt D 61 A4
Gross Warnow D 44 B3
Gross-Weikersdorf A 64 B1
Gross-Welle D 44 B4
Gross Wokern D 44 B4
Grossalmerode D 51 B5
Grossarl A 72 A3
Grossbodungen D 51 B6
Grossburgwedel D 44 C1
Grosschönau D 53 C4
Grossenbrode D 44 A3
Grossenehrich D 51 B6
Grossengottern D 51 B6
Grossenhain D 52 B3
Grossenkneten D 43 C5
Grossenlüder D 51 C5
Grossensee D 44 B2
Grossenzersdorf A 64 B2
Grosseto I 81 D5
Grossgerungs A 63 B5
Grossglobnitz A 63 B6
Grosshabersdorf D 62 A1
Grossharras A 64 B2
Grosshöchstetten CH 70 B2
Grosskrut A 64 B2
Grosslohra D 51 B6
Grossmehring D 62 B2
Grossostheim D 61 A5
Grosspertholz A 63 B5
Grosspetersdorf A 73 A6
Grosspostwitz D 53 B4
Grossraming A 63 C5
Grossräschen D 53 B4
Grossrinderfeld D 61 A5
Grossröhrsdorf D 53 B4
Grossschirma D 52 C3
Grossschweinbarth A 64 B2
Grosssiegharts A 63 B6
Grosssölk A 72 A3
Grosswarasdorf A 74 A1
Grosswilfersdorf A 73 A5
Grostenquin F 60 B2
Grosuplje SLO 73 C4
Grotli N 114 E4
Grötlingbo S 37 E5
Grottáglie I 104 C3
Grottaminarda I 103 B8
Grottammare I 82 D2
Grotte di Castro I 81 D5
Grotteria I 106 C3
Gróttole I 104 C2
Grouw NL 42 B2
Grov N 112 D6
Grova N 33 C5
Grove E 86 B2
Grua N 34 B2
Grube D 44 A3
Grubišno Polje HR 74 C2
Gruda HR 105 A4
Grude BIH 84 C2
Grudovo BG 11 E9
Grudusk PL 47 B6
Grudziądz PL 47 B4
Grue N 34 B4
Gruissan F 78 C2
Grullos E 86 A4
Grumo Áppula I 104 B2
Grums S 35 C5
Grünau im Almtal A 63 C4
Grünberg D 51 C4
Grünburg A 63 C5
Grundarfjörður IS 111 C2
Gründau D 51 C5
Gründelhardt D 61 A5
Grundforsen S 34 A4
Grundlsee A 63 C4
Grundsund S 35 D3
Grunewald D 53 B3
Grungedal N 33 C4
Grunow D 53 A4
Grünstadt D 61 A4
Gruvberget S 36 A3
Gruyères CH 70 B2
Gruža SRB 85 C5
Grybów PL 65 A6
Grycksbo S 36 B2
Gryfice PL 45 B7
Gryfino PL 45 B6
Gryfów Śląski PL 53 B5
Gryllefjord N 112 C6
Grymyr N 34 B2
Gryt S 37 D3
Grytgöl S 37 D2
Grythyttan S 37 C1
Grytnäs S 37 D4
Grzmiąca PL 46 B2
Grzybno PL 45 B6
Grzywna PL 47 B4
Gschnitz A 71 A6
Gschwend D 61 B5
Gstaad CH 70 B2
Gsteig CH 70 B2
Guadahortuna E 100 B2
Guadalajara E 95 B3
Guadalaviar E 95 B5
Guadalcanal E 99 A5
Guadalcázar E 100 B1
Guadalix de la Sierra E 94 B3
Guadálmez E 100 A1
Guadalupe E 93 B5
Guadamur E 94 C2
Guadarrama E 94 B2
Guadiaro E 99 C5
Guadix E 100 B2
Guagnano I 105 C3
Guagno F 102 A1
Guajar-Faragüit E 100 C2
Gualchos E 100 C2
Gualdo Tadino I 82 C1
Gualtieri I 81 B4
Guarcino I 103 B6
Guarda P 92 A3
Guardamar del Segura E 96 C2
Guardão P 92 A2
Guardavalle I 106 C3
Guardea I 102 A5
Guárdia I 103 C8
Guárdia Sanframondi I 103 B7
Guardiagrele I 103 A7
Guardiarégia I 103 B7
Guardias Viejas E 100 C3
Guardiola de Bergueda E 91 A4
Guardo E 88 B2
Guareña E 93 C4
Guaro E 100 C1
Guarromán E 100 A2
Guasila I 110 C2
Guastalla I 81 B4
Gubbhögen S 115 C12
Gúbbio I 82 C1
Guben D 53 B4
Gubin PL 53 B4
Guča SRB 85 C5
Gudå N 114 D8
Gudavac BIH 83 B5
Guddal N 32 A2
Güderup DK 39 E2
Gudhem S 35 D5
Gudhjem DK 41 D4
Gudovac HR 74 C1
Gudow D 44 B2
Güdül TR 118 B7
Gudvangen N 32 B3
Guebwiller F 60 C3
Guéjar-Sierra E 100 B2
Guéméné-Penfao F 57 C4
Guéméné-sur-Scorff F 56 B2
Güeñes E 89 A3
Guer F 57 C3
Guérande F 66 A2
Guéret F 68 B1
Guérigny F 68 A3
Guesa E 76 D1
Gueugnon F 68 B4
Guglionesi I 103 B7
Gühlen Glienicke D 45 B4
Guia P 92 B2
Guichen F 57 C4
Guidizzolo I 71 C5
Guidónia-Montecélio I 102 B5
Guiglia I 81 B4
Guignes F 58 B3
Guijo E 100 A1
Guijo de Coria E 93 A4
Guijo de Santa Bábera E 93 A5
Guijuelo E 93 A5
Guildford GB 31 C3
Guillaumes F 79 B5
Guillena E 99 B4
Guillestre F 79 B5
Guillos F 76 B2
Guilsfield GB 26 C2
Guilvinec F 56 C1
Guimarães P 87 C2
Guincho P 92 C1
Guînes F 48 C2
Guingamp F 56 B2
Guipavas F 56 B1
Guisborough GB 27 A4
Guiscard F 59 A4
Guiscriff F 56 B2
Guise F 59 A4
Guisona E 91 B4
Guitiriz E 86 A3
Guîtres F 76 A2
Gujan-Mestras F 76 B1
Gulbene LV 7 C9
Gulçayır TR 118 C6
Guldborg DK 39 E4
Gullabo S 40 C5
Gullane GB 25 B5
Gullbrå N 32 B3
Gullbrandstorp S 40 C2
Gulleråsen S 36 A2
Gullhaug N 35 C2
Gullringen S 40 B5
Gullspång S 35 D6
Gullstein N 114 D5
Güllük TR 119 E2
Gülnar TR 16 C6
Gülpınar TR 116 C8
Gülşehir TR 16 B7
Gulsvik N 34 B1
Gumiel de Hizán E 88 C3
Gummersbach D 50 B3
Gümüldür TR 119 D2
Gümüşhaciköy TR 16 A7
Gümüşova TR 118 B5

Invergowrie GB 25 B4
Inverkeilor GB 25 B5
Inverkeithing GB 25 B4
Invermoriston GB 22 D4
Inverness GB 23 D4
Inveruno I 70 C3
Inverurie GB 23 D6
Ioannina GR 116 C2
Iolanda di Savoia I 81 B5
Ion Corvin RO 11 D9
Ióppolo I 106 C2
Ios GR 117 F7
Ipati GR 116 D4
Ipsala TR 118 B1
Ipswich GB 30 B5
Iraklia GR 116 A5
Iraklio = Heraklion GR 117 G7
Irdning A 73 A4
Iregszemcse H 74 B3
Irgoli I 110 B2
Irig SRB 85 A4
Ironbridge GB 26 C3
Irpin UA 11 A11
Irrel D 60 A2
Irsina I 104 C2
Irsta S 37 C3
Irthlingborough GB 30 B3
Iruela E 87 B4
Irún E 76 C1
Irurita E 76 C1
Irurzun E 76 D1
Irvine GB 24 C3
Irvinestown GB 19 B4
Is-sur-Tille F 69 A5
Isaba E 76 D2
Isabela E 100 A2
Ísafjörður IS 111 A2
Isane N 114 F2
Isaszeg H 75 A4
Isbister GB 22 A7
Íscar E 88 C2
İscehisar TR 118 D5
Ischgl A 71 A5
Íschia I 103 C6
Ischia di Castro I 102 A4
Ischitella I 104 B1
Isdes F 58 C3
Ise N 35 C3
Iselle I 70 B3
Iseltwald CH 70 B2
Isen D 62 B3
Isenbüttel D 44 C2
Iseo I 71 C5
Iserlohn D 50 B3
Isérnia I 103 B7
Isfjorden N 114 E4
Ishëm AL 105 B5
Isigny-sur-Mer F 57 A4
Işıklı TR 119 D4
Ísili I 110 C2
İskilip TR 16 A7
Isla Canela E 98 B3
Isla Cristina E 98 B3
Islares E 89 A3
Isle Of Whithorn GB 24 D3
Isleham GB 30 B4
Ismaning D 62 B2
Isna P 92 B3
Isnestoften N 113 B11
Isny D 61 C6
Isoba E 88 A1
Isokylä FIN 113 F16
Isokylä S 113 E11
Isola F 79 B6
Isola del Gran Sasso d'Itália I 103 A6
Ísola del Liri I 103 B6
Ísola della Scala I 71 C6
Isola delle Fémmine I 108 A2
Isola di Capo Rizzuto I 107 C4
Isona E 91 A4
Ispagnac F 78 B2
Isparta TR 119 E5
Isperikh BG 11 E9
Íspica I 109 C3
Isselburg D 50 B2
Issigeac F 77 B3
Issogne I 70 C2
Issoire F 68 C3
Issoncourt F 59 B6
Issoudun F 68 B2
Issum D 50 B2
Issy-l'Evêque F 68 B3
Istán E 100 C1
İstanbul TR 118 A3
Istebna PL 65 A4
Ístia d'Ombrone I 81 D5
Istiea GR 116 D5
Istok KOS 85 D5
Istres F 78 C3
Istvándi H 74 B2
Itea GR 116 D4
Ithaki GR 117 D2
Itoiz E 76 D1
Ítrabo E 100 C2
Itri I 103 B6
Ittireddu I 110 B1
Íttiri I 110 B1
Itzehoe D 43 B6
Ivalo FIN 113 D16
Iván H 74 A1
Ivanava BY 7 E8
Ivančice CZ 64 A2
Ivančna Gorica SLO 73 C4
Iváncsa H 74 A3
Ivanec HR 73 B6
Ivanić Grad HR 73 C6
Ivanjica SRB 85 C5
Ivanjska BIH 84 B2
Ivanka SK 64 B4
Ivankovo HR 74 C3
Ivano-Frankivsk UA 11 B8
Ivanovice na Hané CZ 64 A3
Ivanska HR 74 C1
Ivatsevichy BY 7 E8
Ivaylovgrad BG 116 A8
Iveland N 33 D4
Ivoz Ramet B 49 C6
Ivrea I 70 C2
İvrindi TR 118 C2
Ivry-en-Montagne F 69 A4
Ivry-la-Bataille F 58 B2
Ivybridge GB 28 C4
Iwaniska PL 55 C6
Iwiny PL 53 B5
Iwuy F 49 C4
Ixworth GB 30 B4
Izarra E 89 B4
Izbica Kujawska PL 47 C4
Izbište SRB 85 A6
Izeda P 87 C4
Izegem B 49 C4
Izernore F 69 B5
Izmayil UA 11 D10
İzmir TR 119 D2
İzmit = Kocaeli TR 118 B4
Iznájar E 100 B1
Iznalloz E 100 B2
Iznatoraf E 100 A2
İznik TR 118 B4
Izola SLO 72 C3
Izsák H 75 B4
Izsófalva H 65 B6
Izyaslav UA 11 A9

J

Jabalquinto E 100 A2
Jablanac HR 83 B3
Jablanica BIH 84 C2
Jablonec nad Jizerou CZ 53 C5
Jablonec nad Nisou CZ 53 C5
Jablonica SK 64 B3
Jablonka PL 65 A5
Jabłonna PL 55 A5
Jablonné nad Orlicí CZ 54 C1
Jablonne Podještědi CZ 53 C4
Jablonov nad Turňou SK 65 B6
Jabłonowo Pomorskie PL 47 B5
Jablúnka CZ 64 A3
Jablunkov CZ 65 A4
Jabučje SRB 85 B5
Jabugo E 99 B4
Jabuka, *Srbija* SRB 85 C4
Jabuka, *Vojvodina* SRB 85 B5
Jabukovac HR 73 C6
Jaca E 90 A2
Jáchymov CZ 52 C2
Jacobidrebber D 43 C5
Jade D 43 B5
Jäderfors S 36 B3
Jädraås S 36 B3
Jadraque E 95 B4
Jægerspris DK 39 D4
Jaén E 100 B2
Jagare BIH 84 B2
Jagel D 43 A6
Jagenbach A 63 B6
Jagodina SRB 85 C6
Jagodnjak HR 74 C3
Jagodzin PL 53 B5
Jagstheim D 61 A6
Jagstzell D 61 A6
Jahodna SK 64 B3
Jajce BIH 84 B2
Ják H 74 A1
Jakabszálbs H 75 B4
Jäkkvik S 115 A14
Jaklovce SK 65 B6
Jakobsnes N 113 C19
Jakovlje HR 73 C5
Jakšic HR 74 C2
Jakubany SK 65 A6
Jalance E 96 B1
Jalasjärvi FIN 3 E25
Jalhay B 50 C1
Jaligny-sur-Besbre F 68 B3
Jallais F 66 A4
Jalón E 96 C2
Jâlons F 59 B5
Jamena SRB 84 B4
Jamilena E 100 B2
Jämjö S 41 C5
Jamnička Kiselica HR 73 C5
Jamno PL 46 A2
Jamoigne B 59 A6
Jämsä FIN 3 F26
Jämshög S 41 C4
Janakkala FIN 3 F26
Jandelsbrunn D 63 B4
Jänickendorf D 52 A3
Janikowo PL 47 C4
Janja BIH 85 B4
Janjina HR 84 D2
Janki, *Łódzkie* PL 55 B4
Janki, *Mazowieckie* PL 55 A5
Jankov CZ 63 A5
Jankowo Dolne PL 46 C3
Jánoshalma H 75 B4
Jánosháza H 74 A2
Jánoshida H 75 A5
Jánossomorja H 64 C3
Janovice nad Uhlavou CZ 63 A4
Janów PL 55 C4
Janowiec Wielkopolski PL 46 C3
Janowo PL 47 B6
Jänsmässholmen S 115 D10
Janville F 58 B2
Janzé F 57 C4
Jarabá SK 65 B5
Jaraczewo PL 54 B2
Jarafuel E 96 B1
Jaraicejo E 93 B5
Jaraíz de la Vera E 93 A5
Jarak SRB 85 B4
Jarandilla de la Vera E 93 A5
Jaray E 89 C4
Järbo S 36 B3
Jard-sur-Mer F 66 B3
Jaren N 34 B2
Jargeau F 58 C3
Jarkovac SRB 75 C5
Järlåsa S 36 C4
Jarmen D 45 B5
Järna S 37 C4
Jarnac F 67 C4
Järnäs S 115 D16
Järnforsen S 40 B5
Jarny F 60 A1
Jarocin PL 54 B2
Jaroměř CZ 53 C5
Jaroměřice nad Rokytnou CZ 64 A1
Jaroslav CZ 53 C6
Jaroslavice CZ 64 B2
Jarosław PL 11 A7
Jaroslawiec PL 46 A2
Jarošov nad Nežarkou CZ 63 A6
Järpås S 35 D4
Järpen S 115 D10
Jarrow GB 25 D6
Järso FIN 36 B6
Järvenpää FIN 7 A8
Jarvorník CZ 54 C1
Järvsö S 115 F13
Jarzé F 67 A4
Jaša Tomic SRB 75 C5
Jasenak HR 73 C5
Jasenica BIH 83 B5
Jasenice HR 83 B4
Jasenovac HR 74 C1
Jasenovo, *Srbija* SRB 85 C4
Jasenovo, *Vojvodina* SRB 85 B6
Jasień PL 53 B5
Jasienica PL 53 B4
Jasika SRB 85 C6
Jasło PL 10 B6
Jásova SK 65 C4
Jasseron F 69 B5
Jastarnia PL 47 A4
Jastrebarsko HR 73 C5
Jastrowie PL 46 B2
Jastrzębia-Góra PL 47 A4
Jastrzębie Zdrój PL 54 D3
Jászals-Lószentgyörgy H 75 A5
Jászapáti H 75 A5
Jászárokszállás H 65 C5
Jászberény H 75 A4
Jászdózsa H 65 C6
Jászfényszaru H 75 A4
Jászjákóhalma H 75 A5
Jászkarajenő H 75 A5
Jászkisér H 75 A5
Jászladány H 75 A5
Jászszentlászló H 75 B4
Jásztelek H 75 A5
Játar E 100 C2
Jättendal S 115 F14
Jatznick D 45 B5
Jaun CH 70 B2
Jausiers F 79 B5
Jávea E 96 C3
Jävenitz D 44 C3
Javerlhac F 67 C5
Javier E 90 A1
Javorani BIH 84 B2
Javorina SK 65 A6
Javron F 57 B5
Jawor PL 53 B6
Jaworzno PL 55 C4
Jaworzyna Śl. PL 54 C1
Jayena E 100 C2
Jaźow PL 53 B4
Jebel RO 75 C6
Jebjerg DK 38 C2
Jedburgh GB 25 C5
Jedlinsk PL 55 B6
Jedlnia PL 55 B6
Jedlnia Letnisko PL 55 B6
Jedovnice CZ 64 A2
Jędrychow PL 47 B5
Jędrzejów PL 55 C5
Jedwabno PL 47 B6
Jeesiö FIN 113 E15
Jegłownik PL 47 A5
Jegun F 77 C3
Jēkabpils LV 7 C8
Jektevik N 32 C2
Jektvik N 112 F2
Jelakci SRB 85 C5
Jelcz-Laskowice PL 54 B2
Jelenec SK 64 B4
Jelenia Góra PL 53 C5
Jelgava LV 6 C7
Jelka SK 64 B3
Jelling DK 39 D2
Jels DK 39 D2
Jelsa HR 83 C5
Jelsa N 33 C3
Jelšava SK 65 B6
Jemgum D 43 B4
Jemnice CZ 63 A6
Jena D 52 C1
Jenaz CH 71 B4
Jenbach A 72 A1
Jenikow PL 45 B7
Jennersdorf A 73 B6
Jenny S 40 B6
Jerchel D 44 C3
Jeres del Marquesado E 100 B2
Jerez de la Frontera E 99 C4
Jerez de los Caballeros E 99 A4
Jerica E 96 B2
Jerichow D 44 C4
Jerka PL 54 A1
Jermenovci SRB 75 C6
Jerslev DK 38 B3
Jerte E 93 A5
Jerup DK 38 B3
Jerxheim D 51 A6
Jerzmanowice PL 55 C4
Jerzu I 110 C2
Jerzwałd PL 47 B5
Jesberg D 51 C5
Jesenice, *Středočeský* CZ 52 C3
Jesenice, *Středočeský* CZ 53 D4
Jesenice SLO 73 B4
Jeseník CZ 54 C2
Jesenké SK 65 B6
Jesi I 82 C2
Jésolo I 72 C2
Jessen D 52 B2
Jessenitz D 44 B3
Jessheim N 34 B3
Jessnitz D 52 B2
Jesteburg D 44 B1
Jeumont F 49 C5
Jeven-stedt D 43 A6
Jever D 43 B4
Jevičko CZ 64 A2
Jevišovice CZ 64 B1
Jevnaker N 34 B2
Jezerane HR 83 A4
Jezero BIH 84 B2
Jezero HR 83 B4
Jeziorany PL 47 B6
Jeżów PL 55 B4
Jičín CZ 53 C5
Jičiněves CZ 53 C5
Jihlava CZ 63 A6
Jijona E 96 C2
Jilemnice CZ 53 C5
Jilové CZ 53 C4
Jilové u Prahy CZ 63 A5
Jimbolia RO 75 C5
Jimena E 100 B2
Jimena de la Frontera E 99 C5
Jimera de Líbar E 99 C5
Jimramov CZ 64 A2
Jince CZ 63 A4
Jindřichovice CZ 52 C2
Jindřichův Hradec CZ 63 A6
Jirkov CZ 52 C3
Jistebnice CZ 63 A5
Joachimsthal D 45 C5
João da Loura P 92 C2
Jobbágyi H 65 C5
Jochberg A 72 A2
Jockfall S 113 F11
Jódar E 100 B2
Jodoigne B 49 C5
Joensuu FIN 3 E28
Joesjö S 115 B11
Jœuf F 60 A1
Jõgeva EST 7 B9
Johann-georgen-stadt D 52 C2
Johannishus S 41 C5
Johanniskirchen D 62 B3
Johansfors S 40 C5
John o'Groats GB 23 C5
Johnshaven GB 25 B5
Johnstone GB 24 C3
Johnstown IRL 21 B4
Jõhvi EST 7 B9
Joigny F 59 C4
Joinville F 59 B6
Jokkmokk S 112 F8
Jöllenbeck D 51 A4
Jomala FIN 36 B6
Jönåker S 37 D3
Jonava LT 6 D8
Jonchery-sur-Vesle F 59 A4
Jondal N 32 B3
Jondalen N 33 C6
Joniškis LT 6 C7
Jönköping S 40 B4
Jonkowo PL 47 B6
Jønnbu N 33 C6
Jonsberg S 37 D3
Jonsered S 38 B5
Jonstorp S 41 C2
Jonzac F 67 C4
Jorba E 91 B4
Jordanów PL 65 A5
Jordanów Śląski PL 54 C1
Jordanowo PL 46 C1
Jordbro S 37 C5
Jordbrua N 115 A11
Jördenstorf D 45 B4
Jordet N 34 A4
Jordøse DK 39 D3
Jork D 43 B6
Jörlanda S 38 B4
Jormlien S 115 C10
Jormvattnet S 115 C11
Jörn S 115 B17
Jørpeland N 33 C3
Jorquera E 96 B1
Jošan HR 83 B4
Jošanička Banja SRB 85 C5
Jošavka BIH 84 B2
Josipdol HR 73 C5
Josipovac HR 74 C3
Jössefors S 35 C4
Josselin F 56 C3
Jøssund N 114 C7
Jostedal N 114 F4
Jósvafő H 65 B6
Jou P 87 C3
Jouarre F 59 B4
Joué-lès-Tours F 67 A5
Joué-sur-Erdre F 66 A3
Joure NL 42 C2
Joutseno FIN 3 F28
Joutsijärvi FIN 113 F16
Joux-la-Ville F 59 C4
Jouy F 58 B2
Jouy-le-Châtel F 59 B4
Jouy-le-Potier F 58 C2
Joyeuse F 78 B3
Joze F 68 C3
Józefów PL 55 A6
Juan-les-Pins F 79 C6
Juankoski FIN 3 E28
Juban AL 105 A5
Jübek D 43 A6
Jubera E 89 B4
Jubrique E 99 C5
Jüchsen D 51 C6
Judaberg N 33 C2
Judenburg A 73 A4
Juelsminde DK 39 D3
Jugon-les-Lacs F 56 B3
Juillac F 67 C6
Juillan F 76 C3
Juist D 43 B4
Jukkasjärvi S 112 E9
Jule N 115 C10
Julianadorp NL 42 C1
Julianstown IRL 19 C5
Jülich D 50 C2
Jullouville F 57 B4
Jumeaux F 68 C3
Jumièges F 58 A1
Jumilhac-le-Grand F 67 C6
Jumilla E 101 A4
Juncosa E 90 B3
Juneda E 90 B3
Jung S 35 D5
Jungingen D 61 B5
Junglingster L 60 A2
Juniville F 59 A5
Junosuando S 113 E11
Junqueira P 87 C3
Junsele S 115 D13
Juoksengi S 113 F12
Juoksenki FIN 113 F12
Juprelle B 49 C6
Jurata PL 47 A4
Jurbarkas LT 6 D7
Jurjevo HR 83 B3
Jūrmala LV 6 C7
Juromenha P 93 C3
Jursla S 37 D3
Jussac F 77 B5
Jussey F 60 C1
Jussy F 59 A4
Juta H 74 B2
Jüterbog D 52 B3
Juuka FIN 3 E28
Juvigny-le-Terte F 57 B4
Juvigny-sous-Andaine F 57 B5
Juzennecourt F 59 B5
Jyderup DK 39 D4
Jyväskylä FIN 3 E26

K

Kaamanen FIN 113 C16
Kaamasmukka FIN 113 C15
Kaaresuvanto FIN 113 D11
Kaarssen D 44 B3
Kaatscheuvel NL 49 B6
Kaba H 75 A6
Kåbdalis S 115 A17
Kačarevo SRB 85 B5
Kačikol KOS 85 D6
Kács H 65 C6
Kadan CZ 52 C3
Kadarkút H 74 B2
Kadınhanı TR 119 D7
Kaduy RUS 7 B14
Kåfalla S 37 C2
Kåfjord N 113 C12
Kåfjordbotn N 112 C9
Kågeröd S 41 D3
Kahl D 51 C5
Kahla D 52 C1
Kainach bei Voitsberg A 73 A5
Kaindorf A 73 A5
Kainulasjärvi S 113 F11
Kairala FIN 113 E16
Kaisepakte S 112 D8
Kaisersesch D 50 C3
Kaiserslautern D 60 A3
Kaisheim D 62 B1
Kajaani FIN 3 D27
Kajárpéc H 74 A2
Kajdacs H 74 B3
Kakanj BIH 84 B3
Kakasd H 74 B3
Kaklik TR 119 E4
Kakolewo PL 54 B1
Kál H 65 C6
Kalače MNE 85 D5
Kalajoki FIN 3 D25
Kalak N 113 B16
Kalamata GR 117 E4
Kalambaka GR 116 C3
Kalamria GR 116 B4
Kalandra GR 116 C5
Kälarne S 115 E13
Kalavrita GR 117 D4
Kalbe D 44 C3
Kalce SLO 73 C4
Káld H 74 A2
Kale, *Antalya* TR 119 F4
Kale, *Denizli* TR 119 E3
Kalecik TR 16 A6
Kalefeld D 51 B6
Kalenić SRB 85 C5
Kalesija BIH 84 B3
Kalety PL 54 C3
Kalevala RUS 3 D29
Kalhovd N 32 B5
Kalí HR 83 B4
Kalimnos GR 119 F2
Kaliningrad RUS 47 A6
Kalinkavichy BY 7 E10
Kalinovac HR 74 B2
Kalinovik BIH 84 C3
Kalinovo SK 65 B5
Kalirachi GR 116 B6
Kaliska, *Pomorskie* PL 47 B4
Kaliska, *Pomorskie* PL 47 A4
Kalisko PL 55 B4
Kalisz PL 54 B3
Kalisz Pomorski PL 46 B1
Kalix S 3 D25
Kaljord N 112 D4
Kalkan TR 119 F4
Kalkar D 50 B2
Kalkım TR 118 C2
Kall D 50 C2
Kall S 115 D10
Källby S 35 D5
Källered S 38 B5
Källerstad S 40 B3
Kallinge S 41 C5
Kallmeti i Madh AL 105 B5
Kallmünz D 62 A2
Kallo FIN 113 E13
Kallsedet S 115 D9
Källvik S 37 D4
Kalmar S 40 C6
Kalmthout B 49 B5
Kalná SK 65 B4
Kalo Nero GR 117 E3
Kalocsa H 75 B3
Kalokhorio CY 120 B2
Kaloni GR 116 C8
Káloz H 74 B3
Kals A 72 A2
Kalsdorf A 73 B5
Kaltbrunn CH 70 A4
Kaltenbach A 72 A1
Kaltenkirchen D 44 B1
Kaltennordheim D 51 C6
Kaluga RUS 7 D14
Kalundborg DK 39 D4
Kalush UA 11 B8
Kałuszyn PL 55 A6
Kalv S 40 B3
Kalvåg N 114 F1
Kalvehave DK 41 D2
Kalwang A 73 A4
Kalwaria-Zebrzydowska PL 65 A5
Kalyazin RUS 7 C14
Kam H 74 A1
Kaman TR 16 B6
Kamares GR 117 F6
Kambos CY 120 A1
Kamen D 50 B3
Kamenice CZ 64 A1
Kamenice nad Lipou CZ 63 A6
Kameničná SK 64 C4
Kamenný Most SK 65 C4
Kamenny Ujezd CZ 63 B5
Kamenska HR 74 C2
Kamensko HR 84 C1
Kamenz D 53 B4
Kamičak BIH 84 B1
Kamień PL 55 B5
Kamień Krajeński PL 46 B3
Kamień Pomorski PL 45 B6
Kamieniec Zabk PL 54 C1
Kamienka SK 65 A6
Kamienna Góra PL 53 C6
Kamieńsk PL 55 B4
Kaminka UA 11 B12
Kamiros Skala GR 119 F2
Kamnik SLO 73 B4
Kamp-Lintfort D 50 B2
Kampen NL 42 C2
Kampinos PL 55 A5
Kampor HR 83 B3
Kamyanets-Podil's'kyy UA 11 B9
Kamyanka-Buz'ka UA 11 A8
Kamýk nad Vltavou CZ 63 A5
Kanal SLO 72 B3
Kanalia GR 116 C4
Kandalaksha RUS 3 C30
Kandanos GR 117 G5
Kandel D 61 A4
Kandern D 60 C3
Kandersteg CH 70 B2
Kandila GR 117 E4
Kandıra TR 118 A5
Kandyty PL 47 A6
Kanfanar HR 82 A2
Kangasala FIN 3 F26
Kangos S 113 E11
Kangosjärvi FIN 113 E12
Kaninë AL 105 C5
Kaniów PL 53 B4
Kanjiža SRB 75 B5
Kankaanpää FIN 3 F25
Kannus FIN 3 E25
Kanturk IRL 20 B3
Kaonik SRB 85 C6
Kapaklı TR 118 A2
Kapellen A 63 C6
Kapellen B 49 B5
Kapellskär S 37 C6
Kapfenberg A 73 A5
Kapfenstein A 73 B5
Kaplice CZ 63 B5
Kapljuh BIH 83 B5
Kápolna H 65 C6
Kápolnásnyék H 74 A3
Kaposfő H 74 B2
Kaposfüred H 74 B2
Kaposszekcsö H 74 B3
Kaposvár H 74 B2
Kapp N 34 B2
Kappel D 60 B3
Kappeln D 44 A1
Kappelshamn S 37 E5
Kappl A 71 A5
Kappstad S 35 C5
Kaprun A 72 A2
Kaptol HR 74 C2
Kapuvár H 64 C3
Karaadilli TR 119 D5
Karabiğa TR 118 B2
Karabük TR 118 A7
Karaburun TR 118 D1
Karacabey TR 118 B3
Karacaköy TR 118 A3
Karacaören TR 119 D5
Karacasu TR 119 E3
Karachev RUS 7 E13
Karácsond H 65 C6
Karád H 74 B2
Karahallı TR 119 D4
Karaisali TR 16 C7
Karaman, *Balıkesir* TR 118 C3
Karaman, *Karaman* TR 16 C6
Karamanlı TR 119 E4
Karamürsel TR 118 B4
Karan SRB 85 C4
Karancslapujto H 65 B5
Karaova TR 119 E2
Karapınar TR 16 C6
Karasjok N 113 C14
Karasu TR 118 A5
Karataş, *Adana* TR 16 C7
Karataş, *Manisa* TR 119 D3
Karatoprak TR 119 E2
Karavostasi CY 120 A1
Karbenning S 36 B3
Kårberg S 37 D1
Kårböle S 115 F12
Karbunara AL 105 C5
Karby D 44 A1
Karby DK 38 C1
Kårby, *Kalmar* S 40 B6
Karby, *Stockholm* S 37 C5
Karcag H 75 A5
Karczew PL 55 A6
Karczów PL 54 C2
Karczowiska PL 53 B6
Kardamena GR 119 F2
Kardamila GR 116 D8
Kardamili GR 117 F4
Kardašova Rečice CZ 63 A5
Kardis S 113 F12
Karditsa GR 116 C3
Kärdla EST 6 B7
Kardoskút H 75 B5
Karesuando S 113 D11
Kargı TR 16 A7
Kargowa PL 53 A5
Karigasniemi FIN 113 C14
Karise DK 41 D2
Karistos GR 117 D6
Karkkila FIN 6 A8
Karl Liebknecht RUS 7 F13
Karlholmsbruk S 36 B4
Karlino PL 46 A1
Karlobag HR 83 B4
Karlovac HR 73 C5
Karlovasi GR 119 E1
Karlovčic SRB 85 B5
Karlovice CZ 54 C2
Karlovo BG 11 E8
Karlovy Vary CZ 52 C2
Karłowice PL 54 C2
Karlsborg S 37 D1
Karlshamn S 41 C4
Karlshöfen D 43 B6
Karlshus N 35 C2
Karlskoga S 37 C1
Karlskrona S 41 C5
Karlsrud N 32 B5
Karlsruhe D 61 A4
Karlstad S 35 C5
Karlstadt D 51 D5
Karlstetten A 63 B6
Karlstift A 63 B5
Karlstorp S 40 B5
Karmacs H 74 B2
Karmin PL 54 B2
Kärna S 38 B4
Karnobat BG 11 E9
Karojba HR 72 C3
Karow D 44 B4

Kongsvik N 112 D5
Kongsvinger N 34 B4
Konice CZ 64 A2
Konie PL 55 B5
Koniecpol PL 55 C4
Königs Wusterhausen D 52 A3
Königsberg D 51 C6
Königsbronn D 61 B6
Königsbrück D 53 B3
Königsbrunn D 62 B1
Konigsdorf D 62 C2
Königsee D 52 C1
Königshorst D 45 C4
Königslutter D 51 A6
Königssee D 62 C3
Königstein, *Hessen* D 51 C4
Königstein, *Sachsen* D 53 C4
Königstetten A 64 B2
Königswartha D 53 B4
Konigswiesen A 63 B5
Königswinter D 50 C3
Konin PL 54 A3
Konispol AL 116 C2
Konitsa GR 116 B2
Köniz CH 70 B2
Konjevići BIH 85 B4
Konjevrate HR 83 C5
Konjic BIH 84 C2
Konjščina HR 73 B6
Könnern D 52 B1
Konnerud N 35 C2
Konopiska PL 54 C3
Konotop PL 53 B5
Konotop UA 7 F12
Końskie PL 55 B5
Konsmo N 33 D4
Konstancin-Jeziorna PL 55 A6
Konstantynów Łódźki PL 55 B4
Konstanz D 61 C5
Kontich B 49 B5
Kontiolahti FIN 3 E28
Konya TR 119 E7
Konz D 60 A2
Kópasker IS 111 A9
Kópavogur IS 111 C4
Kopčany SK 64 B3
Koper SLO 72 C3
Kopervik N 33 C2
Kópháza H 64 C2
Kopice PL 54 C2
Kopidlno CZ 53 C5
Köping S 37 C2
Köpingebro S 41 D3
Köpingsvik S 41 C6
Koplik AL 105 A5
Köpmanholmen S 115 D15
Koppang N 34 A3
Koppangen N 112 C9
Kopparberg S 36 C1
Koppelo FIN 113 D16
Koppom S 35 C4
Koprivlen BG 116 A5
Koprivna BIH 84 B3
Koprivnica HR 74 B1
Kopřivnice CZ 64 A4
Köprübaşı TR 118 D3
Koprzywnica PL 55 C6
Kopstal L 60 A2
Kopychyntsi UA 11 B8
Kopytkowo PL 47 B4
Korbach D 51 B4
Körbecke D 50 B4
Korçë AL 116 B2
Korčula HR 84 D2
Korczyców PL 53 A4
Korenevo RUS 7 F13
Korenita SRB 85 B4
Korets UA 11 A9
Korfantów PL 54 C2
Körfez TR 118 B4
Korgen N 115 A10
Korinth DK 39 D3
Korinthos = Corinth GR 117 E4
Korita BIH 83 B5
Korita HR 84 D2
Korithi GR 117 E2
Korkuteli TR 119 E5
Körmend H 74 A1
Korne PL 46 A3
Korneuburg A 64 B2
Kornevo RUS 47 A6
Kórnik PL 54 A2
Kornsjø N 35 D3
Környe H 74 A3
Koromačno HR 82 B3
Koroni GR 117 F3
Koronos GR 117 E7
Koronowo PL 46 B3
Körösladány H 75 B6
Köröstarcsa H 75 B6
Korosten UA 11 A10
Korostyshev UA 11 A10
Korpilombolo S 113 F12
Korsberga, *Jönköping* S 40 B5
Korsberga, *Skaraborg* S 35 D6
Korshavn N 35 C2
Korskrogen S 115 F12
Korsnäs S 36 B2
Korsør DK 39 D4
Korsun Shevchenkovskiy UA 11 B11
Kortrijk B 49 C4
Korucu TR 118 C2
Koryčany CZ 64 A3
Koryukovka UA 7 F12
Korzeńsko PL 54 B1
Korzybie PL 46 A2
Kos GR 119 F2
Kosakowo PL 47 A4
Kosanica MNE 85 C4
Kosaya Gora RUS 7 D14
Kösching D 62 B2
Kościan PL 54 A1
Kościelec PL 54 A3
Kościerzyna PL 46 A3
Koserow D 45 A5
Košetice CZ 63 A6
Košice SK 10 B6
Kosjerić SRB 85 C4
Koška HR 74 C3
Koskullskulle S 112 E9
Kosovska Mitrovica KOS 85 D5
Kosta S 40 C5
Kostajnica HR 74 C1
Kostajnik SRB 85 B4
Kostanica MNE 105 A5
Kostanjevica SLO 73 C5
Kostelec na Hané CZ 64 A3
Kostelec nad Černými Lesy CZ 53 D4
Kostice CZ 53 C3
Kostkowo PL 47 A4
Kostojevići SRB 85 B4
Kostolac SRB 85 B6
Kostomłoty PL 54 B1
Kostopil UA 11 A9
Kostów PL 54 B3
Kostrzyn, *Lubuskie* PL 45 C6
Kostrzyn, *Wielkopolskie* PL 46 C3
Koszalin PL 46 A2
Koszęcin PL 54 C3
Kőszeg H 74 A1
Koszwaly PL 47 A4
Koszyce PL 55 C5
Kot SLO 73 C5
Kotala FIN 113 E17
Kotë AL 105 C5
Kötelek H 75 A5
Köthen D 52 B1
Kotka FIN 7 A9
Kotomierz PL 47 B4
Kotor MNE 105 A4
Kotor Varoš BIH 84 B2
Kotoriba HR 74 B1
Kotorsko BIH 84 B3
Kotovsk UA 11 C10
Kotraža SRB 85 C5
Kotronas GR 117 F4
Kötschach A 72 B2
Kötzting D 62 A3
Koudum NL 42 C2
Kouřim CZ 53 C4
Kout na Šumave CZ 62 A4
Kouvola FIN 3 F27
Kovačevac SRB 85 B5
Kovačica SRB 85 A5
Kovdor RUS 3 C29
Kovel' UA 11 A8
Kovilj SRB 75 C5
Kovin SRB 85 B5
Kovren MNE 85 C4
Kowal PL 47 C5
Kowalewo Pomorskie PL 47 B4
Kowalów PL 45 C6
Kowary PL 53 C5
Köyceğiz TR 119 F3
Kozan TR 16 C7
Kozani GR 116 B3
Kozarac BIH 84 B1
Kozarac HR 73 C5
Kozárovce SK 65 B4
Kozelets UA 11 A11
Kozelsk RUS 7 D13
Kozica HR 84 C2
Koziegłowy PL 55 C4
Kozienice PL 55 B6
Kozina SLO 72 C3
Kozje SLO 73 B5
Kozlu TR 118 A6
Kozluk BIH 85 B4
Koźmin PL 54 B2
Koźminek PL 54 B3
Kozolupy CZ 63 A4
Kożuchów PL 53 B5
Kožuhe BIH 84 B3
Kozyatyn UA 11 B10
Kozyürük TR 118 A1
Krackow D 45 B6
Kraddsele S 115 B13
Krąg PL 46 A2
Kragenæs DK 39 E4
Kragerø N 33 D6
Krągi PL 46 B2
Kragujevac SRB 85 B5
Kraiburg D 62 B3
Krajenka PL 46 B2
Krajišnik SRB 75 C5
Krajková CZ 52 C2
Krajné SK 64 B3
Krajnik Dolny PL 45 B6
Krakača BIH 83 A4
Kräklingbo S 37 E5
Kraków = Cracow PL 55 C4
Krakow am See D 44 B4
Králíky CZ 54 C1
Kraljevica HR 73 C4
Kraljevo SRB 85 C5
Kráľov Brod SK 64 B3
Kral'ovany SK 65 A5
Kralovice CZ 52 D3
Kralupy nad Vltavou CZ 53 C4
Králův Dvůr CZ 63 A5
Kramfors S 115 E14
Kramsach A 72 A1
Kramsk PL 54 A3
Kråmvik N 32 C5
Kranenburg D 50 B2
Krania GR 116 C3
Krania Elasonas GR 116 C4
Kranichfeld D 52 C1
Kranidi GR 117 E5
Kranj SLO 73 B4
Kranjska Gora SLO 72 B3
Krapanj HR 83 C4
Krapina HR 73 B5
Krapje HR 74 C1
Krapkowice PL 54 C2
Kraselov CZ 63 A4
Krašić HR 73 C5
Krāslava LV 7 D9
Kraslice CZ 52 C2
Krasna PL 55 B5
Krasna Lipa CZ 53 C4
Kraśnik PL 11 A7
Krašnja SLO 73 B4
Krásno SK 65 A4
Krasno Polje HR 83 B4
Krásnohorské Podhradie SK 65 B6
Krasnozavodsk RUS 7 C15
Krasnystaw PL 11 A7
Krasnyy RUS 7 D11
Krasnyy Kholm RUS 7 B14
Krasocin PL 55 C5
Kraszewice PL 54 B3
Kraszkowice PL 54 B3
Kratigos GR 118 C1
Kraubath A 73 A4
Krausnick D 53 A3
Krautheim D 61 A5
Kravaře, *Severočeský* CZ 53 C4
Kravaře, *Severomoravsky* CZ 64 A4
Kravarsko HR 73 C6
Kraznějov CZ 63 A4
Krčedin SRB 75 C5
Krefeld D 50 B2
Kregme DK 39 D5
Krembz D 44 B3
Kremenchuk UA 11 B12
Kremenets UA 11 A8
Kremmen D 45 C5
Kremna SRB 85 C4
Kremnica SK 65 B4
Krempe D 43 B6
Krems A 63 B6
Kremsbrücke A 72 B3
Kremsmünster A 63 B5
Křemže CZ 63 B5
Křenov CZ 64 A2
Krepa PL 54 B3
Krępa Krajeńska PL 46 B2
Krepsko PL 46 B2
Kreševo BIH 84 C3
Kressbronn D 61 C5
Krestena GR 117 E3
Kretinga LT 6 D6
Krettsy RUS 7 B12
Kreuth D 62 C2
Kreuzau D 50 C2
Kreuzlingen CH 61 C5
Kreuztal D 50 C3
Krewelin D 45 C5
Krezluk BIH 84 B2
Krieglach A 73 A5
Kriegsfeld D 60 A3
Kriens CH 70 A3
Krimml A 72 A2
Krimpen aan de IJssel NL 49 B5
Křinec CZ 53 C5
Kristdala S 40 B6
Kristiansand N 33 D5
Kristianstad S 41 C4
Kristiansund N 114 D4
Kristiinankaupunki FIN 3 E24
Kristinefors S 34 B4
Kristinehamn S 35 C6
Kriváň SK 65 B5
Křivoklát CZ 53 C3
Krivoy Rog = Kryvyy Rih UA 11 C12
Križ HR 74 C1
Křižanov CZ 64 A2
Križevci HR 74 B1
Krk HR 83 A3
Krka SLO 73 C4
Krnjača SRB 85 B5
Krnjak HR 73 C5
Krnjeuša BIH 83 B5
Krnjevo SRB 85 B6
Krnov CZ 54 C2
Krobia PL 54 B1
Kroczyce PL 55 C4
Krøderen N 34 B1
Krokees GR 117 F4
Krokek S 37 D3
Krokom S 115 D11
Krokowa PL 47 A4
Krokstad-elva N 34 C1
Kroksund N 35 C3
Krolevets UA 7 F12
Kroměříž CZ 64 A3
Krommenie NL 42 C1
Krompachy SK 65 B6
Kromy RUS 7 E13
Kronach D 52 C1
Kronshagen D 44 A2
Kronshtadt RUS 7 B10
Kröpelin D 44 A3
Kropp D 43 A6
Kroppenstedt D 52 B1
Kropstädt D 52 B2
Krościenko nad Dunajcem PL 65 A6
Kröslin D 45 A5
Krośnice PL 54 B2
Krośniewice PL 55 A4
Krosno PL 10 B6
Krosno Odrzańskie PL 53 A5
Krostitz D 52 B2
Krotoszyn PL 54 B2
Krottendorf A 73 A5
Krouna CZ 64 A2
Krowiarki PL 54 C3
Krrabë AL 105 B5
Kršan HR 73 C4
Krško SLO 73 C5
Krstac MNE 84 C3
Krstur SRB 75 B5
Křtiny CZ 64 A2
Kruft D 50 C3
Kruishoutem B 49 C4
Krujë AL 105 B5
Krulyewshchyna BY 7 D9
Krumbach A 73 A6
Krumbach D 61 B6
Krumovgrad BG 116 A7
Krün D 71 A6
Krupá CZ 53 C3
Krupa na Vrbasu BIH 84 B2
Krupanj SRB 85 B4
Krupina SK 65 B5
Krupka CZ 53 C3
Krupki BY 7 D10
Kruså DK 39 E2
Krušćica BIH 84 B2
Kruševac SRB 85 C6
Kruševo MK 116 A3
Kruszwica PL 47 C4
Kruszyn PL 47 C5
Krute MNE 105 A5
Krychaw BY 7 E11
Krynica PL 65 A6
Krynica Morska PL 47 A5
Kryvyy Rih = Krivoy Rog UA 11 C12
Krzęcin PL 46 B1
Krzelów PL 54 B1
Krzepice PL 54 C3
Krzepielów PL 53 B6
Krzeszowice PL 55 C4
Krzeszyce PL 45 C7
Krzynowłaga Mała PL 47 B6
Krzywiń PL 54 B1
Krzyż Wielkopolski PL 46 C2
Krzyżanowice PL 54 D3
Krzyżowa PL 65 A5
Ksiaz Wielkopolski, *Małopolskie* PL 55 C5
Książ Wielkopolski, *Wielkopolskie* PL 54 A2
Ktębowiec PL 46 B2
Kübekháza H 75 B5
Küblis CH 71 B4
Kuç AL 105 C5
Kuchary PL 54 B2
Kuchl A 63 C4
Kucice PL 47 C6
Kuciste HR 84 D2
Kućište KOS 85 D5
Kuçovë AL 105 C5
Küçükbahçe TR 118 D1
Küçükköy TR 118 C1
Küçükkuyu TR 118 C1
Kucura SRB 75 C4
Kuczbork-Osada PL 47 B6
Kuddby S 37 D3
Kudowa-Zdrój PL 53 C6
Kufstein A 62 C3
Kuggeboda S 41 C5
Kuggörana S 115 F14
Kühbach D 62 B2
Kuhmo FIN 3 D28
Kuhmoinen FIN 3 F26
Kuhnsdorf A 73 B4
Kuhstedt D 43 B5
Kuinre NL 42 C2
Kuivastu EST 6 B7
Kukës AL 10 E6
Kuklin PL 47 B6
Kukljica HR 83 B4
Kukujevci SRB 85 A4
Kula, *Srbija* SRB 85 B6
Kula, *Vojvodina* SRB 75 C4
Kula TR 119 D3
Kuldīga LV 6 C6
Kulen Vakuf BIH 83 B5
Kulina BIH 84 B3
Kullstedt D 51 B6
Kulmain D 62 A2
Kulmbach D 52 C1
Kulu TR 16 B6
Kumafşarı TR 119 E4
Kumane SRB 75 C5
Kumanovo MK 10 E6
Kumbağ TR 118 B2
Kumdanlı TR 119 D5
Kumkale TR 118 C1
Kumla S 37 C2
Kumlakyrkby S 36 C3
Kumlinge FIN 36 B7
Kumluca TR 119 F5
Kumrovec HR 73 B5
Kunadacs H 75 B4
Kunágota H 75 B6
Kunbaja H 75 B4
Kunda EST 7 B9
Kundl A 72 A1
Kunes N 113 B15
Kunfehértó H 75 B4
Kungälv S 38 B4
Kungs-Husby S 37 C4
Kungsängen S 37 C4
Kungsäter S 40 B2
Kungsbacka S 38 B5
Kungsgården S 36 B3
Kungshamn S 35 D3
Kungsör S 37 C3
Kunhegyes H 75 A5
Kunmadaras H 75 A5
Kunovice CZ 64 A3
Kunów PL 55 C6
Kunowo, *Wielkopolskie* PL 54 B2
Kunowo, *Zachodnio-Pomorskie* PL 45 B6
Kunštát CZ 64 A2
Kunszállás H 75 B4
Kunszentmárton H 75 B5
Kunszentmiklós H 75 A4
Kunžak CZ 63 A6
Künzelsau D 61 A5
Kuolayarvi RUS 113 F18
Kuopio FIN 3 E27
Kuosku FIN 113 E17
Kup H 74 A2
Kup PL 54 C2
Kupa H 65 B6
Kupari HR 84 D3
Kupci SRB 85 C6
Kupferzell D 61 A5
Kupinec HR 73 C5
Kupinečki Kraljevac HR 73 C5
Kupinovo SRB 85 B5
Kupirovo HR 83 B5
Kupjak HR 73 C4
Kuppenheim D 61 B4
Kupres BIH 84 C2
Küps D 52 C1
Kurbnesh AL 105 B6
Kurd H 74 B3
Kŭrdzhali BG 116 A7
Küre TR 16 A6
Kuressaare EST 6 B7
Kurikka FIN 3 E25
Kuřim CZ 64 A2
Kuřivody CZ 53 C4
Kurki PL 47 B6
Kurort Oberwiesenthal D 52 C2
Kurort Schmalkalden D 51 C6
Kurort Stolberg D 51 B6
Kurort Wippra D 52 B1
Kurów PL 11 A7
Kurowice PL 55 B4
Kurravaara S 112 E9
Kursk RUS 7 F14
Kursu FIN 113 F17
Kuršumlija SRB 85 C6
Kuršumlijska Banja SRB 85 C6
Kurşunlu, *Bursa* TR 118 B4
Kurşunlu, *Çankırı* TR 16 A6
Kurtakko FIN 113 E13
Kürten D 50 B3
Kurucaşile TR 16 A6
Kurzelów PL 55 C4
Kusadak SRB 85 B5
Kuşadası TR 119 E2
Kusel D 60 A3
Kusey D 44 C3
Küsnacht CH 70 A3
Kütahya TR 118 C4
Kutenholz D 43 B6
Kutina HR 74 C1
Kutjevo HR 74 C2
Kutná Hora CZ 53 D5
Kutno PL 55 A4
Kuttara FIN 113 D15
Küttingen CH 70 A3
Kúty SK 64 B3
Kuusamo FIN 3 D28
Kuusankoski FIN 3 F27
Kuvshinovo RUS 7 C13
Kuyucak TR 119 E3
Kuzmin SRB 85 A4
Kuźnia Raciborska PL 54 C3
Kuźnica Czarnkowska PL 46 C2
Kuźnica Żelichowska PL 46 C2
Kvænangsbotn N 113 C11
Kværndrup DK 39 D3
Kvaløysletta N 112 C7
Kvalsund N 113 B12
Kvam, *Nord-Trøndelag* N 114 C8
Kvam, *Oppland* N 114 F6
Kvamsøy N 32 A3
Kvanndal N 32 B3
Kvänum S 35 D5
Kvås N 33 D4
Kvasice CZ 64 A3
Kvelde N 35 C1
Kvenna N 114 E5
Kvernaland N 33 D2
Kvibille S 40 C2
Kvicksund S 37 C3
Kvidinge S 41 C3
Kvikkjokk S 112 F6
Kvikne N 114 E7
Kvilda CZ 63 A4
Kville S 35 D3
Kvillsfors S 40 B5
Kvinesdal N 33 D3
Kvinlog N 33 D3
Kvinnherad N 32 C3
Kvissel DK 38 B3
Kvissleby S 115 E14
Kviteseid N 33 C5
Kvitsøy N 33 C2
Kwakowo PL 46 A3
Kwidzyn PL 47 B4
Kwilcz PL 46 C2
Kyjov CZ 64 B3
Kyle of Lochalsh GB 22 D3
Kyleakin GB 22 D3
Kylerhea GB 22 D3
Kylestrome GB 22 C3
Kyllburg D 50 C2
Kyllini GR 117 E3
Kynšperk nad Ohří CZ 52 C2
Kyperounda CY 120 B1
Kyrenia CY 120 A2
Kyritz D 44 C4
Kyrkesund S 38 A4
Kyrkhult S 41 C4
Kyrksæterøra N 114 D6
Kysucké Nové Mesto SK 65 A4
Kythira GR 117 F4
Kythréa CY 120 A2
Kyustendil BG 11 E7
Kyyiv = Kiev UA 11 A11
Kyyjärvi FIN 3 E26

L

La Adrada E 94 B2
La Alameda E 100 A2
La Alberca E 93 A4
La Alberca de Záncara E 95 C4
La Albergueria de Argañán E 93 A4
La Albuera E 93 C4
La Aldea del Portillo del Busto E 89 B3
La Algaba E 99 B4
La Aliseda de Tormes E 93 A5
La Almarcha E 95 C4
La Almolda E 90 B2
La Almunia de Doña Godina E 89 C5
La Antillas E 98 B3
La Arena E 86 A4
La Aulaga E 99 B4
La Balme-de-Sillingy F 69 C6
La Bañeza E 88 B1
La Barca de la Florida E 99 C5
La Barre-de-Monts F 66 B2
La Barre-en-Ouche F 58 B1
La Barrosa E 99 C4
La Barthe-de-Neste F 77 C3
La Bassée F 48 C3
La Bastide-de-Sèrou F 77 C4
La Bastide-des-Jourdans F 79 C4
La Bastide-Puylaurent F 78 B2
La Bathie F 69 C6
La Baule-Escoublac F 66 A2
La Bazoche-Gouet F 58 B1
La Bégude-de-Mazenc F 78 B3
La Bernerie-en-Retz F 66 A2
La Bisbal d'Empordà E 91 B6
La Boissière F 57 A6
La Bourboule F 68 C2
La Bóveda de Toro E 88 C1
La Brède F 76 B2
La Bresse F 60 B2
La Bridoire F 69 C5
La Brillanne F 79 C4
La Bruffière F 66 A3
La Bussière F 58 C3
La Caillère F 66 B4
La Caletta, *Cágliari* I 110 C1
La Caletta, *Núoro* I 110 B2
La Calmette F 78 C3
La Calzada de Oropesa E 93 B5
La Campana E 99 B5
La Cañada E 94 B2
La Canourgue F 78 B2
La Capelle F 49 D4
La Cardanchosa E 99 A5
La Caridad E 86 A4
La Carlota E 100 B1
La Carolina E 100 A2
La Cava E 90 C3
La Cavalerie F 78 B2
La Celle-en-Moravan F 69 A4
La Celle-St. Avant F 67 A5
La Cerca E 89 B3
La Chaise-Dieu F 68 C3
La Chaize-Giraud F 66 B3
La Chaize-le-Vicomte F 66 B3
La Chambre F 69 C6
La Chapelaude F 68 B2
La Chapelle-d'Angillon F 68 A2
La Chapelle-en-Aalgaudémar F 79 B5
La Chapelle-en-Vercors F 79 B4
La Chapelle-Glain F 57 C4
La Chapelle-la-Reine F 58 B3
La Chapelle-Laurent F 68 C3
La Chapelle-St. Luc F 59 B5
La Chapelle-sur-Erdre F 66 A3
La Chapelle-Vicomtesse F 58 C2
La Charce F 79 B4
La Charité-sur-Loire F 68 A3
La Chartre-sur-le-Loir F 58 C1
La Châtaigneraie F 67 B4
La Châtre F 68 B1
La Chaussée-sur-Marne F 59 B5
La Chaux-de-Fonds CH 70 A1
La Cheppe F 59 A5
La Chèze F 56 B3
La Ciotat F 79 C4
La Clayette F 69 B4
La Clusaz F 69 C6
La Codosera E 93 B3
La Concha E 88 A3
La Condamine-Châtelard F 79 B5
La Contienda E 99 A4
La Coquille F 67 C5
La Coronada E 93 C5
La Côte-St. André F 69 C5
La Cotinière F 66 C3
La Courtine F 68 C2
La Crau F 79 C5
La Crèche F 67 B4
La Croix F 67 A5
La Croix-Valmer F 79 C5
La Cumbre E 93 B5
La Douze F 77 A3
La Espina E 86 A4
La Estrella E 94 C1
La Farga de Moles E 91 A4
La Fatarella E 90 B3
La Felipa E 95 C5
La Fère F 59 A4
La Ferrière, *Indre-et-Loire* F 58 C1
La Ferrière, *Vendée* F 66 B3
La Ferrière-en-Parthenay F 67 B4
La-Ferté-Alais F 58 B3
La Ferté-Bernard F 58 B1
La Ferté-Frênel F 58 B1
La Ferté-Gaucher F 59 B4
La Ferté-Imbault F 68 A1
La Ferté-Macé F 57 B5
La Ferté-Milon F 59 A4
La Ferté-St. Aubin F 58 C2
La Ferté-St.Cyr F 58 C2
La Ferté-sous-Jouarre F 59 B4
La Ferté-Vidame F 58 B1
La Ferté Villeneuil F 58 C2
La Feuillie F 58 A2
La Flèche F 57 C5
La Flotte F 66 B3
La Font de la Figuera E 101 A5
La Fouillade F 77 B5
La Fregeneda E 87 D4
La Fresneda E 90 C3
La Fuencubierta E 99 B6
La Fuente de San Esteban E 87 D4
La Fulioala E 91 B4
La Gacilly F 57 C3
La Galera E 90 C3
La Garde-Freinet F 79 C5
La Garnache F 66 B3
La Garriga E 91 B5
La Garrovilla E 93 C4
La Gaubretière F 66 B3
La Gineta E 95 C4
La Granadella, *Alicante* E 96 C3
La Granadella, *Lleida* E 90 B3
La Grand-Combe F 78 B3
La Grande-Croix F 69 C4
La Grande-Motte F 78 C3
La Granja d'Escarp E 90 B3
La Granjuela E 93 C5
La Grave F 79 A5
La Gravelle F 57 B4
La Guardia E 95 C3
La Guardia de Jaén E 100 B2
La Guerche-de-Bretagne F 57 C4
La Guerche-sur-l'Aubois F 68 B2
La Guérinière F 66 B2
La Haba E 93 C5
La Haye-du-Puits F 57 A4
La Haye-Pesnel F 57 B4
La Herlière F 48 C3
La Hermida E 88 A2
La Herrera E 95 D4
La Higuera E 101 A4
La Hiniesta E 88 C1
La Horcajada E 93 A5
La Horra E 88 C3
La Hulpe B 49 C5
La Hutte F 57 B6
La Iglesuela E 94 B2
La Iglesuela del Cid E 90 C2
La Iruela E 100 B3
La Javie F 79 B5
La Jonchère-St. Maurice F 67 B6
La Jonquera E 91 A5
La Lantejuela E 99 B5
La Línea de la Concepción E 99 C5
La Llacuna E 91 B4
La Londe-les-Maures F 79 C5
La Loupe F 58 B2
La Louvière B 49 C5
La Luisiana E 99 B5
La Machine F 68 B3
la Maddalena I 110 A2
La Mailleraye-sur-Seine F 58 A1
La Malène F 78 B2
La Mamola E 100 C2
La Manresana dels Prats E 91 B4
La Masadera E 90 B2
La Mata E 94 C2

le Prese I 71 B5
Le Puy-en-Velay F 78 A2
Le Puy-Ste. Réparade F 79 C4
Le Quesnoy F 49 C4
Le Rayol F 79 C5
Le Rœulx B 49 C5
Le Rouget F 77 B5
Le Rozier F 78 B2
Le Russey F 70 A1
Le Sel-de-Bretagne F 57 C4
Le Sentier CH 69 B6
Le Souquet F 76 C1
Le Teil F 78 B3
Le Teilleul F 57 B5
Le Temple-de-Bretagne F 66 A3
Le Theil F 58 B1
Le Thillot F 60 C2
Le Touquet-Paris-Plage F 48 C2
Le Touvet F 69 C5
Le Translay F 48 D2
Le Tréport F 48 C2
Le Val F 79 C5
Le Val-André F 56 B3
Le Val-d'Ajol F 60 C2
Le Verdon-sur-Mer F 66 C3
Le Vernet F 79 B5
Le Vigan F 78 C2
le Ville I 82 C1
Le Vivier-sur-Mer F 57 B4
Lea GB 27 B5
Leadburn GB 25 C4
Leadhills GB 25 C4
Leap IRL 20 C2
Leatherhead GB 31 C3
Łeba PL 46 A3
Lebach D 60 A2
Lebedyn UA 7 F13
Lebekke B 49 B5
Lébény H 64 C3
Łebno PL 47 A4
Leboreiro E 87 B3
Lębork PL 46 A3
Lebrija E 99 C4
Lebring A 73 B5
Lebus D 45 C6
Lebusa D 52 B3
Leca da Palmeira P 87 C2
Lecce I 105 C4
Lecco I 71 C4
Lécera E 90 B2
Lećevica HR 83 C5
Lech A 71 A5
Lechbruck D 62 C1
Lechena GR 117 E3
Lechlade GB 29 B6
Lechovice CZ 64 B2
Leciñena E 90 B2
Leck D 39 E1
Lectoure F 77 C3
Łęczyca, *Łódzkie* PL 55 A4
Łęczyca, *Zachodnio-Pomorskie* PL 45 B7
Ledaña E 95 C5
Ledbury GB 29 A5
Lede B 49 C4
Ledeč nad Sazavou CZ 63 A6
Ledenice CZ 63 B5
Ledesma E 87 C4
Lédignan F 78 C3
Lédigos E 88 B2
Ledmore GB 22 C4
Lednice CZ 64 B2
Lednicke-Rovné SK 64 A4
Lędyczek PL 46 B2
Lędziny PL 55 C4
Leeds GB 27 B4
Leek GB 26 B3
Leek NL 42 B3
Leenaun IRL 18 C2
Leens NL 42 B3
Leer D 43 B4
Leerdam NL 49 B6
Leerhafe D 43 B4
Leese D 43 C6
Leeuwarden NL 42 B2
Leezen D 44 B2
Lefka CY 120 A1
Lefkada GR 116 D2
Lefkimis GR 116 C2
Lefkoniko CY 120 A2
Leganés E 94 B3
Legau D 61 C6
Legbąd PL 46 B3
Legé F 66 B3
Lège-Cap-Ferret F 76 B1
Legionowo PL 55 A5
Léglise B 60 A1
Legnago I 71 C6
Legnano I 70 C3
Legnaro I 72 C1
Legnica PL 53 B6
Łęgowo PL 47 A4
Legrad HR 74 B1
Léguevin F 77 C4
Legutiano E 89 B4
Lehesten D 52 C1
Lehnice SK 64 B3
Lehnin D 52 A2
Lehrberg D 61 A6
Lehre D 51 A6
Lehrte D 44 C1
Lehsen D 44 B3
Leibnitz A 73 B5
Leicester GB 30 B2
Leiden NL 49 A5
Leidschendam NL 49 A5
Leigh GB 26 B3
Leighlinbridge IRL 21 B5
Leighton Buzzard GB 31 C3
Leignon B 49 C6
Leikanger N 114 E2
Leimen D 61 A4
Leinefelde D 51 B6
Leinesfjord N 112 E4
Leintwardine GB 29 A5
Leipojärvi S 112 E10
Leipzig D 52 B2
Leira, *Nordland* N 115 A10
Leira, *Oppland* N 32 B6
Leirámoen N 112 F3
Leiria P 92 B2
Leirvik, *Hordaland* N 32 C2
Leirvik, *Sogn og Fjordane* N 32 A2
Leisach A 72 B2
Leisnig D 52 B2
Leiston GB 30 B5
Leitholm GB 25 C5
Leitrim IRL 18 C3
Leitza E 76 C1
Leitzkau D 52 A1
Lejkowo PL 46 A2
Lekani GR 116 A6
Łękawa PL 55 B4
Łekawica PL 65 A5
Lekbibaj AL 105 A5
Lekeitio E 89 A4
Lekenik HR 73 C6
Lekeryd S 40 B4
Leknes N 112 D2
Łęknica PL 53 B4
Leksand S 36 B1
Leksvik N 114 D7
Lekunberri E 76 C1
Lekvattnet S 34 B4
Lelkowo PL 47 A6
Lelów PL 55 C4
Lelystad NL 42 C2
Lem, *Ringkøbing* DK 39 C1
Lem, *Viborg Amt.* DK 38 C1
Lembach F 60 A3
Lemberg F 60 A3
Lembèye F 76 C2
Lemelerveld NL 42 C3
Lemförde D 43 C5
Lemgo D 51 A4
Lemland FIN 36 B7
Lemmer NL 42 C2
Lempdes F 68 C3
Lemvig DK 38 C1
Lemwerder D 43 B5
Lena N 34 B2
Lenart SLO 73 B5
Lenartovce SK 65 B6
Lenauheim RO 75 C5
Lencloître F 67 B5
Lend A 72 A3
Lendalfoot GB 24 C3
Lendava SLO 73 B6
Lendery RUS 3 E29
Lendinara I 81 A5
Lendorf A 72 B3
Lendum DK 38 B3
Lengefeld D 52 C3
Lengerich, *Niedersachsen* D 43 C4
Lengerich, *Nordrhein-Westfalen* D 50 A3
Lenggries D 62 C2
Lengyeltóti H 74 B2
Lenhovda S 40 C5
Lenk CH 70 B2
Lennartsfors S 35 C3
Lennestadt D 50 B4
Lennoxtown GB 24 C3
Leno I 71 C5
Lénola I 103 B6
Lens B 49 C4
Lens F 48 C3
Lens Lestang F 69 C5
Lensahn D 44 A2
Lensvik N 114 D6
Lentellais E 87 B3
Lentföhrden D 44 B1
Lenti H 74 B1
Lentini I 109 B3
Lenungshammar S 35 C4
Lenzburg CH 70 A3
Lenzen D 44 B3
Lenzerheide CH 71 B4
Leoben A 73 A5
Leogang A 72 A2
Leominster GB 29 A5
León E 88 B1
Léon F 76 C1
Leonberg D 61 B5
Léoncel F 79 B4
Leonding A 63 B5
Leonessa I 102 A5
Leonforte I 109 B3
Leonidio GR 117 E4
Leopoldsburg B 49 B6
Leopoldsdorf im Marchfeld A 64 B2
Leopoldshagen D 45 B5
Leova MD 11 C10
Lepe E 98 B3
Lepenac MNE 85 D5
Lepenac SRB 85 C6
Lepenou GR 116 D3
Lephin GB 22 D2
L'Epine F 79 B4
Lepoglava HR 73 B6
Leppäjärvi FIN 113 D12
Leppävirta FIN 3 E27
Leppin D 44 C3
Lepsény H 74 B3
Léquile I 105 C4
Lercara Friddi I 108 B2
Lerdal S 35 D3
Leré F 68 A2
Lérici I 81 B3
Lerin E 89 B5
Lerm-et-Musset F 76 B2
Lerma E 88 B3
Lermoos A 71 A5
Lérouville F 60 B1
Lerum S 40 B2
Lervik N 35 C2
Lerwick GB 22 A7
Lés E 77 D3
Les Abrets F 69 C5
Les Aix-d'Angillon F 68 A2
Les Ancizes-Comps F 68 C2
Les Andelys F 58 A2
Les Arcs, *Savoie* F 70 C1
Les Arcs, *Var* F 79 C5
Les-Aubiers F 67 B4
Les Baux-de-Provence F 78 C3
Les Bézards F 58 C3
Les Bois CH 70 A1
Les Bordes F 58 C3
Les Borges Blanques E 90 B3
Les Borges del Camp E 91 B4
Les Brunettes F 68 B3
Les Cabannes F 77 D4
Les Contamines-Montjoie F 70 C1
les Coves de Vinroma E 90 C3
Les Déserts F 69 C5
Les Deux-Alpes F 79 B5
Les Diablerets CH 70 B2
Les Echelles F 69 C5
Les Escaldes AND 91 A4
Les Essarts F 66 B3
Les Estables F 78 B3
Les Eyzies-de-Tayac F 77 B4
Les Gets F 70 B1
Les Grandes-Ventes F 58 A2
Les Haudères CH 70 B2
Les Herbiers F 66 B3
Les Hôpitaux-Neufs F 69 B6
Les Lucs-sur-Boulogne F 66 B3
Les Mages F 78 B3
Les Mazures F 59 A5
Les Mées F 79 B4
Les Mureaux F 58 B2
Les Omergues F 79 B4
Les Ormes-sur-Voulzie F 59 B4
Les Orres F 79 B5
Les Pieux F 57 A4
Les Ponts-de-Cé F 67 A4
Les Ponts-de-Martel CH 70 B1
Les Praz F 70 C1
Les Riceys F 59 C5
Les Roches F 69 C4
Les Rosaires F 56 B3
Les Rosiers F 67 A4
Les Rousses F 69 B6
Les Sables-d'Olonne F 66 B3
Les Settons F 68 A4
Les Ternes F 78 A1
Les Thilliers en-Vexin F 58 A2
Les Touches F 66 A3
Les Trois Moûtiers F 67 A5
Les Vans F 78 B3
Les Verrières CH 69 B6
Les Vignes F 78 B2
Lešak KOS 85 C5
Lesaka E 76 C1
Lesbury GB 25 C6
L'Escala E 91 A6
Lescar F 76 C2
L'Escarène F 80 C1
Lesce SLO 73 B4
Lescheraines F 69 C6
Lesconil F 56 C1
Lesdins F 59 A4
Lesično SLO 73 B5
Lésina I 103 B8
Lesjaskog N 114 E5
Lesjöfors S 34 C6
Leskova Dolina SLO 73 C4
Leskovac SRB 10 E6
Leskovec CZ 64 A3
Leskovec SLO 73 C5
Leskovice CZ 63 A6
Leskovik AL 116 B2
Leslie GB 25 B4
Lesmahagow GB 25 C4
Lesmont F 59 B5
Leśna PL 53 B5
Lesneven F 56 B1
Leśnica PL 54 C3
Lešnica SRB 85 B4
Leśniów Wielkoplski PL 53 B5
Lesnoye RUS 7 B13
Lesparre-Médoc F 66 C4
l'Espérance F 59 A4
l'Esperou F 78 B2
Lesponne F 76 C3
L'Espunyola E 91 A4
Lessach A 72 A3
Lessay F 57 A4
Lessebo S 40 C5
Lessines B 49 C4
L'Estany E 91 B5
Lesterps F 67 B5
Leswalt GB 24 D2
Leszno, *Mazowieckie* PL 55 A5
Leszno, *Wielkopolskie* PL 54 B1
Leszno Górne PL 53 B5
Letchworth GB 31 C3
Letenye H 74 B1
Letino I 103 B7
Letohrad CZ 54 C1
Letovice CZ 64 A2
Letschin D 45 C6
Letterfrack IRL 18 C2
Letterkenny IRL 19 B4
Lettermacaward IRL 18 B3
Lettoch GB 23 D5
Letur E 101 A3
Letux E 90 B2
Letzlingen D 44 C3
Leucate F 78 D2
Leuchars GB 25 B5
Leuglay F 59 C5
Leuk CH 70 B2
Leukerbad CH 70 B2
Leumrabhagh GB 22 C2
Leuna D 52 B2
Leusden NL 49 A6
Leutenberg D 52 C1
Leuterschach D 61 C6
Leutershausen D 61 A6
Leutkirch D 61 C6
Leuven B 49 C5
Leuze-en-Hainaut B 49 C4
Levan AL 105 C5
Levanger N 114 D8
Levanjska Varoš HR 74 C3
Lévanto I 80 B3
Levaré F 57 B5
Levata I 71 C5
Leveld N 32 B5
Leven, *East Yorkshire* GB 27 B5
Leven, *Fife* GB 25 B5
Leverano I 105 C3
Leverkusen D 50 B2
Levern D 43 C5
Levet F 68 B2
Levice SK 65 B4
Lévico Terme I 71 B6
Levie F 102 B2
Levier F 69 B6
Lévignen F 59 A3
Levinovac HR 74 C2
Levoča SK 65 A6
Levroux F 67 B6
Lewes GB 31 D4
Lewin Brzeski PL 54 C2
Lewisham GB 31 C3
Leyburn GB 27 A4
Leyland GB 26 B3
Leysdown-on-Sea GB 31 C4
Leysin CH 70 B2
Lezajsk PL 11 A7
Lézardrieux F 56 B2
Lézat-sur-Léze F 77 C4
Lezay F 67 B4
Lezhë AL 105 B5
Lézignan-Corbières F 78 C1
Lezignan-la-Cèbe F 78 C2
Ležimir SRB 75 C4
Lézinnes F 59 C5
Lezoux F 68 C3
Lezuza E 95 D4
Lgov RUS 7 F13
Lhenice CZ 63 B5
Lherm F 77 C4
Lhommaizé F 67 B5
L'Hospitalet F 91 A4
L'Hospitalet de l'Infant E 90 C3
L'Hospitalet de Llobregat E 91 B5
L'Hospitalet-du-Larzac F 78 C2
Lhuître F 59 B5
Liancourt F 58 A3
Liart F 59 A5
Liatorp S 40 C4
Liatrie GB 22 D4
Libáň CZ 53 C5
Libceves CZ 53 C3
Liběchov CZ 53 C4
Liber E 86 B3
Liberec CZ 53 C5
Libiąż PL 55 C4
Libina CZ 64 A3
Libochovice CZ 53 C4
Libofshë AL 105 C5
Libohovë AL 116 B2
Libourne F 76 B2
Libramont B 59 A6
Librazhd AL 116 A2
Librilla E 101 B4
Libros E 96 A1
Licata I 108 B2
Licciana Nardi I 81 B4
Licenza I 102 A5
Liceros E 89 C3
Lich D 51 C4
Lichères-près-Aigremont F 59 C4
Lichfield GB 27 C4
Lichtenau A 63 B6
Lichtenau D 51 B4
Lichtenberg D 52 C1
Lichtenfels D 52 C1
Lichtensteig CH 71 A4
Lichtenstein D 52 C2
Lichtenvoorde NL 50 B2
Lichtervelde B 49 B4
Lička Jesenica HR 83 A4
Lickershamn S 37 E5
Lički Osik HR 83 B4
Ličko Lešce HR 83 B4
Licodía Eubéa I 109 B3
Licques F 48 C2
Lida BY 7 E8
Lidar N 32 A6
Lidečko CZ 64 A4
Liden S 115 E13
Lidhult S 40 C3
Lidköping S 35 D5
Lido I 72 C2
Lido Azzurro I 104 C3
Lido degli Estensi I 82 B1
Lido degli Scacchi I 82 B1
Lido della Nazioni I 82 B1
Lido di Camaiore I 81 C4
Lido di Casalbordino I 103 A7
Lido di Castél Fusano I 102 B5
Lido di Cincinnato I 102 B5
Lido di Classe I 82 B1
Lido di Fermo I 82 C2
Lido di Fondi I 103 B6
Lido di Jésolo I 72 C2
Lido di Lícola I 103 C7
Lido di Metaponto I 104 C2
Lido di Óstia I 102 B5
Lido di Policoro I 106 A3
Lido di Pomposa I 82 B1
Lido di Savio I 82 B1
Lido di Scanzano I 104 C2
Lido di Siponto I 104 B1
Lido di Squillace I 106 C3
Lido di Volano I 82 B1
Lido Riccio I 103 A7
Lido Silvana I 104 C3
Lidoriki GR 116 D4
Lidsjöberg S 115 C12
Lidzbark PL 47 B5
Lidzbark Warmiński PL 47 A6
Liebenau A 63 B5
Liebenau D 43 C6
Liebenwalde D 45 C5
Lieberose D 53 B4
Liebling RO 75 C6
Lieboch A 73 B5
Liège B 49 C6
Lieksa FIN 3 E29
Lienen D 50 A3
Lienz A 72 B2
Liepāja LV 6 C6
Lier B 49 B5
Lierbyen N 34 C2
Liernais F 69 A4
Liesing A 72 B2
Liestal CH 70 A2
Liétor E 101 A4
Lieurac F 77 D4
Lieurey F 58 A1
Liévin F 48 C3
Liezen A 73 A4
Liffol-le-Grand F 60 B1
Lifford IRL 19 B4
Liffré F 57 B4
Ligardes F 77 B3
Lignano Sabbiadoro I 72 C3
Ligne F 66 A3
Lignières F 68 B2
Ligny-en-Barrois F 59 B6
Ligny-le-Châtel F 59 C4
Ligoła Polska PL 54 B2
Ligourio GR 117 E5
Ligowo PL 47 C5
Ligueil F 67 A5
Lijeva Rijeka MNE 85 D4
Likavka SK 65 A5
Likenäs S 34 B5
Likhoslavl RUS 7 C13
Lild Strand DK 38 B1
L'Île-Bouchard F 67 A5
l'Île-Rousse F 102 A1
Lilienfeld A 63 B6
Lilienthal D 43 B5
Lilla Edet S 35 D4
Lilla Tjärby S 40 C3
Lille B 49 B5
Lille F 49 C4
Lillebonne F 58 A1
Lillehammer N 34 A2
Lillerød DK 41 D2
Lillers F 48 C3
Lillesand N 33 D5
Lillestrøm N 34 C3
Lillhärdal S 115 F11
Lillkyrka S 37 C4
Lillo E 95 C3
Lillögda S 115 C14
Lima S 34 B5
Limanowa PL 65 A6
Limassol CY 120 B2
Limavady GB 19 A5
Limbach-Oberfrohna D 52 C2
Limbaži LV 6 C8
Limbourg B 50 C1
Limburg D 50 C4
Lime DK 39 C3
Limedsforsen S 34 B5
Limenaria GR 116 B6
Limenas Chersonisou GR 117 G7
Limerick IRL 20 B3
Limes I 71 C5
Limésy F 58 A1
Limmared S 40 B3
Limni GR 116 D5
Limoges F 67 C6
Limogne-en-Quercy F 77 B4
Limoise F 68 B3
Limone Piemonte I 80 B1
Limone sul Garda I 71 C5
Limons F 68 C3
Limours F 58 B3
Limoux F 77 C5
Linares E 100 A2
Linares de Mora E 90 C2
Linares de Riofrio E 93 A5
Linaria GR 116 D6
Linas de Broto E 90 A2
Lincoln GB 27 B5
Lind DK 39 C1
Lindås N 32 B2
Lindau D 71 A4
Lindberget N 34 A3
Lindelse DK 39 E3
Lindenberg D 53 A4
Lindenberg im Allgäu D 61 C5
Lindern D 43 C4
Linderöd S 41 D3
Lindesberg S 37 C2
Lindesnäs S 36 B1
Lindesnes N 33 E4
Lindholmen S 37 C5
Lindknud DK 39 D2
Lindlar D 50 B3
Lindö S 37 D3
Lindome S 38 B5
Lindos GR 119 F3
Lindoso P 87 C2
Lindow D 45 C4
Lindsdal S 40 C6
Lindshammar S 40 B5
Lindstedt D 44 C3
Lindved DK 39 D2
Líně CZ 63 A4
Lingbo S 36 A3
Lingen D 43 C4
Linghed S 36 B2
Linghem S 37 D2
Linguaglossa I 109 B4
Linia PL 46 A3
Linie PL 45 B6
Liniewo PL 47 A4
Linkenheim D 61 A4
Linköping S 37 D2
Linksness GB 23 C5
Linlithgow GB 25 C4
Linneryd S 40 C5
Linnes Hammarby S 36 C4
Linnich D 50 C2
Linsell S 115 E10
Linslade GB 31 C3
Linthal CH 70 B4
Linyola E 90 B3
Linz A 63 B5
Linz D 50 C3
Liomseter N 32 A6
Lion-sur-Mer F 57 A5
Lionárisso CY 120 A3
Lioni I 103 C8
Lipany SK 65 A6
Lipar SRB 75 C4
Lípari I 106 C1
Lipcani MD 11 B9
Liperi FIN 3 E28
Liphook GB 31 C3
Lipiany PL 45 B6
Lipik HR 74 C2
Lipka PL 46 B3
Lipki Wielkie PL 46 C1
Lipnica PL 46 B3
Lipnica Murowana PL 65 A6
Lipnik PL 55 C6
Lipník nad Bečvou CZ 64 A3
Lipno, *Kujawsko-Pomorskie* PL 47 C5
Lipno, *Łódzkie* PL 54 B3
Liposthey F 76 B2
Lipovac HR 84 A4
Lipovec CZ 64 A2
Lipovets UA 11 B10
Lipovljani HR 74 C1
Lipowiec PL 47 B6
Lipowina PL 47 A5
Lippborg D 50 B4
Lippó H 74 C3
Lippoldsberg D 51 B5
Lippstadt D 51 B4
Lipsko PL 55 B6
Liptál CZ 64 A3
Liptovská-Lúžna SK 65 B5
Liptovská Osada SK 65 B5
Liptovská-Teplička SK 65 B6
Liptovský Hrádok SK 65 A5
Liptovský Milkuláš SK 65 A5
Lipusz PL 46 A3
Lipůvka CZ 64 A2
Liré F 66 A3
Lis AL 105 B6
Lisa SRB 85 C5
Lisac BIH 84 B2
Lisbellaw GB 19 B4
Lisboa = Lisbon P 92 C1
Lisbon = Lisboa P 92 C1
Lisburn GB 19 B5
Liscannor IRL 20 B2
Lisdoonvarna IRL 20 A2
Lisewo PL 47 B4
Lisia Góra PL 55 C6
Lisięcice PL 54 C2
Lisieux F 57 A6
Lisjö S 37 C3
Liskeard GB 28 C3
L'Isle CH 69 B6
L'Isle-Adam F 58 A3
L'Isle-de-Noé F 77 C3
L'Isle-en-Dodon F 77 C3
L'Isle-Jourdain, *Gers* F 77 C4
L'Isle-Jourdain, *Vienne* F 67 B5
L'Isle-sur-la-Sorgue F 79 C4
L'Isle-sur-le Doubs F 69 A6
L'Isle-sur-Serein F 59 C5
Lisle-sur-Tarn F 77 C4
Lismore IRL 21 B4
Lisnaskea GB 19 B4
Lišov CZ 63 A5
Lisów, *Lubuskie* PL 45 C6
Lisów, *Śląskie* PL 54 C3
Lisse NL 49 A5
Lissycasey IRL 20 B2
List D 39 D1
Listerby S 41 C5
Listowel IRL 20 B2
Listrac-Médoc F 76 A2
Liszki PL 55 C4
Liszkowo PL 46 B3
Lit S 115 D11
Lit-et-Mixe F 76 B1
Litava SK 65 B5
Litcham GB 30 B4
Litija SLO 73 B4
Litke H 65 B5
Litlabø N 32 C2
Litochoro GR 116 B4
Litoměřice CZ 53 C4
Litomyšl CZ 64 A2
Litovel CZ 64 A3
Litschau A 63 B6
Little Walsingham GB 30 B4
Littlehampton GB 31 D3
Littleport GB 30 B4
Littleton IRL 21 B4
Litvinov CZ 52 C3
Livadero GR 116 B3
Livadhia CY 120 B2
Livadi GR 116 B4
Livadia GR 116 D4
Livarot F 57 B6
Liveras CY 120 A1
Livernon F 77 B4
Liverovici MNE 85 D4
Liverpool GB 26 B3
Livigno I 71 B5
Livingston GB 25 C4
Livno BIH 84 C1
Livold SLO 73 C4
Livorno I 81 C4
Livorno Ferraris I 70 C3
Livron-sur-Drôme F 78 B3
Livry-Louvercy F 59 A5
Lixheim F 60 B3
Lixouri GR 117 D2
Lizard GB 28 D2
Lizy-sur-Ourcq F 59 A4
Lizzano I 104 C3
Lizzano in Belvedere I 81 B4
Ljesane KOS 85 D5
Ljig SRB 85 B5
Ljørdalen N 34 A4
Ljosland N 33 D4
Ljubija BIH 83 B5
Ljubinje BIH 84 D3
Ljubljana SLO 73 B4
Ljubno ob Savinji SLO 73 B4
Ljubovija SRB 85 B4
Ljubuški BIH 84 C2
Ljugarn S 37 E5
Ljung S 40 B3
Ljunga S 37 D3
Ljungaverk S 115 E13
Ljungby S 40 C3
Ljungbyhed S 41 C3
Ljungbyholm S 40 C6
Ljungdalen S 115 E9
Ljungsarp S 40 B3
Ljungsbro S 37 D2
Ljungskile S 35 D3
Ljusdal S 115 F13
Ljusfallshammar S 37 D2
Ljusne S 36 A4
Ljusterö S 37 C5
Ljutomer SLO 73 B6
Lladurs E 91 A4
Llafranc E 91 B6
Llagostera E 91 B5
Llanaelhaiarn GB 26 C1
Llanarth GB 28 A3
Llanbedr GB 26 C1
Llanbedrog GB 26 C1
Llanberis GB 26 B1
Llanbister GB 29 A4
Llanbrynmair GB 26 C2
Llançà E 91 A6
Llandeilo GB 28 B4
Llandissilio GB 28 B3
Llandovery GB 28 B4
Llandrillo GB 26 C2
Llandrindod Wells GB 29 A4
Llandudec F 56 B1
Llandudno GB 26 B2
Llandysul GB 28 A3
Llanelli GB 28 B3
Llanerchymedd GB 26 B1
Llanes E 88 A2
Llanfair Caereinion GB 26 C2
Llanfairfechan GB 26 B2
Llanfyllin GB 26 C2
Llangadog GB 28 B4
Llangefni GB 26 B1
Llangollen GB 26 C2
Llangrannog GB 28 A3
Llangurig GB 26 C2
Llanidloes GB 26 C2
Llanilar GB 28 A3
Llanrhystud GB 28 A3
Llanrwst GB 26 B2
Llansannan GB 26 B2
Llansawel GB 28 A3
Llanstephan GB 28 B3

Majavatn N 115 B10
Majs H 74 C3
Majšperk SLO 73 B5
Makarska HR 84 C2
Makkum NL 42 B2
Maklár H 65 C6
Makó H 75 B5
Makoszyce PL 54 C2
Makov SK 65 A4
Makovac KOS 85 D6
Maków Podhalański PL 65 A5
Mąkowarsko PL 46 B3
Makrakomi GR 116 D4
Malå S 115 B15
Mala Bosna SRB 75 B4
Mala Kladuša BIH 73 C5
Mala Krsna SRB 85 B6
Malá Lehota SK 65 B4
Mala Pijace SRB 75 B4
Mala Plana SRB 85 C6
Mala Subotica HR 74 B1
Mala Vyska UA 11 B11
Malacky SK 64 B3
Maladzyechna BY 7 D9
Málaga E 100 C1
Malagón E 94 C3
Malaguilla E 95 B3
Malahide IRL 21 A5
Malalbergo I 81 B5
Malanów PL 54 B3
Malaucène F 79 B4
Malaunay F 58 A2
Malaya Vishera RUS 7 B12
Malborghetto I 72 B3
Malbork PL 47 A5
Malborn D 60 A2
Malbuisson F 69 B6
Malcésine I 71 C5
Malchin D 45 B4
Malching D 63 B4
Malchow D 44 B4
Malcocinado E 99 A5
Malczyce PL 54 B1
Maldegem B 49 B4
Maldon GB 31 C4
Małdyty PL 47 B5
Malè I 71 B5
Malemort F 67 C6
Malente D 44 A2
Målerås S 40 C5
Males GR 117 G7
Malesherbes F 58 B3
Malesina GR 116 D5
Malestroit F 56 C3
Maletto I 109 B3
Malexander S 40 A5
Malfa I 106 C1
Malgrat de Mar E 91 B5
Malhadas P 87 C4
Mali Lošinj HR 83 B3
Malia CY 120 B1
Malia GR 117 G7
Malicorne-sur-Sarthe F 57 C5
Malijai F 79 B5
Malildjoš SRB 75 C4
Målilla S 40 B5
Malin IRL 19 A4
Málinec SK 65 B5
Malingsbo S 36 C2
Maliniec PL 54 A3
Malinska HR 83 A3
Maliq AL 116 B2
Maljevac HR 73 C5
Malkara TR 118 B1
Małki PL 47 B5
Malko Tŭrnovo BG 11 E9
Mallaig GB 22 D3
Mallaranny IRL 18 C2
Mallemort F 79 C4
Mallén E 89 C5
Malléon F 77 C4
Mallersdorf-Pfaffenberg D 62 B3
Málles Venosta I 71 B5
Malling DK 39 C3
Mallnitz A 72 B3
Mallow IRL 20 B3
Mallwyd GB 26 C2
Malm N 114 C8
Malmbäck S 40 B4
Malmberget S 112 E9
Malmby S 37 C4
Malmédy B 50 C2
Malmesbury GB 29 B5
Malmköping S 37 C3
Malmö S 41 D3
Malmon S 35 D3
Malmslätt S 37 D2
Malnate I 70 C3
Malo I 71 C6
Maloarkhangelsk RUS 7 E14
Małogoszcz PL 55 C5
Maloja CH 71 B4
Małomice PL 53 B5
Måløy N 114 F2
Maloyaroslovets RUS 7 D14
Malpartida E 93 B4
Malpartida de la Serena E 93 C5
Malpartida de Plasencia E 93 B4
Malpas E 90 A3
Malpas GB 26 B3
Malpica P 92 B3
Malpica de Bergantiños E 86 A2
Malpica de Tajo E 94 C2
Malsch D 61 B4
Malšice CZ 63 A5
Malta A 72 B3
Maltat F 68 B3
Maltby GB 27 B4
Malung S 34 B5
Malungsfors S 34 B5
Maluszów PL 45 C7
Maluszyn PL 55 C4
Malva E 88 C1
Malvaglia CH 70 B3
Malveira P 92 C1
Malvik N 114 D7
Malyn UA 11 A10
Mamarrosa P 92 A2
Mamer L 60 A2
Mamers F 58 B1
Mamirolle F 69 A6
Mammendorf D 62 B2
Mámmola I 106 C3
Mamoiada I 110 B2
Mamonovo RUS 47 A5
Mamuras AL 105 B5
Maňa SK 64 B4
Manacor E 97 B3
Manavgat TR 119 F6
Mancera de Abajo E 94 B1
Mancha Real E 100 B2
Manchester GB 26 B3
Manching D 62 B2
Manchita E 93 C4
Manciano I 102 A4
Manciet F 76 C3
Mandal N 33 D4
Mandanici I 109 A4
Mándas I 110 C2
Mandatoriccio I 107 B3
Mandayona E 95 B4
Mandelieu-la-Napoule F 79 C5
Mandello del Lário I 71 C4
Mandelsloh D 43 C6
Manderfeld B 50 C2
Manderscheid D 50 C2
Mandino Selo BIH 84 C2
Mandoudi GR 116 D5
Mandra GR 117 D5
Mandraki GR 119 F2
Mandúria I 104 C3
Mane, *Alpes-de-Haute-Provence* F 79 C4
Mane, *Haute-Garonne* F 77 C3
Manérbio I 71 C5
Mañeru E 89 B5
Manetin CZ 52 D3
Manfredónia I 104 B1
Mangalia RO 11 E10
Manganeses de la Lampreana E 88 C1
Manganeses de la Polvorosa E 88 B1
Mangen N 34 C3
Manger N 32 B2
Mangiennes F 60 A1
Mangotsfield GB 29 B5
Mångsbodarna S 34 A5
Mangualde P 92 A3
Maniago I 72 B2
Manilva E 99 C5
Manisa TR 118 D2
Manises E 96 B2
Mank A 63 B6
Månkarbo S 36 B4
Manlleu E 91 B5
Manna DK 38 B2
Männedorf CH 70 A3
Mannersdorf am Leithagebirge A 64 C2
Mannheim D 61 A4
Manningtree GB 31 C5
Manoppello I 103 A7
Manorbier GB 28 B3
Manorhamilton IRL 18 B3
Manosque F 79 C4
Manowo PL 46 A2
Manresa E 91 B4
Månsarp S 40 B4
Månsåsen S 115 D11
Manschnow D 45 C6
Mansfeld D 52 B1
Mansfield GB 27 B4
Mansilla de Burgos E 88 B3
Mansilla de las Mulas E 88 B1
Manskog S 35 C4
Mansle F 67 C5
Manso F 102 A1
Manteigas P 92 A3
Mantel D 62 A3
Mantes-la-Jolie F 58 B2
Mantes-la-Ville F 58 B2
Manthelan F 67 A5
Mantorp S 37 D2
Mántova I 71 C5
Mänttä FIN 3 E26
Manuel E 96 B2
Manyas TR 118 B2
Manzanal de Arriba E 87 B4
Manzanares E 95 C3
Manzanares el Real E 94 B3
Manzaneda, *León* E 87 B4
Manzaneda, *Orense* E 87 B3
Manzanedo E 88 B3
Manzaneque E 94 C3
Manzanera E 96 A2
Manzanilla E 99 B4
Manzat F 68 C2
Manziana I 102 A5
Manziat F 69 B4
Maó E 97 B4
Maoča BIH 84 B3
Maqueda E 94 B2
Mara E 89 C5
Maramaraereğlisi TR 118 B2
Maraña E 88 A1
Maranchón E 95 A4
Maranello I 81 B4
Marano I 103 C7
Marano Lagunare I 72 C3
Marans F 66 B3
Maratea I 106 B2
Marateca P 92 C2
Marathokambos GR 119 E1
Marathonas GR 117 D5
Marathóvouno CY 120 A2
Marazion GB 28 C2
Marbach, *Baden-Württemberg* D 61 B5
Marbach, *Hessen* D 51 C5
Marbach F 60 B2
Marbäck S 40 B3
Mårbacka S 34 C5
Marbella E 100 C1
Marboz F 69 B5
Marburg D 51 C4
Marcali H 74 B2
Marčana HR 82 B2
Marcaria I 81 A4
Marcelová SK 64 C4
Marcenat F 68 C2
March GB 30 B4
Marchamalo E 95 B3
Marchaux F 69 A6
Marche-en-Famenne B 49 C6
Marchegg A 64 B2
Marchena E 99 B5
Marchenoir F 58 C2
Marcheprime F 76 B2
Marciac F 76 C3
Marciana Marina I 81 D4
Marcianise I 103 B7
Marcigny F 68 B4
Marcilla E 89 B5
Marcillac-la-Croisille F 68 C2
Marcillac-Vallon F 77 B5
Marcillat-en-Combraille F 68 B2
Marcille-sur-Seine F 59 B4
Marcilloles F 69 C5
Marcilly-le-Hayer F 59 B4
Marcinkowice PL 46 B2
Marciszów PL 53 C6
Marck F 48 C2
Marckolsheim F 60 B3
Marco de Canevezes P 87 C2
Mårdsele S 115 C16
Mårdsjö S 115 D12
Mareham le Fen GB 27 B5
Marek S 40 B5
Marennes F 66 C3
Maresquel F 48 C2
Mareuil F 67 C5
Mareuil-en-Brie F 59 B4
Mareuil-sur-Arnon F 68 B2
Mareuil-sur-Lay F 66 B3
Mareuil-sur-Ourcq F 59 A4
Margam GB 28 B4
Margariti GR 116 C2
Margate GB 31 C5
Margaux F 76 A2
Margerie-Hancourt F 59 B5
Margès F 69 C5
Margherita di Savóia I 104 B2
Margita SRB 75 C6
Margone I 70 C2
Margonin PL 46 C3
Marguerittes F 78 C3
Margut F 59 A6
Maria E 101 B3
Maria Neustift A 63 C5
Maria Saal A 73 B4
Mariager DK 38 C2
Mariana E 95 B4
Mariannelund S 40 B5
Marianópoli I 108 B2
Mariánské Lázně CZ 52 D2
Mariapfarr A 72 A3
Mariazell A 63 C6
Maribo DK 39 E4
Maribor SLO 73 B5
Marieberg S 37 C2
Mariefred S 37 C4
Mariehamn FIN 36 B6
Marieholm S 41 D3
Mariembourg B 49 C5
Marienbaum D 50 B2
Marienberg D 52 C3
Marienheide D 50 B3
Mariental D 51 A6
Mariestad S 35 D5
Marieux F 48 C3
Marigliano I 103 C7
Marignane F 79 C4
Marigny, *Jura* F 69 B5
Marigny, *Manche* F 57 A4
Marigny-le-Châtel F 59 B4
Marija Bistrica HR 73 B6
Marijampolė LT 6 D7
Marín E 87 B2
Marina HR 83 C5
Marina del Cantone I 103 C7
Marina di Acquappesa I 106 B2
Marina di Alberese I 81 D5
Marina di Amendolara I 106 B3
Marina di Árbus I 110 C1
Marina di Campo I 81 D4
Marina di Carrara I 81 B4
Marina di Castagneto-Donorático I 81 C4
Marina di Cécina I 81 C4
Marina di Gáiro I 110 C2
Marina di Ginosa I 104 C2
Marina di Gioiosa Iónica I 106 C3
Marina di Grosseto I 81 D4
Marina di Léuca I 107 B5
Marina di Massa I 81 B4
Marina di Nováglie I 107 B5
Marina di Pisa I 81 C4
Marina di Ragusa I 109 C3
Marina di Ravenna I 82 B1
Marina di Torre Grande I 110 C1
Marina Romea I 82 B1
Marinaleda E 100 B1
Marine de Sisco F 102 A2
Marinella I 108 B1
Marinella di Sarzana I 81 B4
Marineo I 108 B2
Marines F 58 A2
Maringues F 68 C3
Marinha das Ondas P 92 A2
Marinha Grande P 92 B2
Marinhas P 87 C2
Marino I 102 B5
Marjaliza E 94 C3
Markabygd N 114 D8
Markaryd S 40 C3
Markdorf D 61 C5
Markelo NL 50 A2
Market Deeping GB 30 B3
Market Drayton GB 26 C3
Market Harborough GB 30 B3
Market Rasen GB 27 B5
Market Warsop GB 27 B4
Market Weighton GB 27 B5
Markethill GB 19 B5
Markgröningen D 61 B5
Markhausen D 43 C4
Marki PL 55 A6
Markina-Xemein E 89 A4
Markinch GB 25 B4
Märkische Buchholz D 53 A3
Markitta S 113 E10
Markkleeberg D 52 B2
Marklohe D 43 C6
Marknesse NL 42 C2
Markneukirchen D 52 C2
Markopoulo GR 117 E5
Markovac SRB 85 B6
Markowice PL 54 C3
Markranstädt D 52 B2
Marksuhl D 51 C6
Markt Allhau A 73 A6
Markt Bibart D 61 A6
Markt Erlbach D 62 A1
Markt-heidenfeld D 61 A5
Markt Indersdorf D 62 B2
Markt Rettenbach D 61 C6
Markt Schwaben D 62 B2
Markt-Übelbach A 73 A5
Marktbreit D 61 A6
Marktl D 62 B3
Marktleuthen D 52 C1
Marktoberdorf D 62 C1
Marktredwitz D 52 C2
Markusica HR 74 C3
Markušovce SK 65 B6
Marl D 50 B3
Marlborough, *Devon* GB 28 C4
Marlborough, *Wiltshire* GB 29 B6
Marle F 59 A4
Marlieux F 69 B5
Marlow D 45 A4
Marlow GB 31 C3
Marma S 36 B4
Marmagne F 69 B4
Marmande F 76 B3
Marmara TR 118 B2
Marmaris TR 119 F3
Marmelete P 98 B2
Marmolejo E 100 A1
Marmoutier F 60 B3
Marnay F 69 A5
Marne D 43 B6
Marnheim D 61 A4
Marnitz D 44 B3
Maroldsweisach D 51 C6
Marolles-les-Braults F 58 B1
Maromme F 58 A2
Marone I 71 C5
Maronia GR 116 B7
Maroslele H 75 B5
Maróstica I 72 C1
Marotta I 82 C2
Marpisa GR 117 E7
Marquion F 49 C4
Marquise F 48 C2
Marradi I 81 B5
Marrasjärvi FIN 113 F14
Marraskoski FIN 113 F14
Marratxi E 97 B2
Marrúbiu I 110 C1
Marrum NL 42 B2
Marrupe E 94 B2
Mars-la-Tours F 60 A1
Marsac F 77 C5
Marsac-en-Livradois F 68 C3
Marságlia I 80 B3
Marsala I 108 B1
Marsberg D 51 B4
Marsciano I 82 D1
Marseillan F 78 C2
Marseille = Marseilles F 79 C4
Marseille en Beauvaisis F 58 A2
Marseilles = Marseille F 79 C4
Mársico Nuovo I 104 C1
Marske-by-the-Sea GB 27 A4
Marsliden S 115 B12
Marson F 59 B5
Märsta S 37 C4
Marstal DK 39 E3
Marstrand S 38 B4
Marta I 102 A4
Martano I 107 A5
Martel F 77 B4
Martelange B 60 A1
Martfeld D 43 C6
Martfű H 75 A5
Martham GB 30 B5
Marthon F 67 C5
Martiago E 93 A4
Martigné-Briand F 67 A4
Martigné-Ferchaud F 57 C4
Martigne-sur-Mayenne F 57 B5
Martigny CH 70 B2
Martigny-les-Bains F 60 B1
Martigues F 79 C4
Martim-Longo P 98 B3
Martin SK 65 A4
Martin de la Jara E 100 B1
Martin Muñoz de las Posadas E 94 A2
Martina CH 71 B5
Martina Franca I 104 C3
Martinamor E 94 B1
Martinengo I 71 C4
Martinsberg A 63 B6
Martinšćica HR 82 B3
Martinshöhe D 60 A3
Martinsicuro I 82 D2
Martinszell D 61 C6
Mártis I 110 B1
Martofte DK 39 D3
Martonvásár H 74 A3
Martorell E 91 B4
Martos E 100 B2
Martres Tolosane F 77 C3
Martti FIN 113 E17
Marugán E 94 B2
Marúggio I 104 C3
Marvão P 92 B3
Marvejols F 78 B2
Marville F 60 A1
Marwałd PL 47 B6
Marykirk GB 25 B5
Marypark GB 23 D5
Maryport GB 26 A2
Marytavy GB 28 C3
Marzabotto I 81 B5
Marzahna D 52 B2
Marzahne D 45 C4
Marzamemi I 109 C4
Marzocca I 82 C2
Mas-Cabardès F 77 C5
Mas de Barberáns E 90 C3
Mas de las Matas E 90 C2
Masa E 88 B3
Mascali I 109 B4
Mascaraque E 94 C3
Mascarenhas P 87 C3
Mascioni I 103 A6
Masegoso E 101 A3
Masegoso de Tajuña E 95 B4
Masera I 70 B3
Masevaux F 60 C2
Masfjorden N 32 B2
Masham GB 27 A4
Masi N 113 C12
Maside E 87 B2
Maslacq F 76 C2
Maslinica HR 83 C5
Maslovare BIH 84 B2
Masone I 80 B2
Massa I 81 B4
Massa Fiscáglia I 81 B6
Massa Lombarda I 81 B5
Massa Lubrense I 103 C7
Massa Marittima I 81 C4
Massa Martana I 82 D1
Massafra I 104 C3
Massamagrell E 96 B2
Massanassa E 96 B2
Massarosa I 81 C4
Massat F 77 D4
Massay F 68 A1
Massbach D 51 C6
Masseret F 67 C6
Masseube F 77 C3
Massiac F 68 C3
Massignac F 67 C5
Massing D 62 B3
Massmechelen B 50 C1
Masterud N 34 B4
Mästocka S 40 C3
Masty BY 6 E8
Masúa I 110 C1
Masueco E 87 C4
Masugnsbyn S 113 E11
Mašun SLO 73 C4
Maszewo, *Lubuskie* PL 53 A4
Maszewo, *Zachodnio-Pomorskie* PL 45 B7
Mata de Alcántara E 93 B4
Matala GR 117 H6
Matalebreras E 89 C4
Matallana de Torio E 88 B1
Matamala E 89 C4
Mataporquera E 88 B2
Matapozuelos E 88 C2
Mataró E 91 B5
Matarocco I 108 B1
Mataruge MNE 85 C4
Mataruška Banja SRB 85 C5
Matélica I 82 C2
Matera I 104 C2
Mateševo MNE 85 D4
Mátészalka H 11 C7
Matet E 96 B2
Matfors S 115 E14
Matha F 67 C4
Mathay F 70 A1
Matignon F 57 B3
Matilla de los Caños del Rio E 94 B1
Matlock GB 27 B4
Matosinhos P 87 C2
Matour F 69 B4
Mátrafüred H 65 C5
Mátraterenye H 65 B5
Matre, *Hordaland* N 32 B2
Matre, *Hordaland* N 32 C2
Matrei am Brenner A 71 A6
Matrei in Osttirol A 72 A2
Matrice I 103 B7
Matsdal S 115 B12
Mattarello I 71 B6
Mattersburg A 64 C2
Mattighofen A 62 B4
Mattinata I 104 B2
Mattos P 92 B2
Mattsee A 62 C4
Mattsmyra S 36 A2
Matulji HR 73 C4
Maubert-Fontaine F 59 A5
Maubeuge F 49 C4
Maubourguet F 76 C3
Mauchline GB 24 C3
Maud GB 23 D6
Mauer-kirchen A 62 B4
Mauern D 62 B2
Mauguio F 78 C3
Maulbronn D 61 B4
Maule F 58 B2
Mauléon F 67 B4
Mauléon-Barousse F 77 D3
Mauléon-Licharre F 76 C2
Maulévrier F 67 A4
Maum IRL 18 C2
Maurach A 72 A1
Maure-de-Bretagne F 57 C4
Maureilhan F 78 C2
Mauriac F 68 C2
Mauron F 57 B3
Maurs F 77 B5
Maury F 77 D5
Maussane-les-Alpilles F 78 C3
Mautern A 63 B6
Mautern im Steiermark A 73 A4
Mauterndorf A 72 A3
Mauthausen A 63 B5
Mauthen A 72 B2
Mauvezin F 77 C3
Mauzé-sur-le-Mignon F 67 B4
Maxent F 57 C3
Maxey-sur-Vaise F 60 B1
Maxial P 92 B1
Maxieira P 92 B2
Maxwellheugh GB 25 C5
Mayalde E 88 C1
Maybole GB 24 C3
Mayen D 50 C3
Mayenne F 57 B5
Mayet F 58 C1
Maylough IRL 18 C3
Mayorga E 88 B1
Mayres F 78 B3
Mayrhofen A 72 A1
Mazagón E 99 B4
Mazaleón E 90 B3
Mazamet F 77 C5
Mazan F 79 B4
Mazara del Vallo I 108 B1
Mazarambroz E 94 C2
Mazarete E 95 B4
Mazaricos E 86 B2
Mazarrón E 101 B4
Mažeikiai LT 6 C7
Mazères F 77 C4
Mazères-sur-Salat F 77 C3
Mazières-en-Gâtine F 67 B4
Mazin HR 83 B4
Mazuelo E 88 B3
Mazyr BY 7 E10
Mazzarino I 109 B3
Mazzarrà Sant'Andrea I 109 A4
Mazzo di Valtellina I 71 B5
Mchowo PL 47 B6
Mdzewo PL 47 C6
Mealabost GB 22 C2
Mealhada P 92 A2
Méan B 49 C6
Meana Sardo I 110 C2
Meaulne F 68 B2
Meaux F 59 B3
Mebonden N 114 D8
Mecerreyes E 89 B3
Mechelen B 49 B5
Mechernich D 50 C2
Mechnica PL 54 C3
Mechowo PL 45 B7
Mechterstädt D 51 C6
Mecidiye TR 118 B1
Mecikal PL 46 B3
Mecina-Bombarón E 100 C2
Mecitözü TR 16 A7
Meckenbeuren D 61 C5
Meckenheim, *Rheinland-Pfalz* D 50 C3
Meckenheim, *Rheinland-Pfalz* D 61 A4
Meckesheim D 61 A4
Mecseknádasd H 74 B3
Meda I 71 C4
Meda P 87 D3
Medak HR 83 B4
Mede I 80 A2
Medebach D 51 B4
Medelim P 93 A3
Medemblik NL 42 C2
Medena Selista BIH 84 B1
Medesano I 81 B4
Medevi S 37 D1
Medgidia RO 11 D10
Medgyesháza H 75 B6
Medhamn S 35 C5
Mediaş RO 11 C8
Medicina I 81 B5
Medina de las Torres E 93 C4
Medina de Pomar E 89 B3
Medina de Rioseco E 88 C1
Medina del Campo E 88 C2
Medina Sidonia E 99 C5
Medinaceli E 95 A4
Medinilla E 93 A5
Medja SRB 75 C5
Medjedja BIH 85 C4
Medulin HR 82 B2
Meduno I 72 B2
Medveda SRB 85 B6
Medvedja SRB 85 C6
Medvedov SK 64 C3
Medvide HR 83 B4
Medvode SLO 73 B4
Medzev SK 65 B6
Medžitlija MK 116 B3
Meerane D 52 C2
Meerle B 49 B5
Meersburg D 61 C5
Meeuwen B 49 B6
Megalo Horio GR 119 F2
Megalopoli GR 117 E4
Megara GR 117 D5
Megève F 69 C6
Meggenhofen A 63 B4
Megra RUS 7 A14
Mehamn N 113 A16
Mehedeby S 36 B4
Méhkerék H 75 B6
Mehun-sur-Yèvre F 68 A2
Meigle GB 25 B4
Meijel NL 50 B1
Meilen CH 70 A3
Meilhan F 76 C2
Meimôa P 93 A3
Meina I 70 C3
Meine D 44 C2
Meinersen D 44 C2
Meinerzhagen D 50 B3
Meiningen D 51 C6
Meira E 86 A3
Meiringen CH 70 B3
Meisenheim D 60 A3
Meissen D 52 B3
Meitingen D 62 B1
Meix-devant-Virton B 60 A1
Męka PL 54 B3
Meka Gruda BIH 84 C3
Mel I 72 B2
Melbu N 112 D3
Melč CZ 64 A3
Meldal N 114 D6
Méldola I 82 B1
Meldorf D 43 A6
Melegnano I 71 C4
Melenci SRB 75 C5
Melendugno I 105 C4
Melfi I 104 C1
Melfjordbotn N 112 F2
Melgaço P 87 B2
Melgar de Arriba E 88 B1
Melgar de Fernamental E 88 B2
Melgar de Yuso E 88 B2
Melhus N 114 D7
Meliana E 96 B2
Melide CH 70 C3
Melide E 86 B2
Melides P 98 A2
Meligales GR 117 E3
Melilli I 109 B4
Melinovac HR 83 B4
Melisenda I 110 C2
Melisey F 60 C2
Mélito di Porto Salvo I 109 B4
Melk A 63 B6
Melksham GB 29 B5
Mellanström S 115 B15
Mellbystrand S 40 C2
Melle B 49 B4
Melle D 50 A4
Melle F 67 B4
Mellendorf D 43 C6
Mellerud S 35 D4
Mellieha M 107 C5
Mellösa S 37 C3
Mellrichstadt D 51 C6
Mělnické Vtelno CZ 53 C4
Mělník CZ 53 C4
Melón E 87 B2
Melrose GB 25 C5
Mels CH 71 A4
Melsungen D 51 B5
Meltaus FIN 113 F14
Meltham GB 27 B4
Melton Mowbray GB 30 B3
Meltosjärvi FIN 113 F13
Melun F 58 B3

Melvaig GB 22 D3
Melvich GB 23 C5
Mélykút H 75 B4
Melzo I 71 C4
Memaliaj AL 116 B1
Membrilla E 95 D3
Membrio E 93 B3
Memer F 77 B4
Memmelsdorf D 51 D6
Memmingen D 61 C6
Memoria P 92 B2
Mena UA 7 F12
Menággio I 71 B4
Menai Bridge GB 26 B1
Menasalbas E 94 C2
Menat F 68 B2
Mendavia E 89 B4
Mendaza E 89 B4
Mende F 78 B2
Menden D 50 B3
Menderes TR 119 D2
Mendig D 50 C3
Mendiga P 92 B2
Mendrisio CH 70 C3
Ménéac F 56 B3
Menemen TR 118 D2
Menen B 49 C4
Menesjärvi FIN 113 D15
Menetou-Salon F 68 A2
Menfi I 108 B1
Ménföcsanak H 64 C3
Mengamuñoz E 94 B2
Mengen D 61 B5
Mengen TR 118 B7
Mengeš SLO 73 B4
Mengíbar E 100 B2
Mengkofen D 62 B3
Menou F 68 A3
Mens F 79 B4
Menslage D 43 C4
Mensträsk S 115 B16
Mentana I 102 A5
Menton F 80 C1
Méntrida E 94 B2
Méobecq F 67 B6
Méounes-les-Montrieux F 79 C4
Meppel NL 42 C3
Meppen D 43 C4
Mequinenza E 90 B3
Mer F 58 C2
Mera, *Coruña* E 86 A2
Mera, *Coruña* E 86 A3
Meråker N 114 D8
Merano I 71 B6
Merate I 71 C4
Mercadillo E 89 A3
Mercatale I 82 C1
Mercatino Conca I 82 C1
Mercato San Severino I 103 C7
Mercato Saraceno I 82 C1
Merching D 62 B1
Merchtem B 49 C5
Merdrignac F 56 B3
Merdžanići BIH 84 C2
Meré E 88 A2
Mere GB 29 B5
Meréville F 58 B3
Merfeld D 50 B3
Méribel F 69 C6
Méribel Motraret F 69 C6
Meriç TR 118 A1
Mérida E 93 C4
Mérignac F 76 B2
Měřín CZ 64 A1
Mering D 62 B1
Merkendorf D 62 A1
Merklin CZ 63 A4
Merksplas B 49 B5
Merlånna S 37 C3
Merlimont Plage F 48 C2
Mern DK 39 D5
Mernye H 74 B2
Mers-les-Bains F 48 C2
Mersch L 60 A2
Merseburg D 52 B1
Merthyr Tydfil GB 29 B4
Mertingen D 62 B1
Mértola P 98 B3
Méru F 58 A3
Merufe P 87 B2
Mervans F 69 B5
Merville F 48 C3
Méry-sur-Seine F 59 B4
Merzen D 43 C4
Merzifon TR 16 A7
Merzig D 60 A2
Mesagne I 105 C3
Mesão Frio P 87 C3
Mesas de Ibor E 93 B5
Meschede D 50 B4
Meschers-sur-Gironde F 66 C4
Meshchovsk RUS 7 D13
Meslay-du-Maine F 57 C5
Mesna N 34 A2
Mesnalien N 34 A2
Mesocco CH 71 B4
Mésola I 82 B1
Mesologi GR 116 D3
Mesopotamo GR 116 C2
Mesoraca I 107 B3
Messac F 57 C4
Messancy B 60 A1
Messdorf D 44 C3
Messei F 57 B5
Messejana P 98 B2
Messelt N 34 A3
Messina I 109 A4
Messingen D 43 C4
Messini GR 117 E4
Messkirch D 61 C5
Messlingen S 115 E9
Messtetten D 61 B4
Mesta GR 117 D7
Mestanza E 100 A1
Městec Králové CZ 53 C5
Mestlin D 44 B3
Město Albrechłice CZ 54 C2
Město Libavá CZ 64 A3
Město Touškov CZ 63 A4
Mestre I 72 C2
Mesvres F 69 B4
Mesztegnyő H 74 B2
Meta I 103 C7
Metajna HR 83 B4
Metelen D 50 A3
Methana GR 117 E5
Methlick GB 23 D6
Methven GB 25 B4
Methwold GB 30 B4
Metković HR 84 C2
Metlika SLO 73 C5
Metnitz A 73 B4
Metslawier NL 42 B3
Metsovo GR 116 C3
Metten D 62 B3
Mettendorf D 50 D2
Mettet B 49 C5
Mettingen D 50 A3
Mettlach D 60 A2
Mettlen CH 70 B2
Mettmann D 50 B2
Metz F 60 A2
Metzervisse F 60 A2
Metzingen D 61 B5
Meulan F 58 A2
Meung-sur-Loire F 58 C2
Meuselwitz D 52 B2
Meuzac F 67 C6
Mevagissey GB 28 C3
Mexborough GB 27 B4
Meximieux F 69 C5
Mey GB 23 C5
Meyenburg D 44 B4
Meyerhöfen D 43 C5
Meylan F 69 C5
Meymac F 68 C2
Meyrargues F 79 C4
Meyrueis F 78 B2
Meyssac F 77 A4
Meysse F 78 B3
Meyzieu F 69 C4
Mèze F 78 C2
Mézériat F 69 B5
Mežica SLO 73 B4
Mézidon-Canon F 57 A5
Mézières-en-Brenne F 67 B6
Mézières-sur-Issoire F 67 B5
Mézilhac F 78 B3
Mézilles F 59 C4
Mézin F 76 B3
Mezöberény H 75 B6
Mezőcsát H 65 C6
Mezöfalva H 74 B3
Mezöhegyes H 75 B5
Mezökeresztes H 65 C6
Mezökomárom H 74 B3
Mezökövácsháza H 75 B5
Mezökövesd H 65 C6
Mezöörs H 74 A2
Mézos F 76 B1
Mezöszilas H 74 B3
Mezötúr H 75 A5
Mezquita de Jarque E 90 C2
Mezzano, *Emilia Romagna* I 81 B6
Mezzano, *Trentino Alto Adige* I 72 B1
Mezzojuso I 108 B2
Mezzoldo I 71 B4
Mezzolombardo I 71 B6
Mgarr M 107 C5
Mglin RUS 7 E12
Miajadas E 93 B5
Miały PL 46 C2
Mianowice PL 46 A3
Miasteczko Krajeńskie PL 46 B3
Miasteczko Sł. PL 54 C3
Miastko PL 46 A2
Michalovce SK 10 B6
Michałowice PL 55 C4
Michelau D 61 A6
Michelbach D 61 A6
Micheldorf A 63 C5
Michelhausen A 64 B1
Michelsneukirchen D 62 A3
Michelstadt D 61 A5
Michendorf D 52 A3
Michurin BG 11 E9
Mickleover GB 27 C4
Mid Yell GB 22 A7
Midbea GB 23 B6
Middelburg NL 49 B4
Middelfart DK 39 D2
Middelharnis NL 49 B5
Middelkerke B 48 B3
Middelstum NL 42 B3
Middlesbrough GB 27 A4
Middleton GB 24 B1
Middleton Cheney GB 30 B2
Middleton-in-Teesdale GB 26 A3
Middletown GB 19 B5
Middlewich GB 26 B3
Middlezoy GB 29 B5
Midhurst GB 31 D3
Midleton IRL 20 C3
Midlum D 43 B5
Midsomer Norton GB 29 B5
Midtgulen N 114 F2
Midtskogberget N 34 A4
Midwolda NL 43 B4
Miechów PL 55 C5
Miedes de Aragón E 89 C5
Miedes de Atienza E 95 A3
Międzybodzie Bielskie PL 65 A5
Międzybórz PL 54 B2
Międzychód PL 46 C1
Międzylesie PL 54 C1
Międzyrzec Podlaski PL 6 F7
Międzyrzecz PL 46 C1
Międzywodzie PL 45 A6
Międzyzdroje PL 45 B6
Miejska Górka PL 54 B1
Miélan F 76 C3
Mielec PL 55 C6
Mielęcin PL 45 B6
Mielno, *Warmińsko-Mazurskie* PL 47 B6
Mielno, *Zachodnio-Pomorskie* PL 46 A2
Miengo E 88 A3
Mieraslompolo FIN 113 C16
Miercurea Ciuc RO 11 C8
Mieres, *Asturias* E 88 A1
Mieres, *Girona* E 91 A5
Mieroszów PL 53 C6
Mierzyn PL 55 B4
Miesau D 60 A3
Miesbach D 62 C2
Mieścisko PL 46 C3
Mieste D 44 C3
Miesterhorst D 44 C3
Mieszków PL 54 A2
Mieszkowice PL 45 C6
Mietków PL 54 C1
Migennes F 59 C4
Miggiano I 107 B5
Migliánico I 103 A7
Migliarino I 81 B5
Migliónico I 104 C2
Mignano Monte Lungo I 103 B6
Migné F 67 B6
Miguel Esteban E 95 C3
Miguelturra E 94 D3
Mihajlovac SRB 85 B5
Miháld H 74 B2
Mihalgazi TR 118 B5
Mihaliçcik TR 118 C6
Mihályi H 74 A2
Mihla D 51 B6
Mihohnić HR 83 A3
Miholjsko HR 73 C5
Mihovljan HR 73 B5
Mijares E 94 B2
Mijas E 100 C1
Mijoska MNE 85 D4
Mike H 74 B2
Mikhnevo RUS 7 D14
Mikines GR 117 E4
Mikkeli FIN 3 F27
Mikkelvik N 112 B8
Mikleuš HR 74 C2
Mikołajki Pomorskie PL 47 B5
Mikolów PL 54 C3
Mikonos GR 117 E7
Mikorzyn PL 54 B3
Mikro Derio GR 116 A8
Mikstat PL 54 B2
Mikulášovice CZ 53 C4
Mikulov CZ 64 B2
Mikulovice CZ 54 C2
Milagro E 89 B5
Miłakowo PL 47 A6
Milan = Milano I 71 C4
Miland N 32 C5
Milano = Milan I 71 C4
Milano Marittima I 82 B1
Milas TR 119 E2
Milazzo I 109 A4
Mildenhall GB 30 B4
Milejewo PL 47 A5
Milelín CZ 53 C5
Miletić SRB 75 C4
Miletićevo SRB 75 C6
Mileto I 106 C3
Milevsko CZ 63 A5
Milford IRL 19 A4
Milford Haven GB 28 B2
Milford on Sea GB 31 D2
Milhão P 87 C4
Milići BIH 84 B4
Miličin CZ 63 A5
Milicz PL 54 B2
Milín CZ 63 A5
Militello in Val di Catánia I 109 B3
Miljevina BIH 84 C3
Milkowice PL 53 B6
Millançay F 68 A1
Millares E 96 B2
Millas F 91 A5
Millau F 78 B2
Millesimo I 80 B2
Millevaches F 68 C2
Millom GB 26 A2
Millport GB 24 C3
Millstatt A 72 B3
Millstreet, *Cork* IRL 20 B2
Millstreet, *Waterford* IRL 21 B4
Milltown, *Galway* IRL 18 C3
Milltown, *Kerry* IRL 20 B1
Milltown Malbay IRL 20 B2
Milly-la-Forêt F 58 B3
Milmarcos E 95 A5
Milmersdorf D 45 B5
Milna HR 83 C5
Milnthorpe GB 26 A3
Miločaj SRB 85 C5
Milogórze PL 47 A6
Miłomłyn PL 47 B5
Milos GR 117 F6
Miloševo SRB 85 B6
Miłosław PL 54 A2
Milot AL 105 B5
Milówka PL 65 A5
Miltach D 62 A3
Miltenberg D 61 A5
Milton Keynes GB 31 B3
Miltzow D 45 A5
Milutovac SRB 85 C6
Milverton GB 29 B4
Milzyn PL 47 C4
Mimice HR 84 C1
Mimizan F 76 B1
Mimizan-Plage F 76 B1
Mimoň CZ 53 C4
Mina de Juliana P 98 B2
Mina de São Domingos P 98 B3
Minas de Riotinto E 99 B4
Minateda E 101 A4
Minaya E 95 C4
Minde P 92 B2
Mindelheim D 61 B6
Mindelstetten D 62 B2
Minden D 51 A4
Mindszent H 75 B5
Minehead GB 29 B4
Mineo I 109 B3
Minerbe I 71 C6
Minérbio I 81 B5
Minervino Murge I 104 B2
Minglanilla E 95 C5
Mingorria E 94 B2
Minnesund N 34 B3
Miño E 86 A2
Miño de San Esteban E 89 C3
Minsen D 43 B4
Minsk BY 7 E9
Mińsk Mazowiecki PL 55 A6
Minsterley GB 26 C3
Mintlaw GB 23 D6
Minturno I 103 B6
Mionica BIH 84 B3
Mionica SRB 85 B5
Mios F 76 B2
Mira E 96 B1
Mira I 72 C2
Mira P 92 A2
Mirabel E 93 B4
Mirabel-aux-Baronnies F 79 B4
Mirabella Eclano I 103 B8
Mirabella Imbáccari I 109 B3
Mirabello I 81 B5
Miradoux F 77 B3
Miraflores de la Sierra E 94 B3
Miralrio E 95 B4
Miramar P 87 C2
Miramare I 82 B1
Miramas F 78 C3
Mirambeau F 67 C4
Miramont-de-Guyenne F 77 B3
Miranda de Arga E 89 B5
Miranda de Ebro E 89 B4
Miranda do Corvo P 92 A2
Miranda do Douro P 87 C4
Mirande F 77 C3
Mirandela P 87 C3
Mirandilla E 93 C4
Mirándola I 81 B5
Miranje HR 83 B4
Mirano I 72 C2
Miras AL 116 B2
Miravet E 90 B3
Miré F 57 C5
Mirebeau F 67 B5
Mirebeau-sur-Bèze F 69 A5
Mirecourt F 60 B2
Mirepoix F 77 C4
Mires GR 117 G6
Miribel F 69 C4
Miričina BIH 84 B3
Mirina GR 116 C7
Mirna SLO 73 C5
Miroslav CZ 64 B2
Mirosławice PL 54 C1
Mirosławiec PL 46 B2
Mirošov CZ 63 A4
Mirotice CZ 63 A5
Mirovice CZ 63 A5
Mirow D 45 B4
Mirsk PL 53 C5
Mirzec PL 55 B6
Misi FIN 113 F15
Misilmeri I 108 A2
Miske H 75 B4
Miskolc H 65 B6
Mislinja SLO 73 B5
Missanello I 104 C2
Missillac F 66 A2
Mistelbach A 64 B2
Mistelbach D 62 A2
Misten N 112 E3
Misterbianco I 109 B4
Misterhult S 40 B6
Mistretta I 109 B3
Misurina I 72 B2
Mitchelstown IRL 20 B3
Mithimna GR 116 C8
Mithoni GR 117 F3
Mitilini GR 118 C1
Mitilinii GR 119 E1
Mittelberg, *Tirol* A 71 B5
Mittelberg, *Vorarlberg* A 71 A5
Mittenwald D 71 A6
Mittenwalde D 52 A3
Mitter-Kleinarl A 72 A3
Mitterback A 63 C6
Mitterdorf im Mürztal A 73 A5
Mittersheim F 60 B2
Mittersill A 72 A2
Mitterskirchen D 62 B3
Mitterteich D 62 A3
Mitton F 76 B2
Mittweida D 52 C2
Mitwitz D 52 C1
Mizhhir'ya UA 11 B7
Mjällby S 41 C4
Mjåvatn N 33 D5
Mjöbäck S 40 B2
Mjölby S 37 D2
Mjølfjell N 32 B3
Mjøndalen N 35 C2
Mjørlund N 34 B2
Mladá Boleslav CZ 53 C4
Mladá Vožice CZ 63 A5
Mladé Buky CZ 53 C5
Mladenovac SRB 85 B5
Mladenovo SRB 75 C4
Mladikovine BIH 84 B2
Mława PL 47 B6
Mlinište BIH 84 B1
Młodzieszyn PL 55 A5
Mlogoszyn PL 55 A4
Młynary PL 47 A5
Mnichóvice CZ 63 A5
Mnichovo Hradiště CZ 53 C4
Mniów PL 55 B5
Mnisek nad Hnilcom SK 65 B6
Mníšek pod Brdy CZ 63 A5
Mniszek PL 55 B5
Mniszków PL 55 B5
Mo, *Hedmark* N 34 B3
Mo, *Hordaland* N 32 B2
Mo, *Møre og Romsdal* N 114 E5
Mo, *Telemark* N 33 C4
Mo, *Gävleborg* S 36 A3
Mo, *Västra Götaland* S 35 D3
Mo i Rana N 115 A11
Moaña E 87 B2
Moate IRL 21 A4
Mocejón E 94 C3
Močenok SK 64 B3
Mochales E 95 A4
Mochowo PL 47 C5
Mochy PL 53 A6
Mockern D 52 A1
Mockfjärd S 36 B1
Möckmühl D 61 A5
Mockrehna D 52 B2
Moclin E 100 B2
Mocsa H 64 C4
Möcsény H 74 B3
Modane F 70 C1
Modbury GB 28 C4
Módena I 81 B4
Möðrudalur IS 111 B10
Módica I 109 C3
Modigliana I 81 B5
Modlin PL 47 C6
Mödling A 64 B2
Modliszewice PL 55 B5
Modliszewko PL 46 C3
Modogno I 104 B2
Modra SK 64 B3
Modran BIH 84 B2
Modriča BIH 84 B3
Modrý Kamen SK 65 B5
Moëlan-sur-Mer F 56 C2
Moelfre GB 26 B1
Moelv N 34 B2
Moen N 112 C7
Moena I 72 B1
Moerbeke B 49 B4
Moers D 50 B2
Móes P 87 D3
Moffat GB 25 C4
Mogadouro P 87 C4
Mogata S 37 D3
Móggio Udinese I 72 B3
Mogielnica PL 55 B5
Mogilany PL 65 A5
Mogilno PL 46 C3
Mogliano I 82 C2
Mogliano Véneto I 72 C2
Mogor E 87 B2
Mógoro I 110 C1
Moguer E 99 B4
Mohács H 74 C3
Moheda S 40 B4
Mohedas E 93 A4
Mohedas de la Jara E 93 B5
Mohelnice CZ 64 A2
Mohill IRL 19 C4
Möhlin CH 70 A2
Moholm S 35 D6
Mohorn D 52 B3
Mohyliv-Podil's'kyy UA 11 B9
Moi N 33 D3
Moià E 91 B5
Móie I 82 C2
Moimenta da Beira P 87 D3
Moirans F 69 C5
Moirans-en-Montagne F 69 B5
Moisaküla EST 7 B8
Moisdon-la-Rivière F 57 C4
Moissac F 77 B4
Moita, *Coimbra* P 92 A2
Moita, *Guarda* P 93 A3
Moita, *Santarém* P 92 B2
Moita, *Setúbal* P 92 C1
Moita dos Ferreiros P 92 B1
Moixent E 101 A5
Mojacar E 101 B4
Mojados E 88 C2
Mojkovac MNE 85 D4
Mojmírovce SK 64 B4
Mojtin SK 65 B4
Möklinta S 36 B3
Mokošica HR 84 D3
Mokra Gora SRB 85 C4
Mokro Polje HR 83 B5
Mokronog SLO 73 C5
Mokrzyska PL 55 C5
Møkster N 32 B2
Mol B 49 B6
Mol SRB 75 C5
Mola di Bari I 104 B3
Molai GR 117 F4
Molare I 80 B2
Molaretto I 70 C2
Molas F 77 C3
Molassano I 80 B2
Molbergen D 43 C4
Mold GB 26 B2
Molde N 114 E4
Møldrup DK 38 C2
Moledo do Minho P 87 C2
Molfetta I 104 B2
Molfsee D 44 A2
Moliden S 115 D15
Molières F 77 B4
Molina de Aragón E 95 B5
Molina de Segura E 101 A4
Molinar E 89 A3
Molinaseca E 86 B4
Molinella I 81 B5
Molinet F 68 B3
Molini di Tures I 72 B1
Molinicos E 101 A3
Molinos de Duero E 89 C4
Molins de Rei E 91 B5
Moliterno I 104 C1
Molkom S 35 C5
Mollas AL 105 C6
Möllbrücke A 72 B3
Mölle S 41 C2
Molledo E 88 A2
Möllenbeck D 45 B5
Mollerussa E 90 B3
Mollet de Perelada E 91 A5
Mollina E 100 B1
Mölln D 44 B2
Molló E 91 A5
Mollösund S 35 D3
Mölltorp S 37 D1
Mölnbo S 37 C4
Mölndal S 38 B5
Mölnlycke S 38 B5
Molompize F 68 C3
Moloy F 69 A4
Molsheim F 60 B3
Moltzow D 45 B4
Molve HR 74 B2
Molveno I 71 B5
Molvizar E 100 C2
Molzbichl A 72 B3
Mombaróccio I 82 C1
Mombeltrán E 94 B1
Mombris D 51 C5
Mombuey E 87 B4
Momchilgrad BG 116 A7
Mommark DK 39 E3
Momo I 70 C3
Monaghan IRL 19 B5
Monar Lodge GB 22 D4
Monasterace Marina I 106 C3
Monasterevin IRL 21 A4
Monasterio de Rodilla E 89 B3
Monastir I 110 C2
Monbahus F 77 B3
Monbazillac F 77 B3
Moncada E 96 B2
Moncalieri I 80 A1
Moncalvo I 80 A2
Monção P 87 B2
Moncarapacho P 98 B3
Moncel-sur-Seille F 60 B2
Monchegorsk RUS 3 C30
Mönchen-gladbach = Munchen-Gladbach D 50 B2
Mónchio della Corti I 81 B4
Monchique P 98 B2
Monclar-de-Quercy F 77 C4
Moncofa E 96 B2
Moncontour F 56 B3
Moncoutant F 67 B4
Monda E 100 C1
Mondariz E 87 B2
Mondavio I 82 C1
Mondéjar E 95 B3
Mondello I 108 A2
Mondim de Basto P 87 C3
Mondolfo I 82 C2
Mondoñedo E 86 A3
Mondorf-les-Bains L 60 A2
Mondoubleau F 58 C1
Mondovì I 80 B1
Mondragon F 78 B3
Mondragone I 103 B6
Mondsee A 63 C4
Monéglia I 80 B3
Monegrillo E 90 B2
Monein F 76 C2
Monemvasia GR 117 F5
Mónesi I 80 B1
Monesiglio I 80 B2
Monesterio E 99 A4
Monestier-de-Clermont F 79 B4
Monestiés F 77 B5
Monéteau F 59 C4
Moneygall IRL 21 B4
Moneymore GB 19 B5
Monfalcone I 72 C3
Monfero E 86 A2
Monflanquin F 77 B3
Monflorite E 90 A2
Monforte P 92 B3
Monforte da Beira E 92 B3
Monforte da Beira P 92 B3
Monforte d'Alba I 80 B1
Monforte de Lemos E 86 B3
Monforte de Moyuela E 90 B1
Monforte del Cid E 96 C2
Monghidoro I 81 B5
Mongiana I 106 C3
Monguelfo I 72 B2
Monheim D 62 B1
Moniaive GB 25 C4
Monifieth GB 25 B5
Monikie GB 25 B5
Monistrol-d'Allier F 78 B2
Monistrol de Montserrat E 91 B4
Monistrol-sur-Loire F 68 C4
Mönkebude D 45 B5
Monkton GB 24 C3
Monmouth GB 29 B5
Monnaie F 67 A5
Monnerville F 58 B3
Monnickendam NL 42 C2
Monolithos GR 119 F2
Monópoli I 104 C3
Monor H 75 A4
Monóvar E 101 A5
Monpazier F 77 B3
Monreal D 50 C3
Monreal E 76 D1
Monreal del Campo E 95 B5
Monreale I 108 A2
Monroy E 93 B4
Monroyo E 90 C2
Mons B 49 C4
Monsaraz P 92 C3
Monschau D 50 C2
Monségur F 76 B3
Monsélice I 72 C1
Mønshaug N 32 B3
Monster NL 49 A5
Mönsterås S 40 B6
Monsummano Terme I 81 C4
Mont-de-Marsan F 76 C2
Mont-Louis F 91 A5
Mont-roig del Camp E 90 B3
Mont-St. Aignan F 58 A2
Mont-St. Vincent F 69 B4
Mont-sous-Vaudrey F 69 B5
Montabaur D 50 C3
Montafia I 80 B2
Montagnac F 78 C2
Montagnana I 71 C6
Montaigu F 66 B3
Montaigu-de-Quercy F 77 B4
Montaiguët-en-Forez F 68 B3
Montaigut F 68 B2
Montaigut-sur-Save F 77 C4
Montainville F 58 B2
Montalbán E 90 C2
Montalbán de Córdoba E 100 B1
Montalbano Elicona I 109 A4
Montalbano Iónico I 104 C2
Montalbo E 95 C4
Montalcino I 81 C5
Montaldo di Cósola I 80 B3
Montalegre P 87 C3
Montalieu-Vercieu F 69 C5
Montalivet-les-Bains F 66 C3
Montallegro I 108 B2
Montalto delle Marche I 82 D2
Montalto di Castro I 102 A4
Montalto Pavese I 80 B3
Montalto Uffugo I 106 B3
Montalvão P 92 B3
Montamarta E 88 C1
Montana BG 11 E7
Montana-Vermala CH 70 B2
Montánchez E 93 B4
Montanejos E 96 A2
Montano Antilia I 106 A2
Montans F 77 C4
Montargil P 92 B2
Montargis F 58 C3
Montastruc-la-Conseillère F 77 C4
Montauban F 77 B4
Montauban-de-Bretagne F 57 B3
Montbard F 59 C5
Montbarrey F 69 A5
Montbazens F 77 B5
Montbazon F 67 A5
Montbéliard F 70 A1
Montbenoit F 69 B6
Montbeugny F 68 B3
Montblanc E 91 B4
Montbozon F 69 A6
Montbrison F 68 C4
Montbron F 67 C5
Montbrun-les-Bains F 79 B4
Montceau-les-Mines F 69 B4

Montcenis F 69 B4
Montchanin F 69 B4
Montcornet F 59 A5
Montcuq F 77 B4
Montdardier F 78 C2
Montdidier F 58 A3
Monte-Carlo MC 80 C1
Monte Clara P 92 B3
Monte Clérigo P 98 B2
Monte da Pedra P 92 B3
Monte de Goula P 92 B3
Monte do Trigo P 92 C3
Monte Gordo P 98 B3
Monte Juntos P 92 C3
Monte Porzio I 82 C2
Monte Real P 92 B2
Monte Redondo P 92 B2
Monte Romano I 102 A4
Monte San Giovanni Campano I 103 B6
Monte San Savino I 81 C5
Monte Sant'Ángelo I 104 B1
Monte Vilar P 92 B1
Monteagudo E 101 A4
Monteagudo de las Vicarias E 89 C4
Montealegre E 88 C2
Montealegre del Castillo E 101 A4
Montebello Iónico I 109 B4
Montebello Vicentino I 71 C6
Montebelluna I 72 C2
Montebourg F 57 A4
Montebruno I 80 B3
Montecarotto I 82 C2
Montecassiano I 82 C2
Montecastrilli I 102 A5
Montecatini Terme I 81 C4
Montécchio I 82 C1
Montécchio Emilia I 81 B4
Montécchio Maggiore I 71 C6
Montech F 77 C4
Montechiaro d'Asti I 80 A2
Montecórice I 103 C7
Montecorvino Rovella I 103 C7
Montederramo E 87 B3
Montedoro I 108 B2
Montefalco I 82 D1
Montefalcone di Val Fortore I 103 B8
Montefalcone nel Sánnio I 103 B7
Montefano I 82 C2
Montefiascone I 102 A5
Montefiorino I 81 B4
Montefortino I 82 D2
Montefranco I 102 A5
Montefrío E 100 B2
Montegiordano Marina I 106 A3
Montegiórgio I 82 C2
Montegranaro I 82 C2
Montehermoso E 93 A4
Montejicar E 100 B2
Montejo de la Sierra E 95 A3
Montejo de Tiermes E 89 C3
Montel-de-Gelat F 68 C2
Monteleone di Púglia I 103 B8
Monteleone di Spoleto I 102 A5
Monteleone d'Orvieto I 81 D6
Montelepre I 108 A2
Montelibretti I 102 A5
Montelier F 79 B4
Montélimar F 78 B3
Montella E 91 A4
Montella I 103 C8
Montellano E 99 B5
Montelupo Fiorentino I 81 C5
Montemaggiore Belsito I 108 B2
Montemagno I 80 B2
Montemayor E 100 B1
Montemayor de Pinilla E 88 C2
Montemésola I 104 C3
Montemilletto I 103 B7
Montemilone I 104 B1
Montemolín E 99 A4
Montemónaco I 82 D2
Montemor-o-Novo P 92 C2
Montemor-o-Velho P 92 A2
Montemurro I 104 C1
Montendre F 67 C4
Montenegro de Cameros E 89 B4
Montenero di Bisáccia I 103 B7
Monteneuf F 57 C3
Monteparano I 104 C3
Montepescali I 81 D5
Montepiano I 81 B5
Montepulciano I 81 C5
Montereale I 103 A6
Montereale Valcellina I 72 B2
Montereau-Faut-Yonne F 59 B3
Monterénzio I 81 B5
Monteroni d'Arbia I 81 C5
Monteroni di Lecce I 105 C4
Monterosso al Mare I 80 B3
Monterosso Almo I 109 B3
Monterosso Grana I 79 B6
Monterotondo I 102 A5
Monterotondo Maríttimo I 81 C4
Monterrey E 87 C3
Monterroso E 86 B3
Monterrubio de la Serena E 93 C5
Monterubbiano I 82 C2
Montes Velhos P 98 B2
Montesa E 96 C2
Montesalgueiro E 86 A2
Montesano sulla Marcellana I 104 C1
Montesárchio I 103 B7
Montescaglioso I 104 C2
Montesclaros E 94 B2
Montesilvano I 103 A7
Montespértoli I 81 C5
Montesquieu-Volvestre F 77 C4
Montesquiou F 77 C3
Montestruc-sur-Gers F 77 C3
Montevarchi I 81 C5
Montéveglio I 81 B5
Montfaucon F 66 A3
Montfaucon-d'Argonne F 59 A6
Montfaucon-en-Velay F 69 C4
Montferrat, *Isère* F 69 C5
Montferrat, *Var* F 79 C5
Montfort-en-Chalosse F 76 C2
Montfort-l'Amaury F 58 B2
Montfort-le-Gesnois F 58 B1
Montfort-sur-Meu F 57 B4
Montfort-sur-Risle F 58 A1
Montgai E 90 B3
Montgaillard F 76 C3
Montgenèvre F 79 B5
Montgiscard F 77 C4
Montgomery GB 26 C2
Montguyon F 67 C4
Monthermé F 59 A5
Monthey CH 70 B1
Monthois F 59 A5
Monthureux-sur-Saône F 60 B1
Monti I 110 B2
Monticelli d'Ongina I 81 A3
Montichiari I 71 C5
Monticiano I 81 C5
Montiel E 100 A3
Montier-en-Der F 59 B5
Montieri I 81 C5
Montiglio I 80 A2
Montignac F 77 A4
Montigny-le-Roi F 60 C1
Montigny-lès-Metz F 60 A2
Montigny-sur-Aube F 59 C5
Montijo E 93 C4
Montijo P 92 C2
Montilla E 100 B1
Montillana E 100 B2
Montilly F 68 B3
Montivilliers F 57 A6
Montjaux F 78 B1
Montjean-sur-Loire F 66 A4
Montlhéry F 58 B3
Montlieu-la-Gard F 67 C4
Montlouis-sur-Loire F 67 A5
Montluçon F 68 B2
Montluel F 69 C5
Montmarault F 68 B2
Montmartin-sur-Mer F 57 B4
Montmédy F 59 A6
Montmélian F 69 C6
Montmeyan F 79 C5
Montmeyran F 78 B3
Montmirail, *Marne* F 59 B4
Montmirail, *Sarthe* F 58 B1
Montmiral F 69 C5
Montmirat F 78 C3
Montmirey-le-Château F 69 A5
Montmoreau-St. Cybard F 67 C5
Montmorency F 58 B3
Montmorillon F 67 B5
Montmort-Lucy F 59 B4
Montoir-de-Bretagne F 66 A2
Montoire-sur-le-Loir F 58 C1
Montoito P 92 C3
Montolieu F 77 C5
Montório al Vomano I 103 A6
Montoro E 100 A1
Montpellier F 78 C2
Montpezat-de-Quercy F 77 B4
Montpezat-sous-Bouzon F 78 B3
Montpon-Ménestérol F 76 A3
Montpont-en-Bresse F 69 B5
Montréal, *Aude* F 77 C5
Montréal, *Gers* F 76 C3
Montredon-Labessonnié F 77 C5
Montréjeau F 77 C3
Montrésor F 67 A6
Montresta I 110 B1
Montret F 69 B5
Montreuil, *Pas de Calais* F 48 C2
Montreuil, *Seine St. Denis* F 58 B3
Montreuil-aux-Lions F 59 A4
Montreuil-Bellay F 67 A4
Montreux CH 70 B1
Montrevault F 66 A3
Montrevel-en-Bresse F 69 B5
Montrichard F 67 A6
Montricoux F 77 B4
Montrond-les-Bains F 69 C4
Montrose GB 25 B5
Montroy E 96 B2
Monts-sur-Guesnes F 67 B5
Montsalvy F 77 B5
Montsauche-les-Settons F 68 A4
Montseny E 91 B5
Montsoreau F 67 A5
Montsûrs F 57 B5
Montuenga E 94 A2
Montuïri E 97 B3
Monturque E 100 B1
Monza I 71 C4
Monzón E 90 B3
Monzón de Campos E 88 B2
Moorbad Lobenstein D 52 C1
Moordorf D 43 B4
Moorslede B 49 C4
Moos D 61 C4
Moosburg D 62 B2
Moosburg im Kärnten A 73 B4
Mór H 74 A3
Mora E 94 C3
Mora P 92 C2
Móra S 36 A1
Mora de Rubielos E 96 A2
Mòra d'Ebre E 90 B3
Mòra la Nova E 90 B3
Moraby S 36 B2
Moradillo de Roa E 88 C3
Morąg PL 47 B5
Mórahalom H 75 B4
Moraime E 86 A1
Morais P 87 C4
Moral de Calatrava E 100 A2
Moraleda de Zafayona E 100 B2
Moraleja E 93 A4
Moraleja del Vino E 88 C1
Morales de Toro E 88 C1
Morales de Valverde E 88 C1
Morales del Vino E 88 C1
Moralina E 87 C4
Morano Cálabro I 106 B3
Mörarp S 41 C2
Morasverdes E 93 A4
Morata de Jalón E 89 C5
Morata de Jiloca E 89 C5
Morata de Tajuña E 95 B3
Moratalla E 101 A4
Moravče SLO 73 B4
Moravec CZ 64 A2
Moraviţa RO 75 C6
Morávka CZ 65 A4
Moravská Třebová CZ 64 A2
Moravské Budějovice CZ 64 A1
Moravské Lieskové SK 64 B3
Moravske Toplice SLO 73 B6
Moravský-Beroun CZ 64 A3
Moravský Krumlov CZ 64 A2
Moravský Svätý Ján SK 64 B3
Morawica PL 55 C5
Morawin PL 54 B3
Morbach D 60 A3
Morbegno I 71 B4
Morbier F 69 B6
Mörbisch am See A 64 C2
Mörbylånga S 41 C6
Morcenx F 76 B2
Morciano di Romagna I 82 C1
Morcone I 103 B7
Morcuera E 89 C3
Mordelles F 57 B4
Mordoğan TR 119 D1
Moréac F 56 C3
Morebattle GB 25 C5
Morecambe GB 26 A3
Moreda, *Granada* E 100 B2
Moreda, *Oviedo* E 88 A1
Morée F 58 C2
Moreles de Rey E 88 B1
Morella E 90 C2
Moreruela de los Infanzones E 88 C1
Morés E 89 C5
Móres I 110 B1
Morestel F 69 C5
Moret-sur-Loing F 58 B3
Moreton-in-Marsh GB 29 B6
Moretonhampstead GB 28 C4
Moretta I 80 B1
Moreuil F 58 A3
Morez F 69 B6
Mörfelden D 51 D4
Morgat F 56 B1
Morges CH 69 B6
Morgex I 70 C2
Morgongåva S 36 C3
Morhange F 60 B2
Morhet B 49 D6
Mori I 71 C5
Morialmé B 49 C5
Morianes P 98 B3
Moriani Plage F 102 A2
Mórichida H 74 A2
Moriles E 100 B1
Morille E 94 B1
Moringen D 51 B5
Morjärv S 3 C25
Morkarla S 36 B4
Mørke DK 39 C3
Mørkøv DK 39 D4
Morkovice-Slížany CZ 64 A3
Morlaàs F 76 C2
Morlaix F 56 B2
Morley F 59 B6
Mörlunda S 40 B5
Mormanno I 106 B2
Mormant F 59 B3
Mornant F 69 C4
Mornay-Berry F 68 A2
Morokovo MNE 85 D4
Morón de Almazán E 89 C4
Morón de la Frontera E 99 B5
Morović SRB 85 A4
Morozzo I 80 B1
Morpeth GB 25 C6
Morphou CY 120 A1
Mörrum S 41 C4
Morsbach D 50 C3
Mörsch D 61 B4
Mörsil S 115 D10
Morsum D 39 E1
Mørsvikbotn N 112 E4
Mortagne-au-Perche F 58 B1
Mortagne-sur-Gironde F 66 C4
Mortagne-sur-Sèvre F 66 B4
Mortágua P 92 A2
Mortain F 57 B5
Mortara I 70 C3
Morteau F 69 A6
Mortegliano I 72 C3
Mortelle I 109 A4
Mortemart F 67 B5
Mortimer's Cross GB 29 A5
Mortrée F 57 B6
Mörtschach A 72 B2
Mortsel B 49 B5
Morud DK 39 D3
Morwenstow GB 28 C3
Moryń PL 45 C6
Morzeszczyn PL 47 B4
Morzewo PL 47 B5
Morzine F 70 B1
Mosalsk RUS 7 D13
Mosbach D 61 A5
Mosbjerg DK 38 B3
Mosby N 33 D4
Mosca P 87 C4
Moscavide P 92 C1
Moščenica HR 73 C6
Mošćenice HR 73 C4
Moščenicka Draga HR 73 C4
Mosciano Sant'Ángelo I 82 D2
Mościsko PL 54 C1
Moscow = Moskva RUS 7 D14
Mosina PL 54 A1
Mosjøen N 115 B10
Moskog N 32 A3
Moskorzew PL 55 C4
Moskosel S 115 B16
Moskuvarra FIN 113 E15
Moskva = Moscow RUS 7 D14
Moslavina Podravska HR 74 C2
Moşniţa Nouă RO 75 C6
Moso in Passíria I 71 B6
Mosonmagyaróvár H 64 C3
Mošorin SRB 75 C5
Mošovce SK 65 B4
Mosqueruela E 90 C2
Moss N 35 C2
Mossfellsbær IS 111 C4
Mössingen D 61 B5
Møsstrand N 32 C5
Most CZ 52 C3
Most na Soči SLO 72 B3
Mosta M 107 C5
Mostar BIH 84 C2
Mosterhamn N 33 C2
Mostki PL 53 A5
Móstoles E 94 B3
Mostová SK 64 B3
Mostowo PL 46 A2
Mostuéjouls F 78 B2
Mosty PL 45 B6
Mostys'ka UA 11 B7
Mosvik N 114 D7
Mota del Cuervo E 95 C4
Mota del Marqués E 88 C1
Motala S 37 D2
Motherwell GB 25 C4
Möthlow D 45 C4
Motilla del Palancar E 95 C5
Motnik SLO 73 B4
Motovun HR 72 C3
Motril E 100 C2
Motta I 71 C6
Motta di Livenza I 72 C2
Motta Montecorvino I 103 B8
Motta Visconti I 70 C3
Mottisfont GB 31 C2
Móttola I 104 C3
Mou DK 38 C3
Mouchard F 69 B5
Moudon CH 70 B1
Moudros GR 116 C7
Mougins F 79 C5
Mouilleron en-Pareds F 66 B4
Mouliherne F 67 A5
Moulinet F 80 C1
Moulins F 68 B3
Moulins-Engilbert F 68 B3
Moulins-la-Marche F 58 B1
Moulismes F 67 B5
Moult F 57 A5
Mount Bellew Bridge IRL 20 A3
Mountain Ash GB 29 B4
Mountfield GB 19 B4
Mountmellick IRL 21 A4
Mountrath IRL 21 A4
Mountsorrel GB 30 B2
Moura P 98 A3
Mourão P 92 C3
Mourenx F 76 C2
Mouriés F 78 C3
Mourmelon-le-Grand F 59 A5
Mouronho P 92 A2
Mouscron B 49 C4
Mousehole GB 28 C2
Moussac F 78 C3
Moussey F 60 B2
Mousteru F 56 B2
Moustey F 76 B2
Moustiers-Ste. Marie F 79 C5
Mouthe F 69 B6
Mouthier-Haute-Pierre F 69 A6
Mouthoumet F 77 D5
Moutier CH 70 A2
Moûtiers F 69 C6
Moutiers-les-Mauxfaits F 66 B3
Mouy F 58 A3
Mouzaki GR 116 C3
Mouzon F 59 A6
Møvik N 32 B2
Moville IRL 19 A4
Moy, *Highland* GB 23 D4
Moy, *Tyrone* GB 19 B5
Moycullen IRL 20 A2
Moyenmoutier F 60 B2
Moyenvic F 60 B2
Mózar E 88 C1
Mozhaysk RUS 7 D14
Mozirje SLO 73 B4
Mözs H 74 B3
Mozzanica I 71 C4
Mramorak SRB 85 B5
Mrčajevci SRB 85 C5
Mrkonjić Grad BIH 84 B2
Mrkopalj HR 73 C4
Mrmoš SRB 85 C6
Mrocza PL 46 B3
Mroczeń PL 54 B2
Mroczno PL 47 B5
Mrozy PL 55 A6
Mrzezyno PL 45 A7
Mšec CZ 53 C3
Mšeno CZ 53 C4
Mstów PL 55 C4
Mstsislaw BY 7 D11
Mszana Dolna PL 65 A6
Mszczonów PL 55 B5
Mtsensk RUS 7 E14
Muć HR 83 C5
Múccia I 82 C2
Much D 50 C3
Much Marcle GB 29 B5
Much Wenlock GB 26 C3
Mücheln D 52 B1
Muchów PL 53 B6
Mucientes E 88 C2
Muckross IRL 20 B2
Mucur TR 16 B7
Muda P 98 B2
Mudanya TR 118 B3
Mudau D 61 A5
Müden D 44 C2
Mudersbach D 50 C3
Mudurnu TR 118 B6
Muel E 90 B1
Muelas del Pan E 88 C1
Muess D 44 B3
Muff IRL 19 A4
Mugardos E 86 A2
Muge P 92 B2
Mügeln, *Sachsen-Anhalt* D 52 B3
Mügeln, *Sachsen* D 52 B3
Múggia I 72 C3
Mugla TR 119 E3
Mugnano I 82 C1
Mugron F 76 C2
Mugueimes E 87 C3
Muhi H 65 C6
Mühlacker D 61 B4
Mühlbach am Hochkönig A 72 A3
Mühlberg, *Brandenburg* D 52 B3
Mühlberg, *Thüringen* D 51 C6
Mühldorf A 72 B3
Mühldorf D 62 B3
Muhleberg CH 70 B2
Mühleim D 61 B4
Muhlen-Eichsen D 44 B3
Mühlhausen, *Bayern* D 62 A1
Mühlhausen, *Thüringen* D 51 B6
Mühltroff D 52 C1
Muhos FIN 3 D27
Muhr A 72 A3
Muine Bheag IRL 21 B5
Muir of Ord GB 23 D4
Muirkirk GB 24 C3
Muirteira P 92 B1
Mukacheve UA 11 B7
Muker GB 26 A3
Mula E 101 A4
Mulben GB 23 D5
Mulegns CH 71 B4
Mules I 71 B6
Mülheim D 50 B2
Mulhouse F 60 C3
Muljava SLO 73 C4
Mullanys Cross IRL 18 B3
Müllheim D 60 C3
Mullhyttan S 37 C1
Mullinavat IRL 21 B4
Mullingar IRL 21 A4
Mullion GB 28 C2
Müllrose D 53 A4
Mullsjö S 40 B3
Mulseryd S 40 B3
Munaðarnes IS 111 A4
Munana E 94 B1
Muñás E 86 A4
Münchberg D 52 C1
Müncheberg D 45 C6
München = Munich D 62 B2
München-Gladbach = Mönchen-gladbach D 50 B2
Münchhausen D 51 C4
Mundaka E 89 A4
Münden D 51 B5
Munderfing A 63 B4
Munderkingen D 61 B5
Mundesley GB 30 B5
Munera E 95 C4
Mungia E 89 A4
Munich = München D 62 B2
Muñico E 94 B1
Muniesa E 90 B2
Munka-Ljungby S 41 C2
Munkebo DK 39 D3
Munkedal S 35 D3
Munkflohögen S 115 D11
Munkfors S 34 C5
Munktorp S 37 C3
Münnerstadt D 51 C6
Muñopepe E 94 B2
Muñotello E 94 B1
Münsingen CH 70 B2
Münsingen D 61 B5
Munsö S 37 C4
Münster CH 70 B3
Münster, *Hessen* D 61 A4
Münster, *Niedersachsen* D 44 C2
Münster, *Nordrhein-Westfalen* D 50 B3
Munster F 60 B3
Muntibar E 89 A4
Münzkirchen A 63 B4
Muodoslompolo S 113 E12
Muonio FIN 113 E12
Muotathal CH 70 B3
Mur-de-Barrez F 77 B5
Mur-de-Bretagne F 56 B2
Mur-de-Sologne F 67 A6
Muradiye TR 118 D2
Murakeresztúr H 74 B1
Murán SK 65 B6
Murano I 72 C2
Muras E 86 A3
Murat F 78 A1
Murat-sur-Vèbre F 78 C1
Muratlı TR 118 A2
Murato F 102 A2
Murau A 73 A4
Muravera I 110 C2
Murazzano I 80 B2
Murça P 87 C3
Murchante E 89 B5
Murchin D 45 B5
Murcia E 101 B4
Murczyn PL 46 C3
Mureck A 73 B5
Mürefte TR 118 B2
Muret F 77 C4
Murg CH 71 A4
Murguia E 89 B4
Muri CH 70 A3
Murias de Paredes E 86 B4
Muriedas E 88 A3
Muriel Viejo E 89 C4
Murillo de Rio Leza E 89 B4
Murillo el Fruto E 89 B5
Murino MNE 85 D4
Muriqan AL 105 A5
Murlaggan GB 22 E3
Murmansk RUS 3 B30
Murmashi RUS 3 B30
Murnau D 62 C2
Muro E 97 B3
Muro F 102 A1
Muro de Alcoy E 96 C2
Muro Lucano I 103 C8
Murol F 68 C2
Muron F 66 B4
Muros E 86 B1
Muros de Nalón E 86 A4
Murowana Goślina PL 46 C3
Mürren CH 70 B2
Murrhardt D 61 B5
Murska Sobota SLO 73 B6
Mursko Središće HR 73 B6
Murtas E 100 C2
Murten CH 70 B2
Murter HR 83 C4
Murtiçi TR 119 F6
Murtosa P 87 D2
Murvica HR 83 B4
Murviel-lès-Béziers F 78 C2
Mürzsteg A 63 C6
Murzynowo PL 46 C1
Mürzzuschlag A 63 C6
Musculdy F 76 C2
Mushqeta AL 105 B5
Muskö S 37 C5
Mušov CZ 64 B2
Musselburgh GB 25 C4
Musselkanaal NL 43 C4
Mussidan F 77 A3
Mussomeli I 108 B2
Musson B 60 A1
Mussy-sur-Seine F 59 C5
Mustafakemalpaşa TR 118 B3
Muszaki PL 47 B6
Muszyna PL 65 A6
Mut TR 16 C6
Muta SLO 73 B5
Muthill GB 25 B4
Mutné SK 65 A5
Mutriku E 89 A4
Muttalip TR 118 C5
Mutterbergalm A 71 A6
Muxía E 86 A1
Muxilka-Ugarte E 89 A4
Muzillac F 66 A2
Mužla SK 65 C4
Muzzano del Turgnano I 72 C3
Mybster GB 23 C5
Myckelgensjö S 115 D14
Myennes F 68 A2
Myjava SK 64 B3
Myking N 32 B2
Mykland N 33 D5
Mykolayiv = Nikolayev UA 11 C12
Myra N 33 D6
Myrdal N 32 B4
Myre, *Nordland* N 112 D4
Myre, *Nordland* N 112 C4
Myresjö S 40 B4
Myrhorod UA 11 B12
Mýri IS 111 B8
Myrtou CY 120 A2
Mysen N 35 C3
Mysłakowice PL 53 C5
Myślenice PL 65 A5
Myślibórz PL 45 C6
Mysłowice PL 55 C4
Myszków PL 55 C4
Mytishchi RUS 7 D14
Mýtna SK 65 B5
Mýtne Ludany SK 65 B4
Mýto CZ 63 A4

N

N Unnaryd S 40 B3
Nå N 32 B3
Naaldwijk NL 49 B5
Naantali FIN 6 A6
Naas IRL 21 A5
Nabais P 92 A3
Nabbelund S 41 B7
Nabburg D 62 A3
Načeradec CZ 63 A5
Náchod CZ 53 C6
Nacław PL 46 A2
Nadarzyce PL 46 B2
Nadarzyn PL 55 A5
Nádasd H 74 B1
Nădlac RO 75 B5
Nádudvar H 75 A6
Nadvirna UA 11 B8
Nærbø N 33 D2
Næsbjerg DK 39 D1
Næstved DK 39 D4
Näfels CH 70 A4
Nafpaktos GR 116 D3
Nafplio GR 117 E4
Nagel D 52 D1
Nagele NL 42 C2
Naggen S 115 E13
Nagłowice PL 55 C5
Nagold D 61 B4
Nagore E 76 D1
Nagyatád H 74 B2
Nagybajom H 74 B2
Nagybaracska H 74 B3
Nagybátony H 65 C5
Nagyberény H 74 B3
Nagybörzsöny H 65 C4
Nagycenk H 64 C2
Nagydorog H 74 B3
Nagyfüged H 65 C6
Nagyhersány H 74 C3
Nagyigmánd H 64 C4
Nagyiván H 75 A5
Nagykanizsa H 74 B1
Nagykáta H 75 A4
Nagykonyi H 74 B3
Nagykőrös H 75 A4
Nagykörü H 75 A5
Nagylóc H 65 B5
Nagymágocs H 75 B5
Nagymányok H 74 B3
Nagymaros H 65 C4
Nagyoroszi H 65 B5
Nagyrábé H 75 A6
Nagyréde H 65 C5
Nagyszékely H 74 B3
Nagyszénás H 75 B5
Nagyszokoly H 74 B3
Nagytöke H 75 B5
Nagyvázsony H 74 B2
Nagyvenyim H 74 B3
Naharros E 95 B4
Nahe D 44 B2
Naidăş RO 85 B6
Naila D 52 C1
Nailloux F 77 C4
Nailsworth GB 29 B5
Naintré F 67 B5
Nairn GB 23 D5
Najac F 77 B4
Nájera E 89 B4
Nak H 74 B3
Nakksjø N 33 C6
Nakło nad Notecią PL 46 B3
Nakskov DK 39 E4
Nalda E 89 B4
Nälden S 115 D11
Nálepkovo SK 65 B6
Nalliers F 66 B3
Nallıhan TR 118 B6
Nalzen F 77 D4
Nalžouské Hory CZ 63 A4
Namdalseid N 114 C8
Náměšť nad Oslavou CZ 64 A2
Námestovo SK 65 A5

Namnå N 34 B4
Namsos N 114 C8
Namsskogan N 115 C10
Namur B 49 C5
Namysłów PL 54 B2
Nançay F 68 A2
Nanclares de la Oca E 89 B4
Nancy F 60 B2
Nangis F 59 B4
Nannestad N 34 B3
Nant F 78 B2
Nanterre F 58 B3
Nantes F 66 A3
Nanteuil-le-Haudouin F 58 A3
Nantiat F 67 B6
Nantua F 69 B5
Nantwich GB 26 B3
Naoussa, *Imathia* GR 116 B4
Naoussa, *Cyclades* GR 117 E7
Napajedla CZ 64 A3
Napiwoda PL 47 B6
Naples = Nápoli I 103 C7
Nápoli = Naples I 103 C7
Nar S 37 E5
Nara N 32 A1
Naraval E 86 A4
Narberth GB 28 B3
Narbonne F 78 C1
Narbonne-Plage F 78 C2
Narbuvollen N 114 E8
Narcao I 110 C1
Nardò I 107 A5
Narken S 113 F11
Narmo N 34 B3
Narni I 102 A5
Naro I 108 B2
Naro Fominsk RUS 7 D14
Narón E 86 A2
Narros del Castillo E 94 B1
Narta HR 74 C1
Naruszewo PL 47 C6
Narva EST 7 B10
Narvik N 112 D6
Narzole I 80 B1
Näs FIN 36 B7
Nås, *Dalarnas* S 36 B1
Näs, *Gotland* S 37 E5
Näsåker S 115 D13
Năsăud RO 11 C8
Nasavrky CZ 64 A1
Nasbinals F 78 B2
Näshull S 40 B5
Našice HR 74 C3
Nasielsk PL 47 C6
Naso I 109 A3
Nassau D 50 C3
Nassenfels D 62 B2
Nassenheide D 45 C5
Nassereith A 71 A5
Nässjö S 40 B4
Nastätten D 50 C3
Näsum S 41 C4
Näsviken S 115 D12
Natalinci SRB 85 B5
Nater-Stetten D 62 B2
Naters CH 70 B3
Nattavaara S 112 F9
Natters A 71 A6
Nattheim D 61 B6
Nättraby S 41 C5
Naturno I 71 B5
Naucelle F 77 B5
Nauders A 71 B5
Nauen D 45 C4
Naul IRL 19 C5
Naumburg D 52 B1
Naundorf D 52 C3
Naunhof D 52 B2
Naustdal N 32 A2
Nautijaur S 112 F8
Nautsi RUS 113 D18
Nava E 88 A1
Nava de Arévalo E 94 B2
Nava de la Asunción E 94 A2
Nava del Rey E 88 C1
Navacerrada E 94 B2
Navaconcejo E 93 A5
Navafriá E 94 A3
Navahermosa E 94 C2
Navahrudak BY 7 E8
Naval E 90 A3
Navalacruz E 94 B2
Navalcán E 94 B1
Navalcarnero E 94 B2
Navaleno E 89 C3
Navalmanzano E 94 A2
Navalmoral E 94 B2
Navalmoral de la Mata E 93 B5
Naválón E 96 C2
Navalonguilla E 93 A5
Navalperal de Pinares E 94 B2
Navalpino E 94 C2
Navaltalgordo E 94 B2
Navaltoril E 94 C2
Navaluenga E 94 B2
Navalvillar de Pela E 93 B5
Navan IRL 19 C5
Navaperal de Tormes E 93 A5
Navapolatsk BY 7 D10
Navarclés E 91 B4
Navarredonda de Gredos E 93 A5
Navarrenx F 76 C2
Navarrés E 96 B2
Navarrete E 89 B4
Navarrevisca E 94 B2
Navás E 91 B4
Navas de Oro E 94 A2
Navas de San Juan E 100 A2
Navas del Madroño E 93 B4
Navas del Rey E 94 B2
Navas del Sepillar E 100 B1
Navascués E 76 D1
Navasfrias E 93 A4
Nave I 71 C5
Nave de Haver P 93 A4
Nävekvarn S 37 D3
Navelli I 103 A6
Navenby GB 27 B5
Näverkärret S 37 C2
Naverstad S 35 D3
Navés E 91 B4
Navezuelas E 93 B5
Navia E 86 A4
Navia de Suarna E 86 B4
Navilly F 69 B5
Navlya RUS 7 E13
Năvodari RO 11 D10
Naxos GR 117 E7
Nay F 76 C2
Nazaré P 92 B1
Nazarje SLO 73 B4
Nazilli TR 119 E3
Nazza D 51 B6
Ndroq AL 105 B5
Nea Anchialos GR 116 C4
Nea Epidavros GR 117 E5
Nea Flippias GR 116 C2
Nea Kalikratia GR 116 B5
Nea Makri GR 117 D5
Nea Moudania GR 116 B5
Nea Peramos GR 116 B6
Nea Stira GR 117 D6
Nea Visa GR 118 A1
Nea Zichni GR 116 A5
Neap GB 22 A7
Neapoli, *Kozani* GR 116 B3
Neapoli, *Kriti* GR 117 G7
Neapoli, *Lakonia* GR 117 F5
Neath GB 28 B4
Nebljusi HR 83 B4
Neblo SLO 72 B3
Nebolchy RUS 7 B12
Nebra D 52 B1
Nebreda E 88 C3
Nechanice CZ 53 C5
Neckargemünd D 61 A4
Neckarsulm D 61 A5
Neda E 86 A2
Neded SK 64 B3
Nedelišće HR 73 B6
Nederweert NL 50 B1
Nedre Gärdsjö S 36 B2
Nedre Soppero S 113 D10
Nedreberg N 34 B3
Nedstrand N 33 C2
Nedvědice CZ 64 A2
Nędza PL 54 C3
Neede NL 50 A2
Needham Market GB 30 B5
Needingworth GB 30 B3
Neermoor D 43 B4
Neeroeteren B 50 B1
Neerpelt B 49 B6
Neesen D 51 A4
Neetze D 44 B2
Nefyn GB 26 C1
Negbina SRB 85 C4
Negotin SRB 11 D7
Negotino MK 116 A4
Negrar I 71 C5
Negredo E 95 A4
Negreira E 86 B2
Nègrepelisse F 77 B4
Negru Vodă RO 11 E10
Negueira de Muñiz E 86 A4
Neheim D 50 B3
Neila E 89 B4
Néive I 80 B2
Nejdek CZ 52 C2
Nekla PL 46 C3
Neksø DK 41 D5
Nelas P 92 A3
Nelaug N 33 D5
Nelidovo RUS 7 C12
Nelim FIN 113 D17
Nellingen D 61 B5
Nelson GB 26 B3
Neman RUS 6 D7
Nemea GR 117 E4
Nemesgörzsöny H 74 A2
Nemeskér H 74 A1
Nemesnádudvar H 75 B4
Nemesszalók H 74 A2
Németkér H 74 B3
Nemours F 58 B3
Nemška Loka SLO 73 C5
Nemšová SK 64 B4
Nenagh IRL 20 B3
Nenince SK 65 B5
Nenita GR 117 D8
Nenzing A 71 A4
Neo Chori GR 116 C3
Neochori GR 116 C3
Neon Petritsi GR 116 A5
Nepi I 102 A5
Nepomuk CZ 63 A4
Nérac F 77 B3
Neratovice CZ 53 C4
Nerchau D 52 B2
Néré F 67 C4
Neresheim D 61 B6
Nereto I 82 D2
Nerezine HR 82 B3
Nerežišća HR 83 C5
Neringa LT 6 D6
Néris-les Bains F 68 B2
Nerito I 103 A6
Nerja E 100 C2
Néronde F 69 C4
Nérondes F 68 B2
Nerpio E 101 A3
Nersingen D 61 B6
Nerva E 99 B4
Nervesa della Battáglia I 72 C2
Nervi I 80 B3
Nes, *Buskerud* N 34 B1
Nes, *Hedmark* N 34 B2
Nes N 114 D6
Nes NL 42 B2
Nesbyen N 32 B6
Neset N 114 F7
Nesflaten N 33 C3
Nesjahverfi IS 111 C10
Neskaupstaður IS 111 B12
Nesland N 33 C4
Neslandsvatn N 33 D6
Nesle F 59 A3
Nesna N 115 A10
Nesoddtangen N 34 C2
Nesovice CZ 64 A3
Nesselwang D 61 C6
Nesslau CH 71 A4
Nessmersiel D 43 B4
Nesso I 71 C4
Nesterov UA 11 A7
Nestorio GR 116 B3
Nesttun N 32 B2
Nesvady SK 64 C4
Nesvatstemmen N 33 D5
Nether Stowey GB 29 B4
Netland N 33 D3
Netolice CZ 63 A5
Netphen D 50 C4
Netstal CH 70 A4
Nettancourt F 59 B5
Nettetal D 50 B2
Nettlingen D 51 A6
Nettuno I 102 B5
Neu Darchau D 44 B2
Neu-Isenburg D 51 C4
Neu Kaliss D 44 B3
Neu Lübbenau D 53 A3
Neu-Ulm D 61 B6
Neualbenreuth D 52 D2
Neubeckum D 50 B4
Neubrandenburg D 45 B5
Neubruch-hausen D 43 C5
Neubukow D 44 A3
Neuburg D 62 B2
Neuchâtel CH 70 B1
Neudau A 73 A6
Neudietendorf D 51 C6
Neudorf D 61 A4
Neuenbürg, *Baden-Württemberg* D 61 B4
Neuenburg, *Niedersachsen* D 43 B4
Neuendorf D 45 A5
Neuenhagen D 45 C5
Neuenhaus D 42 C3
Neuenkirchen, *Niedersachsen* D 43 C5
Neuenkirchen, *Niedersachsen* D 43 B6
Neuenkirchen, *Nordrhein-Westfalen* D 50 A3
Neuenkirchen, *Nordrhein-Westfalen* D 50 C3
Neuenrade D 50 B3
Neuenwalde D 43 B5
Neuerburg D 50 C2
Neuf-Brisach F 60 B3
Neufahrn, *Bayern* D 62 B2
Neufahrn, *Bayern* D 62 B3
Neufchâteau B 60 A1
Neufchâteau F 60 B1
Neufchâtel-en-Bray F 58 A2
Neufchâtel-sur-Aisne F 59 A5
Neuflize F 59 A5
Neugersdorf D 53 C4
Neuhardenberg D 45 C6
Neuharlingersiel D 43 B4
Neuhaus, *Bayern* D 62 A2
Neuhaus, *Bayern* D 63 B4
Neuhaus, *Niedersachsen* D 44 B2
Neuhaus, *Niedersachsen* D 51 B5
Neuhaus, *Niedersachsen* D 43 B6
Neuhaus a Rennweg D 52 C1
Neuhausen CH 61 C4
Neuhausen ob Eck D 61 C4
Neuhof, *Bayern* D 62 A1
Neuhof, *Hessen* D 51 C5
Neuhofen an der Krems A 63 B5
Neuillé-Pont-Pierre F 67 A5
Neuilly-en-Thelle F 58 A3
Neuilly-le-Réal F 68 B3
Neuilly-l'Évêque F 60 C1
Neuilly-St. Front F 59 A4
Neukalen D 45 B4
Neukirch D 53 B4
Neukirchen A 62 B4
Neukirchen, *Hessen* D 51 C5
Neukirchen, *Schleswig-Holstein* D 39 E1
Neukirchen am Grossvenediger A 72 A2
Neukirchen bei Heiligen Blut D 62 A3
Neukloster D 44 B3
Neulengbach A 64 B1
Neulise F 68 C4
Neum BIH 84 D2
Neumagen D 60 A2
Neumarkt D 62 A2
Neumarkt am Wallersee A 63 C4
Neumarkt im Hausruckkreis A 63 B4
Neumarkt im Mühlkreis A 63 B5
Neumarkt im Steiermark A 73 A4
Neumarkt Sankt Veit D 62 B3
Neumünster D 44 A1
Neunburg vorm Wald D 62 A3
Neung-sur-Beuvron F 68 A1
Neunkirch, *Luzern* CH 70 A3
Neunkirch, *Schaffhausen* CH 61 C4
Neunkirchen A 64 C2
Neunkirchen, *Nordrhein-Westfalen* D 50 C3
Neunkirchen, *Saarland* D 60 A3
Neunkirchen am Brand D 62 A2
Neuötting D 62 B3
Neupetershain D 53 B4
Neuravensburg D 61 C5
Neureut D 61 A4
Neuruppin D 45 C4
Neusäss D 62 B1
Neusiedl A 64 C2
Neuss D 50 B2
Neussargues-Moissac F 68 C2
Neustadt, *Bayern* D 62 A1
Neustadt, *Bayern* D 62 B2
Neustadt, *Bayern* D 62 A3
Neustadt, *Brandenburg* D 44 C4
Neustadt, *Hessen* D 51 C5
Neustadt, *Niedersachsen* D 43 C6
Neustadt, *Rheinland-Pfalz* D 61 A4
Neustadt, *Sachsen* D 53 B4
Neustadt, *Schleswig-Holstein* D 44 A2
Neustadt, *Thüringen* D 52 C1
Neustadt, *Thüringen* D 52 C1
Neustadt-Glewe D 44 B3
Neustift im Stubaital A 71 A6
Neustrelitz D 45 B5
Neutal A 73 A6
Neutrebbin D 45 C6
Neuves-Maisons F 60 B2
Neuvic, *Corrèze* F 68 C2
Neuvic, *Dordogne* F 77 A3
Neuville-aux-Bois F 58 B3
Neuville-de-Poitou F 67 B5
Neuville-les-Dames F 69 B5
Neuville-sur-Saône F 69 C4
Neuvy-le-Roi F 58 C1
Neuvy-St. Sépulchre F 68 B1
Neuvy-Santour F 59 B4
Neuvy-sur-Barangeon F 68 A2
Neuwied D 50 C3
Neuzelle D 53 A4
Névache F 79 A5
Neveklov CZ 63 A5
Nevel RUS 7 D10
Neverfjord N 113 B12
Nevers F 68 B3
Nevesinje BIH 84 C3
Névez F 56 C2
Nevlunghavn N 35 D1
Nevşehir TR 16 B7
New Abbey GB 25 D4
New Aberdour GB 23 D6
New Alresford GB 31 C2
New Costessey GB 30 B5
New Cumnock GB 24 C3
New Galloway GB 24 C3
New Mills GB 27 B4
New Milton GB 31 D2
New Pitsligo GB 23 D6
New Quay GB 28 A3
New Radnor GB 29 A4
New Romney GB 31 D4
New Ross IRL 21 B5
New Scone GB 25 B4
Newark-on-Trent GB 27 B5
Newbiggin-by-the-Sea GB 25 C6
Newbliss IRL 19 B4
Newborough GB 26 B1
Newbridge IRL 21 A5
Newbridge on Wye GB 29 A4
Newburgh, *Aberdeenshire* GB 23 D6
Newburgh, *Fife* GB 25 B4
Newbury GB 31 C2
Newby Bridge GB 26 A3
Newcastle GB 19 B6
Newcastle Emlyn GB 28 A3
Newcastle-under-Lyme GB 26 B3
Newcastle-Upon-Tyne GB 25 D6
Newcastle West IRL 20 B2
Newcastleton GB 25 C5
Newchurch GB 29 A4
Newent GB 29 B5
Newham GB 31 C4
Newhaven GB 31 D4
Newington GB 31 C5
Newinn IRL 21 B4
Newlyn GB 28 C2
Newmachar GB 23 D6
Newmarket, *Suffolk* GB 30 B4
Newmarket, *Western Isles* GB 22 C2
Newmarket IRL 20 B3
Newmarket-on-Fergus IRL 20 B3
Newport, *Isle of Wight* GB 31 D2
Newport, *Newport* GB 29 B5
Newport, *Pembrokeshire* GB 28 A3
Newport, *Telford & Wrekin* GB 26 C3
Newport, *Mayo* IRL 18 C2
Newport, *Tipperary* IRL 20 B3
Newport-on-Tay GB 25 B5
Newport Pagnell GB 30 B3
Newquay GB 28 C2
Newry GB 19 B5
Newton Abbot GB 29 C4
Newton Arlosh GB 25 D4
Newton Aycliffe GB 27 A4
Newton Ferrers GB 28 C3
Newton Stewart GB 24 D3
Newtonhill GB 23 D6
Newtonmore GB 23 D4
Newtown, *Herefordshire* GB 29 A5
Newtown, *Powys* GB 26 C2
Newtown Cunningham IRL 19 B4
Newtown Hamilton GB 19 B5
Newtown St. Boswells GB 25 C5
Newtown Sands IRL 20 B2
Newtownabbey GB 19 B6
Newtownards GB 19 B6
Newtownbutler GB 19 B4
Newtownmountkennedy IRL 21 A5
Newtownshandrum IRL 20 B3
Newtownstewart GB 19 B4
Nexon F 67 C6
Neyland GB 28 B3
Nibbiano I 80 B3
Nibe DK 38 C2
Nicaj-Shalë AL 105 A5
Nicastro I 106 C3
Niccone I 82 C1
Nice F 80 C1
Nickelsdorf A 64 C3
Nicolosi I 109 B4
Nicosia CY 120 A2
Nicosia I 109 B3
Nicótera I 106 C2
Nidda D 51 C5
Nidzica PL 47 B6
Niebla E 99 B4
Nieborów PL 55 A5
Niebüll D 39 E1
Niechanowo PL 46 C3
Niechorze PL 45 A7
Niedalino PL 46 A2
Nieder-Olm D 61 A4
Niederaula D 51 C5
Niederbipp CH 70 A2
Niederbronn-les-Bains F 60 B3
Niederfischbach D 50 C3
Niedergörsdorf D 52 B2
Niederkrüchten D 50 B2
Niederndorf A 62 C3
Niedersachs-werfen D 51 B6
Niederstetten D 61 A5
Niederurnen CH 70 A4
Niederwölz A 73 A4
Niedoradz PL 53 B5
Niedzica PL 65 A6
Niegosławice PL 53 B5
Nieheim D 51 B5
Niemcza PL 54 C1
Niemegk D 52 A2
Niemodlin PL 54 C2
Nienburg, *Niedersachsen* D 43 C6
Nienburg, *Sachsen-Anhalt* D 52 B1
Niepołomice PL 55 C5
Nierstein D 61 A4
Niesky D 53 B4
Niestronno PL 46 C3
Nieświń PL 55 B5
Nieszawa PL 47 C4
Nieul-le-Dolent F 66 B3
Nieul-sur-Mer F 66 B3
Nieuw-Amsterdam NL 42 C3
Nieuw-Buinen NL 42 C3
Nieuw-Weerdinge NL 42 C3
Nieuwe Niedorp NL 42 C1
Nieuwe-Pekela NL 42 B3
Nieuwe-schans NL 43 B4
Nieuwegein NL 49 A6
Nieuwerkerken B 49 C6
Nieuwolda NL 42 B3
Nieuwpoort B 48 B3
Niğde TR 16 C7
Nigrita GR 116 B5
Nigüelas E 100 C2
Níjar E 101 C3
Nijemci HR 75 C4
Nijkerk NL 49 A6
Nijlen B 49 B5
Nijmegen NL 50 B1
Nijverdal NL 42 C3
Nikel RUS 113 C19
Nikinci SRB 85 B4
Nikiti GR 116 B5
Nikitsch A 74 A1
Nikkaluokta S 112 E8
Nikla H 74 B2
Niklasdorf A 73 A5
Nikolayev = Mykolayiv UA 11 C12
Nikšić MNE 84 D3
Nilivaara S 113 E10
Nîmes F 78 C3
Nimis I 72 B3
Nimtofte DK 39 C3
Nin HR 83 B4
Nindorf D 43 A6
Ninemilehouse IRL 21 B4
Ninove B 49 C5
Niort F 67 B4
Niš SRB 10 E6
Nisa P 92 B3
Niscemi I 109 B3
Nissafors S 40 B3
Nissan-lez-Ensérune F 78 C2
Nissedal N 33 C5
Nissumby DK 38 C1
Nisterud N 33 C6
Niton GB 31 D2
Nitra SK 64 B4
Nitrianske-Pravno SK 65 B4
Nitrianske Rudno SK 65 B4
Nitry F 59 C4
Nittedal N 34 B2
Nittenau D 62 A3
Nittendorf D 62 A2
Nivala FIN 3 E26
Nivelles B 49 C5
Nivenskoye RUS 47 A6
Nivnice CZ 64 B3
Nizhyn UA 11 A11
Nižná SK 65 A5
Nižná Boca SK 65 B5
Nižne Repaše SK 65 A6
Nizza Monferrato I 80 B2
Njarðvík IS 111 D3
Njegůsevo SRB 75 C4
Njivice HR 73 C4
Njurundabommen S 115 E14
Njutånger S 115 F14
Noailles F 58 A3
Noain E 76 D1
Noale I 72 C2
Noalejo E 100 B2
Noblejas E 95 C3
Noceda E 86 B4
Nocera Inferiore I 103 C7
Nocera Terinese I 106 B3
Nocera Umbra I 82 C1
Noceto I 81 B4
Noci I 104 C3
Nociglia I 107 A5
Nodeland N 33 D4
Nödinge S 38 B5
Nods F 69 A6
Noé F 77 C4
Noépoli I 106 A3
Noeux-les-Mines F 48 C3
Noez E 94 C2
Nogales E 93 C4
Nogara I 71 C6
Nogarejas E 87 B4
Nogaro F 76 C2
Nogent F 59 B6
Nogent l'Artaud F 59 B4
Nogent-le-Roi F 58 B2
Nogent-le-Rotrou F 58 B1
Nogent-sur-Seine F 59 B4
Nogent-sur-Vernisson F 58 C3
Nogersund S 41 C4
Noguera E 95 B5
Nogueruelas E 96 A2
Nohfelden D 60 A3
Nohn D 50 C2
Noia E 86 B2
Noicáttaro I 104 B2
Noirétable F 68 C3
Noirmoutier-en-l'Île F 66 A2
Noja E 89 A3
Nojewo PL 46 C2
Nokia FIN 3 F25
Nol S 38 B5
Nola I 103 C7
Nolay F 69 B4
Noli I 80 B2
Nolnyra S 36 B4
Nombela E 94 B2
Nomeny F 60 B2
Nomexy F 60 B2
Nonancourt F 58 B2
Nonant-le-Pin F 57 B6
Nonántola I 81 B5
Nonaspe E 90 B3
None I 80 B1
Nontron F 67 C5
Nonza F 102 A2
Noordhorn NL 42 B3
Noordwijk NL 49 A5
Noordwijkerhout NL 49 A5
Noordwolde NL 42 C3
Noppikoski S 36 A1
Nora S 37 C2
Nørager DK 38 C2
Norberg S 36 B2
Norboda S 36 B5
Nórcia I 82 D2
Nord-Odal N 34 B3
Nordagutu N 33 C6
Nordanås S 115 C15
Nordausques F 48 C3
Nordborg DK 39 D2
Nordby, *Aarhus Amt.* DK 39 D3
Nordby, *Ribe Amt.* DK 39 D1
Norddeich D 43 B4
Norddorf D 43 A5
Norden D 43 B4
Nordenham D 43 B5
Norderhov N 34 B2
Norderney D 43 B4
Norderstapel D 43 A6
Norderstedt D 44 B2
Nordfjord N 113 B19
Nordfjordeid N 114 F3
Nordfold N 112 E4
Nordhalben D 52 C1
Nordhausen D 51 B6
Nordheim vor der Rhön D 51 C6
Nordholz D 43 B5
Nordhorn D 43 C4
Nordingrå S 115 E15
Nordkjosbotn N 112 C8
Nordli N 115 C10
Nördlingen D 61 B6
Nordmaling S 115 D16
Nordmark S 34 C6
Nordmela N 112 C4
Nordre Osen N 34 A3
Nordsinni N 34 B1
Nørdstedalsseter N 114 F4
Nordstemmen D 51 A5
Nordvågen N 113 B15
Nordwalde D 50 A3
Noreña E 88 A1
Noresund N 34 B1
Norg NL 42 B3
Norheimsund N 32 B3
Norie S 41 C4
Norma I 102 B5
Nornäs S 34 A5
Norra Vi S 40 B5
Norrahammar S 40 B4
Norråker S 115 C12
Norrala S 36 A3
Nørre Aaby DK 39 D2
Nørre Alslev DK 39 E4
Nørre Lyndelse DK 39 D3
Nørre Nebel DK 39 D1
Nørre Snede DK 39 D2
Nørre Vorupør DK 38 C1
Norrent-Fontes F 48 C3
Nørresundby DK 38 B2
Norrhult Klavreström S 40 B5
Norrköping S 37 D3
Norrskedika S 36 B5
Norrsundet S 36 B4
Norrtälje S 36 C5
Nors DK 38 B1
Norsbron S 35 C5
Norsholm S 37 D2
Norsjö S 115 C16
Nort-sur-Erdre F 66 A3
Nörten-Hardenberg D 51 B5
North Berwick GB 25 B5
North Charlton GB 25 C6
North Frodingham GB 27 B5
North Kessock GB 23 D4
North Molton GB 28 B4
North Petherton GB 29 B4
North Somercotes GB 27 B6
North Tawton GB 28 C4
North Thoresby GB 27 B5
North Walsham GB 30 B5
Northallerton GB 27 A4
Northampton GB 30 B3
Northeim D 51 B6
Northfleet GB 31 C4
Northleach GB 29 B6
Northpunds GB 22 B7
Northwich GB 26 B3
Norton GB 27 A5
Nortorf D 44 A1
Nörvenich D 50 C2
Norwich GB 30 B5
Norwick GB 22 A8
Nøsen N 32 B5
Nosivka UA 11 A11
Nossa Senhora do Cabo P 92 C1
Nossebro S 35 D4
Nössemark S 35 C3
Nossen D 52 B3
Notaresco I 103 A6
Noto I 109 C4
Notodden N 33 C6
Nottingham GB 27 C4
Nottuln D 50 B3
Nouan-le-Fuzelier F 68 A2
Nouans-les-Fontaines F 67 A6
Nougaroulet F 77 C3
Nouvion F 48 C2
Nouzonville F 59 A5
Nova H 74 B1
Nová Baňa SK 65 B4
Nová Bystrica SK 65 A5
Nová Bystřice CZ 63 A6
Nova Crnja SRB 75 C5
Nova Gorica SLO 72 C3
Nova Gradiška HR 74 C2
Nova Levante I 71 B6
Nova Odesa UA 11 C11
Nová Paka CZ 53 C5
Nova Pazova SRB 85 B5
Nová Pec CZ 63 B4
Nova Siri I 106 A3
Nova Topola BIH 84 A2
Nova Varoš SRB 85 C4
Nova Zagora BG 11 E8
Novafeltria I 82 C1
Nováky SK 65 B4

Novalaise F 69 C5
Novales E 90 A2
Novalja HR 83 B3
Novara I 70 C3
Novara di Sicilia I 109 A4
Novate Mezzola I 71 B4
Novaya Ladoga RUS 7 A12
Nové Hrady CZ 63 B5
Nové Mésto SK 64 B3
Nové Město na Moravě CZ 64 A2
Nové Město nad Metují CZ 53 C6
Nové Město pod Smrkem CZ 53 C5
Nové Mitrovice CZ 63 A4
Nové Sady SK 64 B3
Nové Strašeci CZ 53 C3
Nové Zámky SK 64 C4
Novelda E 101 A5
Novellara I 81 B4
Noventa di Piave I 72 C2
Noventa Vicentina I 71 C6
Novés E 94 B2
Noves F 78 C3
Novés de Segre E 91 A4
Novgorod RUS 7 B11
Novhorod-Siverskyy UA 7 F12
Novi Bečej SRB 75 C5
Novi di Módena I 81 B4
Novi Kneževac SRB 75 B5
Novi Ligure I 80 B2
Novi Marof HR 73 B6
Novi Pazar BG 11 E9
Novi Pazar SRB 85 C5
Novi Sad SRB 75 C4
Novi Slankamen SRB 75 C5
Novi Travnik BIH 84 B2
Novi Vinodolski HR 83 A3
Novigrad, *Istarska* HR 72 C3
Novigrad, *Zadarsko-Kninska* HR 83 B4
Novigrad Podravski HR 74 B1
Noville B 50 C1
Novion-Porcien F 59 A5
Novo Brdo KOS 85 D6
Novo Mesto SLO 73 C5
Novo Miloševo SRB 75 C5
Novo Selo BIH 84 A2
Novo Selo KOS 85 D5
Novo Selo SRB 85 C5
Novohrad-Volynskyy UA 11 A9
Novomirgorod UA 11 B11
Novorzhev RUS 7 C10
Novoselë AL 105 C5
Novoselytsya UA 11 B9
Novosil RUS 7 E14
Novosokolniki RUS 7 C10
Novoukrayinka UA 11 B11
Novoveská Huta SK 65 B6
Novovolynsk UA 11 A8
Novozybkov RUS 7 E11
Novska HR 74 C1
Nový Bor CZ 53 C4
Nový Bydžov CZ 53 C5
Novy-Chevrières F 59 A5
Novy Dwór Mazowiecki PL 47 C6
Nový-Hrozenkov CZ 64 A4
Nový Jičín CZ 64 A4
Nový Knín CZ 63 A5
Novyy Buh UA 11 C12
Nowa Cerekwia PL 54 C2
Nowa Karczma PL 47 A4
Nowa Kościoł PL 53 B5
Nowa Ruda PL 54 C1
Nowa Słupia PL 55 C6
Nowa Sól PL 53 B5
Nowa Wieś PL 47 B5
Nowa-Wieś Wielka PL 47 C4
Nowe PL 47 B4
Nowe Brzesko PL 55 C5
Nowe Grudze PL 55 A4
Nowe Miasteczko PL 53 B5
Nowe Miasto, *Mazowieckie* PL 55 B5
Nowe Miasto, *Mazowieckie* PL 47 C6
Nowe Miasto Lubawskie PL 47 B5
Nowe Miasto nad Wartą PL 54 A2
Nowe Skalmierzyce PL 54 B3
Nowe Warpno PL 45 B6
Nowica PL 47 A5
Nowogard PL 45 B7
Nowogród Bobrzanski PL 53 B5
Nowogrodziec PL 53 B5
Nowosolna PL 55 B4
Nowy Dwór Gdański PL 47 A5
Nowy Korczyn PL 55 C5
Nowy Sącz PL 65 A6
Nowy Staw PL 47 A5
Nowy Targ PL 65 A6
Nowy Tomyśl PL 46 C2
Nowy Wiśnicz PL 65 A6
Noyal-Pontivy F 56 B3
Noyalo F 56 C3
Noyant F 67 A5
Noyelles-sur-Mer F 48 C2
Noyen-sur-Sarthe F 57 C5
Noyers F 59 C4
Noyers-sur-Cher F 67 A6
Noyers-sur-Jabron F 79 B4
Noyon F 59 A3
Nozay F 66 A3
Nuaillé F 66 A4
Nuaillé-d'Aunis F 66 B4
Nuars F 68 A3
Nubledo E 88 A1
Nuéno E 90 A2
Nuestra Señora Sa Verge des Pilar E 97 C1
Nueva E 88 A2
Nueva Carteya E 100 B1
Nuevalos E 95 A5
Nuits F 59 C5
Nuits-St. Georges F 69 A4
Nule I 110 B2
Nules E 96 B2
Nulvi I 110 B1
Numana I 82 C2
Numansdorp NL 49 B5
Nümbrecht D 50 C3
Nunchritz D 52 B3
Nuneaton GB 30 B2
Nunnanen FIN 113 D13
Nuñomoral E 93 A4
Nunspeet NL 42 C2
Nuorgam FIN 113 B16
Núoro I 110 B2
Nurallao I 110 C2
Nuremberg = Nürnberg D 62 A2
Nurmes FIN 3 E28
Nürnberg = Nuremberg D 62 A2
Nurri I 110 C2
Nürtingen D 61 B5
Nus I 70 C2
Nusnäs S 36 B1
Nusplingen D 61 B4
Nuštar HR 74 C3
Nyåker S 115 D16
Nyáregyháza H 75 A4
Nyarlörinc H 75 B4
Nyasvizh BY 7 E9
Nybble S 35 C6
Nybergsund N 34 A4
Nybøl DK 39 E2
Nyborg DK 39 D3
Nybro S 40 C5
Nybster GB 23 C5
Nyby DK 39 E5
Nye S 40 B5
Nyékládháza H 65 C6
Nyergesujfalu H 65 C4
Nyhammar S 36 B1
Nyhyttan S 37 C1
Nyirád H 74 A2
Nyirbátor H 11 C7
Nyíregyháza H 10 C6
Nyker DK 41 D4
Nykil S 37 D2
Nykirke N 34 B2
Nykøbing, *Falster* DK 39 E4
Nykøbing, *Vestsjællands Amt.* DK 39 D4
Nykøbing M DK 38 C1
Nyköping S 37 D4
Nykroppa S 35 C6
Nykvarn S 37 C4
Nykyrke S 37 D1
Nyland S 115 D14
Nylars DK 41 D4
Nymburk CZ 53 C5
Nynäshamn S 37 D4
Nyon CH 69 B6
Nyons F 79 B4
Nýřany CZ 63 A4
Nýrsko CZ 62 A4
Nyrud N 113 C18
Nysa PL 54 C2
Nysäter S 35 C4
Nyseter N 114 E5
Nyskoga S 34 B4
Nysted DK 44 A3
Nystrand N 35 C1
Nyúl H 64 C3
Nyvoll N 113 B12

O

O Barco E 86 B4
O Bolo E 87 B3
O Carballiño E 86 B2
O Corgo E 86 B3
Ö Lagnö S 37 C5
O Näsberg S 34 B5
O Páramo E 86 B3
O Pedrouzo E 86 B2
O Pino E 86 B2
O Porriño E 87 B2
O Rosal E 87 C2
Oadby GB 30 B2
Oakengates GB 26 C3
Oakham GB 30 B3
Oanes N 33 D3
Obalj BIH 84 C3
Oban GB 24 B2
Obdach A 73 A4
Obejo E 100 A1
Ober Grafendorf A 63 B6
Ober-Morlen D 51 C4
Oberammergau D 62 C2
Oberasbach D 62 A1
Oberau D 62 C2
Oberaudorf D 62 C3
Oberbruck F 60 C2
Oberdiessbach CH 70 B2
Oberdorf CH 70 A2
Oberdrauburg A 72 B2
Obere Stanz A 73 A5
Oberelsbach D 51 C6
Obergünzburg D 61 C6
Obergurgl A 71 B6
Oberhausen D 50 B2
Oberhof D 51 C6
Oberkirch D 61 B4
Oberkirchen D 51 B4
Oberkochen D 61 B6
Obermassfeld-Grimmenthal D 51 C6
Obermünchen D 62 B2
Obernai F 60 B3
Obernberg A 63 B4
Obernburg D 61 A5
Oberndorf D 61 B4
Oberndorf bei Salzburg A 62 C3
Obernkirchen D 51 A5
Oberort A 73 A5
Oberpullendorf A 74 A1
Oberriet CH 71 A4
Oberröblingen D 52 B1
Oberrot D 61 A5
Oberstaufen D 61 C6
Oberstdorf D 71 A5
Obertauern A 72 A3
Obertilliach A 72 B2
Obertraubling D 62 B3
Obertraun A 72 A3
Obertrubach D 62 A2
Obertrum A 62 C4
Oberursel D 51 C4
Obervellach A 72 B3
Oberviechtach D 62 A3
Oberwart A 73 A6
Oberwesel D 50 C3
Oberwinter D 50 C3
Oberwölzstadt A 73 A4
Oberzell D 63 B4
Obice PL 55 C5
Óbidos P 92 B1
Obilić KOS 85 D6
Obing D 62 C3
Objat F 67 C6
Objazda PL 46 A3
Öblarn A 73 A4
Obninsk RUS 7 D14
Oborniki PL 46 C2
Oborniki Śląskie PL 54 B1
Obornjača SRB 75 C4
Oboyan RUS 7 F14
Obrenovac SRB 85 B5
Obrež, *Srbija* SRB 85 C6
Obrež, *Vojvodina* SRB 85 B4
Obrigheim D 61 A5
Obrov SLO 73 C4
Obrovac HR 83 B4
Obrovac SRB 75 C4
Obrovac Sinjski HR 83 C5
Obruk TR 16 B6
Obrzycko PL 46 C2
Obudovac BIH 84 B3
Ocaña E 95 C3
Occhiobello I 81 B5
Occimiano I 80 A2
Očevlja BIH 84 B3
Ochagavía E 76 D1
Ochakiv UA 11 C11
Ochiltree GB 24 C3
Ochla PL 53 B5
Ochotnica-Dolna PL 65 A6
Ochotnica-Górna PL 65 A6
Ochsenfurt D 61 A6
Ochsenhausen D 61 B5
Ochtendung D 50 C3
Ochtrup D 50 A3
Ocieka PL 55 C6
Ockelbo S 36 B3
Öckerö S 38 B4
Ocniţa MD 11 B9
Očová SK 65 B5
Ócsa H 75 A4
Öcseny H 74 B3
Öcsöd H 75 B5
Octeville F 57 A4
Ocypel PL 47 B4
Ödåkra S 41 C2
Odby DK 38 C1
Odda N 32 B3
Odder DK 39 D3
Ödeborg S 35 D3
Odeceixe P 98 B2
Odechów PL 55 B6
Odeleite P 98 B3
Odemira P 98 B2
Ödemiş TR 119 D2
Ödensbacken S 37 C2
Odense DK 39 D3
Odensjö, *Jönköping* S 40 B4
Odensjö, *Kronoberg* S 40 C3
Oderberg D 45 C6
Oderzo I 72 C2
Odesa = Odessa UA 11 C11
Ödeshög S 37 D1
Odessa = Odesa UA 11 C11
Odiáxere P 98 B2
Odie GB 23 B6
Odiham GB 31 C3
Odintsovo RUS 7 D14
Odivelas P 98 A2
Odolanów PL 54 B2
Odón E 95 B5
Odorheiu Secuiesc RO 11 C8
Odoyevo RUS 7 E14
Odrowaz PL 55 B5
Odry CZ 64 A3
Odrzywół PL 55 B5
Ødsted DK 39 D2
Odžaci SRB 75 C4
Odžak BIH 84 A3
Oebisfelde D 44 C2
Oederan D 52 C3
Oeding D 50 B2
Oegstgeest NL 49 A5
Oelde D 50 B4
Oelsnitz D 52 C2
Oer-Erkenschwick D 50 B3
Oerlinghausen D 51 B4
Oettingen D 62 B1
Oetz A 71 A5
Oeventrop D 50 B4
Offanengo I 71 C4
Offenbach D 51 C4
Offenburg D 60 B3
Offida I 82 D2
Offingen D 61 B6
Offranville F 58 A2
Ofir P 87 C2
Ofte N 33 C5
Ofterschwang D 71 A5
Oggiono I 71 C4
Ogihares E 100 B2
Ogliastro Cilento I 103 C8
Ogliastro Marina I 103 C7
Ogmore-by-Sea GB 29 B4
Ogna N 33 D2
Ogre LV 6 C8
Ogrodzieniec PL 55 C4
Ogulin HR 73 C5
Ögur IS 111 A3
Ohanes E 101 B3
Ohey B 49 C6
Ohlstadt D 62 C2
Ohrdorf D 44 C2
Ohrdruf D 51 C6
Ohrid MK 116 A2
Öhringen D 61 A5
Oia E 87 B2
Oiã P 92 A2
Oiartzun E 76 C1
Oilgate IRL 21 B5
Oimbra E 87 C3
Oiselay-et-Grachoux F 69 A5
Oisemont F 48 D2
Oisterwijk NL 49 B6
Öja S 37 E5
Öje S 34 B5
Ojén E 100 C1
Ojrzeń PL 47 C6
Ojuelos Altos E 99 A5
Okalewo PL 47 B5
Okány H 75 B6
Okehampton GB 28 C3
Okhtyrka UA 7 F13
Oklaj HR 83 C5
Økneshamn N 112 D4
Okoč SK 64 C3
Okoličné SK 65 A5
Okonek PL 46 B2
Okonin PL 47 B4
Okřisky CZ 64 A1
Oksa PL 55 C5
Oksbøl DK 39 D1
Oksby DK 39 D1
Øksfjord N 113 B11
Øksna N 34 B3
Okučani HR 74 C2
Okulovka RUS 7 B12
Ólafsfjörður IS 111 A7
Ólafsvík IS 111 C2
Olagüe E 76 D1
Oland N 33 D5
Olargues F 78 C1
Oława PL 54 C2
Olazagutia E 89 B4
Olbernhau D 52 C3
Ólbia I 110 B2
Olching D 62 B2
Old Deer GB 23 D6
Oldbury GB 29 B5
Oldcastle IRL 19 C4
Oldeberkoop NL 42 C3
Oldeboorn NL 42 B2
Olden N 114 F3
Oldenbrok D 43 B5
Oldenburg, *Niedersachsen* D 43 B5
Oldenburg, *Schleswig-Holstein* D 44 A2
Oldenzaal NL 50 A2
Olderdalen N 112 C9
Olderfjord N 113 B14
Oldersum D 43 B4
Oldervik N 112 C7
Oldham GB 26 B3
Oldisleben D 52 B1
Oldmeldrum GB 23 D6
Olea E 88 B2
Oleby S 34 B5
Olechów PL 55 B6
Oledo P 92 B3
Oléggio I 70 C3
Oleiros, *Coruña* E 86 A2
Oleiros, *Coruña* E 86 B1
Oleiros P 92 B3
Oleksandriya, *Kirovohrad* UA 11 B12
Oleksandriya, *Rivne* UA 11 A9
Oleksandrovka UA 11 B12
Olen B 49 B5
Ølen N 33 C2
Olenegorsk RUS 3 B30
Olenino RUS 7 C12
Olesa de Montserrat E 91 B4
Oleśnica PL 54 B2
Olešnice CZ 64 A2
Olesno PL 54 C3
Oletta F 102 A2
Olette F 91 A5
Olevsk UA 11 A9
Olfen D 50 B3
Olgiate Comasco I 70 C3
Olginate I 71 C4
Ølgod DK 39 D1
Olgrinmore GB 23 C5
Olhão P 98 B3
Olhavo P 92 B1
Oliana E 91 A4
Olias del Rey E 94 C3
Oliena I 110 B2
Oliete E 90 C2
Olimbos GR 119 G2
Olite E 89 B5
Oliva E 96 C2
Oliva de la Frontera E 99 A4
Oliva de Mérida E 93 C4
Oliva de Plasencia E 93 A4
Olivadi I 106 C3
Olival P 92 B2
Olivar E 100 C2
Olivares E 99 B4
Olivares de Duero E 88 C2
Olivares de Júcar E 95 C4
Oliveira de Azeméis P 87 D2
Oliveira de Frades P 87 D2
Oliveira do Conde P 92 A3
Oliveira do Douro P 87 C2
Oliveira do Hospital P 92 A3
Olivenza E 93 C3
Olivet F 58 C2
Olivone CH 70 B3
Öljehult S 41 C5
Olkusz PL 55 C4
Ollerton GB 27 B4
Ollerup DK 39 D3
Olliergues F 68 C3
Ölmbrotorp S 37 C2
Ölme S 35 C5
Olmedilla de Alarcón E 95 C4
Olmedillo de Roa E 88 C3
Olmedo E 88 C2
Olmedo I 110 B1
Olmeto F 102 B1
Olmillos de Castro E 87 C4
Olmos de Ojeda E 88 B2
Olney GB 30 B3
Ołobok PL 54 B3
Olocau del Rey E 90 C2
Olofström S 41 C4
Olomouc CZ 64 A3
Olonets RUS 3 F30
Olonne-sur-Mer F 66 B3
Olonzac F 78 C1
Oloron-Ste. Marie F 76 C2
Olost E 91 B5
Olot E 91 A5
Olovo BIH 84 B3
Olpe D 50 B3
Olsberg D 51 B4
Olsene B 49 C4
Olserud S 35 C5
Olshammar S 37 D1
Olshanka UA 11 B11
Olszanica PL 53 B5
Olsztyn, *Śląskie* PL 55 C4
Olsztyn, *Warmińsko-Mazurskie* PL 47 B6
Olsztynek PL 47 B6
Olszyna PL 53 B5
Olszyny PL 47 B6
Oltedal N 33 D3
Olten CH 70 A2
Olteniţa RO 11 D9
Olula del Rio E 101 B3
Ølve N 32 B2
Olvega E 89 C5
Olvera E 99 C5
Olympia GR 117 E3
Olzai I 110 B2
Omagh GB 19 B4
Omalos GR 117 G5
Omegna I 70 C3
Omiš HR 83 C5
Omišalj HR 73 C4
Ommen NL 42 C3
Omodhos CY 120 B1
Omoljica SRB 85 B5
On B 49 C6
Oña E 89 B3
Onano I 81 D5
Oñati E 89 A4
Onda E 96 B2
Ondara E 96 C3
Ondarroa E 89 A4
Onesse-et-Laharie F 76 B1
Onești RO 11 C9
Onhaye B 49 C5
Onich GB 24 B2
Onil E 96 C2
Onis E 88 A2
Önnestad S 41 C4
Onsala S 38 B5
Ontinyent E 96 C2
Ontur E 101 A4
Onzain F 67 A6
Onzonilla E 88 B1
Oost-Vlieland NL 42 B2
Oostburg NL 49 B4
Oostende B 48 B3
Oosterend NL 42 B2
Oosterhout NL 49 B5
Oosterwolde NL 42 C3
Oosterzele B 49 C4
Oosthuizen NL 42 C2
Oostkamp B 49 B4
Oostmalle B 49 B5
Oostvoorne NL 49 B5
Ootmarsum NL 42 C3
Opalenica PL 54 A1
Opařany CZ 63 A5
Oparić SRB 85 C6
Opatija HR 73 C4
Opatów, *Śląskie* PL 54 C3
Opatów, *Świętokrzyskie* PL 55 C6
Opatów, *Wielkopolskie* PL 54 B3
Opatówek PL 54 B3
Opatowiec PL 55 C5
Opava CZ 64 A3
Opeinde NL 42 B3
Oper Thalkirchdorf D 61 C6
Opglabbeerk B 49 B6
Opicina I 72 C3
Oplotnica SLO 73 B5
Opmeer NL 42 C1
Opochka RUS 7 C10
Opočno CZ 53 C6
Opoczno PL 55 B5
Opole PL 54 C2
Oporów PL 55 A4
Opovo SRB 85 A5
Oppach D 53 B4
Oppdal N 114 E6
Oppeby, *Östergötland* S 40 A5
Oppeby, *Södermanland* S 37 D3
Oppedal N 32 A2
Oppegård N 34 C2
Oppenau D 61 B4
Oppenberg A 73 A4
Oppenheim D 61 A4
Óppido Lucano I 104 C1
Óppido Mamertina I 106 C2
Opponitz A 63 C5
Oppstad N 34 B3
Oprtalj HR 72 C3
Opsaheden S 34 B5
Ópusztaszer H 75 B5
Opuzen HR 84 C2
Ora CY 120 B2
Ora I 71 B6
Orada P 92 C3
Oradea RO 10 C6
Oradour-sur-Glane F 67 C6
Oradour-sur-Vayres F 67 C5
Oragonja SLO 72 C3
Orah BIH 84 C3
Orahova BIH 84 B2
Orahovica HR 74 C2
Orahovo BIH 74 C2
Oraison F 79 C4
Orajärvi FIN 113 F13
Orange F 78 B3
Orani I 110 B2
Oranienbaum D 52 B2
Oranienburg D 45 C5
Oranmore IRL 20 A3
Orašac SRB 85 B5
Orašje BIH 84 A3
Oravská Lesná SK 65 A5
Oravská Polhora SK 65 A5
Oravské Veselé SK 65 A5
Oravsky-Podzámok SK 65 A5
Orba E 96 C2
Orbacém P 87 C2
Ørbæk DK 39 D3
Orbais F 59 B4
Orbassano I 80 A1
Orbe CH 69 B6
Orbec F 58 A1
Orbetello I 102 A4
Orbetello Scalo I 102 A4
Orbigny F 67 A6
Ørby DK 39 C3
Örbyhus S 36 B4
Orce E 101 B3
Orcera E 101 A3
Orchamps-Vennes F 69 A6
Orches F 67 B5
Orchete E 96 C2
Orchies F 49 C4
Orchowo PL 47 C4
Orcières F 79 B5
Ordes E 86 A2
Ordhead GB 23 D6
Ordino AND 91 A4
Ordizia E 89 A4
Orduña E 89 B4
Ore S 36 A2
Orea E 95 B5
Orebić HR 84 D2
Örebro S 37 C2
Öregcsertő H 75 B4
Öregrund S 36 B5
Orehoved DK 39 E4
Orel RUS 7 E14
Orellana E 93 B5
Orellana de la Sierra E 93 B5
Ören TR 119 E2
Örencik TR 118 C4
Orestiada GR 118 A1
Organyà E 91 A4
Orgaz E 94 C3
Orgelet F 69 B5
Ørgenvika N 34 B1
Orgères-en-Beauce F 58 B2
Orgibet F 77 D3
Orgnac-l'Aven F 78 B3
Orgon F 79 C4
Orgósolo I 110 B2
Orhaneli TR 118 C3
Orhangazi TR 118 B4
Orhei MD 11 C10
Orhomenos GR 116 D4
Oria E 101 B3
Ória I 104 C3
Origny-Ste. Benoite F 59 A4
Orihuela E 101 A5
Orihuela del Tremedal E 95 B5
Orikum AL 105 C5
Oriola P 92 C3
Oriolo I 106 A3
Oriovac HR 74 C2
Orissaare EST 6 B7
Oristano I 110 C1
Öriszentpéter H 73 B6
Ørje N 35 C3
Orjiva E 100 C2
Orkanger N 114 D6
Örkelljunga S 41 C3
Örkény H 75 A4
Orlamünde D 52 C1
Orlane KOS 85 D6
Orléans F 58 C2
Orlová CZ 65 A4
Orlovat SRB 75 C5
Ormea I 80 B1
Ormelet N 35 C2
Ormemyr N 33 C6
Ormilia GR 116 B5
Ormos GR 117 E6
Ormož SLO 73 B6
Ormskirk GB 26 B3
Ornans F 69 A6
Ornäs S 36 B2
Ørnes N 112 F2
Orneta PL 47 A6
Ørnhøj DK 39 C1
Ornö S 37 C5
Örnsköldsvik S 115 D15
Orolik HR 75 C3
Orom SRB 75 C4
Oron-la-Ville CH 70 B1
Oronsko PL 55 B5
Oropa I 70 C2
Oropesa, *Castellón de la Plana* E 96 A3
Oropesa, *Toledo* E 93 B5
Orosei I 110 B2
Orosháza H 75 B5
Oroslavje HR 73 C5
Oroszlány H 74 A3
Oroszlo H 74 B3
Orotelli I 110 B2
Orozko E 89 A4
Orphir GB 23 C5
Orpington GB 31 C4
Orreaga-Roncesvalles E 76 C1
Orrefors S 40 C5
Orrviken S 115 D11
Orsa S 36 A1
Orsara di Púglia I 103 B8
Orsay F 58 B3
Orscholz D 60 A2
Orsennes F 67 B6
Orserum S 40 A4
Orsha BY 7 D11
Orsières CH 70 B2
Orsjö S 40 C5
Ørslev DK 39 D4
Örslösa S 35 D4
Orsogna I 103 A7
Orsomarso I 106 B2
Orşova RO 11 D7
Ørsta N 114 E3
Ørsted DK 38 C3
Örsundsbro S 37 C4
Orta Nova I 104 B1
Ortaca TR 119 F3
Ortakent TR 119 E2
Ortaklar TR 119 E2
Ortaköy TR 16 B7
Orte I 102 A5
Ortenburg D 63 B4
Orth A 64 B2
Orthez F 76 C2
Ortigueira E 86 A3
Ortilla E 90 A2
Ortisei I 72 B1
Orţişoara RO 75 C6
Ortnevik N 32 A3
Orton GB 26 A3
Ortona I 103 A7
Ortrand D 53 B3
Orubica HR 74 C2
Ørum DK 38 C2
Orune I 110 B2
Orusco E 95 B3
Orvalho P 92 A3
Orvault F 66 A3
Ørvella N 33 C6
Orvieto I 82 D1
Orvínio I 102 A5
Oryakhovo BG 11 E7
Orzesze PL 54 C3
Orzinuovi I 71 C4
Orzivécchi I 71 C4
Os, *Hedmark* N 114 E8
Os, *Hedmark* N 34 B3
Os Peares E 86 B3
Osann-Monzel D 60 A2
Osaonica SRB 85 C5
Osbruk S 40 B4
Øsby DK 39 D2
Osby S 41 C3
Oščadnica SK 65 A4
Oschatz D 52 B3
Oschersleben D 52 A1
Óschiri I 110 B2
Osciłowo PL 47 C6
Osdorf D 44 A2
Osečina SRB 85 B4
Osečná CZ 53 C4

Pontenx-les-Forges F 76 B1
Ponterwyd GB 26 C2
Pontevedra E 86 B2
Pontevico I 71 C5
Pontfaverger-Moronvillers F 59 A5
Pontgibaud F 68 C2
Ponticino I 81 C5
Pontigny F 59 C4
Pontijou F 58 C2
Pontínia I 102 B6
Pontinvrea I 80 B2
Pontivy F 56 B3
Pontlevoy F 67 A6
Pontoise F 58 A3
Pontones E 101 A3
Pontonx-sur-l'Abour F 76 C2
Pontoon IRL 18 C2
Pontorson F 57 B4
Pontrémoli I 81 B3
Pontresina CH 71 B4
Pontrhydfendigaid GB 28 A4
Pontrieux F 56 B2
Ponts E 91 B4
Ponts-aux-Dames F 59 B3
Pöntsö FIN 113 E13
Pontvallain F 57 C6
Pontypool GB 29 B4
Pontypridd GB 29 B4
Ponza I 102 C5
Poo E 88 A2
Poole GB 29 C6
Poolewe GB 22 D3
Poperinge B 48 C3
Pópoli I 103 A6
Popovac SRB 85 C6
Popovača HR 74 C1
Popow PL 55 A4
Poppel B 49 B6
Poppenhausen, *Bayern* D 51 C6
Poppenhausen, *Hessen* D 51 C5
Poppi I 81 C5
Poprad SK 65 A6
Popučke SRB 85 B4
Pópulo P 87 C3
Populónia I 81 D4
Pörböly H 74 B3
Porcuna E 100 B1
Pordenone I 72 C2
Pordic F 56 B3
Poręba PL 55 C4
Poreč HR 72 C3
Pori FIN 3 F24
Porjus S 112 F8
Porkhov RUS 7 C10
Porlezza I 71 B4
Porlock GB 29 B4
Pörnbach D 62 B2
Pornic F 66 A2
Pornichet F 66 A2
Porodin SRB 85 B6
Poronin PL 65 A5
Poros, *Attiki* GR 117 E5
Poros, *Kefalonia* GR 117 D2
Poroszló H 65 C6
Porozina HR 82 A3
Porquerolles F 79 D5
Porrentruy CH 70 A2
Porreres E 97 B3
Porretta Terme I 81 B4
Porsgrunn N 35 C1
Porspoder F 56 B1
Port-a-Binson F 59 A4
Port Askaig GB 24 C1
Port Bannatyne GB 24 C2
Port-Barcarès F 78 D2
Port-Camargue F 78 C3
Port Charlotte GB 24 C1
Port d'Andratx E 97 B2
Port-de-Bouc F 78 C3
Port-de-Lanne F 76 C1
Port de Pollença E 97 B3
Port de Sóller E 97 B2
Port-des-Barques F 66 C3
Port Ellen GB 24 C1
Port-en-Bessin F 57 A5
Port Erin GB 26 A1
Port Eynon GB 28 B3
Port Glasgow GB 24 C3
Port Henderson GB 22 D3
Port Isaac GB 28 C3
Port-Joinville F 66 B2
Port-la-Nouvelle F 78 C2
Port Logan GB 24 D3
Port Louis F 56 C2
Port Manech F 56 C2
Port Nan Giuran GB 22 C2
Port-Navalo F 66 A2
Port Nis GB 22 C2
Port-St.-Louis-du-Rhône F 78 C3
Port St. Mary GB 26 A1
Port-Ste. Marie F 77 B3
Port-sur-Saône F 60 C2
Port Talbot GB 28 B4
Port-Vendres F 91 A6
Port William GB 24 D3
Portacloy IRL 18 B2
Portadown GB 19 B5
Portaferry GB 19 B6
Portaje E 93 B4
Portalegre P 92 B3
Portarlington IRL 21 A4
Portavadie GB 24 C2
Portavogie GB 19 B6
Portbail F 57 A4
Portbou E 91 A6
Portegrandi I 72 C2
Portel P 92 C3
Portela P 92 A2
Portelo P 87 C4
Portemouro E 86 B2
Port'Ercole I 102 A4
Portes-lès-Valence F 78 B3
Portets F 76 B2
Portezuelo E 93 B4
Portglenone GB 19 B5
Porthcawl GB 28 B4
Porthleven GB 28 C2
Porthmadog GB 26 C1
Porticcio F 102 B1
Portici I 103 C7
Portico di Romagna I 81 B5
Portilla de la Reina E 88 A2
Portillo E 88 C2
Portimao P 98 B2
Portinatx E 97 B1
Portinho da Arrabida P 92 C1
Portishead GB 29 B5
Portknockie GB 23 D6
Portlaoise IRL 21 A4
Portlethen GB 23 D6
Portmagne IRL 20 C1
Portmahomack GB 23 D5
Portman E 101 B5
Portnacroish GB 24 B2
Portnahaven GB 24 C1
Porto F 102 A1
Porto P 87 C2
Porto-Alto P 92 C2
Porto Azzurro I 81 D4
Porto Cerésio I 70 C3
Porto Cervo I 110 A2
Porto Cesáreo I 107 A4
Porto Colom E 97 B3
Porto Covo P 98 B2
Porto Cristo E 97 B3
Porto d'Áscoli I 82 D2
Porto de Lagos P 98 B2
Porto de Mos P 92 B2
Porto de Rei P 98 A2
Porto do Son E 86 B2
Porto Empédocle I 108 B2
Porto Garibaldi I 82 B1
Porto Petro E 97 B3
Porto Pino I 110 D1
Porto Potenza Picena I 82 C2
Porto Recanati I 82 C2
Porto San Giórgio I 82 C2
Porto Sant'Elpídio I 82 C2
Porto Santo Stéfano I 102 A4
Porto Tolle I 82 B1
Porto Tórres I 110 B1
Porto-Vecchio F 102 B2
Portocannone I 103 B8
Portoferráio I 81 D4
Portofino I 80 B3
Portogruaro I 72 C2
Portokhelion GR 117 E5
Portomaggiore I 81 B5
Portomarin E 86 B3
Porton GB 29 B6
Portonovo E 87 B2
Portopalo di Capo Passero I 109 C4
Portør N 33 D6
Portoscuso I 110 C1
Portovénere I 81 B3
Portpatrick GB 24 D2
Portreath GB 28 C2
Portree GB 22 D2
Portroe IRL 20 B3
Portrush GB 19 A5
Portsall F 56 B1
Portsmouth GB 31 D2
Portsoy GB 23 D6
Portstewart GB 19 A5
Portugalete E 89 A4
Portumna IRL 20 A3
Porvoo FIN 7 A8
Porzuna E 94 C2
Posada, *Oviedo* E 88 A2
Posada, *Oviedo* E 88 A1
Posada I 110 B2
Posada de Valdeón E 88 A2
Posadas E 99 B5
Poschiavo CH 71 B5
Posedarje HR 83 B4
Positano I 103 C7
Possagno I 72 C1
Posseck D 52 C2
Possesse F 59 B5
Pössneck D 52 C1
Posta I 102 A6
Posta Piana I 104 B1
Postal I 71 B6
Postbauer-Heng D 62 A2
Posterholt NL 50 B2
Postioma I 72 C2
Postira HR 83 C5
Postojna SLO 73 C4
Postoloprty CZ 53 C3
Postomino PL 46 A2
Posušje BIH 84 C2
Potamos, *Attiki* GR 117 G5
Potamos, *Attiki* GR 117 F4
Potegowo PL 46 A3
Potenza I 104 C1
Potenza Picena I 82 C2
Potes E 88 A2
Potigny F 57 B5
Potkrajci MNE 85 C4
Potočari BIH 85 B4
Potoci BIH 84 C2
Potoci BIH 83 B5
Potony H 74 C2
Potries E 96 C2
Potsdam D 45 C5
Potštát CZ 64 A3
Pottenbrunn A 63 B6
Pottendorf A 64 C2
Pottenstein A 64 C2
Pottenstein D 62 A2
Potters Bar GB 31 C3
Pöttmes D 62 B2
Pöttsching A 64 C2
Potworów PL 55 B5
Pouancé F 57 C4
Pougues-les-Eaux F 68 A3
Pouilly-en-Auxois F 69 A4
Pouilly-sous Charlieu F 68 B4
Pouilly-sur-Loire F 68 A2
Poujol-sur-Orb F 78 C2
Poullaouen F 56 B2
Poulton-le-Fylde GB 26 B3
Poundstock GB 28 C3
Pourcy F 59 A4
Pourrain F 59 C4
Pouy-de-Touges F 77 C4
Pouyastruc F 76 C3
Pouzauges F 66 B4
Pova de Santa Iria P 92 C1
Považská Bystrica SK 65 A4
Povedilla E 101 A3
Povlja HR 84 C1
Povljana HR 83 B4
Póvoa, *Beja* P 98 A3
Póvoa, *Santarém* P 92 B2
Póvoa de Lanhosa P 87 C2
Póvoa de Varzim P 87 C2
Póvoa e Meadas P 92 B3
Powidz PL 46 C3
Poyales del Hoyo E 93 A5
Poynton GB 26 B3
Poyntz Pass GB 19 B5
Poysdorf A 64 B2
Poza de la Sal E 89 B3
Pozaldez E 88 C2
Pozán de Vero E 90 A3
Pozanti TR 16 C7
Požarevac SRB 85 B6
Požega HR 74 C2
Požega SRB 85 C5
Poznań PL 46 C2
Pozo Alcón E 100 B3
Pozo Cañada E 101 A4
Pozo de Guadalajara E 95 B3
Pozo de la Serna E 100 A2
Pozoantiguo E 88 C1
Pozoblanco E 100 A1
Pozohondo E 101 A4
Pozondón E 95 B5
Poźrzadło Wielkie PL 46 B1
Pozuel del Campo E 95 B5
Pozuelo de Alarcón E 94 B3
Pozuelo de Calatrava E 100 A2
Pozuelo de Zarzón E 93 A4
Pozuelo del Páramo E 88 B1
Pozzallo I 109 C3
Pozzo San Nicola I 110 B1
Pozzomaggiore I 110 B1
Pozzuoli I 103 C7
Pozzuolo I 81 C5
Prabuty PL 47 B5
Prača BIH 84 C3
Prachatice CZ 63 A4
Prada E 87 B3
Pradelle F 79 B4
Pradelles F 78 B2
Prades E 90 B3
Prades F 91 A5
Pradła PL 55 C4
Prado E 88 A1
Prado P 87 C2
Prado del Rey E 99 C5
Pradoluengo E 89 B3
Præstø DK 39 D5
Pragelato I 79 A5
Pragersko SLO 73 B5
Prägraten A 72 A2
Prague = Praha CZ 53 C4
Praha = Prague CZ 53 C4
Prahecq F 67 B4
Praia P 92 B1
Práia a Mare I 106 B2
Praia da Rocha P 98 B2
Praia da Viera P 92 B2
Praia de Mira P 92 A2
Praiano I 103 C7
Pralboino I 71 C5
Pralognan-la-Vanoise F 70 C1
Pramanda GR 116 C3
Pranjani SRB 85 B5
Prapatnica HR 83 C5
Praszka PL 54 B3
Prat F 77 C3
Prat de Compte E 90 C3
Prata I 81 C4
Prata di Pordenone I 72 C2
Pratau D 52 B2
Pratdip E 90 B3
Pratella I 103 B7
Prato I 81 C5
Prátola Peligna I 103 A6
Pratola Serra I 103 C7
Prats-de-Mollo-la-Preste F 91 A5
Prauthoy F 59 C6
Pravia E 86 A4
Praxmar A 71 A6
Prayssac F 77 B4
Prazzo I 79 B6
Pré-en-Pail F 57 B5
Prebold SLO 73 B5
Préchac F 76 B2
Précy-sur-Thil F 69 A4
Predáppio I 81 B5
Predazzo I 72 B1
Předin CZ 63 A6
Preding A 73 B5
Predjame SLO 73 C4
Predlitz A 72 A3
Predmeja SLO 72 C3
Predoi I 72 A2
Prees GB 26 C3
Preetz D 44 A2
Préfailles F 66 A2
Pregarten A 63 B5
Pregrada HR 73 B5
Preignan F 77 C3
Preiļi LV 7 C9
Preitenegg A 73 B4
Prekaja BIH 83 B5
Preko HR 83 B4
Preljina SRB 85 C5
Prelog HR 74 B1
Prelošćica HR 74 C1
Přelouč CZ 53 C5
Prem SLO 73 C4
Premantura HR 82 B2
Prémery F 68 A3
Prémia I 70 B3
Premià de Mar E 91 B5
Premnitz D 44 C4
Prémont F 49 C4
Prenzlau D 45 B5
Preodac BIH 83 B5
Přerov CZ 64 A3
Prerow D 45 A4
Presencio E 88 B3
Presicce I 107 B5
Presly F 68 A2
Prešov SK 10 B6
Pressac F 67 B5
Pressath D 62 A2
Pressbaum A 64 B2
Prestatyn GB 26 B2
Prestebakke N 35 D3
Presteigne GB 29 A4
Přeštice CZ 63 A4
Preston, *Lancashire* GB 26 B3
Preston, *Scottish Borders* GB 25 C5
Prestonpans GB 25 C5
Prestwick GB 24 C3
Prettin D 52 B2
Preturo I 103 A6
Pretzchendorf D 52 C3
Pretzier D 44 C3
Pretzsch D 52 B2
Preuilly-sur-Claise F 67 B5
Prevalje SLO 73 B4
Prevenchères F 78 B2
Préveranges F 68 B2
Preveza GR 116 D2
Prevršac HR 73 C6
Prezid HR 73 C4
Priaranza del Bierzo E 86 B4
Priay F 69 B5
Pribeta SK 64 C4
Priboj BIH 84 B3
Priboj SRB 85 C4
Příbor CZ 64 A4
Příbram CZ 63 A5
Pribylina SK 65 A5
Přibyslav CZ 63 A6
Pričević SRB 85 B4
Pridjel BIH 84 B3
Priego E 95 B4
Priego de Córdoba E 100 B1
Priekule LV 6 C6
Prien D 62 C3
Prienai LT 6 D7
Prievidza SK 65 B4
Prigradica HR 84 D1
Prigrevica SRB 75 C4
Prijeboj HR 83 B4
Prijedor BIH 83 B5
Prijepolje SRB 85 C4
Prilep MK 116 A3
Priluka BIH 84 C1
Primda CZ 62 A3
Primel-Trégastel F 56 B2
Primišje HR 73 C5
Primorsk, *Kaliningrad* RUS 47 A6
Primorsk, *Severo-Zapadnyy* RUS 7 A10
Primošten HR 83 C4
Primstal D 60 A2
Princes Risborough GB 31 C3
Princetown GB 28 C3
Principina a Mare I 81 D5
Priolo Gargallo I 109 B4
Prioro E 88 B2
Priozersk RUS 3 F29
Prirechnyy RUS 113 C19
Prisoje BIH 84 C2
Pristen RUS 7 F14
Priština KOS 85 D6
Pritzerbe D 44 C4
Pritzier D 44 B3
Pritzwalk D 44 B4
Privas F 78 B3
Priverno I 102 B6
Privlaka, *Vukovarsko-Srijemska* HR 74 C3
Privlaka, *Zadarska* HR 83 B4
Prizna HR 83 B3
Prizren KOS 10 E6
Prizzi I 108 B2
Prnjavor BIH 84 B2
Prnjavor HR 73 C5
Prnjavor SRB 85 B4
Proaza E 86 A4
Probstzella D 52 C1
Probus GB 28 C3
Prócchio I 81 D4
Prochowice PL 54 B1
Prócida I 103 C7
Prodhromos CY 120 B1
Prodo I 82 D1
Proença-a-Nova P 92 B3
Proença-a-Velha P 92 A3
Profondeville B 49 C5
Prokuplje SRB 10 E6
Propriano F 102 B1
Prosec CZ 64 A2
Prösen D 52 B3
Prosenjakovci SLO 73 B6
Prosotsani GR 116 A5
Prostějov CZ 64 A3
Prószków PL 54 C2
Proszowice PL 55 C5
Protić BIH 84 B1
Protivanov CZ 64 A2
Protivín CZ 63 A5
Prötzel D 45 C5
Provins F 59 B4
Prozor BIH 84 C2
Prrenjas AL 116 A2
Prudhoe GB 25 D6
Prudnik PL 54 C2
Pruggern A 72 A3
Prüm D 50 C2
Pruna E 99 C5
Prunelli-di-Fiumorbo F 102 A2
Prunetta I 81 B4
Pruniers F 68 B2
Prusice PL 54 B1
Pruské SK 64 A4
Pruszce PL 47 B4
Pruszcz Gdański PL 47 A4
Pruszków PL 55 A5
Prutz A 71 A5
Prüzen D 44 B4
Pruzhany BY 6 E8
Pružina SK 65 A4
Pryluky UA 11 A12
Pryzlęg PL 46 C1
Przechlewo PL 46 B3
Przecław PL 55 C6
Przedbórz PL 55 B4
Przedecz PL 54 A3
Przejęslav PL 53 B5
Przemków PL 53 B5
Przemocze PL 45 B6
Przemyśl PL 11 B7
Przerąb PL 55 B4
Przewodnik PL 47 B4
Przewóz PL 53 B4
Przezmark PL 47 B5
Przodkowo PL 47 A4
Przybiernów PL 45 B6
Przyborowice PL 47 C6
Przybyszew PL 55 B5
Przybyszów PL 55 B4
Przylęg PL 46 C1
Przysucha PL 55 B5
Przytóczna PL 46 C1
Przytyk PL 55 B5
Przywidz PL 47 A4
Psachna GR 116 D5
Psara GR 116 D7
Psary PL 54 B3
Pskov RUS 7 C10
Pszczew PL 46 C1
Pszczółki PL 47 A4
Pszczyna PL 54 D3
Pszów PL 54 C3
Pteleos GR 116 C4
Ptolemaida GR 116 B3
Ptuj SLO 73 B5
Ptusza PL 46 B2
Puch A 62 C4
Puchberg am Schneeberg A 64 C1
Puchevillers F 48 C3
Puchheim D 62 B2
Púchov SK 64 A4
Pučišća HR 83 C5
Puck PL 47 A4
Puçol E 96 B2
Puconci SLO 73 B6
Pudasjärvi FIN 3 D27
Puderbach D 50 C3
Puebla de Albortón E 90 B2
Puebla de Alcocer E 93 C5
Puebla de Beleña E 95 B3
Puebla de Don Fadrique E 101 B3
Puebla de Don Rodrigo E 94 C2
Puebla de Guzmán E 98 B3
Puebla de la Calzada E 93 C4
Puebla de la Reina E 93 C4
Puebla de Lillo E 88 A1
Puebla de Obando E 93 B4
Puebla de Sanabria E 87 B4
Puebla de Sancho Pérez E 93 C4
Puebla del Maestre E 99 A4
Puebla del Principe E 100 A3
Puente Almuhey E 88 B2
Puente de Domingo Flórez E 86 B4
Puente de Génave E 101 A3
Puente de Montañana E 90 A3
Puente del Congosto E 93 A5
Puente Duero E 88 C2
Puente-Genil E 100 B1
Puente la Reina E 89 B5
Puente la Reina de Jaca E 90 A2
Puente Mayorga E 99 C5
Puente Viesgo E 88 A3
Puentelarra E 89 B3
Puertas, *Asturias* E 88 A2
Puertas, *Salamanca* E 87 C4
Puerto de Mazarrón E 101 B4
Puerto de San Vicente E 94 C1
Puerto de Santa Cruz E 93 B5
Puerto-Lápice E 95 C3
Puerto Lumbreras E 101 B4
Puerto Moral E 99 B4
Puerto Real E 99 C4
Puerto Rey E 94 C1
Puerto Seguro E 87 D4
Puerto Serrano E 99 C5
Puertollano E 100 A1
Puget-Sur-Argens F 79 C5
Puget-Théniers F 79 C5
Puget-ville F 79 C5
Pugnochiuso I 104 B2
Puig Reig E 91 B4
Puigcerdà E 91 A4
Puigpunyent E 97 B2
Puillon F 76 C2
Puimichel F 79 C5
Puimoisson F 79 C5
Puiseaux F 58 B3
Puisieux F 48 C3
Puisserguier F 78 C2
Puivert F 77 D5
Pujols F 76 B2
Pukanec SK 65 B4
Pukavik S 41 C4
Pukë AL 105 A5
Pula HR 82 B2
Pula I 110 C1
Puławy PL 10 A6
Pulborough GB 31 D3
Pulfero I 72 B3
Pulgar E 94 C2
Pulheim D 50 B2
Pulkau A 64 B1
Pulpi E 101 B4
Pulsano I 104 C3
Pulsnitz D 53 B4
Pułtusk PL 6 E6
Pumpsaint GB 28 A4
Punat HR 83 A3
Punta Marina I 82 B1
Punta Prima E 97 B4
Punta Sabbioni I 72 C2
Punta Umbria E 99 B4
Puntas de Calnegre E 101 B4
Puolanka FIN 3 D27
Puoltikasvaara S 112 E10
Puoltsa S 112 E8
Puračić BIH 84 B3
Purbach am Neusiedler See A 64 C2
Purchena E 101 B3
Purfleet GB 31 C4
Purgstall A 63 B6
Purkersdorf A 64 B2
Purmerend NL 42 C1
Purullena E 100 B2
Pushkin RUS 7 B11
Pushkino RUS 7 C14
Püspökladány H 75 A6
Pusté Ulany SK 64 B3
Pustelnik PL 55 A6
Pustoshka RUS 7 C10
Puszcza Mariańska PL 55 B5
Puszczykowo PL 54 A1
Pusztamagyaród H 74 B1
Pusztamonostor H 75 A4
Pusztaszabolcs H 74 A3
Pusztavám H 74 A3
Putanges-Pont-Ecrepin F 57 B5
Putbus D 45 A5
Putignano I 104 C3
Putlitz D 44 B4
Putnok H 65 B6
Putte B 49 B5
Puttelange-aux-Lacs F 60 A2
Putten NL 49 A6
Puttgarden D 44 A3
Püttlingen D 60 A2
Putzu Idu I 110 B1
Puy-Guillaume F 68 C3
Puy-l'Évêque F 77 B4
Puylaroque F 77 B4
Puylaurens F 77 C5
Puymirol F 77 B3
Puyôo F 76 C2
Puyrolland F 67 B4
Pwllheli GB 26 C1
Pyatykhatky UA 11 B12
Pyetrikaw BY 7 E10
Pyhäjärvi FIN 3 E26
Pyla CY 120 A2
Pyla-sur-Mer F 76 B1
Pyryatyn UA 11 A12
Pyrzyce PL 45 B6
Pysely CZ 63 A5
Pyskowice PL 54 C3
Pytalovo RUS 7 C9
Pyzdry PL 54 A2

Q

Quakenbrück D 43 C4
Quargnento I 80 B2
Quarré-les-Tombes F 68 A3
Quarteira P 98 B2
Quartu Sant'Élena I 110 C2
Quatre-Champs F 59 A5
Quedlinburg D 52 B1
Queensferry, *Edinburgh* GB 25 C4
Queensferry, *Flintshire* GB 26 B2
Queige F 69 C6
Queipo E 99 B4
Queixans E 91 A4
Quel E 89 B4
Quelaines-St-Gault F 57 C5
Queljada P 87 C2
Quemada E 89 C3
Queralbs E 91 A5
Quercianella I 81 C4
Querfurt D 52 B1
Quérigut F 77 D5
Quero E 95 C3
Quero I 72 C1
Querqueville F 57 A4
Quesada E 100 B2
Questembert F 56 C3
Quettehou F 57 A4
Quevauvillers F 58 A3
Quevy B 49 C5
Quiaois P 92 A2
Quiberon F 66 A1
Quiberville F 58 A1
Quickborn D 44 B1
Quiévrain B 49 C4
Quillan F 77 D5
Quillebeuf F 58 A1
Quimper F 56 B1
Quimperlé F 56 C2
Quincampoix F 58 A2
Quincoces de Yuso E 89 B3
Quincy F 68 A2
Quinéville F 57 A4
Quingey F 69 A5
Quinson F 79 C5
Quinssaines F 68 B2
Quinta-Grande P 92 C2
Quintana de la Serena E 93 C5
Quintana del Castillo E 86 B4
Quintana del Marco E 88 B1
Quintana del Puenta E 88 B2
Quintana-Martin Galindez E 89 B3
Quintanaortuño E 88 B3
Quintanapalla E 89 B3
Quintanar de la Orden E 95 C3
Quintanar de la Sierra E 89 C3
Quintanar del Rey E 95 C5
Quintanilla de la Mata E 88 C3
Quintanilla de Onésimo E 88 C2
Quintanilla de Somoza E 87 B4
Quintanilla del Coco E 89 C3
Quintas de Valdelucio E 88 B2
Quintela P 87 D3
Quintin F 56 B3
Quinto E 90 B2
Quinzano d'Oglio I 71 C5
Quiroga E 86 B3
Quismondo E 94 B2
Quissac F 78 C2
Quistello I 81 A4

R

Raab A 63 B4
Raabs an der Thaya A 63 B6
Raahe FIN 3 D26
Raajärvi FIN 113 F15
Raalte NL 42 C3
Raamsdonksveer NL 49 B5
Raanujarvi FIN 113 F13
Raattama FIN 113 D13
Rab HR 83 B3
Rabac HR 82 A3
Rábade E 86 A3
Rábafüzes H 73 B6
Rábahidvég H 74 A1
Rabanales E 87 C4
Rábapatona H 64 C3
Rabapordány H 74 A2
Rabastens F 77 C4
Rabastens-de-Bigorre F 76 C3
Rabat = Victoria, *Gozo* M 107 C5
Rabat, *Malta* M 107 C5
Rabča SK 65 A5
Rabe SRB 75 B5
Rabi CZ 63 A4
Rabino PL 46 B1
Rabka PL 65 A5
Rabrovo SRB 85 B6
Rača, *Srbija* SRB 85 B6
Rača, *Srbija* SRB 85 C6
Racale I 107 B5
Rácalmás H 75 A3
Racalmuto I 108 B2
Racconigi I 80 B1
Rače SLO 73 B5
Rachecourt-sur-Marne F 59 B6
Raciąż PL 47 C6
Racibórz PL 54 C3
Račinovci HR 84 B3
Ráckeve H 75 A3
Racławice PL 55 C5
Racławice Sląskie PL 54 C2
Racot PL 54 A1

Råda, *Skaraborg* S 35 D5
Råda, *Värmland* S 34 B5
Radalj SRB 85 B4
Rădăuți RO 11 C8
Radda in Chianti I 81 C5
Raddusa I 109 B3
Radeberg D 53 B3
Radebeul D 52 B3
Radeburg D 53 B3
Radeče SLO 73 B5
Radekhiv UA 11 A8
Radenci SLO 73 B6
Radenthein A 72 B3
Radevormwald D 50 B3
Radicófani I 81 D5
Radicóndoli I 81 C5
Radišići BIH 84 C2
Radizel SLO 73 B5
Radków PL 54 C1
Radlje ob Dravi SLO 73 B5
Radłów PL 55 C5
Radmer an der Stube A 73 A4
Radnejaur S 115 B15
Radnice CZ 63 A4
Radohova BIH 84 B2
Radojevo SRB 75 C5
Radolfzell D 61 C4
Radom PL 55 B6
Radomice PL 47 C5
Radomin PL 47 B5
Radomsko PL 55 B4
Radomyshl UA 11 A10
Radomyśl Wielki PL 55 C6
Radošina SK 64 B3
Radošovce SK 64 B3
Radostowo PL 47 B6
Radoszewice PL 54 B3
Radoszyce PL 55 B5
Radotin CZ 53 D4
Radoviš MK 116 A4
Radovljica SLO 73 B4
Radowo Wielkie PL 46 B1
Radstadt A 72 A3
Radstock GB 29 B5
Raduc HR 83 B4
Radviliškis LT 6 D7
Radzanów, *Mazowieckie* PL 47 C6
Radzanów, *Mazowieckie* PL 55 B5
Radziejów PL 47 C4
Radziejowice PL 55 A5
Radzovce SK 65 B5
Radzymin PL 55 A6
Radzyń Chełmiński PL 47 B4
Raeren B 50 C2
Raesfeld D 50 B2
Raffadali I 108 B2
Rafina GR 117 D5
Rafsbotn N 113 B12
Ragachow BY 7 E11
Ragály H 65 B6
Rågeleje DK 41 C2
Raglan GB 29 B5
Ragnitz A 73 B5
Ragusa I 109 C3
Rahden D 43 C5
Råholt N 34 B3
Raiano I 103 A6
Raigada E 87 B3
Rain D 62 B1
Rainbach im Mühlkreis A 63 B5
Rainham GB 31 C4
Rairiz de Veiga E 87 B3
Raisdorf D 44 A2
Raisio FIN 6 A7
Raiva, *Aveiro* P 87 C2
Raiva, *Coimbra* P 92 A2
Raja-Jooseppi FIN 113 D17
Rajala FIN 113 E15
Rajcza PL 65 A5
Rajec SK 65 A4
Rájec-Jestřebi CZ 64 A2
Rajecké Teplice SK 65 A4
Rajevo Selo HR 84 B3
Rajhrad CZ 64 A2
Rajić HR 74 C2
Rajka H 64 C3
Rakaca H 65 B6
Rakek SLO 73 C4
Rakhiv UA 11 B8
Rakitna SLO 73 C4
Rakkestad N 35 C3
Rákóczifalva H 75 A5
Rakoniewice PL 53 A6
Rakoszyce PL 54 B1
Raková SK 65 A4
Rakovac BIH 84 A2
Rakovica HR 83 B4
Rakovník CZ 53 C3
Rakow D 45 A5
Raków PL 55 C6
Rakvere EST 7 B9
Ralja SRB 85 B5
Rälla S 41 C6
Ramacastañas E 94 B1
Ramacca I 109 B3
Ramales de la Victoria E 89 A3
Ramberg N 112 D2
Rambervillers F 60 B2
Rambouillet F 58 B2
Rambucourt F 60 B1
Ramdala S 41 C5
Ramerupt F 59 B5
Ramingstein A 72 A3
Ramirás E 87 B2
Ramiswil CH 70 A2
Ramkvilla S 40 B4
Ramme DK 38 C1
Rämmen S 34 B6
Ramnäs S 36 C3
Ramnes N 35 C2
Râmnicu Vâlcea RO 11 D8
Ramonville-St. Agne F 77 C4
Rampside GB 26 A2
Ramsau D 62 C3
Ramsbeck D 51 B4
Ramsberg S 36 C2
Ramsele S 115 D13
Ramsey, *Cambridgeshire* GB 30 B3
Ramsey, *Isle of Man* GB 26 A1
Ramseycleuch GB 25 C4
Ramsgate GB 31 C5
Ramsjö S 115 E12
Ramstein-Meisenbach D 60 A3
Ramsund N 112 D5
Ramundberget S 114 E9
Ramvik S 115 E14
Ranalt A 71 A6
Rånäs S 36 C5
Rånåsfoss N 34 B3
Rance B 49 C5
Ránchio I 82 C1
Randaberg N 33 D2
Randalstown GB 19 B5
Randan F 68 B3
Randazzo I 109 B3
Rånddalen S 115 E10
Randegg A 63 B5
Randers DK 38 C3
Randijaur S 112 F8
Randin E 87 C3
Randsverk N 114 F6
Rånes F 57 B5
Rångedala S 40 B3
Ranis D 52 C1
Rankweil A 71 A4
Rånnaväg S 40 B3
Ränneslöv S 40 C3
Rannoch Station GB 24 B3
Ranovac SRB 85 B6
Ransäter S 34 C5
Ransbach-Baumbach D 50 C3
Ransta S 36 C3
Ranttila FIN 113 C14
Ranua FIN 3 D27
Ranum DK 38 C2
Ranvalhal P 92 B1
Raon-l'Étape F 60 B2
Ráossi I 71 C6
Rapallo I 80 B3
Rapla EST 6 B8
Rapness GB 23 B6
Rapolano Terme I 81 C5
Rapolla I 104 C1
Raposa P 92 B2
Rapperswil CH 70 A3
Raša HR 82 A3
Rasal E 90 A2
Rascafria E 94 B3
Rasdorf D 51 C5
Raseiniai LT 6 D7
Rašica SLO 73 C4
Rasines E 89 A3
Raška SRB 85 C5
Rasquera E 90 B3
Rássina I 81 C5
Rastatt D 61 B4
Rastede D 43 B5
Rastenberg D 52 B1
Rastošnica BIH 84 B3
Rastovac MNE 84 D3
Rasueros E 94 A1
Rasy PL 55 B4
Raszków PL 54 B2
Rataje SRB 85 C6
Rätan S 115 E11
Rateče SLO 72 B3
Ratekau D 44 B2
Ratež SLO 73 C5
Rathangan IRL 21 A5
Rathcoole IRL 21 A5
Rathcormack IRL 20 B3
Rathdrum IRL 21 B5
Rathebur D 45 B5
Rathenow D 44 C4
Rathfriland GB 19 B5
Rathkeale IRL 20 B3
Rathmelton IRL 19 A4
Rathmolyon IRL 21 A5
Rathmore IRL 20 B2
Rathmullan IRL 19 A4
Rathnew IRL 21 B5
Rathvilly IRL 21 B5
Ratibořské Hory CZ 63 A5
Ratingen D 50 B2
Ratková SK 65 B6
Ratkovo SRB 75 C4
Ratne UA 6 F8
Ratoath IRL 21 A5
Rattelsdorf D 51 C6
Ratten A 73 A5
Rattosjärvi FIN 113 F13
Rattray GB 25 B4
Rättvik S 36 B2
Ratvika N 114 D7
Ratzeburg D 44 B2
Rätzlingen D 44 C3
Raucourt-et-Flaba F 59 A5
Raudeberg N 114 F2
Raufarhöfn IS 111 A10
Raufoss N 34 B2
Rauhala FIN 113 E13
Rauland N 33 C5
Raulhac F 77 B5
Raulia N 115 B11
Rauma FIN 3 F24
Raundal N 32 B3
Raunds GB 30 B3
Rauris A 72 A3
Rautas S 112 E8
Rautavaara FIN 3 E28
Rauville-la-Bigot F 57 A4
Rauzan F 76 B2
Rava-Rus'ka UA 11 A7
Ravanusa I 108 B2
Ravča HR 84 C2
Ravels B 49 B5
Rävemåla S 40 C5
Ravenglass GB 26 A2
Ravenna I 82 B1
Ravensburg D 61 C5
Rävlanda S 40 B2
Ravna Gora HR 73 C4
Ravne na Koroškem SLO 73 B4
Ravnište SRB 85 C6
Ravnje SRB 85 B4
Ravno BIH 84 D2
Ravno Selo SRB 75 C4
Rawa Mazowiecka PL 55 B5
Rawicz PL 54 B1
Rawtenstall GB 26 B3
Rayleigh GB 31 C4
Ražana SRB 85 B4
Ražanac HR 83 B4
Razboj BIH 84 A2
Razbojna SRB 85 C6
Razes F 67 B6
Razgrad BG 11 E9
Razkrižje SLO 73 B6
Razo E 86 A2
Reading GB 31 C3
Réalmont F 77 C5
Rebais F 59 B4
Reboly RUS 3 E29
Rebordelo P 87 C3
Recanati I 82 C2
Recas E 94 B3
Recaş RO 10 D6
Recco I 80 B3
Recess IRL 18 C2
Recey-sur-Ource F 59 C5
Recezinhos P 87 C2
Rechnitz A 73 A6
Rechytsa BY 7 E11
Recke D 43 C4
Recklinghausen D 50 B3
Recoaro Terme I 71 C6
Recogne B 59 A6
Recoules-Prévinquières F 78 B1
Recsk H 65 C6
Recz PL 46 B1
Red Point GB 22 D3
Reda PL 47 A4
Redalen N 34 B2
Redange L 60 A1
Redcar GB 27 A4
Redditch GB 29 A6
Redefin D 44 B3
Redhill GB 31 C3
Redics H 74 B1
Redkino RUS 7 C14
Redland GB 23 B5
Redlin D 44 B4
Redon F 57 C3
Redondela E 87 B2
Redondo P 92 C3
Redruth GB 28 C2
Redzikowo PL 46 A3
Reepham GB 30 B5
Rees D 50 B2
Reeth GB 27 A4
Reetz D 44 B3
Reftele S 40 B3
Regalbuto I 109 B3
Regen D 62 B4
Regensburg D 62 A3
Regenstauf D 62 A3
Reggello I 81 C5
Réggio di Calábria I 109 A4
Réggio nell'Emília I 81 B4
Reggiolo I 81 B4
Reghin RO 11 C8
Régil E 89 A4
Regna S 37 D2
Regniéville F 60 B1
Regny F 69 C4
Rego da Leirosa P 92 A2
Regöly H 74 B3
Regueiro E 86 B2
Reguengo, *Portalegre* P 92 B3
Reguengo, *Santarém* P 92 B2
Reguengos de Monsaraz P 92 C3
Rehau D 52 C2
Rehburg D 43 C6
Rehden D 43 C5
Rehna D 44 B3
Reichelsheim D 61 A4
Reichelshofen D 61 A6
Reichenau A 64 C1
Reichenbach, *Sachsen* D 52 C2
Reichenbach, *Sachsen* D 53 B4
Reichenfels A 73 A4
Reichensachsen D 51 B6
Reichertshofen D 62 B2
Reichshoffen F 60 B3
Reiden CH 70 A2
Reigada E 86 A4
Reigada P 87 D4
Reigate GB 31 C3
Reillanne F 79 C4
Reillo E 95 C5
Reims F 59 A5
Reinach CH 70 A3
Reinbek D 44 B2
Reinberg D 45 A5
Reine N 112 E2
Reinfeld D 44 B2
Reinheim D 61 A4
Reinli N 32 B6
Reinosa E 88 A2
Reinstorf D 44 B3
Reinsvoll N 34 B2
Reisach A 72 B3
Reiss GB 23 C5
Reit im Winkl D 62 C3
Reitan N 114 E8
Rejmyre S 37 D2
Rekavice BIH 84 B2
Rekovac SRB 85 C6
Relleu E 96 C2
Rém H 75 B4
Remagen D 50 C3
Rémalard F 58 B1
Rembercourt-aux-Pots F 59 B6
Remedios P 92 B1
Remels D 43 B4
Remetea Mare RO 75 C6
Remich L 60 A2
Rémilly F 60 A2
Remiremont F 60 C2
Remolinos E 90 B1
Remoulins F 78 C3
Remscheid D 50 B3
Rémuzat F 79 B4
Rena N 34 A3
Renaison F 68 B3
Renazé F 57 C4
Renchen D 61 B4
Rencurel F 79 A4
Rende I 106 B3
Rendina GR 116 C3
Rendsburg D 43 A6
Renedo E 88 C2
Renens CH 69 B6
Renfrew GB 24 C3
Rengsjö S 36 A3
Reni UA 11 D10
Rennebu N 114 E6
Rennerod D 50 C4
Rennertshofen D 62 B2
Rennes F 57 B4
Rennes-les-Bains F 77 D5
Rennweg A 72 A3
Rens DK 39 E2
Rensjön S 112 D8
Rentería E 76 C1
Rentjärn S 115 B15
Répcelak H 74 A2
Repojoki FIN 113 D14
Repvåg N 113 B14
Requena E 96 B1
Réquista F 77 B5
Rerik D 44 A3
Resana I 72 C1
Resarö S 37 C5
Reschen = Résia I 71 B5
Resen MK 116 A3
Resende P 87 C3
Résia = Reschen I 71 B5
Reşiţa RO 10 D6
Resko PL 46 B1
Resnik SRB 85 B5
Ressons-sur-Matz F 58 A3
Restábal E 100 C2
Resuttano I 109 B3
Retamal E 93 C4
Retford GB 27 B5
Rethel F 59 A5
Rethem D 43 C6
Rethimno GR 117 G6
Retie B 49 B6
Retiers F 57 C4
Retortillo E 87 D4
Retortillo de Soria E 89 C3
Retournac F 68 C4
Rétság H 65 C5
Rettenegg A 73 A5
Retuerta del Bullaque E 94 C2
Retz A 64 B1
Retzbach D 61 A5
Reuden D 52 A2
Reuilly F 68 A2
Reus E 91 B4
Reusel NL 49 B6
Reuterstadt Stavenhagen D 45 B4
Reuth D 62 A3
Reutlingen D 61 B5
Reutte A 71 A5
Reuver NL 50 B2
Revel F 77 C4
Revello I 80 B1
Revenga E 94 B2
Revest-du-Bion F 79 B4
Révfülöp H 74 B2
Revigny-sur-Ornain F 59 B5
Revin F 59 A5
Řevnice CZ 63 A5
Řevničov CZ 53 C3
Revo I 71 B6
Revsnes N 32 A4
Revúca SK 65 B6
Rewa PL 47 A4
Rewal PL 45 A7
Rexbo S 36 B2
Reyðarfjörður IS 111 B11
Reyero E 88 B1
Reykhólar IS 111 B3
Reykholt, *Árnessýsla* IS 111 C5
Reykholt, *Borgarfjarðarsýsla* IS 111 C4
Reykjahlið IS 111 B9
Reykjavík IS 111 C4
Rezé F 66 A3
Rēzekne LV 7 C9
Rezovo BG 11 F10
Rezzato I 71 C5
Rezzoáglio I 80 B3
Rhade D 43 B6
Rhaunen D 60 A3
Rhayader GB 29 A4
Rheda-Wiedenbrück D 50 B4
Rhede, *Niedersachsen* D 43 B4
Rhede, *Nordrhein-Westfalen* D 50 B2
Rheinau D 60 B3
Rheinbach D 50 C2
Rheinberg D 50 B2
Rheine D 50 A3
Rheinfelden D 70 A2
Rheinsberg D 45 B4
Rhêmes-Notre-Dame I 70 C2
Rhenen NL 49 B6
Rhens D 50 C3
Rheydt D 50 B2
Rhiconich GB 22 C4
Rhinow D 44 C4
Rhiw GB 26 C1
Rho I 70 C4
Rhoden D 51 B5
Rhodes GR 119 F3
Rhondda GB 29 B4
Rhosllanerchrugog GB 26 B2
Rhosneigr GB 26 B1
Rhossili GB 28 B3
Rhubodach GB 24 C2
Rhuddlan GB 26 B2
Rhyl GB 26 B2
Rhynie GB 23 D6
Riala S 37 C5
Riallé F 66 A3
Riaño E 88 B1
Riano I 102 A5
Rians F 79 C4
Rianxo E 86 B2
Riaza E 89 C3
Riba E 89 A3
Riba de Saelices E 95 B4
Riba-Roja de Turia E 96 B2
Riba-roja d'Ebre E 90 B3
Ribadavia E 87 B2
Ribadeo E 86 A3
Ribadesella E 88 A1
Ribaflecha E 89 B4
Ribaforada E 89 C5
Ribare SRB 85 B6
Ribariće SRB 85 D5
Ribe DK 39 D1
Ribeauvillé F 60 B3
Ribécourt-Dreslincourt F 59 A3
Ribeira da Pena P 87 C3
Ribeira de Piquín E 86 A3
Ribemont F 59 A4
Ribera I 108 B2
Ribera de Cardós E 91 A4
Ribera del Fresno E 93 C4
Ribérac F 67 C5
Ribes de Freser E 91 A5
Ribesalbes E 96 A2
Ribiers F 79 B4
Ribnica BIH 84 B3
Ribnica SLO 73 C4
Ribnica SRB 85 C5
Ribnica na Potorju SLO 73 B5
Ribnik HR 73 C5
Rîbniţa MD 11 C10
Ribnitz-Damgarten D 44 A4
Ribolla I 81 D5
Říčany, *Jihomoravský* CZ 64 A2
Říčany, *Středočeský* CZ 53 D4
Riccia I 103 B7
Riccione I 82 B1
Ricco Del Golfo I 81 B3
Richebourg F 59 B6
Richelieu F 67 A5
Richisau CH 70 A3
Richmond, *Greater London* GB 31 C3
Richmond, *North Yorkshire* GB 27 A4
Richtenberg D 45 A4
Richterswil CH 70 A3
Rickling D 44 A2
Rickmansworth GB 31 C3
Ricla E 89 C5
Riddarhyttan S 36 C2
Ridderkerk NL 49 B5
Riddes CH 70 B2
Ridjica SRB 75 C4
Riec-sur-Bélon F 56 C2
Ried A 63 B4
Ried im Oberinntal A 71 A5
Riedenburg D 62 B2
Riedlingen D 61 B5
Riedstadt D 61 A4
Riegersburg A 73 B5
Riego de la Vega E 88 B1
Riego del Camino E 88 C1
Riello E 88 B1
Riemst B 49 C6
Rienne B 49 D5
Riénsena E 88 A2
Riesa D 52 B3
Riese Pio X I 72 C1
Riesi I 109 B3
Riestedt D 52 B1
Rietberg D 51 B4
Rieti I 102 A5
Rietschen D 53 B4
Rieumes F 77 C4
Rieupeyroux F 77 B5
Rieux F 77 C4
Riez F 79 C5
Rīga LV 6 C8
Riggisberg CH 70 B2
Rignac F 77 B5
Rignano Gargánico I 104 B1
Rigolato I 72 B2
Rigside GB 25 C4
Rigutino I 81 C5
Riihimäki FIN 3 F26
Rijeka HR 73 C4
Rijeka Crnojeviča MNE 105 A5
Rijen NL 49 B5
Rijkevorsel B 49 B5
Rijssen NL 50 A2
Rilić BIH 84 C2
Rilievo I 108 B1
Rillé F 67 A5
Rillo de Gallo E 95 B5
Rimavská Baňa SK 65 B5
Rimavská Seč SK 65 B6
Rimavská Sobota SK 65 B6
Rimbo S 36 C5
Rimforsa S 37 D2
Rímini I 82 B1
Rîmnicu Sărat RO 11 D9
Rimogne F 59 A5
Rimpar D 61 A5
Rimske Toplice SLO 73 B5
Rincón de la Victoria E 100 C1
Rincón de Soto E 89 B5
Rindal N 114 D6
Rinde N 32 A3
Ringarum S 37 D3
Ringaskiddy IRL 20 C3
Ringe DK 39 D3
Ringebu N 34 A2
Ringkøbing DK 39 C1
Ringsaker N 34 B2
Ringsted DK 39 D4
Ringwood GB 29 C6
Rinkaby S 41 D4
Rinkabyholm S 40 C6
Rinlo E 86 A3
Rinn A 71 A6
Rinteln D 51 A5
Rio E 86 B3
Rio do Coures P 92 B2
Rio Douro P 87 C3
Rio Frio P 92 C2
Rio frio de Riaza E 95 A3
Rio Maior P 92 B2
Rio Marina I 81 D4
Rio Tinto P 87 C2
Riobo E 86 B2
Riodeva E 96 A1
Riofrio E 94 B2
Riofrio de Aliste E 87 C4
Riogordo E 100 C1
Rioja E 101 C3
Riola I 81 B5
Riola Sardo I 110 C1
Riolobos E 93 B4
Riom F 68 C3
Riom-ès-Montagnes F 68 C2
Riomaggiore I 81 B3
Rion-des-Landes F 76 C2
Rionegro del Puente E 87 B4
Rionero in Vúlture I 104 C1
Riopar E 101 A3
Riós E 87 C3
Rioseco E 88 A1
Rioseco de Tapia E 88 B1
Riotord F 69 C4
Riotorto E 86 A3
Rioz F 69 A6
Ripač BIH 83 B4
Ripacándida I 104 C1
Ripanj SRB 85 B5
Ripatransone I 82 D2
Ripley GB 27 B4
Ripoll E 91 A5
Ripon GB 27 A4
Riposto I 109 B4
Ripsa S 37 D3
Risan MNE 105 A4
Risbäck S 115 C12
Risca GB 29 B4
Rischenau D 51 B5
Riscle F 76 C2
Risebo S 40 A6
Risnes N 32 A2
Rišňovce SK 64 B3
Risør N 33 D6
Risøyhamn N 112 D4
Rissna S 115 D12
Ritsem S 112 E6
Ritterhude D 43 B5
Riutula FIN 113 D15
Riva del Garda I 71 C5
Riva Ligure I 80 C1
Rivanazzano I 80 B3
Rivarolo Canavese I 70 C2
Rivarolo Mantovano I 81 A4
Rive-de-Gier F 69 C4
Rivedoux-Plage F 66 B3
Rivello I 106 A2
Rivergaro I 80 B3
Rives F 69 C5
Rivesaltes F 78 D1
Rivignano I 72 C3
Rivne UA 11 A9
Rívoli I 80 A1
Rivolta d'Adda I 71 C4
Rixheim F 60 C3
Rixo S 35 D3
Riza GR 116 B5
Rizokarpaso CY 120 A3
Rjukan N 32 C5
Rø DK 41 D4
Rö S 37 C5
Roa E 88 C3
Roa N 34 B2
Roade GB 30 B3
Roager DK 39 D1
Roaldkvam N 33 C3
Roanne F 68 B4
Robakowo PL 47 B4
Róbbio I 70 C3
Röbel D 45 B4
Roberton GB 25 C5
Robertville B 50 C2
Robin Hood's Bay GB 27 A5
Robleda E 93 A4
Robledillo de Trujillo E 93 B5
Robledo, *Albacete* E 101 A3
Robledo, *Orense* E 86 B4
Robledo de Chavela E 94 B2
Robledo del Buey E 94 C2
Robledo del Mazo E 94 C2
Robledollano E 93 B5
Robles de la Valcueva E 88 B1
Robliza de Cojos E 87 D5
Robres E 90 B2
Robres del Castillo E 89 B4
Rocafort de Queralt E 91 B4
Rocamadour F 77 B4
Rocca di Mezzo I 103 A6
Rocca di Papa I 102 B5
Rocca Imperiale I 106 A3
Rocca Priora I 82 C2
Rocca San Casciano I 81 B5
Rocca Sinibalda I 102 A5
Roccabernarda I 107 B3
Roccabianca I 81 A4
Roccadáspide I 103 C8
Roccagorga I 102 B6
Roccalbegna I 81 D5
Roccalumera I 109 B4
Roccamena I 108 B2
Roccamonfina I 103 B6
Roccanova I 106 A3
Roccapalumba I 108 B2
Roccapassa I 103 A6
Roccaraso I 103 B7
Roccasecca I 103 B6
Roccastrada I 81 C5
Roccatederighi I 81 C5
Roccella Iónica I 106 C3
Rocchetta Sant'António I 103 B8
Rocester GB 27 C4
Rochdale GB 26 B3
Roche-lez-Beaupré F 69 A6
Rochechouart F 67 C5
Rochefort B 49 C6
Rochefort F 66 C4
Rochefort-en-Terre F 56 C3
Rochefort-Montagne F 68 C2
Rochefort-sur-Nenon F 69 A5
Rochemaure F 78 B3
Rocheservière F 66 B3
Rochester, *Medway* GB 31 C4
Rochester, *Northumberland* GB 25 C5
Rochlitz D 52 B2
Rociana del Condado E 99 B4
Rockenhausen D 60 A3
Rockhammar S 37 C2
Rockneby S 40 C6
Ročko Polje HR 73 C4
Ročov CZ 53 C3
Rocroi F 59 A5
Roda de Bara E 91 B4
Roda de Ter E 91 B5
Rodach D 51 C6
Rodalben D 60 A3
Rødberg N 32 B5
Rødby DK 44 A3
Rødbyhavn DK 44 A3
Rødding, *Sønderjyllands Amt.* DK 39 D2
Rødding, *Viborg Amt.* DK 38 C1
Rödeby S 41 C5
Rodeiro E 86 B3
Rødekro DK 39 D2
Roden NL 42 B3
Ródenas E 95 B5
Rodenkirchen D 43 B5
Rödental D 52 C1
Rödermark D 51 D4
Rodewisch D 52 C2
Rodez F 77 B5
Rodi Gargánico I 104 B1
Roding D 62 A3
Rödjebro S 36 B4
Rødkærsbro DK 39 C2
Rodolivas GR 116 B5
Rodoñá E 91 B4
Rødvig DK 41 D2
Roermond NL 50 B1
Roesbrugge B 48 C3
Roeschwoog F 61 B4
Roeselare B 49 C4
Roetgen D 50 C2
Roffiac F 78 A2

St. Germain-du-Bois F 69 B5
St. Germain-du-Plain F 69 B4
St. Germain-du Puy F 68 A2
St. Germain-en-Laye F 58 B3
St. Germain-Laval F 68 C4
St. Germain-Lembron F 68 C3
St. Germain-les-Belles F 67 C6
St. Germain-Lespinasse F 68 B3
St. Germain-l'Herm F 68 C3
St. Gervais-d'Auvergne F 68 B2
St. Gervais-les-Bains F 70 C1
St. Gervais-sur-Mare F 78 C2
St. Gildas-de-Rhuys F 66 A2
St. Gildas-des-Bois F 66 A2
St. Gilles, *Gard* F 78 C3
St. Gilles, *Ille-et-Vilaine* F 57 B4
St. Gilles-Croix-de-Vie F 66 B3
St. Gingolph F 70 B1
St. Girons, *Ariège* F 77 D4
St. Girons, *Landes* F 76 C1
St. Girons-Plage F 76 C1
St. Gobain F 59 A4
St. Gorgon-Main F 69 A6
St. Guénolé F 56 C1
St. Harmon GB 29 A4
St. Helens GB 26 B3
St. Helier GB 57 A3
St. Herblain F 66 A3
St. Hilaire, *Allier* F 68 B3
St. Hilaire, *Aude* F 77 C5
St. Hilaire-de-Riez F 66 B3
St. Hilaire-de-Villefranche F 67 C4
St. Hilaire-des-Loges F 67 B4
St. Hilaire-du-Harcouët F 57 B4
St. Hilaire-du-Rosier F 79 A4
St. Hippolyte, *Aveyron* F 77 B5
St. Hippolyte, *Doubs* F 70 A1
St. Hippolyte-du-Fort F 78 C2
St. Honoré-les-Bains F 68 B3
St. Hubert B 49 C6
St. Imier CH 70 A2
St. Issey GB 28 C3
St. Ives, *Cambridgeshire* GB 30 B3
St. Ives, *Cornwall* GB 28 C2
St. Izaire F 78 C1
St. Jacques-de-la-Lande F 57 B4
St. Jacut-de-la-Mer F 57 B3
St. James F 57 B4
St. Jaume d'Enveja E 90 C3
St. Jean-Brévelay F 56 C3
St. Jean-d'Angély F 67 C4
St. Jean-de-Belleville F 69 C6
St. Jean-de-Bournay F 69 C5
St. Jean-de-Braye F 58 C2
St. Jean-de-Côle F 67 C5
St. Jean-de-Daye F 57 A4
St. Jean de Losne F 69 A5
St. Jean-de-Luz F 76 C1
St. Jean-de-Maurienne F 69 C6
St. Jean-de-Monts F 66 B2
St. Jean-d'Illac F 76 B2
St. Jean-du-Bruel F 78 B2
St. Jean-du-Gard F 78 B2
St. Jean-en-Royans F 79 A4
St. Jean-la-Riviere F 79 C6
St. Jean-Pied-de-Port F 76 C1
St. Jean-Poutge F 77 C3
St. Jeoire F 69 B6
St. Joachim F 66 A2
St. Johnstown IRL 19 B4
St. Jorioz F 69 C6
St. Joris Winge B 49 C5
St. Jouin-de-Marnes F 67 B4
St. Juéry F 77 C5
St. Julien F 69 B5
St. Julien-Chapteuil F 78 A3
St. Julien-de-Vouvantes F 57 C4
St. Julien-du-Sault F 59 B4
St. Julien-du-Verdon F 79 C5
St. Julien-en-Born F 76 B1
St. Julien-en-Genevois F 69 B6
St. Julien la-Vêtre F 68 C3
St. Julien-l'Ars F 67 B5
St. Julien-Mont-Denis F 69 C6
St. Julien-sur-Reyssouze F 69 B5
St. Junien F 67 C5
St. Just F 78 B3
St. Just GB 28 C2
St. Just-en-Chaussée F 58 A3
St. Just-en-Chevalet F 68 C3
St. Just-St. Rambert F 69 C4
St. Justin F 76 C2
St. Keverne GB 28 C2
St. Lary-Soulan F 77 D3
St. Laurent-d'Aigouze F 78 C3
St. Laurent-de-Chamousset F 69 C4
St. Laurent-de-Condel F 57 A5
St. Laurent-de-la-Cabrerisse F 78 C1
St. Laurent-de-la-Salanque F 78 D1
St. Laurent-des-Autels F 66 A3
St. Laurent-du-Pont F 69 C5
St. Laurent-en-Caux F 58 A1
St. Laurent-en-Grandvaux F 69 B5
St. Laurent-Médoc F 76 A2
St. Laurent-sur-Gorre F 67 C5
St. Laurent-sur-Mer F 57 A5
St. Laurent-sur-Sèvre F 66 B4
St. Leger B 60 A1
St. Léger-de-Vignes F 68 B3
St. Léger-sous-Beuvray F 68 B4
St. Léger-sur-Dheune F 69 B4
St. Léonard-de-Noblat F 67 C6
St. Leonards GB 31 D4
St. Lô F 57 A4
St. Lon-les-Mines F 76 C1
St. Louis F 60 C3
St. Loup F 68 B3
St. Loup-de-la-Salle F 69 B4
St. Loup-sur-Semouse F 60 C2
St. Lunaire F 57 B3
St. Lupicin F 69 B5
St. Lyphard F 66 A2
St. Lys F 77 C4
St. Macaire F 76 B2
St. Maclou F 58 A1
St. Maixent-l'École F 67 B4
St. Malo F 57 B3
St. Mamet-la-Salvetat F 77 B5
St. Mandrier-sur-Mer F 79 C4
St. Marcel, *Drôme* F 78 B3
St. Marcel, *Saône-et-Loire* F 69 B4
St. Marcellin F 69 C5
St. Marcellin sur Loire F 68 C4
St. Marcet F 77 C3
St. Mards-en-Othe F 59 B4
St. Margaret's-at-Cliffe GB 31 C5
St. Margaret's Hope GB 23 C6
St. Mars-la-Jaille F 66 A3
St. Martin-d'Ablois F 59 B4
St. Martin-d'Auxigny F 68 A2
St. Martin-de-Belleville F 69 C6
St. Martin-de-Bossenay F 59 B4
St. Martin-de-Crau F 78 C3
St. Martin-de-Londres F 78 C2
St. Martin-de-Queyrières F 79 B5
St. Martin-de-Ré F 66 B3
St. Martin-de-Valamas F 78 B3
St. Martin-d'Entraunes F 79 B5
St. Martin des Besaces F 57 A5
St. Martin-d'Estreaux F 68 B3
St. Martin-d'Hères F 69 C5
St. Martin-du-Frêne F 69 B5
St. Martin-en-Bresse F 69 B5
St. Martin-en-Haut F 69 C4
St. Martin-la-Méanne F 68 C1
St. Martin-sur-Ouanne F 59 C4
St. Martin-Valmeroux F 77 A5
St. Martin-Vésubie F 79 B6
St. Martory F 77 C3
St. Mary's GB 23 C6
St. Mathieu F 67 C5
St. Mathieu-de-Tréviers F 78 C2
St. Maurice CH 70 B1
St. Maurice-Navacelles F 78 C2
St. Maurice-sur-Moselle F 60 C2
St. Mawes GB 28 C2
St. Maximin-la-Ste. Baume F 79 C4
St. Méard-de-Gurçon F 76 B3
St. Médard-de-Guizières F 76 A2
St. Médard-en-Jalles F 76 B2
St. Méen-le-Grand F 57 B3
St. Menges F 59 A5
St. Merløse DK 39 D4
St. Město CZ 54 C1
St. M'Hervé F 57 B4
St. Michel, *Aisne* F 59 A5
St. Michel, *Gers* F 77 C3
St. Michel-Chef-Chef F 66 A2
St. Michel-de-Castelnau F 76 B2
St. Michel-de-Maurienne F 69 C6
St. Michel-en-Grève F 56 B2
St. Michel-en-l'Herm F 66 B3
St. Michel-Mont-Mercure F 66 B4
St. Mihiel F 60 B1
St. Monance GB 25 B5
St. Montant F 78 B3
St. Moritz CH 71 B4
St. Nazaire F 66 A2
St. Nazaire-en-Royans F 79 A4
St. Nazaire-le-Désert F 79 B4
St. Nectaire F 68 C2
St. Neots GB 30 B3
St. Nicolas-de-Port F 60 B2
St. Nicolas-de-Redon F 57 C3
St. Nicolas-du-Pélem F 56 B2
St. Niklaas B 49 B5
St. Omer F 48 C3
St. Pair-sur-Mer F 57 B4
St. Palais F 76 C1
St. Palais-sur-Mer F 66 C3
St. Pardoux-la-Rivière F 67 C5
St. Paul-Cap-de-Joux F 77 C4
St. Paul-de-Fenouillet F 77 D5
St. Paul-de-Varax F 69 B5
St. Paul-le-Jeune F 78 B3
St. Paul-lès-Dax F 76 C1
St. Paul-Trois-Châteaux F 78 B3
St. Paulien F 68 C3
St. Pé-de-Bigorre F 76 C2
St. Pée-sur-Nivelle F 76 C1
St. Péravy-la-Colombe F 58 C2
St. Péray F 78 B3
St. Père-en-Retz F 66 A2
St. Peter Port GB 56 A3
St. Petersburg = Sankt-Peterburg RUS 7 B11
St. Philbert-de-Grand-Lieu F 66 A3
St. Pierre F 78 C1
St. Pierre-d'Albigny F 69 C6
St. Pierre-d'Allevard F 69 C6
St. Pierre-de-Chartreuse F 69 C5
St. Pierre-de-Chignac F 77 A3
St. Pierre-de-la-Fage F 78 C2
St. Pierre-d'Entremont F 69 C5
St. Pierre-d'Oléron F 66 C3
St. Pierre-Eglise F 57 A4
St. Pierre-en-Port F 58 A1
St. Pierre-le-Moûtier F 68 B3
St. Pierre Montlimart F 66 A3
St. Pierre-Quiberon F 66 A1
St. Pierre-sur-Dives F 57 A5
St. Pierreville F 78 B3
St. Pieters-Leeuw B 49 C5
St. Plancard F 77 C3
St. Poix F 57 C4
St. Pol-de-Léon F 56 B2
St. Pol-sur-Ternoise F 48 C3
St. Polgues F 68 C3
St. Pons-de-Thomières F 78 C1
St. Porchaire F 66 C4
St. Pourçain-sur-Sioule F 68 B3
St. Priest F 69 C4
St. Privat F 68 C2
St. Quay-Portrieux F 56 B3
St. Quentin F 59 A4
St. Quentin-la-Poterie F 78 B3
St. Quentin-les-Anges F 57 C5
St. Rambert-d'Albon F 69 C4
St. Rambert-en-Bugey F 69 C5
St. Raphaël F 79 C5
St. Rémy-de-Provence F 78 C3
St. Rémy-du-Val F 57 B6
St. Remy-en-Bouzemont F 59 B5
St. Renan F 56 B1
St. Révérien F 68 A3
St. Riquier F 48 C2
St. Romain-de-Colbosc F 58 A1
St. Rome-de-Cernon F 78 B1
St. Rome-de-Tarn F 78 B1
St. Sadurní d'Anoia E 91 B4
St. Saëns F 58 A2
St. Sampson GB 56 A3
St. Samson-la-Poterie F 58 A2
St. Saturnin-de-Lenne F 78 B2
St. Saturnin-lès-Apt F 79 C4
St. Sauflieu F 58 A3
St. Saulge F 68 A3
St. Sauveur, *Finistère* F 56 B2
St. Sauveur, *Haute-Saône* F 60 C2
St. Sauveur-de-Montagut F 78 B3
St. Sauveur-en-Puisaye F 59 C4
St. Sauveur-en-Rue F 69 C4
St. Sauveur-le-Vicomte F 57 A4
St. Sauveur-Lendelin F 57 A4
St. Sauveur-sur-Tinée F 79 B6
St. Savin, *Gironde* F 76 A2
St. Savin, *Vienne* F 67 B5
St. Savinien F 67 C4
St. Savournin F 79 C4
St. Seine-l'Abbaye F 69 A4
St. Sernin-sur-Rance F 77 C5
St. Sevan-sur-Mer F 57 B3
St. Sever F 76 C2
St. Sever-Calvados F 57 B4
St. Sorlin-d'Arves F 69 C6
St. Soupplets F 58 A3
St. Sulpice F 77 C4
St. Sulpice-Laurière F 67 B6
St. Sulpice-les-Feuilles F 67 B6
St. Symphorien F 76 B2
St. Symphorien-de-Lay F 69 C4
St. Symphorien d'Ozon F 69 C4
St. Symphorien-sur-Coise F 69 C4
St. Teath GB 28 C3
St. Thégonnec F 56 B2
St. Thiébault F 60 B1
St. Trivier-de-Courtes F 69 B5
St. Trivier sur-Moignans F 69 B4
St. Trojan-les-Bains F 66 C3
St. Tropez F 79 C5
St. Truiden B 49 C6
St. Vaast-la-Hougue F 57 A4
St. Valérien F 59 B4
St. Valery-en-Caux F 58 A1
St. Valéry-sur-Somme F 48 C2
St. Vallier, *Drôme* F 69 C4
St. Vallier, *Saône-et-Loire* F 69 B4
St. Vallier-de-Thiey F 79 C5
St. Varent F 67 B4
St. Vaury F 68 B1
St. Venant F 48 C3
St. Véran F 79 B5
St. Vincent I 70 C2
St. Vincent-de-Tyrosse F 76 C1
St. Vit F 69 A5
St. Vith B 50 C2
St. Vivien-de-Médoc F 66 C3
St. Yan F 68 B4
St. Ybars F 77 C4
St. Yorre F 68 B3
St. Yrieix-la-Perche F 67 C6
Ste. Adresse F 57 A6
Ste. Anne F 58 B1
Ste. Anne-d'Auray F 56 C3
Ste. Croix CH 69 B6
Ste. Croix-Volvestre F 77 C4
Ste. Engrâce F 76 C2
Ste. Enimie F 78 B2
Ste. Foy-de-Peyrolières F 77 C4
Ste. Foy-la-Grande F 76 B3
Ste. Foy l'Argentiere F 69 C4
Ste. Gauburge-Ste. Colombe F 58 B1
Ste. Gemme la Plaine F 66 B3
Ste. Geneviève F 58 A3
Ste. Hélène F 76 B2
Ste. Hélène-sur-Isère F 69 C6
Ste. Hermine F 66 B3
Ste. Jalle F 79 B4
Ste. Livrade-sur-Lot F 77 B3
Ste. Marie-aux-Mines F 60 B3
Ste. Marie-du-Mont F 57 A4
Ste. Maure-de-Touraine F 67 A5
Ste. Maxime F 79 C5
Ste. Menéhould F 59 A5
Ste. Mère-Église F 57 A4
Ste. Ode B 49 C6
Ste. Savine F 59 B5
Ste. Sévère-sur-Indre F 68 B2
Ste. Sigolène F 69 C4
Ste. Suzanne F 57 B5
Ste. Tulle F 79 C4
Sainteny F 57 A4
Saintes F 67 C4
Stes. Maries-de-la-Mer F 78 C3
Saintfield GB 19 B6
Saissac F 77 C5
Saja E 88 A2
Sajan SRB 75 C5
Šajkaš SRB 75 C5
Sajókaza H 65 B6
Sajószentpéter H 65 B6
Sajóvámos H 65 B6
Sakarya TR 118 B5
Šakiai LT 6 D7
Sakskøbing DK 39 E4
Sakule SRB 75 C5
Sala S 36 C3
Šal'a SK 64 B3
Sala Baganza I 81 B4
Sala Consilina I 104 C1
Salakovac SRB 85 B6
Salamanca E 94 B1
Salamina GR 117 E5
Salandra I 104 C2
Salaparuta I 108 B1
Salar E 100 B1
Salardú E 90 A3
Salas E 86 A4
Salas de los Infantes E 89 B3
Salau F 77 D4
Salavaux CH 70 B2
Salbertrand I 79 A5
Salbohed S 36 C3
Salbris F 68 A2
Salbu N 32 A2
Salce E 86 B4
Salching D 62 B3
Salcombe GB 28 C4
Saldaña E 88 B2
Saldus LV 6 C7
Sale I 80 B2
Saleby S 35 D5
Salem D 61 C5
Salemi I 108 B1
Salen, *Argyll & Bute* GB 24 B2
Salen, *Highland* GB 24 B2
Salen N 114 C8
Sälen S 34 A5
Salernes F 79 C5
Salerno I 103 C7
Salers F 68 C2
Salford GB 26 B3
Salgótarján H 65 B5
Salgueiro P 92 B3
Salhus N 32 B2
Sali HR 83 C4
Sálice Salentino I 105 C3
Salientes E 86 B4
Salies-de-Béarn F 76 C2
Salies-du-Salat F 77 C3
Salignac-Eyvigues F 77 B4
Saligney-sur-Roudon F 68 B3
Salihli TR 119 D3
Salihorsk BY 7 E9
Salinas, *Alicante* E 101 A5
Salinas, *Huesca* E 90 A3
Salinas de Medinaceli E 95 A4
Salinas de Pisuerga E 88 B2
Salindres F 78 B3
Saline di Volterra I 81 C4
Salins-les-Bains F 69 B5
Salir P 98 B2
Salisbury GB 29 B6
Salla A 73 A4
Salla FIN 113 F17
Sallachy GB 23 C4
Sallanches F 70 C1
Sallent E 91 B4
Sallent de Gállego E 76 D2
Salles F 76 B2
Salles-Curan F 78 B1
Salles-sur-l'Hers F 77 C4
Sallins IRL 21 A5
Sällsjö S 115 D10
Salmerón E 95 B4
Salmiech F 77 B5
Salmivaara FIN 113 F17
Salmoral E 94 B1
Salo FIN 6 A7
Salò I 71 C5
Salobreña E 100 C2
Salon-de-Provence F 79 C4
Salonica = Thessaloniki GR 116 B4
Salonta RO 10 C6
Salorino E 93 B3
Salornay-sur-Guye F 69 B4
Salorno I 71 B6
Salou E 91 B4
Šalovci SLO 73 B6
Salsbruket N 114 C8
Salses-le-Chateau F 78 D1
Salsomaggiore Terme I 81 B3
Salt E 91 B5
Saltaire GB 27 B4
Saltara I 82 C1
Saltash GB 28 C3
Saltburn-by-the-Sea GB 27 A5
Saltcoats GB 24 C3
Saltfleet GB 27 B6
Salto P 87 C3
Saltrød N 33 D5
Saltsjöbaden S 37 C5
Saltvik FIN 36 B7
Saltvik S 40 B6
Saludécio I 82 C1
Salussola I 70 C3
Saluzzo I 80 B1
Salvacañete E 95 B5
Salvada P 98 B3
Salvagnac F 77 C4
Salvaleon E 93 C4
Salvaterra de Magos P 92 B2
Salvaterra do Extremo P 93 B4
Salvatierra, *Avila* E 89 B4
Salvatierra, *Badajoz* E 93 C4
Salvatierra de Santiago E 93 B4
Salviac F 77 B4
Salz-hemmendorf D 51 A5
Salzburg A 62 C4
Salzgitter D 51 A6
Salzgitter Bad D 51 A6
Salzhausen D 44 B2
Salzkotten D 51 B4
Salzmünde D 52 B1
Salzwedel D 44 C3
Samadet F 76 C2
Samandıra TR 118 B4
Samassi I 110 C1
Samatan F 77 C3
Sambiase I 106 C3
Sambir UA 11 B7
Samborowo PL 47 B5
Sambuca di Sicília I 108 B2
Samedan CH 71 B4
Samer F 48 C2
Sami GR 117 D2
Şamlı TR 118 C2
Sammichele di Bari I 104 C2
Samnaun CH 71 B5
Samobor HR 73 C5
Samoëns F 70 B1
Samogneux F 59 A6
Samokov BG 11 E7
Samora Correia P 92 C2
Šamorín SK 64 B3
Samos E 86 B3
Samos GR 119 E1
Samoš SRB 75 C5
Samothraki GR 116 B7
Samper de Calanda E 90 B2
Sampéyre I 79 B6
Sampieri I 109 C3
Sampigny F 60 B1
Samplawa PL 47 B5
Samproniano I 81 D5
Samtens D 45 A5
Samugheo I 110 C1
San Adrián E 89 B5
San Agustín E 101 C3
San Agustin de Guadalix E 94 B3
San Alberto I 82 B1
San Amaro E 87 B2
San Andrês del Rabanedo E 88 B1
San Antanio di Santadi I 110 C1
San Antolín de Ibias E 86 A4
San Arcángelo I 104 C2
San Asensio E 89 B4
San Bartolomé de la Torre E 99 B3
San Bartolomé de las Abiertas E 94 C2
San Bartolomé de Pinares E 94 B2
San Bartolomeo in Galdo I 103 B8
San Benedetto del Tronto I 82 D2
San Benedetto in Alpe I 81 C5
San Benedetto Po I 81 A4
San Benito E 100 A1
San Benito de la Contienda E 93 C3
San Biágio Plátani I 108 B2
San Biágio Saracinisco I 103 B6
San Bonifacio I 71 C6
San Calixto E 99 B5
San Cándido I 72 B2
San Carlo CH 70 B3
San Carlo I 108 B2
San Carlos del Valle E 100 A2
San Casciano dei Bagni I 81 D5
San Casciano in Val di Pesa I 81 C5
San Cataldo, *Puglia* I 105 C4
San Cataldo, *Sicilia* I 108 B2
San Cebrián de Castro E 88 C1
San Cesário di Lecce I 105 C4
San Chírico Raparo I 106 A3
San Cibrao das Viñas E 87 B3
San Cipirello I 108 B2
San Ciprián E 86 A3
San Clemente E 95 C4
San Clodio E 86 B3
San Colombano al Lambro I 71 C4
San Costanzo I 82 C2
San Crisóbal de Entreviñas E 88 B1
San Cristóbal de la Polantera E 88 B1
San Cristóbal de la Vega E 94 A2
San Cristovo E 87 C3
San Damiano d'Asti I 80 B2
San Damiano Macra I 79 B6
San Daniele del Friuli I 72 B3
San Demétrio Corone I 106 B3
San Demétrio né Vestini I 103 A6
San Donà di Piave I 72 C2
San Dónaci I 105 C3
San Donato Val di Comino I 103 B6
San Emiliano E 86 B5
San Enrique E 99 C5
San Esteban E 86 A4
San Esteban de Gormaz E 89 C3
San Esteban de la Sierra E 93 A5
San Esteban de Litera E 90 B3
San Esteban de Valdueza E 86 B4
San Esteban del Molar E 88 C1
San Esteban del Valle E 94 B2
San Fele I 104 C1
San Felice Circeo I 102 B6
San Felice sul Panaro I 81 B5
San Felices E 88 B3
San Felices de los Gallégos E 87 D4
San Ferdinando di Púglia I 104 B2
San Fernando E 99 C4
San Fernando de Henares E 95 B3
San Fili I 106 B3
San Foca I 105 C4
San Fratello I 109 B3
San Gavino Monreale I 110 C1
San Gémini Fonte I 102 A5
San Germano Vercellese I 70 C3
San Giácomo, *Trentino Alto Adige* I 72 B1
San Giácomo, *Umbria* I 82 D1
San Gimignano I 81 C5
San Ginésio I 82 C2
San Giórgio a Liri I 103 B6
San Giórgio del Sánnio I 103 B7
San Giorgio della Richinvelda I 72 B2
San Giórgio di Lomellina I 70 C3
San Giórgio di Nogaro I 72 C3
San Giorgio di Piano I 81 B5
San Giórgio Iónico I 104 C3
San Giovanni a Piro I 106 A2
San Giovanni Bianco I 71 C4
San Giovanni di Sinis I 110 C1
San Giovanni in Croce I 81 A4
San Giovanni in Fiore I 106 B3
San Giovanni in Persiceto I 81 B5
San Giovanni Reatino I 102 A5
San Giovanni Rotondo I 104 B1
San Giovanni Suérgiu I 110 C1
San Giovanni Valdarno I 81 C5
San Giuliano Terme I 81 C4
San Giustino I 82 C1
San Godenzo I 81 C5
San Gregorio Magno I 103 C8
San Guiseppe Jato I 108 B2
San Javier E 101 B5
San Jorge P 92 B2
San José E 101 C3
San Juan E 89 B3
San Juan de Alicante E 96 C2
San Juan de la Nava E 94 B2
San Justo de la Vega E 86 B4
San Lazzaro di Sávena I 81 B5
San Leo I 82 C1
San Leonardo de Yagüe E 89 C3
San Leonardo in Passiria I 71 B6
San Lorenzo a Merse I 81 C5
San Lorenzo al Mare I 80 C1
San Lorenzo Bellizzi I 106 B3
San Lorenzo de Calatrava E 100 A2
San Lorenzo de El Escorial E 94 B2
San Lorenzo de la Parrilla E 95 C4
San Lorenzo di Sebato I 72 B1
San Lorenzo in Campo I 82 C1
San Lorenzo Nuovo I 81 D5
San Lourenco P 98 A2
San Luca I 106 C3
San Lúcido I 106 B3
San Marcello I 82 C2
San Marcello Pistoiese I 81 B4
San Marcial E 88 C1
San Marco I 103 C7
San Marco Argentano I 106 B3
San Marco dei Cavoti I 103 B7
San Marco in Lámis I 104 B1
San Marino RSM 82 C1
San Martín de Castañeda E 87 B4
San Martín de la Vega E 95 B3
San Martin de la Vega del Alberche E 93 A5
San Martín de Luiña E 86 A4
San Martin de Montalbán E 94 C2
San Martin de Oscos E 86 A4
San Martin de Pusa E 94 C2
San Martin de Unx E 89 B5
San Martín de Valdeiglesias E 94 B2
San Martín del Tesorillo E 99 C5
San Martino di Campagna I 72 B2
San Martino di Castrozza I 72 B1
San-Martino-di-Lota F 102 A2
San Martino in Pénsilis I 103 B8
San Mateo de Gallego E 90 B2
San Máuro Forte I 104 C2
San Michele all'Adige I 71 B6
San Michele di Ganzaria I 109 B3
San Michele Mondovì I 80 B1
San Miguel de Aguayo E 88 A2
San Miguel de Bernuy E 88 C3
San Miguel de Salinas E 101 B5
San Miguel del Arroyo E 88 C2
San Millán de la Cogolla E 89 B4
San Miniato I 81 C4
San Muñoz E 87 D4
San Nicola del'Alto I 107 B3
San Nicolás del Puerto E 99 B5
San Nicolò I 81 B5
San Nicolò Gerrei I 110 C2
San Pablo de los Montes E 94 C2
San Pancrázio Salentino I 105 C3
San Pantaleo I 110 A2
San Páolo di Civitate I 103 B8
San Pawl il-Bahar M 107 C5
San Pedro, *Albacete* E 101 A3
San Pedro, *Oviedo* E 86 A4
San Pedro de Alcántara E 100 C1
San Pedro de Cadeira P 92 B1
San Pedro de Ceque E 87 B4
San Pedro de Latarce E 88 C1
San Pedro de Merida E 93 C4
San Pedro de Valderaduey E 88 B2
San Pedro del Arroyo E 94 B2
San Pedro del Pinatar E 101 B5
San Pedro del Romeral E 88 A3
San Pedro Manrique E 89 B4
San Pellegrino Terme I 71 C4
San Piero a Sieve I 81 C5
San Piero in Bagno I 81 C5
San Piero Patti I 109 A3
San Pietro I 109 B3

Savières F 59 B4
Savigliano I 80 B1
Savignac-les-Eglises F 67 C5
Savignano Irpino I 103 B8
Savignano sul Rubicone I 82 B1
Savigny-sur-Braye F 58 C1
Saviñán E 89 C5
Savines-le-lac F 79 B5
Savino Selo SRB 75 C4
Savio I 82 B1
Sävja S 36 C4
Šavnik MNE 85 D4
Savognin CH 71 B4
Savona I 80 B2
Savonlinna FIN 3 F28
Savournon F 79 B4
Sävsjö S 40 B4
Savsjön S 36 C1
Sävsjöström S 40 B5
Savudrija HR 72 C3
Savukoski FIN 113 E17
Sawbridgeworth GB 31 C4
Sawtry GB 30 B3
Sax E 101 A5
Saxdalen S 36 B1
Saxilby GB 27 B5
Saxmundham GB 30 B5
Saxnäs S 115 C12
Saxthorpe GB 30 B5
Sayalonga E 100 C1
Sayatón E 95 B4
Sayda D 52 C3
Säytsjärvi FIN 113 C16
Śazava, *Jihomoravský* CZ 64 A1
Sázava, *Středočeský* CZ 63 A5
Scaër F 56 B2
Scafa I 103 A7
Scalasaig GB 24 B1
Scalby GB 27 A5
Scalea I 106 B2
Scaletta Zanclea I 109 A4
Scalloway GB 22 A7
Scamblesby GB 27 B5
Scandale I 107 B3
Scandiano I 81 B4
Scandicci I 81 C5
Scandolara Ravara I 81 A4
Scanno I 103 B6
Scansano I 81 D5
Scanzano Jónico I 104 C2
Scarborough GB 27 A5
Scardovari I 82 B1
Scardoy GB 22 D4
Scarinish GB 24 B1
Scarperia I 81 C5
Scarriff IRL 20 B3
Scey-sur-Saône et St. Albin F 60 C1
Schachendorf A 73 A6
Schaffhausen CH 61 C4
Schafstädt D 52 B1
Schafstedt D 43 A6
Schäftlarn D 62 C2
Schagen NL 42 C1
Schalkau D 51 C7
Schangnau CH 70 B2
Schapbach D 61 B4
Scharbeutz D 44 A2
Schärding A 63 B4
Scharnitz A 71 A6
Scharrel D 43 B4
Schattendorf A 64 C2
Scheemda NL 42 B3
Scheessel D 43 B6
Schéggia I 82 C1
Scheibbs A 63 B6
Scheibenberg D 52 C2
Scheidegg D 61 C5
Scheifling A 73 A4
Scheinfeld D 61 A6
Schelklingen D 61 B5
Schenefeld, *Schleswig-Holstein* D 43 A6
Schenefeld, *Schleswig-Holstein* D 44 B1
Schenklengsfeld D 51 C5
Scherfede D 51 B5
Schermbeck D 50 B2
Scherpenzeel NL 49 A6
Schesslitz D 52 D1
Scheveningen NL 49 A5
Schiedam NL 49 B5
Schieder-Schwalenberg D 51 B5
Schierling D 62 B3
Schiers CH 71 B4
Schildau D 52 B2
Schillingen D 60 A2
Schillingsfürst D 61 A6
Schilpário I 71 B5
Schiltach D 61 B4
Schiltigheim F 60 B3
Schio I 71 C6
Schirmeck F 60 B3
Schirnding D 52 C2
Schkeuditz D 52 B2
Schkölen D 52 B1
Schlabendorf D 53 B3
Schladen D 51 A6
Schladming A 72 A3
Schlangen D 51 B4
Schleiden D 50 C2
Schleiz D 52 C1
Schleswig D 43 A6
Schleusingen D 51 C6
Schlieben D 52 B3
Schliengen D 60 C3
Schliersee D 62 C2
Schlitz D 51 C5
Schloss Neuhans D 51 B4
Schlossvippach D 52 B1
Schlotheim D 51 B6
Schluchsee D 61 C4
Schlüchtern D 51 C5
Schmallenberg D 50 B4
Schmelz D 60 A2
Schmidmühlen D 62 A2
Schmiedeberg D 53 C3
Schmiedefeld D 51 C6
Schmirn A 72 A1
Schmölln, *Brandenburg* D 45 B6
Schmölln, *Sachsen* D 52 C2
Schnaittach D 62 A2
Schneeberg D 52 C2
Schneizlreuth D 62 C3
Schneverdingen D 44 B1
Schöder A 73 A4
Schoenburg B 50 C2
Schollene D 44 C4
Schöllkrippen D 51 C5
Schomberg D 61 B4
Schönach D 62 B3
Schönau, *Baden-Württemberg* D 60 C3
Schönau, *Bayern* D 62 B3
Schönbeck D 45 B5
Schönberg, *Bayern* D 63 B4
Schönberg, *Mecklenburg-Vorpommern* D 44 B2
Schönberg, *Schleswig-Holstein* D 44 A2
Schönebeck D 52 A1
Schöneck D 52 C2
Schönecken- D 50 C2
Schönermark D 45 B5
Schönewalde D 52 B3
Schongau D 62 C1
Schöngrabern A 64 B2
Schönhagen D 51 B5
Schönhausen D 44 C4
Schöningen D 51 A6
Schönkirchen D 44 A2
Schönsee D 62 A3
Schöntal D 61 A5
Schönthal D 62 A3
Schonungen D 51 C6
Schönwalde D 44 A2
Schoondijke NL 49 B4
Schoonebeek NL 42 C3
Schoonhoven NL 49 B5
Schopfheim D 60 C3
Schöppenstedt D 51 A6
Schörfling A 63 C4
Schorndorf D 61 B5
Schortens D 43 B4
Schotten D 51 C5
Schramberg D 61 B4
Schraplau D 52 B1
Schrattenberg A 64 B2
Schrecksbach D 51 C5
Schrems A 63 B6
Schrobenhausen D 62 B2
Schröcken A 71 A5
Schrozberg D 61 A5
Schruns A 71 A4
Schüpfheim CH 70 B3
Schüttorf D 50 A3
Schwaan D 44 B4
Schwabach D 62 A2
Schwäbisch Gmünd D 61 B5
Schwäbisch Hall D 61 A5
Schwabmünchen D 62 B1
Schwadorf A 64 B2
Schwagstorf D 43 C4
Schwaigern D 61 A5
Schwalmstadt D 51 C5
Schwanberg A 73 B5
Schwanden CH 70 B4
Schwandorf D 62 A3
Schwanebeck D 52 B1
Schwanenstadt A 63 B4
Schwanewede D 43 B5
Schwanfeld D 61 A6
Schwangau D 62 C1
Schwarmstedt D 43 C6
Schwarz-heide D 53 B3
Schwarza D 51 C6
Schwarzach im Pongau A 72 A3
Schwarzau im Gebirge A 63 C6
Schwarzenau A 63 B6
Schwarzenbach D 52 C1
Schwarzenbach am Wald D 52 C1
Schwarzenbek D 44 B2
Schwarzenberg D 52 C2
Schwarzenburg CH 70 B2
Schwarzenfeld D 62 A3
Schwaz A 72 A1
Schwechat A 64 B2
Schwedt D 45 B6
Schwei D 43 B5
Schweich D 60 A2
Schweighausen D 60 B3
Schweinfurt D 51 C6
Schweinitz D 52 B3
Schweinrich D 45 B4
Schwelm D 50 B3
Schwemsal D 52 B2
Schwendt A 62 C3
Schwenningen D 61 B4
Schwepnitz D 53 B3
Schwerin D 44 B3
Schwerte D 50 B3
Schweskau D 44 C3
Schwetzingen D 61 A4
Schwyz CH 70 A3
Sciacca I 108 B2
Scicli I 109 C3
Ściechów PL 45 C6
Scigliano I 106 B3
Scilla I 109 A4
Ścinawa PL 54 B1
Scionzier F 69 B6
Scoglitti I 109 C3
Scole GB 30 B5
Sconser GB 22 D2
Scopello, *Piemonte* I 70 C3
Scopello, *Sicilia* I 108 A1
Scordia I 109 B3
Scorzè I 72 C2
Scotch Corner GB 27 A4
Scotter GB 27 B5
Scourie GB 22 C3
Scousburgh GB 22 B7
Scrabster GB 23 C5
Screeb IRL 20 A2
Scremerston GB 25 C6
Scritto I 82 C1
Scunthorpe GB 27 B5
Scuol CH 71 B5
Scúrcola Marsicana I 103 A6
Seaford GB 31 D4
Seaham GB 25 D6
Seahouses GB 25 C6
Seascale GB 26 A2
Seaton GB 29 C4
Sebazac-Concourès F 77 B5
Sebečevo SRB 85 C5
Seben TR 118 B6
Sebersdorf A 73 A5
Sebezh RUS 7 C10
Sebnitz D 53 C4
Seborga I 80 C1
Seby S 41 C6
Seč, *Vychodočeský* CZ 63 A6
Seč, *Západočeský* CZ 63 A4
Sečanj SRB 75 C5
Secemin PL 55 C4
Séchault F 59 A5
Seckau A 73 A4
Seclin F 49 C4
Secondigny F 67 B4
Seda P 92 B3
Sedan F 59 A5
Sedano E 88 B3
Sedbergh GB 26 A3
Sedella E 100 C1
Séderon F 79 B4
Sedgefield GB 27 A4
Sedico I 72 B2
Sédilo I 110 B1
Sédini I 110 B1
Sedlarica HR 74 C2
Sedlčany CZ 63 A5
Sedlec-Prčice CZ 63 A5
Sedlice CZ 63 A4
Sędziejowice PL 55 B4
Sędziszów PL 55 C5
Sędziszów Małapolski PL 55 C6
Seebach F 60 B3
Seeboden A 72 B3
Seefeld, *Brandenburg* D 45 C5
Seefeld, *Niedersachsen* D 43 B5
Seefeld in Tirol A 71 A6
Seeg D 62 C1
Seehausen, *Sachsen-Anhalt* D 44 C3
Seehausen, *Sachsen-Anhalt* D 52 A1
Seeheim-Jugenheim D 61 A4
Seelbach D 60 B3
Seelow D 45 C6
Seelze D 43 C6
Seerhausen D 52 B3
Sées F 57 B6
Seesen D 51 B6
Seeshaupt D 62 C2
Seewalchen A 63 C4
Seferihisar TR 119 D1
Sefkerin SRB 85 A5
Segård N 34 B2
Segerstad S 35 C5
Segesd H 74 B2
Seglinge FIN 36 B7
Segmon S 35 C5
Segonzac F 67 C4
Segorbe E 96 B2
Segovia E 94 B2
Segré F 57 C5
Ségur-les-Villas F 68 C2
Segura E 89 B4
Segura P 93 B3
Segura de León E 99 A4
Segura de los Baños E 90 C2
Segurrilla E 94 B2
Sehnde D 51 A5
Seia P 92 A3
Seiches-sur-le-Loir F 67 A4
Seifhennersdorf D 53 C4
Seignelay F 59 C4
Seijo E 87 C2
Seilhac F 68 C1
Seilles B 49 C6
Seim N 32 B2
Seinäjoki FIN 3 E25
Seissan F 77 C3
Seitenstetten Markt A 63 B5
Seixal P 92 C1
Seiz A 73 A4
Seizthal A 73 A4
Sejerslev DK 38 C1
Seksna RUS 7 B15
Selárdalur IS 111 B1
Selárgius I 110 C2
Selb D 52 C2
Selby GB 27 B4
Selca HR 84 C1
Selcë AL 105 A5
Selce HR 73 C4
Selçuk TR 119 E2
Selde DK 38 C2
Selenča SRB 75 C4
Selendi, *Manisa* TR 118 D3
Selendi, *Manisa* TR 118 D2
Selenicë AL 105 C5
Sélestat F 60 B3
Seleuš SRB 75 C5
Selevac SRB 85 B5
Selfoss IS 111 D5
Selgua E 90 B3
Selice SK 64 B3
Seligenstadt D 51 C4
Seligenthal D 51 C6
Selimiye TR 119 E2
Selizharovo RUS 7 C12
Selja S 36 A1
Selje N 114 E2
Seljelvnes N 112 C8
Seljord N 33 C5
Selkirk GB 25 C5
Sellano I 82 D1
Selles-St. Denis F 68 A1
Selles-sur-Cher F 67 A6
Sellières F 69 B5
Sellin D 45 A5
Sellye H 74 C2
Selm D 50 B3
Selnica ob Dravi SLO 73 B5
Selongey F 59 C6
Selonnet F 79 B5
Selow D 44 B3
Selsey GB 31 D3
Selsingen D 43 B6
Selters D 50 C3
Seltso RUS 7 E13
Seltz F 61 B4
Selva E 97 B2
Selva di Cadore I 72 B2
Selva di Val Gardena I 72 B1
Selvik, *Sogn og Fjordane* N 32 A2
Selvik, *Vestfold* N 35 C2
Selvino I 71 C4
Selyatyn UA 11 C8
Sem N 35 C2
Semeljci HR 74 C3
Semenovka, *Chernihiv* UA 7 E12
Semenovka, *Kremenchuk* UA 11 B12
Semič SLO 73 C5
Semide F 59 A5
Semide P 92 A2
Semily CZ 53 C5
Seminara I 106 C2
Semlac RO 75 B5
Semmen-stedt D 51 A6
Šempeter SLO 73 B5
Semriach A 73 A5
Semur-en-Auxois F 69 A4
Sena E 90 B2
Sena de Luna E 88 B1
Senarpont F 58 A2
Sénas F 79 C4
Senćanski Trešnjevac SRB 75 C4
Sencelles E 97 B2
Senčur SLO 73 B4
Senden, *Bayern* D 61 B6
Senden, *Nordrhein-Westfalen* D 50 B3
Sendenhorst D 50 B3
Sendim P 87 C4
Senec SK 64 B3
Seneffe B 49 C5
Séneghe I 110 B1
Senés E 101 B3
Senez F 79 C5
Senftenberg D 53 B3
Sengouagnet F 77 D3
Sengwarden D 43 B5
Senica SK 64 B3
Senice na Hané CZ 64 A3
Senigállia I 82 C2
Senirkent TR 119 D5
Sénis I 110 C1
Senise I 106 A3
Senj HR 83 B3
Senje SRB 85 C6
Senjehopen N 112 C6
Senjski Rudnik SRB 85 C6
Senlis F 58 A3
Sennan S 40 C2
Sennecey-le-Grand F 69 B4
Sennen GB 28 C2
Senno BY 7 D10
Sénnori I 110 B1
Sennwald CH 71 A4
Sennybridge GB 29 B4
Senohrad SK 65 B5
Senonches F 58 B2
Senones F 60 B2
Senorbì I 110 C2
Senovo SLO 73 B5
Senožeče SLO 73 C4
Senožeti SLO 73 B4
Sens F 59 B4
Sens-de-Bretagne F 57 B4
Senta SRB 75 C5
Senterada E 90 A3
Sentilj SLO 73 B5
Šentjernej SLO 73 C5
Šentjur SLO 73 B5
Senumstad N 33 D5
Seoane E 86 B3
Seon CH 70 A3
Sépeaux F 59 C4
Sépey CH 70 B2
Sepino I 103 B7
Sępólno Krajeńskie PL 46 B3
Seppenrade D 50 B3
Seppois F 70 A2
Septeuil F 58 B2
Sepúlveda E 88 C3
Sequals I 72 B2
Sequeros E 93 A4
Seraincourt F 59 A5
Seraing B 49 C6
Seravezza I 81 C4
Sered' SK 64 B3
Seredka RUS 7 B10
Şereflikoçhisar TR 16 B6
Seregélyes H 74 A3
Seregno I 71 C4
Sérent F 56 C3
Serfaus A 71 A5
Sergiyev Posad RUS 7 C15
Seriate I 71 C4
Sérifontaine F 58 A2
Serifos GR 117 E6
Sérignan F 78 C2
Serik TR 119 F6
Serina I 71 C4
Serinhisar TR 119 E4
Sermaises F 58 B3
Sermaize-les-Bains F 59 B5
Sérmide I 81 B5
Sermoneta I 102 B5
Sernache de Bonjardim P 92 B2
Sernancelhe P 87 D3
Serón E 101 B3
Serón de Najima E 89 C4
Serooskerke NL 49 B4
Seròs E 90 B3
Serpa P 98 B3
Serpukhov RUS 7 D14
Serra de Outes E 86 B2
Serra San Bruno I 106 C3
Serra San Quirico I 82 C2
Serracapriola I 103 B8
Serrada E 88 C2
Serradifalco I 108 B2
Serradilla E 93 B4
Serradilla del Arroyo E 93 A4
Serradilla del Llano E 93 A4
Serramanna I 110 C1
Serramazzoni I 81 B4
Serranillos E 94 B2
Serrapetrona I 82 C2
Serrastretta I 106 B3
Serravalle, *Piemonte* I 70 C3
Serravalle, *Umbria* I 82 D2
Serravalle di Chienti I 82 C1
Serravalle Scrívia I 80 B2
Serre I 103 C8
Serrejón E 93 B5
Serres F 79 B4
Serres GR 116 A5
Serrières F 69 C4
Serrières-de-Briord F 69 C5
Sersale I 106 B3
Sertã P 92 B2
Sertig Dörfli CH 71 B4
Servance F 60 C2
Serverette F 78 B2
Servia GR 116 B4
Servian F 78 C2
Serviers F 78 B3
Servigliano I 82 C2
Serzedelo P 87 C2
Ses Salines E 97 B3
Seseña Nuevo E 95 B3
Sesimbra P 92 C1
Seskinore GB 19 B4
Sesma E 89 B4
Sessa Aurunca I 103 B6
Sesta Godano I 80 B3
Šestanovac HR 84 C1
Sestao E 89 A4
Sestino I 82 C1
Sesto I 72 B2
Sesto Calende I 70 C3
Sesto Fiorentino I 81 C5
Sesto San Giovanni I 71 C4
Séstola I 81 B4
Sestri Levante I 80 B3
Sestriere I 79 B5
Sestroretsk RUS 7 A11
Sestu I 110 C2
Sesvete HR 73 C6
Setcases E 91 A5
Sète F 78 C2
Setenil E 99 C5
Setermoen N 112 D7
Šetonje SRB 85 B6
Setskog N 34 C3
Settalsjølia N 114 E7
Séttimo Torinese I 70 C2
Settimo Vittone I 70 C2
Settle GB 26 A3
Setúbal P 92 C2
Seubersdort D 62 A2
Seùi I 110 C2
Seùlo I 110 C2
Seurre F 69 B5
Sevaster AL 105 C5
Sevel DK 38 C1
Sevenoaks GB 31 C4
Sever do Vouga P 87 D2
Sévérac-le-Château F 78 B2
Severin HR 73 C5
Severomorsk RUS 3 B30
Séveso I 71 C4
Ševětin CZ 63 A5
Sevettijärvi FIN 113 C17
Sévigny F 59 A5
Sevilla = Seville E 99 B5
Sevilla la Nueva E 94 B2
Seville = Sevilla E 99 B5
Sevilleja de la Jara E 94 C2
Sevlievo BG 11 E8
Sevnica SLO 73 B5
Sevojno SRB 85 C4
Sevrier F 69 C6
Sevsk RUS 7 E13
Sexdrega S 40 B3
Seyches F 76 B3
Seyda D 52 B2
Seyðisfjörður IS 111 B12
Seydişehir TR 119 E6
Seyitgazi TR 118 C5
Seyitömer TR 118 C4
Seymen TR 118 A2
Seyne F 79 B5
Seynes F 78 B3
Seyssel F 69 C5
Sežana SLO 72 C3
Sézanne F 59 B4
Sezulfe P 87 C3
Sezze I 102 B6
Sfântu Gheorghe RO 11 D8
Sforzacosta I 82 C2
Sgarasta Mhor GB 22 D1
Shaftesbury GB 29 B5
Shaldon GB 29 C4
Shanagolden IRL 20 B2
Shanklin GB 31 D2
Shap GB 26 A3
Sharpness GB 29 B5
Shawbury GB 26 C3
Shchekino RUS 7 D14
Shchigry RUS 7 F14
Shchors UA 7 F11
Sheerness GB 31 C4
Sheffield GB 27 B4
Shefford GB 31 B3
Shenfield GB 31 C4
Shëngjergj AL 116 A2
Shëngjin AL 105 B5
Shepetivka UA 11 A9
Shepshed GB 27 C4
Shepton Mallet GB 29 B5
Sherborne GB 29 C5
Shercock IRL 19 C5
Sheringham GB 30 B5
Shiel Bridge GB 22 D3
Shieldaig GB 22 D3
Shijak AL 105 B5
Shillelagh IRL 21 B5
Shimsk RUS 7 B11
Shipston-on-Stour GB 29 A6
Shirgjan AL 105 B6
Shklow BY 7 D11
Shkodër AL 105 A5
Shoeburyness GB 31 C4
Shoreham-by-Sea GB 31 D3
Shostka UA 7 F12
Shotley Gate GB 31 C5
Shpola UA 11 B11
Shrewsbury GB 26 C3
Shugozero RUS 7 B13
Shumen BG 11 E9
Siabost GB 22 C2
Siamanna I 110 C1
Sianów PL 46 A2
Siatista GR 116 B3
Siauges-St. Romain F 78 A2
Šiauliai LT 6 D7
Sibari I 106 B3
Sibbhult S 41 C4
Šibenik HR 83 C4
Sibinj HR 74 C2
Sibiu RO 11 D8
Sibnica SRB 85 B5
Sibsey GB 27 B6
Siculiana I 108 B2
Šid SRB 85 A4
Sidari GR 116 C1
Siddeburen NL 42 B3
Sidensjö S 115 D15
Siderno I 106 C3
Sidirokastro GR 116 A5
Sidmouth GB 29 C4
Sidzina PL 65 A5
Siebe N 113 D12
Siebenlehn D 52 B3
Siedlce PL 6 E7
Siedlice PL 46 B1
Siedlinghausen D 51 B4
Siedlisko PL 46 C2
Siegburg D 50 C3
Siegen D 50 C4
Siegenburg D 62 B2
Sieghartskirchen A 64 B2
Siegsdorf D 62 C3
Siekierki PL 45 C6
Sielpia PL 55 B5
Siemiany PL 47 B5
Siena I 81 C5
Sieniawka PL 53 C4
Siennica PL 55 A6
Sienno PL 55 B6
Sieppijärvi FIN 113 E13
Sieradz PL 54 B3
Sieraków, *Śląskie* PL 54 C3
Sieraków, *Wielkopolskie* PL 46 C2
Sierakowice PL 46 A3
Sierck-les-Bains F 60 A2
Sierentz F 60 C3
Sierning A 63 B5
Sierpc PL 47 C5
Sierra de Fuentes E 93 B4
Sierra de Luna E 90 A2
Sierra de Yeguas E 100 B1
Sierre CH 70 B2
Siestrzeń PL 55 A5
Sietamo E 90 A2
Siewierz PL 55 C4
Sigdal N 34 B1
Sigean F 78 C1
Sigerfjord N 112 D4
Sighetu-Marmatiei RO 11 C7
Sighişoara RO 11 C8
Sigillo I 82 C1
Siglufjörður IS 111 A7
Sigmaringen D 61 B5
Signa I 81 C5
Signes F 79 C4
Signy-l'Abbaye F 59 A5
Signy-le-Petit F 59 A5
Sigogne F 67 C4
Sigri GR 116 C7
Sigtuna S 37 C4
Sigueiro E 86 B2
Sigüenza E 95 A4
Sigües E 90 A1
Sigulda LV 6 C8
Siilinjärvi FIN 3 E27
Sikenica SK 65 B4
Sikia GR 116 B5
Sikinos GR 117 F7
Sikkilsdalseter N 32 A6
Siklós H 74 C3
Sikórz PL 47 C5
Sikselet S 115 A14
Silandro I 71 B5
Silánus I 110 B1
Silbaš SRB 75 C4
Silbersted D 43 A6
Şile TR 118 A4
Siles E 101 A3
Silgueiros P 92 A3
Silifke TR 16 C6
Siliqua I 110 C1
Silistra BG 11 D9
Silivri TR 118 A3
Siljan N 35 C1
Siljansnäs S 36 B1
Silkeborg DK 39 C2
Silla E 96 B2
Sillamäe EST 7 B9
Sillé-le-Guillaume F 57 B5
Silleda E 86 B2
Sillenstede D 43 B4
Sillerud S 35 C4
Sillian A 72 B2
Silloth GB 25 D4
Silno PL 46 B3
Silnowo PL 46 B2
Silo HR 73 C4
Sils E 91 B5
Silsand N 112 C6
Silte S 37 E5
Šilute LT 6 D6
Silvalen N 114 B9
Silvaplana CH 71 B4
Silvares P 92 A3
Silvberg S 36 B2
Silverdalen S 40 B5
Silvermines IRL 20 B3
Silverstone GB 30 B2
Silverton GB 29 C4
Silves P 98 B2
Silvi Marina I 103 A7
Simandre F 69 B4
Šimanovci SRB 85 B5
Simard F 69 B5
Simat de Valldigna E 96 B2
Simav TR 118 C3
Simbach, *Bayern* D 62 B4
Simbach, *Bayern* D 62 B3
Simbário I 106 C3
Simeria RO 11 D7
Simi GR 119 F2
Simićevo SRB 85 B6
Simlångsdalen S 40 C3
Simmerath D 50 C2
Simmerberg D 61 C5
Simmern D 50 D3
Simo FIN 3 D26
Šimonovce SK 65 B6
Simonsbath GB 28 B4
Simonstorp S 37 D3
Simontornya H 74 B3
Simplon CH 70 B3
Simrishamn S 41 D4
Sinaia RO 11 D8
Sinalunga I 81 C5
Sinanaj AL 105 C5
Sinarcas E 96 B1
Sincan TR 118 C7
Sincanlı TR 118 D5
Sindal DK 38 B3
Sindelfingen D 61 B5
Sindia I 110 B1
Sındırgı TR 118 C3
Sinekli TR 118 A3
Sines P 98 B2
Sinetta FIN 113 F14
Sineu E 97 B3
Singen D 61 C4

Spišský-Štvrtok SK 65 B6
Spital A 63 C5
Spital am Semmering A 63 C6
Spittal an der Drau A 72 B3
Spittle of Glenshee GB 25 B4
Spitz A 63 B6
Spjærøy N 35 C2
Spjald DK 39 C1
Spjelkavik N 114 E3
Spjutsbygd S 41 C5
Split HR 83 C5
Splügen CH 71 B4
Spodsbjerg DK 39 E3
Spofforth GB 27 B4
Spohle D 43 B5
Spoleto I 82 D1
Spoltore I 103 A7
Spondigna I 71 B5
Sponvika N 35 C3
Spornitz D 44 B3
Spotorno I 80 B2
Spraitbach D 61 B5
Sprakensehl D 44 C2
Spręcowo PL 47 B6
Spremberg D 53 B4
Spresiano I 72 C2
Sprimont B 49 C6
Springe D 51 A5
Sproatley GB 27 B5
Spuž MNE 105 A5
Spydeberg N 35 C3
Spytkowice PL 55 D4
Squillace I 106 C3
Squinzano I 105 C4
Sračinec HR 73 B6
Srbac BIH 84 A2
Srbica KOS 85 D5
Srbobran SRB 75 C4
Srebrenica BIH 85 B4
Srebrenik BIH 84 B3
Središče SLO 73 B6
Śrem PL 54 A2
Sremska Mitrovica SRB 85 B4
Sremski Karlovci SRB 75 C4
Srní CZ 63 A4
Srnice Gornje BIH 84 B3
Srock PL 55 B4
Środa Śląska PL 54 B1
Środa Wielkopolski PL 54 A2
Srpska Crnja SRB 75 C5
Srpski Itebej SRB 75 C5
Srpski Miletić SRB 75 C4
Staatz A 64 B2
Stabbursnes N 113 B13
Staberdorf D 44 A3
Stabroek B 49 B5
Stachy CZ 63 A4
Stade D 43 B6
Staden B 49 C4
Staðarfell IS 111 B3
Stadl an der Mur A 72 A3
Stadskanaal NL 42 C3
Stadtallendorf D 51 C5
Stadthagen D 51 A5
Stadtilm D 52 C1
Stadtkyll D 50 C2
Stadtlauringen D 51 C6
Stadtlengsfeld D 51 C6
Stadtlohn D 50 B2
Stadtoldendorf D 51 B5
Stadtroda D 52 C1
Stadtsteinach D 52 C1
Stäfa CH 70 A3
Staffanstorp S 41 D3
Staffelstein D 51 C6
Staffin GB 22 D2
Stafford GB 26 C3
Stainach A 73 A4
Staindrop GB 27 A4
Staines GB 31 C3
Stainville F 59 B6
Stainz A 73 B5
Staithes GB 27 A5
Staíti I 106 D3
Stäket S 37 C4
Stakroge DK 39 D1
Stalać SRB 85 C6
Štalcerji SLO 73 C4
Stalden CH 70 B2
Stalham GB 30 B5
Stalheim N 32 B3
Stallarholmen S 37 C4
Ställberg S 36 C1
Ställdalen S 36 C1
Stallhofen A 73 A5
Stalon S 115 C12
Stalowa Wola PL 11 A7
Stamford GB 30 B3
Stamford Bridge GB 27 B5
Stamnes N 32 B2
Stams A 71 A5
Stamsried D 62 A3
Stamsund N 112 D3
Stanford le Hope GB 31 C4
Stånga S 37 E5
Stange N 34 B3
Stanghella I 72 C1
Stanhope GB 25 D5
Stanišić SRB 75 C4
Stanisławów PL 55 A6
Staňkov CZ 62 A4
Stankovci HR 83 C4
Stanley GB 25 D6
Stans CH 70 B3
Stansted Mountfitchet GB 31 C4
Stanzach A 71 A5
Stapar SRB 75 C4
Staphorst NL 42 C3
Staplehurst GB 31 C4
Stąporków PL 55 B5
Stara Baška HR 83 B3
Stara Fužina SLO 72 B3
Stara Kamienica PL 53 C5
Stara Kiszewa PL 47 B4
Stará L'ubovňa SK 65 A6
Stara Moravica SRB 75 C4
Stara Novalja HR 83 B3
Stara Pazova SRB 85 B5
Stará Turá SK 64 B3
Stara Zagora BG 11 E8
Starachowice PL 55 B6
Staraya Russa RUS 7 C11
Stårbsnäs S 36 C6
Starčevo SRB 85 B5
Stare Dłutowo PL 47 B5
Staré Hamry CZ 65 A4
Stare Jabłonki PL 47 B6
Staré Město CZ 64 A3
Stare Pole PL 47 A5
Stare Sedlo CZ 63 A5
Stare Strącze PL 53 B6
Stargard Szczeciński PL 45 B7
Stårheim N 114 F2
Stari Banovci SRB 85 B5
Stari Bar MNE 105 A5
Stari Gradac HR 74 C2
Stari Jankovci HR 75 C3
Stari Majdan BIH 83 B5
Stari-Mikanovci HR 74 C3
Stari Raušić KOS 85 D5
Starigrad, *Ličko-Senjska* HR 83 B3
Starigrad, *Splitsko-Dalmatinska* HR 83 C5
Starigrad-Paklenica HR 83 B4
Staritsa RUS 7 C13
Starkenbach A 71 A5
Starnberg D 62 C2
Staro Petrovo Selo HR 74 C2
Staro Selo HR 73 C5
Staro Selo SRB 85 B6
Starodub RUS 7 E12
Starogard PL 46 B1
Starogard Gdański PL 47 B4
Starokonstyantyniv UA 11 B9
Stary Brzozów PL 55 A5
Stary Dzierzgoń PL 47 B5
Starý Hrozenkov CZ 64 B3
Stary Jaroslaw PL 46 A2
Stary Plzenec CZ 63 A4
Stary Sącz PL 65 A6
Starý Smokovec SK 65 A6
Staryy Chartoriysk UA 11 A8
Staškov SK 65 A4
Stassfurt D 52 B1
Staszów PL 55 C6
Stathelle N 35 C1
Staufen D 60 C3
Staunton GB 29 B5
Štavalj SRB 85 C5
Stavang N 32 A2
Stavanger N 33 D2
Stavåsnäs S 34 B4
Stavby S 36 B5
Staveley GB 27 B4
Stavelot B 50 C1
Stavenisse NL 49 B5
Stavern N 35 D2
Stavnäs S 35 C4
Stavoren NL 42 C2
Stavros CY 120 A1
Stavros GR 116 B5
Stavroupoli GR 116 A6
Stavseng N 32 A6
Stavsiø N 34 B2
Stavsnäs S 37 C5
Stawiszyn PL 54 B3
Steane N 33 C5
Steblevë AL 116 A2
Stechelberg CH 70 B2
Štěchovice CZ 63 A5
Stechow D 44 C4
Steckborn CH 61 C4
Stede Broek NL 42 C2
Steeg A 71 A5
Steenbergen NL 49 B5
Steenvoorde F 48 C3
Steenwijk NL 42 C3
Štefanje HR 74 C1
Steffisburg CH 70 B2
Stegaurach D 62 A1
Stege DK 41 E2
Stegelitz D 45 B5
Stegersbach A 73 A6
Stegna PL 47 A5
Steimbke D 43 C6
Stein GB 22 D2
Stein an Rhein CH 61 C4
Steinach A 71 A6
Steinach, *Baden-Württemberg* D 61 B4
Steinach, *Bayern* D 51 C6
Steinach, *Thüringen* D 52 C1
Steinau, *Bayern* D 51 C5
Steinau, *Niedersachsen* D 43 B5
Steinbeck D 45 C5
Steinberg am Rofan A 72 A1
Steindorf A 73 B4
Steine N 32 B2
Steinen D 60 C3
Steinfeld A 72 B3
Steinfeld D 43 C5
Steinfurt D 50 A3
Steingaden D 62 C1
Steinhagen D 51 A4
Steinheid D 52 C1
Steinheim, *Bayern* D 61 B6
Steinheim, *Nordrhein-Westfalen* D 51 B5
Steinhöfel D 45 C6
Steinhorst D 44 C2
Steinigtwolmsdorf D 53 B4
Steinkjer N 114 C8
Steinsholt N 35 C1
Stekene B 49 B5
Stelle D 44 B2
Stellendam NL 49 B5
Stenåsa S 41 C6
Stenay F 59 A6
Stenberga S 40 B5
Stendal D 44 C3
Stenhammar S 35 D5
Stenhamra S 37 C4
Stenhousemuir GB 25 B4
Stenlose DK 41 D2
Stensätra S 36 B3
Stensele S 115 B14
Stenstorp S 35 D5
Stenstrup DK 39 D3
Stenudden S 112 F6
Stenungsund S 38 A4
Štěpánov CZ 64 A3
Stephanskirchen D 62 C3
Stepnica PL 45 B6
Stepojevac SRB 85 B5
Stepping DK 39 D2
Sterbfritz D 51 C5
Sternberg D 44 B3
Šternberk CZ 64 A3
Sterup D 44 A1
Stęszew PL 54 A1
Štětí CZ 53 C4
Stevenage GB 31 C3
Stewarton GB 24 C3
Steyerburg D 43 C6
Steyning GB 31 D3
Steyr A 63 B5
Stężyca PL 46 A3
Stezzano I 71 C4
Stia I 81 C5
Stibb Cross GB 28 C3
Sticciano Scalo I 81 D5
Stidsvig S 41 C3
Stiens NL 42 B2
Stige DK 39 D3
Stigen S 35 D4
Stigliano I 104 C2
Stigtomta S 37 D3
Stilida GR 116 D4
Stilla N 113 C12
Stillington GB 27 A4
Stilo I 106 C3
Stintino I 110 B1
Stio I 103 C8
Štip MK 116 A4
Stira GR 117 D6
Stirling GB 25 B4
Štítnik SK 65 B6
Štíty CZ 54 D1
Stjärnhov S 37 C4
Stjärnsund S 36 B3
Stjørdalshalsen N 114 D7
Stobnica PL 55 B4
Stobno PL 46 B2
Stobreč HR 83 C5
Stochov CZ 53 C3
Stockach D 61 C5
Stöckalp CH 70 B3
Stockaryd S 40 B4
Stockbridge GB 31 C2
Stockerau A 64 B2
Stockheim D 52 C1
Stockholm S 37 C5
Stockport GB 26 B3
Stocksbridge GB 27 B4
Stockton-on-Tees GB 27 A4
Stod CZ 62 A4
Stöde S 115 E13
Stöðvarfjörður IS 111 C12
Stødi N 112 F4
Stoer GB 22 C3
Stoholm DK 38 C2
Stoke Ferry GB 30 B4
Stoke Fleming GB 29 C4
Stoke Mandeville GB 31 C3
Stoke-on-Trent GB 26 B3
Stokesley GB 27 A4
Stokke N 35 C2
Stokkemarke DK 39 E4
Stokken N 33 D5
Stokkseyri IS 111 D4
Stokkvågen N 115 A10
Stokmarknes N 112 D3
Štoky CZ 63 A6
Stolac BIH 84 C2
Stølaholmen N 32 A3
Stolberg D 50 C2
Stolin BY 7 F9
Stollberg D 52 C2
Stöllet S 34 B5
Stollhamm D 43 B5
Stolno PL 47 B4
Stolpen D 53 B4
Stolzenau D 43 C6
Stompetoren NL 42 C1
Ston HR 84 D2
Stonařov CZ 63 A6
Stone GB 26 C3
Stonehaven GB 25 B5
Stonehouse GB 25 C4
Stongfjorden N 32 A2
Stonndalen N 32 B4
Stony Stratford GB 30 B3
Stopanja SRB 85 C6
Stopnica PL 55 C5
Storå S 37 C2
Storås N 114 D6
Storby FIN 36 B6
Stordal, *Møre og Romsdal* N 114 E4
Stordal, *Nord-Trøndelag* N 114 D8
Store GB 23 B6
Store Damme DK 41 E2
Store Heddinge DK 41 D2
Store Herrestad S 41 D3
Store Levene S 35 D4
Store Molvik N 113 B17
Store Skedvi S 36 B2
Store Vika S 37 D4
Storebø N 32 B2
Storebro S 40 B5
Storelv N 113 B11
Støren N 114 D7
Storfjellseter N 114 F7
Storfjord N 112 C8
Storfjorden N 114 E3
Storfors S 35 C6
Storforshei N 112 F3
Storhøliseter N 32 A6
Storjord N 112 F4
Storkow, *Brandenburg* D 53 A3
Storkow, *Mecklenburg-Vorpommern* D 45 B6
Storli N 114 E6
Storlien S 114 D9
Stornara I 104 B1
Stornoway GB 22 C2
Storo I 71 C5
Storozhynets UA 11 B8
Storrington GB 31 D3
Storseleby S 115 C13
Storsjön S 36 A3
Storslett N 112 C10
Storsteinnes N 112 C8
Storuman S 115 B14
Störvattnet S 115 E9
Storvik N 112 F2
Storvik S 36 B3
Storvreta S 36 C4
Štos SK 65 B6
Stössen D 52 B1
Stotel D 43 B5
Stötten D 62 C1
Stotternheim D 52 B1
Stouby DK 39 D2
Stourbridge GB 26 C3
Stourport-on-Severn GB 29 A5
Støvring DK 38 C2
Stow GB 25 C5
Stow-on-the-Wold GB 29 B6
Stowbtsy BY 7 E9
Stowmarket GB 30 B5
Straach D 52 B2
Strabane GB 19 B4
Strachan GB 23 D6
Strachur GB 24 B2
Stracholt D 43 B4
Stradbally IRL 20 B1
Stradella I 80 A3
Straelen D 50 B2
Stragari SRB 85 B5
Strakonice CZ 63 A4
Strålsnäs S 37 D2
Stralsund D 45 A5
Strand N 34 A3
Stranda N 114 E3
Strandby DK 38 B3
Strandebarm N 32 B3
Strandhill IRL 18 B3
Strandlykkja N 34 B3
Strandvik N 32 B2
Strangford GB 19 B6
Strängnäs S 37 C4
Strångsjö S 37 D3
Stráni CZ 64 B3
Stranice SLO 73 B5
Stranorlar IRL 19 B4
Stranraer GB 24 D2
Strasatti I 108 B1
Strasbourg F 60 B3
Strasburg D 45 B5
Strašice CZ 63 A4
Strass im Steiermark A 73 B5
Stråssa S 37 C2
Strassburg A 73 B4
Strasskirchen D 62 B3
Strasswalchen A 63 C4
Stratford-upon-Avon GB 29 A6
Strathaven GB 24 C3
Strathdon GB 23 D5
Strathkanaird GB 22 D3
Strathpeffer GB 23 D4
Strathy GB 23 C5
Strathyre GB 24 B3
Stratinska BIH 84 B1
Stratton GB 28 C3
Straubing D 62 B3
Straulas I 110 B2
Straume N 33 C6
Straumen, *Nord-Trøndelag* N 114 D8
Straumen, *Nordland* N 112 E4
Straumsjøen N 112 D3
Straumsnes N 112 E4
Straupitz D 53 B4
Strausberg D 45 C5
Straussfurt D 51 B7
Strawczyn PL 55 C5
Straž nad Nezárkou CZ 63 A5
Stráž Pod Ralskem CZ 53 C4
Straža SLO 73 C5
Straža SRB 85 B6
Strážnice CZ 64 B3
Strážný CZ 63 B4
Štrbské Pleso SK 65 A6
Strečno SK 65 A4
Street GB 29 B5
Strehla D 52 B3
Strekov SK 65 C4
Strem A 73 A6
Stremska-Rača SRB 85 B4
Strengberg A 63 B5
Strengelvåg N 112 D4
Streoci KOS 85 D5
Stresa I 70 C3
Streufdorf D 51 C6
Strib DK 39 D2
Striberg S 37 C1
Stříbro CZ 62 A3
Strichen GB 23 D6
Strigno I 71 B6
Štrigova HR 73 B6
Strijen NL 49 B5
Strizivojna HR 74 C3
Strmica HR 83 B5
Strmilov CZ 63 A6
Ströhen D 43 C5
Strokestown IRL 18 C3
Stromberg, *Nordrhein-Westfalen* D 50 B4
Stromberg, *Rheinland-Pfalz* D 60 A3
Stromeferry GB 22 D3
Strömnäs S 115 C13
Stromness GB 23 C5
Strömsberg S 36 B4
Strömsbruk S 115 F14
Strömsfors S 37 D3
Strömsnäsbruk S 40 C3
Strömstad S 35 D3
Strömsund, *Jämtland* S 115 D12
Strömsund, *Västerbotten* S 115 B13
Stronachlachar GB 24 B3
Stróngoli I 107 B4
Stronie Śląskie PL 54 C1
Strontian GB 24 B2
Stroppiana I 70 C3
Stroud GB 29 B5
Stroumbi CY 120 B1
Stróża PL 65 A5
Strücklingen D 43 B4
Struer DK 38 C1
Struga MK 116 A2
Strugi Krasnyye RUS 7 B10
Strumica MK 116 A4
Strumien PL 65 A4
Struy GB 22 D4
Stružec HR 74 C1
Stryków PL 55 B4
Stryn N 114 F3
Stryy UA 11 B7
Strzałkowo PL 54 A2
Strzegocin PL 47 C6
Strzegom PL 54 C1
Strzegowo PL 47 C6
Strzelce PL 55 A4
Strzelce Krajeńskie PL 46 C1
Strzelce Kurowo PL 46 C1
Strzelce Opolskie PL 54 C3
Strzelin PL 54 C2
Strzelno PL 47 C4
Strzepcz PL 47 A4
Strzybnica PL 54 C3
Strzygi PL 47 B5
Stubal SRB 85 C5
Stubbekøbing DK 39 E5
Stuben A 71 A5
Stubenberg A 73 A5
Stubline SRB 85 B5
Studená CZ 63 A6
Studenci HR 84 C2
Studenica SRB 85 C5
Studénka CZ 64 A4
Studenzen A 73 A5
Studienka SK 64 B3
Studland GB 29 C6
Studley GB 29 A6
Studzienice PL 46 A3
Stuer D 44 B4
Stugudal N 114 E8
Stugun S 115 D12
Stuhr D 43 B5
Stukenbrock D 51 B4
Stülpe D 52 A3
Stupava SK 64 B3
Stupnik HR 73 C5
Stupsk PL 47 B6
Sturkö S 41 C5
Sturminster Newton GB 29 C5
Štúrovo SK 65 C4
Sturton GB 27 B5
Stuttgart D 61 B5
Stvolny CZ 52 C3
Stykkishólmur IS 111 B3
Styri N 34 B3
Stysö S 38 B4
Suances E 88 A2
Subbiano I 81 C5
Subiaco I 102 B6
Subotica SRB 75 B4
Subotište SRB 85 B4
Sučany SK 65 A4
Suceava RO 11 C9
Sucha-Beskidzka PL 65 A5
Suchacz PL 47 A5
Suchań PL 46 B1
Suchdol nad Lužnice CZ 63 B5
Suchedniów PL 55 B5
Suchorze PL 46 A3
Suchteln D 50 B2
Sucina E 101 B5
Suckow D 44 B3
Sućuraj HR 84 C2
Sudbury GB 30 B4
Suddesjaur S 115 B16
Suden D 43 A5
Süderbrarup D 44 A1
Süderlügum D 39 E1
Súðavík IS 111 A3
Suðureyri IS 111 A2
Sudoměřice u Bechyně CZ 63 A5
Sudovec HR 73 B6
Sudzha RUS 7 F13
Sueca E 96 B2
Suelli I 110 C2
Sugenheim D 61 A6
Sugères F 68 C3
Sugny B 59 A5
Suhl D 51 C6
Suhlendorf D 44 C2
Suho Polje BIH 85 B4
Suhopolje HR 74 C2
Şuhut TR 119 D5
Šuica BIH 84 C2
Suippes F 59 A5
Sukhinichi RUS 7 D13
Sukobin MNE 105 A5
Sukošan HR 83 B4
Sükösd H 75 B3
Suków PL 55 C5
Šul'a SK 65 B5
Suldalsosen N 33 C3
Suldrup DK 38 C2
Sulechów PL 53 A5
Sulęcin PL 45 C7
Sulęczyno PL 46 A3
Sulejów PL 55 B4
Sulejówek PL 55 A6
Süleymanlı TR 118 D2
Sulgen CH 71 A4
Sulibórz PL 46 B1
Sulina RO 11 D10
Sulingen D 43 C5
Suliszewo PL 46 B1
Sulitjelma N 112 E5
Sułkowice PL 65 A5
Süller TR 119 D4
Sully-sur-Loire F 58 C3
Sulmierzyce, *Łódzkie* PL 55 B4
Sulmierzyce, *Wielkopolskie* PL 54 B2
Sulmona I 103 A6
Süloğlu TR 118 A1
Sułoszowa PL 55 C4
Sulów PL 54 B2
Sulsdorf D 44 A3
Sultandağı TR 119 D6
Sülüklü TR 118 D7
Suluova TR 16 A7
Sulvik S 35 C4
Sülysáp H 75 A4
Sülz D 61 B4
Sulzbach, *Baden-Württemberg* D 61 B5
Sulzbach, *Baden-Württemberg* D 61 A5
Sulzbach, *Bayern* D 61 A5
Sulzbach, *Saarland* D 60 A3
Sulzbach-Rosenberg D 62 A2
Sülze D 44 C2
Sulzfeld D 51 C6
Sumartin HR 84 C1
Sumburgh GB 22 B7
Sümeg H 74 B2
Sumiswald CH 70 A2
Šumná CZ 64 B1
Šumperk CZ 54 D1
Šumvald CZ 64 A3
Sumy UA 7 F13
Sunbilla E 76 C1
Sünching D 62 B3
Sund FIN 36 B7
Sund S 35 C3
Sundborn S 36 B2
Sundby DK 38 C1
Sunde N 32 C2
Sunde bru N 33 D6
Sunderland GB 25 D6
Sundern D 50 B4
Sundhultsbrunn S 40 B4
Sundnäs S 115 A14
Sunds DK 39 C2
Sundsfjord N 112 F3
Sundsvall S 115 E14
Sungurlu TR 16 A7
Suni I 110 B1
Sunja HR 74 C1
Sunnansjö S 36 B1
Sunnaryd S 40 B3
Sunndalsøra N 114 E5
Sunne S 34 C5
Sunnemo S 34 C5
Sunnersberg S 35 D5
Suolovuopmio N 113 C12
Suomussalmi FIN 3 D28
Suoyarvi RUS 3 E30
Super Sauze F 79 B5
Supetar HR 83 C5
Supetarska Draga HR 83 B3
Supino I 102 B6
Šuplja Stijena MNE 84 C4
Surahammar S 37 C3
Šurany SK 64 B4
Surazh BY 7 D11
Surazh RUS 7 E12
Surbo I 105 C4
Surčin SRB 85 B5
Surgères F 66 B4
Surhuisterveen NL 42 B3
Sùria E 91 B4
Surin F 67 B5
Surka N 34 B2
Surnadalsøra N 114 E5
Sursee CH 70 A3
Surte S 38 B5
Surwold D 43 C4
Sury-le-Comtal F 69 C4
Susa I 70 C2
Šušara SRB 85 B6
Susch CH 71 B5
Susegana I 72 C2
Süsel D 44 A2
Sušice CZ 63 A4
Šušnjevica HR 73 C4
Sussen D 61 B5
Susurluk TR 118 C3
Susz PL 47 B5
Sütçüler TR 119 E5
Sutivan HR 83 C5
Sutjeska SRB 75 C5
Sutomore MNE 105 A5
Sutri I 102 A5
Sutton GB 31 C3
Sutton Coldfield GB 27 C4
Sutton-in-Ashfield GB 27 B4
Sutton-on-Sea GB 27 B6
Sutton-on-Trent GB 27 B5
Sutton Scotney GB 31 C2
Sutton Valence GB 31 C4
Suvaja BIH 83 B5
Suvereto I 81 C4
Suvorov RUS 7 D14
Suwałki PL 6 D7
Suze-la-Rousse F 78 B3
Suzzara I 81 B4
Svabensverk S 36 A2
Svalbarð IS 111 A10
Svalöv S 41 D3
Svanabyn S 115 C13
Svanberga S 36 C5
Svaneke DK 41 D5
Svanesund S 35 D3
Svängsta S 41 C4
Svannäs S 115 A15
Svanskog S 35 C4
Svanstein S 113 F12
Svappavaara S 112 E10
Svärdsjö S 36 B2
Svarstad N 35 C1
Svartå, *Örebro* S 37 C1
Svärta, *Södermanland* S 37 D4
Svartå, *Värmland* S 34 C5
Svartinge S 37 D3
Svartnäs S 36 B3
Svartnes N 112 E3
Svarttjärn S 115 B13
Svatsum N 34 A1
Svätý Jur SK 64 B3
Svätý Peter SK 64 C4
Svedala S 41 D3
Sveg S 115 E11
Sveindal N 33 D4
Sveio N 33 C2
Svejbæk DK 39 C2
Svelgen N 114 F2
Svelvik N 35 C2
Svendborg DK 39 D3
Svene N 32 C6
Svenljunga S 40 B3
Svennevad S 37 C2
Svenstavik S 115 E11
Svenstrup DK 38 C2
Švermov CZ 53 C4
Sveti Ivan Zabno HR 74 C1
Sveti Ivan Zelina HR 73 C6
Sveti Nikola MNE 105 B5
Sveti Rok HR 83 B4
Sveti Stefan MNE 105 A4
Světla nad Sázavou CZ 63 A6
Svetlyy RUS 47 A6
Svetvinčenat HR 82 A2
Švica HR 83 B4
Svidník SK 10 B6
Švihov CZ 63 A4
Svilajnac SRB 85 B6
Svilengrad BG 11 F9
Svindal N 35 C3
Svinhult S 40 B5
Svinna SK 64 B4
Svinninge DK 39 D4
Svinninge S 37 C5
Sviritsa RUS 7 A12
Svishtov BG 11 E8
Svislach BY 6 E8
Svit SK 65 A6
Svitavy CZ 64 A2
Svitlovodsk UA 11 B12
Svodín SK 65 C4
Svolvær N 112 D3
Svortemyr N 32 A2
Svortland N 32 C2
Svratka CZ 64 A2
Svrčinovec SK 65 A4
Svullrya N 34 B4
Svyetlahorsk BY 7 E10
Swadlincote GB 27 C4
Swaffham GB 30 B4
Swanage GB 29 C6
Swanley GB 31 C4
Swanlinbar IRL 19 B4
Swansea GB 28 B4

Swarzędz PL 46 C3
Swatragh GB 19 B5
Świątki PL 47 B6
Świdnica, *Dolnośląskie* PL 54 C1
Świdnica, *Lubuskie* PL 53 B5
Świdnik PL 11 A7
Świdwin PL 46 B1
Świebodzice PL 53 C6
Świebodzin PL 53 A5
Świecie PL 47 B4
Świedziebnia PL 47 B5
Świeradów Zdrój PL 53 C5
Świerki PL 54 C1
Swierzawa PL 53 B5
Swierzno PL 45 B6
Swięta PL 45 B6
Swieta Anna PL 55 C4
Świętno PL 53 B4
Swifterbant NL 42 C2
Swindon GB 29 B6
Swineshead GB 30 B3
Swinford IRL 18 C3
Świnoujście PL 45 B6
Swinton GB 25 C5
Swobnica PL 45 B6
Swords IRL 21 A5
Swornegacie PL 46 B3
Sya S 37 D2
Syasstroy RUS 7 A12
Sycewice PL 46 A2
Sychevka RUS 7 D13
Syców PL 54 B2
Sycowice PL 53 A5
Sydnes N 33 C2
Syfteland N 32 B2
Syke D 43 C5
Sykkylven N 114 E3
Sylling N 34 C2
Sylte N 114 E4
Symbister GB 22 A7
Symington GB 25 C4
Symonds Yat GB 29 B5
Sypniewo, *Kujawsko-Pomorskie* PL 46 B3
Sypniewo, *Wielkopolskie* PL 46 B2
Sysserum S 40 B6
Sysslebäck S 34 B4
Syväjärvi FIN 113 E14
Szabadbattyán H 74 A3
Szabadegyháza H 74 A3
Szabadszállás H 75 B4
Szadek PL 54 B3
Szajol H 75 A5
Szakály H 74 B3
Szakcs H 74 B3
Szakmár H 75 B4
Szalánta H 74 C3
Szałas PL 55 B5
Szalkszentmárton H 75 B4
Szalonna H 65 B6
Szamocin PL 46 B3
Szamotuły PL 46 C2
Szany H 74 A2
Szarvas H 75 B5
Szarvaskö H 65 C6
Szászvár H 74 B3
Százhalombatta H 74 A3
Szczawa PL 65 A6
Szczawnica PL 65 A6
Szczecin PL 45 B6
Szczecinek PL 46 B2
Szczekociny PL 55 C4
Szczerców PL 55 B4
Szczucin PL 55 C6
Szczuczarz PL 46 B2
Szczurkowo PL 47 A6
Szczurowa PL 55 C5
Szczyrk PL 65 A5
Szczytna PL 54 C1
Szczytno PL 6 E6
Szczyty PL 54 B3
Szécsény H 65 B5
Szederkény H 74 C3
Szedres H 74 B3
Szeged H 75 B5
Szeghalom H 75 A6
Szegvár H 75 B5
Székesfehérvár H 74 A3
Székkutas H 75 B5
Szekszárd H 74 B3
Szemplino Czarne PL 47 B6
Szemud PL 47 A4
Szendehely H 65 C5
Szendrö H 65 B6
Szentendre H 65 C5
Szentes H 75 B5
Szentgotthárd H 73 B6
Szentlászló H 74 B2
Szentlörinc H 74 B2
Szentmártonkáta H 75 A4
Szenyér H 74 B2
Szeremle H 74 B3
Szerep H 75 A6
Szigetszentmiklós H 75 A4
Szigetvár H 74 B2
Szikáncs H 75 B5
Szikszó H 65 B6
Szil H 74 A2
Szilvásvárad H 65 B6
Szklarska Poreba PL 53 C5
Szlichtyngowa PL 53 B6
Szob H 65 C4
Szolnok H 75 A5
Szombathely H 74 A1
Szorosad H 74 B3
Szpetal Graniczny PL 47 C5
Szprotawa PL 53 B5
Szreńsk PL 47 B6
Sztum PL 47 B5
Sztutowo PL 47 A5
Szubin PL 46 B3
Szücsi H 65 C5
Szulmierz PL 47 C6
Szulok H 74 B2
Szumanie PL 47 C5
Szwecja PL 46 B2
Szydłów, *Łódzkie* PL 55 B4
Szydłów, *Świętokrzyskie* PL 55 C6
Szydłowiec PL 55 B5
Szydlowo, *Mazowieckie* PL 47 B6
Szydłowo, *Wielkopolskie* PL 46 B2
Szymanów PL 55 A5
Szynkielów PL 54 B3
Szynwald PL 55 D6

T

Taastrup DK 41 D2
Tab H 74 B3
Tabanera la Luenga E 94 A2
Tabaqueros E 96 B1
Tábara E 88 C1
Tabenera de Cerrato E 88 B2
Taberg S 40 B4
Tabernas E 101 B3
Tabiano Bagni I 81 B4
Taboada E 86 B3
Taboadela E 87 B3
Tábor CZ 63 A5
Táborfalva H 75 A4
Taborište HR 73 C6
Tábua P 92 A2
Tabuaco P 87 C3
Tabuenca E 89 C5
Tabuyo del Monte E 87 B4
Täby S 37 C5
Tác H 74 A3
Tachov CZ 62 A3
Tadcaster GB 27 B4
Tadley GB 31 C2
Tafalla E 89 B5
Tafjord N 114 E4
Taganheira P 98 B2
Tågarp S 41 D2
Tággia I 80 C1
Tagliacozzo I 102 A6
Táglio di Po I 82 A1
Tagnon F 59 A5
Tahal E 101 B3
Tahitótfalu H 65 C5
Tahtaköprü TR 118 C4
Tailfingen D 61 B5
Taillis F 57 B4
Tain GB 23 D4
Tain-l'Hermitage F 78 A3
Taipadas P 92 C2
Taivalkoski FIN 3 D28
Takene S 35 C5
Takovo SRB 85 C5
Taksony H 75 A4
Tal E 86 B2
Tal-Y-Llyn GB 26 C2
Talachyn BY 7 D10
Talamello I 82 C1
Talamone I 102 A4
Talant F 69 A4
Talarrubias E 93 B5
Talas TR 16 B7
Taleván E 93 B4
Talavera de la Reina E 94 C2
Talavera la Real E 93 C4
Talayuela E 93 B5
Talayuelas E 96 B1
Talgarth GB 29 B4
Talgje N 33 C2
Talhadas P 92 A2
Táliga E 93 C3
Talizat F 78 A2
Tálknafjörður IS 111 B2
Talla I 81 C5
Talladale GB 22 D3
Tallaght IRL 21 A5
Tallard F 79 B5
Tällberg S 36 B1
Tallinn EST 6 B8
Talloires F 69 C6
Tallow IRL 21 B4
Tallsjö S 115 C15
Talmay F 69 A5
Talmont-St. Hilaire F 66 B3
Talmont-sur-Gironde F 66 C4
Talne UA 11 B11
Talsano I 104 C3
Talsi LV 6 C7
Talvik N 113 B11
Talybont GB 26 C2
Tamajón E 95 B3
Tamame E 88 C1
Tamames E 93 A4
Tamarit de Mar E 91 B4
Tamarite de Litera E 90 B3
Tamariu E 91 B6
Tamási H 74 B3
Tambach-Dietharz D 51 C6
Tameza E 86 A4
Tammisaari FIN 6 A7
Tampere FIN 3 F25
Tamsweg A 72 A3
Tamurejo E 94 D2
Tamworth GB 27 C4
Tana bru N 113 B17
Tañabueyes E 89 B3
Tanakajd H 74 A1
Tananger N 33 D2
Tanaunella I 110 B2
Tancarville F 58 A1
Tandsjöborg S 115 F11
Tånga S 41 C2
Tangelic H 74 B3
Tangen N 34 B3
Tangerhütte D 44 C3
Tangermünde D 44 C3
Tanhua FIN 113 E16
Taninges F 69 B6
Tankavaara FIN 113 D16
Tann D 51 C6
Tanna D 52 C1
Tannadice GB 25 B5
Tannåker S 40 C3
Tännäs S 115 E9
Tannay, *Ardennes* F 59 A5
Tannay, *Nièvre* F 68 A3
Tannenbergsthal D 52 C2
Tännesberg D 62 A3
Tannheim A 71 A5
Tanowo PL 45 B6
Tanum S 35 D3
Tanumshede S 35 D3
Tanus F 77 B5
Tanvald CZ 53 C5
Taormina I 109 B4
Tapa EST 7 B8
Tapfheim D 62 B1
Tapia de Casariego E 86 A4
Tapio F 77 C4
Tápióbicske H 75 A4
Tápiógyörgye H 75 A4
Tápióság H 75 A4
Tápiószecsö H 75 A4
Tápiószele H 75 A4
Tápiószentmárton H 75 A4
Tapolca H 74 B2
Tapolcafö H 74 A2
Tar HR 72 C3
Tarabo S 40 B2
Taradell E 91 B5
Taraklı TR 118 B5
Taramundi E 86 A3
Tarancón E 95 B3
Táranto I 104 C3
Tarare F 69 C4
Tarascon F 78 C3
Tarascon-sur-Ariège F 77 D4
Tarashcha UA 11 B11
Tarazona E 89 C5
Tarazona de la Mancha E 95 C5
Tarbena E 96 C2
Tarbert GB 24 C2
Tarbert IRL 20 B2
Tarbes F 76 C3
Tarbet GB 24 B3
Tarbolton GB 24 C3
Tarcento I 72 B3
Tarčin BIH 84 C3
Tarczyn PL 55 B5
Tardajos E 88 B3
Tardelcuende E 89 C4
Tardets-Sorholus F 76 C2
Tardienta E 90 B2
Tärendö S 113 E11
Targon F 76 B2
Târgovişte RO 11 D8
Târgu-Jiu RO 11 D7
Târgu Mureş RO 11 C8
Târgu Ocna RO 11 C9
Târgu Secuiesc RO 11 D9
Tarifa E 99 C5
Tariquejas E 98 B3
Tarján H 65 C4
Tárkany H 64 C4
Tarland GB 23 D6
Tarłów PL 55 B6
Tarm DK 39 D1
Tarmstedt D 43 B6
Tärnaby S 115 B12
Tarnalelesz H 65 B6
Tarnaörs H 65 C6
Târnăveni RO 11 C8
Tärnet N 113 C19
Tarnobrzeg PL 55 C6
Tarnos F 76 C1
Tarnów, *Lubuskie* PL 45 C6
Tarnów, *Małopolskie* PL 55 C5
Tarnowo Podgórne PL 46 C2
Tarnowskie Góry PL 54 C3
Tärnsjö S 36 B3
Tårnvik N 112 E4
Tarouca P 87 C3
Tarp D 43 A6
Tarquínia I 102 A4
Tarquínia Lido I 102 A4
Tarragona E 91 B4
Tàrrega E 91 B4
Tarrenz A 71 A5
Tårs, *Nordjyllands* DK 38 B3
Tårs, *Storstrøms* DK 39 E4
Tarsia I 106 B3
Tarsus TR 16 C7
Tartas F 76 C2
Tartu EST 7 B9
Tarussa RUS 7 D14
Tarves GB 23 D6
Tarvísio I 72 B3
Taşağıl TR 119 F6
Täsch CH 70 B2
Taşköprü TR 16 A7
Tasov CZ 64 A2
Tasovčići BIH 84 C2
Taşucuo TR 16 C6
Tát H 65 C4
Tata H 65 C4
Tatabánya H 74 A3
Tataháza H 75 B4
Tatarbunary UA 11 D10
Tatárszentgyörgy H 75 A4
Tatranská-Lomnica SK 65 A6
Tau N 33 C2
Tauber-bischofsheim D 61 A5
Taucha D 52 B2
Taufkirchen D 62 B3
Taufkirchen an der Pram A 63 B4
Taulé F 56 B2
Taulignan F 78 B3
Taulov DK 39 D2
Taunton GB 29 B4
Taunusstein D 50 C4
Tauragė LT 6 D7
Taurianova I 106 C3
Taurisano I 107 B5
Tauste E 90 B1
Tauves F 68 C2
Tavankut SRB 75 B4
Tavannes CH 70 A2
Tavarnelle val di Pesa I 81 C5
Tavas TR 119 E4
Tavaux F 69 A5
Tävelsås S 40 C4
Taverna I 106 B3
Taverne CH 70 B3
Tavernelle I 82 C1
Tavernes de la Valldigna E 96 B2
Tavérnola Bergamasca I 71 C5
Taverny F 58 A3
Tavescan E 91 A4
Taviano I 107 B5
Tavira P 98 B3
Tavistock GB 28 C3
Tavnik SRB 85 C5
Tavşanlı TR 118 C4
Tayinloan GB 24 C2
Taynuilt GB 24 B2
Tayport GB 25 B5
Tázlár H 75 B4
Tazones E 88 A1
Tczew PL 47 A4
Tczów PL 55 B6
Teangue GB 22 D3
Teano I 103 B7
Teba E 100 C1
Tebay GB 26 A3
Techendorf A 72 B3
Tecklenburg D 50 A3
Tecko-matorp S 41 D3
Tecuci RO 11 D9
Tefenni TR 119 E4
Tegelsmora S 36 B4
Tegernsee D 62 C2
Teggiano I 104 C1
Tegoleto I 81 C5
Teichel D 52 C1
Teignmouth GB 29 C4
Teillay F 57 C4
Teillet F 77 C5
Teisendorf D 62 C3
Teistungen D 51 B6
Teixeiro E 86 A2
Tejada de Tiétar E 93 A5
Tejado E 89 C4
Tejares E 94 B1
Tejn DK 41 D4
Teke TR 118 A4
Tekirdağ TR 118 B2
Tekovské-Lužany SK 65 B4
Telavåg N 32 B1
Telč CZ 63 A6
Telese Terme I 103 B7
Telford GB 26 C3
Telfs A 71 A6
Telgárt SK 65 B6
Telgte D 50 B3
Tellingstedt D 43 A6
Telšiai LT 6 D7
Telti I 110 B2
Teltow D 45 C5
Tembleque E 95 C3
Temelin CZ 63 A5
Temerin SRB 75 C4
Temiño E 89 B3
Témpio Pausánia I 110 B2
Temple Sowerby GB 26 A3
Templederry IRL 20 B3
Templemore IRL 21 B4
Templin D 45 B5
Temse B 49 B5
Ten Boer NL 42 B3
Tenay F 69 C5
Tenbury Wells GB 29 A5
Tenby GB 28 B3
Tence F 78 A3
Tende F 80 B1
Tenhult S 40 B4
Tenja HR 74 C3
Tenneville B 49 C6
Tennevoll N 112 D6
Tensta S 36 B4
Tenterden GB 31 C4
Teo E 86 B2
Teora I 103 C8
Tepasto FIN 113 E13
Tepelenë AL 116 B2
Teplá CZ 52 D2
Teplice CZ 53 C3
Teplička nad Váhom SK 65 A4
Tepsa FIN 113 E14
Ter Apel NL 43 C4
Tera E 89 C4
Téramo I 103 A6
Terborg NL 50 B2
Terchová SK 65 A5
Terebovlya UA 11 B8
Teremia Mare RO 75 C5
Terena P 92 C3
Teresa de Cofrentes E 96 B1
Terešov CZ 63 A4
Terezín CZ 53 C4
Terezino Polje HR 74 C2
Tergnier F 59 A4
Teriberka RUS 3 B31
Terlizzi I 104 B2
Termas de Monfortinho P 93 A4
Terme di Súio I 103 B6
Terme di Valdieri I 79 B6
Termens E 90 B3
Termes F 78 B2
Términi Imerese I 108 B2
Terminillo I 102 A5
Térmoli I 103 B8
Termonfeckin IRL 19 C5
Ternberg A 63 C5
Terndrup DK 38 C3
Terneuzen NL 49 B4
Terni I 102 A5
Ternitz A 64 C2
Ternopil UA 11 B8
Terpan AL 105 C6
Terpni GR 116 B5
Terracina I 102 B6
Terråk N 115 B9
Terralba I 110 C1
Terranova di Pollino I 106 B3
Terranova di Sibari I 106 B3
Terras do Bouro P 87 C2
Terrasini I 108 A2
Terrassa E 91 B5
Terrasson-la-Villedieu F 77 A4
Terrazos E 89 B3
Terriente E 95 B5
Terrugem P 92 C3
Tertenía I 110 C2
Teruel E 90 C1
Tervola FIN 3 C26
Tervuren B 49 C5
Terzaga E 95 B5
Tešanj BIH 84 B2
Tesáske-Mlyňany SK 65 B4
Teslić BIH 84 B2
Tessin D 44 A4
Tessy-sur-Vire F 57 B4
Tét H 74 A2
Tetbury GB 29 B5
Teterchen F 60 A2
Teterow D 45 B4
Teteven BG 11 E8
Tetiyev UA 11 B10
Tetovo MK 10 E6
Tettau D 52 C1
Tettnang D 61 C5
Teublitz D 62 A3
Teuchern D 52 B2
Teulada E 96 C3
Teulada I 110 D1
Teupitz D 52 A3
Teurajärvi S 113 F11
Teutschenthal D 52 B1
Tevel H 74 B3
Teviothead GB 25 C5
Tewkesbury GB 29 B5
Thale D 52 B1
Thalfang D 60 A2
Thalgau A 63 C4
Thalkirch CH 71 B4
Thalmässing D 62 A2
Thalwil CH 70 A3
Thame GB 31 C3
Thann F 60 C3
Thannhausen D 61 B6
Thaon-les-Vosges F 60 B2
Tharandt D 52 C3
Tharsis E 99 B3
Thasos GR 116 B6
Thatcham GB 31 C2
Thaxted GB 31 C4
Thayngen CH 61 C4
The Barony GB 23 B5
The Hague = 's-Gravenhage NL 49 A5
The Mumbles GB 28 B4
Theale GB 31 C2
Thebes = Thiva GR 117 D5
Theding-hausen D 43 C6
Theessen D 52 A2
Themar D 51 C6
Thénezay F 67 B4
Thenon F 67 C6
Therouanne F 48 C3
Thessaloniki = Salonica GR 116 B4
Thetford GB 30 B4
Theth AL 105 A5
Theux B 50 C1
Thézar-les-Corbières F 78 C1
Thèze F 76 C2
Thiberville F 58 A1
Thibie F 59 B5
Thiéblemont-Farémont F 59 B5
Thiendorf D 53 B3
Thiene I 71 C6
Thierrens CH 70 B1
Thiers F 68 C3
Thiesi I 110 B1
Thiessow D 45 A5
Thiezac F 77 A5
Þingeyri IS 111 B2
Þingvellir IS 111 C4
Thionville F 60 A2
Thira GR 117 F7
Thiron-Gardais F 58 B1
Thirsk GB 27 A4
Thisted DK 38 C1
Thiva = Thebes GR 117 D5
Thivars F 58 B2
Thiviers F 67 C5
Thizy F 69 B4
Tholen NL 49 B5
Tholey D 60 A3
Thomas Street IRL 20 A3
Thomastown IRL 21 B4
Thônes F 69 C6
Thonnance-les-Joinville F 59 B6
Thonon-les-Bains F 69 B6
Thorame-Basse F 79 B5
Thorame-Haute F 79 B5
Thorens-Glières F 69 C6
Thorigny-sur-Oreuse F 59 B4
Thörl A 73 A5
Þorlákshöfn IS 111 D4
Thornaby on Tees GB 27 A4
Thornbury GB 29 B5
Thorne GB 27 B5
Thornhill, *Dumfries & Galloway* GB 25 C4
Thornhill, *Stirling* GB 24 B3
Thornthwaite GB 26 A2
Thornton-le-Dale GB 27 A5
Þórshöfn IS 111 A10
Thouarcé F 67 A4
Thouars F 67 B4
Thrapston GB 30 B3
Threlkeld GB 26 A2
Thrumster GB 23 C5
Thueyts F 78 B3
Thuin B 49 C5
Thuir F 91 A5
Thumau D 52 C1
Thun CH 70 B2
Thuret F 68 C3
Thurey F 69 B5
Thüringen A 71 A4
Thurins F 69 C4
Thürkow D 45 B4
Thurles IRL 21 B4
Thurmaston GB 30 B2
Thurø By DK 39 D3
Thursby GB 25 D4
Thurso GB 23 C5
Thury-Harcourt F 57 B5
Thusis CH 71 B4
Thyborøn DK 38 C1
Þykkvibær IS 111 D5
Thyregod DK 39 D2
Tibi E 96 C2
Tibro S 35 D6
Tidaholm S 35 D5
Tidan S 35 D6
Tidersrum S 40 B5
Tiedra E 88 C1
Tiefenbach D 62 A3
Tiefencastel CH 71 B4
Tiefenort D 51 C6
Tiefensee D 45 C5
Tiel NL 49 B6
Tielmes E 95 B3
Tielt B 49 B4
Tienen B 49 C5
Tiengen D 61 C4
Tiercé F 57 C5
Tierga E 89 C5
Tiermas E 90 A1
Tierp S 36 B4
Tierrantona E 90 A3
Tighina MD 11 C10
Tighnabruaich GB 24 C2
Tignes F 70 C1
Tigy F 58 C3
Tihany H 74 B2
Tijnje NL 42 B2
Tijola E 101 B3
Tikhvin RUS 7 B12
Til Châtel F 69 A5
Tilburg NL 49 B6
Tilh F 76 C2
Tillac F 76 C3
Tillberga S 37 C3
Tille F 58 A3
Tillicoultry GB 25 B4
Tilloy Bellay F 59 A5
Tilly F 67 B6
Tilly-sur-Seulles F 57 A5
Tim DK 39 C1
Timau I 72 B3
Timbaki GR 117 G6
Timi CY 120 B1
Timişoara RO 75 C6
Timmele S 40 B3
Timmendorfer Strand D 44 B2
Timmernabben S 40 C6
Timmersdala S 35 D5
Timoleague IRL 20 C3
Timolin IRL 21 B5
Timrå S 115 E14
Timsfors S 40 C3
Timsgearraidh GB 22 C1
Tinajas E 95 B4
Tinalhas P 92 B3
Tinchebray F 57 B5
Tincques F 48 C3
Tineo E 86 A4
Tinglev DK 39 E2
Tingsryd S 40 C4
Tingstäde S 37 E5
Tingvoll N 114 E5
Tinlot B 49 C6
Tinnoset N 33 C6
Tinos GR 117 E7
Tintagel GB 28 C3
Tinténiac F 57 B4
Tintern GB 29 B5
Tintigny B 60 A1
Tione di Trento I 71 B5
Tipperary IRL 20 B3
Tiptree GB 31 C4
Tirana = Tiranë AL 105 B5
Tiranë = Tirana AL 105 B5
Tirano I 71 B5
Tiraspol MD 11 C10
Tire TR 119 D2
Tires I 71 B6
Tiriez E 95 D4
Tirig E 90 C3
Tiriolo I 106 C3
Tirnavos GR 116 C4
Tirrénia I 81 C4
Tirschenreuth D 62 A3
Tirstrup DK 39 C3
Tirteafuera E 100 A1
Tishono RUS 47 A6
Tisno HR 83 C4
Tišnov CZ 64 A2
Tisovec SK 65 B5
Tisselskog S 35 D4
Tistedal N 35 C3
Tistrup DK 39 D1
Tisvildeleje DK 39 C5
Tiszaalpár H 75 B4
Tiszabö H 75 A5
Tiszadorogma H 65 C6
Tiszaföldvár H 75 B5
Tiszafüred H 65 C6
Tiszajenö H 75 A5
Tiszakécske H 75 B5
Tiszakürt H 75 B5
Tiszanána H 75 A5
Tiszaörs H 75 A5
Tiszaroff H 75 A5
Tiszasüly H 75 A5
Tiszasziget H 75 B5
Tiszaszőlős H 75 A5
Titaguas E 96 B1
Titel SRB 75 C5
Titisee-Neustadt D 61 C4
Tito I 104 C1
Titova Korenica HR 83 B4
Titran N 114 D5
Tittling D 63 B4
Tittmoning D 62 B3
Titz D 50 B2
Tiurajärvi FIN 113 E13
Tivat MNE 105 A4
Tived S 37 D1
Tiverton GB 29 C4
Tivisa E 90 B3
Tívoli I 102 B5
Tjæreborg DK 39 D1
Tjällmo S 37 D2
Tjåmotis S 112 F7
Tjautjas S 112 E9
Tjøme N 35 C2
Tjong N 112 F2
Tjonnefoss N 33 D5
Tjörn IS 111 B5
Tjörnarp S 41 D3
Tjøtta N 115 B9
Tkon HR 83 C4
Tleń PL 47 B4
Tlmače SK 65 B4
Tłuchowo PL 47 C5
Tlumačov CZ 64 A3
Tóalmas H 75 A4
Toano I 81 B4
Toba D 51 B6
Tobarra E 101 A4
Tobercurry IRL 18 B3
Tobermore GB 19 B5
Tobermory GB 24 B1
Toberonochy GB 24 B2
Tobha Mor GB 22 D1
Tobo S 36 B4
Tocane-St. Apre F 67 C5
Tocha P 92 A2
Tocina E 99 B5
Töcksfors S 35 C3
Tocón E 100 B2
Todal N 114 E5
Todi I 82 D1
Todmorden GB 26 B3
Todorici BIH 84 B2
Todtmoos D 61 C4
Todtnau D 60 C3
Toén E 87 B3
Tofta, *Gotland* S 37 E5
Tofta, *Skaraborg* S 35 D5
Toftbyn S 36 B2
Tofte N 35 C2
Töftedal S 35 D3
Tofterup DK 39 D1
Toftlund DK 39 D2
Tófű H 74 B3
Tohmo FIN 113 F16
Tokarnia PL 55 C5
Tokary PL 54 B3
Tokod H 65 C4
Tököl H 75 A3
Tolastadh bho Thuath GB 22 C2
Toledo E 94 C2
Tolentino I 82 C2
Tolfa I 102 A4
Tolg S 40 B4

Tolga N 114 E8
Tolkmicko PL 47 A5
Tolko PL 47 A6
Tollarp S 41 D3
Tollered S 40 B2
Tølløse DK 39 D4
Tolmachevo RUS 7 B10
Tolmezzo I 72 B3
Tolmin SLO 72 B3
Tolna H 74 B3
Tolnanémedi H 74 B3
Tolob GB 22 B7
Tolosa E 89 A4
Tolosa P 92 B3
Tolox E 100 C1
Tolpuddle GB 29 C5
Tolva E 90 A3
Tolve I 104 C2
Tomar P 92 B2
Tomarza TR 16 B7
Tomaševac SRB 75 C5
Tomašica BIH 83 B5
Tomášikovo SK 64 B3
Tomašouka BY 6 F7
Tomášovce SK 65 B5
Tomaszów Mazowiecki PL 55 B5
Tomatin GB 23 D5
Tombeboeuf F 77 B3
Tomdoun GB 22 D3
Tomelilla S 41 D3
Tomellosa E 95 B4
Tomelloso E 95 C3
Tomiño E 87 C2
Tomintoul GB 23 D5
Tomislavgrad BIH 84 C2
Tomisław PL 53 B5
Tomisławice PL 47 C4
Tomnavoulin GB 23 D5
Tompa H 75 B4
Tompaládony H 74 A1
Tomra N 114 E3
Tomter N 35 C2
Tona E 91 B5
Tonara I 110 B2
Tonbridge GB 31 C4
Tondela P 92 A2
Tønder DK 39 E1
Tongeren B 49 C6
Tongue GB 23 C4
Tönisvorst D 50 B2
Tønjum N 32 A4
Tonkopuro FIN 113 F17
Tonnay-Boutonne F 67 C4
Tonnay-Charente F 66 C4
Tonneins F 77 B3
Tonnerre F 59 C4
Tonnes N 115 A10
Tönning D 43 A5
Tonsåsen N 32 B6
Tønsberg N 35 C2
Tonstad N 33 D3
Toomyvara IRL 20 B3
Toormore IRL 20 C2
Topares E 101 B3
Topas E 94 A1
Toplița RO 11 C8
Topola SRB 85 B5
Topolčani MK 116 A3
Topoľčany SK 64 B4
Topoľčianky SK 65 B4
Topolje HR 73 C6
Topólka PL 47 C4
Topoľníky SK 64 C3
Toponár H 74 B2
Toporów PL 53 A5
Topsham GB 29 C4
Topusko HR 73 C5
Toques E 86 B3
Tor Vaiánica I 102 B5
Torà E 91 B4
Toral de los Guzmanes E 88 B1
Toral de los Vados E 86 B4
Torbalı TR 119 D2
Torbjörntorp S 35 D5
Torbole I 71 C5
Torchiarolo I 105 C4
Torcross GB 29 C4
Torcy-le-Petit F 58 A2
Torda SRB 75 C5
Tørdal N 33 C5
Tordehumos E 88 C1
Tordera E 91 B5
Tordesillas E 88 C1
Tordesilos E 95 B5
Töre S 3 D25
Töreboda S 35 D6
Toreby DK 39 E4
Torekov S 41 C2
Torella dei Lombardi I 103 C8
Torellò E 91 A5
Toreno E 86 B4
Torfou F 66 A3
Torgau D 52 B3
Torgelow D 45 B6
Torgueda P 87 C3
Torhamn S 41 C5
Torhop N 113 B16
Torhout B 49 B4
Torigni-sur-Vire F 57 A5
Torija E 95 B3
Toril E 95 B5
Torino = Turin I 80 A1
Toritto I 104 C2
Torkovichi RUS 7 B11
Torla E 90 A2
Törmänen FIN 113 D16
Tormestorp S 41 C3
Tórmini I 71 C5
Tornada P 92 B1
Tornal'a SK 65 B6
Tornavacas E 93 A5
Tornby DK 38 B2
Tornesch D 43 B6
Torness GB 23 D4
Torniella I 81 C5
Tornimparte I 103 A6
Torning DK 39 C2
Tornio FIN 3 D26
Tornjoš SRB 75 C4
Tornos E 95 B5
Toro E 88 C1
Törökszentmiklós H 75 A5
Toropets RUS 7 C11
Torpa S 40 C3
Torpè I 110 B2
Torphins GB 23 D6
Torpo N 32 B5
Torpoint GB 28 C3
Torpsbruk S 40 B4
Torquay GB 29 C4
Torquemada E 88 B2
Torralba de Burgo E 89 C4
Torralba de Calatrava E 94 C3
Torrão P 98 A2
Torre Annunziata I 103 C7
Torre Canne I 104 C3
Torre Cardela E 100 B2
Torre das Vargens P 92 B3
Torre de Coelheiros P 92 C3
Torre de Dom Chama P 87 C3
Torre de Juan Abad E 100 A2
Torre de la Higuera E 99 B4
Torre de Miguel Sesmero E 93 C4
Torre de Moncorvo P 87 C3
Torre de Santa Maria E 93 B4
Torre del Bierzo E 86 B4
Torre del Burgo E 95 B3
Torre del Campo E 100 B2
Torre del Greco I 103 C7
Torre del Lago Puccini I 81 C4
Torre del Mar E 100 C1
Torre dell'Orso I 105 C4
Torre do Terranho P 87 D3
Torre Faro I 109 A4
Torre la Ribera E 90 A3
Torre los Negros E 90 C1
Torre Orsáia I 106 A2
Torre-Pacheco E 101 B5
Torre Péllice I 79 B6
Torre Santa Susanna I 105 C3
Torreblacos E 89 C4
Torreblanca E 96 A3
Torreblascopedro E 100 A2
Torrecaballeros E 94 A2
Torrecampo E 100 A1
Torrecilla E 95 B4
Torrecilla de la Jara E 94 C2
Torrecilla de la Orden E 94 A1
Torrecilla del Pinar E 88 C2
Torrecilla en Cameros E 89 B4
Torrecillas de la Tiesa E 93 B5
Torredembarra E 91 B4
Torredonjimeno E 100 B2
Torregrosa E 90 B3
Torreira P 87 D2
Torrejón de Ardoz E 95 B3
Torrejón de la Calzada E 94 B3
Torrejón del Rey E 95 B3
Torrejon el Rubio E 93 B4
Torrejoncillo E 93 B4
Torrelaguna E 95 B3
Torrelapaja E 89 C5
Torrelavega E 88 A2
Torrelobatón E 88 C1
Torrelodones E 94 B3
Torremaggiore I 103 B8
Torremanzanas E 96 C2
Torremayor E 93 C4
Torremezzo di Falconara I 106 B3
Torremocha E 93 B4
Torremolinos E 100 C1
Torrenieri I 81 C5
Torrenostra E 96 A3
Torrenova I 102 B5
Torrent E 96 B2
Torrente de Cinca E 90 B3
Torrenueva, *Ciudad Real* E 100 A2
Torrenueva, *Granada* E 100 C2
Torreorgaz E 93 B4
Torreperogil E 100 A2
Torres E 100 B2
Torres-Cabrera E 100 B1
Torres de la Alameda E 95 B3
Torres Novas P 92 B2
Torres Vedras P 92 B1
Torresandino E 88 C3
Torrevieja E 96 D2
Torri del Benaco I 71 C5
Torricella I 104 C3
Torridon GB 22 D3
Torriglia I 80 B3
Torrijos E 94 C2
Tørring DK 39 D2
Torrita di Siena I 81 C5
Torroal P 92 C2
Torroella de Montgrì E 91 A6
Torrox E 100 C2
Torrskog S 35 C4
Torsåker S 36 B3
Torsang S 36 B2
Torsås S 41 C6
Torsby S 34 B4
Torsetra N 34 B2
Torshälla S 37 C3
Tórshavn FO 2 E10
Torslanda S 38 B4
Torsminde DK 39 C1
Törtel H 75 A4
Tórtoles E 93 A5
Tórtoles de Esgueva E 88 C2
Tortoli I 110 C2
Tortona I 80 B2
Tórtora I 106 B2
Tortoreto Lido I 82 D2
Tortorici I 109 A3
Tortosa E 90 C3
Tortosendo P 92 A3
Tortuera E 95 B5
Tortuero E 95 B3
Toruń PL 47 B4
Torup S 40 C3
Torver GB 26 A2
Tørvikbygde N 32 B3
Torviscón E 100 C2
Torzhok RUS 7 C13
Torzym PL 53 A5
Tosbotn N 115 B9
Toscelanor-Maderno I 71 C5
Tosno RUS 7 B11
Tossa de Mar E 91 B5
Tossåsen S 115 E10
Tosse F 76 C1
Tösse S 35 D4
Tossicía I 103 A6
Tostedt D 43 B6
Tosya TR 16 A7
Tószeg H 75 A5
Toszek PL 54 C3
Totana E 101 B4
Totebo S 40 B6
Tôtes F 58 A2
Tótkomlós H 75 B5
Totland N 114 F2
Tøtlandsvik N 33 C3
Totnes GB 28 C4
Tótszerdahely H 74 B1
Tøttdal N 114 C8
Totton GB 31 D2
Touça P 87 C3
Toucy F 59 C4
Toul F 60 B1
Toulon F 79 C4
Toulon-sur-Allier F 68 B3
Toulon-sur-Arroux F 68 B4
Toulouse F 77 C4
Tour de la Parata F 102 B1
Tourcoing F 49 C4
Tourlaville F 57 A4
Tournai B 49 C4
Tournan-en-Brie F 58 B3
Tournay F 76 C3
Tournon-d'Agenais F 77 B3
Tournon-St. Martin F 67 B5
Tournon-sur-Rhône F 78 A3
Tournus F 69 B4
Touro E 86 B2
Touro P 87 D3
Tourouvre F 58 B1
Tourriers F 67 C5
Tours F 67 A5
Tourteron F 59 A5
Tourves F 79 C4
Toury F 58 B2
Touvedo P 87 C2
Touvois F 66 B3
Toužim CZ 52 C2
Tovačov CZ 64 A3
Tovariševo SRB 75 C4
Tovarnik HR 75 C4
Tovdal N 33 D5
Tovrljane SRB 85 C6
Towcester GB 30 B3
Town Yetholm GB 25 C5
Tråastølen N 32 B4
Trabada E 86 A3
Trabadelo E 86 B4
Trabanca E 87 C4
Trabazos E 87 C4
Traben-Trarbach D 50 D3
Trabia I 108 B2
Tradate I 70 C3
Trädet S 40 B3
Trafaria P 92 C1
Tragacete E 95 B5
Tragwein A 63 B5
Traiguera E 90 C3
Trainel F 59 B4
Traisen A 63 B6
Traismauer A 64 B1
Traitsching D 62 A3
Trákhonas CY 120 A2
Tralee IRL 20 B2
Tramacastilla de Tena E 76 D2
Tramagal P 92 B2
Tramariglio I 110 B1
Tramatza I 110 B1
Tramelan CH 70 A2
Tramonti di Sopra I 72 B2
Tramore IRL 21 B4
Trampot F 60 B1
Trana I 80 A1
Tranås S 40 A4
Tranbjerg DK 39 C3
Tranby N 34 C2
Trancoso P 87 D3
Tranebjerg DK 39 D3
Tranekær DK 39 E3
Tranemo S 40 B3
Tranent GB 25 C5
Tranevåg N 33 D3
Trängslet S 34 A5
Tranhult S 40 B3
Trani I 104 B2
Trans-en-Provence F 79 C5
Transtrand S 34 A5
Tranum DK 38 B2
Tranvik S 37 C5
Trápani I 108 A1
Trappes F 58 B3
Traryd S 40 C3
Trasacco I 103 B6
Trasierra E 99 A4
Träslövsläge S 40 B2
Trasmiras E 87 B3
Traspinedo E 88 C2
Trate SLO 73 B5
Trauchgau D 62 C1
Traun A 63 B5
Traunreut D 62 C3
Traunstein D 62 C3
Traunwalchen D 62 C3
Tråvad S 35 D5
Travemünde D 44 B2
Traversétolo I 81 B4
Travnik BIH 84 B2
Travnik SLO 73 C4
Travo F 102 B2
Travo I 80 B3
Trawsfynydd GB 26 C2
Trbovlje SLO 73 B5
Trbušani SRB 85 C5
Treban F 68 B3
Třebařov CZ 64 A2
Trebatsch D 53 A4
Trebbin D 52 A3
Třebechovice pod Orebem CZ 53 C5
Trebel D 44 C3
Třebenice CZ 53 C3
Trébeurden F 56 B2
Třebíč CZ 64 A1
Trebinje BIH 84 D3
Trebisacce I 106 B3
Trebitz D 52 B2
Trebnje SLO 73 C5
Třeboň CZ 63 A5
Třebovice CZ 64 A2
Trebsen D 52 B2
Trebujena E 99 C4
Trecastagni I 109 B4
Trecate I 70 C3
Trecenta I 81 A5
Tredegar GB 29 B4
Tredózio I 81 B5
Treffen A 72 B3
Treffort F 69 B5
Treffurt D 51 B6
Trefnant GB 26 B2
Tregaron GB 28 A4
Trégastel-Plage F 56 B2
Tregnago I 71 C6
Tregony GB 28 C3
Tréguier F 56 B2
Trégunc F 56 C2
Treharris GB 29 B4
Trehörningsjö S 115 D15
Tréia I 82 C2
Treignac F 68 C1
Treignat F 68 B2
Treignes B 49 C5
Treis-Karden D 50 C3
Trekanten S 40 C6
Trélazé F 67 A4
Trelech GB 28 B3
Trélissac F 67 C5
Trelleborg S 41 D3
Trélon F 49 C5
Trélou-sur-Marne F 59 A4
Tremblay-le-Vicomte F 58 B2
Tremés P 92 B2
Tremezzo I 71 C4
Třemošná CZ 63 A4
Tremp E 90 A3
Trenčianska Stankovce SK 64 B3
Trenčianska Turná SK 64 B4
Trenčianske Teplá SK 64 B4
Trenčianske Teplice SK 64 B4
Trenčín SK 64 B4
Trendelburg D 51 B5
Trengereid N 32 B2
Trensacq F 76 B2
Trent D 45 A5
Trento I 71 B6
Treorchy GB 29 B4
Trepča KOS 85 D5
Trept F 69 C5
Trepuzzi I 105 C4
Trescore Balneário I 71 C4
Tresenda I 71 B5
Tresfjord N 114 E4
Tresigallo I 81 B5
Trešnjevica SRB 85 C6
Tresnurághes I 110 B1
Trespaderne E 89 B3
Třešť CZ 63 A6
Trestina I 82 C1
Tretower GB 29 B4
Trets F 79 C4
Tretten N 34 A2
Treuchtlingen D 62 B1
Treuen D 52 C2
Treuenbrietzen D 52 A2
Treungen N 33 C5
Trevelez E 100 C2
Trevi I 82 D1
Trevi nel Lázio I 102 B6
Treviana E 89 B3
Trevíglio I 71 C4
Trevignano Romano I 102 A5
Treviso I 72 C2
Trévoux F 69 C4
Treysa D 51 C5
Trézelles F 68 B3
Trezzo sull'Adda I 71 C4
Trhová Kamenice CZ 64 A1
Trhové Sviny CZ 63 B5
Triacastela E 86 B3
Triaize F 66 B3
Trianda GR 119 F3
Triaucourt-en-Argonne F 59 B6
Tribanj Kruščica HR 83 B4
Triberg D 61 B4
Tribsees D 45 A4
Tribuče SLO 73 C5
Tricárico I 104 C2
Tricase I 107 B5
Tricésimo I 72 B3
Trie-sur-Baïse F 77 C3
Trieben A 73 A4
Triebes D 52 C2
Triepkendorf D 45 B5
Trier D 60 A2
Trieste I 72 C3
Triggiano I 104 B2
Triglitz D 44 B4
Trignac F 66 A2
Trigueros E 99 B4
Trigueros del Valle E 88 C2
Trijebine SRB 85 C4
Trikala GR 116 C3
Trikeri GR 116 C5
Trikomo CY 120 A2
Trilj HR 83 C5
Trillo E 95 B4
Trilport F 59 B3
Trim IRL 21 A5
Trimdon GB 25 D6
Trindade, *Beja* P 98 B3
Trindade, *Bragança* P 87 C3
Třinec CZ 65 A4
Tring GB 31 C3
Trinità d'Agultu I 110 B1
Trinitápoli I 104 B2
Trino I 70 C3
Trinta P 92 A3
Triora I 80 C1
Tripoli GR 117 E4
Triponzo I 82 D1
Triptis D 52 C1
Triste E 90 A2
Trittau D 44 B2
Trivento I 103 B7
Trivero I 70 C3
Trivigno I 104 C1
Trn BIH 84 B2
Trnava HR 74 C3
Trnava SK 64 B3
Trnovec SK 64 B3
Trnovo BIH 84 C3
Trnovska vas SLO 73 B5
Troarn F 57 A5
Trochtelfingen D 61 B5
Trödje S 36 B4
Trœnse DK 39 D3
Trofa P 87 C2
Trofaiach A 73 A4
Trofors N 115 B10
Trogir HR 83 C5
Trøgstad N 35 C3
Tróia I 103 B8
Troia P 92 C2
Troina I 109 B3
Trois-Ponts B 50 C1
Troisdorf D 50 C3
Troisvierges L 50 C2
Trojane SLO 73 B4
Trojanów PL 55 B6
Troldhede DK 39 D1
Trollhättan S 35 D4
Trolog BIH 84 C1
Tromello I 70 C3
Tromøy N 33 D5
Tromsø N 112 C8
Trondheim N 114 D7
Tronget F 68 B3
Trönninge S 40 C2
Trönningeby S 40 B2
Trönö S 36 A3
Tronzano-Vercellese I 70 C3
Trôo F 58 C1
Troon GB 24 C3
Tropea I 106 C2
Tropojë AL 105 A6
Tropy Sztumskie PL 47 B5
Trosa S 37 D4
Trösken S 36 B3
Trosly-Breuil F 59 A4
Trossingen D 61 B4
Trostberg D 62 B3
Trostyanets UA 7 F13
Trouville-sur-Mer F 57 A6
Trowbridge GB 29 B5
Troyes F 59 B5
Trpanj HR 84 C2
Trpezi MNE 85 D5
Trpinja HR 74 C3
Tršće HR 73 C4
Tršice CZ 64 A3
Trstená SK 65 A5
Trstenci BIH 84 A2
Trstenik KOS 85 D5
Trstenik SRB 85 C6
Trsteno HR 84 D2
Trstice SK 64 B3
Trstin SK 64 B3
Trubchevsk RUS 7 E12
Trubia E 88 A1
Trubjela MNE 84 D3
Truchas E 87 B4
Trujillanos E 93 C4
Trujillo E 93 B5
Trumieje PL 47 B5
Trun CH 70 B3
Trun F 57 B6
Truro GB 28 C2
Trusetal D 51 C6
Truskavets' UA 11 B7
Trustrup DK 39 C3
Trutnov CZ 53 C5
Tryserum S 37 D3
Trysil N 34 A4
Tryszczyn PL 46 B3
Trzcianka PL 46 B2
Trzciel PL 46 C1
Trzcińsko Zdrój PL 45 C6
Trzebiatów PL 45 A7
Trzebiel PL 53 B4
Trzebielino PL 46 A3
Trzebień PL 53 B5
Trzebiez PL 45 B6
Trzebinia PL 55 C4
Trzebnica PL 54 B2
Trzebnice PL 53 B6
Trzeciewiec PL 47 B4
Trzemeszno PL 46 C3
Trzemeszno-Lubuskie PL 46 C1
Trzetrzewina PL 65 A6
Tržič SLO 73 B4
Tsamandas GR 116 C2
Tschagguns A 71 A4
Tschernitz D 53 B4
Tsebrykove UA 11 C11
Tsvetkovo UA 11 B11
Tsyelyakhany BY 7 E8
Tua P 87 C3
Tuam IRL 20 A3
Tubbergen NL 42 C3
Tubilla del Lago E 89 C3
Tübingen D 61 B5
Tubize B 49 C5
Tučapy CZ 63 A5
Tučepi HR 84 C2
Tuchan F 78 D1
Tüchen D 44 B4
Tuchola PL 46 B3
Tuchomie PL 46 A3
Tuchów PL 65 A7
Tuczno PL 46 B2
Tuddal N 32 C5
Tudela E 89 B5
Tudela de Duero E 88 C2
Tudweiliog GB 26 C1
Tuejar E 96 B1
Tuffé F 58 B1
Tufsingdalen N 114 E8
Tuhaň CZ 53 C4
Tui E 87 B2
Tukums LV 6 C7
Tula I 110 B1
Tula RUS 7 D14
Tulcea RO 11 D10
Tul'chyn UA 11 B10
Tulette F 78 B3
Tuliszków PL 54 A3
Tulla IRL 20 B3
Tullamore IRL 21 A4
Tulle F 68 C1
Tullins F 69 C5
Tulln A 64 B2
Tullow IRL 21 B5
Tułowice PL 54 C2
Tulppio FIN 113 E18
Tulsk IRL 18 C3
Tumba S 37 C4
Tummel Bridge GB 24 B3
Tun S 35 D4
Tuna, *Kalmar* S 40 B6
Tuna, *Uppsala* S 36 B5
Tuna Hästberg S 36 B2
Tunçbilek TR 118 C4
Tunes P 98 B2
Tungelsta S 37 C5
Tunje AL 105 C6
Tunnerstad S 40 A4
Tunnhovd N 32 B5
Tunstall GB 30 B5
Tuohikotti FIN 3 F27
Tuoro sul Trasimeno I 82 C1
Tupadły PL 47 C4
Tupanari BIH 84 B3
Tupik RUS 7 D12
Tuplice PL 53 B4
Tura H 65 C5
Turanj HR 83 C4
Turany SK 65 A5
Turbe BIH 84 B2
Turbenthal CH 70 A3
Turcia E 88 B1
Turčianske Teplice SK 65 B4
Turcifal P 92 B1
Turckheim F 60 B3
Turda RO 11 C7
Turégano E 94 A3
Turek PL 54 A3
Tŭrgovishte BG 11 E9
Turgutlu TR 119 D2
Turi I 104 C3
Turin = Torino I 80 A1
Turis E 96 B2
Türje H 74 B2
Turka UA 11 B7
Túrkeve H 75 A5
Türkheim D 62 B1
Türkmenli TR 118 C1
Turku FIN 6 A7
Turleque E 94 C3
Turňa nad Bodvou SK 65 B6
Turnberry GB 24 C3
Turnhout B 49 B5
Türnitz A 63 C6
Turnov CZ 53 C5
Turnu RO 75 B6
Turnu Măgurele RO 11 E8
Turón E 100 C2
Turoszów PL 53 C4
Turowo PL 47 B6
Turquel P 92 B1
Turri I 110 C1
Turries F 79 B5
Turriff GB 23 D6
Tursi I 104 C2
Turtmann CH 70 B2
Turtola FIN 113 F12
Turze PL 54 B2
Turzovka SK 65 A4
Tusa I 109 B3
Tuscánia I 102 A4
Tuse DK 39 D4
Tušilovic HR 73 C5
Tuszyn PL 55 B4
Tutin SRB 85 D5
Tutow D 45 B5
Tutrakan BG 11 D9
Tuttlingen D 61 C4
Tutzing D 62 C2
Tuzi MNE 105 A5
Tuzla BIH 84 B3
Tuzla TR 16 C7
Tuzlukçu TR 119 D6
Tvååker S 40 B2
Tvärålund S 115 C16
Tvärskog S 40 C6
Tvedestrand N 33 D5
Tveit, *Hordaland* N 32 B4
Tveit, *Rogaland* N 33 C3
Tver RUS 7 C13
Tverrelvmo N 112 D8
Tversted DK 38 B3
Tving S 41 C5
Tvrdošin SK 65 A5
Tvrdošovce SK 64 B4
Twardogóra PL 54 B2
Twatt GB 23 B5
Twello NL 50 A2
Twimberg A 73 B4
Twist D 43 C4
Twistringen D 43 C5
Tworóg PL 54 C3
Twyford, *Hampshire* GB 31 C2
Twyford, *Wokingham* GB 31 C3
Tyachiv UA 11 B7
Tychówka PL 46 B2
Tychowo PL 46 B2
Tychy PL 54 C3
Tydal N 114 D8
Týec nad Labem CZ 53 C5
Tyfors S 34 B6
Tygelsjö S 41 D2
Tylldal N 114 E7
Tylstrup DK 38 B2
Tymbark PL 65 A6
Tymowa PL 65 A6
Týn nad Vltavou CZ 63 A5
Tyndrum GB 24 B3
Týnec nad Sázavou CZ 63 A5
Tynemouth GB 25 C6
Tyngsjö S 34 B5
Týniště nad Orlicí CZ 53 C6
Tynset N 114 E7
Tyresö S 37 C5
Tyringe S 41 C3
Tyrislöt S 37 D3
Tyristrand N 34 B2
Tyrrellspass IRL 21 A4
Tysnes N 32 B2
Tysse N 32 B2
Tyssebotn N 32 B2
Tyssedal N 32 B3
Tystberga S 37 D4
Tysvær N 33 C2
Tywyn GB 26 C1
Tzermiado GR 117 G7
Tzummarum NL 42 B2

U

Ub SRB 85 B5
Ubby DK 39 D4
Úbeda E 100 A2
Überlingen D 61 C5
Ubidea E 89 A4
Ubli HR 84 D1
Ubli MNE 105 A5
Ubrique E 99 C5
Ucero E 89 C3
Uchaud F 78 C3
Üchte D 43 C5
Uckerath D 50 C3
Uckfield GB 31 D4
Ucklum S 38 A4
Uclés E 95 C4
Ucria I 109 A3

Udbina HR 83 B4
Uddebo S 40 B3
Uddeholm S 34 B5
Uddevalla S 35 D3
Uddheden S 34 C4
Uden NL 49 B6
Uder D 51 B6
Udiča SK 65 A4
Údine I 72 B3
Udvar H 74 C3
Ueckermünde D 45 B6
Uelsen D 42 C3
Uelzen D 44 C2
Uetendorf CH 70 B2
Uetersen D 43 B6
Uetze D 44 C2
Uffculme GB 29 C4
Uffenheim D 61 A6
Ugarana E 89 A4
Ugento I 107 B5
Ugerldse DK 39 D4
Uggerby DK 38 B3
Uggerslev DK 39 D3
Uggiano la Chiesa I 107 A5
Ugíjar E 100 C2
Ugine F 69 C6
Uglejevik BIH 84 B4
Uglenes N 32 B2
Uglich RUS 7 C15
Ugljane HR 84 C1
Ugod H 74 A2
Uherské Hradiště CZ 64 A3
Uherský Brod CZ 64 A3
Uherský Ostroh CZ 64 B3
Uhingen D 61 B5
Uhliřské-Janovice CZ 63 A6
Uhřiněves CZ 53 C4
Uhyst D 53 B4
Uig GB 22 D2
Uitgeest NL 42 C1
Uithoorn NL 49 A5
Uithuizen NL 42 B3
Uithuizermeeden NL 42 B3
Uivar RO 75 C5
Ujazd, *Łódzkie* PL 55 B4
Ujazd, *Opolskie* PL 54 C3
Ujezd u Brna CZ 64 A2
Ujhartyán H 75 A4
Újkigyós H 75 B6
Ujpetre H 74 C3
Ujście PL 46 B2
Ujsolt H 75 B4
Újszász H 75 A5
Ujué E 89 B5
Ukanc SLO 72 B3
Ukmergė LT 6 D8
Ukna S 40 A6
Ula TR 119 E3
Ul'anka SK 65 B5
Ulaş TR 118 A2
Ulássai I 110 C2
Ulbjerg DK 38 C2
Ulbster GB 23 C5
Ulceby GB 27 B5
Ulcinj MNE 105 B5
Uldum DK 39 D2
Ulefoss N 33 C6
Uleila del Campo E 101 B3
Ulëz AL 105 B5
Ulfborg DK 39 C1
Uljma SRB 85 A6
Ullånger S 115 D15
Ullapool GB 22 D3
Ullared S 40 B2
Ullatti S 113 E10
Ullatun N 33 C3
Ulldecona E 90 C3
Ulldemolins E 90 B3
Ullerslev DK 39 D3
Ullervad S 35 D5
Üllés H 75 B4
Üllö H 75 A4
Ulm D 61 B5
Ulme P 92 B2
Ulmen D 50 C2
Ulnes N 32 B6
Ulog BIH 84 C3
Ulricehamn S 40 B3
Ulrichstein D 51 C5
Ulrika S 37 D2
Ulriksfors S 115 D12
Ulrum NL 42 B3
Ulsberg N 114 E6
Ulsta GB 22 A7
Ulsted DK 38 B3
Ulsteinvik N 114 E2
Ulstrup, *Vestsjællands Amt.* DK 39 D3
Ulstrup, *Viborg Amt.* DK 39 C2
Ulsvåg N 112 D4
Ulubey TR 119 D4
Uluborlu TR 119 D5
Ulukışla TR 16 C7
Ulverston GB 26 A2
Ulvik N 32 B3
Umag HR 72 C3
Uman UA 11 B11
Umba RUS 3 C31
Umbértide I 82 C1
Umbriático I 107 B3
Umčari SRB 85 B5
Umeå S 3 E24
Umgransele S 115 C15
Umhausen A 71 A5
Umka SRB 85 B5
Umljanovic HR 83 C5
Umnäs S 115 B13
Umurbey TR 118 B1
Unaðsdalur IS 111 A3
Unapool GB 22 C3
Unari FIN 113 E14
Uncastillo E 90 A1
Undenäs S 37 D1
Undersaker S 115 D10
Undredal N 32 B4
Unecha RUS 7 E12
Unešić HR 83 C5
Úněšov CZ 62 A4
Ungheni MD 11 C9
Unhais da Serra P 92 A3
Unhošt CZ 53 C4
Unichowo PL 46 A3
Uničov CZ 64 A3
Uniejów PL 54 B3
Unisław PL 47 B4
Unkel D 50 C3
Unken A 62 C3
Unna D 50 B3
Unnaryd S 40 C3
Unquera E 88 A2
Unter Langkampfen A 72 A2
Unter-steinbach D 61 A6
Unterach A 63 C4
Unterägeri CH 70 A3
Unterammergau D 62 C2
Unterhaching D 62 B2
Unteriberg CH 70 A3
Unterkochen D 61 B6
Unterlaussa A 63 C5
Unterlüss D 44 C2
Untermünkheim D 61 A5
Unterschächen CH 70 B3
Unterschleissheim D 62 B2
Unterschwaningen D 62 A1
Untersiemau D 51 C6
Unterweissenbach A 63 B5
Unterzell D 62 A3
Upavon GB 29 B6
Úpice CZ 53 C6
Upiłka PL 46 B3
Upphärad S 35 D4
Uppingham GB 30 B3
Upplands-Väsby S 37 C4
Uppsala S 36 C4
Uppsjøhytta N 34 A1
Upton-upon-Severn GB 29 A5
Ur F 91 A4
Ura e Shtrenjte AL 105 A5
Ura-Vajgurorë AL 105 C5
Uras I 110 C1
Uraz PL 54 B1
Urbánia I 82 C1
Urbino I 82 C1
Urçay F 68 B2
Urda E 94 C3
Urdax E 76 C1
Urdilde E 86 B2
Urdos F 76 D2
Urk NL 42 C2
Úrkút H 74 A2
Urla TR 119 D1
Urlingford IRL 21 B4
Urnäsch CH 71 A4
Urnes N 32 A4
Uroševac KOS 10 E6
Urracal E 101 B3
Urries E 90 A1
Urroz E 76 D1
Ursensollen D 62 A2
Urshult S 40 C4
Uršna Sela SLO 73 C5
Urszulewo PL 47 C5
Ury F 58 B3
Urziceni RO 11 D9
Urzulei I 110 B2
Usagre E 93 C4
Uşak TR 118 D4
Ušće SRB 85 C5
Usedom D 45 B5
Useldange L 60 A1
Usellus I 110 C1
Ushakovo RUS 47 A6
Usingen D 51 C4
Usini I 110 B1
Usk GB 29 B5
Uskedal N 32 C2
Üsküdar TR 118 A4
Uslar D 51 B5
Úsov CZ 64 A3
Usquert NL 42 B3
Ussássai I 110 C2
Ussé F 67 A5
Usséglio I 70 C2
Ussel, *Cantal* F 78 A1
Ussel, *Corrèze* F 68 C2
Usson-du-Poitou F 67 B5
Usson-en-Forez F 68 C3
Usson-les-Bains F 77 D5
Ust Luga RUS 7 B10
Ustaoset N 32 B5
Ustaritz F 76 C1
Uštěk CZ 53 C4
Uster CH 70 A3
Ústi CZ 64 A3
Ústí nad Labem CZ 53 C4
Ústí nad Orlicí CZ 54 D1
Ustibar BIH 85 C4
Ustikolina BIH 84 C3
Ustiprača BIH 84 C4
Ustka PL 46 A3
Ustroń PL 65 A4
Ustronie Morskie PL 46 A1
Ustyuzhna RUS 7 B14
Uszód H 74 B3
Utåker N 32 C2
Utansjö S 115 E14
Utebo E 90 B2
Utena LT 7 D8
Utery CZ 62 A4
Uthaug N 114 D6
Utiel E 96 B1
Utne N 32 B3
Utö S 37 D5
Utrecht NL 49 A6
Utrera E 99 B5
Utrillas E 90 C2
Utsjoki FIN 113 C16
Utstein kloster N 33 C2
Uttendorf A 72 A2
Uttenweiler D 61 B5
Utterslev DK 39 E4
Uttoxeter GB 27 C4
Utvälinge S 41 C2
Utvorda N 114 C7
Uusikaarlepyy FIN 3 E25
Uusikaupunki FIN 3 F24
Uvac BIH 85 C4
Uvaly CZ 53 C4
Uvdal N 32 B5
Uza F 76 B1
Uzdin SRB 75 C5
Uzdowo PL 47 B6
Uzein F 76 C2
Uzel F 56 B3
Uzerche F 67 C6
Uzès F 78 B3
Uzhhorod UA 11 B7
Uzhok UA 11 B7
Užice SRB 85 C4
Uznach CH 70 A3
Uznovë AL 105 C6
Üzümlü, *Konya* TR 119 E6
Üzümlü, *Muğla* TR 119 F4
Uzunköprü TR 118 A1

V

Vaalajärvi FIN 113 E15
Vaas F 58 C1
Vaasa FIN 3 E24
Vaasen NL 50 A1
Vabre F 77 C5
Vác H 65 C5
Vacha D 51 C6
Váchartyán H 65 C5
Väckelsång S 40 C4
Vacqueyras F 78 B3
Vad S 36 B2
Vada I 81 C4
Väddö S 36 C5
Väderstad S 37 D1
Vadheim N 32 A2
Vadillo de la Sierra E 93 A5
Vadillos E 95 B4
Vadla N 33 C3
Vado I 81 B5
Vado Lígure I 80 B2
Vadsø N 113 B18
Vadstena S 37 D1
Vadum DK 38 B2
Vaduz FL 71 A4
Væggerløse DK 44 A3
Vafos N 33 D6
Vág H 74 A2
Vågåmo N 114 F6
Vaggeryd S 40 B4
Vaghia GR 117 D5
Vaglia I 81 C5
Váglio Basilicata I 104 C1
Vagney F 60 B2
Vagnhärad S 37 D4
Vagnsunda S 37 C5
Vagos P 92 A2
Vai GR 117 G8
Vaiano I 81 C5
Vaiges F 57 B5
Vaihingen D 61 B4
Vaillant F 59 C6
Vailly-sur-Aisne F 59 A4
Vailly-sur Sauldre F 68 A2
Vairano Scalo I 103 B7
Vaison-la-Romaine F 79 B4
Vaite F 60 C1
Väjern S 35 D3
Vajszló H 74 C2
Vaksdal N 32 B2
Vál H 74 A3
Val de San Lorenzo E 86 B4
Val de Santo Domingo E 94 B2
Val d'Esquières F 79 C5
Val-d'Isère F 70 C1
Val-Suzon F 69 A4
Val Thorens F 69 C6
Valaam RUS 3 F29
Valada P 92 B2
Vålådalen S 115 D10
Valadares P 87 C2
Valado P 92 B1
Valandovo MK 116 A4
Valaská SK 65 B5
Valaská Belá SK 65 B4
Valaská Dubová SK 65 A5
Valašská Polanka CZ 64 A3
Valašské Klobouky CZ 64 A4
Valašské Meziříčí CZ 64 A3
Valberg F 79 B5
Vålberg S 35 C5
Valbo S 36 B4
Valbom P 87 C2
Valbondione I 71 B5
Valbonë AL 105 A5
Valbonnais F 79 B4
Valbuena de Duero E 88 C2
Vâlcani RO 75 C5
Valdagno I 71 C6
Valdahon F 69 A6
Valdaracete E 95 B3
Valday RUS 7 C12
Valdealgorfa E 90 C2
Valdecaballeros E 93 B5
Valdecabras E 95 B4
Valdecarros E 94 B1
Valdeconcha E 95 B4
Valdeflores E 99 B4
Valdefresno E 88 B1
Valdeganga E 95 C5
Valdelacasa E 93 A5
Valdelacasa de Tajo E 93 B5
Valdelarco E 99 B4
Valdelosa E 94 A1
Valdeltormo E 90 C3
Valdelugeros E 88 B1
Valdemanco de Esteras E 94 D2
Valdemarsvik S 37 D3
Valdemorillo E 94 B2
Valdemoro E 94 B3
Valdemoro Sierra E 95 B5
Valdenoceda E 89 B3
Valdeobispo E 93 A4
Valdeolivas E 95 B4
Valdepeñas E 100 A2
Valdepeñas de Jaén E 100 B2
Valdepiélago E 88 B1
Valdepolo E 88 B1
Valderas E 88 B1
Valdérice I 108 A1
Valderrobres E 90 C3
Valderrueda E 88 B2
Valdestillas E 88 C2
Valdetorres E 93 C4
Valdetorres de Jarama E 95 B3
Valdeverdeja E 93 B5
Valdevimbre E 88 B1
Valdieri I 80 B1
Valdilecha E 95 B3
Valdobbiádene I 72 C1
Valdocondes E 89 C3
Valdoviño E 86 A2
Vale de Açor, *Beja* P 98 B3
Vale de Açor, *Portalegre* P 92 B3
Vale de Agua P 98 B2
Vale de Cambra P 87 D2
Vale de Lobo P 98 B2
Vale de Prazeres P 92 A3
Vale de Reis P 92 C2
Vale de Rosa P 98 B3
Vale de Santarém P 92 B2
Vale de Vargo P 98 B3
Vale do Peso P 92 B3
Valea lui Mihai RO 11 C7
Valega P 87 D2
Valéggio sul Mincio I 71 C5
Valeiro P 92 C2
Valença P 87 B2
Valençay F 67 A6
Valence, *Charente* F 67 C5
Valence, *Drôme* F 78 B3
Valence d'Agen F 77 B3
Valence-d'Albigeois F 77 B5
Valence-sur-Baise F 77 C3
Valencia E 96 B2
Valencia de Alcántara E 93 B3
Valencia de Don Juan E 88 B1
Valencia de las Torres E 93 C4
Valencia de Mombuey E 99 A3
Valencia del Ventoso E 99 A4
Valenciennes F 49 C4
Valensole F 79 C4
Valentano I 102 A4
Valentigney F 70 A1
Valentine F 77 C3
Valenza I 80 A2
Valenzuela E 100 B1
Valenzuela de Calatrava E 100 A2
Våler, *Hedmark* N 34 B3
Våler, *Østfold* N 35 C2
Valera de Abajo E 95 C4
Valeria E 95 C4
Valestrand N 33 C2
Valestrandfossen N 32 B2
Valevåg N 33 C2
Valfabbrica I 82 C1
Valflaunes F 78 C2
Valga EST 7 C9
Valgorge F 78 B3
Valgrisenche I 70 C2
Valguarnera Caropepe I 109 B3
Valhelhas P 92 A3
Valjevo SRB 85 B4
Valka LV 7 C8
Valkeakoski FIN 3 F26
Valkenburg NL 50 C1
Valkenswaard NL 49 B6
Valkó H 75 A4
Vall d'Alba E 96 A2
Valla S 37 C3
Vallada E 96 C2
Vallado E 86 A4
Valladolid E 88 C2
Vallåkra S 41 D2
Vallata I 103 B8
Vallberga S 40 C3
Valldemossa E 97 B2
Valle N 33 C4
Valle Castellana I 82 D2
Valle de Abdalajís E 100 C1
Valle de Cabuérniga E 88 A2
Valle de la Serena E 93 C5
Valle de Matamoros E 93 C4
Valle de Santa Ana E 93 C4
Valle Mosso I 70 C3
Valledolmo I 108 B2
Valledoria I 110 B1
Vallelado E 88 C2
Vallelunga Pratameno I 108 B2
Vallendar D 50 C3
Vallentuna S 37 C5
Vallerås S 34 B5
Valleraugue F 78 B2
Vallermosa I 110 C1
Vallet F 66 A3
Valletta M 107 C5
Valley GB 26 B1
Vallfogona de Riucorb E 91 B4
Valli del Pasúbio I 71 C6
Vallo della Lucánia I 103 C8
Valloire F 69 C6
Vallombrosa I 81 C5
Vallon-Pont-d'Arc F 78 B3
Vallorbe CH 69 B6
Vallouise F 79 B5
Valls E 91 B4
Vallset N 34 B3
Vallsta S 36 A3
Vallstena S 37 E5
Valmadrid E 90 B2
Valmiera LV 7 C8
Valmojado E 94 B2
Valmont F 58 A1
Valmontone I 102 B5
Valö S 36 B5
Valognes F 57 A4
Valongo P 92 A2
Valongo P 87 C2
Válor E 100 C2
Valoria la Buena E 88 C2
Valøy N 114 C7
Valozhyn BY 7 D9
Valpaços P 87 C3
Valpelline I 70 C2
Valpiana I 81 C4
Valpovo HR 74 C3
Valras-Plage F 78 C2
Valréas F 78 B3
Vals CH 71 B4
Vals-les-Bains F 78 B3
Valsavarenche I 70 C2
Vålse DK 39 E4
Valsequillo E 93 C5
Valsjöbyn S 115 C11
Valsonne F 69 C4
Valstagna I 72 C1
Valtablado del Rio E 95 B4
Valþjofsstaður IS 111 B11
Valtice CZ 64 B2
Valtiendas E 88 C3
Valtierra E 89 B5
Valtopina I 82 C1
Valtorta I 71 C4
Valtournenche I 70 C2
Valverde E 89 C5
Valverde de Burguillos E 93 C4
Valverde de Júcar E 95 C4
Valverde de la Vera E 93 A5
Valverde de la Virgen E 88 B1
Valverde de Llerena E 99 A5
Valverde de Mérida E 93 C4
Valverde del Camino E 99 B4
Valverde del Fresno E 93 A4
Vamberk CZ 53 C6
Vamdrup DK 39 D2
Våmhus S 34 A6
Vamlingbo S 37 F5
Vammala FIN 3 F25
Vamos GR 117 G6
Vámosmikola H 65 C4
Vámosszabadi H 64 C3
Vanault-les-Dames F 59 B5
Vandel DK 39 D2
Vandenesse F 68 B3
Vandenesse-en-Auxois F 69 A4
Vandóies I 72 B1
Väne-Åsaka S 35 D4
Vänersborg S 35 D4
Vänersnäs S 35 D4
Vang N 32 A5
Vänge S 36 C4
Vangsnes N 32 A3
Vänjaurbäck S 115 C15
Vännacka S 35 C4
Vannareid N 112 B8
Vännäs S 115 D16
Vannes F 56 C3
Vannsätter S 36 A3
Vannvåg N 112 B8
Vansbro S 34 B6
Vanse N 33 D3
Vantaa FIN 6 A8
Vanviken N 114 D7
Vanyarc H 65 C5
Vaour F 77 B4
Vapnyarka UA 11 B10
Vaprio d'Adda I 71 C4
Vaqueiros P 98 B3
Vara S 35 D4
Varacieux F 69 C5
Varades F 66 A3
Varages F 79 C4
Varaldsøy N 32 B2
Varallo I 70 C3
Varangerbotn N 113 B17
Varano de'Melegari I 81 B4
Varaždin HR 73 B6
Varaždinske Toplice HR 73 B6
Varazze I 80 B2
Varberg S 40 B2
Vardal N 34 B2
Varde DK 39 D1
Vårdö FIN 36 B7
Vardø N 113 B20
Vardomb H 74 B3
Varel D 43 B5
Varėna LT 6 D8
Vårenes N 33 C2
Varengeville-sur-Mer F 58 A1
Varenna I 71 B4
Varennes-en-Argonne F 59 A6
Varennes-le-Grand F 69 B4
Varennes-St. Sauveur F 69 B5
Varennes-sur-Allier F 68 B3
Varennes-sur-Amance F 60 C1
Vareš BIH 84 B3
Varese I 70 C3
Varese Ligure I 80 B3
Vârfurile RO 11 C7
Vårgårda S 40 A2
Vargas E 88 A3
Vargas P 92 B2
Vargön S 35 D4
Varhaug N 33 D2
Variaş RO 75 B5
Variaşu Mic RO 75 B6
Varilhes F 77 C4
Varin SK 65 A4
Väring S 35 D5
Váriz P 87 C4
Varkaus FIN 3 E27
Varmahlíð IS 111 B6
Varmaland IS 111 C4
Värmlands Bro S 35 C5
Värmskog S 35 C4
Varna BG 11 E9
Varna SRB 85 B4
Värnamo S 40 B4
Varnhem S 35 D5
Varnsdorf CZ 53 C4
Värö S 40 B2
Varoška Rijeka BIH 83 A5
Városlöd H 74 A2
Várpalota H 74 A3
Varreddes F 59 B3
Vars F 79 B5
Varsi I 81 B3
Varsseveld NL 50 B2
Vårsta S 37 C4
Vartdal N 114 E3
Vartofta S 35 D5
Varvarin SRB 85 C6
Vårvik S 35 C4
Várvölgy H 74 B2
Varzi I 80 B3
Varzjelas P 92 A2
Varzo I 70 B3
Varzy F 68 A3
Vasad H 75 A4
Väse S 35 C5
Vašica SRB 85 A4
Vasilevichi BY 7 E10
Väskinde S 37 E5
Vaskút H 75 B3
Vaslui RO 11 C9
Vassbotn N 33 D5
Vassenden N 32 A6
Vassieux-en-Vercors F 79 B4
Vassmolösa S 40 C6
Vassy F 57 B5
Västansjö S 115 B12
Västanvik S 36 B1
Västerås S 37 C3
Västerby S 36 B2
Västerfärnebo S 36 C3
Västergarn S 37 E5
Västerhaninge S 37 C5
Västervik S 40 B6
Vasto I 103 A7
Västra Ämtervik S 35 C5
Västra-Bodarne S 40 B2
Västra Karup S 41 C2
Vasvár H 74 A1
Vasylkiv UA 11 A11
Vát H 74 A1
Vatan F 68 A1
Väte S 37 E5
Vathia GR 117 F4
Vatican City = Città del Vaticano I 102 B5
Vatili CY 120 A2
Vatin SRB 75 C6
Vatland N 33 D4
Vatnar N 33 C6
Vatnås N 32 C6
Vatne N 33 D4
Vatnestrøm N 33 D5
Vätö S 36 C5
Vatra-Dornei RO 11 C8
Vatry F 59 B5
Vattholma S 36 B4
Vättis CH 71 B4
Vauchamps F 59 B4
Vauchassis F 59 B4
Vaucouleurs F 60 B1
Vaudoy-en-Brie F 59 B4
Vaulen N 33 D2
Vaulruz CH 70 B1
Vaulx Vraucourt F 48 C3
Vaumas F 68 B3
Vausseroux F 67 B4
Vauvenargues F 79 C4
Vauvert F 78 C3
Vauvillers F 60 C2
Vaux-sur-Sure B 60 A1
Vawkavysk BY 6 E8
Vaxholm S 37 C5
Växjö S 40 C4
Våxtorp S 41 C3
Vayrac F 77 B4
Važec SK 65 A5
Veberöd S 41 D3
Vechelde D 51 A6
Vechta D 43 C5
Vecinos E 94 B1
Vecsés H 75 A4
Vedavågen N 33 C2
Veddige S 40 B2
Vedersø DK 39 C1
Vedeseta I 71 C4
Vedevåg S 37 C2
Vedra E 86 B2
Vedum S 35 D4
Veendam NL 42 B3
Veenendaal NL 49 A6
Vega, *Asturias* E 88 A1
Vega, *Asturias* E 88 A1
Vega de Espinareda E 86 B4
Vega de Infanzones E 88 B1
Vega de Pas E 88 A3
Vega de Valcarce E 86 B4
Vega de Valdetronco E 88 C1
Vegadeo E 86 A3
Vegårshei N 33 D5
Vegas de Coria E 93 A4
Vegas del Condado E 88 B1
Vegby S 40 B3
Vegger DK 38 C2
Veggli N 32 B6
Veghel NL 49 B6
Veglast D 45 A4
Véglie I 105 C3
Veguillas E 95 B3
Vegusdal N 33 D5
Veidholmen N 114 D4
Veidnes N 113 B15
Veikåker N 34 B1
Veinge S 40 C3
Vejbystrand S 41 C2
Vejen DK 39 D2
Vejer de la Frontera E 99 C5
Vejle DK 39 D2
Vejprty CZ 52 C3
Vela Luka HR 83 D5
Velada E 94 B2
Velayos E 94 B2
Velbert D 50 B3
Velburg D 62 A2
Velde N 114 C8
Velden, *Bayern* D 62 A2
Velden, *Bayern* D 62 B3
Velden am Worther See A 73 B4
Velefique E 101 B3
Velen D 50 B2
Velenje SLO 73 B5
Veles MK 116 A3
Velesevec HR 73 C6
Velešin CZ 63 B5
Velestino GR 116 C4
Velez Blanco E 101 B3
Vélez de Benaudalla E 100 C2
Vélez-Málaga E 100 C1
Vélez Rubio E 101 B3
Veli Lošinj HR 83 B3
Veliiki Radinci SRB 85 A4
Velika HR 74 C2
Velika MNE 85 D4
Velika Drenova SRB 85 C6
Velika Gorica HR 73 C6
Velika Grdevac HR 74 C2
Velika Greda SRB 75 C6
Velika Ilova BIH 84 B2
Velika Kladuša BIH 73 C5
Velika Kopanica HR 74 C3
Velika Krsna SRB 85 B5
Velika Obarska BIH 85 B4
Velika Pisanica HR 74 C2
Velika Plana, *Srbija* SRB 85 B6
Velika Plana, *Srbija* SRB 85 C6
Velika Zdenci HR 74 C2
Velike Lašče SLO 73 C4
Veliki Gaj SRB 75 C6
Veliki Popović SRB 85 B6
Veliki Šiljegovac SRB 85 C6
Velikiye Luki RUS 7 C11
Veliko Gradište SRB 85 B6
Veliko Orašje SRB 85 B6
Veliko Selo SRB 85 B6
Veliko Tŭrnovo BG 11 E8
Velilla de San Antonio E 95 B3
Velilla del Río Carrió E 88 B2
Velipojë AL 105 B5
Velizh RUS 7 D11
Veljun HR 73 C5
Velká Bíteš CZ 64 A2
Velká Hleďscbe CZ 52 D2
Velká Lomnica SK 65 A6
Velká nad Veličkou CZ 64 B3
Velké Bystřice CZ 64 A3
Velké Heraltice CZ 54 D2
Velké Karlovice CZ 64 A4
Vel'ké Leváre SK 64 B3
Velké Losiny CZ 54 C2
Velké Meziříčí CZ 64 A2
Velké Pavlovice CZ 64 B2
Vel'ké Rovné SK 65 A4
Vel'ké Uherce SK 65 B4
Vel'ké Zálužie SK 64 B3
Vel'ke'Kostol'any SK 64 B3

Vinga RO 75 B6
Vingåker S 37 C2
Vingnes N 34 A2
Vingrau F 78 D1
Vingrom N 34 A2
Vinhais P 87 C4
Vinica HR 73 B6
Vinica SK 65 B5
Vinica SLO 73 C5
Vinicka MNE 85 D4
Viniegra de Arriba E 89 B4
Vinje, *Hordaland* N 32 B3
Vinje, *Sør-Trøndelag* N 114 D6
Vinje, *Telemark* N 33 C4
Vinkovci HR 74 C3
Vinliden S 115 C14
Vinninga S 35 D5
Vinnytsya UA 11 B10
Vinon F 68 A2
Vinon-sur-Verdon F 79 C4
Vinslöv S 41 C3
Vintjärn S 36 B3
Vintrosa S 37 C1
Viñuela E 100 C1
Viñuela de Sayago E 87 C5
Viñuelas E 95 B3
Vinuesa E 89 C4
Vinzelberg D 44 C3
Viöl D 43 A6
Viola I 80 B1
Violay F 69 C4
Vipava SLO 72 C3
Vipiteno I 71 B6
Vipperow D 45 B4
Vir BIH 84 C2
Vir HR 83 B4
Vira CH 70 B3
Vire F 57 B5
Vireda S 40 B4
Vireux F 49 C5
Virgen A 72 A2
Virgen de la Cabeza E 100 A1
Virginia IRL 19 C4
Virieu F 69 C5
Virieu-le-Grand F 69 C5
Virje HR 74 B1
Virklund DK 39 C2
Virovitica HR 74 C2
Virpazar MNE 105 A5
Virsbo S 36 C3
Virserum S 40 B5
Virtaniemi FIN 113 D17
Virton B 60 A1
Virtsu EST 6 B7
Viry F 69 B6
Vis HR 83 C5
Visbek D 43 C5
Visby DK 39 D1
Visby S 37 E5
Visé B 50 C1
Višegrad BIH 85 C4
Viserba I 82 B1
Viseu P 92 A3
Visiedo E 90 C1
Viskafors S 40 B2
Visland N 33 D3
Vislanda S 40 C4
Visnes N 33 C2
Višnja Gora SLO 73 C4
Višnjan HR 72 C3
Višnové CZ 64 B2
Visnums-Kil S 35 C6
Viso del Marqués E 100 A2
Visoko BIH 84 C3
Visoko SLO 73 B4
Visone I 80 B2
Visp CH 70 B2
Vissefjärda S 40 C5
Visselhövede D 43 C6
Vissenbjerg DK 39 D3
Visso I 82 D2
Vistabella del Maestrat E 96 A2
Vita I 108 B1
Vitanje SLO 73 B5
Vitanovac SRB 85 C5
Vitebsk = Vitsyebsk BY 7 D11
Viterbo I 102 A5
Vitez BIH 84 B2
Vithkuq AL 116 B2
Vitigudino E 87 C4
Vitina BIH 84 C2
Vitina GR 117 E4
Vitis A 63 B6
Vitkov CZ 64 A3
Vitkovac SRB 85 C5
Vitomirica KOS 85 D5
Vitoria-Gasteiz E 89 B4
Vitré F 57 B4
Vitrey-sur-Mance F 60 C1
Vitry-en-Artois F 48 C3
Vitry-le-François F 59 B5
Vitry-sur-Seine F 58 B3
Vitsand S 34 B4
Vitsyebsk = Vitebsk BY 7 D11
Vittangi S 113 E10
Vittaryd S 40 C3
Vitteaux F 69 A4
Vittel F 60 B1
Vittinge S 36 C4
Vittória I 109 C3
Vittório Véneto I 72 C2
Vittsjö S 41 C3
Viù I 70 C2
Viul N 34 B2
Vivario F 102 A2
Viveiro E 86 A3
Vivel del Rio Martin E 90 C2
Viver E 96 B2
Viverols F 68 C3
Viveros E 101 A3
Viviers F 78 B3
Vivonne F 67 B5
Vivy F 67 A4
Vize TR 118 A2
Vizille F 79 A4
Viziñada HR 72 C3
Viziru RO 11 D9
Vizovice CZ 64 A3
Vizvár H 74 B2
Vizzavona F 102 A2
Vizzini I 109 B3
Vlachiotis GR 117 F4
Vlachovice CZ 64 A3
Vlachovo SK 65 B6
Vláchovo Březi CZ 63 A4
Vladimirci SRB 85 B4
Vladimirovac SRB 85 A5
Vladislav CZ 64 A1
Vlagtwedde NL 43 B4
Vlajkovac SRB 85 A6
Vlasenica BIH 84 B3
Vlašim CZ 63 A5
Vlatkovići BIH 84 B2
Vledder NL 42 C3
Vlissingen NL 49 B4
Vlkolínec SK 65 A5
Vlorë AL 105 C5
Vlotho D 51 A4
Vnanje Gorice SLO 73 C4
Vobarno I 71 C5
Voćin HR 74 C2
Vöcklabruck A 63 B4
Vöcklamarkt A 63 C4
Vodanj SRB 85 B5
Voderady SK 64 B3
Vodice, *Istarska* HR 73 C4
Vodice, *Šibenska* HR 83 C4
Vodice SLO 73 B4
Vodňany CZ 63 A5
Vodnjan HR 82 B2
Vodskov DK 38 B3
Voe GB 22 A7
Voerså DK 38 B3
Voghera I 80 B3
Vogogna I 70 B3
Vogošća BIH 84 C3
Vogüé F 78 B3
Vohburg D 62 B2
Vohenstrauss D 62 A3
Vöhl D 51 B4
Vöhrenbach D 61 B4
Vöhringen D 61 B6
Void-Vacon F 60 B1
Voiron F 69 C5
Voise F 58 B2
Voisey F 60 C1
Voiteg RO 75 C6
Voiteur F 69 B5
Voitsberg A 73 A5
Vojens DK 39 D2
Vojka SRB 85 B5
Vojlovica SRB 85 B5
Vojnić HR 73 C5
Vojnice SK 65 C4
Vojnik SLO 73 B5
Vojvoda Stepa SRB 75 C5
Volada GR 119 G2
Volargne I 71 C5
Volary CZ 63 B4
Volče SLO 72 B3
Volda N 114 E3
Volendam NL 42 C2
Volga RUS 7 B15
Volimes GR 117 E2
Volissos GR 116 D7
Volkach D 61 A6
Völkermarkt A 73 B4
Volkhov RUS 7 B12
Völklingen D 60 A2
Volkmarsen D 51 B5
Voll N 114 E4
Vollenhove NL 42 C2
Vollore-Montagne F 68 C3
Vollsjö S 41 D3
Volodymyr-Volyns'kyy UA 11 A8
Volokolamsk RUS 7 C13
Volos GR 116 C4
Volosovo RUS 7 B10
Volovets UA 11 B7
Volta Mantovana I 71 C5
Voltággio I 80 B2
Volterra I 81 C4
Voltri I 80 B2
Volturara Áppula I 103 B8
Volturara Irpina I 103 C7
Volvic F 68 C3
Volx F 79 C4
Volyně CZ 63 A4
Vonitsa GR 116 D2
Vönöck H 74 A2
Vonsild DK 39 D2
Voorschoten NL 49 A5
Vopnafjörður IS 111 B11
Vorau A 73 A5
Vorbasse DK 39 D2
Vorchdorf A 63 C4
Vorden D 43 C5
Vorden NL 50 A2
Vordernberg A 73 A4
Vordingborg DK 39 D4
Vorë AL 105 B5
Voreppe F 69 C5
Vorey F 68 C3
Vorgod DK 39 C1
Vormsund N 34 B3
Voronezh UA 7 F12
Võru EST 7 C9
Voskopojë AL 116 B2
Voss N 32 B3
Votice CZ 63 A5
Voué F 59 B5
Vouillé F 67 B5
Voulx F 59 B3
Voussac F 68 B3
Vouvray F 67 A5
Vouvry CH 70 B1
Vouzela P 87 D2
Vouziers F 59 A5
Voves F 58 B2
Voxna S 36 A2
Voy GB 23 B5
Voynitsa RUS 3 D29
Voznesensk UA 11 C11
Voznesenye RUS 7 A13
Vrå DK 38 B2
Vrå S 40 C3
Vráble SK 64 B4
Vračenovići MNE 84 D3
Vračev Gaj SRB 85 B6
Vraćevsnica SRB 85 B5
Vrådal N 33 C5
Vrakneika GR 117 D3
Vrana HR 83 B4
Vranduk BIH 84 B2
Vrångö S 38 B4
Vrani RO 85 A6
Vranić SRB 85 B5
Vraniči BIH 84 C3
Vranja HR 73 C4
Vranjak BIH 84 B3
Vranje SRB 10 E6
Vranov nad Dyje CZ 64 B1
Vranovice CZ 64 B2
Vransko SLO 73 B4
Vrapčići BIH 84 C2
Vratimov CZ 64 A4
Vratsa BG 11 E7
Vrbanja HR 84 B3
Vrbanjci BIH 84 B2
Vrbas SRB 75 C4
Vrbaška BIH 84 A2
Vrbnik, *Primorsko-Goranska* HR 83 A3
Vrbnik, *Zadarsko-Kninska* HR 83 B5
Vrbno pod Pradědem CZ 54 C2
Vrboska HR 83 C5
Vrbov SK 65 A6
Vrbovce SK 64 B3
Vrbové SK 64 B3
Vrbovec HR 73 C6
Vrbovski SRB 85 B5
Vrbovsko HR 73 C5
Vrchlabí CZ 53 C5
Vrčin SRB 85 B5
Vrdy CZ 63 A6
Vrebac HR 83 B4
Vreden D 50 A2
Vrela KOS 85 D5
Vreoci SRB 85 B5
Vretstorp S 37 C1
Vrginmost HR 73 C5
Vrgorac HR 84 C2
Vrhnika SLO 73 C4
Vrhovine HR 83 B4
Vrhpolje SRB 85 B4
Vriezenveen NL 42 C3
Vrigne-aux-Bois F 59 A5
Vrigstad S 40 B4
Vrlika HR 83 C5
Vrmbaje SRB 85 C5
Vrnjačka Banja SRB 85 C5
Vrnograč BIH 73 C5
Vron F 48 C2
Vroomshoop NL 42 C3
Vroutek CZ 52 C3
Vrpolje HR 74 C3
Vršac SRB 85 A6
Vrsar HR 82 A2
Vrsi HR 83 B4
Vrtoče BIH 83 B5
Vrútky SK 65 A4
Všeruby CZ 62 A3
Všestary CZ 53 C5
Vsetín CZ 64 A3
Vuča MNE 85 D5
Vučitrn KOS 85 D5
Vučkovica SRB 85 C5
Vught NL 49 B6
Vuillafans F 69 A6
Vukovar HR 75 C4
Vuku N 114 D8
Vulcan RO 11 D7
Vulcaneşti MD 11 D10
Vuoggatjålme S 112 F5
Vuojärvi FIN 113 E15
Vuolijoki FIN 3 D27
Vuotso FIN 113 D16
Vuzenica SLO 73 B5
Vy-lès Lure F 60 C2
Vyartsilya RUS 3 E29
Vyazma RUS 7 D13
Vyborg RUS 3 F28
Výčapy CZ 64 A1
Výčapy-Opatovce SK 64 B4
Východna SK 65 A5
Vydrany SK 64 B3
Vyerkhnyadzvinsk BY 7 D9
Vyhne SK 65 B4
Vylkove UA 11 D10
Vynohradiv UA 11 B7
Vyshniy Volochek RUS 7 C13
Vyškov CZ 64 A3
Vysoká nad Kysucou SK 65 A4
Vysoké Mýto CZ 53 D6
Vysokovsk RUS 7 C14
Vyšší Brod CZ 63 B5
Vytegra RUS 7 A14

W

Waabs D 44 A1
Waalwijk NL 49 B6
Waarschoot B 49 B4
Wabern D 51 B5
Wąbrzeźno PL 47 B4
Wąchock PL 55 B6
Wachow D 45 C4
Wachów PL 54 C3
Wächtersbach D 51 C5
Wackersdorf D 62 A3
Waddington GB 27 B5
Wadebridge GB 28 C3
Wadelsdorf D 53 B4
Wädenswil CH 70 A3
Wadern D 60 A2
Wadersloh D 50 B4
Wadlew PL 55 B4
Wadowice PL 65 A5
Wagenfeld D 43 C5
Wageningen NL 49 B6
Waghäusel D 61 A4
Waging D 62 C3
Wagrain A 72 A3
Wagrowiec PL 46 C3
Wahlsdorf D 52 B3
Wahlstedt D 44 B2
Wahrenholz D 44 C2
Waiblingen D 61 B5
Waidhaus D 62 A3
Waidhofen an der Thaya A 63 B6
Waidhofen an der Ybbs A 63 C5
Waimes B 50 C2
Wainfleet All Saints GB 27 B6
Waizenkirchen A 63 B4
Wakefield GB 27 B4
Wałbrzych PL 53 C6
Walchensee D 62 C2
Walchsee A 62 C3
Wałcz PL 46 B2
Wald CH 70 A3
Wald-Michelbach D 61 A4
Waldaschaff D 51 D5
Waldbach A 73 A5
Waldböckelheim D 60 A3
Waldbröl D 50 C3
Waldeck D 51 B5
Waldenburg D 52 C2
Waldfischbach-Burgalben D 60 A3
Waldheim D 52 B3
Waldkappel D 51 B5
Waldkirch D 60 B3
Waldkirchen D 63 B4
Waldkirchen am Wesen A 63 B4
Waldkraiburg D 62 B3
Waldmohr D 60 A3
Waldmünchen D 62 A3
Waldring A 62 C3
Waldsassen D 52 C2
Waldshut D 61 C4
Waldstatt CH 71 A4
Waldwisse F 60 A2
Walenstadt CH 71 A4
Walentynów PL 55 B6
Walichnowy PL 54 B3
Walincourt F 49 C4
Walkenried D 51 B6
Walkeringham GB 27 B5
Wallasey GB 26 B2
Walldürn D 61 A5
Wallenfells D 52 C1
Wallenhorst D 43 C5
Wallers F 49 C4
Wallersdorf D 62 B3
Wallerstein D 61 B6
Wallingford GB 31 C2
Wallitz D 45 B4
Walls GB 22 A7
Wallsbüll D 39 E2
Walmer GB 31 C5
Walsall GB 27 C4
Walshoutem B 49 C6
Walsrode D 43 C6
Waltenhofen D 61 C6
Waltershausen D 51 C6
Waltham Abbey GB 31 C4
Waltham on the Wolds GB 30 B3
Walton-on-Thames GB 31 C3
Walton-on-the-Naze GB 31 C5
Wamba E 88 C2
Wanderup D 43 A6
Wandlitz D 45 C5
Wanfried D 51 B6
Wangen im Allgäu D 61 C5
Wangerooge D 43 B4
Wangersen D 43 B6
Wängi CH 70 A3
Wanna D 43 B5
Wansford GB 30 B3
Wantage GB 31 C2
Wanzleben D 52 A1
Waplewo PL 47 B6
Wapnica PL 46 B1
Wapno PL 46 C3
Warburg D 51 B5
Wardenburg D 43 B5
Ware GB 31 C3
Waregem B 49 C4
Wareham GB 29 C5
Waremme B 49 C6
Waren D 45 B4
Warendorf D 50 B3
Warga NL 42 B2
Warin D 44 B3
Wark GB 25 C5
Warka PL 55 B6
Warkworth GB 25 C6
Warlubie PL 47 B4
Warminster GB 29 B5
Warnemünde D 44 A4
Warnow D 44 B3
Warnsveld NL 50 A2
Warrenpoint GB 19 B5
Warrington GB 26 B3
Warsaw = Warszawa PL 55 A6
Warsingsfehn D 43 B4
Warsow D 44 B3
Warstein D 51 B4
Warszawa = Warsaw PL 55 A6
Warta PL 54 B3
Wartberg A 63 C5
Warth A 71 A5
Warwick GB 30 B2
Warza D 51 C6
Wasbister GB 23 B5
Washington GB 25 D6
Wąsosz PL 54 B1
Wasselonne F 60 B3
Wassen CH 70 B3
Wassenaar NL 49 A5
Wasserauen CH 71 A4
Wasserburg D 62 B3
Wassertrüdingen D 62 A1
Wassy F 59 B5
Wasungen D 51 C6
Watchet GB 29 B4
Waterford IRL 21 B4
Watergrasshill IRL 20 B3
Waterloo B 49 C5
Waterville IRL 20 C1
Watford GB 31 C3
Wathlingen D 44 C2
Watten F 48 C3
Watten GB 23 C5
Wattens A 72 A1
Watton GB 30 B4
Wattwil CH 71 A4
Waunfawr GB 26 B1
Wavignies F 58 A3
Wavre B 49 C5
Wearhead GB 25 D5
Wechadlow PL 55 C5
Wedel D 43 B6
Wedemark D 43 C6
Weedon Bec GB 30 B2
Weener D 43 B4
Weert NL 50 B1
Weesp NL 49 A6
Weeze D 50 B2
Weferlingen D 52 A1
Wegeleben D 52 B1
Weggis CH 70 A3
Węgierska-Górka PL 65 A5
Wegliniec PL 53 B5
Węgorzyno PL 46 B1
Węgrzynice PL 53 A5
Wegscheid D 63 B4
Wehdel D 43 B5
Wehr D 60 C3
Weibersbrunn D 61 A5
Weichering D 62 B2
Weida D 52 C2
Weiden D 62 A3
Weidenberg D 52 D1
Weidenhain D 52 B2
Weidenstetten D 61 B5
Weierbach D 60 A3
Weikersheim D 61 A5
Weil D 62 B1
Weil am Rhein D 60 C3
Weil der Stadt D 61 B4
Weilburg D 50 C4
Weilerswist D 50 C2
Weilheim, *Baden-Württemberg* D 61 B5
Weilheim, *Bayern* D 62 C2
Weilmünster D 51 C4
Weiltensfeld A 73 B4
Weimar D 52 C1
Weinberg D 61 A6
Weinfelden CH 71 A4
Weingarten, *Baden-Württemberg* D 61 A4
Weingarten, *Baden-Württemberg* D 61 C5
Weinheim D 61 A4
Weinstadt D 61 B5
Weismain D 52 C1
Weissbriach A 72 B3
Weissenbach A 71 A5
Weissenberg D 53 B4
Weissenbrunn D 52 C1
Weissenburg D 62 A1
Weissenfels D 52 B1
Weissenhorn D 61 B6
Weissenkirchen A 63 B6
Weissensee D 52 B1
Weissenstadt D 52 C1
Weisskirchen im Steiermark A 73 A4
Weisstannen CH 71 B4
Weisswasser D 53 B4
Weitendorf D 44 B4
Weitersfeld A 64 B1
Weitersfelden A 63 B5
Weitnau D 61 C6
Wéitra A 63 B5
Weiz A 73 A5
Wejherowo PL 47 A4
Welkenraedt B 50 C1
Wellaune D 52 B2
Wellin B 49 C6
Wellingborough GB 30 B3
Wellington, *Somerset* GB 29 C4
Wellington, *Telford & Wrekin* GB 26 C3
Wellingtonbridge IRL 21 B5
Wells GB 29 B5
Wells-next-the-Sea GB 30 B4
Wels A 63 B5
Welschenrohr CH 70 A2
Welshpool GB 26 C2
Welver D 50 B3
Welwyn Garden City GB 31 C3
Welzheim D 61 B5
Welzow D 53 B4
Wem GB 26 C3
Wembury GB 28 C3
Wemding D 62 B1
Wenden D 50 C3
Wendisch Rietz D 53 A4
Wendlingen D 61 B5
Weng A 63 B4
Weng bei Admont A 63 C5
Wengen CH 70 B2
Wenigzell A 73 A5
Wennigsen D 51 A5
Wenns A 71 A5
Wenzenbach D 62 A3
Weppersdorf A 64 C2
Werben D 44 C3
Werbig D 52 B3
Werdau D 52 C2
Werder D 45 C4
Werdohl D 50 B3
Werfen A 72 A3
Werkendam NL 49 B5
Werl D 50 B3
Werlte D 43 C4
Wermelskirchen D 50 B3
Wermsdorf D 52 B2
Wernberg Köblitz D 62 A3
Werne D 50 B3
Werneck D 51 D6
Werneuchen D 45 C5
Wernigerode D 51 B6
Wertach D 61 C6
Wertheim D 61 A5
Wertingen D 62 B1
Weseke D 50 B2
Wesel D 50 B2
Wesenberg D 45 B4
Wesendorf D 44 C2
Wesołowo PL 47 B6
Wesselburen D 43 A5
Wesseling D 50 C2
West Bridgford GB 27 C4
West Bromwich GB 27 C4
West Haddon GB 30 B2
West Kilbride GB 24 C3
West Linton GB 25 C4
West Lulworth GB 29 C5
West Mersea GB 31 C4
West-Terschelling NL 42 B2
West Woodburn GB 25 C5
Westbury, *Shropshire* GB 26 C3
Westbury, *Wiltshire* GB 29 B5
Westbury-on-Severn GB 29 B5
Westendorf A 72 A2
Westensee D 44 A1
Westerbork NL 42 C3
Westerburg D 50 C3
Westerhaar NL 42 C3
Westerholt D 43 B4
Westerkappeln D 50 A3
Westerland D 39 E1
Westerlo B 49 B5
Westerstede D 43 B4
Westheim D 62 A1
Westhill GB 23 D6
Westkapelle B 49 B4
Westkapelle NL 49 B4
Westminster GB 31 C3
Weston GB 26 C3
Weston-super-Mare GB 29 B5
Westport IRL 18 C2
Westruther GB 25 C5
Westward Ho! GB 28 B3
Wetheral GB 25 D5
Wetherby GB 27 B4
Wetter, *Hessen* D 51 C4
Wetter, *Nordrhein-Westfalen* D 50 B3
Wetteren B 49 B4
Wettin D 52 B1
Wettringen D 50 A3
Wetzikon CH 70 A3
Wetzlar D 51 C4
Wewelsfleth D 43 B6
Wexford IRL 21 B5
Weybridge GB 31 C3
Weyer Markt A 63 C5
Weyerbusch D 50 C3
Weyersheim F 60 B3
Weyhe D 43 C5
Weyhill GB 31 C2
Weymouth GB 29 C5
Weyregg A 63 C4
Węzyska PL 53 A4
Whalton GB 25 C6
Whauphill GB 24 D3
Wheatley GB 31 C2
Whickham GB 25 D6
Whipsnade GB 31 C3
Whitburn GB 25 C4
Whitby GB 27 A5
Whitchurch, *Hampshire* GB 31 C2
Whitchurch, *Herefordshire* GB 29 B5
Whitchurch, *Shropshire* GB 26 C3
White Bridge GB 23 D4
Whitegate IRL 20 C3
Whitehaven GB 26 A2
Whitehead GB 19 B6
Whithorn GB 24 D3
Whitley Bay GB 25 C6
Whitstable GB 31 C5
Whittington GB 26 C3
Whittlesey GB 30 B3
Wiązów PL 54 C2
Wiązowna PL 55 A6
Wick GB 23 C5
Wickede D 50 B3
Wickford GB 31 C4
Wickham GB 31 D2
Wickham Market GB 30 B5
Wicklow IRL 21 B5
Wicko PL 46 A3
Widawa PL 54 B3
Widdrington GB 25 C6
Widecombe in the Moor GB 28 C4
Widemouth GB 28 C3
Widnes GB 26 B3
Widuchowo PL 45 B6
Więcbork PL 46 B3
Wiefelstede D 43 B5
Wiehe D 52 B1
Wiehl D 50 C3
Wiek D 45 A5
Większyce PL 54 C2
Wiele PL 46 B3
Wieleń PL 46 C2
Wielgie, *Kujawsko-Pomorskie* PL 47 C5
Wielgie, *Łódzkie* PL 54 B3
Wielgie, *Mazowieckie* PL 55 B6
Wielgomłyny PL 55 B4
Wielichowo PL 54 A1
Wieliczka PL 55 D5
Wielka Łąka PL 47 B4
Wielowies PL 54 C3
Wieluń PL 54 B3
Wien = Vienna A 64 B2
Wiener Neustadt A 64 C2
Wiepke D 44 C3
Wierden NL 42 C3
Wieren D 44 C2
Wieruszów PL 54 B3
Wierzbica PL 55 B6
Wierzbie PL 54 B3
Wierzbięcin PL 45 B7
Wierzbno PL 55 A6
Wierzchowo PL 46 B2
Wierzchucino PL 47 A4
Wierzchy PL 54 B3
Wies A 73 B5
Wiesau D 62 A3
Wiesbaden D 50 C4
Wieselburg A 63 B6
Wiesen CH 71 B4
Wiesenburg D 52 A2
Wiesenfelden D 62 A3
Wiesensteig D 61 B5
Wiesentheid D 61 A6
Wiesloch D 61 A4
Wiesmath A 64 C2
Wiesmoor D 43 B4
Wietmarschen D 43 C4
Wietze D 44 C1
Wigan GB 26 B3
Wiggen CH 70 B2
Wigston GB 30 B2
Wigton GB 25 D4
Wigtown GB 24 D3
Wijchen NL 50 B1
Wijhe NL 42 C3
Wijk bij Duurstede NL 49 B6
Wil CH 70 A4
Wilamowice PL 65 A5
Wilczęta PL 47 A5
Wilczkowice PL 55 A4
Wilczna PL 54 A3
Wilczyn PL 47 C4
Wildalpen A 63 C5
Wildbad D 61 B4
Wildberg, *Baden-Württemberg* D 61 B4
Wildberg, *Brandenburg* D 45 C4
Wildegg CH 70 A3
Wildendürnbach A 64 B2
Wildeshausen D 43 C5
Wildon A 73 B5
Wilfersdorf A 64 B2
Wilga PL 55 B6
Wilhelmsburg A 63 B6
Wilhelmsburg D 45 B5
Wilhelmsdorf D 61 C5
Wilhelmshaven D 43 B5
Wilków PL 47 C6
Willebadessen D 51 B5
Willebroek B 49 B5
Willgottheim F 60 B3
Willhermsdorf D 62 A1

Name	Country	Page	Grid
Willich	D	50	B2
Willingen	D	51	B4
Willington	GB	25	D6
Willisau	CH	70	A3
Wilmslow	GB	26	B3
Wilsdruff	D	52	B3
Wilster	D	43	B6
Wilsum	D	42	C3
Wilton	GB	29	B6
Wiltz	L	50	D1
Wimborne Minster	GB	29	C6
Wimereux	F	48	C2
Wimmenau	F	60	B3
Wimmis	CH	70	B2
Wincanton	GB	29	B5
Winchcombe	GB	29	B6
Winchelsea	GB	31	D4
Winchester	GB	31	C2
Windermere	GB	26	A3
Windisch-eschenbach	D	62	A3
Windischgarsten	A	63	C5
Windorf	D	63	B4
Windsbach	D	62	A1
Windsor	GB	31	C3
Windygates	GB	25	B4
Wingene	B	49	B4
Wingham	GB	31	C5
Winkleigh	GB	28	C4
Winklern	A	72	B2
Winnenden	D	61	B5
Winnigstedt	D	51	A6
Winnweiler	D	60	A3
Winschoten	NL	43	B4
Winsen, Niedersachsen	D	44	B2
Winsen, Niedersachsen	D	44	C1
Winsford	GB	26	B3
Wińsko	PL	54	B1
Winslow	GB	31	C3
Winsum, Friesland	NL	42	B2
Winsum, Groningen	NL	42	B3
Winterberg	D	51	B4
Winterfeld	D	44	C3
Winterswijk	NL	50	B2
Winterthur	CH	70	A3
Wintzenheim	F	60	B3
Winzer	D	62	B4
Wipperdorf	D	51	B6
Wipperfürth	D	50	B3
Wirksworth	GB	27	B4
Wisbech	GB	30	B4
Wischhafen	D	43	B6
Wishaw	GB	25	C4
Wisła	PL	65	A4
Wisła Wielka	PL	54	D3
Wislica	PL	55	C5
Wismar	D	44	B3
Wisniewo	PL	47	B6
Wiśniowa	PL	65	A6
Wissant	F	48	C2
Wissembourg	F	60	A3
Wissen	D	50	C3
Witanowice	PL	65	A5
Witham	GB	31	C4
Withern	GB	27	B6
Withernsea	GB	27	B6
Witkowo	PL	46	C3
Witmarsum	NL	42	B2
Witney	GB	31	C2
Witnica	PL	45	C6
Witonia	PL	55	A4
Witry-les-Reims	F	59	A5
Wittdün	D	43	A5
Wittelsheim	F	60	C3
Witten	D	50	B3
Wittenberge	D	44	B3
Wittenburg	D	44	B3
Wittenheim	F	60	C3
Wittichenau	D	53	B4
Wittighausen	D	61	A5
Wittingen	D	44	C2
Wittislingen	D	61	B6
Wittlich	D	50	D2
Wittmannsdorf	A	73	B5
Wittmund	D	43	B4
Wittorf	D	43	B6
Wittstock	D	44	B4
Witzenhausen	D	51	B5
Wiveliscombe	GB	29	B4
Wivenhoe	GB	31	C4
Władysławowo	PL	47	A4
Wleń	PL	53	B5
Włocławek	PL	47	C5
Włodawa	PL	6	F7
Włodzimierzów	PL	55	B5
Włosień	PL	53	B5
Włostow	PL	55	C6
Włoszakowice	PL	54	B1
Włoszczowa	PL	55	C4
Wöbbelin	D	44	B3
Woburn	GB	31	C3
Wodzisław	PL	55	C5
Wodzisław Śląski	PL	54	D3
Woerden	NL	49	A5
Woerth	F	60	B3
Wohlen	CH	70	A3
Woippy	F	60	A2
Wojciechy	PL	47	A6
Wojcieszow	PL	53	C5
Wojkowice Kościelne	PL	55	C5
Wojnicz	PL	55	D5
Woking	GB	31	C3
Wokingham	GB	31	C3
Wola Jachowa	PL	55	B5
Wola Niechcicka	PL	55	B4
Wolbórz	PL	55	B4
Wolbrom	PL	55	C4
Wołczyn	PL	54	B3
Woldegk	D	45	B5
Wolfach	D	61	B4
Wolfegg	D	61	C5
Wolfen	D	52	B2
Wolfenbüttel	D	51	A6
Wolfersheim	D	51	C4
Wolfhagen	D	51	B5
Wolfratshausen	D	62	C2
Wolf's Castle	GB	28	B3
Wolfsberg	A	73	B4
Wolfsburg	D	44	C2
Wolfshagen	D	45	B5
Wolfstein	D	60	A3
Wolfurt	A	71	A4
Wolgast	D	45	A5
Wolhusen	CH	70	A3
Wolin	PL	45	B6
Wolka	PL	55	B5
Wolkenstein	D	52	C3
Wolkersdorf	A	64	B2
Wöllersdorf	A	64	C2
Wollin	D	52	A2
Wöllstadt	D	51	C4
Wolmirstedt	D	52	A1
Wolnzach	D	62	B2
Wołomin	PL	55	A6
Wołów	PL	54	B1
Wolsztyn	PL	53	A6
Wolvega	NL	42	C2
Wolverhampton	GB	26	C3
Wolverton	GB	31	B3
Wombwell	GB	27	B4
Woodbridge	GB	30	B5
Woodhall Spa	GB	27	B5
Woodstock	GB	31	C2
Wookey Hole	GB	29	B5
Wool	GB	29	C5
Woolacombe	GB	28	B3
Wooler	GB	25	C5
Woolwich	GB	31	C4
Wooperton	GB	25	C6
Worb	CH	70	B2
Worbis	D	51	B6
Worcester	GB	29	A5
Wördern	A	64	B2
Wörgl	A	72	A2
Workington	GB	26	A2
Worksop	GB	27	B4
Workum	NL	42	C2
Wörlitz	D	52	B2
Wormer	NL	42	C1
Wormhout	F	48	C3
Wormit	GB	25	B5
Worms	D	61	A4
Worpswede	D	43	B5
Wörrstadt	D	61	A4
Wörschach	A	73	A4
Worsley	GB	26	B3
Wörth, Bayern	D	62	A3
Wörth, Bayern	D	61	A5
Wörth, Bayern	D	62	B3
Wörth, Rheinland-Pfalz	D	61	A4
Worthing	GB	31	D3
Woudsend	NL	42	C2
Woumen	B	48	B3
Woźniki	PL	55	C4
Wragby	GB	27	B5
Wrangle	GB	27	B6
Wręczyca Wlk.	PL	54	C3
Wredenhagen	D	44	B4
Wremen	D	43	B5
Wrentham	GB	30	B5
Wrexham	GB	26	B3
Wriedel	D	44	B2
Wriezen	D	45	C6
Wrist	D	43	B6
Wróblewo, Mazowieckie	PL	47	C6
Wróblewo, Wielkopolskie	PL	46	C2
Wrocki	PL	47	B5
Wrocław	PL	54	B2
Wronki	PL	46	C2
Wroxham	GB	30	B5
Września	PL	54	A2
Wrzosowo	PL	46	A1
Wschowa	PL	53	B6
Wulfen, Nordrhein-Westfalen	D	50	B3
Wülfen, Sachsen-Anhalt	D	52	B1
Wulkau	D	44	C4
Wünnenberg	D	51	B4
Wünsdorf	D	52	A3
Wunsiedel	D	52	C2
Wunstorf	D	43	C6
Wuppertal	D	50	B3
Wurmannsquick	D	62	B3
Würselen	D	50	C2
Wurzbach	D	52	C1
Würzburg	D	61	A5
Wurzen	D	52	B2
Wust	D	45	C4
Wusterhausen	D	44	C4
Wusterwitz	D	44	C4
Wustrau-Altfriesack	D	45	C4
Wustrow	D	44	A4
Wuustwezel	B	49	B5
Wye	GB	31	C4
Wyględów	PL	55	B6
Wyk	D	43	A5
Wykroty	PL	53	B5
Wylye	GB	29	B6
Wymiarki	PL	53	B5
Wymondham	GB	30	B5
Wyrzysk	PL	46	B3
Wyśmierzyce	PL	55	B5
Wysoka, Dolnośląskie	PL	53	B5
Wysoka, Wielkopolskie	PL	46	B3
Wyszanów	PL	54	B3
Wyszogród	PL	47	C6

X

Name	Country	Page	Grid
Xanten	D	50	B2
Xanthi	GR	116	A6
Xarrë	AL	116	C2
Xàtiva	E	96	C2
Xeraco	E	96	B2
Xert	E	90	C3
Xerta	E	90	C3
Xertigny	F	60	B2
Xilagani	GR	116	A7
Xilokastro	GR	117	D4
Xinzo de Limia	E	87	B3
Xixón = Gijón	E	88	A1
Xove	E	86	A3
Xubia	E	86	A2
Xunqueira de Ambia	E	87	B3
Xunqueira de Espadañedo	E	87	B3
Xylophagou	CY	120	B2

Y

Name	Country	Page	Grid
Y Felinheli	GB	26	B1
Yablanitsa	BG	11	E8
Yağcılar	TR	118	E3
Yahotyn	UA	11	A11
Yahyalı	TR	16	B7
Yalova	TR	118	B4
Yalvaç	TR	119	D6
Yambol	BG	11	E9
Yampil	UA	11	B10
Yaniskoski	RUS	113	D17
Yarbasan	TR	118	D3
Yarcombe	GB	29	C4
Yarm	GB	27	A4
Yarmouth	GB	31	D2
Yarrow	GB	25	C4
Yartsevo	RUS	7	D12
Yasinya	UA	11	B8
Yatağan	TR	119	E3
Yate	GB	29	B5
Yatton	GB	29	B5
Yavoriv	UA	11	B7
Yaxley	GB	30	B3
Yazıca	TR	118	D6
Yazıköy	TR	119	F2
Ybbs	A	63	B6
Ybbsitz	A	63	C5
Ydby	DK	38	C1
Yddal	N	32	B2
Yealmpton	GB	28	C4
Yebra de Basa	E	90	A2
Yecla	E	101	A4
Yecla de Yeltes	E	87	D4
Yelnya	RUS	7	D12
Yelsk	BY	7	F10
Yelverton	GB	28	C3
Yenice, Ankara	TR	16	B6
Yenice, Aydın	TR	119	E3
Yenice, Çanakkale	TR	118	C2
Yenice, Edirne	TR	116	B8
Yenifoça	TR	118	D1
Yenihisar	TR	119	E2
Yeniköy	TR	118	D4
Yeniköy Plaji	TR	118	B4
Yenipazar	TR	119	E3
Yenişarbademli	TR	119	E6
Yenişehir	TR	118	B4
Yenne	F	69	C5
Yeovil	GB	29	C5
Yepes	E	95	C3
Yerköy	TR	16	B7
Yerólakkos	CY	120	A2
Yeroskipos	CY	120	B1
Yerseke	NL	49	B5
Yerville	F	58	A1
Yeşildağ	TR	119	E6
Yeşilhisar	TR	16	B7
Yeşilköy	TR	118	B3
Yeşilova	TR	119	E4
Yeşilyurt	TR	119	D3
Yesnogorsk	RUS	7	D14
Yeste	E	101	A3
Yezerishche	BY	7	D10
Ygos-St. Saturnin	F	76	C2
Ygrande	F	68	B2
Yialousa	CY	120	A3
Yiğilca	TR	118	B6
Yli-Muonia	FIN	113	D12
Ylitornio	FIN	3	C25
Ylivieska	FIN	3	D26
Ylläsjärvi	FIN	113	E13
Ymonville	F	58	B2
Yngsjö	S	41	D4
Yoğuntaş	TR	118	A2
York	GB	27	B4
Youghal	IRL	21	C4
Yozgat	TR	16	B7
Yport	F	58	A1
Ypres = Ieper	B	48	C3
Yssingeaux	F	68	C4
Ystad	S	41	D3
Ystalyfera	GB	28	B4
Ystebrød	N	33	D2
Ystradgynlais	GB	28	B4
Ytre Arna	N	32	B2
Ytre Enebakk	N	35	C3
Ytre Rendal	N	114	F8
Ytterhogdal	S	115	D11
Ytterdal	S	115	E11
Yttermalung	S	34	B5
Yukhnov	RUS	7	D13
Yumurtalık	TR	16	C7
Yunak	TR	118	D6
Yuncos	E	94	B3
Yunquera	E	100	C1
Yunquera de Henares	E	95	B3
Yushkozero	RUS	3	D30
Yverdon-les-Bains	CH	70	B1
Yvetot	F	58	A1
Yvignac	F	57	B3
Yvoir	B	49	C5
Yvonand	CH	70	B1
Yxnerum	S	37	D3
Yzeure	F	68	B3

Z

Name	Country	Page	Grid
Zaamslag	NL	49	B4
Zaanstad	NL	42	C1
Žabalj	SRB	75	C5
Žabar	H	65	B6
Žabari	SRB	85	B6
Zabiče	SLO	73	C4
Zabierzów	PL	55	C4
Ząbki	PL	55	A6
Ząbkowice Śląskie	PL	54	C1
Zablaće	HR	83	C4
Zablače	SRB	85	C5
Žabljak	MNE	85	C4
Zabok	HR	73	B5
Zabokreky	SK	64	B4
Zabor	PL	53	B5
Zabowo	PL	46	B1
Zábřeh	CZ	64	A2
Zabrežje	SRB	85	B5
Zabrowo	PL	46	B1
Zabrze	PL	54	C3
Zabrzeż	PL	65	A6
Zacharo	GR	117	E3
Zadar	HR	83	B4
Zadzim	PL	54	B3
Zafarraya	E	100	C1
Zafferana Etnea	I	109	B4
Zafra	E	93	C4
Žaga	SLO	72	B3
Zagań	PL	53	B5
Zaglav	HR	83	C4
Zaglavak	SRB	85	C4
Zagnańsk	PL	55	C5
Zagora	GR	116	C5
Zagorc	SLO	73	B5
Zagoríčani	BIH	84	C2
Zagorje	SLO	73	B5
Zagórów	PL	54	A2
Zagradje	SRB	85	B5
Zagreb	HR	73	C5
Zagrilla	E	100	B1
Zagvozd	HR	84	C2
Zagwiżdże	PL	54	C2
Zagyvarékas	H	75	A5
Zagyvaróna	H	65	B5
Zahara	E	99	C5
Zahara de los Atunes	E	99	C5
Zahinos	E	93	C4
Zahna	D	52	B2
Záhoří	CZ	63	A5
Zahrádka	CZ	63	A6
Zahrensdorf	D	44	B2
Zaidín	E	90	B3
Zaječar	SRB	11	E7
Zákamenné	SK	65	A5
Zákány	H	74	B1
Zákányszék	H	75	B4
Zakliczyn	PL	65	A6
Zakopane	PL	65	A5
Zakrzew	PL	47	C6
Zakrzewo	PL	47	C4
Zakupy	CZ	53	C4
Zakynthos	GR	117	E2
Zalaapáti	H	74	B2
Zalabaksa	H	74	B1
Zalaegerszeg	H	74	B1
Zalakomár	H	74	B2
Zalakoppány	H	74	B2
Zalalövő	H	74	B1
Zalamea de la Serena	E	93	C5
Zalamea la Real	E	99	B4
Zalaszentgrót	H	74	B2
Zalaszentiván	H	74	B1
Zalău	RO	11	C7
Zalavár	H	74	B2
Zalcsie	PL	55	B4
Zaldibar	E	89	A4
Žalec	SLO	73	B5
Zalesie	PL	47	B6
Zalewo	PL	47	B5
Zalishchyky	UA	11	B8
Zalla	E	89	A3
Zaltbommel	NL	49	B6
Zamárdi	H	74	B2
Zamarte	PL	46	B3
Zamberk	CZ	54	C1
Zambra	E	100	B1
Zambugueira do Mar	P	98	B2
Zámoly	H	74	A3
Zamora	E	88	C1
Zamość	PL	11	A7
Zamostné	PL	55	B4
Zams	A	71	A5
Zandhoven	B	49	B5
Žandov	CZ	53	C4
Zandvoort	NL	42	C1
Zangliveri	GR	116	B5
Zánka	H	74	B2
Zaorejas	E	95	B4
Zaovine	SRB	85	C4
Zapadnaya Dvina	RUS	7	C12
Zapfend	D	51	C6
Zapole	PL	54	B3
Zapolyarnyy	RUS	3	B29
Zapponeta	I	104	B1
Zaprešić	HR	73	C5
Zaragoza	E	90	B2
Zarasai	LT	7	D9
Zarautz	E	89	A4
Zarcilla de Ramos	E	101	B4
Żarki	PL	55	C4
Zarko	GR	116	C4
Žarnovica	SK	65	B4
Zarnow	PL	55	B5
Zarnowiec	PL	47	A4
Zárošice	CZ	64	A2
Zarów	PL	54	C1
Zarren	B	48	B3
Zarrentin	D	44	B2
Żary	PL	53	B5
Zarza Capilla	E	93	C5
Zarza de Alange	E	93	C4
Zarza de Granadilla	E	93	A4
Zarza de Tajo	E	95	B3
Zarza la Mayor	E	93	B4
Zarzadilla de Totana	E	101	B4
Zarzuela del Monte	E	94	B2
Zarzuela del Pinar	E	88	C2
Zas	E	86	A2
Zasavica	SRB	85	B4
Zasieki	PL	53	B4
Zásmuky	CZ	53	D5
Žatec	CZ	52	C3
Zaton	HR	84	D3
Zatonie	PL	53	B5
Zator	PL	55	C4
Zauchwitz	D	52	A3
Zavala	BIH	84	D2
Zavalje	BIH	83	B4
Zavattarello	I	80	B3
Zavidovići	BIH	84	B3
Zavlaka	SRB	85	B4
Zawady	PL	55	B6
Zawadzkie	PL	54	C3
Zawdy	PL	54	B3
Zawidów	PL	53	B5
Zawidz	PL	47	C5
Zawiercie	PL	55	C4
Zawonia	PL	54	B2
Zázrivá	SK	65	A5
Zbarazh	UA	11	B8
Zbąszyń	PL	53	A5
Zbąszynek	PL	53	A5
Zbehy	SK	64	B3
Zbiersk	PL	54	B3
Zblewo	PL	47	B4
Zbójno	PL	47	B5
Zbrachlin	PL	47	C4
Zbraslav	CZ	63	A5
Zbraslavice	CZ	63	A6
Ždala	HR	74	B2
Ždánice	CZ	64	A3
Žďár nad Sázavou	CZ	63	A6
Zdbice	PL	46	B2
Zdenci	HR	74	C2
Ždiar	SK	65	A6
Zdice	CZ	63	A4
Zdirec nad Doubravou	CZ	64	A1
Zdolbuniv	UA	11	A9
Zdounky	CZ	64	A3
Zdravinje	SRB	85	C6
Ždrelo	SRB	85	B6
Zduńska Wola	PL	54	B3
Zduny, Łódzkie	PL	55	A4
Zduny, Wielkopolskie	PL	54	B2
Zdzieszowice	PL	54	C2
Zdziechowice, Opolskie	PL	54	B3
Zdziechowice, Wielkopolskie	PL	54	A2
Zdziszowice	PL	54	C3
Žeberio	E	89	A4
Zebreira	P	93	B3
Zebrzydowa	PL	53	B5
Zebrzydowice	PL	54	D3
Zechlin	D	45	B4
Zechlinerhütte	D	45	B4
Zederhaus	A	72	A3
Žednik	SRB	75	C4
Zeebrugge	B	49	B4
Zehdenick	D	45	C5
Zehren	D	52	B3
Zeil	D	51	C6
Zeilarn	D	62	B3
Zeist	NL	49	A6
Zeithain	D	52	B3
Zeitz	D	52	B2
Želatava	CZ	63	A6
Zelazno, Dolnośląskie	PL	54	C1
Zelazno, Pomorskie	PL	46	A3
Zele	B	49	B4
Zelenoborskiy	RUS	3	C30
Zelenogorsk	RUS	7	A10
Zelenograd	RUS	7	C14
Zelenogradsk	RUS	6	D6
Železná Ruda	CZ	63	A4
Železnice	CZ	53	C5
Železnik	SRB	85	B5
Železniki	SLO	73	B4
Železný Brod	CZ	53	C5
Zelhem	NL	50	A2
Želiezovce	SK	65	B4
Želkowo	PL	46	A3
Zell	CH	70	A2
Zell, Baden-Württemberg	D	60	C3
Zell, Baden-Württemberg	D	61	B4
Zell, Rheinland-Pfalz	D	50	C3
Zell am See	A	72	A2
Zell am Ziller	A	72	A1
Zell an der Pram	A	63	B4
Zell bei Zellhof	A	63	B5
Zella-Mehlis	D	51	C6
Zellerndorf	A	64	B1
Zellingen	D	61	A5
Želovce	SK	65	B5
Zelów	PL	55	B4
Zeltweg	A	73	A4
Zelzate	B	49	B4
Zemberovce	SK	65	B4
Zembrzyce	PL	65	A5
Zemianske-Kostol'any	SK	65	B4
Zemitz	D	45	B5
Zemné	SK	64	C3
Zemst	B	49	C5
Zemun	SRB	85	B5
Zemunik Donji	HR	83	B4
Zennor	GB	28	C2
Žepa	BIH	85	C3
Žepče	BIH	84	B3
Zepponami	I	102	A5
Zerbst	D	52	B2
Zerf	D	60	A2
Żerków	PL	54	B2
Zermatt	CH	70	B2
Zernez	CH	71	B5
Zerpen-schleuse	D	45	C5
Zestoa	E	89	A4
Zetel	D	43	B4
Zeulenroda	D	52	C1
Zeven	D	43	B6
Zevenaar	NL	50	B2
Zevenbergen	NL	49	B5
Zévio	I	71	C6
Zeytinbaği	TR	118	B4
Zeytindağ	TR	118	D2
Zgierz	PL	55	B4
Zgorzelec	PL	53	B5
Zgošča	BIH	84	B3
Zhabinka	BY	6	B8
Zharkovskiy	RUS	7	D12
Zhashkiv	UA	11	B11
Zheleznogorsk	RUS	7	E13
Zhlobin	BY	7	E11
Zhmerynka	UA	11	B10
Zhodzina	BY	7	D10
Zhovti Vody	UA	11	B12
Zhovtneve	UA	11	C12
Zhukovka	RUS	7	E12
Zhytomyr	UA	11	A10
Žiar nad Hronom	SK	65	B4
Zicavo	F	102	B2
Zickhusen	D	44	B3
Zidani Most	SLO	73	B5
Ziddorf	D	45	B4
Židlochovice	CZ	64	A2
Ziębice	PL	54	C2
Ziegendorf	D	44	B3
Ziegenrück	D	52	C1
Zielenic, Dolnośląskie	PL	54	C1
Zielenic, Zachodnio-Pomorskie	PL	46	B1
Zielona	PL	47	B5
Zielona Góra	PL	53	B5
Zielonka	PL	55	A6
Zieluń-Osada	PL	47	B5
Ziemetshausen	D	61	B6
Zierenberg	D	51	B5
Zierikzee	NL	49	B4
Ziersdorf	A	64	B1
Zierzow	D	44	B3
Ziesar	D	52	A2
Ziesendorf	D	44	B4
Ziethen	D	45	B5
Žihle	CZ	52	C3
Zile	TR	16	A7
Žilina	SK	65	A4
Ziltendorf	D	53	A4
Zimandu Nou	RO	75	B6
Zimna Woda	PL	47	B6
Zimnicea	RO	11	E8
Zinal	CH	70	B2
Zinasco	I	70	C4
Zingst	D	45	A4
Zinkgruvan	S	37	D2
Zinnowitz	D	45	A5
Zirc	H	74	A2
Žiri	SLO	73	B4
Zirl	A	71	A6
Zirndorf	D	62	A1
Žirovnica	SRB	85	B6
Žirovnice	CZ	63	A6
Zistersdorf	A	64	B2
Žitište	SRB	75	C5
Zitsa	GR	116	C2
Zittau	D	53	C4
Živinice	BIH	84	B3
Zlatar	HR	73	B6
Zlatar Bistrica	HR	73	B6
Zlate Hory	CZ	54	C2
Zlaté Klasy	SK	64	B3
Zlaté Moravce	SK	65	B4
Zlatná na Ostrove	SK	64	C3
Zlatníky	SK	64	B4
Zlatograd	BG	116	A7
Žlebič	SLO	73	C4
Zlin	CZ	64	A3
Złocieniec	PL	46	B2
Złoczew	PL	54	B3
Zlonice	CZ	53	C4
Złotniki Kujawskie	PL	47	C4
Złotoryja	PL	53	B5
Złotów	PL	46	B3
Złoty Stok	PL	54	C1
Zlutice	CZ	52	C3
Zmajevac	BIH	83	B5
Zmajevo	SRB	75	C4
Żmigród	PL	54	B1
Zmijavci	HR	84	C2
Žminj	HR	72	C3
Znamyanka	UA	11	B12
Żnin	PL	46	C3
Znojmo	CZ	64	B2
Zöblitz	D	52	C3
Zocca	I	81	B4
Zoetermeer	NL	49	A5
Zofingen	CH	70	A2
Zogno	I	71	C4
Zohor	SK	64	B2
Zolling	D	62	B2
Zolochiv	UA	11	B8
Zolotonosha	UA	11	B12
Zomba	H	74	B3
Zomergem	B	49	B4
Zonhoven	B	49	C6
Zonza	F	102	B2
Zörbig	D	52	B2
Zorita	E	93	B5
Żory	PL	54	C3
Zossen	D	52	A3
Zottegem	B	49	C4
Zoutkamp	NL	42	B3
Zovi Do	BIH	84	C3
Zreče	SLO	73	B5
Zrenjanin	SRB	75	C5
Žrnovica	HR	83	C5
Zruč nad Sazavou	CZ	63	A6
Zsámbék	H	65	C4
Zsámbok	H	75	A4
Zsana	H	75	B4
Zschopau	D	52	C3
Zuberec	SK	65	A5
Zubieta	E	76	C1
Zubin Potok	KOS	85	D5
Zubiri	E	76	D1
Zubtsov	RUS	7	C13
Zucaina	E	96	A2
Zudar	D	45	A5
Zufre	E	99	B4
Zug	CH	70	A3
Zuheros	E	100	B1
Zuidhorn	NL	42	B3
Zuidlaren	NL	42	B3
Zuidwolde	NL	42	C3
Zújar	E	101	B3
Żukowo	PL	47	A4
Żuljana	HR	84	D2
Žulová	CZ	54	C2
Zülpich	D	50	C2
Zumaia	E	89	A4
Zumarraga	E	89	A4
Zundert	NL	49	B5
Županja	HR	84	A3
Žurgena	E	101	B3
Zürich	CH	70	A3
Zurzach	CH	70	A3
Zusmarshausen	D	62	B1
Zusow	D	44	B3
Züssow	D	45	B5
Žuta Lovka	HR	83	B4
Žužemberk	SLO	73	C4
Zvečan	KOS	85	D5
Zvenyhorodka	UA	11	B11
Zvikovské Podhradí	CZ	63	A5
Zvolen	SK	65	B5
Zvolenská Slatina	SK	65	B5
Zvornik	BIH	85	B4
Zwartsluis	NL	42	C3
Zweibrücken	D	60	A3
Zweisimmen	CH	70	B2
Zwettl	A	63	B6
Zwettl an der Rodl	A	63	B5
Zwickau	D	52	C2
Zwiefalten	D	61	B5
Zwieryn	PL	46	C1
Zwierzno	PL	47	A5
Zwiesel	D	63	A4
Zwieselstein	A	71	B6
Zwoleń	PL	55	B6
Zwolle	NL	42	C3
Zwönitz	D	52	C2
Zychlin	PL	55	A4
Zydowo, Wielkopolskie	PL	46	C3
Zydowo, Zachodnio-Pomorskie	PL	46	A2
Żyrardów	PL	55	A5
Zytno	PL	55	B4
Żywiec	PL	65	A5
Zyyi	CY	120	B2